P9-BAU-440

CITIZEN HEARST

W. A. SWANBERG

CITIZEN HEARST

A BIOGRAPHY OF
William Randolph Hearst

Galahad Books • New York

Copyright © 1961 by W.A. Swanberg

All rights reserved. No part of this work may be reproduced or transmitted in any form or by any means, electronic or mechanical, including photocopying, recording, or any information storage and retrieval system without permission in writing from the publisher. All requests for permission to reproduce material from this work should be directed to Scribner, a division of Simon and Schuster, Inc., 1230 Avenue of the Americas, New York, NY 10020.

First Galahad Books edition published in 1996.

Galahad Books
A division of Budget Book Service, Inc.
386 Park Avenue South
New York, NY 10016

Galahad Books is a registered trademark of Budget Book Service, Inc.
Published by arrangement with Scribner, a division of Simon and Schuster, Inc.
Library of Congress Catalog Card Number: tk   96-77429
ISBN: 0-88365-970-0

Printed in the United States of America.

QUOTATIONS FROM COPYRIGHTED SOURCES

GRATITUDE is expressed to the following for permission to quote copyrighted material in *Citizen Hearst*:

Mrs. Willis J. Abbot for extracts from *Watching the World Go By*, by Willis J. Abbot, Little, Brown & Co., Boston, 1933; Appleton-Century-Crofts, Inc., New York, for extracts from *William Randolph Hearst, American,* by Mrs. Fremont Older, published by that company in 1936; E.P. Dutton & Co., New York, for extracts from *My Last Million Readers*, by Emile Gauvreau, published by that company in 1941; Holt, Rinehart & Winston, Inc., New York, for extracts from *Hollywood Rajah*, by Bosley Crowther, published by that company in 1960; Simon and Schuster, Inc., New York for extracts from *William Randolph Hearst: A Portrait in His Own Words*, by Edmond D. Coblentz, published by that company in 1952; and the Viking Press, Inc., for extracts from *Hearst: Lord of San Simeon*, by Oliver Carlson and Ernest Sutherland Bates, published by that company in 1936.

PICTURE CREDITS

Author's Collection: 19; Black Star: 22 (ROBERT E. WALTZ), 26 (ROSE MADDEN); Brown Brothers: 1, 2, 3, 5, 7, 11, 13, 14, 15, 24, 29; *Collier's* Magazine: 9; Culver Service: 8, 12, 21, 25, 30, 36; Loomis Dean—*Life*, copyright 1951 *Time Inc.*: 31; Allen Grant—*Life*, copyright 1951 *Time Inc.*: 42; *Harper's Weekly:* 10; Harvard College Library: 4; *New York Journal:* 16, 28; Bob Landry: 40; Dr. Erich Salomon, copyright Peter Hunter, Amsterdam, The Netherlands: 33, 34, 35, 37, 39; Peter Stackpole: 6, 27, 38; United Press International: 17, 18, 20, 32, 41; Wide World: 23.

FOR

J. W · S.

Contents

List of Illustrations

CITIZEN HEARST

BOOK ONE

THE PRODIGY

1. The Pioneers

In 1882, tall, shag-bearded George Hearst rose before his fellow delegates at the California Democratic convention at San Jose and addressed them with his usual disregard for nicety. He was a multi-millionaire, untidy of dress, almost illiterate, an assassin of grammar, a lover of poker and good bourbon, and an inveterate tobacco chewer whose long beard and shirtfront were generally stained with juice. Yet he hoped, and with some reason, that he would be nominated for governor.[1]

"My opponents say that I haven't the book learning that they possess," he rumbled. "They say I can't spell. They say I spell bird, b-u-r-d. If b-u-r-d doesn't spell bird, what in hell does it spell?" [2]

Hearst was exaggerating. He probably *could* spell "bird," although he would have had a struggle with anything over one syllable. He knew well that he was short on education and that rhetoric was a mystery he never would solve. But he also knew that among his listeners was a fair proportion of men who were also desecrators of the idiom and that a humorous dilation on his own shortcomings would appeal to them as well as to the word-splitters in the crowd.

The homely Hearst had a gentle, aristocratic wife, who, although she had long since despaired of rubbing off his rough edges, would have been shocked at his use of even mild profanity in a public speech. He had a son, Willie, who could spell practically anything and was even then preparing for Harvard, but would not have been shocked at all. Together, the three made an amazing family, the son inheriting strength and crudity from his father, strength and delicacy from his mother, and blending these into a unique combination of powerful talents that would shape history and convulse millions with enthusiasm, puzzlement, fright or rage.

Born in 1820 in sparsely settled Franklin County, Missouri, George Hearst was brought up on his parents' small plantation in semi-frontier country where he was lucky to get two years of schooling. A strapping youth, he did his share of the labor along with four slaves, but took far more pleasure in spare-time work at a lead mine near the farm. His home life was not of the happiest, for his father was interested in another woman and Mrs. Hearst would not speak to him except when necessary.[3] Mining fascinated him from

---

[1] N. Y. *Times,* Mar. 1, 1891.
[2] Edmond D. Coblentz, *William Randolph Hearst, a Portrait in His Own Words,* 24.
[3] Mrs. Joseph Marshall Flint to author, Jan. 18, 1960.

3

the start. Slow and painful as reading was for him, he managed to get a few books on geology and digest them thoroughly. He talked with lead miners, haunted the diggings and gained enough savvy to impress neighboring Indians, who called him Boy-That-Earth-Talked-To.[4]

At maturity he was a muscular man over six feet tall, handsome, taciturn, devoid of the social graces but keen and practical, filled with energy and even with ambition in his own quiet way. He avoided women—or possibly women avoided him—but he dabbled in local politics, once being a delegate to a Democratic state convention. When his father died in 1846, George became responsible for his mother, sister, brother and an estate that included a few Negroes and several thousand dollars in debts—an enormous burden at the time. A solid sort, he worked for three years to discharge the debts, putting his family in sound shape—a good thing, because in 1849 came news that drew him like a magnet. Gold had been discovered in California.[5]

The gold fever made fools of many poorly equipped young Americans who plunged unthinkingly into the adventure and ended by inhabiting early graves. It did not make a fool of George Hearst. He had the three requisites of the pioneer—strength, courage and ingenuity—and on top of that he had a rudimentary knowledge of mining. He was a bachelor nearing thirty on May 12, 1850, when he left with a party of fifteen, some of them relatives, on the terrifying trail west that was already marked by bleaching bones. Although they met no hostile Indians, they suffered the usual hardships, and at Fort Laramie Hearst came down with cholera so badly that he wanted to die. Doubtless a less hardy individual would have died, but Hearst recovered, reached Eldorado County, California, by the end of the year and began mining with a pick and shovel.[6]

But the earth was uncommunicative to Boy-That-Earth-Talked-To. Except for one minor strike, he spent nine lean years mingling with boomers and cutthroats, trying his luck in a dozen places, once opening a general store in Nevada City and again in Sacramento, returning always to dig in the dirt. In 1859 he got wind of a strike in the Washoe country across the border in Nevada Territory. Mounting his mule, he headed for Washoe, only to be stopped near Nevada City by a constable who reminded him that he owed a shopkeeper forty dollars and accused him of running out on the debt. Hearst admitted that he was almost penniless, whereupon the constable seized the mule.[7]

At that moment, though Hearst did not know it, the mule was as important to him as a horse to Richard III. Luckily, two good friends, Melville Atwood and A. E. Head, happened along, and one of them paid the forty dollars. With his partners, Hearst rode on to Virginia City, where they

[4] Oliver Carlson and Ernest Bates, *Hearst, Lord of San Simeon,* 5.
[5] Mrs. Fremont Older, *William Randolph Hearst, American,* 5, 13.
[6] Alonzo Phelps, *Contemporary Biography of California's Representative Men,* Vol. II, 10–11; George H. Tinkham, *California Men and Events,* 298.
[7] Rockwell D. Hunt, *California and Californians.* Vol. IV, 46; N. Y. *Times,* Mar. 1, 1891.

scraped up $450 to buy a half-interest in a nearby claim—a mine that turned out to contain no gold at all but plenty of silver. It was part of the Comstock Lode, a strike so rich that it started a silver rush almost as crazed as the gold rush ten years earlier. Hearst, suddenly flush, rode his luck and bought a one-sixth interest in the Ophir, another Comstock mine that came in strong—$2,200 a ton. The earth was talking to him at last. When winter interrupted their labors, Hearst, Head and Atwood went to San Francisco for a saloon celebration.[8]

In 1860, Hearst learned that his mother was ill in Missouri, and returned by boat via Panama, reaching his home in September. Now a rich man, he made his mother's last days "luxuriously happy." He stayed to bury her, and a good while longer, for he took a shine to eighteen-year-old Phoebe Elizabeth Apperson, a school teacher whom he had carried on his shoulder as a pig-tailed girl before he left home in 1850.[9]

Hearst was forty, old enough to be her father. Although kindly, he was uncouth in appearance and manner, his ability at violating the language having if anything been improved by his association with sourdoughs and cardsharps. He drank, chewed tobacco and swore. Randolph and Drusilla Apperson, who were prosperous slave-owners with a handsome farm on the Meramec River and some social pretensions, must have regarded his arrival as a barbarian invasion, especially since it is said that Hearst resolutely forbore from telling anyone of his new wealth.[10] Phoebe herself was a tiny thing, pretty as a Dresden doll, whose only escape from rusticity had been a brief period of study in St. Louis. Her ambition and accomplishment are denoted by the fact that she spoke not only precise English but also passable French—an achievement unusual in rural Missouri at the time. Being a perfectionist, she could not have been other than painfully aware of the Hearstian crudity. But he represented the romance of places far from bucolic Franklin County, and he *was* handsome. Her parents strongly opposed the match—probably forbade it—and for a time matters were at an impasse.[11]

One of the more fabulous might-have-beens of history arises from conjecture at what might *not* have happened had Hearst failed in his suit. For then William Randolph Hearst would never have been born, the United States might not have gone to war with Spain, Theodore Roosevelt might have remained a frustrated minor politician, and the name of Dewey might never have risen out of obscurity. Without William Randolph Hearst, the Presidency would have eluded Franklin Delano Roosevelt, sweeping social changes now accepted might never have been consummated, the newspapers might still be preoccupied with the mere gathering of news, and California would have lost a castle. Phoebe Apperson, with immense, unknown

[8] George D. Lyman, *The Saga of the Comstock Lode*, 53, 74; T. A. Rickard, *A History of American Mining*, 98.
[9] Lyman, 367; Phelps, II, 12.   [10] Mrs. Fremont Older, *op. cit.*, 6.
[11] Mrs. Joseph Marshall Flint to author, Feb. 20, 1960.

power in her hands, could have remolded the nation only by saying a firm "No," and so much more that it staggers the imagination to contemplate —even down to subsidiary consequences including the grievous loss to art dealers, the non-establishment of the Milk Fund, and the possible failure of many people such as Arthur Brisbane, John Hylan, Walter Winchell and Louella Parsons to rise to anything like fame.

All this and much more Miss Apperson held in the balance, unknowing, while George Hearst waited and persisted. It took time, for she was nineteen and Hearst forty-one when they finally eloped and were married at Stedman, Missouri, on June 15, 1862. The long delay probably reflected some misgivings on Phoebe's part about marrying a man who so outraged the amenities. The Appersons were faced by a *fait accompli* while Hearst remained four months longer with his bride, attending to his mother's estate.[12]

While it is likely that Hearst did not boast of his wealth, his rise above his Franklin County poverty must have been evident, and Randolph Apperson would have been a strange parent had he not made pointed inquiries about Hearst's ability to support pretty Phoebe. Furthermore, the newlyweds took the "luxury route" to California in October, going by train to New York, by boat to Panama, crossing the isthmus and boarding another vessel for San Francisco—a journey impossible for the indigent. What with Hearst's age and inelegance, he would have been a triply unwelcome swain had he also been anywhere near penniless. The suspicion arises that Phoebe and the Appersons well knew that he was prosperous and that the story of their ignorance of his wealth might have been invented later to counter the inevitable talk that Phoebe had married the old roughneck for his money.

The Civil War meanwhile had developed into a bitter struggle from which the Hearst couple remained aloof, George being a trifle old for soldiering. The sympathies of both of them, brought up as they were under the slave system, were with the South. Phoebe, in early pregnancy, was in frequent discomfort on the Pacific leg of the journey. Among the passengers were Mr. and Mrs. David Peck and their two-year-old son Orrin, who had left Kingston, New York, to make their home in San Francisco. The friendly Mrs. Peck took a liking to Phoebe, fussing over her, bringing her tea when she felt queasy, and showing a kindliness that Phoebe would repay in later years.[13]

As they sailed through the Golden Gate, Phoebe, the Missouri girl to whom a trip to St. Louis had been an adventure, was thrilled by one of the world's most magnificent prospects.

"I intend," she said, "to live on these hills where I can always see the bay." [14]

The words expressed her quiet determination. San Francisco was a raw, ugly town in a splendid setting, bustling with some 75,000 people on the

[12] Phelps, vol. II, 12.   [13] Mrs. J. M. Flint to author.
[14] Mrs. Fremont Older, *op. cit.*, 6.

make. The Hearsts lived briefly at the ornate Lick House, then moved to the quieter Stevenson House at California and Montgomery Streets. Hearst's mining interests were almost 200 miles away, but he did not want his bride to consort with the madams and faro dealers of Virginia City. San Francisco itself was enough to give a modest woman qualms, since only a half-mile from the hotel was the roaring Barbary Coast and its scores of brothels inhabited by doxies of all hues. But the city at any rate had its quota of respectable women who had already set up a social caste based more on wealth than on breeding.

On April 29, 1863—on the eve of the battle of Chancellorsville far across the nation—Phoebe Hearst, in great torment, gave birth to a boy in her bedroom at the Stevenson.

The boy was named William Randolph, after his paternal and maternal grandfathers, but nobody got around to baptizing him because neither the nominally Presbyterian mother nor the nominally Episcopalian father were overly engrossed in religion. George Hearst bought mother and son a brick house with a garden on fashionable Rincon Hill, then was off to Nevada again.[15]

II. BLESS HIS LITTLE HEART

PHOEBE APPERSON HEARST, the former school teacher who would gain national fame for her gifts to needy students and educational institutions, showed no schoolmarm sternness in rearing her own son. She believed in sweet reason. Enormously maternal and possessive, she wanted more children, several of them. It was a pity that she had no more, for with her husband gone the child became the object of a flood of affection that engulfed him. He was mothered, loved, pampered, praised, protected, instructed, fussed over, waited on and worried about every moment of his infant existence. Phoebe had no doubt that he was a superior child. Her mission was to enhance perfection. She hired an Irish governess, Eliza Pike, who also served as wet-nurse. Eliza was still wet-nursing him when he was fourteen months old, perhaps later—a laggard weaning that may have affected his emotional development. Excerpts from Phoebe's incessant letters to relatives and friends show her preoccupation:

"Bless his little heart. . . . He is a very good boy. . . . He seems to understand everything. He likes his books, can tell all about Cocky Locky and Henny Penny. . . . Willie knows several words in French. . . . He is so cunning. . . . No signs of a little sister yet. . . . His being with me so constantly has made him perfectly devoted to me. He is a real little calf about me. He never wants anyone else to do anything for him, and I think I love him better than ever before. Some days I do very little but amuse

[15] John K. Winkler, *William Randolph Hearst—A New Appraisal,* 20. For information about the family background, see Appendix I.

him. He is very wise and sweet . . . he is a great comfort to me—he talks to me sometimes when we are alone like an old man, he understands so much."[1]

Naturally, Willie adored the mother who gave him such unstinted devotion. He insisted on sleeping with her, and was still her bedfellow when he was three and a half. "He was very much put out when his Papa came home because he could not sleep with me," Phoebe wrote. "I told him when his Papa went away again he could sleep with me. He said, well, he wished he would go." [2]

From the first, Phoebe was determined that he would have every advantage of education, under her own supervision—a thought that made her question her ability to lead the way. She tutored in the humanities, studied painting and went faithfully to the opera and the art museums. The matron from Missouri had a thirst for knowledge that Franklin County had never been able to satisfy, and she absorbed everything that San Francisco had to offer with no companionship whatever from her culture-blind spouse. Hearst was a fond husband who gave her everything she wanted but the thing she most wanted—an interest in the arts. She solved the problem early in her marriage by letting him grub in the dirt and become involved in Democratic politics while she embarked on a cultural career of her own, preparing the way for Willie.[3]

Catholic Eliza was upset because the boy was not baptized and would suffer eternal damnation if he should die uncleansed of sin. Phoebe was unconcerned about eternity. Her parents came to visit, and doubtless because she was lonely with her husband away, she persuaded them to make their home in California, helping them find a ranch near Santa Clara. Once Phoebe returned from Santa Clara to learn that Eliza had seized the opportunity and taken Willie to the parish priest, who baptized him in the Catholic church.

"But, Eliza," Phoebe protested, "I am a Presbyterian."

"No matter, madam," the nurse replied, "the baby is a Christian." [4]

Phoebe burst into laughter at the spectacle of her son being consecrated to popery. Dogma was unimportant to her. Although she was conventionally God-fearing, she found her chief faith in secular self-improvement and her religion in the upbringing of her child. Somewhat shy but never ascetic, she frankly enjoyed the luxuries, the "better things" that money could bring. The Hearst mines were paying handsomely. In 1865 the little family moved to a grander house on hilly Chestnut Street with a spectacular view of ships on the bay, Alcatraz and Yerba Buena, and the Contra Costa hills beyond. That same year, George Hearst, who had been contributing heavily to the Democratic party, was elected to the state legislature. His wife and small son spent the winter with him in Sacramento, where he served on the

[1] Mrs. Fremont Older notes, letters dated June 17, 1864, and Sept. (?) and Nov. 18, 1866.
[2] Mrs. Fremont Older notes, letter dated Dec. 9, 1866.
[3] Mrs. Fremont Older, op. cit., 8.   [4] The same, 9.

mining committee, voted against the Thirteenth Amendment abolishing slavery, but was wise enough to make no speeches.[5]

For all his taciturnity, Hearst was amiable, warm-hearted, had flashes of homely humor and was well liked. He hated to "dress up." He walked and talked slowly. Nothing could hurry him. He liked to play poker for pots as high as $10,000. When in San Francisco, it was his special joy to fill his pockets with twenty-dollar gold pieces and stroll down Market Street, stopping to chat with old mining cronies down on their luck, quietly slipping a double eagle to each of them until his pockets were empty. A gambler in more than cards, he was extending his mining holdings and also spreading into land speculation. He joined with William M. Lent, a San Francisco promoter, in the purchase of large tracts on the outskirts of the city. On his own, in 1865 he moved down the California coast and bought the Piedra Blanca ranch, an old Spanish grant in San Luis Obispo County—48,000 acres at something like sixty cents an acre. He was gripped by a land hunger second only to his passion for mines, and between the two of them he managed to extend himself precariously.[6]

His wife's preoccupation with things literary and artistic was something to be classed with crocheting—incomprehensible and useless but not really subversive so long as he was not expected to become involved. He indulged her foibles and was allowed his own, although Phoebe never gave up her effort to coax him to dress a little less like a prospector. She had become mistress of what amounted to a small salon at the Chestnut Street mansion,[7] having painters, musicians and literary people in to tea with society matrons and encouraging talk on such subjects as Oscar Wilde or the Pre-Raphaelites —affairs Hearst shunned. On one occasion he arrived home during such an entertainment, entering "in his stocking feet, carefully carrying his boots in his right hand while his left supported the regulation crooked cane. He looked neither to right nor to left, but glided through the apartment like a ghost, to the intense amusement of the guests."[8]

The Hearst couple, poles apart in outlook, were alike in being strong, determined characters, unwilling to bend. Although they had reached a *modus vivendi* of sorts, there was no meeting of the minds and their marriage was not idyllic. It appears rather to have settled into a condition approaching polite, sustained armistice. It is scarcely surprising that at some time during this period, Hearst became involved with another woman.[9] The attachment caused a family crisis, and although it was ultimately ended it must have been a cruel blow to the idealistic Phoebe, causing her to focus her love

[5] Carlson and Bates, 9.
[6] Mrs. Flint to author; John Bruce, *Gaudy Century*, 199–200; John K. Winkler, *W. R. Hearst: An American Phenomenon*, 44; San Francisco *Examiner*, Mar. 1, 1891.
[7] Winifred Black Bonfils, *The Life and Personality of Phoebe Apperson Hearst*, 21.
[8] Sacramento *Bee*, quoted in Bruce, 200.
[9] Mrs. J. M. Flint to author, Jan. 18, 1960.

even more firmly in a direction where too much mother-love was already being lavished—on her son.

She continued to broadcast epistolary effusions about him: "When he was sick, he would say often, day or night, 'Mama, I want to tell you something.' I would say 'What?' His answer would be, 'I love you.' . . . I won't trust him with the maid, for her influence is so bad. When he is rude she laughs a big loud laugh and he thinks he has done something smart. She encourages him to deceive me, but he is too honest. He will tell me what happens, be it good or evil. . . . He is a great comfort to me and I hope he will be a good man, they are scarce. . . . He knows all his letters perfectly and will soon learn to spell. I have not made him feel it was tiresome or a task to learn, but make it interesting and funny. . . . He likes his books, you would be astonished to hear him spell and pronounce words of 3 letters, can count 100, and knows what country, State and City he lives in. Also who discovered America and about the world being round." [10]

All this was unusual in a boy of four, but the word "momism" would seem to apply. Phoebe saw no danger in maternalistic excess. Willie Hearst, a stocky, blue-eyed, fair-haired boy, decidedly handsome, grew up with his talents encouraged at the same time that his emotional stability was crippled by an atmosphere of protection and adulation, and he would suffer all his life for it.

He had his first riding lesson while still a baby. Later, he went to the Presbyterian Sunday school and was enrolled at a private school, since his mother felt him too "delicate" for the rough-and-tumble of public school. He had two dogs—the first of hundreds he would own during his lifetime—and he made frequent trips down to Meiggs' Wharf to see the strange birds and animals brought by sailors from all over the world. Immensely fond of animals, he owned rabbits and white mice and always looked forward to trips to the ranch of his grandparents, where he could ride until he was weary of it. [11]

Quiet, intelligent, imaginative, he was at times willful and disobedient. Athletics did not interest him. Sentimentally affectionate, he developed a great fondness for Eliza Pike, and missed her when she returned to her former home in Illinois. Likewise, he was devoted to his grandmother, Drusilla Apperson, so that his adult relationships were mostly with women. Like the girl in the nursery rhyme, when he was bad he was horrid. He could not have failed to sense that to his mother he was the person of supreme importance, and to have agreed that the world did indeed revolve around him. Yet he had friends, most of them from the upper crust. Among them were Orrin Peck, the lad who had come around via Panama when Willie was yet unborn; Eugene Lent, son of George Hearst's land-buying associate; Fred Moody, a near neighbor; and Katherine "Pussy" Soulé, who lived next door and played with him daily.

[10] Mrs. Fremont Older notes, letters dated Feb. 20 and June 19, 1867.
[11] Coblentz, *Hearst*, 13; San Francisco *Examiner*, Oct. 17, 1930.

"When I grow up I'm going to marry Pussy," he once told his mother in the girl's presence.[12]

Pussy was impressed by his ability at remembering rhymes and tunes. He often sang for her. Many years later, Miss Soulé said, "There was never a nicer, kinder, more sensitive boy than Willie Hearst." [13]

Orrin Peck, who lived far off near the Mission Dolores, was devoted to Willie although two years older. Others were less admiring, for the boy could be a terror. On one occasion when he and Fred Moody played hooky from dancing school, a friend of Phoebe's, Miss Estrada, found them in the garden and ordered them sharply to class. Willie stuck out his tongue at her.

"I won't go!" he said.

"You bad boy!" Miss Estrada exclaimed.

Willie picked up the garden hose and showered her with water, ruining her billowy afternoon dress and her temper.[14]

His distaste for dancing swelled into a personal vendetta against Professor Lunt, the *maître de danse*, causing him to lead a group of cronies to the Lunt hall on Polk Street and stone the place. Lunt thereafter refused to have him as a student. Willie created panic at one of his mother's receptions by liberating a mechanical mouse. Even his doting grandparents found him a hard one to discipline.[15]

But mother forgave all. A pioneer in spirit, excited rather than intimidated by travel, she took Willie to Missouri when he was five, visiting relatives, attending the fair and the French opera in St. Louis with him. The next year, the Hearsts took him on a trip to Mexico. When he came down with typhoid on the homeward journey, his mother was almost frantic until he recovered. An epidemic of smallpox in San Francisco terrified her. The "little sister" she hoped for failed to arrive, and Willie alone took the punishment of her love. Her letters were prolonged paeans of praise.

"We feel very proud of our boy," she wrote. "The teacher has 12 little scholars and says Willie is the favorite of them all. He is such a mimic, sings, dances, plays, so as to much amuse them all. . . . We are all amused at him picking up Chinese from our [house] boy—he can count 100 in Chinese and knows a good many words." [16]

She seldom mentioned that he was a genius at mischief. He showed a partiality for pranks causing a maximum of noise, confusion and sensation. Once, while the Hearst home was being redecorated and the family moved temporarily into the Nob Hill home of some friends, the Addisons, Willie bought some Bengal lights—flares that burned with a red glow. After the household was asleep, he set several flares on tin pie plates, touched them off, madly shrieked "Fire!", then locked himself in. The Hearsts and Addisons came on the run, horrified at the red glare filtering under the door and

[12] Mrs. Fremont Older, *op. cit.*, 20.   [13] The same.   [14] The same, p. 23.
[15] Mrs. J. M. Flint to author.
[16] Mrs. Fremont Older notes, letter of Nov. 13, 1870.

certain that the boy was being incinerated. They were trying to batter down the door when Willie opened it and explained merrily that it was all a joke. Mrs. Hearst was so relieved to find him safe that she hardly scolded him, but George Hearst put on a show of menace.

"Were you very warm in that room while the fire was going on, Willie?" he demanded.

"No, Papa, I wasn't warm at all," the boy replied.

"Well," said Hearst, laying Willie across his knee, "you're going to be warmed now, son, where it will do you the most good." [17]

However, as Willie himself later recalled it, this was just a "pretense of severity" and he got very little warming, if any. A succession of such sky-larking marks him as an early prototype of the baleful Katzenjammer Kids his newspapers would later make famous, and although he was often prompt and courteous in apologizing, adults were apt to keep a wary eye on him.[18]

Although the willow switch was then believed indispensable in rearing children, there is no record that Willie ever got a genuine whacking. Phoebe reasoned with the little man. Hearst, likewise indulgent, was not inclined to spend his visits home in dispensing discipline. On the contrary, when Willie once asked him for ice cream money for him and his friends, Hearst gave him not a quarter but a twenty-dollar gold piece that furnished a candy debauch for the whole neighborhood.[19] Willie was given just about every-thing he wanted, including a pony and cart and a Punch and Judy show in the barn. Doubtless the neighbors said the Hearsts spoiled their boy, and doubtless the neighbors were right.

Still holding his interest in the Ophir, Hearst was buying and selling other mines, or pieces of them, getting involved in lawsuits which were en-demic in a region swarming with chiselers who stole claims and bribed judges and juries. One contemporary said of him, "His word . . . was abso-lutely sacred, no matter if millions were involved," and another described him as "one of nature's noblemen." [20] He won admiration because his honesty was well above the average, because he was utterly unpretentious and was warmly generous to those down on their luck. But late in the Sixties his own luck turned sour when, on the heels of a crippling business depression, he took a $400,000 licking in a mining deal and lost a vital lawsuit against the Raymond & Ely mine in Nevada. ". . . he was financially embarrassed," an observer wrote, "and, had his creditors pressed him, would have been insolvent in the amount of several hundred thousands of dollars." [21]

The blow apparently did not impair his confidence in a comeback, for the family continued to live in style on Chestnut Street with servants and a

[17] Coblentz, Hearst, 10–12.
[18] Winkler, William Randolph Hearst—A New Appraisal, 23.
[19] Mrs. Fremont Older, op. cit., 15.
[20] Thomas Edwin Farish, The Gold Hunters of California, 218; Tinkham, 298.
[21] Phelps, II, 12; Farish, 215.

handsome carriage. Even if Hearst was broke, he formed an alliance with two ex-Kentuckians who were not—Lloyd Tevis and James Ben Ali Haggin, the latter's exotic middle names being the gift of his mother, a Turk. Tevis and Haggin had both forsaken the practice of law to become money-lenders, then land speculators and finally mining promoters. The character of the men and also of the times is admirably expressed in a single comment: "They were clever, shrewd, ruthless men . . . and highly respected in San Francisco." [22]

Tevis and Haggin had plenty of money but no mining savvy. The penniless Hearst was known as a man who could smell gold or silver. They pooled their resources, the financiers backing Hearst cautiously at first. Hearst went on a tour of available mining properties, descending into the bowels of the earth, examining quartz veins and taking samples. In 1872 he recommended the purchase of several mines, one of them the Ontario silver mine in Utah which Tevis and Haggin snapped up for $45,000.[23] That same winter occurred one of the West's most gorgeous hoaxes, in which two slippery prospectors salted a remote spot in Colorado with rough gems, convinced San Francisco Banker William Ralston and his experts that they had discovered a mine loaded with diamonds, and swindled Ralston out of a fortune before the fraud was exposed by a brilliant government geologist named Clarence King. This spectacular knavery was the talk of California, and King, suddenly known as the "King of Diamonds," was invited to some of San Francisco's best homes, including that of George Hearst. King was not favorably impressed by his host, later penning an unkind quip:

". . . Hearst was bitten on the privates by a scorpion; the latter fell dead." [24]

This was hardly a fair characterization of Hearst, who was the sort who would close up in contemptuous silence in the presence of such a fashion plate and sparkling conversationalist as King. Apparently he had recouped in some measure, for otherwise Phoebe would not have picked this time to plan a costly tour of Europe with Willie.

A trip to Europe had become one of the status symbols marking the San Francisco elite, but with Phoebe, a sharpshooting huntress of knowledge, the snob attraction carried little weight. She had long yearned to see Europe. Now her son was old enough to profit from it. George Hearst was gone so much that they would scarcely see him if they stayed home. On top of that, Mrs. William Lent and her son Eugene were already in Europe, and the Hearsts could meet them there.

Phoebe hired a young Harvard graduate, Thomas Barry, to tutor Willie on the tour. There was a round of farewell parties for the boy and his friends at the Hearst home, complete with fireworks. Willie was crazy about fireworks.

[22] Gertrude Atherton, *Golden Gate Country*, 186.   [23] Rickard, 98; Farish, 215–16.
[24] Thurman Wilkins, *Clarence King*, 172.

"We will study all the time we are gone and improve all we can," Phoebe wrote a friend. "It keeps me very busy to take 6 lessons a week and entertain in company, visit besides always helping Willie with all his lessons." [25]

In the spring of 1873, Phoebe rented out the Chestnut Street home and left with her ten-year-old son and Barry on the transcontinental railroad that had been completed only four years earlier.[26]

III. THE HEARST INVASION

PEOPLE were marveling at the luxury of crossing the nation by rail in a mere ten days. It was still an adventurous journey, with male passengers shooting buffalo and deer from the windows and keeping a sharp eye for Indians. The party broke it by stopping with relatives of Phoebe in Missouri. Another stop was made at Bloomington, Illinois, where they left the train at 3 o'clock on a miserably wet morning to visit Eliza Pike—an indication of Phoebe's kindliness and the fondness of Willie for his old nurse. They sailed from Boston on the *Adriatic* in April, with Phoebe already engrossed in a diary largely devoted to the activities and bright sayings of her son.[1]

For the average boy of ten, a year and a half in Europe would be a dreary eternity, a yearning for familiar scenes and lost playmates, a frustration at strange languages and customs, a rebellion against exotic cookery, unfamiliar beds and the rootlessness of travel. Willie Hearst was no average boy. He showed a keen interest in what he saw that saved him from boredom and denoted a maturing intellect. He had a lively sense of pity. In Dublin he was troubled by the sight of overworked horses and by a depth of poverty he had never seen in America.

"The poorer classes are so *terribly* poor," Phoebe wrote her husband. "Willie wanted to give away all his money & clothes, too, and really I felt the same way, if we could have relieved even half of them." [2]

He was fascinated by medieval Edinburgh, enjoyed tours through art galleries there and in London, and on seeing Windsor Castle uttered prescient words: "I would like to live there." [3] Despite a bout with whooping cough, he read German legends as he sailed up the Rhine with his mother and Tutor Barry. They stayed for a time in Dresden, where he was given daily German lessons and was required to speak the language at meals. He collected the amusing German *Bilderbücher*—in fact began an orgy of collecting that included stamps, coins, beer steins and porcelain, an augury of the future that Phoebe could not foresee. Far from adopting the normal boy's disdain for art, he was an enthusiastic gallery gazer, even bribing a guard in Vienna to admit him to rooms closed to juveniles. He was a precocious tourist, thoughtful, perceptive, stimulated by the treasures of the Old

[25] Mrs. Fremont Older notes, letter of Feb. 8, 1873.
[26] Bonfils, 34; Mrs. Fremont Older, *op. cit.*, 27.   [1] Bonfils, 36.
[2] Bonfils, 37.   [3] Mrs. Fremont Older, *op. cit.*, 28.

World and given plenty of money to satisfy his whims, unaware that his father meanwhile was in financial straits.[4]

However, his dedication to uplift had its limits. By the time the Hearst party reached Paris to meet Mrs. Lent and Eugene, both Willie and Eugene were spoiling for non-intellectual activity. They lived at a *pension* opposite the Tuileries Gardens. On their first day in Paris a gendarme found them catching goldfish in the Tuileries pools with bent pins, and brought them home by the ears. Confined to quarters for this, they tied a string tightly around the tail of a Persian cat owned by the *pension* keeper, a Mme. Pincée, causing the yowling animal to race around the room with some destruction to draperies. Madame Pincée had hardly been propitiated when the two boys got some alcohol and started a small experimental fire which got out of hand when the burning alcohol spilled on the floor, requiring a visit by brass-helmeted Parisian *pompiers,* who squirted enough water to add to the ruin. This time Mme. Pincée refused to be mollified, and the *sauvages Americains* were requested to pay damages and leave.[5]

The two families moved to the elegant Hôtel d'Albe on the Champs Élysées. Taking advantage of their mothers' absence on a shopping tour, the boys bought a toy *chassepot* that had unsuspected fire power, put in a cartridge and tried an upward shot that surprisingly drove the gun's ramrod deep into the ornately sculptured plaster ceiling. The concierge came upstairs and muttered at what he saw. He got on a chair, pulled hard at the ramrod, and the whole plaster ceiling fell in a cloud of dust.[6]

So there were more damages to pay. Eugene Lent later spoke admiringly of Willie's talent for mischief, crediting him with an imaginative approach that came near virtuosity. The boys toured Paris with Barry, listened to lectures on Napoleon and Charlemagne, and took fencing lessons. Willie, fascinated by the Louvre, asked his mother to buy it. The excursioners moved on to Italy, where the two parties separated, possibly on the theory that the boys were less destructive when apart. The Hearsts visited Verona, Venice, Florence and Rome, haunting the galleries, Phoebe occasionally buying statuary to send home. A letter she wrote her husband from Florence shows the educational pace she set for her son:

"While at Geneva he studied French and progressed well. I also kept up his English studies. Two days after coming here he commenced German, French and arithmetic with splendid teachers. He also takes drawing twice a week and is reading an interesting and instructive book about Italy. He has lessons three hours each day and goes out to galleries, palaces, churches. He prepares his lessons in the evening and for half an hour before dinner. Saturdays we make excursions to the various places a little in the suburbs. Sundays we go to church, in the afternoon take a delightful drive around the city or in the beautiful park. We are always busy. I like it and wish we could remain another year." [7]

[4] Winkler, *Hearst—A New Appraisal*, 25.   [5] Coblentz, *Hearst*, 16–18.
[6] The same, 19.   [7] Mrs. Fremont Older notes, letter of Dec. 10, 1873.

Phoebe's worship for learning was a little overpowering. This small frame concealed a predatory pedagogical instinct. She was absorbing culture at a fast pace and cramming it gently down her son's throat. In Rome, characteristically, she succeeded in arranging an audience with Pope Pius IX. "He was so kind and lovely, spoke altogether in French, asked where we came from," she wrote her spouse. "When he came to Willie he placed his hand on his head and blessed him . . ." [8]

That was on February 7, 1874. It was October before the Hearst pair reached Liverpool and sailed for New York. Willie had conceived a precocious interest in architecture, art and antiquities that would never leave him. He had also displayed a growing shyness with strangers, perhaps because the only person he really understood was his mother.

They reached home to find that George Hearst was at low ebb. Although he had confidence in the Ontario mine, it was still in the development stage, soaking up money instead of paying it. He took a step that must have wounded his pride, for it advertised to the world that he was in straits. He sold the Chestnut Street mansion, sold the horses and carriage, and was off to the mines again while Phoebe and Willie went to board with some friends, the Winns. [9]

Willie returned to grammar school. The fact that he attended four different San Francisco primary schools could indicate desperation among his teachers, but this is conjecture, for the school records were lost in the fire of 1906. In any case, the Hearst pinch ended gloriously in 1875 when the Ontario mine began pouring out a flood of high-grade ore, proving to be one of the most profitable silver mines in the country and making George Hearst richer than ever. [10] With a promptness indicating a distaste for boarding-house life, the Hearsts bought the imposing Graves home on Van Ness Avenue, furnished it in style, acquired a new carriage and moved back into the beau monde.

Phoebe in particular must have blessed the Utah cornucopia, for she immediately added an art gallery to the mansion to accommodate her sculpture, and began to acquire more. [11]

Ready money had a kindling effect on the whole family. George Hearst now had more time to devote to politics, being a strong Tilden-for-President man and entertaining hopes for important office himself. Phoebe, who would have scaled a precipice had Culture been at the top, could not resist the lure of the World's Fair at Philadelphia in 1876. She and Willie made the long train trip in the heat of summer, enjoyed the fair and went on to New York, where they paid a call possibly indicating that Phoebe was not averse to helping her husband's aspirations for office. They visited the Gramercy Park home of Samuel J. Tilden, then in the midst of his campaign against the Republican Hayes.

The great New Yorker talked with them pleasantly, put his hand on

[8] The same, undated letter.
[10] Farish, 216.
[9] Mrs. Fremont Older, op. cit., 35.
[11] Mrs. Fremont Older, op. cit., 36.

Willie Hearst's head and told him to be a good Democrat like his father—advice he would never precisely follow.[12]

Willie Hearst had boyhood advantages given to few, but he paid a price for them. His rearing was in the hands of his devoted but demanding mother, who pushed him too hard, forgiving almost any lapse of discipline as long as his "education" was advancing. To her, education was the answer for everything. Precociousness was forced on him. Certainly his pranks were in part the eruption of his enormous energy, but doubtless also there was in them some rebellion at the domination of his mother. In many of them—drenching Miss Estrada, stoning the Lunt hall, staging the fake fire—there was a common element: extreme aggressiveness.

By the time he was thirteen, Willie had demonstrated traits that would stay with him through life. Under his shyness was an aggressive urge for showmanship and sensation. He had a talent for manipulating people. He had a soft, feminine side—a capacity for sympathy and sentiment. If his emotions were queerly jumbled, his mind was lucid. He had the concentration of a yoga. And he had a marvelous ability at getting what he wanted.

■ The same, 37–38.

2. Willie at Large

I. THE MINERS CAME IN FORTY-NINE

SAN FRANCISCO, a city like none other in the world, had a faculty for producing citizens of marked ability, eccentricity or villainy, but who were seldom merely commonplace. Its unique atmosphere had its effect on the blond young Hearst boy.

Mushrooming from a sleepy village to a boom town in the Fifties, it was so inaccessible that only the hardy and adventurous were able to get there at all in its young years of madness, either by sea or land. Its early inhabitants were pioneers of the stamp of George Hearst, most of them coarse, some of them unprincipled, but all of them virile, aggressive and unafraid. Sheer hardship had weeded out the weak and left only the strong of both sexes, a classic example of the survival of the fittest. The children of these robust people were not inclined to be weaklings. Willie Hearst, the son of a belated Forty-niner and of a woman brimming with the same indomitable spirit, came from excellent stock. Along with the inevitable imperfections, he inherited strength and inflexible will from both.

Profit and adventure later lured to San Francisco professional men, grifters, con men, prostitutes and pimps from the East—a region loosely defined as anywhere beyond Nevada—and an influx of foreigners including Germans, French, Irish, Mexicans, Peruvians, Hawaiians and Chinese, not to mention a contingent of ruffians from the Australian penal colony. Violence, vice and harlotry throve so that San Francisco became known as the wickedest city in the world. Prostitution was regarded indulgently as a civic necessity. Some of the more gilded madams became persons of importance —an easy-going attitude expressed in a popular ditty beginning:

> *The miners came in forty-nine,*
> *The whores in fifty-one;*
> *And when they got together*
> *They produced the native son.*[1]

But if leading citizens tipped their hats to courtesans and occasionally married them, they were forced to take action on another front when the law became a joke and crimes of violence rose to such a peak that legitimate business was threatened. Irate townsmen took the law in their own hands by forming Vigilance Committees—themselves illegal—and in 1851 and 1856 performed some salutary hangings.

Although the San Francisco of Willie Hearst's boyhood had matured some-

[1] Herbert Asbury, *The Barbary Coast*, 31.

what, this is purely a relative term. The city still had a tradition of violence, the law was unreliable, citizens toted six-guns, and wholesale vice still flourished in the wide-open Barbary Coast dives near the slopes of Telegraph Hill, crowded with groggeries, dance halls and cribs where lively girls cavorted semi-nude. Less brazen prostitution resorts had opened nearer the business district, and something new in commercialized vice had been invented—the French restaurant. These haunts were strictly respectable on the ground floors, where fine food was served at high prices. The upper floors were divided into private rooms, each furnished with a table, a bed and an inside lock. The upper floors were reached by a separate entrance so that ladies and gentlemen repairing thither could do so without suffering the embarrassment of passing among the diners on the first floor.[2] Some of these restaurants boasted a cuisine so excellently prepared by French chefs that the best citizens dined there with no reflection on their character so long as they remained on the ground floor—and indeed not too much even should they wander upward.

But if San Francisco shrugged at moral laxity, it achieved a tolerance in directions other than sinful. Truly cosmopolitan if a bit provincial, it accommodated in amity people from dozens of races who had such a light-hearted flair for enjoying life with celebrations of Chinese New Year, St. Patrick's Day, Bastille Day and other festivities that it seemed in perpetual carnival. There was prosperity and a general demand for entertainment that created a thriving trade for saloons, music halls, theaters and even grand opera. The city was a world to itself, with no other town of consequence within a thousand miles. It furnished its own amusement with a zest rarely equalled, supporting a covey of noisily humorous newspapers and sustaining for twenty-one years a harmless lunatic who believed himself a king, styling himself Norton I, who was allowed to stalk the streets in an officer's uniform, to dine free at the best cafes, and to levy his own modest taxes— a straight-faced joke that persisted until the emperor died in 1880 and was buried with real regret.[3]

Willie Hearst grew up in a city sinful but gay, sentimental, vigorous and stimulating—a spirit that left its impress on him, for he remembered San Francisco with fondness all his long life. Given a considerable allowance while in grammar school, he haunted the ornate California Theater on Bush Street, saw Booth's *Hamlet,* Jefferson's *Rip Van Winkle,* Clara Morris' *Camille,* and was so smitten by Adelaide Neilson's *Juliet* that he could not sleep for two nights and was desolated when Neilson died in Paris in 1877.[4] Deeply sentimental, he could project himself into any drama and shed copious tears with the heroine. But his taste was catholic and his sense of humor vivid, for he roared at the antics of Billy Emerson's Minstrels, who appeared at the Bush Street Theater and made barbed comments on local politics, and he memorized many of the songs.[5]

[2] Oscar Lewis, *Bay Window Bohemia,* 26.   [3] Bruce, 180.
[4] Mrs. Fremont Older, *op. cit.,* 41.   [5] Winkler, *Hearst—A New Appraisal,* 28.

The stage-struck young man decided to make acting his career. The idea made Phoebe's flesh creep. To her, the stage was permissible only as an entertainment, and acting as a profession was vulgar and even a shade immoral. She had no intention of letting her son waste himself in such tawdriness. After the Hearst family moved once more, this time to a Spanish-type house on Nob Hill—the seat of the wealthy, called "Snob Hill" by the envious—Willie and his friends built a theater in the stable and presented minstrel shows and dramatic productions attended by their parents. The glamor of the stage gripped Willie like a fever. With Eugene Lent, Orrin Peck or other friends, he often dined at the vast, seven-story Palace Hotel on New Montgomery Street, San Francisco's pride, just to see actors pass through on their way to the greenroom of the California Theater nearby.[6]

George Hearst meanwhile was wandering far afield, taking a look at a new gold claim in South Dakota that excited him enough to make him spend $70,000 for an option and to close the deal for himself and his partners.[7] Occasionally he grub-staked prospectors in whom he had confidence. When three such prospectors whom he had financed went down into New Mexico Territory and found gold at Pinos Altos, Hearst, who always had to see for himself, visited Pinos Altos, gave the claim his blessing and ordered its development.[8] Roaming the lone reaches of the West for weeks at a time, often cooking over a campfire and sleeping under the stars, he yet refused to settle into easy chair and slippers when he returned to San Francisco. Although nearing sixty, he was still restless, energetic, a lover of the open who shrugged at discomforts, a man who saw opportunities in the expanding West and took pleasure in exploiting them. Occasionally he drew fees as high as $50,000 for examining mines for others. Often he took his son and the latter's friends to the Piedra Blanca ranch almost 200 miles south on San Simeon Bay, which he was stocking with cattle. There they rode, shot and fished. The South Dakota mine, now called the Homestake, gave such golden promise that in 1877 Haggin, Hearst and Tevis capitalized it at $10,000,000 and installed crushing mills.[9] Hearst, who would never again have money worries, built a wharf at San Simeon in 1878 and constructed a spacious ranch house on the slope above the sea. With the new wharf and house, the San Simeon ranch was both easier of access and more comfortable to visit, and thereafter Phoebe, the Lents and other friends often joined in excursions there.[10]

The Hearst mine in New Mexico proved a rich producer. Hearst visited it again, this time with Phoebe and Willie, to find that Pinos Altos had become a boom town, long on saloons and short on churches. Phoebe, although her own piety was of a personal sort that seldom impelled her to attend divine services, was distressed enough to find that the village had only one

[6] Mrs. Fremont Older, op. cit., 41–42.
[7] Rickard, 214.
[8] Silver City, N.M., Enterprise, Aug. 20, 1959.
[9] Rickard, 215.
[10] Mrs. Fremont Older, op. cit., 43.

church, and that Catholic, that she promptly gave funds for a community Protestant church.[11]

Indeed, the Hearsts were alike in detesting inaction, all three possessing great physical vitality that drove them in activity that would have exhausted ordinary people—an endless round that indicated also a keen enjoyment of life and a reluctance to miss anything it had to offer. In San Francisco, Phoebe's teas for the intellectuals continued. She formed an endearing habit of making discreet inquiries about poor but promising young men and giving them funds to continue their education. She was also giving thought to her own son's education. While Willie's schooling had been anything but neglected, it had been of a patchwork sort that would offend formalists. Furthermore, his willfulness argued a need for strict supervision. Undoubtedly it was Phoebe who wanted him to go to Harvard, since her husband's ideas about higher education were negligible, and probably it was she who decided to send him away to a private school that would at once curb him, prepare him for college and disengage him from his mother's apron strings—an attachment even she must have realized was too strong for his own good.

But first Europe was beckoning again. Early in 1879, Phoebe and Willie, once more with Tutor Barry in tow, crossed the country and the Atlantic for another look at the galleries. Apparently Phoebe finally overtaxed her energies, for she was ill enough to resign herself to one of Germany's curative baths and stay there while Willie, after adding to his various collections, sailed home in August with Barry and enrolled at St. Paul's School near Concord, New Hampshire.[12]

Willie, now shooting up like a weed at sixteen, hated St. Paul's. This was his first long-term separation from his mother. Although he roomed with a San Francisco friend, Will Tevis, son of his father's associate, he was lonely and homesick. Being partial to baseball, he was irked by the English game of cricket played at the school, writing scornfully about this years later. Even worse was the required attendance at three Episcopal services every day in the week. A letter he wrote his mother, still at the German baths, shows that he missed her even to the point of promising to mend his ways:

> If you get well, you shall never have anything to make you sick again, if I can help it. . . . I often think how bad I have been and how many unkind words I have said, and I am sure that when you come back I will . . . never be so bad again. . . . The only thing that comforts me is that the time is getting shorter every day till you will be here.[13]

Phoebe returned in November, visited him at school, and during the holidays took him to Cambridge for a glimpse of Harvard, then to New York. When she returned to California, the boy found the bleak New Eng-

---

[11] Silver City, N.M., *Enterprise*, Aug. 20, 1959.   [12] Carlson and Bates, 39.
[13] Mrs. Fremont Older, *op. cit.*, 44–45.

land winter endless. Occasionally he went to New York to spend a weekend with an uncle of Orrin Peck's, one Mr. Hughes. He finished his first year and went back for a second only under compulsion. The young man was so accustomed to the benign freedom of San Francisco that the stern Yankee-Episcopalian discipline at St. Paul's outraged him. To escape the master's clutches even briefly was an objective worth any effort. He wrote to Hughes in New York, asking politely if he could be invited there for the holidays. Hughes neglected to reply promptly, and Willie sent him a telegram telling in eight desperate words his horror of St. Paul's:

"For God's sake please ask me to New York." [14]

He was invited. But his exile in New Hampshire was almost over, for he left the school by request early in 1881, probably because of some prank.[15] He returned to San Francisco and resumed his studies under private tutors.

Meanwhile, George Hearst had been contributing to the Democrats, loaning money to the moribund, Democratic San Francisco *Examiner,* and letting it be known that he was not averse to office. In October, 1880, because the *Examiner* could not repay him and also because he felt that outright ownership of a political organ would be beneficial, he bought the paper and took steps to improve it. He hired Emanuel Katz away from the local *Chronicle* as general manager, enlarged the staff, paid his men liberally and moved them from a small shop on Sacramento Street to larger quarters on Market Street. Willie Hearst, now having nothing more formidable than tutors to escape, must have visited the *Examiner* frequently and got his first close whiff of printer's ink, but there is no record that he was instantly fascinated.[16]

For some reason he was opposed to his father's political ambitions. He might as well have tried to stem an avalanche, for George Hearst had set his heart on becoming United States Senator and was ready to roll logs and spend money to get the seat he yearned for. He had secured the support of the San Francisco Democratic machine, bossed by Chris Buckley, a blind politician and saloonkeeper who knew all his friends by their handshake. In June, 1882, Hearst made his bid for the Democratic nomination for the governorship with his quaint remarks about spelling. He looked on the governorship as an easy step into the Senate. California political morality was of the earthiest kind, and it was said that delegates were bought like schooners of beer in the midst of undercover jockeying for the support of the Southern Pacific Railroad, which had emerged as a potent and malign influence. Hearst made a speech opposing the railroad monopoly, but his enemies claimed that this was merely for popular consumption and that his agents were busily wooing the "S.P." If so, the strategy failed, for Hearst was defeated in a close race by General George Stoneman, the former Union cavalry leader.

[14] The same, 45.   [15] *The American Magazine,* Nov., 1906.
[16] John P. Young, *Journalism in California,* 126; G. R. Katz to author, Dec. 15, 1959; *Pearson's Magazine,* Sept., 1906.

It was a bitter disappointment. Hearst supported Stoneman in his successful campaign for the governorship but began a series of attacks on the S.P. in his *Examiner*. It was said that he now aimed to leap into the Senate without any intervening step, and was carefully cementing his political alliances to that end.[17]

Not even money could soothe him, for Homestake was coming in strong, and on the recommendation of an old mining friend, Marcus Daly, he and his partners, Haggin and Tevis, spent $30,000 for a small silver mine in Montana, the Anaconda. In 1882 the busy Hearst visited the mine, which was only sixty feet deep, looked it over, and was so sanguine about its silver-producing possibilities that he "recommended deep development, for which he selected the place of a new shaft." [18] Hearst was as surprised as anyone when the shaft disclosed not only a satisfying amount of silver but also the richest vein of copper anyone had ever set eyes on. This was like tripping and falling into wealth. While it was true that Hearst was an indefatigable worker, intrepid in his roaming of the West when travel meant danger and hardship which his soft, office-sitting partners, Haggin and Tevis, never endured, and was keen in his judgment of mines, he was also one of the luckiest men in creation. Yet he was so well liked that few begrudged him his good fortune. One mining expert commented:

> It is a remarkable fact that this group of enterprising men [Hearst, Haggin and Tevis] should have happened to select three of the best mines in the United States: the Ontario, the Anaconda, and the Homestake.[19]

Willie Hearst was in that awkward stage between childhood and manhood, suffering from a shyness that must have been aggravated by the failure of his soft voice to deepen. He sounded childish while some of his smaller companions were speaking in manly bass. Yet he had something of a connoisseur's eye for girls. On a visit to the Southern Pacific's big resort hotel, the Del Monte, at romantic Monterey, he became infatuated with Sybil Sanderson, daughter of a state supreme court justice who lived in San Francisco. Sybil, a dashing brunette, impetuously became engaged to him.[20]

But the Sandersons had plans for Sybil, whose singing voice showed promise, and they wanted no youthful passion to blight her career. They shipped her off to Paris for further study. Willie took it philosophically, writing his mother after a later trip:

> On the train I saw the prettiest girl. Every love including Sybil sank into the dimness of obscurity when the fair unknown beamed upon me. When she smiled my poor little intoxicated heart butted up against my ribs in a way that I fear has permanently injured it, flattening it out probably till it looks like a Dutch pancake.
> Why can't a fellow go through life without being continually led like a lamb to the slaughter, a sacrifice to beauty? Why can't he see the *prettiest*

[17] Edith Dobie, *The Political Career of Stephen Mallory White*, 40–41.
[18] Rickard, 352.   [19] Rickard, 351.   [20] Mrs. Fremont Older, *op. cit.*, 46.

girl first so that all the others forever after will seem tame and homely . . . ? Whether my battered heart would ever resume its wonted state is a different matter, but after mature deliberation I have concluded that I should not be surprised if it did. It is rather elastic as a rule, and in that respect it is *very much* like a Dutch pancake.[21]

Willie was susceptible, but he could write his mother about it and could even poke fun at his own susceptibility.

II. ALLIGATORS, JACKASSES AND CHAMBER POTS

WHEN William Randolph Hearst entered Harvard at nineteen in the fall of 1882, he was a tall, slender, gangling, pink-and-white young man with big feet and hands and a voice of such girlish timbre that it seemed that there must be a ventriloquist in the offing. He was escorted by his five-foot mother, who was concerned enough to cross the broad continent with him to see him installed. Probably she sensed that in her affection she had failed to prepare him for this crisis. No other children had come to her, which was unfortunate for Willie.

To her, his success at college was of high importance. She knew that he had keen intelligence and that if he applied himself he could sail through his courses with ease. But Willie was different, a nonconformist. He was still Mamma's boy in a way, a devoted son who made no secret of his fondness for the little woman who had dedicated almost two decades to the proposition that he had enormous talent, taught him, traveled with him, molded him for what she felt sure would be greatness of some kind. Yet he also had some of his father's independence of mind and contempt for convention. On top of that was his known willfulness and resentment of discipline—traits that must have given Mrs. Hearst uneasy visions of professors glued to their chairs, and firecrackers popping at chapel.

Harvard took itself seriously and would not put up with that sort of thing. Mrs. Hearst lingered in Cambridge for several days, undoubtedly pouring advice into Willie's ear as she supervised the decoration of his room in Matthews Hall, equipping it with furniture and a choice library. When she returned to San Francisco, Harvard had on its hands a student it would never quite appreciate, even unto his maturity, fame, notoriety and death.[1]

Young Hearst settled down to a period of misery. He was homesick. San Francisco meant a joyous freedom largely woven out of his mother's ability to accede to his whims. Cambridge meant classes on the hour, regulations, rollcalls, assignments, regimentation. Harvard bristled with distinguished professors such as Josiah Royce, William James and Barrett Wendell, but who among them could take the place of Mamma?

"I am beginning to get awfully tired of this place," he wrote his mother after only a few weeks, "and I long to get out west somewhere where I can

---

[21] Mrs. Fremont Older notes, undated letter.   [1] Mrs. Fremont Older, *op. cit.*, 48.

stretch myself without coming in contact with the narrow walls with which the prejudice of the bean eaters has surrounded us. I long to get out in the woods and breathe the fresh mountain air and listen to the moaning of the pines. It makes me almost crazy with homesickness when I think of it. I hate this weak, pretty New England scenery with its gentle rolling hills, its pea green foliage, its vistas, tame enough to begin with but totally disfigured by houses and barns which could not be told apart save for the respective inhabitants. I hate it as I do a weak pretty face without force or character. I long to see our own woods, the jagged rocks and towering mountains, the majestic pines, the grand impressive scenery of the far West. I shall never live anywhere but in California, I like to be away for a while only to appreciate it the more when I return." [2]

Hearst in theory parted his blond hair in the middle, but often it cascaded chrysanthemum fashion. His long-oval face was bisected by a straight blade of a nose that plunged from his high forehead right into his silky mustache. Strangers were startled by his eyes, blue-gray in color but with the irises swimming in whites so large as to give a staring effect—an impression accentuated by his habit of looking directly, with the most unwavering concentration, at anyone speaking with him. Despite his shyness, he ran to showy plaids and screaming neckties. All this, combined with the soprano voice that issued from his deep chest, doubtless brought him a deal of ragging in the Yard. [3]

Luckily, his good friend Eugene Lent, who had helped him test the Paris firemen, was a year ahead of him at Harvard. Another Californian, John Gilbert Follansbee of Oakland, was a classmate. With this cushion of friendship, Hearst gradually formed a small circle of intimates who found him full of generous impulses, not averse to beer, always ready for a lark, and shockingly careless in the way he spent the big allowance that came from home. [4]

He was given more money than was good for any collegian. The openhanded George Hearst, who gave away twenty-dollar gold pieces, bet thousands at poker and gave thousands more to the Democratic party, was not inclined to stint his son, whom he called "Billy Buster." One of the jokes at Harvard was that William Hearst received regularly a fist-sized gold nugget from his father's mines. [5]

An indifferent student, Willie enjoyed the theater and never missed an opportunity to go by carriage with a group of cronies to presentations in Boston. On one such occasion they carried custard pies into their box at the Howard Atheneum and pelted the performers with them. On another, Hearst and Lent returned from Boston in a hack, hurling oranges at policemen they passed en route. Hearst somewhere acquired a small alligator, which he christened Champagne Charlie, occasionally making calls with the reptile in tow. The nickname was not merely jocular, for he gave Charlie

[2] Mrs. Fremont Older notes, undated letter.   [3] Carlson and Bates, 40–41.
[4] Coblentz, Hearst, 23.   [5] Winkler, W. R. Hearst—An American Phenomenon, 55.

libations of wine so that the alligator was frequently drunk, and its erratic locomotion and rakish eye became a campus entertainment. Doubtless Charlie got more attention than the textbooks, for in his first year Hearst took Latin and Greek among other courses, disliking the classic languages so much that he dropped them both and tried Philosophy, which he also disliked and dropped.[6] German, of course, came easy for him. A classmate described him as a young man of "amiable indolence broken by spasms of energy," noting, "Yet he had enormous power of application for a brief period, and he was capable of learning enough of a text-book in a night to pass an examination." [7]

His forte was clearly in the field of practical jokes. But in his second year he demonstrated that he could muster a similar enthusiasm for constructive projects if they challenged his interest.

This came about because of the unhappy dilemma of his friend Lent, who was business manager of the *Lampoon,* a position then regarded as more of a liability than an honor. The humor magazine, then in its early years, was a chronic loser. It was the duty of the business manager to cut its losses as much as possible and pay whatever deficit remained out of his own pocket. Lent, whose wealthy parents gave him only a limited allowance, was in dire financial trouble when Hearst took the job off his hands to help him out. Hearst's huge allowance made him the obvious man for the post, and doubtless the *Lampoon* staff looked on him with satisfaction as nothing more than a droll fellow with a thick wallet.

However, although money meant nothing to him, he refused to be a mere catspaw. He attacked the problem with energy and ingenuity. As a heavy buyer of neckties and other haberdashery, he was already acquainted with several shopkeepers in Cambridge, to whom he sold advertisements. He organized a group of student solicitors, gave them lists of establishments in Cambridge and Boston, and sold more space. He sent promotional letters to Harvard men and to friends, one of them even going to his mother, whom he urged to be a sort of California agent, writing, "The *Lampoon* ought to be supported by Harvard men with contributions and subscriptions." [8] He launched a circulation drive. The Hearst program was so successful that the magazine actually began to show a profit, and "the students had to have frequent banquets to keep the surplus down." [9]

His labors for the *Lampoon* gave him a new curiosity about the *Examiner,* which was sent to him from San Francisco and which he scanned with disapproval, regarding it as badly edited. He developed a keen interest in newspapers, studying the Boston and New York dailies and discovering a real admiration for the noisy New York *World,* which had recently been purchased by Joseph Pulitzer and was striking out in startling journalistic directions. He got a letter of introduction to Colonel Charles H. Taylor, pro-

[6] The same, 58–59; Coblentz, *Hearst,* 22; Mrs. J. M. Flint to author.
[7] *Collier's,* Sept. 22, 1906.   [8] Mrs. Fremont Older, *op. cit.,* 49–50.
[9] *Pearson's Magazine,* Sept., 1906.

prietor of the Boston *Globe,* and visited the *Globe* repeatedly to study it from city room to pressroom.[10]

The shrinking, self-conscious Hearst tried hard for success in the important college realm of good fellowship. He took to smoking cigarettes and even cigars. Follansbee and Lent remained his best friends, and if it took stern effort for him to relax with others, he made the effort, winning acceptance among some of the staff of the *Lampoon,* which numbered such outstanding men as George Santayana, Hammond Lamont and Grover Flint. The discriminating Santayana admired Hearst's business enterprise, but disliked his extravagance. Hearst rented a room, equipped it with a long table, chairs and a stove, as well as the latest issues of the *Vie Parisienne* and other exotic publications, and presented it to the *Lampoon* staff, giving each member a key. Santayana, thinking this a crude effort to buy friends, refused to use his key. Hearst, he said, was "invaluable" to the *Lampoon,* but "He was little esteemed in the College." [11]

But this was the judgment of a choosy intellectual. While Hearst seemed to lack a true sense of taste, and was a trifle obvious in his efforts to push himself forward, his old landlady was utterly charmed by his kindness and courtesy. He was a complex young man, not easily classifiable, who puzzled his mates. No conventional intellectual, he yet had a first-class mind. Occasionally languid, he was frequently driven by seizures of furious energy. His painful shyness could not subdue his urge for self-expression and recognition. He had the courage to wrestle with what must have approximated terror when he appeared in college theatricals, always in comic roles—a big man with such a squeaky voice could hardly have essayed anything serious—ranging from a mock temperance lecture to an impersonation of Sir Henry Irving. His strong sense of humor constantly warred with his reticence and often won out. He could yodel wonderfully. Occasionally he had friends in his room for midnight snacks, cooking Welsh rabbit for them and sometimes unbending enough to sing comic songs, twitching his long legs expertly in a darktown shuffle recalled from the minstrel shows he had seen. He was elected to Hasty Pudding. His athletic ability was nil, but he had decided talents of his own that commanded respect—a capacity for organization and leadership hidden behind a deceptively retiring façade and rendered further attractive because he was so polite, so considerate, so outwardly unimpressed by the fact that he had money to throw away.[12] He threw it away and wrote for more, knowing that he would have his way. One of his letters to his mother read in part:

> And now to end with the customary plea—give me a penny for bread.
> . . . My financial condition is the same as usual. I am busted. And what
> is more I have been busted for days. . . . My trip to New York bored a
> big hole in my allowance and a loan of $70.00 finished me. Gene [Eugene

[10] *Collier's,* Feb. 18, 1911; Winkler, W. R. *Hearst—An American Phenomenon,* 59.
[11] George Santayana, *Persons and Places,* 198.
[12] Mrs. Fremont Older, *op. cit.,* 52; Winkler, *Hearst—An American Phenomenon,* 55.

Lent] and I are in the same boat. Too proud to borrow, too sensible to bet. We were reduced to the last resources of the poor—we spouted our watch. I say we—I should say *he*. And *we* divided the spoils. For twenty—a paltry sum, but it seemed a fortune in our eyes. Ten dollars apiece. Why we were millionaires! We got reckless and went to the theatre afterwards. We got wildly extravagant and had a supper and a bottle of ale—a whole bottle of ale. And we returned to Cambridge busted, and we remained so ever since. But I never had quite so much fun.[13]

Hearst, had he half tried, could have made a spectacular success at Harvard. But the young man who had never been disciplined continued to resent discipline. He gave his attention only to those courses he enjoyed, neglecting the others. He clashed with faculty advisors because they forbade the *Lampoon's* use of a libelous cartoon of Professor Charles Eliot Norton.[14]

Authority of any kind provoked him to automatic protest. He was a shy show-off. Quiet in manner, anything but the typical, noisy campus cut-up, nevertheless he loved to stage roaring political parades replete with beer, firecrackers and music, and he added to his reputation as a practical joker. He went about this work with earnest inventiveness, planning his productions with an eye for theatrical effect and never allowing mere cost to interfere with success. Champagne Charlie, who had succumbed to alcoholism, had been stuffed and hung in his room. Hearst wrote to the Kaiser, describing himself as president of the nonexistent "Medical Faculty Society," informed him that he had been elected an honorary member, and was delighted to receive a "beautiful set of surgical instruments" from the monarch.[15] It was said that on one occasion he bought a jackass, brushed and groomed it, and managed to spirit it into a professor's room so that when the pedagogue returned he found the animal waiting with a ribbon around its neck to which was attached a card reading, "Now there are two of you." [16]

In 1884, in his junior year, Hearst showed his bent for politics by taking his third course in political economy. That fall, he took part in a Hasty Pudding production, *Joan of Arc, or the Old Maid of New Orleans*, playing the role of a German valet named Pretzel, "an interesting cuss with a penchant for legerdemain," and afterwards using more of the limitless Hearst funds to give a party for the Hasty Pudding group.

That same fall, now being twenty-one, he cast his first vote for the Democrat Cleveland against the Republican Blaine. Early reports indicated that Blaine was elected, but when the vote was in, Cleveland was the winner— the first Democratic Presidential victory since the Civil War. Hearst was the moving spirit and the moneybags behind a celebration that went on all night. He hired a brass band from Boston, bought fireworks, had Fred Briggs, a *Lampoon* artist, paint enormous portraits of Cleveland and Hen-

[13] Mrs. Fremont Older notes, undated letter.   [14] Mrs. Fremont Older, *op. cit.*, 52.
[15] N. Y. *Times*, Oct. 3, 1902.   [16] G. R. Katz to author, Dec. 15, 1959.

dricks on a banner which was then strung across the street, and organized a parade and a flag-raising at Holyoke and Mt. Auburn Streets. There was punch, probably not innocent of alcohol, and there was continuous noise. According to one historian, Hearst "bought wagon-loads of beer, set off fireworks in all directions, and raised such a red-blazing, ear-splitting, rip-roaring, all-night racket as to scandalize old Cambridge." [17] During the night, the roysterers somehow obtained several dozens of roosters, which were placed in the Yard, setting up a mass crowing at dawn that awakened students and professors.

Probably there was some impulsive property damage during the night. Willie Hearst, already viewed with disapproval, was rusticated from Harvard.[18]

He loved a good show at any cost, and there is no record that he was conscience-stricken. Having developed a keen interest in politics, he decided that it would be useful to spend the time of his suspension in Washington. His mother, much upset by his conflict with the dean, determined that Willie would have her help. She went to Washington and took a house so that he would be under her wing while he served his penance and pursued his political studies. George Hearst was still frequently absent, once on a trip to Mexico, where he became acquainted with President Porfirio Diaz and cheaply bought title to a thousand square miles of land in Vera Cruz, Campeche and Yucatan, and a million-acre ranch, known as the Babicora, in Chihuahua.[19] Phoebe had San Francisco friends in the capital, among them Senator Leland Stanford and wife. California's other Senator, John T. Miller, was seriously ill, and probably it was already known that Hearst was slated to replace him should he die. In the winter of 1884–1885, Willie and his mother were the advance guard for one of the nation's more picturesque Senators.

From Washington, Willie wrote his father a long letter that had moments of extravagance in expression but demonstrated an astonishing grasp of the newspaper business:

> Dear Father: I have just finished and dispatched a letter to the Editor of the *Examiner* in which I recommended Eugene Lent to his favorable notice, and commented on the illustrations, if you may call them such, which have lately disfigured the paper.
>
> I really believe that the *Examiner* has furnished what is thus far the crowning absurdity in illustrated Journalism, in illustrating an article on the chicken show by means of the identical Democratic roosters used during the late campaign.
>
> In my letter to the editor, however, I did not refer to this for fear of offending him, but I did tell him that in my opinion the cuts that have recently appeared in the paper bore an unquestionable resemblance to the Cuticura

[17] *Pearson's Magazine*, Sept., 1906.
[18] Florence Finch Kelly, *Flowing Stream*, 239–40; Carlson and Bates, 42.
[19] Carlson and Bates, 13–14.

Soap advertisements; and I am really inclined to believe that our editor has illustrated many of his articles from his stock on hand of cuts representing gentlemen before and after using that efficacious remedy.

In case my remarks should have no effect, and he should continue in his career of desolation, let me beg of you to remonstrate with him and thus prevent him from giving the finishing stroke to our miserable little sheet.

I have begun to have a strange fondness for our little paper—a tenderness like unto that which a mother feels for a puny or deformed offspring, and I should hate to see it die now after it had battled so long and so nobly for existence; in fact, to tell the truth, I am possessed of the weakness which at some time or other of their lives pervades most men; I am convinced that I could run a newspaper successfully.

Now if you should make over to me the *Examiner*—with enough money to carry out my schemes—I'll tell you what I would do!

In the first place I would change the general appearance of the paper and make seven wide columns where we now have nine narrow ones, then I would have the type spaced more, and these two changes would give the pages a much cleaner and neater appearance.

Secondly, it would be well to make the paper as far as possible original, to clip only when absolutely necessary and to imitate only some such leading journal as the New York *World* which is undoubtedly the best paper of that class to which the *Examiner* belongs—that class which appeals to the people and which depends for its success upon enterprise, energy and a certain startling originality and not upon the wisdom of its political opinions or the lofty style of its editorials: And to accomplish this we must have—as the *World* has—active, intelligent and energetic young men; we must have men who come out West in the hopeful buoyancy of youth for the purposes of making their fortunes and not a worthless scum that has been carried there by the eddies of repeated failures.

Thirdly, we must advertise the paper from Oregon to New Mexico and must also increase our number of advertisements if we have to lower our rates to do it, thus we can put on the first page that our circulation is such and our advertisements so and so and constantly increasing.

And now having spoken of the three great essential points let us turn to details.

The illustrations are a detail, though a very important one. Illustrations embellish a page; illustrations attract the eye and stimulate the imagination of the masses and materially aid the comprehension of an unaccustomed reader and thus are of particular importance to that class of people which the *Examiner* claims to address. Such illustrations, however, as have heretofore appeared in the paper nauseate rather than stimulate the imagination and certainly do anything but embellish a page.

Another detail of questionable importance is that we actually or apparently establish some connection between ourselves and the New York *World,* and obtain a certain prestige in bearing some relation to that paper. We might contract to have important private telegrams forwarded or something of that sort, but understand that the principal advantage we are to derive is from the attention that such a connection would excite and from the advertisement we could make of it. Whether the *World* would consent to such an arrangement for any reasonable sum is very doubtful, for its net profit is over one thousand dollars a day and no doubt it would consider the *Examiner* is beneath its notice. Just think, over one thousand dollars a day and four years ago it belonged to Jay Gould and was losing money rapidly.

And now to close with a suggestion of great consequence, namely, that all these changes be made not by degrees but at once so that the improvement will be very marked and noticeable and will attract universal attention and comment.

There is little to be said about my studies. . . . Congress is as stupid as it is possible to conceive of. . . .

Well, good-by. I have given up all hope of having you write to me. . . . By the way, I heard you had bought 2,000 acres of land the other day and I hope some of it was the land adjoining our ranch that I begged you to buy in my last letter.

> Your affectionate son,
> W. R. Hearst [20]

If George Hearst read the letter carefully, he must have been aware that Billy Buster had put more serious thought on newspapers than on anything else in his life.

William attended sessions of Congress. He visited Mount Vernon and Monticello. He boned up on American history, developing a devotion to Jefferson that persisted throughout his life. With his mother he saw the inauguration of Cleveland, the new President being unaware of the collegian's Cambridge sacrifice for him.

Another visitor in Washington was Eleanor Calhoun, a Californian from Tulare County who had gone to San Francisco, scored some success as a dramatic actress, and become a protégée of the Haggins and Tevises. Naturally she was a guest at the Hearst home. Miss Calhoun was a slender, poised beauty, a descendant of the great John C. Calhoun, so determined to win fame in Shakespearean roles that she wanted to go to London for further study. The susceptible William, always fascinated by the theater, eyed her with interest. He enjoyed Washington enough to feel that a second Hearst home there would be pleasant, especially since his father would eventually be a Senator. Indeed, he was considering the idea of running for Congress himself. He scouted around the city for a suitable dwelling, found one he liked, and wrote his father about it in half-humorous vein:

> . . . . I have been on the lookout for a suitable residence for the Senator and Congressman that are to be and I think I have succeeded in finding the very thing. . . . It must be imposing but unassuming. . . . the interior must possess comfort, and yet not display that arrogance of wealth that is so offensive to the people. And here again our house is marvelously complete. Moreover, it possesses still another attraction. It is surrounded on all sides by land belonging to us, and this gives the impression that we might have

[20] Reprinted in N. Y. *Journal-American*, Mar. 4, 1947.

built a larger house had we so desired, but that with true democratic humility we have limited ourselves to the existing, modest structure. . . .

But seriously, if our affairs have reached a condition such that we may afford the luxury of a home there is no better place for the location of that home than Washington. The climate is delightful, and then the society there is composed neither of wealthy boors nor of aristocratic imbeciles, but of men of science and letters and is therefore well worth cultivating. . . . there is no house in the city which is so admirably adapted to our wants or so completely satisfying to our ideas of perfection as the one in question.

The property includes the lot on which the house stands (106 x 106 feet), the house and furniture, the stable and the lot on which the stable stands, all of which may be had for the disgustingly small sum of $159,000. Or if you would bargain over a mere trifle, perhaps for $150,000. If sold three per cent ought to accrue to your affectionate son—

W. R. Hearst [21]

In both letters to his father, the young man betrayed a touch of cynicism and expediency in his maneuvers to satisfy "the people." Meanwhile, he had fallen in love with Eleanor Calhoun. He sent her a barrage of flowers, called on her incessantly, and so charmed her that they became engaged.

Phoebe was alarmed. Miss Calhoun was three years older than William and was an actress, a profession regarded as not far removed from sinfulness. Mrs. Hearst had an impression that the girl was more interested in the Hearst millions than in Willie himself. Phoebe set her son on a high pedestal, and doubtless envisioned his later marriage to some young lady of distinguished family and high cultural attainments. Miss Calhoun, for all her charm and talent, did not fulfill the specifications.

Mrs. Hearst knew better than to put her foot down. Instead, she arranged a tête-à-tête with William and Eleanor reminiscent of a Victorian novel, spoke to them with sweet logic and suggested that their love would keep if they postponed marriage until her son finished college. It was said that, unknown to William, she added an incentive by subsidizing Miss Calhoun's trip to Europe for dramatic study. The arrangement was agreed on, and the infatuated William unhappily went along with a compromise that sounded the knell of his second "serious" romance.[22]

Returning to Harvard in the spring of 1885, he continued his off-campus study of newspapers. He chanced to read about an incident that stuck in his mind. A hotel saloonkeeper of East Cambridge named Sullivan and his son had a scuffle with an abusive drinker, who fell heavily, later died, and both Sullivans were charged with manslaughter.

Tall, black-haired, pleasure-loving Jack Follansbee was being sent to Harvard by his uncle, James R. Keene, a California mining promoter who had become a spectacular Wall Street operator. Follansbee lived luxuriously at college, even to the extent of taking a mistress, a pretty thing named Tessie

[21] Mrs. Fremont Older notes, undated letter.
[22] Mrs. J. M. Flint to author, Jan. 18, 1960.

Powers, who had been a waitress in a Cambridge restaurant. When Keene suffered a speculative disaster, Follansbee's handsome allowance was cut off. Hearst wrote his father pleading for financial support for Follansbee that was not forthcoming, and Follansbee was forced to leave college. This left Miss Powers unprovided for, so Hearst took over her care and maintenance. It was said that Follansbee himself, concerned about the girl, suggested this, and in any case Hearst developed a real fondness for her. Tessie had been stricken by repeated family misfortunes which touched his sympathies. Since he was in arrears in course credits and also eyed warily by the college authorities, much like a convict on parole, this romantic affair was academically unsound.

He had established a reputation for horseplay that he perhaps felt it a point of pride to maintain. His pranks in his last year at Harvard are not specifically recorded, but it is said that he put creative thought on them. When he telegraphed his father urgently requesting $2000, the elder Hearst, fearful that his son was in a scrape, sent it at once—a further example of his gambler's carelessness with money. He learned with relief that Willie was in no scrape at all just then, but wanted the money to buy a rare edition of Alexander Hamilton's *Federalist Papers* to add to his collection of books.[23]

The scrape came soon thereafter. A messenger called at the home of each of his instructors, leaving a large package which, when opened, proved to contain a chamber pot with the recipient's name ornamentally lettered on the inside bottom. Perhaps Hearst did not deliberately plan his dismissal from Harvard, but it cannot be said that he tried earnestly to stay, and the effect was the same. He was expelled without quite having finished his junior year.[24]

III. LAYING THE PIPES

EXPULSION from college was the first of a series of occasional disappointments and shocks Phoebe Hearst would suffer at the hands of her unpredictable son. She wept bitterly over it. She tried vainly to get him reinstated. George Hearst was less upset until William made it plain once more that his chief interest was journalism.

"I want the San Francisco *Examiner*," he said.

"Great God!" Hearst exploded. "Haven't I spent money enough on that paper already? I took it for a bad debt and it's a sure loser. Instead of holding it for my own son, I've been saving it up to give to an enemy." [1]

In real annoyance, he consulted Thomas Williams, business manager of the *Examiner*.

[23] Mrs. William Randolph Hearst to author, May 15, 1959.
[24] *Social Frontier*, Feb., 1935. It has been erroneously published that Hearst was expelled in his senior year. Kimball C. Elkins of the Harvard University Archives, without giving details, informs me that Hearst did not return for his senior year.
[1] *Pearson's Magazine*, Sept., 1906.

"Tom," he said, "suppose a man made a success of a newspaper; a great success, greater than anybody else—how much would he make at it?"

"Oh," Williams hazarded, "a hundred thousand a year."

"Hell!" Hearst snapped. "That ain't no money." [2]

He took his son, along with Eugene Lent and Jack Follansbee, on a trip to the vast Babicora ranch in Mexico. Babicora, located on four high plateaus separated by mountain ranges, employed hundreds of vaqueros to care for its herds. Hearst offered the ranch to William and a supervisory job to Follansbee. Follansbee accepted with alacrity, but William declined.

"I could never learn to manage that business better than anybody else," he said.[3]

He likewise refused the managership of any of the other Hearst ranches, or of the great Anaconda and Homestake mines. In George Hearst's eyes, his son was rejecting certain success in favor of certain failure. Often puzzled by him, Hearst had once uttered a homely truth:

"There's only one thing that's sure about my boy Bill. I've been watching him and notice that when he wants cake, he wants cake, and he wants it now. And I notice that after a while he gets the cake." [4]

Hearst touched on one of the young man's basic traits. William was not one of those who want something vaguely but recognize it as beyond reach and give up the quest. He refused to let obstacles deter him. When he wanted anything, he wanted it insistently, heart and soul, with a downright craving that made him resort to extremes of labor, planning and maneuvering to get it. His admirers would later call this determination. His enemies would call it selfishness. His whole life would be a series of wants which he labored to fulfill, some of them seemingly extravagant and unplausible, such as the Presidency and a castle of his own, but none of them in his own highly aggressive and optimistic mind at all beyond reach.

Now his want was comparatively modest: the *Examiner*. An expert at getting his own way, he had no doubt that he could eventually bring his father around. He wanted the *Examiner* because he felt supremely confident of his ability to handle it, light it like a huge firecracker, wake up San Francisco with a series of explosions, and incidentally do some good. Realizing that all he lacked was newspaper experience, he set out to get it with that directness of action that always marked him. In what should have been his senior year at Harvard, he went to New York and got a job as a reporter for the *World*.[5]

If a man can be in love with a newspaper, Hearst was downright passionate about the *World*. Pulitzer had aimed it straight at the masses, infusing it with a strange blend of sensationalism and idealism, plugging murder and scandal but at the same time exposing monopolies, hammering at injustice and corruption and maintaining a liberal attitude in politics. Conservative New Yorkers thought it abysmally cheap and vulgar. Hearst thought it so brilliant

[2] *American Magazine*, Nov., 1906.   [3] The same.   [4] The same.
[5] Coblentz, *Hearst*, 31.

that it made other papers look antique—particularly since Pulitzer in three years had raised its circulation from 15,000 to 250,000 and brought it out of the red to pay enormous profits.

It irked him that the *Examiner* should be a loser. He blamed this on his father's willingness to take the loss in return for the paper's help as his personal political organ, and also on the old man's amateurishness in journalism.

He seems to have spent about a year in New York, a period for which the records are skimpy. Whether he had Tessie Powers with him is unknown, but it seems likely that he did, for their affair was far from finished. Like his father, he had a maverick disregard for convention which in him was most noticeable in his relations with women. A cheerful hedonist, he took Tessie just as he would take anything he wanted or enjoyed, but apparently he was faithful and kind to her.

When Senator Miller died in mid-March, 1886, Governor Stoneman appointed George Hearst to fill the post. He hastened to Washington with Phoebe to take the seat he so prized, even though it would be only for a few months. Willie went down from New York to visit his parents, and the proud new Senator made it a point to take his son with him to call on President Cleveland.[6]

If Tessie was with Hearst in New York, she doubtless had plenty of leisure, for he possessed astonishing energy and dedication for any project that interested him. At the *World,* he conceived a reverence for the ability of Ballard Smith, one of the editors. Immediately he wrote his father urging that he hire Smith to run the *Examiner,* admitting that he would command at least $7,000 a year. George Hearst replied that such an expense was out of the question. His son demolished this argument in another letter:

> . . . The objection to Mr. Ballard Smith is, that he is high-priced. You must reconcile yourself to paying the salary or give up the *Examiner.* It has been conclusively proven that poor wages and mediocre talent will not do, and the only thing that remains to be tried is first-class talent and corresponding wages. You could not even sell the paper at present, so I think this is the only thing to be done. Mr. Ballard Smith will state his terms and I would say, "Mr. Smith, I guarantee you this amount and I promise you a certain interest in the paper in case you make a glittering success. You are to have entire control of the paper, Mr. Smith, with the privilege of employing whomever you please." [7]

That is, Mr. Smith could employ anyone he pleased with the exception of William Hearst, who would most certainly boss Mr. Smith. But George Hearst still resisted the expensive Smith—in fact, still resisted the idea of his son undertaking the hare-brained business of journalism. As for Phoebe, she entertained hopes that Willie would become a diplomat. Willie held his ground, sending written propaganda to his father as he continued his New York apprenticeship. He persuaded his father to broaden the *Examiner's*

[6] Edith Dobie, 64; Coblentz, 31.   [7] Mrs. Fremont Older, *op. cit.,* 64.

news coverage by subscribing to the New York *Herald* telegraph service. He studied the witty New York *Sun,* the conservative *Tribune,* the peppery *Herald,* the thoughtful *Evening Post,* and above all the noisy *World,* always with an eye for the formula that would cure the ailing *Examiner.*[8] In the face of the opposition of both his parents, and despite his knowledge that he could choose a hand-me-down career of certain ease and profit in mining, ranching or real estate, he showed an independence of mind unusual in rich men's sons when he picked the riskiest and least honored profession of all, journalism, because he loved it and would continue to love it for sixty-six years.

In 1885, shortly before Hearst joined the staff, the *World* had moved him to admiration with a demonstration of what energetic journalism could do. The Statue of Liberty, France's gift to America, had arrived, only to have a laggard Congress fail to appropriate enough funds for a pedestal. While the copper goddess lay unassembled in packing cases, the *World* launched a blaring five-month campaign for funds, even collecting nickels and dimes from children to raise the needed $100,000. Hearst may well have witnessed the unveiling of the statue in New York harbor on October 28, 1886, and viewed it as a revelation of the power of the press.

The college jokester was charmed by Pulitzer's circus-parade tactics, but he saw honest purpose underneath. For a young man who had spent $2000 for a book and sizeable sums for fireworks, brass bands, donkeys and chamber pots, he had an incongruous ideal of public service and a sympathy for the underdog. The Hearstian social consciousness was impulsive and immature, arising from compassionate observation rather than from the hard experience of one who had been an underdog himself, but it was sincere, springing from a heart easily touched. Unfortunately, it would have to grapple with a compulsive ego, a vaulting ambition and a passion for display so that there would always be some question which would win out.

But young Hearst, at twenty-three, was quite satisfied to picture himself as the Pulitzer of the West, leading the *Examiner* in a crusade for the purification of California, and incidentally having plenty of fun at it.

In January, 1887, George Hearst was elected to a full term as Senator by a legislature described as "bought and paid for." One correspondent, calling him "Boodler Hearst" and terming him "illiterate," observed that "for six years California will be represented in the United States Senate by a man whose sole claim to preferment . . . is that he is rich," adding, "At a moderate estimate it may be stated that Hearst's Senatorial seat has cost him a cool half million." [9] If true, this was routine, since in corruption-ridden California Senators were expected to pay handsomely for their seats.

With a six-year tenure in Washington ahead of him, he reluctantly gave in and wrote his son that he could have the *Examiner,* still nursing the hope

---

[8] Carlson and Bates, 44–45.   [9] N. Y. *Times,* Jan. 19, 1887.

that William would see the futility of journalism and turn to something sensible.

Young Hearst was overjoyed. To Ballard Smith he said, "I have the San Francisco *Examiner*. Will you be its editor?"

Smith refused. He was satisfied at the *World*.

"Do you mind if I give you some advice?" he said. ". . . You understand the work pretty well. Be your own editor." [10]

Hearst wrote his father a letter reflecting some confidence that Smith knew what he was talking about:

> Dear Father: . . . I shall be through here on the 10th of February, and I shall go immediately to San Francisco if I can catch you before you come here. I am anxious to begin work on the *Examiner*. I have all my pipes laid, and it only remains to turn on the gas. One year from the day I take hold of the thing our circulation will have increased ten thousand.
>
> It is necessary that the *Examiner* destroy every possibility of being considered an organ. I know it is not an organ devoted exclusively to your interests, but there are many people who do not know this, and so, the influence and accordingly the sale of the paper is thus largely affected. . . .
>
> We must be alarmingly enterprising, and we must be startlingly original. We must be honest and fearless. We must have greater variety than we have ever had. We must print more matter than we have printed. We must increase our force, and enlarge our editorial building. . . .
>
> There are some things that I intend to do new and striking which will constitute a revolution in the sleepy journalism of the Pacific slope and will focus the eyes of all that section on the *Examiner*. I am not going to write you what these are, for the letter might get lost, or you might leak. . . . In a year we will have increased at least ten thousand in circulation. In two years we will be paying. And in five years we will be the biggest paper on the Pacific slope. We won't be paying for two years because up to that time I purpose turning back into the improvement of the paper every cent that comes in.
>
> Your affectionate son,
> W. R. Hearst [11]

---

[10] Mrs. Fremont Older, *op. cit.*, 68.   [11] The same.

BOOK TWO

THE HEDONIST

1. Startling, Amazing, and Stupefying

SHORTLY after mid-February, Hearst arrived in San Francisco, doubtless just in time to see his parents before they left for Washington. The Senator, who had lost over $250,000 on the *Examiner*, was grudgingly willing to stake his son's effort to succor the invalid but made it plain that there were limitations to his patience and his largesse.[1] When the Hearst couple left, they took with them Phoebe's niece, nine-year-old Anne Drusilla Apperson, who would live with them for years as a daughter in all but blood.[2]

William took a house on the steep hillside at Sausalito across the bay, having a fortnight to study the *Examiner in situ* before he took charge officially. San Franciscans noted that he was over six feet tall, slender, racily dressed with especially dazzling cravats, very blond, with a small golden mustache and a high-pitched voice that had refused to grow up with him. He had a large collection of walking sticks, one of them a trick one that whistled as he walked up Market Street. It was a city-wide joke, especially relished by the men of the *Chronicle* and *Call*, to think of bashful Willie running a newspaper. But Willie was happy. He had what he wanted.[3]

The *Examiner*, a morning paper, now occupied offices at 10 Montgomery Street, had two telephones, 1804 for the editorial rooms and 1805 for the business department, and one creaky single-web press. It claimed a circulation of 23,914, but this was heavily weighted with "give-aways" during George Hearst's efforts to publicize his candidacy, and it was said that many were used solely for kindling fires. Although it had been handicapped by its known status as a Hearst-praiser, it had some able men on its staff who were up against vigorous competition. But to the new boss it was dull, commonplace, a steady loser for seven years, a proven failure. General Manager Emanuel Katz, Editor Clarence Greathouse and Managing Editor E. B. Henderson were a trifle nervous. On March 4, 1887—the same day George Hearst was sworn in for a full Senate term—William, not yet twenty-four, stayed up all night to put out his first issue, with a modest announcement on the editorial page:

> The *Examiner* with this issue has become the exclusive property of William Randolph Hearst, the son of its former proprietor. It will be conducted

---

[1] Bruce, 200; Coblentz, *Hearst*, 34.

[2] 82-year-old Mrs. Joseph Marshall Flint, who has contributed to this narrative, was that little girl.

[3] *Pearson's Magazine*, Sept., 1906.

in the future on the same lines and policies which characterized its career under the control of Senator Hearst.

This was hardly to be taken seriously, since it was Hearst's intention to revolutionize everything. He had already learned a few hard facts, one of them being that his announced intention to astonish the city with an overnight transformation was impossible with the staff and equipment he had. The March 4 issue was much like earlier ones except for one windy front-page exposé about the pathetic condition of foundlings brought into the Lying-In Hospital, and a divorce-court yarn featuring the testimony of one Job Cram about the excessive drinking of his wife—topics more spicy than the paper was wont to use. But Hearst was on the move. He enlarged the paper to eight pages and called for more news, local, national and foreign, using more of the costly New York *Herald* dispatches to widen the *Examiner's* horizon and give it a cosmopolitan air. He invariably stayed up most of the night to see the paper to bed. He disconcerted sedate Managing Editor Henderson with story ideas Henderson thought undignified.

They *were* undignified. Hearst wanted them that way. He introduced a disturbing practice—putting sporting news on Page One. When the aging Edwin Booth played *Hamlet* in his first San Francisco appearance in ten years, Hearst gave him two enthusiastic front-page columns, along with society notes describing the brilliant audience, even tossing a bouquet at the wife of his sternest competitor, M. H. De Young of the *Chronicle:* "Mrs. De Young was radiant in jetted net. . . ." [4] Kaiser Wilhelm, who under the old regime might have got a few paragraphs, was splashed all over the front page on the occasion of his ninetieth birthday, with a history of his reign and numerous gay sidelights such as an account of German students celebrating with beer, the whole under a monstrous headline:

"HOCH! HOCH!" [5]

This unrefinement must have made Greathouse and Henderson reel. Young Mr. Hearst was very polite with them, but determined to have his way. The line under the masthead, "W. R. Hearst, Proprietor," was changed on March 12 to "Proprietor and Editor," and again on March 14 to "Editor and Proprietor"—an indication that he was running the show in the editorial room and not merely warming a swivel chair in the front office. Shrinking personally, he was a braggart in print. He set aside large blocks of space wherein the *Examiner* praised the *Examiner*. He gave it a new tagline— "Monarch of the Dailies"—and trumpeted in big type that it was "THE LARGEST, BRIGHTEST AND BEST NEWSPAPER ON THE PACIFIC COAST," with "Thousands of New Readers" because it had "THE MOST ELABORATE LOCAL NEWS, THE FRESHEST SOCIAL NEWS, THE LATEST AND MOST ORIGINAL SENSATIONS." [6]

Managing Editor Henderson, feeling responsible to the Senator, took to

[4] San Francisco *Examiner*, Mar. 8, 1887.   [5] *Examiner*, Mar. 23, 1887.
[6] *Examiner*, Mar. 12, 1887.

writing careful directions for each day's issue, knowing that Hearst would not follow them but keeping them on record to show the Senator that he was not to be blamed for the paper's ruin.[7] Hearst, contrary to his earlier inclination, had the good sense not to houseclean his staff, but he improved it. He hired his good friend Eugene Lent to report society and financial news. An admirer of Ambrose Bierce, he sailed across to Oakland to call on the writer, who had recently worked for the San Francisco *Argonaut*. The handsome, fastidious Bierce, then forty-five, was a polished master of satire and invective who saw the world and all its works through such jaundiced eyes that it was said that the sight of blooming roses merely moved him to comment about the manure around the roots of the bush. Since he habitually attacked and belittled people in print, he carried a pistol for protection and possibly had it with him when he answered Hearst's knock. According to his classic description of the scene, he saw "the youngest man, it seemed to me, that I had ever confronted," standing on the stoop. Bierce, with his customary cordiality, said, "Well?"

" 'I am from the San Francisco Examiner,' [Hearst] explained in a voice like the fragrance of violets made audible, and backed a little away.

" 'Oh,' I said, 'you come from Mr. Hearst?'

"Then that unearthly child lifted his blue eyes and cooed, 'I *am* Mr. Hearst.' " [8]

He made Bierce such a flattering offer that he accepted at once, starting a biting column called "Prattle" in the March 27 issue. A few days later, on April 2, Hearst was agonized to discover that the *Chronicle* and *Call* had scooped him on a fire that gutted the big Del Monte Hotel at Monterey— the place where he had lost his heart to Sybil Sanderson. Thinking fast, he hired a Southern Pacific train, sped to the scene with a carload of artists and writers, and hurried back to produce a fourteen-page special edition—an unheard-of size—on April 3. This extravaganza had illustrations three columns wide—also unheard-of—and devoted Page One and most of Page Two not only to thorough coverage of the fire but also to a rousing pat of the *Examiner's* hand on the *Examiner's* back for the *Examiner's* enterprise in getting a special train and the admirable efficiency of the whole staff. San Francisco was amazed, but perhaps the most startling thing was the main headline on the fire, two whole columns wide (likewise a departure), and written by Hearst himself:

HUNGRY, FRANTIC FLAMES

"LEAPING HIGHER, HIGHER, HIGHER,
WITH DESPERATE DESIRE"
RUNNING MADLY RIOTOUS THROUGH CORNICE,
ARCHWAY AND FACADE.
RUSHING IN UPON THE TREMBLING
GUESTS WITH SAVAGE FURY . . .

[7] Mrs. Fremont Older, *op. cit.*, 72.
[8] Walter Neale, *The Life of Ambrose Bierce*, 89–90.

—and several more lines of the same. This was a headline such as had never been seen before. It was moonshine, but it was *lively* moonshine. It quoted a bit of rhyme and built up suspense after the manner of the Nick Carter novels then coming into vogue. It treated the fire as a circus spectacle, and gave an impression that young Mr. Hearst would like to see the hotel burn down every day, which perhaps some thought lacking in taste since the destruction of the building was a disaster even if it did belong to the Southern Pacific.

Nevertheless, the "fire special" sold out fast, as did an extra edition, and a second extra edition. Hearst had turned his competitors' scoop into victory for himself, and he bragged about it next day in a lead editorial headed "A GREAT PAPER." [9] Modesty was eschewed in the *Examiner*. Every day the two front-page ears were devoted to puffs from other papers, the New York *World* saying, "THE EXAMINER has been modernized in every way and turned into a LIVE NEWSPAPER of the present era," the Chicago *Tribune* contributing, "THE EXAMINER has shaked [sic] up the dry bones of newspaperdom in San Francisco." [10] If Senator Hearst was reading the paper in Washington, he could scarcely help concluding that his son was calling him a fossil.

"I don't suppose that I shall live more than three or four years if this strain keeps up," Hearst wrote his mother. "I don't get to bed until two o'clock and I wake up about seven in the morning and can't get to sleep again, for I must see the paper and compare it with the *Chronicle*. If we are best, I can turn over and go to sleep with quiet satisfaction, but if the *Chronicle* happens to scoop us, that lets me out of all sleep for the day . . .

"Thank Heaven for one thing, our efforts are appreciated. The great and good people of California want the *Examiner*. They don't want it very bad; they don't want it much harder than at the rate of thirty additional copies a day, but in time this will count. If we can manage to keep ahead we will have in a year from thirty to thirty-two thousand subscribers. That will put us well ahead of the *Call* and well up with the *Chronicle*." [11]

He was indeed working hard, enjoying every minute of it. He got rid of Editor Greathouse by having Senator Hearst snare for him the consul-general post in Tokyo. He unloaded a few other staff men who did not shake the dry bones loudly enough. But he kept on Managing Editor Henderson, City Editor Joseph Ward, writers Al "Blinker" Murphy and Andrew M. Lawrence, and others, some of whom remained with him all their lives. He called in the "Harvard Brigade," three men who had worked with him on the *Lampoon*—cartoonist Fred Briggs, whom he made head of the art department, Frank L. H. Noble, who became Sunday editor, and writer E. L. Thayer. He ordered a costly new press from New York. By offering handsome salaries,

[9] *Examiner*, April 4, 1887.   [10] *Examiner*, May 4, 1887.
[11] Mrs. Fremont Older, *op. cit.*, 79–80.

he lured away from other local papers solid talent including Arthur McEwen, William H. Hart and Edward "Pop" Hamilton.[12]

There was talk in San Francisco about the way Wasteful Willie was spending the Senator's money. De Young of the *Chronicle* snorted that the kid was a flash in the pan, a college cut-up.[13]

Examiner men, who had first viewed the new editor with amusement, were grudgingly impressed. He worked with them, not over them. He got his hands dirty setting type with the compositors. He was a crank on headlines. He sprouted ideas for features. He wrote out suggestions for each of his writers, couched in the most courteous phraseology, but it soon became apparent that a Hearst "suggestion" was an order. He regarded his newspaper as the most important enterprise in the world, and expected his men to take the same view. If there was one thing Willie Hearst could not abide, it was a routine, perfunctory attitude toward the news. He got excited about it. He wanted his men to get excited too, so that their product would be exciting even if not always rigidly accurate.[14]

The *Examiner*'s advertisements were meager and undistinguished, its biggest space being taken by one Dr. Prentice, who boasted of "138 Cross-Eyes Straightened In One Month," claimed also to cure catarrh and piles, and yet called himself a "specialist"; and Professor Shipley, who announced that "He has removed 1,200 tapeworms in the last five years." Hearst reduced the rates to bring in more advertisements. He began publishing popular songs on Sundays—a real innovation—beginning with "Ho! Molly Grogan!", aimed at San Francisco's large Irish population. Since the city was strongly unionized, he reached out for the labor element with a column called "The Workingman," devoted to activities of the unions. He opened a branch office on Broadway in Oakland to stir up advertising and circulation across the bay. Above all, he made use of a Ballard Smith-*World* tactic, seeking a smash front-page story every day that would startle, amaze or stupefy the reader and let him know that he could depend on being startled, amazed or stupefied daily simply by buying the *Examiner*.[15]

Here he was confronted by a journalistic fact known to all circulation-conscious editors—namely, that stupefying things do not happen every day. He solved this by creating them. When Sarah Bernhardt arrived in May to appear in *La Dame aux Camélias*—a theatrical event in itself—she unwittingly became the property of the *Examiner*. A Hearst reporter traveled 374 miles east to meet her train in Nevada, interview her, escort her in triumph to the city and accompany her to the Palace Hotel. The next thing Madame Sarah knew, she was captured by the cordial *Examiner* men who beat off opposing reporters as they took her and a few of her Parisian com-

[12] Jerome A. Hart, *In Our Second Century*, 83; Bruce, 202.
[13] Hart, 89.   [14] *Pearson's Magazine*, Sept., 1906.
[15] Items noted in the *Examiner* for Mar. 6, 18 and 27, and May 4 and 14, 1887.

panions on a tour of Chinatown highlighted—if one can believe the printed word—by a visit to a genuine opium den. Said the *Examiner:*

> On the low bunks around the room lay Chinamen, whose faces stood out in the cloud of smoke with ghastly pallor.
> "*C'est horrible!*" gasped the ladies.
> "*C'est magnifique!*" exclaimed Madame Sarah, pushing into the room with eager curiosity.
> A victim lay in a stupor before her. He was evidently marked for an early death. The tight skin seemed green and mouldy.
> His fingers were mechanically preparing a ball of opium for his pipe. . . .
> "*Il rêve!*" exclaimed Bernhardt, leaning over him and peering into his countenance, as if to read his dreams.[16]

It would be surprising if competing newsmen did not feel that Hearst and his crew were far gone on the pipe themselves. Four days later, when Bernhardt had been wrung dry, the front-page stunner came from W. B. Drew of Oakland, whom several relatives and friends had planned to murder in the hope of sharing his insurance. Writers Andrew Lawrence and William Hart built this up to eleven columns—more space than would normally be given to a cataclysm—with vivid details and breathless nonsense:

> The famous case of the Burkers in Edinburgh, who killed men and women for the dissecting table, does not contain the hideous elements of the awful conspiracy which has existed in our city for Heaven knows how long.
> The great plot of the sixteenth century in Florence, where women were banded together for wholesale poisoning, did not involve the sickening tragedies which our modern plot conceals. . . .
> The thugs of India are the only parallel in the history of the world. . . .
> The *Examiner,* in the face of a league strong as the terrible *Vehmgericht* of Germany, feared not to tear away the veil that hid the festering charnel-house.[17]

Since the plot against Drew was clumsily contrived and failed, so that Drew emerged unharmed, all this seemed excessive. Yet the readers seemed to like it. The next sensation was self-propelled. The *Examiner* announced that it had engaged special trains, one going south to Santa Cruz, the other northeast to Sacramento, to carry Sunday papers during the summer and "provide its many subscribers with the best news at the earliest hour." [18] The *Examiner* gave its own innovation front-page headlines.

On Sunday, May 22, Hearst made it a gala promotional event by taking with him Eugene Lent, Edward Townsend, William Hart and other staff men in the southbound special train to Santa Cruz, tossing out flowers at towns along the route. At Santa Cruz, Hearst was host at a breakfast of rum omelets, chicken and trout at the Pacific Ocean House. Among the guests were Mayor Robert Effey and other local leaders, who then followed

---

[16] *Examiner,* May 16, 1887.   [17] *Examiner,* May 20, 1887.
[18] *Examiner,* May 21.

Hearst and his entourage to his private railroad car for champagne and speeches. Mayor Effey spoke, as did *Examiner* man Townsend and several others, but not Hearst, who was too painfully shy for public speaking. But there was nothing shy about the *Examiner*'s exploitation of the affair—five columns on the front page, with maps showing the routes taken by the *Examiner* trains, statements from Mayor Eugene Gregory and other officials congratulating the paper on its enterprise, and much ado about the speed of the *Examiner*'s northern train, which covered the forty miles from Suisun to Sacramento in a record thirty-eight minutes.[19]

The *Examiner* soon added a third special Sunday train going north to Cloverdale. The *Chronicle*, stung by all this ballyhoo, was forced to copy it and engage special trains of its own—a move causing the *Examiner* to jeer, ". . . and every time the *Examiner* has reached the four quarters of the State before its imitative contemporaries." [20]

Hearst always planned his next sensation before the current one played out. On July 1, *Examiner* readers learned that all they had to do was clip a coupon from the paper to get a free seven-hour excursion on the bay next day. Four thousand people waved coupons and stormed the gangplank of the *Examiner*-chartered *James M. Donohue*, which could accommodate barely 1000. There was some difficulty as 3000 disgruntled citizens were turned away with police help, but those who got aboard had a glorious day. The Third Regiment Band played. The boat was decorated with bunting and many advertisements for the *Examiner*, the two paddle-boxes bearing vast signs lettered, "MONARCH OF THE DAILIES." The *Donohue* cruised around the bay, stopping at Angel Island, where it was met at the dock by the commandant at the military post there, a corpulent soldier named Colonel W. R. Shafter, and his staff—a circumstance that seemed to place even the United States Army in the position of giving a free testimonial to the *Examiner*.[21]

By midsummer of 1887, four months after Hearst took over, the paper was losing money at a far greater rate than when his father had it. But it was rising noticeably both in circulation and advertising. The *Chronicle* and *Call* had a formidable competitor on their hands. The attitude of the whole city toward the *Examiner* was epitomized by a remark made by Grove L. Johnson, a well-known Sacramento lawyer. Johnson was quoted (in the *Examiner*, to be sure) as saying:

"Well, what will you people do next?" [22]

II. WHAT WILL YOU PEOPLE DO NEXT?

With the *Examiner*, Hearst was employing the same tactics as he did at Harvard when hiring brass bands, throwing pies or filling the Yard with roosters. He was a shy fellow expressing himself in his own oblique way,

[19] *Examiner*, May 23 and 24, 1887.
[20] June 13 issue.
[21] *Examiner*, July 1 and 3, 1887.
[22] May 30 issue.

creating a public furor and enjoying it. He was a gifted amateur at stage-craft, putting on a show. He was also a gambler, betting that he could make the *Examiner* pay before his father's patience ran out, knowing that the answer lay in circulation, circulation and more circulation. And he was a young man with a towering will for leadership, so tongue-tied and embar-rassed among strangers that he sought that leadership through the power of the press, an extension of himself that was neither tongue-tied nor embar-rassed.[1]

The show he put on was a carnival pitch to get the people inside his tent. Once they were inside, he knew he had to show them something worthwhile or they would not return. He did this with intelligence, courage and a sense of public service that puzzled those who thought him a mere exhibitionist. San Francisco was a corrupt, boss-dominated city badly needing a voice of reform. Hearst furnished the voice, strident but effective. The noise he made reached clear to New York, where there was already some speculation about the upstart in the West. In the fall of 1887, Allen Kelly, city editor of the New York *Evening Sun* and an old friend of Arthur McEwen's, got such an attractive offer to become city editor of the *Examiner* that he quit and crossed the nation. With him went his pretty wife, Florence, also a writer, who went to work for the *Examiner* "on space." Thereafter the Kelly couple observed the Hearst operations with wonderment and sometimes with dis-approval. Mrs. Kelly noted that Hearst was "boyish and slightly diffident in manner and still a bit under the influence of the impish high spirits of youth." [2] She soon began to feel that he did not have a due sense of responsi-bility toward the news.

But she could scarcely quarrel with his reforming zeal, for in his first year Hearst launched a dozen-odd crusades, all of them laudable and at least three of them of first importance: a drive to defeat a mischievous new city charter; a battle for lower water rates; and a long campaign against the strangling, unscrupulous power of the Southern Pacific Railroad.

The proposed charter was the combined work of the Republican boss, William Higgins, and the Democratic boss, blind Chris Buckley, the Bush Street saloonkeeper who had helped send George Hearst to the Senate. It was aimed at strengthening boss control, and the *Examiner* led the opposi-tion that defeated it—a signal achievement for the young editor.[3]

The water-rate fight won him new laurels. San Francisco got its water from a private monopoly, the Spring Valley Water Company. For years the boss-influenced city board of supervisors, who fixed the rate, had been sus-pected of accepting bribes from the company to hike the rate profitably high.[4] The *Examiner* set up such a protest that the water company's presi-dent, uneasy, called at the office, spoke privately to one of the editors and offered him a handsome honorarium to stop his infernal campaign. The out-raged editor cursed him for a scoundrel, showed him the door and told Hearst

[1] R. L. Duffus in *World's Work*, Oct., 1922.   [2] Florence Finch Kelly, 239.
[3] Carlson and Bates, 49.   [4] Walton Bean, *Boss Ruef's San Francisco*, 140.

about it. Hearst's icy-blue eyes widened when he learned the size of the bribe.

"We must have them on the run if they are scared that much!" he exclaimed. "What did you tell him?"

The editor said he had ordered him to leave.

"You're a fool!" Hearst laughed. "Why didn't you take the money and keep up the fight just the same? He would never have dared to say a word about it." [5]

Although it may have been a Hearstian joke, it troubled Mrs. Kelly because she could not decide whether he meant it or not. But she had to cheer when the *Examiner* campaign finally won a sixteen percent reduction in water rates—relief that every taxpayer could feel in his own pocket.[6]

These were as minor skirmishes when compared with Hearst's crusade against the Southern Pacific, which also owned the Central Pacific and enjoyed a monopoly not only in California but in California's connection with the East and was determined to maintain it. The real government of the state was not in Sacramento but at the railroad's office at Fourth and Townsend Streets in San Francisco, where railroad money and influence decided all important national and state offices from Senator and governor on down, controlling also the San Francisco city bosses who in turn ran the city. The power behind the S.P. was huge, Yankee-born Collis P. Huntington, a miserly millionaire who had been a gold-rush hardware dealer in Sacramento with a genius for cornering the supply of such necessities as nails or shovels and then charging all the traffic would bear. Later branching into railroad building with the aid of stupendous government grants, he had cornered transportation and followed the same policy.[7] Farmers and shippers all over the state groaned under exorbitant rates and poor service. Nothing was done about it because the railroad made the rules by bribery so general and long-continued that it became almost respectable. It also controlled most of California's important newspapers by what were politely known as "subsidies," and by a monopolistic power over industry and advertisers that could cripple any editor so headstrong as to fight back.

This was the sort of challenge that delighted Hearst, who, according to one who knew him well, regarded journalism as "an enchanted playground in which giants and dragons were to be slain simply for the fun of the thing." [8] Considering his financial dependence on his father, his decision to fight the S.P. was downright daring. Characteristically, he fought not only in the editorial page but in the news columns, and also with the aid of Ambrose Bierce, an S.P.-hater of long standing who took pleasure in such comments as: "The Overland arrived at midnight last night, more than nine hours late, and twenty passengers descended from the snow-covered cars. All were frozen and half-starved, but thankful they had escaped with their lives."

[5] Florence Finch Kelly, 494.   [6] Mrs. Fremont Older, *op. cit.*, 78.
[7] Oscar Lewis, *The Big Four*, 221.
[8] James Creelman in *Pearson's Magazine,* Sept. 1906.

The trains were invariably so late, said Bierce, that "the passenger is exposed to the perils of senility." [9]

The Monarch of the Dailies, declaring that in return for exorbitant rates the railroad furnished equipment in the last stages of decay, said the public should be able to ride in it with a chance for survival "at least equal to that of a soldier on the battlefield." [10] Whenever the S.P. had a wreck of even minor proportions, Hearst sent out a battery of reporters and artists who filled the *Examiner* with frightening pictures of destruction and interviews with "survivors," along with tart editorial comment about murderous railroad laxity.[11] All this was doubtless embarrassing to Senator Hearst, whose good friend in Washington was Senator Leland Stanford, Huntington's partner in mismanagement of the S.P., especially when Bierce wrote: "Let Leland Stanford remove his dull face from the United States Senate and exert some of his boasted 'executive ability' disentangling the complexities in which his frankly brainless subordinates have involved the movements of his trains." [12]

Bierce liked to print his name as "£eland $tanford." Huntington, Stanford and their fellow moguls, who had borrowed millions from the government to build their line, supplying little capital themselves, were now taking the stand that the road was in poverty and would be bankrupted if required to repay the loan. The *Examiner* noted that Stanford thoughtlessly picked this time to buy his wife a $100,000 necklace, commenting also on the poverty that allowed him to spend millions on race horses, paintings and California estates, and to set aside an endowment of $30,000,000 to found a university in memory of his son.[13]

The *Examiner's* war against the S.P. would go on for years with no immediate victory except in circulation. Other newspapers had taken occasional shots at the railroad, but it was Hearst who launched the first determined, sustained campaign, hammering steadily through months and years, informing the people of the facts and starting a groundswell of public opinion that in the end would count. By the time he had been editor a year, the pink-cheeked young playboy, heir to a mining fortune, was recognized as the spokesman for "the people," the voiceless masses with whom he had not the slightest apparent kinship. Nominally Democratic, his maverick independence made him blast the Democrats when he thought them in the wrong. His independence was going pretty far when he assailed Chris Buckley, his father's old crony. Loyal Democrats protested, pointing to the Senator's party regularity. Hearst had a pat answer, letting it be known that he was running the *Examiner,* not his father.

"My father is reputed well-to-do," he said in his formal way. "I know he is fully able to pay his own debts. I must refer you to him for the satisfaction of all his obligations." [14]

Hearst, so shy and shut-mouthed among strangers, felt what was for his

[9] Oscar Lewis, *The Big Four,* 349.   [10] The same, 350.   [11] The same.
[12] *Examiner,* Aug. 4, 1888.   [13] Lewis, *The Big Four,* 190–91.
[14] *American Magazine,* Nov., 1906.

withdrawn nature a sense of relaxation among his newspapermen, with whom he could discuss the day's sensation as man to man. It was impossible for him to be loquacious, but he could be companionable. He was a good listener. He gave a speaker his full attention, eyeing him with that straight, unwavering, bug-eyed gaze that some found a bit unnerving. His manners were formal, well-drilled but charming. He addressed everybody as "Mister." He would not allow anyone to follow him through a door. He leaped to his feet when a woman entered. He never swore. His conversation was filled with polite consideration for those spoken to. His voice, if not precisely like violets, was uncommonly high-pitched for such a big man. Newcomers to the *Examiner* who feared that the rich Senator's son might be a painful popinjay were charmed by his quaint courtesy and the absence of anything top-lofty or condescending about him. His sense of democracy, like that of his father, was no studied veneer but came from within, and he won further admiration because he worked harder than anyone else and was often pawing over forms at midnight, changing headlines, getting himself smeared with ink.[15]

Yet he never succeeded in becoming "one of the boys." He was always "Mr. Hearst," never becoming "Willie" or "Bill." There was something strange about Hearst that would grow stranger with the years—a built-in failure of communication, an aloofness of temperament, an air of secrecy and loneliness, an inability to unbend into the true, easy spontaneity and exchange of confidences that bring men together. The victim of an abnormal childhood, he was hedged in by inhibitions. Now and then he would seem close to breaking through, only to recede again, like a turtle withdrawing into its shell. His men respected him, admired him, were even enthusiastic about him; but it is doubtful that any of them understood him.[16]

One whose admiration began to flag was Allen Kelly. Kelly, who had a strong sense of news propriety, became disillusioned after a few months as city editor because he felt that Hearst expected him to slant the news and color it with "unwarranted insinuations." Kelly asked for a change, and Hearst agreeably switched him to feature assignments.[17] There seems no record that other staff members were offended by the Hearst news manipulation. Most of them were San Franciscans, accustomed to the city's freewheeling journalistic code, and to them the *Examiner* was an exciting place to work, with a boss who paid wonderfully, loved a fight and was always looking for new injustices to attack. Will Irwin, a journalist who later became acquainted with many members of the original *Examiner* staff, wrote that "those who knew Hearst best in this early era declare that . . . he kept a real sympathy for the submerged man and woman, a real feeling of his own mission to plead their cause." [18]

Hearst, enjoying himself thoroughly, would occasionally come out of his

[15] James Swinnerton to author, Nov. 2, 1959.
[16] Charles E. Tebbs to author, May 3, 1960.   [17] Florence Finch Kelly, 241.
[18] Will Irwin in *Collier's*, Feb. 18, 1911.

office with a grave face and execute a jig for the benefit of newsmen in the editorial room. He liked to chat with the more jocular members of the staff— the Harvard Brigade, the witty Arthur McEwen, a screwball reporter named George Bruton, even the acid Bierce—not infrequently contributing a morsel of first-rate humor himself. There were two things that could make him show genuine warmth—a good joke, which would send him into a girlish giggle, and a good news story, which would galvanize him into excitement. Although he should rightly have been worrying about money, he never did so then nor would he for precisely fifty years. Money had always come to him. He seemed incapable of believing it would ever stop.

Tessie Powers was with him again, installed for a long stay at the place in Sausalito. Tessie, who came from a poor family and had been beset by troubles, was apparently anything but the typical adventuress. She is described as pretty, quietly genteel in manner, and it is said that she was extremely fond of Hearst, but her other attributes seem unrecorded.[19] Hearst bought an expensive yacht, the *Aquila,* for his journeys across the bay, and with his usual generosity he often entertained the *Examiner* men in a manner suggesting his belief that the Senator's indulgence would continue forever. He made no secret whatever of his liaison with Tessie. He was the most sociable of persons, liking to have gay people around him, yet always remaining slightly aloof from the sociability he had created. At times he even took parties down the coast to the great ranch at San Simeon. On lazy afternoons when the news pressure was off, he would seize a few reporters for a quick boat ride in the bay, just to be doing something.[20]

He could not endure idleness. He was driven by a need for work, action, pleasure, planning. He worked hard and played hard, with no time for mere loafing. At work, he had a capacity for intense concentration that shut out all extraneous thought. Most of the ideas that caused the *Examiner* to become an object of civic amazement were Hearst ideas.

One of these came on Washington's birthday, 1888, when he took half of his crew with him to Washington to publish a special edition of the *Examiner* urging that the Democratic national convention be held that summer in San Francisco. Senator and Mrs. Hearst were delighted to find the *Examiner* on the doorstep of their splendid home at 1400 New Hampshire Avenue, which may have been part of their son's strategy, for the exploit cost him $80,000.[21]

The Senator had become a Washington curiosity, a frequenter of Chamberlain's bar, where he took his whisky neat and foregathered with cronies who called him "Uncle George." Despite his tobacco stains and his villainous English, he was prized for his kindliness and lack of pretense in a city where pretense was common. Partly because of the malign influence of his turfman friend, Senator Stanford, he had fallen prey to a new vice—horse-racing. Over the strong protests of his wife, who regarded the sport as a vulgar waste

[19] Mrs. J. M. Flint to author.   [20] Carlson and Bates, 57.
[21] Mrs. Fremont Older, *op. cit.,* 90.

of money, he had bought an imported mare, Gorgo, who promptly won two races. Delighted, he spent $47,000 for a yearling colt, King Thomas, who came highly recommended but to date had failed even to place in several races.[22] The Senator had a tendency to go whole-hog for anything that pleased him—a weakness in which his son would later excel him. He raced his horses at Sheepshead Bay and other tracks, and he bought a 500-acre horse ranch near the racetrack at Pleasanton, California, east of San Francisco Bay. If he complained to William about his attacks on £eland $tanford, it had no effect, for they continued.

Hearst considered his $80,000 Washington demonstration a good investment, for the other San Francisco papers, much as they disliked taking their cue from the *Examiner,* were forced to fall in line in the convention-in-San Francisco boom. Even though the Democrats ungratefully chose St. Louis instead, the *Examiner* had made a magnificent noise and won national publicity. Returning to California, Hearst on the night of March 3 gave a party for his staff to commemorate his first year in charge. His present to the paper was another new press, paid for by the Senator.[23]

Although by this time the Monarch's circulation had risen to nearly 40,000, and its advertising had doubled, the tremendous cost of new presses and equipment, higher salaries, a larger staff, and above all huge promotional expenses had cost Senator Hearst around $300,000 in one year, which was something more than he had lost in the entire seven years he had run the paper himself. Hearst, undisturbed by the deficit, was looking for more brilliant men to brighten his pages, and particularly for a high-priced editor. His intention was not to lighten his own load, for he enjoyed the load. He needed a man who could translate his ideas into the kind of dazzling action he sought. He had become addicted to the belief that his newspaper could not have too much talent.

That summer he went to New York and registered at the Hoffman House, the traditional Democratic headquarters in the metropolis. In the hotel bar he met his man—Samuel S. Chamberlain, as much of a fashion plate as Hearst, with the added distinction of a monocle gripped in his eye and a gardenia in his lapel. Chamberlain, nearing forty, was a tall, urbane individual, a veteran newsman whose bouts with the bottle were widely spaced but determined. He had worked for the *Herald,* the *World,* and in Paris had edited Bennett's *Herald* before establishing *Le Matin*—precisely the lively experience Hearst was looking for. The two men took an immediate liking to each other. When Hearst returned to San Francisco, Chamberlain followed soon thereafter to become managing editor of the *Examiner.*[24]

[22] N. Y. *Herald,* Mar. 1, 1891.   [23] Mrs. Fremont Older, *op. cit.,* 90–91.
[24] Charles Tebbs to author; Willard G. Bleyer, *Main Currents in the History of American Journalism,* 355.

III. THE LONE WOLF

ONE of the puzzles of the Hearst personality is that while he possessed qualities that should have attracted companions innumerable, he had few close friends. Normally it would be expected that anyone with his rare gifts of intelligence, wit, charm, generosity and sympathy for misfortune would be popular to the point of satiety. Yet he was lonely.

One obvious reason was his shyness, his retreats into a cool reserve that kept others at a distance. Yet even in those instances when he became so well acquainted with another person that his shyness was conquered, there arose another bar to lasting friendship. This was his powerful will, which made it necessary for him to dictate the terms of friendship, to call the tune, to have his own way—in short, to exercise supervisory authority over a companion.

Although he could do this in the most genial and subtle ways, the Hearst dictation would eventually offend independent spirits. Only pliable, easy-going personalities would accept it without annoyance.

It is significant that Orrin Peck and Jack Follansbee, who remained lifelong friends, both saw Hearst only intermittently. Peck for years had been in Munich, where he had originally been sent at Phoebe Hearst's expense, a token of her gratitude for the kindness of Orrin's mother on the boat from Panama in 1862. He was now an accomplished portrait and landscape painter. Follansbee was in Mexico, supervising the Hearst Babicora ranch [1]

As a result, Hearst had only the Harvard Brigade—Eugene Lent, Frank "Cozy" Noble, Fred Briggs and E. L. "Phinney" Thayer—as available friends of long standing. Lent soon left the *Examiner* to study law. Briggs returned East for reasons unknown, and Thayer did likewise for reasons of health, continuing to contribute occasional pieces, one of them the immortal "Casey at the Bat." Although Hearst was a member of the Bohemian Club, whose Pine Street rooms were a meeting place for the gay and literate, he was uncomfortable among strangers and seldom attended.

Possibly motivated in part by loneliness, he decided that he needed a private secretary to handle letters and office detail. His method of selecting one was unique. A newcomer to the *Examiner*, a young printer named George E. Pancoast, played a harmless practical joke on Ike Allen, a copy editor, that amused Hearst. Always attracted by humor, he called Pancoast to his office and asked if he knew shorthand.

"No," Pancoast admitted, "but I can take longhand if you don't talk too fast."

"That's good enough for me," Hearst said.[2]

Pancoast found Hearst's method of answering mail casual. He would simply hand Pancoast a letter and say, "Tell them no," or "Tell them to see about that." Pancoast was slow on the typewriter, but being a mechanical

[1] Mrs. J. M. Flint to author.
[2] N. Y. *Times*, Mar. 16, 1939; *Editor & Publisher*, Mar. 14, 1936.

wizard he rearranged the type bars and keys on his machine to correspond with a type case and soon became a proficient typist. A lean, neat Yankee from New Hampshire, he had barnstormed for six years as song-and-dance man with rural road shows. His pixie smile, his fund of jokes and his ability to cut a caper were qualities that appealed to Hearst, who was never far removed from the vaudeville stage, and he fulfilled another Hearst require-ment—a willingness to be on the job with the boss any hour of the day or night. It turned out that Pancoast was interested in photography. Hearst, curious, bought a camera and quickly became fascinated.[3]

It was a confirmed trait with him to explore any subject catching his inter-est somewhat in the way a research scientist explores a promising new theory. He could drop it or relegate it to a side-issue if investigation showed it to be of minor importance, but if it continued to stimulate his imagination, he would pour endless concentration and effort into it, unable to stop as long as possibilities for pleasure or profit remained unplumbed. Adept at technical matters, he easily grasped the principles of photography. He was impressed by its immense usefulness in journalism if a satisfactory way could be found to translate photographs into type metal. Hearst and Pancoast became fellow picture fanatics. Hearst bought the best equipment available in San Francisco and wired New York for more. His Sausalito house proved inadequate, so he bought a bigger one nearby, converting the entire second floor into work-room, darkroom and a room for showing slides.[4] When he wanted anything, he wanted it in a hurry and was consumed by impatience at delay. The whole photographic installation was accomplished with such speed that it must have thrust Tessie momentarily into the background.

Hearst and Pancoast embarked on a friendship that would continue—intermittently—for life. Pancoast, who remained with the Hearst organiza-tion until he died, was never in a position to complain of the demands the boss made on his friends.

Monocled Sam Chamberlain, the new managing editor, proved an ideal Hearst lieutenant, a practical psychologist whose New York and Paris experi-ence had taught him what it took to startle, amaze and stupefy the public. Possibly he was amazed himself to discover that an *Examiner* sensation could find its inception in casual office chatter. Hearst one day had a discussion with Allen Kelly on the question of whether there were any grizzly bears left in California. Kelly, a confirmed outdoorsman, was convinced that there were. The idea grew on Hearst. He commissioned Kelly to go forth, regard-less of time and expense, trap a grizzly alive and bring it back to San Fran-cisco as a roaring example of *Examiner* enterprise. Kelly trekked to the Tehachapi range in southern California, hired a dozen woodsmen, built a network of pit traps baited with meat, and after almost three months of effort caught a grizzly. The animal was chained and hauled to the railroad, loaded into a boxcar and shipped to San Francisco. There it was transferred to a beer wagon and paraded through the city with great fanfare. Christened

[3] *Editor & Publisher*, Mar. 18, 1939.   [4] Mrs. Fremont Older, *op. cit.*, 87.

"Monarch" to honor the Monarch of the Dailies, the beast was eventually installed in a pen at Golden Gate Park.[5]

All of this was exploited in a series of *Examiner* stories telling of the difficulties involved, the hazards encountered, and the disappointments preceding the triumphant capture. Hearst, with instinctive theatrical skill, built up suspense that carried on from day to day like a serial thriller, exclusive with the *Examiner* because no other paper would touch it. He loved "created news" that could be spun out from day to day into a circulation-building sensation. He would also settle for a one-day stunner, such as when he sent a young couple up in a balloon emblazoned with the *Examiner* name in large letters, with a clergyman who married them above the city. He gave a personal demonstration of his theories of journalism militant when a fisherman was wrecked in a storm and marooned on a rock near Point Bonita, outside the Golden Gate. The Coast Guard, finding the seas too rough, elected to let the man cling there until morning if he could. The *Examiner* elected otherwise.

Hearst and some of his younger men, among them George Bruton and H. R. Haxton, hired a tug and steamed out to the scene. Haxton, a powerful swimmer, disrobed and carried a line to the chilled fisherman, who was hauled into the tug, bundled into blankets and taken to the *Examiner* office. There he was given hot coffee while an artist sketched him along with Hero Haxton for an exclusive story in the morning paper that did not fail to criticize the Coast Guard at the same time that it lauded the *Examiner's* dash and enterprise. Its sniping resulted in the establishment of a new Coast Guard station. Hearst meanwhile was off in full cry with a new idea making further use of his swimmer.[6]

Haxton took a ride in the *Oakland*, one of the bay ferries operated by the hated S.P., accompanied by a reporter and an artist. Near Yerba Buena Island, Haxton toppled off and howled for help, while his mates likewise bellowed as they observed and timed the rescue operations with a stopwatch. It took three minutes and forty seconds for the ferry to stop and put out a small boat. The *Examiner* next morning poured sarcasm on the inefficiency of the crew, pointed out that Haxton would have drowned several times over had he been a non-athletic old lady, and warned, "The general public is recommended not to fall overboard too often."[7] The embarrassed ferry company promptly inaugurated new life-saving standards.[8]

In 1888, Emanuel Katz, the holdover general manager of the *Examiner*, saw clearly that Hearst was his own general manager. Katz resigned. With Hearst's blessing he moved to New York and opened an office in the gold-domed new Pulitzer Building as Eastern advertising representative for the *Examiner* and other Western newspapers. In his wake Hearst sent Ike Allen to New York as the first full-time eastern correspondent for any newspaper

[5] Florence Finch Kelly, 257–60; Bruce, 206–7.
[6] Coblentz, *Hearst*, 47–48; Bruce, 208.   [7] *Examiner*, Sept. 2, 1888.
[8] Bruce, 209.

west of the Rockies.[9] The fact that Allen used Katz's office at night indicates that Hearst, under pressure, was trying to exercise something foreign to his nature—economy. Senator Hearst was on the warpath. For one thing, talk about Tessie Powers had spread in widening circles from Sausalito to San Francisco, and some letter-writing friend had apprised the Hearst couple about Tessie. For another, the *Examiner* was costing a fortune. Although it had made striking gains and had emerged as a powerful and progressive force in California, its deficit was still so fearful that in 1889 the Senator flatly refused to subsidize it any further.

His attitude was not illogical. He had poured about $750,000 into the paper since his son took it over.[10] The young man was devoid of any money sense, hiring men as if he were gathering an army, paying them enormous salaries, and spending large sums for such things as special trains, balloons, grizzly bears and a young woman who lived in. Even the Senator's indulgence had its limits. Moreover, he had not changed his opinion that journalism was a refuge for tricksters and political adventurers. He was sixty-nine, not feeling well, and he still hoped that his son would take charge of his properties.

For the first time in his life, William Hearst had a money problem—a downright crisis. To lose the *Examiner* was unthinkable, after so many wiseacres had predicted that he would fail. Furthermore, he was on the verge of making the newspaper pay. Only a small further financial push was needed.

This unfamiliar experience of not having his own way, of being forced to face fiscal unpleasantness, must have driven him frantic. He begged for another $50,000. The Senator was obdurate.

William mentioned his dilemma to Michael Francis Tarpey, Democratic committeeman for California and an old friend of the Senator's. Tarpey was likewise distressed, for the party could not afford to lose its most stentorian voice. He had a solution.

"We were in the heat of a campaign," Tarpey later recalled. "I went to the Senator and told him that the party needed contributions, and that he was down for $100,000 . . . The Senator didn't hesitate. I received his check for that amount.

"Half of the sum went into our campaign fund. The other $50,000 I turned over to young William for his and the paper's espousal of the Democratic principles . . ."[11]

There are other scattered evidences that William was practicing what he felt was painful parsimony. Outside of occasional journeys to Washington and New York, he had stayed on the job. He had made no trips to Europe. He had missed the Paris Exposition of 1889. And there is no record that he expended any large amount for objects of art to add to his collection.

These were Hearstian sacrifices for the cause of journalism. They were

[9] G. R. Katz to author, Dec. 15, 1959.   [10] *Pearson's Magazine*, Sept., 1906.
[11] Coblentz, *Hearst*, 34–35.

enough, for by 1890 the *Examiner* was on its own feet, showing a profit, and Senator Hearst's last chance of redeeming his son from the newspaper business was gone.[12]

Nevertheless, William was undoubtedly green with envy when Pulitzer's *World* sent a twenty-two-year-old girl called Nellie Bly on a race around the world to beat the eighty-day effort of Jules Verne's fictional hero. Nellie made it in seventy-two days, six hours and eleven minutes. For seventy-two days and more the *World* daubed its pages with running accounts of the story it had made, manufactured, created out of its own ingenuity. On January 21, 1890, Nellie arrived in San Francisco on the last leg of her journey. The *Examiner* suffered the humiliation of sending a reporter to interview Miss Bly and to publicize the creation of the *World*.

[12] Mrs. Fremont Older, *op. cit.,* 104.

2. The Gee-Whiz Emotion

I. DISINHERITED

"WHAT we're after," said Arthur McEwen, the tall, goateed Scot who gave brilliance to the *Examiner* editorial page, "is the gee-whiz emotion." [1]

This appraisal was too conservative. Any issue that did not cause its reader to rise out of his chair and cry, "Great God!" was counted a failure. Although McEwen was a sincere crusader and not a cynic, his words had a cynical tinge. Yet Hearst, who was the author of the policy and who labored steadfastly to convulse his readers with excitement, seemed utterly serious and is not on record as having uttered a cynical word about his methods. San Francisco was an excitement-loving city that demanded racy fare. Jerome Hart, who edited the local *Argonaut,* was downright admiring, writing:

> . . . *Examiner* young men go up in balloons . . . *Examiner* young men jump off ferryboats to test the crews. *Examiner* young men swim to save fisherman marooned on rocks. In brief, *Examiner* men are doing many things these days, and some fine and brave things. I am inclined to believe that many of their exploits are performed more for the love of adventure than for the love of advertising.[2]

Hearst not only surrounded himself with able young men but also had a faculty for instilling into them a loyalty and *esprit de corps* that made them plunge without hesitation into bizarre exploits in search of the gee-whiz emotion. His skilled lieutenant in this daily quest was Sam Chamberlain.

Chamberlain assigned reporter Frank Peltret to have himself committed to the insane asylum at Stockton, which he accomplished by jumping off a steamer en route to that city and talking wildly when fished out. Peltret spent a month in the asylum, then wrote a blood-curdling account of his experiences.[3] Chamberlain hired a handsome, red-headed girl reporter, Wisconsin-born Winifred Sweet, who had arrived in San Francisco as a chorus girl in a touring theatrical troupe, and gave her careful instructions in the Hearst method.

"We don't want fine writing in a newspaper," he said. "Remember that. There's a gripman on the Powell Street line—he takes his car out at three o'clock in the morning, and while he's waiting for the signals he opens the morning paper . . . Think of him when you're writing a story. Don't write a single line he can't understand and wouldn't read." [4]

Miss Sweet, who would become famous as the nation's first sob sister

[1] *World's Work,* Oct., 1922.
[2] Lewis, *Bay Window Bohemia,* 139.
[3] Jerome Hart, 87.
[4] Ishbel Ross, *Ladies of the Press,* 61–62.

under her *nom de guerre* of "Annie Laurie," fell in easily with the mad *Examiner* spirit. There had been some criticism of the city's facilities for caring for the stricken. She was assigned to test them. Dressed in shabby clothes, she collapsed on Market Street and waited for an interminable time while a crowd gathered and a policeman with a bourbon breath tried to smell whisky on her own. She was finally carried in a jolting express wagon to the City Receiving Hospital on Washington Street where, according to her indignant exposé in the *Examiner,* she was insulted and pawed by vulgar internes, given an emetic of hot water and mustard and turned loose. Her front-page story resulted in a shakeup at the hospital and the suspension of the physician in charge. The physician called at the *Examiner* office bent on vengeance, was knocked flat by a burly reporter, and, said the *Examiner* story, "lay on his back whining like a whipped cur." [5] Enemies of the *Examiner* generally wound up whining like whipped curs, according to the *Examiner.* In truth, Hearst was not a newsman at all in the conventional sense. He was an inventor, a producer, an arranger. The news that actually happened was too dull for him, and besides it was also available to the other papers. He lived in a childlike dream world, imagining wonderful stories and then going out and creating them, so that the line between fact and fancy was apt to be fuzzy.

An occupational hazard he had to make provision for was insobriety. Chamberlain could go for weeks in admirable temperance, then fall with a crash. McEwen was another whose periods of abstinence usually ended drastically. He was a brother-in-law of Charles Michelson, a young *Examiner* staffer who, decades later, would become director of publicity for the Democratic party. When McEwen was reported missing, Michelson would lead a rescue squad to search the saloons for the fallen editorialist. On one occasion, Hearst, seeking to confer with McEwen about an editorial, finally found him stretched comatose under the half-closed rolltop of his desk. San Francisco was a city of two-fisted drinkers, with a jam-packed Home for Inebriates on Stockton Street, but as a class newsmen easily won first rank as imbibers. The *Examiner* had drinkers of all categories, moderate, steady, intermittent and inert, and the staff was so flexibly arranged that when a member fell from grace another would take his place without comment.[6]

Virtually the only sobersides was Hearst himself, who, if he had occasionally been a trifle gay at Harvard, had since decided that hard liquor was not for him and would touch nothing stronger than beer or wine. Likewise, after becoming a steady smoker he had come to view the habit as unwholesome and had quit cold—a fair indication of his strength of will. These decisions were not motivated by moral considerations. He simply disliked the giddiness induced by alcohol, and cigarettes struck him as time-wasting and harmful. Unlike some abstainers who condemn the vice they secretly wish they could

[5] Lewis, *Bay Window Bohemia,* 138–39.
[6] James Swinnerton to author, Nov. 2, 1959; Charles Tebbs to author, May 3, 1960.

enjoy, he was never the spoilsport. He was remarkably indulgent with his prodigals—so much so that the staff often took advantage of his lenience. If a man was handed an unpleasant assignment, he might disappear for a few days and return, pleading intoxication, knowing that this would excuse everything. One day Hearst met a reporter who was perfectly sober, yet was supposed to be on a spree. "On the scamp's assurance that he had honestly intended to get drunk, but lacked the price," Bierce recalled, "Mr. Hearst gave him enough money to reestablish his character for veracity and passed on." [7]

Bierce, who frequently eyed his employer with a mixture of admiration and puzzlement, admitted that he was baffled when Hearst, having found that one of his managerial men was stealing *Examiner* money, kept the man on in the same position.

"I have a new understanding with him," Hearst said with a straight face. "He is to steal only small sums hereafter; the largest are to come to me." [8]

While he could grow irked if the *Examiner* was scooped, Hearst seemed disinclined to let dishonesty bother him, or to take a high moral stand against any of the immemorial personal vices. He was tolerant toward them. He never sponsored any all-out campaign against the Barbary Coast iniquities. This trait was further illustrated by his openness in maintaining Tessie at Sausalito. To worldly San Franciscans there was nothing surprising about the son of a millionaire having a *petite amie*, but it was expected that he would keep the affair reasonably well concealed. This Hearst refused to do, being completely indifferent about the bourgeois conception of respectability.

Meanwhile, Senator Hearst, who had been unwell in Washington, went to New York to consult Dr. Charles Ward, who diagnosed his illness as "a complication of diseases, resulting primarily from a serious derangement of the bowels." [9] The seventy-year-old Senator returned to Washington and grew worse. Resigned to his fate, he summoned Dr. Ward to the capital and said, "Doctor, I want you to stay with me and see me through this." [10] William Hearst arrived from California. Jack Follansbee arrived from Mexico. Old George Hearst was upset about William's Sausalito affair, and "on his deathbed he exhorted his son to lead a serious life." [11] On February 28, 1891, as William Hearst and Follansbee stood by, Phoebe Hearst held one of the dying man's hands and Dr. Ward the other, "and so quietly and easily did he pass away that Mrs. Hearst did not know he was dead until so informed by the physician." [12]

No one would have called Uncle George a statesman, but his unassuming kindness had won him warm friends. Senator Stanford was one of many who eulogized him in the Senate and House. Speaker Reed appointed a group of

[7] Quoted in Carlson and Bates, 51.
[9] San Francisco *Examiner*, Mar. 1, 1891.
[11] *Pearson's Magazine*, Sept., 1906.
[8] The same.
[10] The same.
[12] *Examiner*, Mar. 1, 1891.

Representatives to attend the funeral, among them a handsome Congress-man from Ohio, William McKinley. President and Mrs. Harrison were among those at the ceremony on March 5, after which the body was shipped west via a dozen railroads, the last one being Stanford and Huntington's Central Pacific. William Hearst and his mother made the week-long rail trip back to California, accompanied by Follansbee, to attend the second service at Grace Church in San Francisco on March 15. The *Examiner*'s floral tribute was a likeness of its front page done in blue and white flowers. It turned out to be a dismal day, but the governor of California and the mayor of San Francisco were among the pallbearers as some 15,000 citizens stood in the rain to watch Uncle George's cortege pass by on the way to Cypress Lawn Cemetery.[13]

The *Examiner* on the day after the Senator's death devoted its black-bordered front page to an account of his career, mentioning proudly that he had "started mining with a pick and shovel on his shoulder." On the day of the San Francisco funeral, however, there was a crisis in the office. An anxious Sam Chamberlain summoned a new member of the staff, Edward Morphy, formerly of the New York *Sun*.

"Ed, can you do a good feature lead on the Senator's funeral?" he asked. "The boys who covered it are drunk. We need a stirring yet dignified account. Can you do it, Ed?"

"Sure thing," Morphy replied. "I'll do a masterpiece for you. But tell me something about the length of the procession and what the old man looked like. Did he have pink whiskers? Was he tall and thin or short and fat?"

Chamberlain was making signs at him. Someone had come into the office. "By the way," Chamberlain said, "meet your boss, Mr. Hearst."

Morphy turned and shook hands with the tall publisher, who said he hoped Mr. Morphy would do a good job on the funeral.[14]

There was speculation that the estate of the free-spending Senator must be $40,000,000 or more. It turned out to be $18,000,000. This was deceptive, however, most of it being in land and in mines now sharply increasing in value, particularly the Homestake and Anaconda mines, which had gone through costly expansion and were just beginning to pour out riches that would break all records.[15]

In his will, Senator Hearst left every penny to his widow, who was still only forty-eight. Some interpreted this as a slap at his twenty-seven-year-old son. It was. It reflected George Hearst's realization that William had no money sense whatever, and could doubtless go through $18,000,000 with ease.

But if he had no money sense, he did have an astonishing newspaper sense. At the time the Senator was buried, the *Examiner* had a daily circulation of 57,352, having passed the *Call* and caught up with the *Chronicle*.[16]

[13] *Examiner*, Mar. 16, 1891.   [14] Carlson and Bates, 53.   [15] Rickard, 216 ff.
[16] San Francisco *Examiner*, Mar. 14, 1891.

II. WANT BEANS CHOWDER CODFISH

To Phoebe Hearst, her niece, Anne Drusilla Apperson, took the place of the daughter she had always hoped for. Anne Drusilla, who was thirteen when she attended the Senator's funeral, is a vigorous eighty-two as this is written. She remembers her cousin Willie vividly as a handsome, charming young man with a nimble sense of humor and a determination to have his own way. She had lived with Senator and Mrs. Hearst for four years in Washington, enjoying Willie's propensity for fun on his visits there. She would remain with Phoebe for another fifteen years, living with her, traveling with her, serving as companion and confidante. A member of the family, she was privy to family affairs. She would see and hear plenty about Willie, who was at once his mother's greatest pride and greatest problem. She recalls that he was "much upset" about his father's will.[1]

The will deprived him of moneys he felt he needed. It gave people the impression that his late father had little respect for his acumen, which, though precisely the case, was humiliating.

He was already fixed in that bizarre attitude toward money that dogged him through life, and which was indeed partly the fault of the mother and father who had never disciplined him dollar-wise or in any other way. To him, money was a commodity to be taken for granted and spent according to whim on the theory that the supply was endless, like water from a tap. It was only when the flood dwindled to a trickle that he became aware of money as such. He was in the habit of doing what he wanted, and the things he did invariably cost money. The *Examiner,* while profitable enough to keep several ordinary men in luxury, was a faucet which, for one of his thirst, merely dribbled. During most of 1889 and 1890, his parched tongue had been hanging out. Now, with the reading of the will, it was close to cracking.

He let his mother know discreetly about his disappointment. But she was well aware of his fiscal failings, and she also had a bone to pick with him about Tessie. Doubtless her San Francisco friends had filled her with colorful details about the girl. She was as shocked as a woman of her stern virtue could have been. In her view it was high time for William to settle down and marry. She had in fact suggested a few eligible young ladies, one of them the daughter of a former ambassador, but he showed no interest. The starchy social circle in which his mother revolved moved him to boredom. It is a safe assumption that she spoke to him seriously about the scandal, and begged him to stop it. But in matters of morality, she and her son did not speak the same language, and the chances are that William, who was genuinely fond of her, tried to soothe her without committing himself, for he never lied to her. The chances are as good that Phoebe, who found it hard

[1] Mrs. J. M. Flint to author, Jan. 18, 1960.

to refuse him anything, relieved his financial pinch and told him to be a good boy.

Senator Hearst's business affairs in San Francisco had long been handled by one I. N. Stump, for whom Phoebe, for some reason, held little regard. Now, with her late husband's estate to worry about, she called in her second cousin, Edwin Hardy Clark, a young Missourian who for some time had operated a Fresno grocery and in whom she had great confidence. She made Clark Stump's assistant, with the intention that Clark would soon displace Stump and serve as her personal business manager. Probably she expected Clark to keep an eye on her son's expenditures and also on his behavior. With Anne Drusilla, Phoebe at last returned to Washington, where she now had so many friends and charities that she considered it her home. Later in 1891, she sailed for Europe with her niece.[2]

Soon thereafter, Hearst likewise left for Europe, taking with him Tessie Powers and George Pancoast. He was quite free from hypocrisy about his affair, seeming to feel that whatever he did should be accepted without question. Phoebe was in Paris when she got word from a San Francisco friend that her son was en route to Europe with "that woman" in tow. She was distressed. She even had fears of a chance meeting with William and his mistress.[3]

She was spared the encounter. Hearst and his odd party roamed England, Scotland and Wales, photographing castles and celebrities and sending occasional stories to Chamberlain at the *Examiner*. Hearst, who followed the news like a hawk, must have known that his former sweetheart, Eleanor Calhoun, had scored a smashing dramatic success in London, starring as "Dora" in *Diplomacy* and becoming a darling of fashion, the friend of Whistler and Browning. Sybil Sanderson, his earlier love, had made her debut as a soprano at The Hague, then had charmed Paris as Manon at the Opéra Comique, her name now being linked romantically with the composer Massenet. The two young ladies of Hearst's salad days had become international artistic sensations, and yet he was perfectly content with Tessie, whose background was an unglamorous Cambridge restaurant.[4]

Hearst and Pancoast had brought duplicate photographic equipment, knowing that in case of breakage it would be difficult to replace in Europe. If Miss Powers was bored by the incessant Hearst-Pancoast talk of photography, she was at any rate getting a pleasant, all-expenses-paid tour, with cultural opportunities formerly undreamed of. The group moved across to the continent and called on Orrin Peck in Munich, grown fat and as jolly as ever. Hearst spent much of his time visiting the museums, attending sales and buying curios, painting and statuary—an indication that his mother had not denied his plea for funds. In Verona, he passed a courtyard in whose center was an old circular stone wellhead that transfixed him.

[2] Mrs. Flint to author, Feb. 20, 1960.   [3] The same.
[4] Winkler, *Hearst—An American Phenomenon*, 89.

"Look at that well!" he exclaimed joyfully.[5]

He bought it and arranged for its transportation to sea and shipment to San Francisco—no small task, since it weighed five tons. Eventually it was decided that Pancoast should return to San Francisco alone, with Hearst and Tessie to follow him later.

When Pancoast reached San Francisco after an arduous ocean and rail trip, he found a cablegram from Hearst awaiting him:

"Going to Egypt. Would you like to go? Please suit your own convenience entirely." [6]

Pancoast knew that a Hearst request was equivalent to an order, and that disregarding it would cause displeasure. Wearily he made the long journey back to Paris, where he was to meet his employer at the Hotel Continental. Hearst was not there, nor was there any message. Pancoast fidgeted for a fortnight before he got a message from Chamonix:

"Come here at once. Bring two thousand dollars. —Hearst." [7]

In Hearst's best of all possible worlds, people were expected to do his bidding, accede to his whims. With some difficulty, Pancoast secured the money from the Paris agent of Wells, Fargo, and joined his chief and his consort at Chamonix. The Yankee-born Pancoast confessed some trepidation about Egyptian food. He longed for good New England fare. The generous Hearst dashed off another cablegram, this one to Ike Allen, his representative in the Pulitzer Building in New York:

"Rush dozen cans Boston beans dozen cans clam chowder two codfish Alexandria Egypt. —Hearst." [8]

The message baffled Allen. The code was unfamiliar. He cabled Hearst asking what code he was using, and got an annoyed reply:

"No code. Want beans chowder codfish." [9]

As always, Hearst gave to play the same all-out application he did to work. He kept in close touch with his newspaper by cable. He and his two companions steamed up the Nile and visited the tombs of the Egyptian kings, Hearst and Pancoast taking pictures with such abandon that one can only wonder whether Miss Powers took up knitting in self-defense. The two men made 3200 negatives. Hearst wrote his mother enthusiastically about their photographic prowess. An ominous message came from Henderson, the *Examiner*'s stiff-necked editorial manager:

"Chamberlain drunk again. May I dismiss him?"

Hearst, who was fond of Chamberlain, replied: "If he is sober one day in thirty that is all that I require." [10]

He bought and shipped back a collection of mummies before he and his guests finally returned to San Francisco in 1892. Decorating his office at the *Examiner* with sculpture and mummies, he resumed shaking the dry bones of newspaperdom. He wanted to expand. He saw no reason why he could

[5] Mrs. Fremont Older, *op. cit.*, 107.   [6] Winkler, *Phenomenon*, 89.
[7] The same, 90.   [8] The same, 91.   [9] The same.   [10] Carlson and Bates, 59.

not shake the bones with equal success elsewhere. He added up the circulation of the existing New York newspapers, compared the figure with the population, and decided there was room for another.[11] He sent his business manager, Charles M. Palmer, on an exploratory trip east, but Palmer found that it would cost $1,250,000 to buy the fading New York *Times*, and $2,000,000 for the Chicago *Morning Record*. Both were much too high. In fact, Hearst knew that he could make no new metropolitan journalistic plunge without heavy financial help from his mother. He besieged her for a loan. It may be that his continued harboring of Tessie was one reason for Phoebe's refusal, and that Miss Powers thus was a determining factor in rescuing New York from the Hearst invasion that eventually struck the city. Still, he was confident that he would ultimately have his way. Taking a map of the United States, he circled the principal cities, drawing a double circle around New York.

"George," he said to his *fidus Achates*, Pancoast, "some day, a paper here and here and here." [12]

In the fall of 1892, scores of deputies and Southern Pacific officers were searching the mountains north of Visalia for two outlaws, Chris Evans and John Sontag. Evans and Sontag had made a practice of robbing S.P. trains in the vicinity and shooting holes in lawmen seeking to arrest them. The railroad was so unpopular because of its ruthless disregard for the public that the fugitives become folk heroes. Citizens guffawed at the platoons of officers who made safari into the wilds only to return empty-handed. The S.P. angrily offered large rewards. It did no good, for the outlaws eluded the searchers with laughable ease. It was at this time that an *Examiner* reporter, tall, elegant Henry "Petey" Bigelow, made his way alone into the mountains, found Evans and Sontag, stayed with them overnight and took down a long interview which he carried back to San Francisco for front-page publication. It was a clear scoop, delighting Hearst and the public alike because it caused irate S.P. executives to demand why, if an *Examiner* writer could find the gunmen, the law could not.[13]

When Arthur McEwen took the Keeley cure, it supplied the idea for another sensation. The paper's most outstanding alcoholic, Robert Duncan Milne, was persuaded to take the cure at Hearst's expense. He came out cold sober to write a full-page shocker about the mental and physical pangs of a drunkard undergoing dehydration. He praised and recommended the cure. A fortnight later his feet sought the familiar brass rail and he was drunk again.[14]

His downfall provoked sneers in the opposition press, which bore no love for Hearst and his fast-gaining daily. The *Examiner* replied with an editorial declaring that the Keeley cure was not responsible for Milne's backsliding, since "he took the bichloride treatment merely as an experiment . . . No desire for sobriety prompted him to seek relief from alcoholic craving." In

[11] James Melvin Lee, *A History of American Journalism*, 372.
[12] Winkler, *Phenomenon*, 92.   [13] *Examiner*, Oct. 7, 1892.   [14] Jerome Hart, 187.

an adjoining column was a letter from Dr. G. E. Gussdorf, manager of the local Keeley Institute, defending the treatment.

"[Milne] seems to have had no wish to be cured," Gussdorf wrote, ". . . . thinking that all the pleasure he had in life was gotten while under the influence of liquor and believing that he could have more pleasure in the future drunk than sober . . . according to his ideas, a state of drunkenness is preferable to a state of sobriety." [15]

Milne proved the contention. Some regarded this journalistic airing of a man's personal weakness as lacking in taste, which indeed it was. In the bright lexicon of Hearst and Chamberlain, the all-important word was "circulation," and "taste" lurked far in the background. This had been bothering the high-minded bear hunter, Allen Kelly, and his wife for some time. After five years on the *Examiner* they resigned, Mrs. Kelly later commenting, "From the beginning of his journalistic career [Hearst] had a very sure instinct about the seamy underside of life and what it would feed on with gusto. And the consequent rapid increase in the *Examiner's* circulation he considered ample proof that he was right." [16]

Hearst had taken a fancy to the ranch his father had bought beyond the bay near Pleasanton. He often spent weekends there with Tessie and such guests as Lent, Chamberlain, Bigelow or Cozy Noble. It was a lovely spot, but the Senator's death had halted his improvements on the place, where he had intended to keep his race horses. Hearst loved horses—in fact, all animals—but had no interest in racing. His quick imagination pictured the ranch as a luxurious country place. He had once told his mother that he would like to live in Windsor Castle, and had asked her to buy the Louvre, which were early indications of his penchant for palaces. He sincerely wanted to own palaces. With most people such thoughts are kept in the safe realm of daydreams never expected to come true, but to his optimistic nature there seemed no reason why they should not be realized. He had an eye for architecture and a genuine, if unorthodox, flair for design. Many of the happiest later years of his life would be spent in buying, designing and building palaces, or buying their contents. Now, although he had to be satisfied with something less, he approached the idea with the same seignorial spirit.

In his enthusiasm he quite forgot that the ranch was his mother's property and that she might have plans of her own for it. Calling in an architect, he modernized the old ranch house. The five-ton stone wellhead from Italy was hauled from San Francisco and installed in the dooryard. He took such a fancy to two baby bears he saw at the San Francisco Midwinter Fair that he bought them and had Pancoast bring them to the ranch by wagon. Hearst and the architect discussed plans for a new and grander house higher on the hillside which, among other things, would accommodate his rapidly growing collection of art objects.[17]

Phoebe's San Francisco friends (could it have been Edward Hardy Clark?)

[15] Quoted in Lewis, *Bay Window Bohemia*, 141.   [16] Florence Finch Kelly, 240.
[17] Mrs. Fremont Older, *op. cit.*, 106–7.

were keeping her well informed. The news reached her in Washington that William was still maintaining Miss Powers and was planning a new ranch house. It aroused her to desperation.

"He is going too far," she said in the hearing of her niece.[18]

One of the things Phoebe Hearst stood for with all her might was propriety, an adherence to the conventional moral code which she considered essential to decency and goodness. For a time years earlier, her husband had strayed and in her opinion had been saved from ruin only by his return to the fold. In Washington she had become a genuinely great lady, known for good works, among them the founding and maintenance of a kindergarten for white children and another for Negro children. To have her son carry on in San Francisco was a double disaster that threatened his own future and also made a travesty of her efforts to improve the opportunities and morals of others. In some way, perhaps from Orrin Peck or from the frank William himself, she had learned that his affair with Tessie had begun at Harvard and continued for eight years. Meanwhile, he had refused to marry and "settle down." To Phoebe, Tessie represented the fatal temptation that was leading him to destruction.

For all her sweetness, Phoebe was not lacking either in decision or in some mastery of the subtle arts. Late in 1893 she arrived with Anne Drusilla in San Francisco and put up at the new California Hotel on Bush Street, determined by hook or crook to scuttle Miss Powers.[19]

How she accomplished this delicate mission is not entirely known, but accomplish it she did, and without her son's knowledge. She managed to get word to Tessie, either in person or through an emissary. One can only speculate about this melodramatic interview. It is possible that Phoebe used a combination of warning and cajolery, letting Tessie know that she was living in illegal cohabitation that might even land her in jail. The girl was devoted to Hearst, but she knew the vulnerability of her position. She left Hearst as if it were her own decision entirely, telling him among other things that her health was failing and she must end their affair with finality and return east. It is said by some in San Francisco today that when she left she took with her $150,000 of Phoebe's money, which is doubtless an exaggeration.[20]

In taking this action, Phoebe thought herself justified by all considerations of righteousness as well as William's welfare. Actually, she was carrying interference quite far in the life of a son who was nearing thirty-one and, whatever his failings, should have been past such motherly meddling.

Hearst was dumfounded at Tessie's departure. He became disconsolate. He was so unhappy that his mother grew concerned. Taking pity on him, she cabled to Munich asking Orrin Peck to come and save Willie from melancholia. The rotund Peck, who had always delighted Hearst with his humor, was the sort who could tell a droll story at a crowded table and have every diner in stitches. A true friend, he arrived in San Francisco within a month. Hearst sadly gave up his house in Sausalito and moved into a suite at the vast, seven-story Palace Hotel with his mother, his cousin and Peck. What had happened to him had thwarted his wish to have his own way, and there seemed nothing that he could do about it. All winter his depression was so acute that Phoebe and Peck made it a point to take him frequently to dinner and the theater. Peck served as court jester, making occasional use of his famous impersonation of Queen Victoria. Draping a towel over his head in imitation of her traditional snood, and distending his fat cheeks and pursing his lips in a ludicrous likeness, he would mouth sonorous absurdities about the goodness of Prince Albert and the glories of the "Empah." Never was such sustained effort expended to save a lovelorn young man from the doldrums. Anne Drusilla, who was fifteen, still remembers the long campaign to rehabilitate the crushed Cousin Willie.[21]

Peck, now a painter of distinction, spent weeks at sittings and executed a portrait in oils of his friend. It shows Hearst as a handsome man with a pale, trailing mustache and large blue eyes that stare straight at the observer with a gaze so cool, direct and penetrating as to be somewhat unnerving.

But if Hearst was depressed, he was still running the *Examiner*, still slaying the dragons, and pressing the assault on the S.P., whose Collis P. Huntington was still in charge although Senator Stanford had recently died. His busy brain was constantly hatching what his staff called "brainwaves." One of these he sprang on Morphy, asking him to do a full-page Sunday feature on seven interesting San Francisco personalities, giving a column to each person. He suggested a few of the personalities and left Morphy to find the rest. Morphy, who was inclined to be leisurely, wrote six of the columns but found himself up against the Sunday deadline without having achieved the seventh. He invented No. 7. It was a pathetic yarn titled "The Last of the McGintys," about an orphan newsboy of that name who was the sole support of his two younger brothers.

Phoebe Hearst read the story and was in tears. She sent Morphy a note containing five twenty-dollar bills to purchase food and clothing for the suffering McGintys.

"I was in a dilemma," Morphy later recalled. "There *were* no McGintys. When I told the city editor about the problem, he suggested, 'We'd better go over to the Mint [a nearby saloon] to break one of these twenties and think things over.'"

Several reporters joined them at the Mint. Most of one twenty was in the till by the time they decided that a story so touching to Mrs. Hearst obviously had human-interest qualities that should be exploited further. They rounded up three ragged urchins, had an *Examiner* artist draw pictures of them, then bought them new clothing and had them sketched again. This before-and-after picture appeared in next Sunday's paper along with a story telling how the generosity of Mrs. Hearst and the *Examiner* had saved the McGintys from squalor. The McGintys made such a hit that they appeared in yet another feature, and possibly would have continued indefinitely had not a reporter for the rival *News-Letter* learned the truth and blazoned the fraud in a stinging exposé.

Fanciful writing of this kind did not offend Hearst, but Morphy did his best to dodge Mrs. Hearst thereafter. Finally she encountered him and fixed him with a reproachful eye.

"Oh, Mr. Morphy," she exclaimed, "how could you do such a thing!"

He was at a loss to reply.

"Well, anyway, Mr. Morphy," she conceded, "that was a wonderful story you wrote . . . It had me weeping for several hours." [22]

When she returned to Washington in the spring with her niece, and Peck left for Munich, William seemed almost to have recovered his equanimity.

III. THE MADHOUSE

ONE night in the *Examiner* office, fiery Assistant City Editor Jake Dressler, a tall man with fierce mustachios and a bass voice, exploded over some delinquency of reporter Alfonso "Blinker" Murphy.

"You're fired!" Dressler bellowed across the room at him.

Murphy, a holdover from the George Hearst regime, spoke with a trace of brogue. "That's all ver-ry well," he said, "but you cannot fire me."

"The hell I can't!" Dressler roared.

While the entire staff watched with interest, Murphy moved into the gorgeous, antique-furnished office of Hearst. Dressler likewise strode in. Hearst, in his shirtsleeves at his desk, looked up inquiringly. Murphy and Dressler, with some heat, each gave his own version of the quarrel. Hearst nodded.

"Mr. Murphy," he said hesitantly, "it has always been my understanding that it was the right of the editor to discharge a man if he felt it necessary. Do you have any reason for suggesting that we make an exception?"

"I have, Mr. Hearst," Murphy replied. "The reason is that *I refuse to be fired.*"

Hearst gazed at him impassively for a moment. Then he turned to Dressler, lifting his hands in resignation.

"In the circumstances, Mr. Dressler," he said, smiling, "I don't see what we can do about this." [1]

Murphy stayed on, to remain an *Examiner* man for many years. Even Dressler saw the comedy of the situation. The enigmatic Hearst charm pervaded the office and gave it a character like none other, particularly appealing to men with a sense of humor and a taste for adventure. "To talk

[22] Carlson and Bates, 55–56.   [1] James Swinnerton to author, Nov. 2, 1959.

with one of the survivors of that crew," a San Francisco newsman wrote thirty-five years later, "is to get the flavor of a happy and extravagant world, now gone forever. The *Examiner* office was a madhouse inhabited by talented and erratic young men, drunk with life in a city that never existed before or since. They had a mad boss, one who flung away money, lived like a ruler of the late Empire . . . and cheered them on as they made newspaper history." [2]

There were few sensitive staff members like the Kellys who were offended by Hearst's liberties with the news. In San Francisco the sky was the limit, journalistically and otherwise. The *Examiner* merely soared higher than the rest. True, Hearst paid the best salaries and was lavish with bonuses for good work. Yet the remarkable solidarity of the staff was not the result of mere pay. Hearst, the practical joker, seemed to take journalism as a glorious lark. Hearst, the showman, seemed to regard the *Examiner* as a thing of flesh and blood acting on a vast stage with the people of California as audience, and unless it made them laugh or cry it was a failure. Hearst, the reformer, thought he was Galahad ridding the world of evil. Hearst, the circulation man, conceived incessant brainwaves—ideas for news stories, features, advertising. Hearst, the collector, could get lost in contemplation of an art catalogue. Hearst, the playboy, took his mistress to the Nile and returned with 3200 negatives.

His quiet enthusiasm and energy were infectious. There was an intriguing sense of suspense in the newsroom, since no one knew what would happen next. The atmosphere was mad, but exciting. The Chief, as he was coming to be called, was a shrewd judge of men and had a lively appreciation for loyalty. He was quick to give praise for a job well done. Courteous in a courtly, old-world way, he never gave a blunt order but always expressed his wishes in the form of a polite suggestion, saying "please," and "if you don't mind." He never got angry. He never raised his voice.[3] He showed great patience in his frequent conciliation of Ambrose Bierce, a firebrand who would fly into a fury if a word of his copy was changed. And he was sentimental enough to save the job of an expendable reporter, Blinker Murphy.

None of that wild crew understood him, but almost to a man they admired him and in some cases loved him. He would never discharge anyone, even with ample cause. He paid Bierce $100 a week, a huge salary at the time, particularly since the satirist was given a free hand and was often over the heads of many *Examiner* readers. The testy Bierce occasionally quit in unreasonable rage. Hearst always went to great lengths to lure him back, using good humor and clever flattery, and even calling on Bierce with olive branches. On one of these occasions he wrote Bierce:

> Write about anything you like if you will only write. . . . Don't for
> Heaven's sake stop "Prattle." I shall think myself a terrible "hoodoo" if im-

---

[2] George P. West in *American Mercury*, Nov., 1930.
[3] Charles E. Tebbs to author, Feb. 6, 1960.

mediately on my return the *Examiner* should lose what is to me its very best feature. I hope you will continue. I don't want to have to stop my subscription to my own paper for lack of interest in the damned old sheet. Shall I appoint myself a committee of one to come up and persuade you? [4]

Bierce, who found it hard to praise anyone, later wrote of his employer, "He did not once direct nor request me to write an opinion that I did not hold, and only two or three times suggested that I refrain for a season from expressing opinions that I did hold, when they were antagonistic to the policy of the paper, as they commonly were." [5]

Bierce was a constant problem, a chronic libeler who sometimes involved the *Examiner* in troublesome lawsuits; yet Hearst ignored the trouble because he prized his wit. Bierce once infuriated the great California wine producer, Arpad Haraszthy, by writing:

> The wine of Arpad Haraszthy has a bouquet all its own. It tickles and titillates the palate. It gurgles as it slips down the alimentary canal. It warms the cockles of the heart, and it burns the sensitive lining of the stomach.

Haraszthy's lawyer demanded a retraction. It came in Bierce's "Prattle" column the next day:

> The wine of Arpad Haraszthy does not have a bouquet all its own. It does not tickle and titillate the palate. It does not gurgle as it slips down the alimentary canal. It does not warm the cockles of the heart, and it does not burn the sensitive lining of the stomach. [6]

Some San Franciscans said that Sam Chamberlain, or Arthur McEwen, or Charles M. Palmer were responsible for the paper's success. The *Examiner* men knew better. Hearst was there before any of them. To be sure, he had gathered the best newspaper staff west of the Rockies, but it was Hearst who had the ideas, called the tune, ran the show and deserved whatever praise or blame was merited.

The general tendency was to give the praise to others and hand the blame to Hearst. He was of a strange, maverick breed which no one could quite fathom, a son of wealth who fought the interests of his own moneyed class. Like his late father, he had no use for boiled-shirt society, but unlike his father who believed that Democratic policies would solve all ills, he was even a maverick Democrat who often taxed his own party as too reactionary. He favored union labor, the eight-hour day, the income tax, the exclusion of cheap Chinese labor, the popular election of United States Senators, some of them measures then regarded as downright radical. The San Francisco upper crust eyed him with suspicion and began to fasten on him what was then a dirty word: Socialist. [7]

[4] Carey McWilliams, *Ambrose Bierce*, 209.
[5] Walter Neale, *The Life of Ambrose Bierce*, 91.
[6] E. D. Coblentz, *Ambrose Bierce, Stepfather of The Family* (pamphlet).
[7] Carlson and Bates, 57; Mrs. Fremont Older, *op. cit.*, 92, 118–19.

Hearst's ability for ignoring abuse was unmatched. He was wooing the masses, not the rich. With an unerring instinct for popular taste, he made his headlines bigger and decorated his pages with more illustrations. Jimmy Swinnerton, only seventeen when he joined the *Examiner,* was soon drawing a comic strip featuring the adventures of some little bears. Homer Davenport, a former Northern Pacific brakeman from Oregon who reached San Francisco as nursemaid for animals belonging to a small circus, joined the *Examiner* as an artist and demonstrated skill as a political cartoonist, although his spelling was as unreliable as that of the late Senator Hearst. Charles E. Tebbs quit cowpunching to join the art department. George Palmer (unrelated to Charles M. Palmer) arrived in town as first mate of a tramp steamer, and although he could not draw a line was made head of the art department—a reward, it was said, for extricating Hearst from some perilous Barbary Coast scrape.[8]

The *Examiner* harbored a crew of Bohemians probably regarded by the sober element as subversive, not the least of them being the huge, yellow-haired, whisky-drinking poet, Joaquin Miller, who had already written his own eulogy and built his own funeral pyre beyond Oakland. Hearst had surrounded himself with a gallery of talented eccentrics who required the most gentle and understanding supervision. His success in keeping them reasonably in hand was itself an achievement.

One of the few who gave him trouble was the gifted editorialist, Arthur McEwen, a militant reformer whose hot temper could explode with slight cause. Early in 1894 he quarreled with Hearst and quit. He started his own paper, the weekly *Letter,* began blasting the rascals of California, and was broke in three months. Hearst took him back immediately as editorial chief. Five months later, Hearst, out of town at the time, wired McEwen a precautionary suggestion:

> I would prefer somewhat fewer editorials. Be careful not to be drawn into too many fights. We are now after the Democrats and the Republicans, the lawyers and the businessmen, with occasional sideswipes at the people. This sort of limits our sympathizers and will also make the editorial page too truculent to be interesting. I think a more calm and judicial tone on politics and a greater variety of subjects would improve the page. Think it over.

The McEwen temper blew. "The public judgment," he replied, "is that the editorial columns of the *Examiner* now have what they very much needed— brains, courage and character. I have given all my energies and sixteen hours a day to your paper and placed it on a higher level than it has ever held before. You don't deserve such work, for you are unable to appreciate it. Your telegram is equally ungrateful and stupid. Accept my resignation." [9]

San Francisco was treated to a family quarrel when McEwen resumed

[8] Lewis, *Bay Window Bohemia,* 226–27; Willis J. Abbot, *Watching The World Go By,* 140.
[9] Bruce, 241–46.

his *Letter* and wrote of Hearst, ". . . he is a humbug in journalism. He is but a clever amateur." [10]

The *Examiner* went on, moving into a fine new building at Third and Market Streets. Annie Laurie, a favorite of Hearst because she was game for anything, continued such exploits as living with Mormons in Utah and exposing polygamy; getting a job in a fruit cannery and publicizing the low wages and miserable working conditions; and interviewing the madam of one of the leading local brothels. Annie's talent for the sob story could at times be constructive. When "Little Jim," the crippled son of a prostitute, was born in City Prison Hospital, Annie pulled out all the stops in a series of pathetic stories that had housewives weeping over back fences. She started a "Little Jim fund" drive that raised $20,000 toward a hospital for crippled children that eventually became a reality.[11] These titillating sensations were balanced by long-range drives for reform such as the campaign for municipal ownership of the water system and street railways, and the never-ending assault on the S.P.

In attacking Huntington and his Southern Pacific–Central Pacific monopoly, which owned many legislators and newspapers and was politically supreme in the West, Hearst for all his money was a puny David pitted against a corporate Goliath. The time was drawing near when the S.P. would be required to repay its thirty-year, $27,500,000 loan from the government, which with interest now totaled almost $60,000,000. Huntington was lobbying energetically in Washington for a measure that would spread the payments over another fifty years on the ground that the road would otherwise be bankrupted.

The *Examiner* was unsympathetic. According to one observer:

> . . . the *Examiner*'s ridicule . . . was so damaging that Huntington gave his personal attention to the matter of how the paper might be silenced. Nothing could be done, for the young man who owned the *Examiner* had the backing of a multi-millionaire mother, and arguments that had proved effective elsewhere [meaning bribes] were found to be useless.[12]

The *Examiner* circulated a petition against the S.P. funding bill and advocating government ownership. It got 194,663 signatures. Although there were occasional anti-Huntington blasts from other editors, no paper in California had carried on such a long, steadfast, brilliant and violent campaign as the *Examiner*, informing and arousing the public about issues concerning every person living west of the Rockies. As it became apparent that the *Examiner* drive was popular and winning it more circulation, other journals joined in the tocsin.[13]

True, the subtler citizens noticed that the *Examiner* was an orchestra composed mainly of horns and drums. Conductor Hearst, in his aim for a new

[10] The same, 246.   [11] Carlson and Bates, 56.   [12] Lewis, *The Big Four*, 349–50.
[13] Stuart Daggett, *Chapters in the History of the Southern Pacific*, 402; San Francisco *Examiner*, Sept. 21, 1894.

fanfare every day, kept waving at the percussionists and brasses, neglecting the violins. His policy was excitement fortissimo, which grew deafening. When a young Sunday school superintendent named Theodore Durrant murdered two pretty girls at Emmanuel Baptist Church in the spring of 1895, the *Examiner's* rendition was a series of crashing crescendoes that went on for weeks. Headline writers labeled it "THE CRIME OF A CENTURY," Annie Laurie dwelled tearfully on its tragic aspects, and artists drew faithful sketches of the church, the killer, the victims, and—especially—the skirts and undergarments of the victims.[14]

When Arthur McEwen failed a second time with his *Letter,* Hearst took him back into the fold again despite his hard words. Another who came back to the fold was Tessie Powers. In some way the determined Hearst reestablished communication with her and she rejoined him. From Tessie he learned of his mother's meddling, and was angry about it. But he could not indulge his anger overmuch, for he needed a sizeable share of her fortune to establish himself in New York. Although Phoebe had helped him financially, she had resisted his requests for the large loan he thought necessary. In 1895 she capitulated in the grand manner.

In a deal handled through the National City Bank of New York, Phoebe sold her seven-sixteenths interest in the Anaconda Copper Mining Company to the Rothschilds of London for $7,500,000, and handed the money over to her son, with the provision that Edward Hardy Clark exercise some supervisory jurisdiction.[15]

At last a multi-millionaire in his own right, Hearst that summer went to Europe, probably taking Tessie with him, certainly buying *objets d'art* and calling on Orrin Peck in Munich. His business manager on the *Examiner,* C. M. Palmer, was also on a European vacation. Hearst, meeting him in Paris, asked him to canvass New York for available newspapers. Palmer reached New York in August, shortly before Hearst, to whom he reported that the *Times, Advertiser, Recorder* and *Morning Journal* were for sale. The first three, however, had high price-tags. While price never made Hearst retreat from anything he wanted, he had a sublime confidence in his own ability to breathe life into any newspaper that had so much as a faint pulse. He told Palmer to dicker for the *Journal.*[16]

The *Journal,* a spicy sheet known as the "chambermaids' delight" when it was owned by Albert Pulitzer, brother of Joseph, had been sold for $1,000,000 in 1894 to John R. McLean, wealthy publisher of the Cincinnati *Enquirer.* McLean had made it a more substantial Democratic newspaper, thereby losing his chambermaid readers and gaining precious few above-stairs. The *Journal's* pulse was indeed flickering. Its circulation had sagged to 77,000, its advertising was meager and deficits were mounting. McLean, having heard of the Hearst circulation magic, offered him a half interest in the paper for $360,000—a suggestion that made Palmer smile.

[14] *Examiner,* April 13, 1895, ff.   [15] Ferdinand Lundberg, *Imperial Hearst,* 50.
[16] Mrs. Fremont Older, *op. cit.,* 129.

"Mr. Hearst believes in going it alone," he said. "If you knew him as I do, you'd realize you could never work with him in running a newspaper." [17]

Palmer offered half the sum, $180,000, for the *Journal*, lock, stock and barrel. McLean accepted with so little parley that Palmer realized he could have got it for less, later admitting as much to Hearst.

The jubilant Hearst laughed off a few thousand dollars. He did not know until some time later that he had also acquired in the deal a German-language edition of the paper, *Das Morgen Journal*. He acquired formal title on September 25, keeping the transaction so quiet that not until almost a fortnight later did the Republican New York *Tribune* learn of the sale and show its ignorance of the radical Democratic Californian by commenting, ". . . Its [the *Journal's*] entire tone will be changed, and it is even hinted that as Mr. Hearst is a Republican the political character of the paper may be altered." [18]

[17] Winkler, *Hearst—An American Phenomenon*, 94–95.
[18] N. Y. *Tribune*, Oct. 6, 1895.

BOOK THREE

THE WAR-MAKER

1. The Invasion

I. SCIENCE, MURDER AND SEX

IN 1895, New York City, counting Brooklyn and other areas not yet technically assimilated, had ten times San Francisco's population. It was a city
of elevated lines, cable cars and four-in-hands, but bicycles were suddenly
the rage and were creating a grave traffic problem. A few horseless carriages
were making their appearance, their drivers being called "engineers." Architecture and interior decorating leaned heavily to the ornate, and women
wore cartwheel hats and seven-yard skirts over fraudulently outjutting undergarments. Men sported derbies, celluloid collars and used mustache cups.
The New York Giants were in seventh place that fall. Well-known products
were Ivory Soap ("99 44/100 Percent Pure"), Beecham's Pills, Budweiser
Beer and Sweet Caporal Cigarettes.

New York looked prosperous enough to the casual observer, but there were
breadlines that the casual did not see. The nation was in economic torment.
The army of unemployed was growing, farmers were burning wheat they
could not sell, and a groundswell of protest was rising far west of Fifth
Avenue. A cry for free silver was gaining in volume. There had been sign-
posts of trouble—Coxey's Army, the Homestead riot, the Pullman strike—
but New York was relatively ignorant of the scope of the discontent. Perhaps
even the Westerner William Randolph Hearst was not fully aware of it as
yet, for he had business problems that tended to diminish externals, but he
would not remain unaware for long.

Hearst took a bachelor apartment in Madison Square near the Hoffman
House at Broadway and Twenty-fifth Street. The tenuous saga of Tessie
Powers, the girl who had woven in and out of his life since Harvard, came
to its end around this time. Tessie's health had really given way, and he had
provided her with funds and a home somewhere in upstate New York. He
summoned Chamberlain, McEwen, Pancoast, Cozy Noble, Annie Laurie,
and others of his San Francisco stars and began publication of the *Morning
Journal* in October, although he did not announce his ownership until the
November 8 issue. Once again he had got his way and was happy. His
hunger for leadership would be satisfied temporarily by exploits in journalism, for he had abandoned the thought of becoming involved personally in
politics, and indeed the idea that such a shy man might seek office was
laughable.[1]

[1] *Pearson's Magazine*, Sept., 1906.

Hearst, at thirty-two, was at a crossroads in his career. He was expanding, invading the nation's largest city, risking disaster. What he did in journalism would give clues to his character, which no one professed to understand. His selfishness and egoism, which could be more kindly described as an iron will to do the things he wanted in the way he wished to do them, would find greater avenues of expression. His contradictory streak of generosity and his sympathy for the common people would likewise be given wider scope. The story of the real Hearst would be told by the road he would take —whether he would strike out into expediency or would choose the lane into generosity and public service.

The fact that he never stayed on either road very long, but would shuttle from a selfishness to generosity and back again, would contribute to the "Hearst puzzle" and denote a basic instability that he seemed unable to conquer.

He would be accused of many things, but never of laziness. Unlike most heirs to millions, he deliberately chose hard work—because he liked newspaper work, it is true, but mostly because he had a kingly dream of a newspaper empire "here and here and here" that would give him, a man unable to speak in public, limitless power without speaking a word. It could be argued that his journalistic strides were the logical extension of his pranks at Harvard, the determined efforts of a bashful man to gain recognition. His natural optimism had been swollen by his success with the *Examiner* until he saw himself holding the key to a kingdom all his own, safely above the reverses and failures of ordinary men because he knew precisely where he was going and how to get there.

The *Journal* occupied a rickety plant in the second and third floors of the Tribune Building, at Park Row and Spruce Street on Printing House Square, where the statue of Ben Franklin adjured newspapermen to high purpose. The proud *Sun* was across the street, the lagging *Times* was nearby, and a short block north was the glittering Pulitzer Building, where the presses spewed out a half million copies of the *World* every day, and where Hearst's correspondent Ike Allen now had an eleventh-floor office furnished in California redwood. Across Park Row was the cupolaed City Hall Hearst would one day set his heart on. Now he was intent only on pitting his puny *Journal* in a war for circulation and power against Joseph Pulitzer, another millionaire, and his puissant *World*—a rash presumption that would be equaled in world affairs should Luxembourg set out to invade Germany.

At first Pulitzer was not even aware of the gnat buzzing around his head. Hearst dropped the *Journal's* price to one cent and enlarged it to sixteen pages, thereby assuring himself of great financial loss. Sam Chamberlain, the managing editor, had somewhat lost contact with New York, the other San Francisco imports were strangers, and the holdover employes from the McLean regime had to be taught how to shake the dry bones, so there were difficulties. The *Journal* imitated the *World* format, gave loving attention to crime and scandal, and immediately showed sympathy for the Cuban rebels fighting their Spanish overlords.[2] It gained in circulation, but since at a penny it was losing on every copy, the loss was greater the more copies were sold. This inherent deficit would continue until greater efficiency and more advertising were obtained. It bothered Hearst not at all. He was ready to lose millions. He was aware that the most intellectual paper in the city was the *Evening Post,* and that it had the lowest circulation. The *Post* could have the intellectuals. He cultivated the masses with a style of schoolboy simplicity and with his characteristic orgy of promotion. Pennies were mailed to registered voters along with strong arguments that the best purchase a penny could make was the *Journal.* Billboards, advertising in elevated railroads and street cars, and brass bands got across the idea that the *Journal* gave more for a penny than the *World* did for double the price. The *Journal* sent out wagons to give free coffee and sweaters to the jobless.[3]

Hearst was looking for more talent, offering large salaries. Liberal, goateed Willis J. Abbot was lured east from the Chicago *Record.* Hearst shook hands with him and told him to take charge of the editorial page next day. Abbot reported as instructed in Hearst's absence, but the assistant editor in charge did not know him and refused him admittance. Abbot would have been sent packing had he not known Business Manager Palmer, who finally got him a desk. He found the *Journal* office a shambles of disorganized endeavor and wrote a friend that he had "secured very remunerative employment in a lunatic asylum." [4]

By year's end the *Journal* had passed 100,000 circulation and the *World* was beginning to notice the competition. Hearst evolved the idea that by raiding the *World's* able staff he would at once cripple Pulitzer and strengthen his own sheet. He cast envious eyes on the Sunday *World,* an immense profit-maker, selling a half million copies at five cents. The editor of its magazine section was a scholarly, irascible young Dartmouth graduate named Morrill Goddard, who had a lunatic style all his own. Goddard had made a calculating study of the mass mind. He appealed to it with wild essays in pseudo-science ("Are Sea Serpents Real?"); excursions into the morbid ("How It Feels to Be a Murderer"); and into sex ("Eight Stage Beauties on Broadway"). He had a popular cartoon called "The Yellow Kid," the adventures of an engaging slum urchin, drawn by R. F. Outcault. Hearst was particularly impressed with Goddard's handling of the racy "Girl-in-the-Pie" stag party given by Stanford White in his studio in the tower of Madison Square Garden. A huge pie had been borne in, and from it stepped a toothsome model "covered only by the ceiling"—a scene Goddard splashed with an enormous drawing.[5]

The Hearst summons soon became an institution in New York journalism. Newsmen knew that if they received a card reading, "Mr. Hearst would be

[2] Don C. Seitz, *Joseph Pulitzer: His Life and Letters,* 210–11.
[3] Lundberg, 52; Mrs. Fremont Older, *op. cit.,* 140–41.
[4] Abbot, *Watching The World Go By,* 136–37.
[5] Winkler, *Hearst—An American Phenomenon,* 103–4.

pleased to have you call," they would be offered employment at flattering salaries. Goddard got his summons late in January, 1896, and met Hearst at the Hoffman House. Goddard had misgivings, since it was widely believed in New York that Hearst would bankrupt himself in time, but he capitulated when Hearst handed him a check in five figures.

"That ought to convince you that I intend to remain in New York quite some time," Hearst said.[6]

Goddard explained that he would be handicapped without his staff of writers and artists.

"All right," Hearst replied. "Let's take the whole staff."[7]

Tall, blind Joseph Pulitzer was a tyrannical genius, so nervous that the mere sound of rattling paper could react on him like an explosion, causing him to weep or curse. The theft of his Sunday specialists enraged him. He ordered his business manager, Solomon S. Carvalho, to lure them back with a higher offer. Carvalho did so, rescuing them for twenty-four hours, until Hearst went still higher and got them for good, doing much of his dickering from his office in the Pulitzer Building.[8]

"I won't have my building used for purposes of seduction!" Pulitzer snapped.[9]

Hearst was evicted, but the raid continued. In the reorganization made necessary by Goddard's departure, Pulitzer raised City Editor Richard A. Farrelly to direction of the morning edition and arranged a banquet to honor Farrelly. Farrelly went over to Hearst the day before the banquet, which was suspended.[10] With Outcault now drawing yellow kids for the *Journal,* and another artist, George Luks, drawing yellow kids for the *World,* the term "yellow journalism" was born. Among the many *World* men Hearst kidnaped was a cartoonist, T. E. Powers. Pulitzer immediately rehired Powers on a contract, whereupon Hearst got him back again on a better contract. Resolving to settle the issue with the Western guerilla, Pulitzer sued for Powers' services, and the cartoonist was enjoined from working for either. Both Pulitzer and Hearst paid him his salary during the litigation, so that Powers became the envy of newspaperdom, a man paid two handsome salaries for doing nothing. When Hearst finally won the suit, Powers stood for drinks in a Park Row saloon, a convivial affair that inspired a skit paraphrasing a line from *Uncle Tom's Cabin.* While a friend belabored him harmlessly with a roll of paper, Powers, on his knees, groaned, "You can beat this poor old body but my soul belongs to William Randolph Hearst."[11]

By now the *Journal* was nearing 150,000 circulation and gaining on the *World.* Carvalho, growing nervous, urged Pulitzer to drop his price to one cent and smash the interloper once and for all. This was done on February 10, 1896, with exultant predictions among *World* executives that the *Journal* would be crushed. Surprisingly, the *Journal* was not hurt, although two

[6] The same, 104.   [7] James W. Barrett, *Joseph Pulitzer and His World,* 172.
[8] Seitz, *Pulitzer,* 212.   [9] Barrett, 173.   [10] Seitz, 215.
[11] Silas Bent, *Ballyhoo,* 154.

smaller sheets, the *Advertiser* and *Press,* were badly wounded. While the *World* gained more than 80,000 readers at its lower price, it was forced to raise its advertising rates, thereby alienating advertisers, some of whom went over to the *Journal.* To halt a huge drop in earnings, Pulitzer reduced his number of pages—a move causing Hearst to believe he had his antagonist staggering and to step up his bandwagon and billboard campaign into a furious assault. The Pulitzer price drop was ill-advised, bringing hardship on Carvalho, who had urged it, for now he had to cope with disgruntled advertisers. Carvalho quit Pulitzer in disgust at the end of March and went over to Hearst. Jokesters said that the sidewalk between the *World* and the *Journal* was growing thin.[12]

Willis Abbot, the Chicago import who had been given the title of "editor-in-chief" because he was in charge of the *Journal* editorial page, found that the title meant nothing. Abbot wrote:

> . . . [Hearst's] greatest joy in life was to attend the theater, follow it up with a lively supper and, at about 1:30 A.M., turn up at the office full of scintillating ideas and therewith rip my editorial page to pieces. Other pages were apt to suffer equally, and it was always an interesting spectacle to me to watch this young millionaire, usually in irreproachable evening dress, working over the forms, changing a head here, shifting the position of an article there, clamoring always for more pictures and bigger type. Any veteran newspaperman will testify that the time of closing in the composing room is always one that tests severely the nerves of the workers. . . . I can testify that not once did [Hearst] ever show signs of irritation or lose his temper . . .[13]

Edward Hardy Clark, Mrs. Hearst's financial manager, had moved his office to New York, part of the reason doubtless being to give him a better view of the Hearst expenditures. It was said that the view was making him nervous. Hearst occasionally visited his mother and cousin in Washington, once taking Cozy Noble with him, and Anne Drusilla Apperson found him in jovial spirits.[14] With a Presidential election looming, the *Journal* conducted a poll of states indicating that McKinley would be the Republican nominee but leaving great doubt as to the Democratic choice.[15] Always on the move, Hearst visited San Francisco in the spring on a "vacation." He dispatched Ambrose Bierce to Washington so that Bierce could keep an eye on the Southern Pacific's lobbying efforts in the capital to shuck off its debt to the government. Hearst was having trouble getting a new managing editor of the *Examiner* to replace Chamberlain. He took Petey Bigelow and Jerome Hart to dine at the splendid Maison Riche. Hart, still with the *Argonaut,* drank claret and Bigelow polished off a whole bottle of champagne while Hearst contented himself with water as he urged Hart for a whole hour to become managing editor of the *Examiner.* "He even said that I could

[12] Seitz, *Pulitzer,* 212–14, 217.   [13] Abbot, 145.
[14] Mrs. J. M. Flint to author, Feb. 20, 1960.   [15] N. Y. *Tribune,* April 20, 1896.

set the amount of my own salary," Hart recalled, but he refused because of the nervous strain he knew would be involved.[16]

When Hearst returned, he was concerned about the strong sentiment he found in the West in favor of unlimited coinage of silver. Hard times and deprivation had caused millions of voters of all political creeds—especially those in and near the silver-producing states—to hit on "free silver" as the remedy. Although his mother held interests in silver mines, and he had already embraced many "radical" theories, Hearst correctly dismissed this one as a delusion. He did not want the Democrats to fall into the silver trap. Having become acquainted with William C. Whitney, the millionaire New York Democrat who had been in Cleveland's cabinet and was a potential nominee for President, Hearst sent Editor Abbot to call on Whitney and offer the *Journal's* help in opposing the silver heresy. Whitney unhappily said it was too late—that the Democrats already were in the hands of the silver faction. In June the Republicans nominated McKinley at St. Louis, as had been expected. In July Hearst sent Abbot, a political specialist, to the Democratic convention in Chicago with instructions to work for the nomination of a gold-standard Democrat like Whitney.[17]

This was the convention which was intoxicated by the personality of William Jennings Bryan, the handsome, thirty-six-year-old ex-Congressman from Nebraska, whose voice had such a spine-tingling, organ quality. His famous "cross of gold" peroration, which he had polished to perfection in many renditions before smaller audiences, hypnotized the convention. He was a walkaway Democratic choice.

Abbot knew that in the conservative East the silver craze was regarded as such fatal folly that most Eastern Democratic papers would bolt the party. If Hearst would embrace Bryan, the *Journal* might gain national stature as the leading Democratic paper in the East. Bryan likewise knew his need for a strong editorial voice in New York. Bryan and Abbot got together in a hotel bathroom, away from frenzied delegates, and composed a telegram urging Hearst to support the Nebraskan.[18]

Hearst had already received news of the Bryan nomination and called a hurried editorial conference. Although he was a Democrat, his independence of thought was well known. All of his top men with one exception—McEwen—begged him to ditch Bryan. The respected business manager, Palmer, felt that support of Bryan would mean the ruin of the *Journal*. The hatred of Bryan and silver in New York City was so bitter that Hearst knew the decision would be crucial. "I had everything to lose and nothing to gain by supporting him," he said later, "for I did not believe in free silver. . . . I came to the conclusion that the man might not be sound, but at least he was sincere, and that the cause he stood for was the people's cause."[19]

This was not quite correct. Hearst, the gambler, knew that he was risking

[16] Hart, 85–86.   [17] Abbot, 157.   [18] The same, 168.
[19] *World's Work*, Oct., 1922.

disaster, but he also knew that with a little luck he stood a chance of great gain.

He said to his men, "Unlimber the guns; we are going to fight for Bryan." [20]

The decision took courage. It was motivated in large part by Hearst's belief that Bryan was the best candidate despite his one misguided plank. The silver issue soon split the Democratic party, caused the nomination of a Gold Democratic ticket and blew up a storm of bitterness seldom seen in American politics. In New York, the financial center, even the solid ranks of Tammany were split by discord. Bryan, whose personal life was blameless except for an inordinate fondness for a third helping of food, was reviled as an anarchist and criminal. New York's crusading Rev. C. H. Parkhurst called his ideas "accursed and treasonable." Brooklyn's Rev. Cortland Myers shouted, "[Bryan's] platform was made in Hell!" A favorite platitude of David B. Hill, the balding Democratic leader of New York State, was, "I am a Democrat." Hill, who had fought Bryan at the convention and lost, was asked if he was still a Democrat. "I am a Democrat still," he nodded. Then he added, "Very still." [21]

Pulitzer and his World, usually Democratic, bolted Bryan. The liberal Times did likewise. Hearst's Journal remained the only important newspaper in the East supporting Bryan. He was roundly abused for abetting anarchy and treason and was described as a traitor to his class.

Yet Hearst, who was already accused of being motivated entirely by expediency and of having no firm principles of his own, was troubled by something his enemies said never embarrassed him—a matter of principle. The nation was shaken by a confused, multitudinous demand for reform, and he, like Bryan, considered himself one of the reformers. His thinking on the issue was clear. He was in accord with Bryan in his espousal of the income tax and the regulation of railroads and corporations. But he considered Bryan dead wrong on the silver plank, which was the overriding issue of the campaign. He knew that free silver was a delusion.

He compromised the dilemma by ordering his editors in New York and San Francisco to boom Bryan but avoid all mention of silver. This was like diving into the water with the hope of staying dry. Silver was what everybody was talking about. For the Journal and the Examiner to ignore it was patently ridiculous. For three weeks they followed this ambivalent course. At last Willis Abbot, who as editorialist was suffering real anguish in trying to make the policy sound reasonable, spoke to Hearst about the absurdity of the stand. Hearst knew it. As Abbot recalled it, "At last with a sigh, he yielded, called a conference of his editors, and informed them that although he personally disbelieved in free coinage, he had been convinced that he must subordinate his principles to those of the party." [22] He instructed that free silver as well as the candidate be given hearty support.

[20] The same. [21] Harry Thurston Peck, Twenty Years of the Republic, 504.
[22] Abbot, 169.

The editor of his German newspaper, *Das Morgen Journal,* was present. This newspaper had been considered a "throw-in" with the purchase of the *Journal,* and Hearst had not given it serious attention.

"Vy, Mr. Hearst," the editor said proudly, "I haf been doing that already these three weeks!" [23]

II. THE YELLOW FELLOWS

Oh, McKinley he is sold for that yellow shining gold,
And Mark Hanna is the one that holds the notes;
He can talk about Inflation and Protection to Perfection,
But Bryan, he's a-goin' to get the votes.[1]

EDWARD Hardy Clark, who had gained stature and influence as Phoebe Hearst's adviser, opposed Bryan and exerted pressure against Hearst's adoption of the lunacy.[2] Hearst ignored him. He balanced his editorial praise for Bryan with vitriolic assault on McKinley and Mark Hanna.

McKinley, a good man without greatness, had served as Congressman and governor of Ohio, and had more than once gone on record as favoring free silver—something he now regretted. Three years earlier he had gone bankrupt by unwisely endorsing $130,000 in notes for a friend. Facing political ruin, he had been saved by the most unlikely-looking of good fairies, the square-faced, jug-eared Hanna. A hearty, roughneck, millionaire industrialist from Cleveland, Hanna had conceived something approaching infatuation for McKinley, although the two were direct opposites in almost everything but political acumen. He had picked up the $130,000 tab for McKinley, making it up with contributions of his own and many friends—an act of generosity without which McKinley would have been forced to quit politics and devote himself to paying his debts. Hanna was now McKinley's closest adviser and campaign manager. Despite McKinley's rigid honesty, the settlement of his debt was something that could be misconstrued by those inclined to misconstrue.[3]

The *Journal* had started to misconstrue as early as April, when it became apparent that McKinley would be nominated. He was labeled the "syndicate-owned candidate." But the cunning Hearst strategy was to center the attack on Hanna. McKinley was described as a nonentity, a puppet in the control of the powerful, unscrupulous Hanna. Into the hands of cartoonist Homer Davenport was thrust an opportunity that made him famous. The big, easygoing Davenport was weak on ideas, which usually had to be supplied by Hearst, McEwen or Abbot, but was a master draughtsman. He drew a series of cartoons always depicting Hanna as a gross, sordid monster covered with dollar signs, and McKinley as his pygmy slave. One of Hearst's ablest writers, Alfred Henry Lewis, was assigned to write articles of maximum injury to

[23] The same.   [1] N. Y. *Times,* Nov. 2, 1896.   [2] Abbot, 169.
[3] James Ford Rhodes, *The McKinley and Roosevelt Administrations,* 11; Herbert Croly, *Marcus Alonzo Hanna,* 170.

Hanna. Few could be as maliciously injurious as Lewis. Day after day, Hanna was heaped with abuse. Enraged, he wrote Hearst in protest, without result. He thought of suing for libel, but was dissuaded by friends who argued that this was precisely what Hearst wanted, since it would give an appearance of persecution.[4] Bryan meanwhile was the victim of insult almost as vengeful and far more general, but, always the gentleman, he stuck to the issues. With him on his record-breaking speechmaking tour were the sob sister, Annie Laurie, and other Hearst reporters.

In August, Bryan arrived in New York on an invasion regarded by his supporters with mingled cheer and anxiety. The metropolis' traditional Democratic supremacy had been shaken, and it was hoped that the magnetism of the Boy Orator of the Platte would arouse the city. Unhappily, he spoke in Madison Square Garden on a day so hot that both he and his audience were bathed in sweat. Inspiring as an extemporaneous speaker, Bryan on this occasion cautiously chose to read his speech, which, added to the fact that he spoke for two solid hours, caused a large exodus. The *Journal* spoke of the "whirlwind of enthusiasm" for him, but the *Times* more truthfully headlined, "BRYAN SPOKE AND HIS AUDIENCE FLED." [5]

On the following Sunday, Bryan was honored at the home of John Brisben Walker, a prominent Democrat and the publisher of *Cosmopolitan* magazine. One of the guests was Hearst, without whom Bryan would have been virtually blacked out newswise in the metropolitan area. Apparently it was their first meeting.[6] Doubtless Bryan thanked him for his support, and doubtless Hearst replied with his typical self-effacing modesty. Never was there a more striking example of the "strange bedfellow" truism—the devout, puritanical Bryan and the amoral, nonreligious Hearst, utter opposites but linked in the same strenuous crusade. For more than a quarter century they would continue to meet on many political stages, sometimes as enemies, alike only in being chronic losers.

The Hearst-Bryan entente had a queer two-way effect on the publisher's fortunes, boosting his circulation and losing him money. With the nearest Bryan paper of any size located in Buffalo, the *Journal* was the only loyal organ available to Bryanites in a radius of several hundred miles, and was being shipped as far as Boston, Philadelphia and Washington. The campaign was so bitter that it split families. Hearst was cold-shouldered at his clubs and subjected to social ostracism that bothered him not at all. Perhaps more painful was the withdrawal of advertising by gold-standard merchants.

". . . Hearst smiled that inscrutable smile of his," Abbot recorded, "and let them go." [7] His paper was losing $100,000 a month. Business Manager Palmer foresaw ruin. Instead of retrenching, Hearst launched a drive for campaign funds, magnificently offering to match every dollar subscribed with a dollar of his own.[8]

[4] Croly, 224–25.   [5] N. Y. *Journal*, Aug. 13, 1896; N. Y. *Times*, same date.
[6] J. C. Long, *Bryan, the Great Commoner*, 96.   [7] Abbot, 180.
[8] N. Y. *Journal*, Sept. 28, 1896.

Even his own editors were aghast at the financial loss. According to Abbot, "It seemed to some of us who day after day inhaled the fumes of his burning money, that he was mad, but he was only, as a matter of fact, shrewd and daring." [9]

The *Journal* office was truly a madhouse, succeeding lukewarm Tammany Hall as Eastern headquarters of the Bryan campaign. Reporters stumbled over politicians. The canny McEwen, a Bryan zealot, invented a character called "The Gentleman" who commented with burlesque snobbery in the *Journal* on the folly of people so ignorant that they believed the uncouth Bryan, who came from Nebraska and graduated from a college no Easterner had ever heard of, could possibly become President. Some unsophisticated Democrats took this seriously, and every mail contained furious threats that The Gentleman, whoever he was, would be murdered.[10] Through all this turmoil Hearst was as calm and unruffled as ever. A master puppeteer, he was pulling strings that exhibited comic interludes right along with the tense political drama. One of them was the "*Journal-Examiner* Yellow Fellow Transcontinental Bicycle Relay."

On August 25, a cyclist clad in yellow left the *Examiner* building on Market Street with a dispatch pouch to be handed successively to other riders on the long eastward grind. The stretch over the Sierras was ridden almost entirely through the snowsheds of the Southern Pacific. Other cyclists endured prairie cloudbursts and came near drowning in mud, but pedaled grimly on. Over the front of the *Journal* office was a huge map showing the course the riders followed, on which spectators could trace the daily progress by the movement of a miniature cyclist. On September 7, the last rider, a racer named Fred Titus, rode the final stretch from Kingsbridge to the *Journal* office at such a pace that bicycle policemen sought to arrest him for scorching but were left far in the rear. A flag-festooned stand had been erected in front of the *Journal* building. In it stood Hearst, a timekeeper, several *Journal* editors, and Postmaster Charles Dayton. A cheering crowd saw the perspiring, yellow-clad Titus ride up like the horseman from Ghent to Aix, to be timed at thirteen days, twenty-nine minutes, four and one-fifth seconds, and to be congratulated gravely by Hearst. The pouch he handed over with a flourish contained nothing more urgent than a friendly letter from the postmaster in San Francisco and another from Colonel William Shafter in the same city.[11]

Hearst seized on his Yellow Fellows to blow up a hurricane of publicity, turning the term "yellow journalism" from opprobrium to praise and capitalizing shrewdly on the bicycle craze. The *Journal* sponsored a great Bicycle Carnival to honor the relay riders, building it up daily with excited headlines and persuading scores of New York wheel clubs to participate. On the night of September 12, hundreds of cyclists gathered at Columbus Circle and pa-

[9] Abbot, 147.   [10] Abbot, 138.
[11] N. Y. *Journal*, Sept. 8, 1896; N. Y. *Times*, same date.

raded northward along Central Park between rows of Japanese lanterns, to the tune of the Seventh Regiment Band and the inspiration of Hearst fireworks. There were bicycles decorated with flowers, with flags, with colored paper, with pictures. There were cycle clubs bearing floats. There were cyclists dressed as Bryan, as McKinley, as Uncle Sam, as clowns, devils, angels. There was Professor Bimberg and his Olympic Mounted Bicycle Band, composed of well-balanced musicians who tooted as they rode. The hard-working participants, cheered by 50,000 spectators along the route, seemed unaware that their efforts were being exploited to boost the *Journal*. More publicity came later when the *Journal* took over the Herald Square Theatre and commissioned tempestuous Anna Held, starring in *A Parlor Match,* to hand out prizes to the winning cyclists.[12]

The Sunday *Journal* under Morrill Goddard had meanwhile attained a luridness rivaled only by the Sunday *World*. The latter was now edited by a handsome young dilettante, Arthur Brisbane, who had put humanity under a microscope and made the same discovery Goddard had—that the masses were stimulated by sex, scandal and other forms of excitement, and at the same time were animated by a humble yearning to learn. Goddard and Brisbane, aided by new color presses, were trying to outdo each other in fulfilling the demand. This contest of yellow journalism reached a pitch of distaste that caused clubs to ban both papers and civic groups to demand that they be curbed. The circulation of both continued to rise. In September, Brisbane became annoyed by Pulitzer's dictatorial ways. He quit and went over to Hearst on an unusual salary arrangement. He was to be paid $150 a week plus a bonus for every 1000 increase in circulation.[13]

Hearst needed Brisbane, because on September 28 he came out with his first evening newspaper, the *Evening Journal,* aimed at doing battle with Pulitzer's *Evening World*. Brisbane, a Bryan partisan, took charge of the *Evening Journal* and joined the Hearst chorus of praise for the Nebraskan. The campaign rode into its last weeks with a bitterness entirely avoided by the two gentlemanly candidates themselves.

The Davenport cartoons representing Hanna as a ruthless capitalist were not too wide of the mark. Hanna had a ferociously realistic belief in the power of money. He used money and propaganda as brutally as did Hearst. By leveling threats that Bryan's election would mean the ruin of business, Hanna got bankers and industrialists to disgorge tremendous sums for the McKinley war chest, raising a total of $3,500,000. As election day neared, the Republican strategy of fear took on a sinister tinge. Capitalists gave large orders to manufacturers, warning them that they were to be executed only if McKinley was elected. Some insurance companies hinted that mortgage payments would be eased—if McKinley was elected. On the weekend before

[12] N. Y. *Journal,* Sept. 13 and 25, 1896.
[13] Oliver Carlson, *Brisbane,* 109–11; Hearst letter to James Brown, April 29, 1935, N.-Y. Historical Society.

the election, many employers throughout the country told their workmen they need not come back to their jobs if Bryan won.[14]

The Democrats by comparison were poor in money and weapons. Hearst's newspapers collected $40,000 in contributions from their readers, which Hearst doubled out of his own pocket. On the day before election, Bryan sent a grateful telegram: "The *Journal* deserves great credit for its splendid fight in behalf of bimetallism and popular government. Its influence has been felt in the West as well as in the East." [15] Its influence was not enough, for McKinley won with a popular vote of 7,111,607 against 6,509,052 for Bryan.

Hearst, who later said he lost $158,000 in the month of October alone, had conceived a genuine admiration for Bryan. He still had money to spend. He sent Mrs. Bryan $5000 worth of orchids.[16]

III. "OUR WILLIE" ACCUSED

ON the day after election, the *Journal* claimed it printed a record 1,506,634 copies—956,921 of the morning edition, 437,401 of the evening paper and 112,312 of *Das Morgen Journal*.[1] While this was a "hot press" day and the average circulation was only a fraction of this, Hearst's skillful use of the Bryan campaign and his fond employment of the journalistic recipe known as "crime and underwear" had succeeded if one computes success in terms of bulk. Suddenly he had become one of the biggest publishers in New York. In a year's time he had outstripped revered old monuments of journalism—the *Sun*, the *Tribune*, the *Times*, the *Herald*. Now he was second only to the *World*. He did not intend to stay second. In a "first birthday" editorial, he did a little bragging:

> What is the explanation of the Journal's amazing and wholly unmatched progress? . . . When the paper was purchased by its present proprietor, a year ago to-day, the work contemplated was at once begun. . . . the Journal realized what is frequently forgotten in journalism, that if news is wanted it often has to be sent for. . . .
> No other journal in the United States includes in its staff a tenth of the number of writers of reputation and talent. It is the Journal's policy to engage brains as well as to get the news, for the public is even more fond of entertainment than it is of information. . . .[2]

Mark well the last sentence—a Hearst credo until he died, one that explains much about him and his newspapers.

For all his sizeable accomplishment, New York still refused to take him seriously. It was well known that his deficits were immense. They could not continue forever. He was regarded by many in the trade as a freak windstorm that had come howling out of the West and would subside when the

[14] Croly, *Hanna*, 220; Peck, 511.
[16] *American Mercury*, Nov., 1930.
[2] *Journal*, Nov. 8, 1896.

[15] N. Y. *Journal*, Nov. 3, 1896.
[1] N. Y. *Journal*, Nov. 5, 1896.

Hearst millions were gone. No one seemed to *know* him. He had joined the fashionable Union and Metropolitan clubs but was seldom seen at either. The crusty, gold-standard members viewed him with aversion as a dangerous absurdity, a millionaire Bryan-silver fanatic who kept attacking capital. He did not belong.

He did not seem to care. He pictured himself as a lone warrior against injustice and outmoded tradition. Once, when Willis Abbot pointed out that a newspaper policy he contemplated would embarrass him if it did not succeed, he replied with a rare tinge of annoyance:

"What the devil do I care about that? I've been in an embarrassing position ever since I came to New York and I've thrived on it." [3]

He preferred a lone hand, or almost alone. The opera bored him, as did serious drama, but he was mad about the frothier footlight fancies. The theaters were having lean times, one critic blaming it on the bicycle craze, commenting, "People ride in the evening and do not care to go to the theater." Hearst was doing his best to fill the breach. No bicyclist, he was now driving a speedy French automobile. He loved Weber & Fields, vaudeville and light musical productions. The convivial Ike Allen, who had been the *Examiner's* representative in New York for seven years, familiarized him with the entertainment places. Hearst worried about Allen's drinking. Pancoast was often his companion as he left his apartment of evenings in dress clothing to attend one of the many theaters bordering Broadway between Twenty-third and Forty-second Streets. Jack Follansbee was now in New York much of the time, leaving subordinates in charge of the Babicora ranch. Like Hearst, the tall, polished Follansbee was a bachelor and a devotee of the theater. The pair were frequent bright-lights cronies.[4]

Hearst, the abstemious, the unsocial, became a regular midnight diner at the gilded resorts of the Nineties where society met and liquor flowed—Delmonico's, Martin's, Sherry's—a "regular" but not an accepted member. Doubtless his exclusion solidified the contempt for the *bon ton* which he had inherited from his father.

His anger at Spain for trying to put down the Cuban rebellion was growing. Two *Journal* "commissioners"—the name he gave his men to distinguish them from ordinary reporters—Charles Michelson and C. B. Pendleton, had been held briefly by Spanish officials in Cuba, something Hearst regarded as an outrage. The Democratic Hearst was disgusted at the Democratic President Cleveland's policy of strict neutrality, the *Journal* growling, "No surer road is open for popularity of the new President [McKinley] than the abandonment of the cold-blooded indifference to Cuba to which Cleveland has committed our government." Hearst was beginning to think of war. In December, the *Journal* sent questionnaires to the governors of every state asking their opinion on United States intervention in Cuba and how many volunteers each state might supply. At the same time the *Journal* fought for the common people of New York, defeating with large headlines and a

[3] Abbot, 143. [4] Mrs. J. M. Flint to author.

timely injunction an effort by the board of aldermen to slip a valuable gas franchise to some favored friends.[5]

The Hearst papers were always fighting something, and fighting as if they were the public's only defenders. Out in San Francisco, the *Examiner* was still blasting the Southern Pacific. In the fall it had conducted a bitter campaign against the reelection of Congressman Grove L. Johnson, a representative from Sacramento who had fought tooth and nail for Huntington and his railroad in the House. Johnson, who had once served Hearst as an attorney, had the distinction of being the only remaining S.P. partisan in the California delegation—House and Senate—a reflection of the massive public opinion against the monopoly which the *Examiner* had helped to arouse.[6] Johnson was snowed under by a whopping 5000 votes. He rightly blamed the *Examiner* for it. With a lame-duck session still ahead of him, he planned revenge on Hearst.

In January, 1897, Congress was considering a new funding bill sponsored by the S.P. which would relieve the railroad from paying its debt to the government when due and would spread it over an additional eighty-three years. The snowy-bearded Huntington had been personally active in the capital, communing with Congressmen. Naturally there was talk of bribes. Ambrose Bierce was also in Washington, sending dispatches that dripped with ridicule of the railroad's declared inability to pay. Huntington, with the defeat of his bill looming, was enraged at the *Examiner,* which had daily cartoons picturing him as a dollar-sign plunderer with his hand in the public's pocket. Hearst had been his mortal enemy for years. When a reporter asked him what motivated Hearst's enmity, Huntington dropped a bombshell.

"We won't keep him on the payroll," he growled.[7]

He declared that for a time, Hearst and the *Examiner* had accepted S.P. "influence money." Significantly, he did not say this under oath, and he refused to amplify his statement.

In saying this, Huntington was admitting publicly what was already well known—that the S.P. had subsidized or bribed many newspapers in California. The San Francisco *Bulletin,* for one, was getting $175 monthly in S.P. money, soon to be raised to $375.[8] Huntington was confessing his own corruption in order to implicate Hearst on the receiving end.

On January 8, Congressman Johnson followed this up with a speech of well-planned virulence. The sixty-six-year-old Johnson, the father of Hiram Johnson, was the man who had once said glowingly of the *Examiner*, "What will you people do next?" He addressed the House in defense of the Southern Pacific bill, following this up with an attack on Mayor Adolph Sutro of San Francisco, an S.P. enemy, and finishing off with the *pièce de résistance*, Hearst. He said in part:

[5] N. Y. *Journal,* Nov. 6, Dec. 13 and Dec. 18, 1896.   [6] N. Y. *Herald,* Jan. 9, 1897.
[7] N. Y. *Herald,* Oct. 30, 1906.   [8] Carlson and Bates, 72.

The *Examiner* has a very large circulation . . . It has done great good in California. It has exposed corruption, denounced villainy, unearthed wickedness, pursued criminals, and rewarded virtue.

At first, we Californians were suspicious of "Our Willie," as Hearst is called on the Pacific Coast. We did not know what he meant. But we came to believe in him and his oft-repeated boasts of independence and honesty. Daily editorials, written by "Our Willie," hired men praising his motives and proclaiming his honesty, had their effect. Besides, "Our Willie" through his paper was doing some good.

We knew him to be a debauchee, a dude in dress, an Anglomaniac in language and manners, but we thought he was honest.

We knew him to be licentious in his tastes, regal in his dissipations, unfit to associate with pure women or decent men, but we thought "Our Willie" was honest.

We knew he was erotic in his tastes, erratic in his moods, of small under-standing and smaller views of men and measures, but we thought "Our Willie," with his English plaids, his cockney accent, and his middle-parted hair, was honest.

We knew he had sought on the banks of the Nile relief from loathsome disease contracted only by contagion in the haunts of vice, and had rivalled the Khedive in the gorgeousness of his harem in the joy of restored health, but we still believed him honest, though low and depraved.

We knew he was debarred from society in San Francisco because of his delight in flaunting his wickedness, but we believed him honest, though tattooed with sin.

We knew he was ungrateful to his friends, unkind to his employes, un-faithful to his business associates, but we believed he was trying to publish an honest paper. . . .

When William R. Hearst commenced his abusive tirades against C. P. Huntington and the Southern Pacific Company and the Central Pacific Rail-road Company and all who were friendly to them, and to denounce the funding bill and all who favored it as thieves and robbers, we thought his course was wrong, his methods bad, and his attacks brutal, but we believed "Our Willie" to be honest.

When C. P. Huntington told the truth about "Our Willie" and showed that he was simply fighting the railroad funding bill because he could get no more blackmail from the Southern Pacific Company, we were dazed with the charge, and as Californians we were humiliated.

We looked eagerly for "Our Willie's" denial, but it came not. On the con-trary he admitted that he had blackmailed the Southern Pacific Company into a contract whereby they were to pay him $30,000 to let them alone, and that he had received $22,000 of his blackmail, and that C. P. Huntington had cut it off as soon as he knew of it, and that he was getting even now on Huntington and the railroad company because he had not received the other $8,000 of his bribe. He admitted by silence that the Southern Pacific Company was financially responsible, but that he dared not sue it for the $8,000 he claimed to be due because of fear that his blackmail would be exposed in court.

With brazen effrontery only equalled by the lowest denizen in the haunts of vice "Our Willie" knows so well in every city of the globe, he unblushingly admitted he had blackmailed the railroad company, but pleaded in extenuation that he did not keep his contract, but swindled them out of their money. . . .

To learn "Our Willie" was nothing but a common, ordinary, everyday blackmailer—a low highwayman of the newspaper world—grieved the people of California, myself included. . . .[9]

The scurrility of the attack had listening Congressmen pop-eyed. No newspaper dared to print more than excerpts. The *Examiner* let it go with brief reference to Johnson's "shameful" and "virulent" speech.[10] Johnson, of course, spoke under Congressional immunity. His charge that Hearst "admitted" blackmail was untrue, as were his remarks about Hearst's health, which had never been other than excellent.

A Hearst-supported Congressman, James G. Maguire of San Francisco, undertook to reply, saying in part:

I say that I am the personal and political friend of Mr. William Randolph Hearst. I have known him personally since his childhood and know him to be a man of honorable character and strong human sympathy . . . He loves justice and contends for it . . . He has done more than any other hundred men to purify the politics of California. . . .

Now, sir, I . . . heard with mingled feelings of horror and disgust the scurrilous attack made by the gentleman from California upon Mr. Hearst. That attack was false in every sentence—false in every charge. I brand it now as false in whole and false in every detail . . .

I will not further notice any of the contemptible falsehoods concerning Mr. Hearst's private life, but the charge that he levied blackmail on the Southern Pacific Company is tangible and requires some attention. The facts upon which the charge is based, as nearly as I can remember them, are these: About five or six years ago, the Southern Pacific Company made a contract with the San Francisco *Examiner* for advertising, during the World's Fair period, for thirty months, at the rate of $1,000 per month.

The advertising matter was published and the agreed price paid by the company for twenty-two months. Then a controversy arose. The *Examiner* had occasion to editorially denounce some schemes in which the company was interested. The company insisted that because of its advertising patronage the *Examiner* should refrain from attacking its interests editorially.

Mr. Hearst, through his business manager, immediately replied, repudiating that principle of business, and stating that under no circumstances would the advertising patrons . . . control the editorial or news columns of the paper. There the matter ended, until Mr. Huntington . . . in a moment of impotent anger, stated that he, or the company, had paid the $22,000 to the *Examiner* as blackmail. Mr. Hearst immediately published the contract and the correspondence concerning it. The gentleman from California

[9] Congressional Record, Vol. 29, Part 1, 54th Congress, 2d Session, pp. 592–93.
[10] *Examiner*, Jan. 10, 1897.

[Johnson] said that Mr. Hearst had admitted receiving $22,000 from Mr. Huntington as blackmail. That statement is simply false. . . .[11]

Maguire could not finish his speech in the time allotted to him, so he made use of his privilege to insert in the Congressional Record the unspoken part as well as the portion he had actually delivered. In the unspoken part, he attacked Johnson's character, declaring among other things that thirty-four years earlier Johnson had been indicted for forgery in Syracuse, New York, and had turned up in California under an assumed name. Maguire's speech was telegraphed to the *Examiner* and published.

Johnson evidently learned of this by telegraph, for he rose again in the House to admit that he had once been indicted. But he said with some justice, "I say, is it right, is it proper to go back thirty-four years in the life of a man and bring out the follies and crimes of his youth . . . ?" (Johnson was thirty-two when indicted.) He had not taken an assumed name, he said, and furthermore he had paid back every cent he owed. As evidence of his reformed character, he pointed to his membership in the Odd Fellows, the Red Men, the Knights of Pythias and the Exempt Firemen's Association of Sacramento.[12]

No one questioned his lodge affiliations. The House, however, voted down the Southern Pacific bill 168–102. The most interesting point at issue was the charge that Hearst had blackmailed the road. "Blackmail" was indeed a self-serving word, for the S.P.'s bribery was notorious and generally voluntary. As an ingratiating final touch, the railroad always gave legislators free passes on the road. But Maguire had not spiked the charge, for the San Francisco *Call* later took it up with equal vehemence.

Under the headline, "Paid to Silence His Blackguardism; Hearst's Secret Compact with the Southern Pacific Company," the *Call* used four full columns in charging that Hearst had "sold out" to the railroad. It published three documents to support the charge. The facts that emerged were these:

On June 29, 1892, while Hearst was abroad, his business department negotiated a contract with the S.P. for the publication of twenty pages of advertising in the *Examiner's* special Columbian Exposition issue at a price of $30,000. Along with the formal contract, the *Call* alleged, was an agreement reading:

> The company is to enjoy immunity from hostility in the columns of the *Examiner*, and it is not to be the victim of malicious attack or criticisms or misrepresentations; that the *Examiner* will not seek to create hostile sentiment in the minds of the community against the Southern Pacific Company, or any of the interests it represents, and that while not stipulating as against all criticism, it agrees that criticism shall not proceed from any motive of malice or malignity and that such criticism as may be found necessary to keep and maintain the confidence of the public to the extent that any public sentiment may have been created from other sources, is to be avoided as much as possible.

[11] Congressional Record (see note 9), 620.   [12] The same, 730.

This was signed by three officials of the railroad, Charles F. Crocker, A. N. Towne and W. H. Mills. The *Examiner's* purported signer was Frank Gassaway of the business department. Gassaway placed parentheses around the words "is to enjoy immunity from hostility in the columns of the *Examiner,* and it," indicating a rejection of that stipulation, but approved the rest. Although the remainder was less sweeping, it still represented an agreement of the paper to keep its criticism in low key. The *Call,* published by John D. Spreckels, said triumphantly that here was clear proof that Hearst had taken tainted railroad money.[13]

The *Examiner* replied furiously that the "secret agreement" was a forgery, saying:

> John Degenerate Spreckels, fool and failure, evilly envious of the success of "The Examiner," and William H. Mills, malevolent mouthpiece of the Southern Pacific, have gone into partnership to traduce this newspaper because of its continued opposition to their corrupt political programmes.
>
> Between them they have concocted a forged document, which Spreckels has presented in his paper as evidence that "The Examiner" is all that the "Call" is believed to be.

Since Crocker and Towne, the other two signers, were dead, the *Examiner* trained its guns on Mills, calling him repeatedly "forger, if responsible for the above," and ending, "Now, William H. Mills, forger if responsible for the above, here is the opportunity of your life. Sue 'The Examiner' for libel . . ."[14]

Mills did not sue. Instead, he was quoted in an *Examiner* interview next day as declaring that Crocker's signature was not affixed to the agreement and adding:

> If the "Call" attached Mr. Crocker's indorsement to this so-called secret agreement consciously and for purposes of deception, it was guilty of a great wrong.[15]

While this suggested some tampering on the part of the *Call,* Mills did not deny the existence of the agreement. If the agreement was indeed a forgery, there were still some puzzling aspects to the transaction.

It was true that Hearst was abroad when the $30,000 advertising deal was made. Although the advertising was printed entirely in the big World's Fair issue of the *Examiner,* the railroad was permitted to pay in thirty monthly installments of $1000 each—an arrangement, it was said, that was often followed, so that the railroad could make sure it was getting value received. These payments were still in progress when Hearst returned. The records showed that Hearst personally hypothecated the contract—traded it for cash—at the First National Bank in San Francisco on July 24, 1893. At this time $11,000 had been paid and $19,000 were still due. He needed money, as he always did, for he was then busy improving the Pleasanton ranch he had forgotten belonged to his mother.

[13] *Call,* Oct. 22, 1898.   [14] *Examiner,* Oct. 23, 1898.   [15] *Examiner,* Oct. 24.

"He may have been listening to the crocodiles on the Nile or listening to the bulbul in Cashmere when his agents were selling the *Examiner* to the Southern Pacific," declared the *Call*, "but when he personally hypothecated that contract . . . Hearst could not be ignorant of the conditions of the sale nor of the time lock it had upon his lying and blackguardism for the space of thirty months." [16]

The monthly payments were still continuing in June, 1894, at which time the bitter Pullman strike in Chicago reached out to California when the S.P. insisted on attaching Pullman cars to its trains as usual. S.P. workers, refusing to handle Pullman cars, went on strike and service was disrupted. The *Examiner*, although supposedly taking a monthly bribe from the road, aggressively took the striker's side and assailed the S.P. At this time $8000 was still due on the advertising contract. According to the *Call*, the S.P. thereupon rescinded the contract, refusing to pay the remaining $8000 because the *Examiner* did not give it "fair treatment." Hearst did not sue for the money because, said the *Call*, he knew that to do so would bring to light the bribe.

It was true that he did not sue, and this was taken by some as proof of his perfidy. Nor did he sue the *Call*. For decades—right up to the present—his failure to bring suit left a cloud over him. As recently as 1936, when Hearst was still living, a biographer mistaken in some vital details painted him inferentially as a bribetaker.[17]

In considering these charges, one must take into account the character and motives of Hearst's three accusers. The unscrupulous Huntington and his S.P., fighting in Washington for millions, were itching to smear their arch-enemies in the fight, Hearst and his *Examiner*. The somewhat blemished Grove Johnson—who later was elected to the state legislature and continued there to fight energetically for the S.P.—had two reasons for seeking revenge. The *Call*, badly beaten by the *Examiner* in the circulation struggle, was also a bitter political enemy aching to discredit Hearst. Although Mills' statement made it appear that there had been some doctoring of at least one of the documents published in support of the charges against the *Examiner*, it is even possible that the *Call* sincerely believed Hearst guilty.

Surprisingly, until now there has never been an investigation of this odd journalistic mystery. Bias against Hearst has increased the disposition to assume his guilt because he did not sue. If any Hearst letters on the case existed, they are not available. The present writer, seeking to get at the truth if possible, sponsored a minor sleuthing project. He persuaded Ronald A. Bergman of the University of California to act as a scholarly detective in gathering evidence in the case. There seemed only one way to do this: to pore through hundreds of issues of the *Examiner*, tabulating all stories and editorials concerning the S.P., and thus determine whether the paper had

[16] *Call*, Oct. 24, 1898.　　　　[17] Lundberg, *Imperial Hearst*, 36–42.

sold out—had ceased its attacks on the railroad for money. Mr. Bergman read the *Examiner*'s issues for four periods of two months each:

Period 1: April and May, 1892—the two months preceding the *Examiner*'s sale of $30,000 in advertising to the S.P.
Period 2: July and August, 1892—the two months following the sale.
Period 3: August and September, 1893—the two months immediately following Hearst's hypothecation of the contract, when he must have known of it.
Period 4: August and September, 1894—the two months following the S.P.'s rescinding of the contract and their refusal to pay the $8000 still due.

It would reasonably be expected that if the *Examiner* had sold out, this would be reflected in the paper's gentler treatment of the railroad after the deal. In Period 1, before the contract, Mr. Bergman found 261 column inches of editorial and news comment on the Southern Pacific, all of it critical.

In Period 2, he found 273 inches, *equally and universally critical*. In fact, there was not one item favorable to the railroad in any of the four periods. There was no change in tone in Period 2—no subtle relaxing of the assault. Typical were editorials and news stories attacking the S.P.'s excessive rates, the road's guilt when a train killed a boy riding in a wagon without sounding any warning, a vigorous editorial blasting the S.P.'s unscrupulous control of San Francisco city bosses, and another virulent attack on the railroad and its control of the Republican party.[18]

This seems a queer way of selling out. Instead of easing the attack after making the deal, the *Examiner* printed somewhat more anti-S.P. material. If the road paid for gentle treatment, it failed to get it.

One recalls Hearst's comment to his editor who had refused a bribe from the water company, saying, "Why didn't you take the money and keep up the fight just the same?" Hearst, never delicate in dealing with those he considered rogues, would have been quite capable of doing that to the S.P. and regarding it as a huge joke.

However, it may be said that at the date of the contract and for some time after, Hearst was excursioning on the Nile with Tessie and Pancoast, bearing cameras, beans, chowder and codfish. It is conceivable that he knew nothing of the contract and had nothing to do with the cavalier treatment of the railroad in Period 2. This is possible but highly improbable, for he kept a remarkably close watch on his paper even while wandering among the Egyptian tombs. He was proud of his World's Fair issue, and would almost certainly have known of the great twenty-page Southern Pacific advertisement. In any case he obviously knew about the arrangement when he hypothecated the contract on July 24, 1893. Here was his opportunity, if he wished to curry favor with the railroad, to tone down the attacks.

Instead, he stepped them up. During Period 3, the *Examiner* printed 348 inches about the railroad, all critical. This was eighty-seven inches more

[18] *Examiner,* July 9, 20, 26 and 28, 1892.

than in Period 1, before the deal. Typical were articles assailing the S.P. for firing 4000 men because of a business depression, for its ruthless attempts to crush a rival ferry line, and for careless operations in Oakland resulting in injuries to citizens.[19]

The S.P. wrote at least two letters to the *Examiner,* complaining about this treatment. One of them, undated, was sent to Thomas T. Williams of the business office. It gave a clear idea of the railroad's conception of the agreement:

> You admit that in consideration of the sum of $30,000 . . . the company was to receive certain advertising and fair treatment. There can be no question that the chief consideration to inure to the Southern Pacific Company in its transaction was the fair treatment to be accorded by your paper; that it would not have entered into an agreement to pay $30,000 for advertising merely, as the benefit to accrue from such advertising alone was grossly inadequate to the sum of money involved.
>
> It is now assumed, on behalf of the *Examiner,* that the question of fair treatment is one which could be determined by the *Examiner* management only, and could not possibly be a question of debate or arbitration. . . . Had we been apprised of such intention, it is not likely that the contract proposed would have been entered into.[20]

The S.P.'s temper finally snapped in 1894, when the *Examiner* became positively violent in its assaults on the road for its activities during the strike, using far more space than ever in its anti-railroad propaganda. The road canceled the contract, refusing to pay the final $8000.

In Period 4, after the cancellation, the *Examiner* used what offhand seems an amazing amount of anti-S.P. space—3010 inches, or an average of about fifty inches a day. It would be easy to jump to the conclusion that this reflected Hearst's anger. But it was not appreciably more than had been used during the earlier strike period, when the contract was still being paid, and the increase was perfectly justified news-wise by a dramatic upturn in events concerning the road. The strike, still in progress, gained in violence so that troops had to be called to restore order, all of which the *Examiner* treated with sympathy for the strikers. The S.P.'s funding bill battle began in earnest in Period 4, and the *Examiner* unlimbered all its guns in opposing this. It began circulating its anti-funding bill petition, which it kept booming for weeks. Furthermore, it was backing Adolph Sutro for mayor and James Budd for governor, both of them strongly anti-S.P. As a result, the railroad became the biggest issue in the election and in the news.

Hearst, the much maligned, was entirely innocent of selling out to the S.P. There is no evidence that his news treatment was affected in the slightest by the advertising deal. He accepted $22,000 in railroad money, which he doubtless regarded as having earned by the advertising he printed. One can picture him watching the entire drama with amusement at the expense of

---

[19] *Examiner,* Aug. 8, 10, and Sept. 23, 1893. [20] *Call,* Oct. 24, 1898.

the corporation he so detested, wondering how long it would be before the railroad caught on.

Why then did he not sue for the remaining $8000? There are at least three possible reasons:

1. He had had $22,000 worth of fun already, probably more than he expected.

2. Many California courts were influenced or controlled by the S.P. A fair trial might have been impossible. Also, a trial might produce documents suggesting that he *had* sold out, although the fact was otherwise.

3. Hearst was vulnerable on another count—Tessie Powers. His affair with her was the talk of the town. He had been with her in Egypt at the time of the advertising deal. The hatred toward him would have gone to any length. Tessie may have been dragged into the trial, possibly called as a witness. This was something the sentimental Hearst could not allow, both for Tessie's sake and his own. For at that very time, he was using all his blandishments on his mother for a huge "loan" that would enable him to invade New York.

Had his affair with Tessie been emblazoned in the newspapers as a result of a nasty court case, he never would have received $7,500,000 from Phoebe in 1895.

2. I'll Furnish the War

ONE of the ingredients of the Hearst enigma was an outer demeanor entirely at variance with his inner self. His disguise was complete. His shyness, modesty, courtesy and high voice were attributes ordinarily associated with men of indecisive, retiring and timid dispositions. People who took him at face value were utterly astounded at the contradiction between his appearance and his acts. Willis Abbot, an intelligent, discerning editor, kept his eye on the *rara avis* and admitted bafflement.

"Even . . . when I was seeing him every night," he wrote, "Hearst was to me a puzzle. Conducting the most brazen and blatant newspapers, he was personally almost shy. It was a real ordeal to introduce him to a public man, even when he himself sought the introduction, for he would invariably sit silent, with downcast eyes, leaving me to carry on the conversation." [1]

The external Hearst was a fraud, unintentional and therefore all the more deceiving. His inferiority complex manifested itself only in his outward manner. Inwardly he was Caesar, Charlemagne and Napoleon combined. He was the most megalomaniac of men, supremely sure of his own greatness. Megalomania, which is merely ridiculous in persons of small abilities, can be either dangerous or beneficent in a man of Hearst's superior, though uneven, endowments. Ever since college, he had read intensively about Napoleon, Caesar, Washington and other immortals. A painting of Napoleon hung over his desk. He owned busts or likenesses of Lincoln, Jefferson, Franklin and others of similar dimensions. He revered greatness and felt a kinship with the great. Behind his helpless disguise he thought and planned in large, lavish ways, uninhibited by the difficulties, obstacles and minor moral considerations that turned back normal men. This regal mode of thought was implemented by qualities of daring, determination, courage and ruthlessness that were hard to stop, particularly since they were backed by several millions of dollars.

The president of the New York police board in 1897 was another unusual man, also of somewhat megalomaniac tendencies. He was toothy, shrill-voiced Theodore Roosevelt, then thirty-nine, who had graduated from Harvard a year before Hearst appeared there with Champagne Charlie and whose path would cross Hearst's in odd ways and places. As head of the police, T. R. was a terror. He delighted in prowling the streets at night to check on his bluecoats. A typical exploit was when he spied Patrolman

[1] Abbot, 142.

Joseph Meyers sneaking a schooner of beer from the side door of a saloon on West Forty-second Street. Roosevelt pounced on Meyers, snapping, "Officer, give me that glass." Meyers, affrighted, dropped the beer and took to his heels, but Roosevelt was after him in full cry and nabbed him in fifty yards, to bring him up on departmental charges next day.[2]

Supervision of this sort was what the easy-going police badly needed, but Hearst's *Journal* had a poor opinion of Roosevelt. Although Hearst himself had a partiality for dazzling clothing, the *Journal* was offended by Roosevelt's pink shirts, and his habit of wearing a tasseled silk sash instead of a vest. Roosevelt was too high-and-mighty, too "aristocratic" in attitude to sympathize with the common people. "He has a very poor opinion of the majority," the *Journal* finished. "But there is one compensation: The majority has a very poor opinion of Mr. Roosevelt." [3]

The *Journal* frankly catered to the majority, "the people," including some who could barely read but could decipher billboard headlines and mural illustrations. If the *World* was the organ of the underdog, the *Journal* fought for the *under* underdog. It flew to the defense of Mrs. Elizabeth Sommers when she was jailed for allegedly accosting a policeman while in a drunken condition. It produced seventeen witnesses who swore that she was a poor but respectable woman, and hired an attorney who secured a writ of habeas corpus for her. Even when later evidence suggested that Mrs. Sommers was no better than she should be, the *Journal* made so much noise that she was released. It took up the cudgels for Mrs. Catherine Brooks, who was arrested for shoplifting although she was, the *Journal* affirmed, "a woman of culture." It gave a benefit vaudeville performance at the Olympia Theater for families made homeless by a tenement fire, not forgetting to include "Five *Journal* Yellow Kids" in the program. Another *Journal* benefit at the Metropolitan Opera House featured such stars as Mlle. Olitzka and Anna Held, raising $5,303.65 for the poor.[4] In doing these things, the *Journal* never failed to point with admiration at its own ingenuity and benevolence.

These attentions made many of the underprivileged *Journal* boosters. So, too, did the free soup kitchen for the unemployed which the *Journal* advertised in its own columns and on large posters. Elsie L. Hess, who had the misfortune to live next to the *Journal* soup kitchen at Grand and Willett Streets, thought otherwise. She complained to Roosevelt's police board that "All the filthiest tramps, the laziest, lowest and most degraded denizens of the east side for miles around, congregate in the vicinity . . . Many of the creatures who come here are filthy in the extreme, and half drunken, and the language they use, and the quarreling in which they indulge, is such as to almost terrorize the neighborhood." [5]

R. W. De Forest of the Charity Organization Society agreed, saying, "No

[2] N. Y. *Tribune*, May 20, 1896.   [3] *Journal*, Jan. 1, 1897.
[4] *Journal*, Jan. 9 and 10 and June 4, 1897; *Evening Journal*, Jan. 1, 1897; *Journal*, Feb. 10, 1897.
[5] N. Y. *Times*, Feb. 11, 1897.

attempt is made even to take the names of applicants . . . The indiscriminate character of the relief is enough of itself to condemn it. [It is] the most direct encouragement to vagrancy." To which Nathaniel Rosenau, manager of the United Hebrew Charities, added amen: "It is unthinking assistance . . . The whole thing has a bad and demoralizing effect." [6]

These attacks, the *Journal* suggested, were inspired by newspapers satisfied to let people starve, adding, "Nor does the *Journal* purpose to be stayed in its work by the voice of envy, hatred and malice." [7]

In the midst of the soup-kitchen debate, Mr. and Mrs. Bradley Martin gave their famous fancy-dress ball at the Waldorf for 700 of the purple. Mrs. Martin, clad as Mary Stuart, wore $50,000 worth of jewels as she perched on a throne while a liveried lackey announced the guests, many of whom wore costumes costing thousands. The *Journal* did not take offense. It treated this precisely as if it were a gala entertainment put on by high society for the poor. It gave its readers an approximation of actual attendance by giving four pages to descriptions and illustrations, noting that the ball was estimated to cost $369,200.[8] Although the Martins had naïvely thought the ball would spur trade and aid the poor, other newspapers were so critical that the Martins eventually left New York to reside in Paris.[9]

By 1897, the *Journal* was as firmly entrenched in its role of purveyor to the underprivileged as was the *Herald* in its acceptance by society of the Bradley Martin set. At the same time, Hearst was applauding another underdog people, the rebels in Cuba. The *Journal* had become known as a good place of employment for daring young men willing to risk their lives by accompanying filibuster expeditions to Cuba as reporters. One such adventurer was Ralph D. Paine, two years out of Yale, who walked into the *Journal* office, talked with Hearst and was hired on the spot. Paine was to accompany a vessel endeavoring to smuggle arms and men into Cuba.

"You may get nowhere," Hearst told him casually, "and if you do the Spaniards will probably scupper you." He was sitting on his desk, swinging his long legs. "By the way, you remember the big fair held in Madison Square Garden to raise money for the Cuban cause. They voted on a sword, at so much a vote, to be given to the greatest living soldier. Of course General Maximo Gomez won in a walk. Then I gave them two thousand dollars for the sword, to help the cause along, and of course I intend to present it to Maximo Gomez. Do you want to see it?"

He hauled it out of its mahogany case. It was the glittering work of a Fifth Avenue jeweler, the hilt gold-plated and sparkling with diamonds. Hearst pointed to the inscriptions on it: "*To Maximo Gomez, Commander-in-Chief of the Army of the Cuban Republic,*" and "*Viva Cuba Libre.*"

"Very handsome," Paine said. "Old Gomez will be tickled to death, when he gets it."

"That is the idea, *when he gets it,*" Hearst observed. "I have been trying

[6] N. Y. *Times,* Feb. 12.   [7] *Journal,* Feb. 12, 1897.
[8] *Journal,* Feb. 11, 1897.   [9] Lloyd Morris, *Incredible New York,* 239–42.

to find somebody foolish enough to carry this elegant sword to Gomez. I am perfectly frank with you. These inscriptions would be devilishly hard to explain to the Spanish army, if you happened to be caught, wouldn't they?"

"And you want me to try to present this eighteen-karat sword to Gomez, with your compliments?" Paine inquired.

"If you don't mind. I swear I don't know what else to do with the confounded thing. Of course, if you are nabbed at sea, you can probably chuck it overboard in time—"

"And if I get surrounded on land, perhaps I can swallow it, Mr. Hearst," Paine grinned. "Never mind that. I am the damn fool you have been looking for . . ." [10]

Paine took the sword and left for Florida. Hearst, who had been brought up on action and had an incurable fear of boredom, was happy. Interesting events were occurring everywhere. One of them was his acquaintance with two very lovely young sisters, Millicent and Anita Willson. The Misses Willson were members of the dancing group called "The Merry Maidens" in "The Girl From Paris," at the Herald Square Theater, a musical extravaganza starring Clara Lipman and featuring high-kicking dances in which shapely, silk-clad legs emerged from fleecy ruffles. Broadway was amazed and a bit amused to see Mr. Hearst squiring not one but *both* of the Willson sisters, one on each arm. When "The Girl From Paris" celebrated its fiftieth performance on January 18, 1897, giving away china clocks as souvenirs, Hearst's reviewer, James L. Ford, gave it a splendid notice, and the chances are that Hearst acquired a china clock. [11]

Another event—on the news side—was the *affaire Seeley*, which had the city goggle-eyed. Herbert Barnum Seeley, a man on the outer fringes of society seeking to get closer to the middle, had given a stag party for fifty of the elite at Sherry's snooty restaurant on Fifth Avenue and Thirty-seventh Street. Police Captain George Chapman of the Tenderloin district, hearing rumors of indecency, raided the place with six detectives. They found the diners applauding three dancers, Minnie Renwood, Cora Routt and Ashea Wabe, who were not quite nude but were "indecently exposed." Captain Chapman read a stern lesson to the group but made no arrests, doubtless being intimidated by the importance of the guests. The *Journal* and its contemporaries seized on this, particularly when it was learned that Ashea Wabe, a slinky Algerian, was the identical "Little Egypt" who had thrilled visitors at the Chicago World's Fair with her stomach dance. It was said that but for Captain Chapman's interruption she would have presented the stomach dance in the altogether. The names of the diners were published, becoming nationally notorious. Some who were married suffered domestic trouble. It was rumored that Mr. Roosevelt, head of the police, had been invited as a guest—a rumor he heatedly denied.

[10] Ralph D. Paine, *Roads of Adventure*, 62–63.   [11] N. Y. *Journal*, Jan. 19, 1897.

Here was a story the *Journal* could and did treat with exhaustive word-and-picture attention without bothering to seek any social implications.[12]

But there were plenty of social implications in Cuba. Hearst was jealous of the *World*, whose correspondent Sylvester Scovel had been jailed by the Spaniards, giving the *World* its opportunity for a loud "free Scovel" campaign. Although Hearst already had several "commissioners" in Cuba, he now sent two more, Richard Harding Davis and Frederick Remington. The thirty-three-year-old Davis, who looked like a matinee idol and talked like an ambassador, was a high-priced man. The *Journal* had paid him $500 the previous fall merely to cover the Harvard-Yale football game. His salary for the Cuban assignment was said to be $3000 a month. Remington, equally famous as an illustrator, commanded a similar fee. In cloak-and-dagger style, the two sailed from New York secretly in the dead of night to conceal their movements from "Spanish spies." [13]

Even while gorged with current sensations, Hearst always sought more. The Dreyfus case had been reopened in France, and he was so indignant at the treatment of the captain that he was formulating a plan whereby Dreyfus would be spirited away to freedom by *Journal* emissaries.[14] Other news crises intervened, however, one of them a gem of the crime-and-underwear genre.

In the summer of 1897, sections of a male human being were found in the East River and elsewhere in New York. They were wrapped in oilcloth with a chaste cabbage-rose design. The parts were assembled in the morgue, but since the head was missing, identification was a problem. Here the *Journal* entered the case. Hearst, always expecting his men to be more intelligent and energetic than city detectives, had formed a special "murder squad" of sleuth-reporters. One of them, George Arnold, visited the morgue and scrutinized the headless body. It happened that Arnold had been a patron of the Murray Hill Turkish baths. The big man on the slab looked vaguely familiar. Arnold was quite sure when he saw that the hands and fingers were heavily calloused, as would be expected of a Turkish bath rubber. He went to the Murray Hill establishment and learned that one of their masseurs, a man with the improbable name of Willie Guldensuppe, was missing. The *Journal* printed its scoop on the identification of the victim before it bothered to inform the police. Hearst paid Arnold a $1000 bonus on the spot.[15]

Hearst threw himself into the case as if he were Police Commissioner Roosevelt. In his Sunday supplement he printed a reproduction in color of the roseate oilcloth design, appealing to the public to help trace the oilcloth. He sent out thirty reporters to canvass dry-goods shops. Once again the *Journal* men outdistanced the police. In Astoria they found the dealer who had sold the oilcloth, and got a description of the woman who had bought

[12] N. Y. *Journal*, Jan. 3, 1897, ff.
[13] Joseph E. Wisan, *The Cuban Crisis as Reflected in the New York Press*, 187; Bleyer, 363.
[14] George Clarke Musgrave, *Under Three Flags in Cuba*, 104.
[15] Mrs. Fremont Older, *op. cit.*, 154–55.

it. From there it was only a short step to her identification. She was Augusta Nack, a woman of operatic contours who had been Guldensuppe's mistress. By now, the police were grateful to get leads provided by the *Journal*. In order to protect his scoop and keep rival newspapers out, Hearst rented the entire East Side building in which Mrs. Nack lived. *Journal* men guarded the entrances and cut telephone wires while detectives questioned Mrs. Nack. In this manner, for a time the *Journal* actually owned the case, printing editions which people fought to buy on the streets. The triumph was complete when Mrs. Nack confessed that she and her new lover, a handsome barber named Martin Thorn, had murdered Guldensuppe because of his jealous interference. Hearst had been in the thick of it, leaping into a hack to aid the investigation at the Turkish bath, and serving as field general in the siege of the Nack home.[16]

"MURDER MYSTERY SOLVED BY THE JOURNAL," was the *Journal's* headline, along with drawings of the different sections of Guldensuppe, the murder knife, Mrs. Nack and her lover. "The *Journal*, as usual, ACTS while the representatives of ancient journalism sit idly by and wait for something to turn up." [17]

His men noticed that when stop-press news of this kind occurred, the usually quiet Hearst got as excited as a cub reporter. Such events tickled his taste for impact and sensation. "When peace brooded over the city and nobody was being robbed or murdered," noted the *Journal* writer, James Ford, "he would come down to the office with despondency written on his face . . . but the tidings of some new crime or disaster would rouse him to instant action." [18] When things were going well, he was apt to break into a vaudeville caper. Another employe, Harry Coleman, entered Hearst's magnificent office on the second floor of the Tribune building to find him studying some proofs. "Hearst suddenly spread the proofs in precise order upon the floor," Coleman wrote, "and began a sort of tap dance around and between them . . . with lively castanet accompaniments produced by his snapping fingers." [19]

He also had his troubles. Sam Chamberlain, after months of reasonable sobriety, would disappear, board a transatlantic steamer and make for a certain waterfront saloon in Antwerp. Hearst's London representative would go to Antwerp and coax him to return. Arthur McEwen, when he strayed, was apt to head for South America.[20] Arthur Brisbane was abstemious, but Ambrose Bierce in Washington was not. Hearst prized Bierce's acid wit, but feared his utter lack of discretion. He asked Abbot to watch the Bierce copy for dangerous passages. Abbot soon found one that made him blanch. Bierce, in writing of a much beloved actress who had recently died, observed, "always famous for her composed manner, she is now quite decomposed."

[16] *Collier's*, Sept. 20, 1906.   [17] Quoted in Lundberg, *Imperial Hearst*, 60–61.
[18] James L. Ford, *Forty-odd Years in the Literary Shop*, 260.
[19] Harry J. Coleman, *Give Us a Little Smile, Baby*, 22.   [20] Coleman, 26; Abbot, 146.

Abbot blue-penciled it. Bierce, on learning that his copy had been changed, immediately resigned. Hearst's patience with him was endless. He lured Bierce back, as Abbot surmised, "probably at an increased salary." [21]

Hearst's constant effort was to get the biggest, the best, the unexpected, the bizarre, in any kind of news coverage, regardless of expense. He spent thousands to send seven correspondents, including Stephen Crane and Julian Ralph, to cover the brief Greco-Turkish war. He engaged Mark Twain to write an account of the sixtieth anniversary of Queen Victoria's coronation. He dispatched a whole boatload of writers, headed by Joaquin Miller, to describe the Klondike gold rush. He was exultant over the ultimate in freakish editorial whims—the signing of ex-Senator John J. Ingalls to cover the Corbett-Fitzsimmons fight in Nevada, sending Ingalls and other representatives to the scene in a *"Journal* special" private railroad car.[22]

He declared open war on Pulitzer, who was incensed over Hearst's theft of his best men although this was precisely what Pulitzer had done when he invaded New York a dozen years earlier. Hearst felt that Pulitzer had plotted to deprive him of an Associated Press franchise. He denounced his rival editorially in terms which in part applied to himself:

> [Pulitzer is] a journalist who made his money by pandering to the worst tastes of the prurient and horror-loving, by dealing in bogus news . . . and by affecting a devotion to the interests of the people while never really hurting those of their enemies, and sedulously looking out for his own.[23]

Henry Klein, a *Journal* writer, later noted, "I remember the Willson sisters, actresses, coming to the office nightly with Mr. Hearst after eleven o'clock, and W. R., kneeling on the floor nightly studying and changing the proposed 'make-up' of the pages." [24]

There was speculation in New York about Hearst's double-barreled romance, the inevitable question being: Which of the sisters is he really interested in? Insiders declared it was Millicent, but that since she was only sixteen, and was devoted to her sister Anita, it was thought best for Anita to accompany them as chaperone. Phoebe Hearst, still living in Washington between trips to Europe, occasionally visited her son in New York. Her prejudice against people of the stage persisted. She strongly opposed anything deeper than friendship with the Willson girls. Hearst, at thirty-four, felt mature enough to make such decisions himself.[25]

Down in Havana, Frederick Remington was growing bored. He sent Hearst a telegram:

> Everything is quiet. There is no trouble here. There will be no war. I wish to return.—Remington.

[21] Abbot, 139.
[23] N. Y. *Journal*, Mar. 29, 1897.
[25] Mrs. J. M. Flint to author.
[22] Bleyer, 367–69; Abbot, 211.
[24] Henry H. Klein, *My Last Fifty Years*, 14.

Hearst's reply was Napoleonic:

> Please remain. You furnish the pictures and I'll furnish the war.—W. R. Hearst.[26]

II. THE PEANUT CLUB

> No man's life, no man's property is safe. American citizens are imprisoned or slain without cause. American property is destroyed on all sides . . . Blood on the roadsides, blood in the fields, blood on the doorsteps, blood, blood, blood! . . . A new Armenia lies within 80 miles of the American coast. Not a word from Washington! Not a sign from the president! [1]

THE above dispatch was written for the *World* by James Creelman, an able, dashing, black-bearded correspondent in Cuba, and was one reason why the Spanish authorities requested him to leave. It was also one reason why Hearst determined to get him. Not long after Creelman returned to the United States, Hearst lured him away, adding to the long list of skilled performers he had purloined from Pulitzer.

To Hearst, with his weakness for reducing complex phenomena to terms of sheerest simplicity, the struggle in Cuba was purely a case of hero *vs.* villain. Spain represented tyranny. The Cuban rebels represented a cause as holy in its yearning for liberty as that of the American Revolution. When a few ragged Cuban fighters met in the island's interior and elected a "president of the republic" at a time when they controlled no port, no city, and in fact were dodging their Spanish pursuers, the *Journal* promptly recognized the new republic even though Washington did not, saying its citizens were "animated by the same fearless spirit that inspired the counsel of the patriot fathers who sat in Philadelphia on the 4th of July, 1776." [2]

Hearst's own editors knew him to be sincere in his sympathy for the rebels and his feeling that Spain should be driven out of the hemisphere.[3] He had supported the Cubans in the *Examiner* before coming to New York. Their plight touched him. But he also saw in the Cuban struggle a source of exciting news that would help him in his struggle with Pulitzer. He was still losing money at a ghastly rate. He swore that he would use up all the *Examiner's* profits and his mother's millions before he gave up the battle with Pulitzer.[4] The Cuban conflict gave him a simultaneous opportunity to support what he considered a noble cause and to advance his own interests. It is probable that by now he was concerned about his continuing losses and ready for desperate measures. The result would be the most disgraceful example of journalistic falsehood ever seen.

It was true that Spain, almost bankrupt, had failed to maintain order in

[26] James Creelman, *On the Great Highway*, 177–78.   [1] N. Y. *World*, May 17, 1896.
[2] *Journal*, Oct. 11, 1895.   [3] Abbot, 212.   [4] Abbot, 147.

Cuba for a quarter century and that this endless wrangle, with cruelty on both sides and some destruction of American property, had long been a trial and a vexation to the United States. It was also true that many Cubans favored Spanish rule, that the rebels often used barbarous methods, and that they were less interested in fighting the Spaniards than in drawing the United States in to haul their chestnuts out of the fire. The insurrecto leaders were early masters of modern propaganda. Their aim was to convince the American people that the fondest sport of the Spaniards was to murder Cuban children, rape their mothers, poke out Cubans' eyes and to sate their blood-lust with other Spanish refinements of torture.[5]

Thousands of Cuban nationalists had left the island after the failure of the previous revolt, to settle in the United States and plan further resistance. Many of them cigar makers, they lived in Key West, Jacksonville, New Orleans, New York and other centers. They formed a stout cadre of revolutionists who loyally gave their money and efforts to the cause, smuggling arms to Cuba and above all fostering intrigue to embroil the United States. They managed to organize an efficient propaganda arm. They sent Gonzalo de Quesada as "Cuban Revolutionary Chargé D'Affaires" to Washington to lobby among legislators there. But the man who shook the nation was earnest, silver-mustached Tomas Estrada Palma, a former school teacher who headed the new York "Junta," a center of revolutionary intrigue.

Estrada Palma lived humbly on Bleecker Street and did not have funds to maintain his own office. He used the office of Horatio Rubens, a New York lawyer sympathetic with the Cubans, at 66 Broadway. This office became a place where furtive, olive-skinned men with flaring mustachios stole in and out at all hours, holding whispered conversations about filibuster expeditions. It also became a "news agency" where Cuban "victories" over the Spaniards were manufactured as well as bloodcurdling tales of Spanish cruelty.[6]

The United States press was at a disadvantage because it was almost impossible to get authentic news from Cuba. The rebellion was a minor affair at first, existing only in the jungle interior of the eastern end of the island. The Spanish authorities had been angered by early Yankee reporters who sat in comfortable Havana hotel chairs and wrote "eyewitness stories" supplied them by Cubans who pictured the Spaniards as beasts without parallel. As a result, the Spaniards had rigidly circumscribed the movements of correspondents and subjected their dispatches to censorship. It was forbidden, of course, for them to travel inland and join the rebel "army," which was in reality an unkempt mob of brave but disorganized bushwhackers, some of them armed only with machetes. The few writers who managed to reach the rebel force had little chance of getting dispatches out to civilization. The war was almost literally incommunicado. The chief sources of information to United States newspapers were writers in Havana or Key West

[5] Walter Millis, *The Martial Spirit*, 31–32.
[6] Wisan, 69; Horatio S. Rubens, *Liberty: The Story of Cuba*, 195.

who might as well have been in New York, and the busy, imaginative Junta.[7]

Every afternoon, New York reporters would gather at the Junta office in what was called the "Peanut Club," because Lawyer Rubens always supplied a large box of peanuts. There, along with peanuts, Estrada Palma gravely gave them "news releases" telling of the latest smashing Cuban triumph and the newest Spanish atrocity. Estrada Palma said he had his own infallible news sources, most of them heroic Cubans who had taken their lives in their hands to steal through the Spanish lines to give the truth to the outside world.

The majority of these heroes did not exist. At rare intervals the Cubans would send to New York a genuine, flesh-and-blood rebel emissary to maintain the illusion. Although he would naturally be biased, his stories would be recorded by the papers as true. Reports from Madrid telling of Spanish victories and Cuban atrocities, however, were given short shrift as "prejudiced."[8]

For two years, while the rebellion gained momentum, the New York newspapers published accounts of battles that never occurred, while remaining ignorant of real battles. They narrated a succession of Spanish atrocities entirely unauthenticated. They dealt in the feeblest of rumor. Several times they reported the death of one of the rebel "generals," Antonio Maceo, and once his suicide, while Maceo was still alive and healthy. Another "general," Maximo Gomez, who had yet to receive Hearst's gem-studded sword, was periodically reported as killed in battle. Havana was repeatedly "captured" by the insurgents when no insurgents were within miles of the city.[9]

Most of the New York papers were guilty of these fabrications, but the greatest offenders were the Cuba-loving *Sun,* the *World,* and the *Journal.* Hearst's *Journal,* vigorously following the hero-villain line, led all the rest.

The *Journal* said, "Spanish troops have resumed the inhuman practice of beating Cuban prisoners to death." The *Journal* said it was "the daily practice of the Spanish jailers to take several prisoners from the forts and prisons and shoot them." Under the heading, "FEEDING PRISONERS TO SHARKS," the *Journal* told how the Spaniards drowned their prisoners at night. The *Journal* constantly denounced the Spaniards for attacking hospitals, outraging women, poisoning wells, imprisoning nuns, and "roasting twenty-five Catholic priests alive."[10] When the rebellion gained despite these repressive measures, the Spanish government removed its easy-going captain-general, Martinez Campos, and replaced him with the tougher General Valeriano Weyler. Weyler must have been amazed to find the *Journal* promptly dubbing him "Butcher" Weyler and greeting him with this character sketch:

> Weyler the brute, the devastator of haciendas, the destroyer of families, and the outrager of women . . . Pitiless, cold, an exterminator of men . . .

[7] M. A. Wilkerson, *Public Opinion and the Spanish-American War,* 8–9.
[8] Wisan, 47.   [9] Millis, 42; Wisan, 56.
[10] *Journal,* Nov. 25, Oct. 23, 1895; Oct. 7, 1896.

There is nothing to prevent his carnal, animal brain from running riot with itself in inventing tortures and infamies of bloody debauchery. . . .[11]

Weyler began to view United States newspapers with suspicion. The Spanish minister in Washington, alarmed by a brand of journalism new to him, tried to combat it. He pointed to the Junta in New York as a hotbed of insurgent propaganda inspired by the single aim of antagonizing the United States toward Spain.

". . . the rebels," he said, ". . . hope in some way to create bad blood, and, ultimately, war between Spain and the United States, with the idea of having their fighting done by American troops." [12]

Although few believed him, this was the simple truth. The rebels never had any idea of winning military victory over the far stronger Spaniards. They were content to fight a sporadic, hit-and-run guerilla warfare, meanwhile depending on Señor Estrada Palma and his Peanut Club to bring the United States to their aid. They knew that Americans were naive about foreign matters but had a natural inclination to dislike monarchies such as Spain and to sympathize with any people fighting for their independence against such a monarchy.

When Richard Harding Davis and Frederick Remington reached Havana, they joined other newsmen in the position of being forbidden to visit the "war zone" and being forced to pick up their news by telepathy or faith. They registered at the handsome Hotel Inglaterra, on the ocean-front Prado, the favorite haunt of correspondents who never saw the war. Nearby was the American consulate in the Casa Nueva, the city's most modern office building. The United States consul-general was white-haired, portly General Fitzhugh Lee, a nephew of Robert E. Lee and a former governor of Virginia, who was in sympathy with the revolution. Lee had his hands full defending the interests of Yankee correspondents whom the Spaniards had either jailed for illegalities or ejected from the island.

Davis, like his colleagues, found news hard to come by in peaceful Havana. Among the few news sources were rebel sympathizers who swore they had just returned from the fighting zone, or had friends who had, and were willing to impart "news" for a few pesos. Davis managed to smuggle out a few atrocity stories gleaned from these dubious sources, but he found himself closely watched by the Spaniards. The *Journal* had represented him as being "with the insurgents" and had published a large picture of him, mounted on a horse loaded down with rifles and cartridges. Copies of the newspaper had reached Havana shortly after he did, causing the Spaniards to keep him under surveillance.[13] He did not begin to earn his $3000 a month until he sent out the tale about the three girls stripped naked by the Spaniards.

The *Journal* featured this under a five-column headline: "DOES OUR

[11] *Journal*, Feb. 23, 1896.　　　[12] N. Y. *World*, Jan. 2, 1896.
[13] George Bronson Rea, *Facts and Fakes About Cuba*, 201-2.

FLAG PROTECT WOMEN?" It related how three pretty Cuban girls had boarded the American vessel *Olivette,* leaving Havana for New York. As the ship was about to sail, Spanish policemen rushed aboard, declaring that the trio were suspected of carrying insurgent dispatches and must be searched. Despite the protests of the captain—this on a vessel flying the Stars and Stripes—the girls were stripped to their skins in a vain search for illegal documents. The story was illustrated by a half-page drawing by Remington, showing one of the girls stark naked, surrounded by interested policemen who were searching her clothing.[14]

The story caused a storm of protest in the United States. Congressman Amos Cummings introduced a resolution in the House, "Resolved . . . that the Honorable Secretary of State . . . give to the House of Representatives any information he may have concerning the incident of the stripping of three lady passengers . . . as related by the correspondent of the 'New York Journal' . . ." Senator Don Cameron drafted a similar resolution in the Senate.[15] Hearst, riding the wave of sensation, went to his own alma mater for an expert opinion on the legality of the search. Joseph H. Beale, professor of international law at Harvard, gravely told the *Journal:*

> However unwise or inhuman the action of the Spanish authorities may have been in searching the women on board the *Olivette,* they appear to have been within their legal rights.[16]

The *World,* disgruntled at being scooped, sent reporters to interview the Cuban girls when they arrived in New York, and got a scoop of its own. The young women were indignant when they saw the story printed about them. They had not been undressed by men, they said. Women matrons had searched them in a stateroom while the officers waited outside. The delighted *World* ran the story under the headline, "The Unclothed Women Searched by Men was an Invention of a New York Newspaper." [17]

Davis, embarrassed by the reflection on his integrity, sent an explanatory letter:

> I never wrote that she was searched by men . . . Mr. Frederick Remington, who was not present, and who drew an imaginary picture of the scene, is responsible for the idea that the search was conducted by men. Had I seen the picture before it appeared, I should never have allowed it to accompany my article . . .[18]

The resolutions of Representative Cummings and Senator Cameron were dropped. The *Journal* was publicly exposed as irresponsible. Hearst was unruffled. He knew the shortness of public memory, and that new sensations would obliterate the *Journal's* momentary shame. He issued no reprimands. Willis Abbot, who had a strong sense of newspaper responsibility, wrote:

[14] *Journal,* Feb. 12, 1897.   [15] Rea, 230.   [16] *Journal,* Feb. 14, 1897.
[17] N. Y. *World,* Feb. 17, 1897.   [18] Rea, 231.

It was characteristic of Hearst methods that no one suffered for what in most papers would have been an unforgivable offense, and I never heard the owner of the paper, in public or in private, express the slightest regret for the scandalous "fake."

Indeed, it soon became the fixed policy of the paper to exaggerate and misconstrue every military act of the Spanish commander in Cuba. "Butcher Weyler" was the figure created out of an honorable soldier who, after the war was over, was recognized as having tried to do his duty in as humane a fashion as the difficult situation would permit.[19]

The next stop-press story came a few days later when Dr. Ricardo Ruiz, a Cuban dentist who had become a naturalized United States citizen, was found dead in his cell at Guanabacoa, a few miles east of Havana. Ruiz, a revolutionist who had fled Cuba during a previous insurrection, had later returned and was one of those "American citizens" who were still Cubans and still revolutionists and who used their American citizenship as a protection while aiding the revolt.[20] He had been arrested for train robbery, not an unusual charge in Cuba, where one of the activities of the rebels was to wreck or raid trains. After two weeks in jail, he committed suicide, the Spaniards said, by pounding his head against the wall of his cell.

A *Journal* correspondent, George Eugene Bryson, was permitted to see Ruiz's body and also his cell. He was suspicious. His suspicions, however, were translated into fact by a *Journal* headline, "American Slain in Spanish Jail," over a story saying there was "strong evidence to show that this man was murdered." [21]

Hearst demanded war to avenge Dr. Ruiz. He telegraphed Ruiz's widow money to enable her to come to the United States as a *Journal* representative. One of his Washington correspondents was Alfred Henry Lewis, the man who had so effectively smeared Hanna. Lewis, a former drunkard, had once taken a number of drinks when he was a Cleveland attorney and had lost touch with reality until he regained consciousness and found himself working as a cowboy on a ranch in New Mexico, an experience that made him take the pledge. Now a sober coffee drinker, he received telegraphed orders from Hearst. He secured an interview with Senator John Sherman of Ohio, soon to become McKinley's Secretary of State. This resulted in a *Journal* headline, "SHERMAN FOR WAR WITH SPAIN FOR MURDERING AMERICANS," over a story in which the Senator admitted that his only information came from the *Journal* and was quoted as saying, "if the facts are true, as reported, and American citizens are being murdered in Cuba in cold blood, the only way to put an end to the atrocities is to declare war on Spain." [22]

The *Journal* followed this with another dispatch from Bryson, who declared he had examined the chair in Ruiz's cell and found scratched on it "a message from Ruiz as from the grave." The dentist had scrawled on the

[19] Abbot, 213–14.   [20] Wilkerson, 96.   [21] *Journal*, Feb. 20, 1897.
[22] *Journal*, Feb. 22.

chair that "he was being killed." To prove that Ruiz was indeed an American citizen although he lived in Cuba, the *Journal* printed a facsimile of his naturalization papers. Said Hearst in his *Journal:*

> If it is true that the Spaniards murdered Ruiz in his Cuban prison, national self-respect, as well as national honor, demands that the United States declare war against Spain . . . War is a dreadful thing, but there are things more dreadful even than war, and one of them is dishonor . . .[23]

However, Senator Sherman pricked the war balloon with a testy pronouncement disavowing the *Journal* interview. "It is a lie from beginning to end," he said. "I am surprised that the *Journal* should make such a statement." [24] The New York *Post* and the *World* took delight in publicizing this new evidence of *Journal* imagination. Yet it had to be admitted that Sherman was not too reliable himself. One of the oddities of the times was that the seventy-four-year-old Senator had been selected for the most important Cabinet post under McKinley although he was failing mentally. Sherman often forgot what he said, what he did, and on at least one occasion forgot where he was, so it is remotely possible that he forgot what he said to Lewis.

The *Journal* applied war pressure to McKinley even before he took office. It conceived war with Spain as a class issue—something demanded by the justice-loving masses and opposed only by bloated Wall-Streeters who feared that war would upset the market. "McKinley," it complained, "is listening with eager ear to the threats of the big Business Interests . . ." [25]

Actually, McKinley was listening to nothing more sinister than a group of insurance agents. As President-elect, he had incautiously mentioned aloud that he would need more life insurance, with the result that insurance men converged on Canton and filled twenty suites at the town's best hotel. McKinley bought $50,000 worth of insurance, choosing the company that had insured his friend Hanna. By coincidence, it was also the same company that had paid off on the deaths of Presidents Garfield and Arthur. McKinley took office on March 5, 1897, avoiding specific reference to Cuba in his inaugural but saying, "We want no wars of conquest. We must avoid the temptation of territorial aggression."

". . . vague and sapless," snapped the *Journal*.[26] It filled a full page with pictures of Mrs. Ruiz, announcing her imminent arrival. When she reached New York, Hearst sent her on to Washington with her children. There, with the aid of the *Journal* Washington staff, she secured interviews with McKinley, Secretary of State Sherman and Representative R. R. Hitt, chairman of the House Committee on Foreign Affairs.

Although she was received politely, and Sherman even ordered an investigation of Dr. Ruiz's death, Hearst must have seen that the country was not ready to go to war for the Ruiz family. Something more dramatic and compelling was needed.

[23] The same.
[25] *Journal*, Jan. 17, 1897.
[24] N. Y. *Evening Post*, Feb. 22, 1897.
[26] *Journal*, Mar. 6, 1897.

The Junta was so pleased at Hearst's cooperation that the *Journal* offices were now haunted by swarthy Cubans whose password was *"Cuba Libre!"* and who explained to reporters the military situation and the villainies of the Spaniards.[27] Ralph Paine was still trying to deliver the jeweled sword to General Gomez. In Key West were several Hearst "commissioners" under Charles Michelson vainly hatching schemes for eluding the Spaniards and joining Gomez in the interior of Cuba. With them was a physician, sent by Hearst, with chests filled with medicines and surgical equipment paid for by Hearst, intended for the rebels but unable to get to Cuba. Sam Chamberlain, generalissimo of the Hearst forces, was shuttling between New York and Key West, urging his men to mount a genuine offensive. In Key West were several speedy Hearst-chartered yachts that proved useless because of the close watch kept by United States gunboats charged with maintaining neutrality.[28]

Hearst was spending large sums to cover the war, but was succeeding in doing little more than furnishing a corps of writers and artists with room and board in Florida and Havana. He was holding policy conferences daily with a dozen of his top editors, but, suffering from stage-fright in such a large group, cut the number down to five or six.[29] Almost every night in the week he went to the theater, usually returning to the *Journal* around midnight with the glamorous Willson sisters. They waited patiently among the statuary in his office while Hearst, always perfectly calm, created frenzy among his men by tearing apart next morning's paper just before deadline.

[27] Abbot, 213.   [28] Rea, 200; Rubens, 316.
[29] Mrs. Fremont Older, *op. cit.*, 181–82.

3. The Cuban Joan of Arc

I. THE POWER OF THE PRESS

THE two loudest warmongers in the United States, Hearst and Pulitzer, were both six feet two inches tall, both millionaires who spent money royally while they espoused the causes of the masses. Both were singularly shy. The similarity ended there. Hearst was in a perfect health, placid and courteous. Pulitzer was blind, a nervous wreck who could fly into profane rages. Hearst was at his office daily, exercising personal control. Pulitzer was rarely at his proud, gold-domed skyscraper. He was only occasionally at his New York home on East Fifty-fifth Street, which was equipped with soundproof rooms to shield his quaking nerves. The rest of the time he was either at one of his four other mansions in Maine, New Jersey, Georgia and France, or aboard his palatial ocean-going yacht *Liberty*, keeping in touch with his editors by telegram or cable. Hearst believed in fighting Spain almost from the start of the Cuban trouble. Pulitzer, at first opposed to United States involvement, came around reluctantly for war, as he later candidly admitted, because it meant circulation.[1]

It is safe to say that had not Pulitzer been locked in a bitter circulation struggle with Hearst, and had he not witnessed the added circulation Hearst's frenetic treatment of the Cuban news brought him, Pulitzer and his mighty *World* would have remained on the side of peace. Thus Hearst, in addition to his own potent newspapers, was responsible for dragging the morning and evening *World*, with the largest circulation in the nation, into the pro-war camp.

These two men addressed literally millions of Americans. In 1897, the circulation of Pulitzer's two papers was more than 800,000 daily. Hearst's morning and evening *Journal* were hardly 100,000 behind, and his San Francisco *Examiner* had 80,000. They had on their pro-war side the influential New York *Sun*, with about 150,000. Through the Associated Press and other news-service affiliations, the *Journal*, *World* and *Sun* dispatches were reprinted in many other important papers across the nation.

Against them they had the strongly anti-war *Herald* (100,000), the *Evening Post* (25,000), the conservative *Tribune* (75,000) and the high-priced *Times* (three cents, under 25,000 circulation). The remaining several New York papers were even smaller, had no funds for coverage of the Cuban rebellion, and exercised small weight.[2]

The total circulation of New York's pro-war newspapers was about 1,560,-000, against the anti-war total of 225,000.

[1] Bleyer, 342. [2] Wisan, 24, 26, 27, 28, 29, 30, 31, 32.

However, all of these papers were of much more than local moment. The prestige of the large New York dailies on either side was a strong and determining influence on hundreds of fresh-water editors throughout the country who knew little of foreign affairs and traditionally had looked to the New York journals for guidance since the days of Greeley, Bennett and Raymond. Since the newspapers were the greatest mass medium then existing, their influence in shaping public opinion would be decisive. And since the New York newspapers in one way or another swayed most of the rest, it could be said that—given a situation where war or peace hung in almost equal balance—the clacking Underwoods and Remingtons in the grubby warrens around Printing House Square would decide whether it would be the olive branch or the sword.

No one could discount the national influence of the anti-war *Herald, Post, Tribune* and *Times.* Yet the plain fact was that their relatively quiet, sensible columns were dull newswise. They were like reasonable men speaking in normal tones. Naturally they were outshouted by the screams of the *Journal* and *World.* The majority of the public found it more exciting to read about the murder of Cuban babies and the rape of Cuban women by the Spaniards than to read conscientious accounts of complicated political problems and injustices on both sides. The hero-villain concept of the war was simple, easy to grasp and satisfying. In addition to having the loudest voices and the most money, Hearst and Pulitzer had the best writers and illustrators and had many more dispatch boats, jeweled swords and correspondents in Key West and Cuba than all the other papers combined. Hearst alone sent a total of at least thirty-five writers and artists to "cover the war" at various times.

During the early stages of the insurrection, the *World* had William Shaw Bowen as its first correspondent in Cuba. Bowen wrote admirably balanced, fair-minded accounts showing the complexities of the struggle and giving Spain its due. Later, the *World* sent Sylvester Scovel, a fiery University of Michigan graduate, to the scene. Scovel was enthusiastically pro-Cuban, an expert delineator of atrocities who could cap a vivid description of murdered and mutilated Cubans with the remark, "the Spanish soldiers habitually cut off the ears of the Cuban dead and retain them as trophies." [3]

The unbiased Bowen was easily the superior correspondent. But Scovel made more exciting reading, and Bowen was summoned back to New York.

Significantly, Bowen, because of his fairness, was permitted by the Spaniards to travel through Cuba and to visit the rebel camp. But Scovel, Creelman and other exponents of the severed-ear school began the fashion of one-sided reporting that caused the angry Spaniards to restrict reporters and censor their dispatches more rigidly. The result was that from 1896 on, the "Cuban correspondents" were kept remote from the fray and were forced to rely on rumor and the ever-present "eyewitness reports" of Span-

[3] N. Y. *World,* May 29, 1896.

ish treachery, which they smuggled out and which in turn often were exaggerated by editors in the New York offices with the aid of the industrious Peanut Club. The official curb on American writers incensed them further against the Spaniards and led them into all manner of deceit and subterfuge.[4]

The New York newspapers, which to a large degree spoke for the nation, actually knew little of what was happening in Cuba. What little they knew was twisted one way or the other by prejudice.

Most ironic of all, the United States administration, which had to base top-level policy on the facts of the Cuban situation, knew scarcely more than was printed in the newspapers. The nation's highest official in Cuba was Consul-General Lee in Havana. Lee himself knew only what he could learn in Havana. He was strongly sympathetic with the rebels and was said to be working quietly for American intervention. His reports to Washington usually belittled the abilities of the Spaniards to suppress the rebellion. Lee lived and dined at the Hotel Inglaterra, where most of the American correspondents also lived. The consulate staff and the writers formed something of an anti-Spanish club. The New York *Journal* news bureau in Havana was in the Casa Nueva, where Lee also had his offices. Since neither Lee nor many United States newspapers of influence paid any attention to official Spanish news releases, believing them lies, the Spanish side of the story was almost unheard in the United States.[5]

From the standpoint of propaganda, the situation could not have been better rigged in favor of the insurgents had Hearst or the Peanut Club itself done the arranging. In Washington, publicity-seeking Senators and Representatives were constantly guilty of indignant statements about Spanish cruelty and oppression based wholly on New York newspaper reports which were highly biased or downright fictitious. The Secretary of State listened gravely to testimony about Spanish atrocities by the *Journal's* Frederick Lawrence, one of the greatest of Munchausens, who had spent his time in Havana without seeing the war and who admitted that he got his information from rebel sympathizers whom he believed truthful.[6]

In the circumstances, one can pity General Valeriano Weyler, who had been sent to Cuba by the Queen Regent of Spain with orders to put down the rebellion. He arrived to find himself described by New York newspapers as a butcher, rapist, and a Torquemada of torture. A fifty-nine-year-old professional soldier, short and broad-shouldered, Weyler as a young officer had been military attaché at the Spanish legation in Washington during the Civil War, and as an observer had accompanied Sherman on his march through Georgia. He had admired Sherman, but his liking for things American was dwindling. He read things in the American papers he could scarcely credit. Miss Nellie Bly, the *World* reporter who had gone around the world in seventy-two days, announced that she planned to recruit a regiment of volunteers, officered by women, to fight for Cuban independ-

[4] Wilkerson, 8–9.   [5] Millis, 74.   [6] Millis, 43; Rea, 170–71.

ence.[7] The Youngstown Chamber of Commerce struck a blow at Spain by voting to boycott the Spanish onion.[8]

"The Cubans are fighting us openly," Weyler said. "The Americans are fighting us secretly . . . The American newspapers are responsible. They poison everything with falsehood." [9]

The Spanish government in Cuba had been autocratic but not oppressive. The rebellion was in large part inspired by revolutionists in New York, encouraged by unrest caused by economic depression and poverty. It had gained in strength because of a ruthless rebel decree that all Cubans who did not aid them would be considered allies of Spain and enemies of the "republic," causing many citizens to help the insurgents out of fear. Weyler, like the majority of Spaniards, believed that the rebels would long since have been crushed but for the incitement of the New York press and the arms, men and supplies sent by filibuster ships that slipped into Cuba. Now Weyler commanded some 80,000 Spanish soldiers whose presence in Cuba was bleeding Spain white. Yet they could not achieve a finished fight because the rebels invariably dodged them. The rebel strategy was to burn sugar plantations and towns, wreck railroads and flee, always avoiding pitched battles. As a result, the sugar industry was all but paralyzed, thousands were homeless, and what had been mere poverty in the island was now ghastly destitution and famine. The hatred between the contending parties had grown so bitter that when men were captured by either side, hangings and disembowelings were common.

Amid such incidents as rebel plotters trying to blow up his Havana palace and succeeding only in destroying a downstairs toilet, Weyler employed the stern measures expected of him. To neutralize the thousands of Cubans in the interior who were secretly aiding and supplying the rebels while posing as loyal citizens, he issued a "reconcentration" order. This required all citizens of the interior not openly with the rebels to leave their villages and move within the Spanish lines. Spanish forces then proceeded to clear the interior of supplies, applying a "scorched earth" program to starve out the rebels. This brought great suffering and privation to the *reconcentrados*, or uprooted families, many of whom were near starvation themselves. But the measure, along with renewed Spanish military activity, proved effective and the insurgents for a time lost ground.

Weyler had almost as much trouble with the New York *Journal* and a pretty Cuban girl named Evangelina Cosio y Cisneros as he did with the rebels.

Señorita Cosio, who came to be known in the United States as Miss Cisneros, or "The Cuban Joan of Arc," or "The Flower of Cuba," was a languorous-eyed, eighteen-year-old Latin beauty. Her father, a revolutionist from Camaguey, had been sentenced to death by the Spaniards for forming a rebel cavalry company. The sentence was later commuted to life imprison-

[7] N. Y. *World*, Mar. 8, 1896.   [8] N. Y. *Tribune*, Mar. 14, 1896.
[9] Creelman, 160.

ment at the Spanish penal colony in Ceuta, Africa. Still later, Evangelina went to Weyler in person to plead for her father, with the result that he was sent instead to mild confinement at the Isle of Pines, south of Cuba.

Evangelina, whose mother was dead, went voluntarily to the Isle of Pines to be near him. While there, she hit on a plan to free him. She succeeded in luring the Spanish commander on the island, Colonel José Berriz, to her cottage, where he was set upon by several rebel sympathizers, beaten and tied. The plot was quickly foiled by Spanish soldiers who rescued the colonel and arrested the girl. She was sent to the Recojidas prison in Havana to await trial for sedition.

At the time, her case received no publicity. It was not until months later, in August, 1897, that the *Journal* correspondent George Eugene Bryson, who had written so touchingly of Dr. Ruiz, came upon Miss Cisneros at the prison. Either through the imaginative efforts of Bryson or Miss Cisneros herself, the facts about her arrest were altered. Bryson telegraphed the *Journal* an indignant dispatch declaring that the sole reason for her imprisonment was her brave defense of her chastity against the lustful advances of Colonel Berriz. Now, said Bryson, she was confined among degenerates in the filthy Recojidas prison and in all probability was doomed to a twenty-year term at Ceuta as a reward for her purity.[10]

Hearst was lolling in his editorial chair when Bryson's dispatch arrived. The summer heat had made interest in Cuba flag. Hearst read the account. Then he slapped his knee and laughed aloud.

"Sam!" he called.

The tall, elegant Chamberlain came in.

"We've got Spain now!" Hearst said.[11]

II. ENLIST THE WOMEN OF AMERICA

> The unspeakable fate to which Weyler has doomed an innocent girl whose only crime is that she had defended her honor against a beast in uniform has sent a shudder of horror through the American people.
>
> —The New York *Journal.*[1]

PROPAGANDIST Hearst had aroused American resentment over the "murder" of Dr. Ruiz in his cell, but a maiden in distress, particularly if she was beautiful, would stir the American imagination better than a hundred Ruizes. Showman Hearst intuitively grasped the emotional possibilities inherent in the spectacle of a wronged girl in the clutches of the decadent Spanish Empire. He half believed in her wronging himself. He became producer, director and stage manager for the greatest of journalistic melodramas as he rattled off orders to Chamberlain.

"Telegraph to our correspondent in Havana to wire every detail of this

[10] *Journal,* Aug. 17, 1897.   [11] Creelman, 179–80.   [1] Aug. 19, 1897.

case," he said. "Get up a petition to the Queen Regent of Spain for this girl's pardon. Enlist the women of America. Have them sign the petition. Wake up our correspondents all over the country. Have distinguished women sign first. Cable the petition and the names to the Queen Regent."

So far, the Cisneros case was a *Journal* exclusive, and he meant to keep it that way. It was his intention to make Miss Cisneros the *Journal's* own property.

"Notify our minister in Madrid," he went on to Chamberlain. "We can make a national issue of this case. It will do more to open the eyes of the country than a thousand editorials or political speeches. The Spanish minister can attack our correspondents, but we'll see if he can face the women of America when they take up the fight. The girl must be saved if we have to take her out of prison by force or send a steamer to meet the vessel that carries her away—but that would be piracy, wouldn't it?" [2]

Creelman was placed in overall charge of the Cisneros campaign. A petition was drawn up asking Queen Regent Maria Christina's intercession for the girl's pardon. With no regard for telegraphic tolls, the petition was wired to more than 200 Hearst correspondents and "stringers" throughout the United States. Each of them was instructed to hire a carriage and call on local women—the most influential women first—and get their signatures on the petition. Meanwhile the *Journal*, under massive headlines, told America of the plight of Miss Cisneros:

> This tenderly nurtured girl was imprisoned at eighteen among the most depraved Negresses of Havana, and now she is about to be sent in mockery to spend twenty years in a servitude that will kill her in a year . . . This girl, delicate, refined, sensitive, unused to hardship, absolutely ignorant of vice, unconscious of the existence of such beings as crowd the cells of the Casa de Recojidas, is seized, thrust into a prison maintained for the vilest class of abandoned women of Havana, and shattered in health until she is threatened with an early death.[3]

The *Journal* also telegraphed General Weyler suggesting that he be merciful. The general could hardly have forgotten that one of the kinder things the *Journal* had called him was "the prince of all cruel generals this century has seen," and was now misrepresenting the Cisneros case as well as accusing him of brutality in his treatment of the girl. As the *Journal's* impassioned Cisneros headlines spewed off the presses, and the *Journal's* descriptions of Miss Cisneros' pitiful plight went out over Associated Press wires to newspapers all over the nation, the *World* was in a jealous pet at having been scooped. It attacked the *Journal* for sensationalism, saying, "The Spanish in Cuba have sins enough to answer for, as the *World* was first to show, but nothing is gained for the Cuban cause by inventions and exaggerations that are past belief." [4]

[2] Creelman, 180.   [3] *Journal*, Aug. 18, 1897.   [4] N. Y. *World*, Aug. 21, 1897.

The *Journal* came back with, ". . . the women of America will save her [Evangelina] yet in spite of Weyler and the *World*."[5]

The women of America were doing their best. Petitions poured in from all parts of the country in response to the energetic work of the Hearst correspondents. Many of them came from women of intelligence and prestige who should have known better than to act on an unconfirmed newspaper report. Some were married or related to important officials so that their signatures carried a hint of governmental authority. Among them were the elderly mother of President McKinley, the wife of Secretary of State Sherman, Mrs. Mark Hanna, the widow of President Grant, the widow of Jefferson Davis, Julia Ward Howe, Frances Hodgson Burnett, Mrs. John A. Logan and Clara Barton. To these were added the names of hundreds of women of only local prominence, and thousands more of no prominence at all. The Sisters of Notre Dame and the Superior of the Order of Visitation joined in the appeal. The *Journal* filled twelve columns with names of women petitioners, by states. It published a "Roll of Honor" of noted women whose hearts bled for Miss Cisneros.[6]

The *Journal* had to grind out extra editions to meet the demand. Hearst widened his drive, calling for action in England. Mrs. Ormiston Chant, the well-known London temperance worker, joined with Lady Rothschild in circulating the *Journal* petition, securing some 200,000 signatures. Julia Ward Howe introduced a new element by addressing a petition to Pope Leo XIII, which the *Journal* promptly cabled, along with others, to Rome. The sentiments of the American and English women were likewise cabled to the Queen Regent in Spain. The United States, along with a good part of Europe, was in a condition of mass indignation over the treatment given a Cuban girl about whom its information was entirely erroneous. It is doubtful whether all history can present another instance wherein so many well-intentioned women—and men—have been so gloriously, angrily wrong.[7]

"At last the ruffians who rule Cuba in the name of Spain have gone too far," said the *Journal*. "They have roused America from its apathy . . . In Washington and Havana the excitement aroused by the *Journal*'s recital of the infamy perpetrated against Señorita Cisneros is so great that the Spanish authorities are alarmed, and are appealing to the bestial commandant to withdraw his charge."[8]

In Havana, the bestial commandant, General Weyler, banished Correspondent Bryson, who had started all the fuss. In Washington, Spanish Minister Dupuy de Lome, who had long recognized the *Journal* as the greatest enemy of any clear-headed American understanding of the Cuban situation, vainly tried to stem the avalanche of misguided passion. He wrote an open

[5] *Journal*, Aug. 22, 1897.
[6] *Journal*, Aug. 22, 1897, ff.; Karl Decker, *The Story of Evangelina Cisneros*, 45–47; Wisan, 87.
[7] Wisan, 326; Millis, 83.   [8] *Journal*, Aug. 19, 1897.

letter to Mrs. Sherman, Mrs. Davis and other grieving women explaining that the *Journal* had misled them, that Miss Cisneros had indeed fomented an uprising and that far from being sentenced to twenty years in Ceuta she had not yet been sentenced at all.[9]

But Evangelina Cisneros had become a symbol of wronged innocence in the United States. Hundreds of mass meetings were held over the nation, at which speakers demanded her rescue from the Spanish rapists. At the Spanish summer palace in San Sebastian, Queen Regent Maria Christina was frightened by the thousands of names cabled her by Señor Hearst, by a cabled appeal from His Holiness Leo XIII, and by the public excitement reported by Minister De Lome. How could one comprehend the Americanos, who called the Spaniards excitable people? Even if she was guilty, Miss Cisneros was not worth offending the United States, England and the Pope. The Queen Regent cabled General Weyler suggesting that the girl be placed in a convent and treated gently. Weyler, who would have been inhuman had he not been angry, did not follow the suggestion. He kept Evangelina in the Casa Recojidas despite protests from Consul General Lee.[10]

The *Journal* kept up the assault for a fortnight, dwelling on the lecherous Colonel Berriz and the horrors of the Recojidas prison. It hinted broadly that Miss Cisneros might be rescued despite all the chains and iron bars of the Spanish Empire.[11]

This was Hearst at his most Napoleonic. Public frenzy could be maintained for only so long. He could see that despite the *Journal* campaign the interest in Miss Cisneros was gradually subsiding. He was contemplating a scheme for the girl's liberation which, if successful, would give him the greatest scoop of all time. The man he selected for the job was Karl Decker, a burly, adventurous writer now connected with the Hearst Washington bureau. Decker had previously served a tour of duty in Cuba, and was familiar with Havana. Late in August he was summoned to New York, where Sam Chamberlain gave him general instructions to perform an international jailbreak.

"I want you to go to Havana, get this girl out of the Recojidas and send her to the United States," Chamberlain was reported to have said. ". . . I can assure you of Mr. Hearst's ample appreciation of your efforts if you succeed." [12]

Decker, his pockets full of Hearst money, left for Havana to replace the banished Bryson. Meanwhile, other New York editors were fuming at Hearst's Cisneros crusade, so fraudulent and yet so successful. The *World*, whose record of exaggeration was second only to the *Journal*'s, truly said that the *Journal*'s campaign might damage the girl's interests because of the insults heaped on Weyler. A *World* reporter who interviewed Miss Cisneros admitted that the Recojidas prison was an unpleasant place whose inmates include prostitutes, criminals and political prisoners. However, the latter,

[9] *Journal*, Aug. 26, 1897.

[11] *Journal*, Aug. 23 and 29, 1897.

[10] Creelman, 181; Decker, 54; Musgrave, 99.

[12] Decker, 64–65.

among them Evangelina, were treated better than the rest, being kept separate in rooms on the second floor, and were allowed to have their meals brought in from outside if they wished.[13]

On September 8, Consul General Lee, who had been indisposed, arrived in New York aboard the Ward liner *Seguranca* for a thirty-day rest. A West Point graduate, Lee was en route to the military academy to visit his son, a cadet there. Although he had little use for the Spaniards, he showed real indignation over the *Journal's* sideshow treatment of the Cisneros affair.

". . . I wish to correct a false and stupid impression which has been created by some newspapers," he said. "I refer to Senorita Cisneros. This young woman has two clean rooms in the Casa Recojidas, and is well clothed and fed. It is all tommy-rot about her scrubbing floors and being subjected to cruelties and indignities. She would have been pardoned long ago if it had not been for the hubbub created by American newspapers.

"I do not believe the Spanish government ever for one moment intended to send her to the penal colony in Africa or elsewhere. I believe her name is now upon the roll for pardon.

"That she was implicated in the insurrection on the Isle of Pines, there can be no question. She herself, in a note to me, acknowledged that fact, and stated she was betrayed by an accomplice named Arias." [14]

Lee, of course, was referring to the *Journal*. The small New York *Commercial Advertiser* editorialized:

"At least nine tenths of the statements about Miss Cisneros printed in this country seem to have been sheer falsehood. The attempt to exalt her case into an issue of international importance is seen to have been merely an audacious scheme of journalistic advertising which took no account of her real interests." [15]

But no one read the *Commercial Advertiser* and innocent Americans across the land still believed that the Cuban girl was a victim of Spanish brutality. The *Journal*, whose own story on the Lee interview conveniently omitted his remarks about "tommyrot," had veered in a new direction—a vendetta against the Spanish minister in Washington, Dupuy de Lome. De Lome's naval attaché, it said, was spying on American forts in preparation for war. Another Spanish spy was inspecting the Atlantic coastal defenses. But the *Journal* assured its readers that if it came to war, the Spanish navy would be easy prey for Uncle Sam's battleships.[16]

In Havana, Karl Decker had put up at the Inglaterra and begun groundwork for his errand of mercy. He was doubtless impelled to haste by the possibility that the Spaniards would release Miss Cisneros voluntarily, which would be a tragic frustration of Mr. Hearst's intention to release her by stealth. But it took some time for Decker to survey the ground around the Recojidas prison, at No. 1 O'Farrell Street. As helpers in his plot he secured William McDonald, an American shipping man in Havana, and Carlos Car-

[13] *World*, Sept. 3, 1897.   [14] Rea, 233.   [15] *Commercial Advertiser*, Sept. 9, 1897.
[16] *Journal*, Sept. 10, 11, 13, 1897.

bonelle, a Cuban rebel. He visited Miss Cisneros at the prison, apprised her of the plan and warned her to be ready. One can only admire the girl's courage. She realized that she had become a flaming, romantic symbol of Spanish oppression and that her deliverance would furnish the Peanut Club and the American newspapers with a useful propaganda coup.

Carrying a .44 caliber revolver and working much like the Spanish spies the *Journal* exposed in America, Decker rented a "secret room" where he could hide the girl after liberating her. By a rare stroke of luck, the house next to the prison was vacant, and, luckier still, its flat roof projected within eight feet of the second-floor parapet of the prison. Decker rented this house also.

Late on the night of October 6, Decker and his mates climbed to the roof, slid a ladder over to the parapet and stole across in stocking feet. They could see Evangelina's white handkerchief tied to one of the cell bars—her signal that she was ready. According to Decker's highly romantic later account, the moment he applied a hacksaw to the bars, "She gave one glad little cry and clasped our hands through the bars, calling upon us to liberate her at once." Also according to Decker, and which may be taken for what it is worth, he had previously supplied her with drugged bonbons which she fed to her cellmates so that they were all safely in narcotic slumber and unable to sound an alarm. Soon Evangelina slipped through the severed bars, teetered across the ladder, descended to the dark street and was off in a carriage with Decker.[17]

All of these thrilling artifices were necessary only for the purposes of making a good story and protecting the guards at the prison. The guards had been bribed in advance with Hearst's money and were conscientiously looking the other way.[18]

The señorita remained in hiding in Decker's rented room until October 9. Then, still keeping the needs of the *Journal*'s romancers in mind, Decker had her dress in a sailor's uniform, plastering her hair under her cap, and gave her a cigar to smoke as she walked down Obispo Street to the wharf, where she boarded the steamer *Seneca* for New York. Decker sent a code cable to the *Journal* telling of her imminent arrival, then boarded another ship, the *Panama,* for New York.[19]

Hearst's reaction to the rescue showed his adolescent removal from reality and his great theatrical gifts. He was elated, of course, and it is a safe bet that Decker received a huge bonus. But never for a moment did Hearst admit any awareness of the preposterousness of the exploit. The Cisneros liberation showed the Harvard practical joker at his zenith. This time he had played a joke on the Spanish Empire and on General Weyler. It was international in scope—in fact, it constituted a gross breach of international law—and it had the whole world for an audience. But no hint of amusement lighted his face, nor did he permit his staff to treat the matter as anything but heroic.

[17] Decker, 75–105.   [18] Abbot, 215–16.   [19] Decker, 117.

"Now is the time to consolidate public sentiment," he said to Chamberlain. "Organize a great open-air reception in Madison Square. Have the two best military bands. Secure orators, have a procession, arrange for plenty of fireworks and searchlights. Announce that Miss Cisneros and her rescuer will appear side by side and thank the people. Send men to all the political leaders in the city, and ask them to work up the excitement. We must have 100,000 people together that night. It must be a whale of a demonstration—something that will make the President and Congress sit up and think." [20]

Editor Abbot, who had watched the Cisneros circus since its inception, admitted bafflement.

"I was at the office during the progress of this comedy and in daily contact with Hearst," he wrote. "He took the whole affair with the utmost seriousness . . . His was the driving force that kept going the prodigious wave of publicity. If ever for a moment he doubted that he was battling a powerful State to save the life and liberty of a sorely persecuted girl martyr, he gave no sign of it. It was the one dominating, all-compelling issue of the moment for him and he brooked no indifference on the part of his employees, most of whom in his absence cursed the whole thing for a false bit of cheap sensationalism. But Hearst felt himself in the role of Sir Galahad rescuing a helpless maiden." [21]

Hearst was showing a psychological aberration that would appear again and again during his career. He could at times become a creature of pure fantasy. He *believed* that he had performed a gallant rescue. He *believed* what his newspapers said about it. He could enter into a dream world and, like a child, live out a heroic role in it, brushing aside humdrum reality. Those who thought him a mere cynical opportunist missed half the point. The Hearst revery could become actuality.

The *Journal's* front page reflected pure knight-errantry. "EVANGELINA CISNEROS RESCUED BY THE JOURNAL—An American Newspaper Accomplishes at a Single Stroke What the Best Efforts of Diplomacy Failed Utterly to Bring About in Many Months," was the headline. The story began, "Evangelina Cosio y Cisneros is at last at liberty, and the *Journal* can place to its credit the greatest journalistic coup of this age." In all history, the account said, the feat was equaled only by the rescue of Mary, Queen of Scots. "Recojidas Prison was none too strong for the *Journal's* determination, and truly did locks not make a prison nor iron bars a cage." The story described exhaustively the perils faced by Decker, his aides and Miss Cisneros herself, and the use of ladders, hacksaws, drugged candy and disguises. It made no mention of the bribing of the jailers, which somehow would have detracted from the romance.[22]

There were before-and-after drawings, showing the marks of emaciation and fear left on her face by brutal Spanish imprisonment. The *Journal* crowed at General Weyler's discomfiture: "BAFFLED WEYLER RAGES

[20] Creelman, 185–86.   [21] Abbot, 216.
[22] *Journal*, Oct. 10, 1897; *Evening Journal*, Oct. 11.

AT THE JOURNAL." It announced proudly, "INTERNATIONAL COM-PLICATIONS MAY RESULT FROM THE CISNEROS RESCUE." [23]

When the girl arrived in New York on October 13, to be greeted by a banner headline, "EVANGELINA CISNEROS REACHES THE LAND OF LIBERTY," she became Hearst's property. In the harbor she was met by a steam launch bearing George Eugene Bryson and a group of enthusiastic *Journal* men. She looked well-nourished. She was whisked away to a suite of rooms in the magnificent new Waldorf-Astoria Hotel. She spoke little English, but Mr. Hearst provided an interpreter as well as flowers for her rooms. She was indeed a beauty—a young lady with a harelip would have been a journalistic disappointment. The first thing to do was to furnish her with raiment for her starring role. She was taken to the city's best shops and provided, at Hearst's expense, "with a superb trousseau which she wore with infinite grace." [24]

For some time the *Journal* devoted itself largely to Miss Cisneros. It reiterated the cruelties of her imprisonment, described the loveliness of her skin, eyes and hair, marveled at her intelligence and social graces, and said she intended to become an American citizen. It kept reminding readers that her liberation had been brought about only through the enterprising and daring of the *Journal* and its Karl Decker, "a modern d'Artagnan." It invited Mayor Robert Van Wyck and hundreds of other prominent citizens to the great reception to be given by the *Journal* to Miss Cisneros on Saturday night, October 16. The Associated Press wires and cables had carried the *Journal's* Cisneros stories all over the nation and to a large part of the world. The *Journal* published congratulations from the wife of the Secretary of State, from Mrs. Grant, Clara Barton, the Bishop of London, numerous Senators and governors, and used many columns to print the names of less famous congratulators. Governor Sadler of Missouri enthusiastically suggested that since one *Journal* man could free Miss Cisneros, the *Journal* ought to send 500 of its reporters to free all of Cuba.[25]

The nation's two highest officials seemed to forget that the girl's "rescue" was a jail delivery, an illegal and unfriendly act. Absent-minded Secretary of State Sherman was quoted as saying that "everyone would sympathize with the *Journal's* enterprise in releasing Miss Cisneros." [26] President Mc-Kinley, the *Journal* said, declared that Sherman's words "correctly voiced the unofficial sentiment of the administration." [27] If they were accurately quoted, McKinley and Sherman were guilty of sorry subserviency to a newspaper publicity campaign as well as a direct insult to Spain. One can well understand the wondering remark of Canovas del Castillo, Prime Minister of Spain, to an American correspondent: "The newspapers of your country seem to be more powerful than the government." [28]

The other New York editors, queasy at the Hearst propaganda, disparaged the Cisneros affair and gave it small space. On the evening of October 16,

[23] *Journal*, Oct. 12, 1897.   [24] Rubens, 240.   [25] *Journal*, Oct. 13, 14.
[26] *Journal*, Oct. 11.   [27] Oct. 13.   [28] Creelman, 187.

Miss Cisneros, gorgeous in a white couturière gown, emerged from the Waldorf on the arm of d'Artagnan Decker, accompanied by Mrs. J. Ellen Foster of the Ladies' Cuban Relief Association of New York. They entered a waiting carriage and were driven slowly downtown as an honor guard of white-clad naval cadets, soldiers and policemen marched in front and behind them and thousands of citizens cheered from the sidewalks. At Madison Square they saw that the electrical transparency over the *Journal* uptown office at Broadway and Twenty-sixth, which usually read "Journal Wants Bring Quick Results," had been cleverly changed to read, "Journal Wants Cuba Free." They entered Delmonico's famous restaurant at Fifth Avenue and Twenty-sixth Street, whose grand ballroom had been reserved by Hearst for the occasion, to find a large crowd there. Mayor Van Wyck had been unable to come, but the room was filled with curious and excited people, including deputations from the D.A.R., the Holland Dames and the Ladies' Cuban Relief Association. They gave Miss Cisneros an ovation when she appeared. Much in evidence were Señor Estrada Palma and other happy members of the Junta, or Peanut Club.[29]

The genius of publicity who had conceived and carried out the affair was absent. Miss Cisneros must have been puzzled that Señor Hearst, of whom she had heard so much, and who had accomplished all these glittering things, had remained out of sight. She had not even met him.

Hearst was like a surgeon who could not bear to have his finger lanced. The blaze of publicity which he had poured on Miss Cisneros, Decker and the *Journal* was too warm for his shrinking nature. Yet he could not avoid it entirely. He rolled up in front of Delmonico's in his French racer and ran inside. As one observer put it, ". . . the man who footed the bills came into the room where [Miss Cisneros] stood among the palms, shyly shook hands with the heroine whom his wonder machine had created, and then excused himself and hastened away in his automobile." [30]

After the dinner, and addresses by Senator Eustis and Dr. Lincoln de Zayas of the "Cuban Legation," both of whom thanked the *Journal* for the blow struck at Spanish oppression in the deliverance of the "Flower of Cuba," the program moved out into the vast, open precincts of Madison Square. Here, many thousands of citizens had been attracted by the *Journal* stories and by the *Journal* searchlights, fireworks and bands. Miss Cisneros, Decker, Estrada Palma and other honored guests mounted a wooden stand erected by the *Journal* in front of the Worth monument to hear a rousing speech by Henry George, who likewise praised the *Journal's* courage and enterprise. Above the monument was a large, electrically-lighted sign, "THE JOURNAL'S WELCOME TO EVANGELINA CISNEROS." [31]

By the time it was over, Miss Cisneros, despite her rudimentary knowledge of English, must have been aware that the *Journal* was not concealing its own role in the affair. Yet she was a dedicated fighter for freedom. Even

[29] *Journal*, Oct. 17, 1897.   [30] *Collier's*, Sept. 29, 1906.
[31] *Journal*, Oct. 17, 1897.

if Mr. Hearst was using her for his own interests, gaining circulation by the thousands, it was still true that he was solidly against Spain and was spreading anti-Spanish feeling over the land.

The Cuban girl was a good soldier. She went along. Hearst supplied her with a chaperone, the energetic, white-haired widow of General John A. Logan, who had written articles for women in the *Journal*. Mrs. Logan took her to Washington, where—again under the *Journal* auspices—Miss Cisneros was presented to President McKinley. Later, she appeared in many United States cities to dramatize her cause. Meanwhile, the Sunday *Journal* was running a highly fictionalized serial story of her life, imprisonment and liberation. At last her news value was played out and she was dropped.[32]

The *Journal* had used a total of some 375 columns of type about her. The *World* used about twelve, the *Times* ten, the *Sun* one column, and the other New York newspapers less than a column each.[33]

Still there was no war with Spain. Indeed, the Cisneros exploit, as Hearst must finally have seen, was psychologically unsuited to stir up war, since it represented an American triumph over Spain. Nevertheless, it boosted circulation and it improved the climate for war in three decisive ways:

It gave millions of Americans a false impression of "Spanish brutality" in Cuba.

It showed the weakness of the President, the Secretary of State and other officials in approving an illegal act insulting to Spain.

It made millions of sensitive Spaniards hate the United States.

[32] Abbot, 216.   [33] Wisan, 331.

4. The Fate of the *Maine*

HEARST must have loved Madison Square, for he hovered around it like a moth around the flame. It was a place of baroque beauty in the Nineties, its sylvan, statue-studded park surrounded by handsome buildings bustling with the activity he craved—the Hoffman House (headquarters of the Democrats), the Fifth Avenue Hotel (headquarters of the Republicans), the Hotel Bartholdi (Bryan's favorite), Delmonico's, the towering Flat-iron Building, and the enormous Madison Square Garden, which accommodated everything from bicycle shows to political meetings. Northward along the Great White Way were the theaters he frequented. Now he moved from his rented apartment but stayed in the same neighborhood, taking over the third floor of the small but fashionable Worth House, across Twenty-fifth Street from the Hoffman House. At the latter establishment he had admired the tact and humor of a waiter named George Thompson, a blond, frog-eyed Irishman, fat but light on his feet. He hired Thompson as his valet, a duty he would perform with devotion for thirty years.[1] Around this time Hearst got rid of his mustache, and thereafter remained clean-shaven.

His French automobile was the first of its kind in New York. Being mechanically inclined, he easily mastered the art of driving it, though at the time driving was regarded as a technological achievement. To charming Millicent Willson, who had no technological pretensions, he presented a shining hansom cab, drawn by a milk-white horse and furnished with a coachman.[2] To Broadway busybodies, this seemed to settle an argument. It was Millicent in whom he was primarily interested, not Anita, although he was still seen with both of them. The sisters lived with their parents in Gramercy Park, conveniently near Madison Square.

Like Caesar and Napoleon, Hearst enjoyed power. He derived pleasure from controlling masses of people, manipulating them to bring about events of national or international importance. Unlike Caesar and Napoleon, the bashful Hearst did his manipulating from behind the scenes with the aid of cylinder presses and tons of newsprint. By now, most other newspaper proprietors in New York regarded him with aversion as a man who would do anything for sensation, devoid of honesty or principle, a Polyphemus of propaganda who ate his enemies and kept his Cyclops eye on circulation. They misjudged the man by his methods. An incurable romantic, swayed by gusts of sentiment, Hearst was sincerely devoted to the Cuban cause and at the same time felt that American interests demanded the expulsion of Spain from the hemisphere. But he had no scruples against linking these defensible

---

[1] Winkler, *Hearst—A New Appraisal*, 68.   [2] Mrs. J. M. Flint to author.

aims with a ruthless and vulgar drive for circulation, so that in the view of people of taste he had no unselfish impulses at all.

Considerations of taste in journalism did not disturb him. He had long since decided that the great majority of people, the masses, had no time or training for such a luxury as taste and could be reached and molded most effectively by the noise, sensation and repetition which he liked himself. Since these are the ingredients of modern mass advertising, Hearst deserves some dubious recognition as a pioneer.

His megalomania had grown. In San Francisco, his campaigns had been largely local, even his feud with the S.P. being inspired by local grievances. In New York he had started with local sensations—murders, public utility franchises, soup kitchens, bicycle carnivals. Now he was expanding his zone of operations into the nation and the world. His enemies were McKinley, Hanna, Weyler, Spain, France. The liberation of Miss Cisneros had been so successful that Hearst now had Karl Decker mapping an expedition to Devil's Island to free the wronged Captain Dreyfus and humiliate France as Spain had been humiliated.[3]

In Spain, the American newspaper outcry, the continuation of the Cuban rebellion and the uprising in the Philippines caused the fall of the government and the formation of a new cabinet. Spain, with only some 18,000,000 people, grievously in debt, naturally feared the rich United States with its 75,000,000. In its anxiety to retain Cuba, its most treasured possession, it pocketed American insults and took steps to mollify the Yankees as well as the Cuban rebels. The new government under Práxedes Mateo Sagasta almost entirely accepted the United States position on Cuba. It promised the Cubans self-government under Spain. It dismissed General Weyler, who left Havana to the accompaniment of a valedictory in Hearst's *Journal* calling him "the monster of the century" who should be hanged for his "innumerable murders." [4] It replaced him with General Ramón Blanco y Erenas, a kindly man not yet known as a murderer. It would be General Blanco's job to install the autonomous Cuban government and restore order.[5]

But Hearst demanded independence for Cuba, not mere autonomy. He wrote a letter dated December 1, 1897, addressed to the unrecognized president of an unrecognized republic.

> His Excellency Bartolomé Masso,
> President of the Republic of Cuba:
> Sir:—Will you kindly state through the New York *Journal*, acting for the people of the United States, the position of the Cuban Government on the offer of autonomy for the island by the Government of Spain?. . . .
> —Yours truly, W. R. Hearst.

Although some would dispute Hearst's right to act for "the people of the United States," Señor Masso did not. Apparently the letter was smuggled through to Masso, who eventually replied from Camaguey in part:

---

[3] Musgrave, 104, fn.   [4] *Journal*, Oct. 2, 1897.   [5] Millis, 87.

. . . We hold ourselves an independent nation, unrecognized though we may be by the civilized world. Autonomy is not for one moment considered by us. We absolutely reject it.

We have no faith left in Spain or her promises. . . .[6]

Along with Hearst, the insurgents with one voice rejected autonomy. Estrada Palma branded the conciliatory measures as ruses to defeat the rebellion by typical Spanish treachery. Rebel army leaders warned that all Cubans who cooperated with the new Spanish schemes would be considered "traitors to the republic," meaning that they would be shot on sight. The militarily feeble rebels could not have taken this intransigent stand had they not seen how American public opinion had already forced the Spaniards to back down. Counting on further American support to drive the Spaniards out entirely, they continued their pillaging of plantations and villages.

The *Journal* agreed that the Cubans "would be fools if they trust Spanish promises," and boasted that "Spain fears the *Journal* and Karl Decker." [7] Not surprisingly, attempts were made to dynamite the *Journal*'s Havana office. But President McKinley, impressed by the conciliatory efforts of the Sagasta government, was disposed to give it every opportunity for success. When Spain agreed to permit American contributions of food and clothing to be distributed to destitute Cubans by the Red Cross, and the relief work got under way, the outlook for peace on the troubled island seemed improved at last.

Meanwhile, a local event of such surpassing interest arose that for an interval it drew a welcome curtain over the repetitious drama in Cuba. This was the incorporation of Brooklyn, Staten Island and sections of Queens and the Bronx into Greater New York, a step which had been authorized by the electorate and would become official with the first moment of the New Year of 1898. It would swell the 234-year-old city from a giant to a colossus, expanding it from thirty-nine square miles to 320 and raising the population from 2,000,000 to 3,388,000. Brooklyn alone would furnish about 1,200,000 of the increase. There were residents there unhappy at the thought of Brooklyn losing its identity as a city and becoming merely a part of New York. Yet the event was so sweeping, accomplishing as it would the feat of making New York the world's second city next to London, that a civic celebration was clearly in order.

But the city authorities could not agree on the festivities. Mayor William Strong suggested holding a "funeral service" over old New York, an idea that was roundly scorned. As the day approached it appeared that no official ceremony would be held other than a prosaic speech or two.

It was typical of Hearst, who loved fanfare and saw opportunity in any event involving the masses, that he proposed that the *Journal* would organize the celebration at its own expense. The offer was gratefully, though unofficially, accepted. Once more the man from California had stolen a march on

[6] *Journal,* Dec. 30, 1897.   [7] *Journal,* Nov. 27, 1897.

his Knickerbocker contemporaries. The *Journal* began a campaign for funds, collecting $500 each from J. P. Morgan, Tammany Boss Richard Croker and Jacob Ruppert, and smaller sums from others, including a paltry ten dollars from the Cuban Junta, which, considering Miss Cisneros, could have done better. *Journal* emissaries enlisted military, civic, marching and bicycle groups, along with bands and singing societies, for a revelry featuring a parade from Union Square to City Hall, where the welkin would ring at midnight.[8]

Imagination and enterprise were shown in the arrangements, although the busy *Journal* staff also had the job of organizing a Christmas dinner for 5000 *Journal* newsboys, compliments of Mr. Hearst, with a speech by Chauncey Depew and songs by Anna Held. Something over $7000 was collected for the city celebration, but Hearst must have contributed much more out of his own pocket. ". . . it is an occasion which ought to be celebrated with all the ceremony which [the *Journal*] is providing," remarked the *Sun* approvingly, "and except for Mr. Hearst's liberality it would have gone unhonored." [9]

Fireworks by the carload were purchased. It was promised that there would be no speeches. The *Journal* offered ten solid silver loving cups as prizes for the best float, the best costume, the best bicycle company, the best singing group, etc. Unattached citizens were invited to join the parade, which was for "ALL THE PEOPLE." Professor F. Fanciulli, leader of the Seventh Regiment Band, set to music an "Ode to Greater New York," beginning:

> *Hail thee, city born today,*
> *Commercial monarch by the sea,*
> *Whose throne is by the Hudson's way,*
> *'Mid thousands' homesteads join'd to thee.*[10]

Unluckily, the evening of December 31 darkened in a downpour of rain that occasionally turned to snow—the worst possible weather for such an occasion. Yet, so well had the *Journal* publicized the event that throngs of hardy celebrants came out nevertheless. Broadway from above looked like a sea of undulating umbrellas. Over in Brooklyn's City Hall—soon to be Borough Hall—Mayor Wurster sadly performed his last official act, turning over almost $10,000,000 in Brooklyn funds to New York and possibly wondering what would become of it. In Manhattan, saloons were packed to the doors, and "liquor flowed . . . in reality like water," but the police were indulgent with staggering roisterers. Fireworks in front of the Broadway Central Hotel frightened horses drawing a float, causing them to bolt into Fanciulli's band, injuring fifteen persons and flattening a tuba and several smaller brasses, but the parade went bravely on. At City Hall Plaza, weirdly illuminated by five hundred magnesium lights, a dozen choral societies vied for singing honors, with a group of judges including Tony Pastor and ex-

[8] N. Y. *Times*, Dec. 21, 23; *Journal*, Dec. 26, 1897.
[9] Quoted in *Journal*, Dec. 30, 1897.   [10] *Journal*, Dec. 26, 1897.

Governor Roswell Flower trying to hear them. They were almost inaudible because of the wind, rain and the noise of bands and aerial bombs.

As midnight approached, the singers switched to *Auld Lang Syne*. Intrepid bicyclists maneuvered up and down the gently sloping City Hall steps. The *Journal* building across the way was bedecked with colored lights, while the dome of the tall Pulitzer Building twinkled with electric lamps hardly perceptible in the mist. At the stroke of 12 came the *Journal's pièce de résistance*. The din ceased for a moment as Mayor James Phelan of San Francisco pressed a button near the Golden Gate that sped an electrical impulse across the continent which sent the new blue-and-white flag of Greater New York whipping up the staff on the City Hall cupola. This was a true Hearst touch, dramatizing the wonders of science and the solidarity of the nation, and giving the San Francisco *Examiner* a news scoop. Then a battery of field guns near the postoffice fired a deafening hundred-gun salute, skyrockets swished upward to become lost in pea soup, and 100,000 spectators cheered as Greater New York became a dripping reality.[11]

It was the "biggest, noisiest and most hilarious New Year's Eve celebration that Manhattan Island has ever known," commented the *Tribune*, which normally had no good to say of anything connected with Hearst. It had to be admitted that no one could hold a Roman candle to Hearst when it came to staging a spectacle.

In Cuba, Consul General Lee kept hearing rumors of an "anti-American plot" in Matanzas. Although this never materialized, he urged protection for American nationals and property in Cuba. It was on Lee's recommendation that the twenty-four-gun battleship *Maine* was moved first to Key West, then to Havana, as a "friendly act of courtesy" to Spain. Spain, not deceived by the polite words, readied its armored cruiser *Vizcaya* to pay a "friendly visit" to New York.[12]

The *Maine*, commanded by solemn, bespectacled Captain Charles D. Sigsbee, passed under the guns of Morro Castle and anchored in Havana harbor on January 25, 1898. The Spanish commander sent a case of fine sherry to Sigsbee and his officers, who later went ashore to dine with General Lee and enjoy a bullfight.

Hearst had hardly been aware of the *Maine* when she was launched in San Francisco in 1890, but now she loomed large. "OUR FLAG IN HAVANA AT LAST," headlined the *Journal*, urging that American vessels occupy all Cuban ports and demand the withdrawal of the Spanish troops, i. e., to make war.[13] Although Captain Sigsbee and his men were enjoying a quiet sojourn in Havana, the *Journal* saw so many war clouds there that it momentarily forgot its *bête noire*, the Spanish minister in Washington, Dupuy de Lome. De Lome, who for three years had conducted himself with dignity in the capital despite painful provocation, chose this moment to commit an error.

[11] N. Y. *Herald, Times,* and *Tribune,* Jan. 1, 1898.
[12] French E. Chadwick, *The Relations of the United States and Spain,* 533–35.
[13] *Journal,* Jan. 26, 27, 1898.

He wrote a letter critical of President McKinley to a friend in Havana, José Canalejas. A rebel sympathizer, Gustavo Escoto, who worked in Canalejas' office, read the letter, saw its propaganda possibilities, and stole it, boarding the next boat for New York.

The letter brought joy to Estrada Palma and the Peanut Club. Palma was so grateful to the *Journal* for its efforts for Cuba that he translated the letter and took it in person to the *Journal* office, handing it in triumph to Sam Chamberlain.[14] In commenting on McKinley's pacific message to Congress, De Lome wrote:

> The message has undeceived the insurgents, who expected something else, and has paralyzed the action of Congress, but I consider it bad . . . Besides the natural and inevitable coarseness with which he [McKinley] repeats all that the press and public opinion of Spain have said of Weyler, it shows once more what McKinley is: weak and catering to the rabble and, besides, a low politician who desires to leave the door open to himself and to stand well with the jingoes of his party . . .[15]

Although this was a private letter, stolen, and although the *Journal* had leveled far worse insults of its own about McKinley multiplied by some 800,000 circulation, it flew into a front-page rage at De Lome that lasted for five days. The letter was too provocative for the Peanut Club to give it exclusively to the *Journal*. It gave it to all the newspapers, handing the *Journal* a beat, however, in giving it exclusive right to publish a facsimile. The *Journal* used *all of its front page* to publicize the letter, headlining it "THE WORST INSULT TO THE UNITED STATES IN ITS HISTORY" and demanding the minister's instant dismissal. It dredged up a book which De Lome had published twenty-two years earlier, stressing critical remarks he had made about American women. It perpetrated an enormity in doggerel:

> *Dupuy de Lome, Dupuy de Lome, what's this I hear of you?*
> *Have you been throwing mud again, is what they're saying true?*
> *Get out, I say, get out before I start to fight.*
> *Just pack your few possessions and take a boat for home.*
> *I would not like my boot to use but—oh—get out, De Lome.*[16]

It ran a huge Davenport cartoon showing an angry Uncle Sam thumbing away a quaking De Lome, with a one-word caption, "Git." "Now let us have action immediate and decisive," it said. "The flag of Cuba Libre ought to float over Morro Castle within a week." [17] All this went out over the Associated Press.

In Washington, De Lome instantly cabled his resignation to Madrid. This took the sting out of the State Department's demand for his dismissal, for he was already packing. The Spanish government promptly disavowed his letter and apologized for it. In a few days, United States officials realized that what the *Journal* and a few other New York newspapers chose to construe

[14] Abbot, 217–18.   [15] *Journal*, Feb. 9, 1898.   [16] *Journal*, Feb. 9.
[17] Feb. 10 and 11 issues, 1898.

as a gross affront was nothing more than a comic diplomatic blunder. In Cuba, the new autonomous government was beginning to function. The outlook was promising. The De Lome incident would have been forgotten had it not been followed almost immediately by an event of violence and tragedy that still poses one of history's impenetrable mysteries.

The *Maine* had now been in Havana for three weeks. Its usefulness there was questionable, since there were no anti-American demonstrations. Navy Secretary John D. Long had contemplated recalling it early in February, only to desist because of Consul General Lee's advice that it stay. On the sultry night of February 15, as the clear bugle notes of "Taps" pealed across the quiet harbor, Captain Sigsbee was in his cabin writing a letter in some embarrassment to his wife. He explained that in a uniform pocket he had discovered a letter to her from an old friend which he had forgotten for ten months. He had just sealed the envelope at 9:40 when the *Maine* blew up all around him.

Though shaken, Sigsbee was unhurt. The vessel's lights blacked out. Screams came from wounded and dying men. Fire broke out forward, causing small-caliber ammunition to start popping like firecrackers. Survivors jumped into the water as the ship began settling slowly into the mud. Dazed bluejackets put out a boat to pick up the swimmers. Other boats came from the Spanish cruiser *Alfonso XII* and an American vessel nearby. Spaniards and Americans joined gallantly in the dangerous rescue work as ammunition continued to explode. At his palace, Spain's General Blanco burst into tears at the news and sent officers to express regret and organize assistance. Of the *Maine*'s 350 officers and men, 260 died in the catastrophe.[18] Sigsbee dispatched a telegram to "Secnav" in Washington, describing it and adding:

> Public opinion should be suspended until further report . . . Many Spanish officers including representatives of General Blanco now with me to express sympathy.[19]

Hearst had left the *Journal* earlier than usual that evening, probably to go to the theater. He returned to his apartment in the Worth House quite late without stopping at his office. He found his man Thompson waiting for him.

"There's a telephone from the office," Thompson said. "They say it's important news."

Hearst telephoned the *Journal*. "Hello," he said. "What is the important news?"

"The battleship *Maine* has been blown up in Havana Harbor," the editor replied.

"Good heavens, what have you done with the story?"

"We have put it on the first page, of course."

"Have you put anything else on the front page?"

"Only the other big news," said the editor.

---

[18] Capt. Charles D. Sigsbee, *The Maine*, 62–63, 69.   [19] The same, 76.

"There is not any other big news," Hearst said. "Please spread the story all over the page. This means war." [20]

II. THERE IS NO OTHER NEWS

HEARST'S coverage of the *Maine* disaster still stands as the orgasmic acme of ruthless, truthless newspaper jingoism. As always, when he wanted anything he wanted it with passionate intensity. The *Maine* represented the fulfillment not of one want but two—war with Spain and more circulation to beat Pulitzer. He fought for these ends with such abandonment of honesty and incitement of hatred that the stigma of it never quite left him even though he still had fifty-three years to live.

Intelligent Americans realized the preposterousness of the idea that Spain had blown up the *Maine*. Proud Spain had swallowed insult to avoid a war she knew she would lose. Her forbearance had borne fruit until the explosion in Havana caused journalistic insanity in New York. The disaster was the worst blow Spain could have suffered. The *Maine* might have been wrecked by an accidental explosion of her own magazines. If she was sunk by plotters, it was most reasonable to suspect those who stood to gain from the crime—the Cuban rebels, whose cause was flagging and would be lost unless the United States could be dragged into the struggle. There was one other possibility: that a group of Spaniards or Cuban loyalists, working off their hatred unknown to the Spanish government, were responsible.[1]

Even the *Journal* admitted disbelief that Spain had officially ordered the explosion.[2] But this was tucked away in small type and later disavowed. The big type, the headlines, the diagrams, the cartoons, the editorials, laid the blame inferentially or flatly on Spain. For a week afterward, the *Journal* devoted a daily average of eight and one-half pages to the *Maine* and war. In the face of Sigsbee's wise suggestion that "public opinion be suspended," the *Journal* lashed public opinion day after day.

Some idea of the *Journal's* enormities, though an inadequate one, is given by a day-by-day recapitulation of its headlines and stories.

February 16: "CRUISER MAINE BLOWN UP IN HAVANA HARBOR." This was simple truth, written before the propaganda machine got into motion. It was the last truthful front-page headline for almost two weeks.

February 17: "THE WARSHIP MAINE WAS SPLIT IN TWO BY AN ENEMY'S SECRET INFERNAL MACHINE." The cause, of course, was unknown. This issue had a seven-column drawing of the ship anchored over mines, and a diagram showing wires leading from the mines to a Spanish fortress on shore—a flight of fancy which many readers doubtless took as fact. The hatred of Spaniards for Americans was mentioned. The caption

[20] Coblentz, *William Randolph Hearst*, 59.
[1] Lundberg, in his antagonistic *Imperial Hearst*, 81, suggests that Hearst may have had some connection with the explosion!
[2] Feb. 21, 1898, issue.

read, "If this [plot] can be proven, the brutal nature of the Spaniards will be shown in that they waited to spring the mine until after all men had retired for the night." The *Journal* said, "Captain Sigsbee Practically Declares that His Ship was Blown Up by a Mine or Torpedo." Sigsbee said no such thing. He later wrote, "A Spanish officer of high rank . . . showed me a New York paper of February 17 in which was pictured the *Maine* anchored over a mine. On another page was a plan showing wires leading from the *Maine* to shore. The officer asked me what I thought of that. It was explained that we had no censorship in the United States . . . Apparently the Spanish officer could not grasp the idea." [3]

February 18: "THE WHOLE COUNTRY THRILLS WITH THE WAR FEVER." This came at a time when Spanish and Cuban military, civil and ecclesiastical leaders were giving the victims a solemn state funeral in Havana, with every mark of respect, dedicating the plots used at Colon Cemetery to the United States in perpetuity. On this day, for the first time, the combined circulation of the morning and evening *Journal* passed a million.

February 20 (over a drawing): "HOW THE MAINE ACTUALLY LOOKS AS IT LIES, WRECKED BY SPANISH TREACHERY, IN HAVANA BAY."

February 21: "HAVANA POPULACE INSULTS THE MEMORY OF THE MAINE VICTIMS." This was over a story alleging that Spanish officers had been overheard to boast that any other American ship visiting Havana would "follow the *Maine.*"

February 23: "THE MAINE WAS DESTROYED BY TREACHERY." Although the *Journal* knew all along who sank the ship, it offered $50,000 reward for the solution of the mystery. It also began a drive for a memorial to be erected to those lost in the explosion, Hearst donating the first $1000. It began as usual by soliciting famous men whose participation could be exploited, among them ex-President Cleveland. Cleveland won some measure of immortality by replying, "I decline to allow my sorrow for those who died on the *Maine* to be perverted to an advertising scheme for the New York *Journal.*" [4] Other "big names" were less percipient, General Nelson Miles, Levi Morton, Chauncey Depew and O. H. P. Belmont being among the many who lent their prestige to the drive.

On February 18, at this most inopportune of times, the Spanish cruiser *Vizcaya* arrived in New York harbor from Cartagena on her "courtesy call." Her commander, Captain Antonio Eulate, shocked when informed of the *Maine* tragedy, ordered his colors half-masted and said he would take no part in any festivities planned in his honor. In view of the public hysteria, the police and naval authorities took strenuous measures to protect the *Vizcaya*, surrounding her with a cordon of patrol boats. The *World*, almost as frenetic in its Hispanophobia as the *Journal*, warned that the *Vizcaya*

[3] Sigsbee, *The Maine*, 125.   [4] N. Y. *Evening Post*, Mar. 28, 1898.

might have treacherous intentions, saying, "While lying off the Battery, her shells will explode on the Harlem River and in the suburbs of Brooklyn." [5] However, the *Vizcaya* did not fire a shot.

The Spanish authorities, incensed by the *Journal's* warmongering, retaliated. *Journal* men were forbidden to board the *Vizcaya*. More important, the *Journal* was denied further use of the cables from Havana. It took cognizance of this with an announcement headed, "SPANISH COURTESIES TO AN AMERICAN NEWSPAPER," and boxed on the front page with a flowing American flag. It read:

> The *Journal* takes great pride in announcing that on account of its too decided Americanism and its work for the patriots of Cuba this newspaper and its reporters have been forbidden entrance on board the Spanish warship *Vizcaya*; its dispatches are refused transmission over the Government cables from Havana.
>
> These Spanish acts, of course, do not prevent the *Journal* from getting all the news. . . . The *Journal* is flattered by these delicate attentions from Spain . . . It expects to merit still more attention when the United States decides to end Spanish misrule and horrors in America.[6]

The *Journal* also presented its readers with a newly-devised "Game of War With Spain," to be played by four persons with cards. Two contestants would portray the crew of the United States battleship *Texas*, doing their best to "sink" the other two, who manned the *Vizcaya*.[7]

Hearst had rounded up a carefully-selected group of jingoistic legislators who were not averse to a free trip to Cuba. Senators Hernando Money of Mississippi, John W. Thurston of Nebraska and J. H. Gallinger of New Hampshire, and Representatives William Alden Smith of Michigan and Amos Cummings of New York, embarked from Fort Monroe on the Hearst yacht *Anita* as "*Journal* Commissioners" to make a survey of conditions on the island and to write reports for the *Journal*, their expenses being paid by Hearst. Representatives Smith and Cummings were members of the House Foreign Affairs and Naval Affairs committees respectively. The *Journal* meanwhile appealed to its readers to write their Congressmen, and said it had so far relayed 15,000 such letters demanding war.[8]

The *Journal* raged at Senator Mark Hanna for deprecating the war talk. It referred to him frequently as "President Hanna," to indicate how completely McKinley was his puppet. The cowardly peace policy of the administration was dictated by a base desire for profits in Wall Street, which could be depressed by war. "President Hanna . . . announced that there will be no war," said the *Journal*. ". . . . This attitude is fairly representative of the eminently respectable porcine citizens who—for dollars in the money-grubbing sty, support 'conservative' newspapers and consider the starvation of . . . inoffensive men, women and children, and the murder of 250 [*sic*]

[5] N. Y. *World*, Feb. 16, 1898.
[7] *Journal*, Feb. 20, 1898.
[6] *Journal*, Feb. 21, 1898.
[8] Feb. 26, 1898.

American sailors . . . of less importance than the fall of two points in a price of stock." [9]

Anyone advocating peace was a traitor or a Wall Street profiteer, probably both. When Navy Secretary Long dared to say that "Spanish official responsibility for the *Maine* explosion might be considered eliminated," Long joined the *Journal's* list of officials who had sold out the nation's honor to Wall Street. This was all part of a money-making coup engineered by Hanna, said the *Journal*, with Long as his pawn, for Hanna had advised his friends before the announcement to buy stocks which rose several points as a result of Long's words and netted them $20,000,000.[10]

The treasonous President McKinley had already publicly stated his opinion that the *Maine* was wrecked by an accidental explosion of her own magazines. The perfidious Secretary of the Navy had defended Spain. In Havana at the time was sitting a United States naval board of inquiry, sending down divers to examine the *Maine's* hull and taking testimony from survivors in an effort to determine the cause of the disaster. Spain had asked, and been promised, that no American newspaper correspondents would take part in the investigation. The *Journal*, with the *World* and *Sun* close behind, was whipping public fury to a point where all these official efforts were rendered useless, a trivial shadow play unheard behind the din of the headlines.

III. THE NEAREST APPROACH TO HELL

IN Cuba, Hearst's junketing group of Senators and Congressmen were finding plenty of destitution, which indeed was so bad that it could scarcely be exaggerated. The *Journal* praised them as "brave congressmen [who] faced death to get at the truth in Cuba." [1] Each of the five legislators wrote articles for the *Journal* describing the suffering they saw. Mrs. Thurston, wife of the Senator from Nebraska, who had accompanied her husband, wrote an especially stirring appeal to *Journal* mothers:

> Oh! Mothers of the Northland, who tenderly clasp your little ones to your loving hearts! Think of the black despair that filled each [Cuban] mother's heart as she felt her life-blood ebb away, and knew that she had left her little ones to perish from the pain of starvation and disease.[2]

While in the harbor of Matanzas, Mrs. Thurston suffered a heart attack and died aboard the Hearst yacht—a misfortune the *Journal* blamed on the destitution she had seen. The five "*Journal* Commissioners" returned to make speeches in Congress praising the *Journal's* patriotic motives and declaring that newspaper reports of conditions in Cuba were not exaggerated. For weeks, while the naval court continued its investigation in Havana, American citizens were conducted into a theater world of Cuban horror, Spanish treachery and United States dishonor staged with primitive efficiency by

[9] Feb. 24 issue.   [10] *Journal*, Mar. 4, 1898.   [1] Mar. 6, 1898, issue.
[2] *Journal*, Mar. 13, 1898.

Producer-Director Hearst and aped by the rabble-rousing Pulitzer (now sadly reduced to the role of imitator) and the respected *Sun*. Edwin Godkin vainly tried to stem the tide in his *Evening Post*, with its puny 25,000 circulation.

". . . when one of [the yellow journals] offers a yacht voyage," Godkin wrote, "with free wine, rum and cigars, and a good bed, under the guise of philanthropy, or gets up a committee for Holy purposes, and promises to puff it, it can get almost any one it pleases to go on the yacht voyage and serve on the committee—senators, lawyers, divines, scholars, poets, presidents and what not. . . . Every one who knows anything about 'yellow journals' knows that everything they do and say is intended to promote sales . . . No one—absolutely no one—supposes a yellow journal cares five cents about the Cubans, the *Maine* victims, or any one else. A yellow journal is probably the nearest approach to hell, existing in any Christian state." [3]

Theodore Roosevelt, who had displeased the *Journal* as head of the New York police, was now Assistant Secretary of the Navy under Long and a jingo after Hearst's own heart. Roosevelt had decided instantly that the *Maine* was sunk by treacherous Spaniards. He privately referred with contempt to McKinley as having "no more backbone than a chocolate eclair." [4] The *Journal*, always doubly glad when it could praise itself as it rapped its enemies, quoted Roosevelt in a front-page interview as saying: "It is cheering to find a newspaper of the great influence and circulation of the *Journal* tell [sic] the facts as they exist and ignore the suggestions of various kinds that emanate from sources that cannot be described as patriotic or loyal to the flag of this country." [5]

Roosevelt immediately repudiated the statement, saying, "The alleged interview with me in today's New York *Journal* is an invention from beginning to end. It is difficult to understand the kind of infamy that resorts to such methods." [6] Roosevelt later won a reputation for occasional denials of indiscreet things he had said, but perhaps in this instance it is safer to trust him than the *Journal*.

Long before the Navy report on the *Maine* was ready, the *Journal* anticipated it with sheer falsehood, saying, "the Court of Inquiry finds that Spanish government officials blew up the *Maine*," and that the warship "was purposely moved where a Spanish mine exploded by Spanish officers would destroy it." "The *Journal* can stake its reputation as a war prophet on this assertion: There will be a war with Spain as certain as the sun shines unless Spain abases herself in the dust and voluntarily consents to the freedom of Cuba." [7] The Spaniards were universally painted as such cowardly, two-faced wretches that Madrid editors not surprisingly began railing at the "Yankee pigs," which in turn was faithfully reported by the *Journal* and its contemporaries.

Under these daily onslaughts, multiplied by many extra editions and news-

---

[3] *Post*, Mar. 17, 1898.   [4] Henry F. Pringle, *Theodore Roosevelt*, 177–78.
[5] Mar. 19 issue.   [6] N. Y. *Post*, Mar. 21, 1898.   [7] *Journal*, Mar. 11 and 13.

service transmission from coast to coast, the nation was seething. The public was deceived, misled and tricked by its only source of information. McKinley, a kindly man of peace, could deal expertly with legislators but lacked the dynamism, the spark of leadership that grips and sways the public mind. The country was getting away from him. The Presidency of the United States was being preempted by batteries of cylinder presses.

On March 28, McKinley handed the report of the naval court to Congress. The court's opinion was that "the *Maine* was destroyed by the explosion of a submarine mine, which caused the partial explosion of two or more of the forward magazines." The court admitted its inability to fix the blame. A Spanish court of inquiry which had made a similar investigation, but which the Americans had denied an opportunity for close inspection, found for an accidental explosion within the ship. This report was ignored. The guilt for the disaster, if guilt there was, was a mystery then as it is today.[8] No one ever collected the *Journal's* $50,000 reward.

However, public sentiment was so inflamed that the United States court's opinion that the explosion came from outside and thus was not accidental was enough to lay the blame on Spain. The *Journal*, dissatisfied, declared that the truth was being hidden from the public, saying, "the suppressed testimony shows Spain is guilty of blowing up the *Maine*." [9] Even the heavens demonstrated the inevitability of war. On the night of April 4, the moon was surrounded by two pale rings. "Many persons insisted," said the *Journal*, "that the contact of the two rings meant nothing short of war; the smaller ring standing for the pretension of Spain in the Island of Cuba and the larger circle for the United States and its immensely superior power." [10]

This whimsy was lost in the prevailing theme of American dishonor. "Write to your Congressmen at once," the *Journal* urged its readers. ". . . Give Congress a chance to know what the people think." The same issue featured a cartoon depicting Hanna, with his puppet McKinley stuck in his back pocket, poking a white feather into the star-studded hat of Uncle Sam, and suggested satirically that the stars on the flag be changed to dollar signs and the stripes to rows of dollar bills. It ran a front-page headline in three-inch type: "HANNA VS. HONOR." When some Ohio politicians charged that Hanna was elected to the Senate by fraud, the *Journal's* cartoon showed him in prison stripes with the caption, "Here is Our 'President-Maker!' How Do You Like Him?" It warned that "Spain's powerful flotilla" was believed to be "stealing toward our shore." Blasting McKinley and his Wall Street bosses for waiting for Spain to strike the first blow, it demanded, in an issue dotted with American flags, "In the name of 266 [*sic*] American seamen, butchered in cold blood by the Spaniards, what is a 'blow' in the McKinley concept of war?" It ran an imaginative drawing showing Spanish soldiers bayoneting helpless Cubans, with the caption, "The wires bring news of the butchery of

[8] Millis, 127.   [9] Issue of April 2, 1898.   [10] April 5.

two hundred more reconcentrados . . . Two hundred murders more or fewer is of little importance in Spain's record, and McKinley can hardly be expected to get excited about this." [11]

The *Journal* pointed out how ridiculously easy it would be to crush Spain. It talked of organizing a regiment of giant athletes including Heavyweights Bob Fitzsimmons and James J. Corbett, Ballplayer Cap Anson, Hammer Thrower Jim Mitchell and Indian Footballer Red Water, all of whom agreed to join. "Think of a regiment composed of magnificent men of this ilk!" glowed the *Journal*. "They would overawe any Spanish regiment by their mere appearance. They would scorn Krag-Jorgensen and Mauser bullets." [12]

According to the *Journal*, volunteers were itching to avenge the *Maine*. Frank James, ex-bandit brother of the legendary Jesse, offered to lead a company of cowboys. Six hundred Sioux Indians were ready and willing to scalp Spaniards in Cuba. The *World* improved on this, reporting the statement of "Buffalo Bill" Cody that 30,000 Indian fighters could clear the Spaniards out of Cuba in sixty days.[13] The *Journal* came back with a report of riots in Havana that had "2,000 AMERICANS IN PERIL," presenting a four-column drawing showing exactly how the Navy would bombard Morro Castle and land men around Havana. *Journal* reporters were sent to interview the mothers of sailors who died in the *Maine* living in the New York area. All made pathetic appeals for vengeance.

"How would President McKinley have felt, I wonder," said one of them, "if he had a son on the *Maine* murdered as was my little boy? Would he then forget the crime and let it go unpunished while the body of his child was lying as food for the sharks in the Spanish harbor of Havana?" Another mother was quoted as saying in part, "I ask that mine and other mothers' sons be avenged . . . I ask it for justice [sic] sake and the honor of the flag." [14]

In Madrid, United States Minister Stewart Woodford was working efficiently for peace, although he was ostracized by Spanish society as De Lome previously had been in Washington. Being out of range of the *Journal*, which attacked his peace efforts as "twaddle," he felt that peace could be preserved. It would have been had not his efforts been junked by the administration. He found the Spanish government ready to go the limit to avoid war. "They cannot go further in open concessions to us," Woodford earlier had informed McKinley, "without being overthrown by their own people here in Spain. . . . They want peace if they can keep peace and save the dynasty. They prefer the chances of war, with the certain loss of Cuba, to the overthrow of the dynasty." [15] On April 9, Woodford cabled that the Queen's government had gone still farther and had surrendered to all the important United States demands, even to the extent of offering to grant an immediate armistice there. Woodford was confident that this last concession meant peace, saying:

[11] *Journal*, Mar. 30, April 2, 4; *Evening Journal*, April 2, 4, 8.   [12] Mar. 29 issue.
[13] *World*, April 3, 1898.   [14] *Journal*, April 9, 1898.   [15] Millis, 113.

I hope that nothing will now be done to humiliate Spain as I am satisfied that the present government is going, and is loyally ready to go, as fast and as far as it can. With your power of action sufficiently free, you will win the fight on your own lines.[16]

Here was the key to an amicable settlement, if the United States wanted it. But McKinley knew that the majority of the American people, misled by their newspapers, wanted war. He knew that many legislators, influenced by their angry constituents, wanted war. And he knew that his administration and the Republican party would suffer unpopularity and loss of confidence if it made a stand for peace.

Mr. McKinley bowed to Mr. Hearst. He went over to the war party. Without taking any stand, he submitted the whole problem to Congress in a message given on April 11. He dramatized his own abandonment of peace by burying the all-important Spanish concessions in the last two paragraphs of his speech.[17] Everybody knew that this meant war, but the *Journal* was impatient at the delay in making it official, as one of its headlines showed:

SUICIDE
LAMENTED
THE MAINE
AGED MRS. MARY WAYT EN-
HALED [sic] GAS THROUGH
A TUBE.
GRIEVED OVER OUR DELAY
"The Government May Live in
Dishonor," Said She,
"I Cannot." [18]

Possibly the President was surprised at the peace sentiment still existing when the Senate on April 19 passed a war resolution by the narrow vote of 42 to 35. Only four more Senators on the peace side would have swung the balance, indicating that determined Presidential leadership might have foiled Hearst. But when the House concurred with the Senate in a 310–6 vote for war, it demonstrated that McKinley, had he won peace, would have won unpopularity along with it.

It was an unnecessary war. It was the newspapers' war. Above all, it was Hearst's war. It is safe to say that had not Hearst, with his magnificently tawdry flair for publicity and agitation, enlisted the women of America in a crusade they misunderstood, made a national heroine of the jail-breaking Miss Cisneros, made a national abomination of Dupuy de Lome, made the *Maine* a mistaken symbol of Spanish treachery, caused thousands of citizens to write their Congressmen, and dragged the powerful *World* along with him into journalistic ill-fame, the public would have kept its sanity, McKinley would have shown more spunk, at least four more Senators would have taken counsel with reason, and there would have been no war.

[16] Chadwick, 575.   [17] Rhodes, 64–66.   [18] *Evening Journal*, Apr. 18, 1898.

"The outbreak of the Spanish-American war found Mr. Hearst in a state of proud ecstasy," recalled James Creelman, who was working with Hearst daily. "He had won his campaign and the McKinley Administration had been forced into war." [19] Willis Abbot wrote: "Hearst was accustomed to refer to the war, in company with his staff, as 'our war.'" [20]

He rallied the United States with a headline in four-inch type:

"NOW TO AVENGE THE MAINE!" [21]

IV. THE FATE OF COLONEL THENUZ

GODKIN was wrong in suggesting that Hearst cared nothing about the Cubans or the victims of the *Maine*—nothing about anything but circulation. Hearst pitied the Cubans. He was appalled at the thought of 260 American sailors killed or drowned in Havana harbor. The womanly side of his nature was shaken by the tragedy. His sympathies were swift and unreasoning. He was emotionally unstable, plunged into horror and indignation by the disaster. Since he wanted to believe the Spaniards guilty, he did. His ability to abandon reality and accept his own fantasies as facts absolved him from any obligation toward truth and led him into wild bypaths of error. Also, the megalomaniac in him delighted in making himself the author of mighty events. His dramatic critic, Ford, observed, ". . . [Hearst] reminded me of a kindly child, thoroughly undisciplined and possessed of a destructive tendency that might lead him to set fire to a house in order to see the engines play water on the flames . . ." [1]

Now that he had his war, his extreme sense of possessiveness drove him to constant effort to manage events so that the war would continue to seem his exclusive property. In both of the *Journal's* front-page ears appeared the blurb "HOW DO YOU LIKE THE JOURNAL'S WAR?" [2]—a sentiment so tasteless that it stayed there only two days, possibly being removed at the plea of some unhappy lieutenant. Characteristically regarding the conflict as a sort of newspaper contest of skills, he offered a $1000 prize for the best idea for getting it off to a good start.

This award rightfully should have gone to Commodore Dewey for his workmanlike thrashing of the Spanish fleet in Manila Bay, an event the *Journal* celebrated with a great spread eagle surmounting the words "VICTORY, Complete! . . . Glorious! . . . THE MAINE IS AVENGED." [3] Hearst and his *Journal* were truly in a state of "proud ecstasy." The whole nation was borne on a wave of headline-inspired romantic militarism that conjured a picture of irresistible American arms. Fifth Avenue was ablaze with flags, sedentary citizens wore patriotic emblems, restaurants served

[19] *Pearson's Magazine*, Sept., 1906.
[20] Abbot, 217.
[21] *Evening Journal*, Apr. 20, 1898.
[1] Ford, 260.
[2] May 2, 1898.
[3] May 9, 10, 1898.

ice cream molded in the form of battleships, and newspapers sold out in minutes. The *Journal* and *World* were each selling a million papers a day.

When a rumor said that a strong Spanish squadron under Admiral Manuel de la Cámara was fitting up at Cadiz to sail to the Philippines via Suez to attack Dewey, Hearst felt his responsibility to save Dewey. His imperial complex came to the fore. James Creelman had recently gone to London on a *Journal* mission, and Hearst sent him an amazing cable:

> I wish you would at once make preparations so that in case the Spanish fleet actually starts for Manila we can buy some big English steamer at the eastern end of the Mediterranean and take her to some part of the Suez Canal where we can then sink her and obstruct the passage of the Spanish warships. . . . I understand that if a British vessel were taken into the canal and sunk under the circumstances outlined above, the British Government would not allow her to be blown up to clear a passage and it might take time enough to raise her to put Dewey in a safe position.[4]

Creelman was a little worried that he might start war with England, but as a loyal *Journal* man he did his best. He had to work cautiously, since few mariners would accept such a hare-brained commission and he could not afford to let the plot become known. By the time he managed to get an option on a British ship, it was too late. Cámara had sailed. The crisis solved itself, however, for Cámara returned in the belief that Spain itself might be attacked by an American fleet.

"That is a good illustration of Mr. Hearst's idea of the privilege as well as the duty of a newspaper," Creelman later observed. "It was a piece of heartfelt, practical patriotism combined with a Napoleonic stroke of advertising. It would have been a grave breach of international law, but, nevertheless, a sensation that even the *Journal's* contemptuous rivals would have had to notice; and the whole country must have acknowledged the service rendered by the despised yellow journalism." [5]

Hearst moved to take another costly personal hand in crushing Spain. The resignation of Assistant Secretary of the Navy Roosevelt to raise a regiment for Cuba had been much admired. He proposed to outdo Roosevelt. He wrote President McKinley, offering to equip, arm and mount *at his own expense* a regiment of cavalry to fight in Cuba.

"While making this offer," he wrote modestly, "I request that you accept my personal services as a member of the regiment suggested. I am conscious of a lack of special qualifications to direct even in a minor capacity such a body of men, and do not, therefore, request any other position in the regiment than that of a man in the ranks." [6]

Hearst, at thirty-four, was anxious to risk his neck in Cuba. An excellent horseman, he doubtless would have been a good cavalryman, although it is hard to picture him taking orders from anyone. McKinley, however, declined the offer with thanks on the ground that if he admitted any additional

[4] Creelman, 190.   [5] *Pearson's Magazine*, Sept., 1906.   [6] *Journal*, June 10, 1898.

regiments outside of state quotas it would cause complaints from states asking to furnish more troops. With his usual determination, Hearst switched to the Navy, writing McKinley again on June 1:

To the President:

Sir: I beg to offer to the United States, as a gift, without any conditions whatever, my steam yacht *Buccaneer*.

This steel boat, designed by E. Burgess, is 138 feet long, 116 feet water line, 20 feet beam. She has triple expansion engines, carries coal and water for a seven days' cruise and is in perfect order. I believe that she would be found a serviceable boat. The yacht is offered to the Government fully equipped, armed and manned. Sailors will be enlisted by me, subject to the approval of the naval authorities. They will be fully armed and uniformed by me in accordance with naval regulations, and their wages paid by me during the continuation of the present war.

As an armament suitable to the vessel I offer the following:

One six-pound gun.

Four two-pound guns.

One one-pound gun.

Two Colt rapid-fire guns.

A suitable supply of ammunition, to be renewed at my expense whenever needed.

I request that you appoint me to a command on this boat, either as commander or second in command. I make this request with the knowledge, of course, that certain examinations are necessary to qualify as commander of a ship, and subject to my ability to pass such examinations. . . . I should acquiesce, of course, in the rejection of any detail in the above offer that might be found unacceptable to the naval authorities. . . . Yours very respectfully, William R. Hearst.[7]

Acting Secretary of the Navy Charles H. Allen accepted the offer June 4 with some qualifications. The Navy would gladly make use of the *Buccaneer*, but it must man it with its own sailors commanded by a regular Navy officer. Hearst, said Allen, would be called before a Navy board for examination as a line officer.

Hearst's feud with Pulitzer had grown more angry when the *World* sued to restrain the Associated Press from furnishing news to the *Journal*, which had secured its A.P. franchise by purchasing the New York *Advertiser*. The two rivals eyed each other pugnaciously. The *Buccaneer* had been used as a *Journal* dispatch boat during the Cuban trouble, and now was at Tampa. With the advent of war, all United States correspondents had left Cuba, many of them congregating in Tampa, where the army was trying with monstrous inefficiency to assemble a striking force. On June 7, a small detachment of soldiers took possession of the *Buccaneer* for the government. A *World* reporter misinterpreted the move, heeding a rumor that may well have been spread by a sly *Journal* man. His story appeared in the *World*

[7] The same.

under the headline, "'Zeal' by Theft in Newsgetting Thwarted at Port Tampa." It read:

> A corporal and guard of three soldiers has been put on the *Buccaneer*, a New York *Journal* dispatch boat, to prevent her leaving the bay. It is said the correspondents on that vessel are suspected of having obtained Government plans and documents and intended to sail for some port where they could send the matter by wire.[8]

Whether or not the *World* was caught in a cunning trap, Hearst immediately sued the paper for $500,000 in libeling his patriotic efforts by accusing him of trying to betray military secrets.

"This is such a malicious falsehood," he said, "and is calculated to do so much injury to the *Journal* and everybody connected with it, that it compels us to publish a correspondence which might not otherwise seem of public interest and of which we had intended to make no mention." [9]

He thereupon printed his correspondence with McKinley, making public his offer of the regiment as well as the boat. The magnificence of the offer was evident when it was estimated that 1300 horses for a regiment of cavalry would cost around $150,000, arms and uniforms as much or more, and incidentals would bring the total to more than $500,000.

"That sum," editorialized the *Times*, "inconsequential to a Government like ours, is big enough to be impressive when held out as a gift to the country by a private citizen, and little sympathy as the *Times* has with many of Mr. Hearst's political ideas and journalistic methods, it does not feel called upon to withhold recognition of his enterprise or his generosity." [10]

The *Journal's* war against the *World* was also carried on by subterfuge. Although the *Journal* had earlier been guilty of cribbing news from the *World*, Brisbane and McEwen now suspected that the *World* was returning the compliment. They set a neat snare, publishing the following imaginative "dispatch" from Cuba:

> Colonel Reflipe W. Thenuz, an Austrian artillerist of European renown, who, with Colonel Ordonez, was defending the land batteries of Aguadores . . . was so badly wounded that he has since died.
> Col. Thenuz was foremost in the attempt to repulse the . . . advance and performed many acts of valor. . . .[11]

The *World* fell heavily into the trap, publishing a rewritten version of the fate of the colonel with an official-looking dateline:

> On board the *World* dispatch boat *Three Friends*, off Santiago de Cuba, via Port Antonio, Jamaica. —Colonel R. W. Thenuz, an Austrian artillerist well known throughout Europe, who, with Colonel Ordonez, was defending

[8] N. Y. *World*, June 8, 1898.   [9] N. Y. *Times*, June 10, 1898.
[10] Issue of June 12, 1898.
[11] *Journal*, June 8, 1898; Charles Edward Russell, *These Shifting Scenes*, 281.

the land batteries of Aguadores . . . was so badly wounded that he has since died.[12]

The *Journal* pounced on its hapless victim, disclosing that Colonel Reflipe W. Thenuz was its own invention and that his name, when somewhat freely rearranged, spelled "We pilfer the news." The *Journal* gave this pleasant coup almost as much publicity as Dewey's victory. It commented on the *World's* criminal ingenuity in datelining the story as if it were original. It published a ridiculous cartoon of Colonel Thenuz, with the legend, "specially taken for the *World,* by the *World's* special photographer." It ran letters from out-of-town editors condemning the *World* for its theft. It published a poem, "In Memoriam," by Cozy Noble, honoring the colonel. It gave ear to a suggestion that a monument be erected to Colonel Thenuz's memory, urging that artists vie in the execution of a suitable design and that the public join in contributions to the Thenuz Memorial Fund. Distinguished artists sent in burlesque sketches showing suggested treatment of the monument. From all over the country came contributions in the form of Chinese money, Confederate currency and repudiated bonds. The ruse became historic in Printing House Square. The *Journal* kept composing variations on the theme for more than a month while the *World,* caught red-handed, maintained a painful silence.[13]

[12] *World,* June 9, 1898.   [13] Abbot, 141.

5. Hearst at the Front

I. UNTERRIFIED 'MID SHOT AND SHELL

THE nation, for weeks in a rosy glow of military glory, was brought up short by the killing of six American sailors by Spanish batteries in the harbor of Cardenas. It appeared that war could be dangerous after all. The report that Rear Admiral Pascual Cervera was sailing for America with a formidable fleet caused panic. The United States was woefully unprepared. The Atlantic defenses were negligible. People who had formerly envisioned the conflict as a punitive expedition safely removed from home, became affrighted. Coastal towns far up in Maine made frantic efforts to meet the Cervera invasion with fishing boats and shotguns. Keepers of summer hotels on the shore, finding their hostelries vacant, howled for Navy protection. Millionaires owning summer mansions on Jekyll Island in Georgia demanded battleships to protect their property. New York City hastily bolstered its defenses. Eastern Congressmen spoke angrily of the danger to their constituents while the bulk of the Navy lay off Florida. The public would have been reassured had it known that Spain had no real hope of winning the war, and that Cervera was sending despairing messages to his Minister of Marine such as the following:

"I beg your Excellency to permit me to insist that the result of our voyage to America must be disastrous for the future of our country." [1]

Hearst was preparing an expedition of his own involving some danger. Although the Navy had quickly taken his *Buccaneer,* it was in no hurry to grant a commission to the Democrat who had heaped abuse on McKinley. Hearst chartered the sizeable steamship *Sylvia* from the Baltimore Fruit Company along with its captain and crew and embarked for the war zone with a staff of newspapermen and typesetters equipped with a lightweight printing press. It was his intention to report the war in person, and also to publish the first American newspaper in Cuba, the *Journal-Examiner,* mainly for the benefit of the soldiers and for the publicity the exploit would arouse back home. Among his companions were his old friend Jack Follansbee; his crony and fellow photography enthusiast, George Pancoast; James Creelman, just back from London; John C. Hemment, a Columbia graduate and professional photographer hired for the expedition; and William Britz, a "biograph" expert who hoped to do something utterly new—take moving pictures of war action.[2]

Before embarking, Hearst went to Washington to clear the way with Secretary of War Russell Alger. Alger obliged, but said later that he told

[1] Millis, 169. [2] John C. Hemment, *Cannon and Camera,* 66.

150

Hearst that "the thing to do with a dirty sheet was to wash it." [3] Alger would hear from Hearst later.

Cervera's flotilla had now taken refuge in Santiago harbor, where he was bottled up by Admiral Sampson's United States fleet. Hearst was determined to get full news and picture coverage. He and Pancoast had each taken along several cameras, to add their talents to those of the professionals. Meanwhile, a United States army force under General William Rufus Shafter had left Tampa in thirty-two transports, intending to land near Santiago. Santiago, on Cuba's southern coast, suddenly became the cynosure of American eyes, a place where hot action could be expected.

The *Sylvia* slid around Cuba and docked at Kingston, Jamaica, in mid-June. The party dined luxuriously at the Crystal Springs Hotel in Kingston, then went to a nearby racecourse, where Hearst and Follansbee, both good judges of horseflesh, bought polo ponies for the Cuban safari and had them driven aboard. On Sunday morning, June 18, the *Sylvia* embarked for Santiago, making the voyage through rough seas in ten hours.[4]

Hearst, always the newsman, sought first to interview the American military leaders. The *Sylvia* located Admiral Sampson's flagship, the *New York*, among the blockading squadron. A launch was sent out in the darkness and Hearst, Creelman and Hemment boarded the *New York* and had a chat with Sampson. Possibly Sampson recalled the *Journal's* coverage of the *Maine* disaster, and in any case he was a man taciturn by nature. Evidently the interview was not a success, for Hearst later wrote of Sampson as a "stiff, severe kind of man" and the *Journal* lampooned him as a "tea-going admiral—a rear admiral, always in the rear." A battalion of Marines had already landed in Guantánamo Bay, forty-five miles east of Santiago, and the *Sylvia* steamed thither. Next day, Hearst and his party found sixty-three-year-old General Shafter aboard the *Seguranca,* a steamship leased by the Navy.[5]

Shafter was the same officer who had formerly been stationed in San Francisco, the one who had sent a message wheeling across the country via the *Journal-Examiner* Yellow Fellow Bicycle Relay, so he had some previous knowledge of Hearst. He was enormously fat, weighing well over 300 pounds, or, as some writers put it, one-sixth of a ton. Stripped to trousers and a blue shirt, he was sweating freely and oppressed by the responsibility of landing safely the 16,000 men of his Fifth Army Corps, but he received Hearst courteously and talked of his prospects. "He expressed himself as satisfied with the men under his command," as Hemment put it, "and added that he would make a very short campaign of it." [6]

After some reconnoitering, Shafter decided to land his men at two places —Daiquirí, eighteen miles southeast of Santiago, and Siboney, ten miles southeast of the city. Following a naval bombardment that scattered whatever Spaniards were there, the landing began on June 22 and was accom-

[3] Margaret Leech, *In the Days of McKinley,* 367.   [4] Hemment, 68–69.
[5] Hemment, 73.   [6] Hemment, 74–76.

plished without opposition at both beachheads. The general got most of his resistance from Richard Harding Davis, who, having quit the *Journal,* was with the army as a *Herald* correspondent. Davis, clad grandly in khakis, helmet and white puggree, took exception to a Shafter order that reporters could not land until the troops had established themselves, saying he was not a reporter but a "descriptive writer." "I don't give a damn who you are," Shafter growled. "I'll treat you all alike." He thereafter received unflattering treatment in Davis' dispatches.[7]

The strategy was to advance on Santiago, take the city, and thus have Cervera's fleet trapped between Shafter's forces and Sampson's battleships. The Spaniards were believed to have about 12,000 men in the vicinity, but since they were defensively deployed, well entrenched and equipped with artillery, it would take sharp work to dislodge them.

Publisher Hearst became War Correspondent Hearst as he watched the landing and the march toward Santiago, writing his impressions of it:

> General Shafter and his officers have accomplished almost a miracle in landing sixteen thousand soldiers with food, arms, ammunition and equipment in small boats through a rough surf on the steep dangerous beach, between ugly reefs in almost killing heat . . . The work was all done and well done in four days . . . The spirit of the army is high.[8]

The *Sylvia* docked at Siboney, where the *Journal* men took over a Cuban dwelling, moved in the printing press and equipment, and made ready for the first issue of the *Journal-Examiner.* Although Hearst was the only American newspaper publisher at the scene, the canebrakes were swarming with reporters from many United States newspapers. Eighty-nine of them had arrived with Shafter's troops, outnumbering the surgeons. Others hovered around in newspaper dispatch boats. The Hearst press had by far the largest staff in Cuba. In addition to the Chief himself, who had with him Creelman, Follansbee, Hemment, Pancoast, Britz and a small corps of editorial and pressroom assistants, the *Journal's* Edward Marshall, J. K. Mumford, Burr McIntosh, William Bengough, Frederick Remington and George Clarke Musgrave had arrived with the army. The *Journal's* Walter Howard and George Coffin were aboard the *Journal's* dispatch boat *Simpson* with Sampson's fleet outside Santiago harbor. Still another *Journal* man was Colonel Honoré Laine, an officer with the Cuban rebels under General Calixto Garcia, who were to cooperate with Shafter in the drive on Santiago. Doubtless there were others.

Siboney was already crowded with emaciated Cuban *pacificos* begging the Yankees for food. Hearst, along with Creelman and Hemment, left their office to seek an interview with General Garcia. The black-bearded Creelman, dapper in khakis and polished leather puttees, had the swagger of a man who had roamed the world for news, interviewed the Pope, Henry

[7] Stewart Holbrook, *Lost Men of American History,* 288–89.
[8] *Evening Journal,* June 29, 1898.

Stanley, Sitting Bull, Count Tolstoy, General Weyler and many others, covered the Japanese-Chinese war, the Greco-Turkish war, and attempted to wreck the Suez Canal. Creelman talked rapidly and fluently. Hearst, on the other hand, wore rumpled flannels and the same Panama hat with its gaily-colored band that he wore on Fifth Avenue. He said little. An obser ver might have got the impression that he was an employe of the slightly older and immensely more self-assured Creelman.[9]

They found General Garcia with several aides on the verandah of a tile-roofed house on the edge of town. Garcia was a tall, sharp-eyed old man with trailing white mustaches and a large hollow scar above the bridge of his nose, a reminder of his attempt at suicide during a previous rebellion when, about to be captured, he shot himself under his jaw, the bullet emerging through his forehead. He wore a white duck suit and a broad straw hat. Well aware of the service given his cause by the *Journal*, he greeted Hearst with real warmth in good English. Famous for his volcanic temper, Garcia had an aide instructed to murmur "Ave Maria" as a warning when he was about to erupt—a chore that brought forth many Aves—but now he was in fine humor, and coffee was served. Passing along Siboney's lone street below were columns of American soldiers. Señor Hearst had put them there.[10]

While Hemment snapped pictures, an officer brought a tattered battle flag bearing the lone star of Cuba, which Garcia took reverently and held out to Hearst.

"I present to the New York *Journal*," he said, "in commemoration of its services to liberty, the headquarters flag of the Second Department of the Republic. You see upon it the marks of Mauser bullets. This flag has been borne through many battles, and hundreds of brave men have died under it. Its colors are faded, but is the best thing the Cuban Republic can offer its best friend." Then he shouted the battle cry of his forces: "Viva Cuba Libre!" which was echoed by all.[11]

The Americans left, ascending higher on the coastal hill. Hearst, who had a notebook and pencil with him as any *Journal* reporter would, surveyed the scene and added to the first bylined story by War Correspondent Hearst. It ran to almost 3000 words, and although it wavered occasionally it gave a vivid picture of the situation that would have done credit to a seasoned writer like Creelman:

> It is satisfactory to be an American and to be here on the soil of Cuba, at the very threshold of what may prove to be the decisive battle of the war. The struggle for the possession of the City of Santiago and the capture of Cervera's fleet seem to be only a few hours away, and from the top of the rough, green ridge where I write this, we can see dimly on the sea the monstrous forms of Sampson's fleet lying in a semi-circle in front of the entrance to Santiago Harbor, while here at our feet masses of American soldiers are

[9] Hemment, 82.
[10] Hemment, 81; Rubens, 300.
[11] *Evening Journal*, June 29, 1898.

pouring from the beach into the scorching valley, where smells of stagnant
and fermented vegetation ground under the feet of thousands of fighting men
rise in the swooning hot mists through which vultures that have already fed
on corpses of slain Spaniards wheel lazily above the thorny, poisonous jungle.
[The *Journal's* editors, thinking it best not to tamper with the Chief's copy,
let this involved, though colorful, sentence pass as written.]

Santiago and the flower of the Spanish fleet are ours, although hundreds
of men may have to die on the field before we take possession of them.

Neither Cervera's crews nor General Linares's battalions or squadrons can
escape, for the American fleet bars the way by sea and our infantry and
dismounted cavalry are gradually encircling the city, driving the Spanish
pickets backward toward the tiers of trenches in which the defenders of
Spanish aggression must make their last stand.

. . . . I have talked with [Sampson, Shafter and Garcia], and each
has assured me that victory is absolutely certain. . . .[12]

II. WE MUST BEAT EVERY PAPER IN THE WORLD

ONE of the things the army had forgotten was ice and ice-making machines
to quell the fever of wounded soldiers. Hearst, who had brought a large
cargo of ice, promptly gave it to the army surgeons along with some food-
stuffs.[1] He and his party then embarked in the *Sylvia* for Port Antonia, Jamaica, with Hemment working like mad in his darkroom to get his plates
developed. Hearst was insistent that the pictures be ready to catch the
next mail boat for New York along with his dispatch, so the *Journal* could
be first. The deadline was met and the *Sylvia* returned to Siboney. There it
was learned that *Journal* Correspondent Edward Marshall, accompanying
the Rough Riders in a sharp skirmish several days earlier at Las Guanimas,
had been shot through the spine.[2] In this action, General Joseph Wheeler, a
former Confederate officer, had had an inspired lapse of memory, shouting,
"Give it to the Yankees!" as his men charged the Spaniards. Hemment went
to visit Marshall, lying in a hospital ship, while Hearst wrote to his mother:

> Dear Mother: I am at the front and absolutely safe, so don't worry. Since
> poor Marshall was shot the General has made strict rules limiting newspaper-
> men to certain localities that are well within the lines so that there is no
> opportunity for any of us to get hurt even if we wanted to.
>
> The landing of troops, guns and horses is most interesting and [the]
> march to the front very impressive. I have interviewed Admiral Sampson,
> General Shafter and General Garcia. The last named gave me his head-
> quarters flag which has seen much service and is riddled by bullets. He said
> the *Journal* had been the most potent influence in bringing the United States
> to the help of Cuba and that they would always remember the *Journal* as
> a friend when friends had been very few. Now he said that they had many
> friends but ranked the *Journal* above all others.
>
> I have been greatly interested in everything and of some service to the

[12] *Evening Journal,* same issue.   [1] Musgrave, 327.   [2] Hemment, 99–105, 111.

hospital ship providing them with ice and delicacies which they lacked. I think the standing of the paper will profit by my being here. Other proprietors are safely at home—and I will be soon. I hope you are well and not at all alarmed about me for honestly there is no occasion.

Lovingly—Will [3]

While he had a newsman's interest in the war, and followed it just as he had chased after the Guldensuppe killers, his other motive is implicit in his words, "I think the standing of the paper will profit by my being here." Despite his assurances to his mother, he was not averse to exposing his large person to danger. Next day, he and Creelman, Follansbee and Hemment mounted and rode out of Siboney toward the front to get the news. They could hear the booming of field pieces ahead. Near El Pozo, shells were whistling as they came upon a detachment of Americans taking cover in trees and sword grass.

"What in hell are you fellows doing?" an officer shouted wrathfully. "Don't you see that you are drawing the fire from those batteries? For God's sake, get off your horses!"

"Well, I guess possibly we are drawing the fire," Hearst admitted.[4]

They dismounted and took refuge on a nearby hill, where they had a good view of the action. Relishing the adventure of "the *Journal's* war," Hearst followed the troops, carrying a revolver in a holster. On July 1 he was with Follansbee and Creelman, watching the attack on the fortified village of El Caney. The Americans had no siege artillery and were forced to rely on four small field pieces to support the attack. The battery crews worked furiously to lay down a thin barrage. Then the infantry rushed the town and its stone fort. Creelman, carried away by glory, joined the charging soldiers and gained the fort, where he was felled by a bullet in the shoulder. Hearst and Follansbee followed at a slightly less foolhardy distance. The heat was scorching as they entered the smoky village. Hearst later found Creelman, who had been carried to the roadside with other wounded. To Hearst, who had a womanly concern for anyone hurt, the sight of these bleeding, groaning men must have been upsetting. Yet he was carried away by the thrill of victory. Creelman subsequently wrote an account of it:

"Some one knelt in the grass beside me and put his hand on my fevered head. Opening my eyes, I saw Mr. Hearst, the proprietor of the New York *Journal*, a straw hat with a bright ribbon on his head, a revolver at his belt, and a pencil and note-book in his hand. The man who had provoked the war had come to see the result with his own eyes and, finding one of his own correspondents prostrate, was doing the work himself. Slowly he took down my story of the fight. Again and again the tinging of Mauser bullets interrupted. But he seemed unmoved. That battle had to be reported somehow.

[3] Undated; copy supplied by Mrs. William Randolph Hearst.   [4] Hemment, 149.

" 'I'm sorry you're hurt, but'—and his face was radiant with enthusiasm— 'wasn't it a splendid fight? We must beat every paper in the world.' " [5]

Follansbee, who spoke fluent Spanish, took a detachment of soldiers and searched the town for stray Spaniards. Hearst was off for Siboney to beat the world with his story—a slow process, for there was no cable or telephone. The *Sylvia* sped with the dispatch to Port Antonio, where it was sent off to New York. The Americans were now closing in on Santiago. Next day, Hearst met his rebel correspondent, Colonel Honoré Laine, who told him how his Cuban forces had been given forty Spanish prisoners taken by the Americans at El Caney.

"And what did you do with them?" Hearst inquired.

"We cut their heads off, of course," Laine replied.

Had Spaniards done this to Cuban prisoners, the *Journal* would have emblazoned the atrocity in four-inch headlines. Hearst, in his dispatch to the *Journal*, excused it as the natural result of Spanish oppression, writing, ". . . the Cuban is tender and gentle. One seldom finds a man of more generous and gracious impulses than this same Laine. His hour has come and he is lost in the almost savage enjoyment of it." [6]

Colonel Theodore Roosevelt, a man with an ego as prominent as Hearst's, had won a victory with his Rough Riders at San Juan Hill on the same day as El Caney. Worried about his poor eyesight, he carried a half-dozen spare sets of glasses sewn to his uniform, one pair inside his hat. He conveyed an impression that he and his cavalry could handle the Spaniards alone if the the rest of the army would get out of their way. Although he was guilty of errors of overzealousness, his courage was undeniable and the New York papers were singing his praises. There was also some comment about Hearst. The spectacle of the millionaire publisher risking fever and bullets in Cuba aroused grudging admiration among some of his rivals, especially at the evidence of his reportorial skill. The *Times*, which had assailed his pre-war jingoism, now complimented him on his first dispatch:

> The editor and proprietor of *The Journal* of this city showed more than usually good judgment when he assigned Mr. W. R. Hearst to duty as a staff correspondent at the campaign of Gen. Shafter, with instructions to interview that grand old soldier and Admiral Sampson, and particularly Gen. Garcia.
>
> We do not know if the assignment was made in order to provide an object lesson to the other correspondents, but the copy turned out is notably superior to that which generally passes the censorship of *The Journal* telegraph desk. It is straightforward, clear, and readable, with the exception of a little nervousness at the start. . . .
>
> We venture to congratulate *The Journal* on its special enterprise, and to express the hope that it indicates similar modification of methods and standards in other departments. [7]

Indeed, the *Journal* itself was the most lavish in its praise of Mr. Hearst. Its Washington bureau rounded up a group of government officials and

[5] Creelman, 210–12.   [6] N. Y. *Journal*, July 6, 1898.   [7] N. Y. *Times*, July 1, 1898.

gathered their plaudits under the headline, "UNITE IN PRAISE OF THE JOURNAL EDITOR'S DISPATCH." Vice President Garret Hobart was quoted as saying, "That the proprietor of a great newspaper should go to the front in a campaign like that against Santiago is surely a departure in journalism . . . An example has thus been set which other newspaper proprietors could well follow." Navy Secretary Long, General Miles, Assistant Secretary of War George Meiklejohn, Senator Stephen B. Elkins, and Assistant Secretary of the Navy Charles Allen added encomiums of Hearst which were also repeated in the San Francisco *Examiner*.[8] Now that two *Journal* correspondents had been wounded in action, and the boss himself was dodging bullets, the *Journal* editors were all the more determined to maintain their ownership of the war. Hearst's dispatch on the capture of El Caney and the wounding of Creelman was given full-page treatment under the heading, "THE HEROIC CAPTURE OF CANEY TOLD BY THE JOURNAL'S EDITOR-IN-CHIEF." Hearst's interview with Laine was headlined, "JOURNAL'S EDITOR-IN-CHIEF DESCRIBES SATURDAY'S FIGHT BEFORE SANTIAGO" and was given similar display.[9]

On July 3, Admiral Sampson left his fleet to confer with General Shafter, who was suffering severely from heat and gout and was spending much of his time in a hammock. Admiral Cervera, caught like a rat in a trap, picked that very time to essay an escape. One by one his six warships slipped out of Santiago harbor at full steam. The heavily superior American fleet, temporarily under the command of Commodore W. S. Schley, was in some confusion for a time, but when its gunners got the range they made short work of the enemy. Before the day was over, all six Spanish ships were smoking ruins and Cervera, with more than 1700 of his officers and men, were prisoners. It was the *coup de grâce* which at once ended Spain's centuries-old sway as a world power and marked the fledgling United States as an international force to be reckoned with. Admiral Sampson returned to find that the great victory of which he had doubtless dreamed during many peaceful years, had been snatched from him by his subordinate, Schley. Feelings between the two men were not cordial.

Hearst and his party steamed out to the scene and rose at 5 next morning to look over the smoking *Vizcaya*. It was the same Spanish cruiser that had made an unhappy call in New York some four months earlier. Hearst, clad in blue flannels and a yachting cap, snapped pictures and then, with Hemment, Pancoast and Follansbee, boarded the *Vizcaya*. Her decks were still almost too hot to touch. "The girders which supported the main deck," Hemment wrote, "were twisted into every conceivable grotesque shape . . . The charred remains of many of the sailors were strewn around . . ."[10] Hearst picked up some Spanish silver money melted into a lump.

"Great heavens!" he wrote in his dispatch. "Is this rent and ruined hull, black and battered, blistered and burned, with the gaping chasm in its bow

[8] *Journal* and *Examiner*, June 30, 1898.   [9] *Journal*, July 4, 6, 1898.
[10] Hemment, 214.

. . . is this the noble boat we all admired so much and dreaded not a little as she lay in New York Harbor just before the war? Is this the deck from from which Captain Eulate trained his guns on the tall buildings of New York?" [11]

They sailed toward another wrecked Spanish warship, the *Oquendo*. She was still burning, shells occasionally exploding aboard her, so they stayed at a distance. A cutter bearing Marines, the *Dixie*, churned up and hailed them.

"What were you doing aboard that ship?" an officer shouted.

"Just looking about, sir, at the results of the battle," Hearst replied meekly.[12]

The officer, learning they were newsmen, warned them of the dangers, and the *Dixie* sped away. Someone aboard the *Sylvia* spied men on the distant shore. Binoculars disclosed at least twenty men, probably Spanish sailors who had swum from their burning craft the day before. Lowering a launch, Hearst, Hemment and a few others headed for the shore.

"We shouted at them and made a demonstration with our firearms," Hearst wrote in his dispatch, "and the poor, cowed fellows, with great alacrity, waved a white handkerchief or shirt as a token of surrender.

"I jumped overboard, swam ashore, and told them we were going to take them aboard our boat to see the Admiral. They appeared rather gratified than otherwise, and seemed to dread the Cubans far more than Americans." [13]

This was not surprising, in view of the Cuban treatment of Spaniards. Hearst, who was widely believed the sort of fellow who would start a war and then keep safely clear, had taken twenty-nine Spanish prisoners. He had them bury a few corpses which had washed up on shore, then took them back aboard the *Sylvia*. It was recalled that this was the Fourth of July. The Spaniards were persuaded to give three cheers for George Washington and President McKinley while they were photographed for the *Journal*. "Mr. Hearst then ordered that these prisoners should have plenty to eat and drink," Hemment recorded. The Spaniards were transferred to the American warship *St. Louis*, where the delighted Hearst demanded and got a receipt: "Received of W. R. Hearst twenty-nine Spanish prisoners." [14]

The *Sylvia* returned to Siboney, where Creelman was resting comfortably. He was taken aboard, and the party steamed for Baltimore. In some seventeen days in Cuba, Hearst had accomplished his purpose, the dispatch about the prisoners being the last under his byline. The war was all over but the shouting, Creelman was glad to escape Siboney's scorpions and tarantulas, the Cuban heat was fierce and there was always yellow fever to worry about. In fact, Burr McIntosh had come down with fever, making the third *Journal* casualty.

The *Sylvia* docked in Baltimore on July 18. Britz's pictures apparently turned out poorly, for nothing further was heard of them. Back in New

[11] *Journal*, July 6, 1898.   [12] Coblentz, *Hearst*, 65.   [13] *Journal*, July 6, 1898.
[14] Coblentz, *Hearst*, 67.

York, Hearst had his receipt for twenty-nine prisoners framed and hung on his office wall along with the bullet-torn flag given him by Garcia. The lump of silver from the *Vizcaya* became his paperweight.[15]

III. THE HORRORS OF PEACE

". . . the proprietor of our esteemed and enterprising yellow contemporary, *The Journal*," said the *Times*, "has captured some twenty survivors of the *Maria Theresa* . . . This is the most genuine as well as the most legitimate increase of circulation, so to speak, which he has of late achieved . . . We admit that we cannot imagine Mr. Pulitzer in the act of corraling shipwrecked Spaniards for the glory of his journal and the country. . . ." [1]

Not counting his Spaniards, Hearst was claiming a daily morning-evening circulation of 1,250,000 for the *Journal*, and the *World* claimed the same. Yet the chances are that the *Journal*, with its smaller advertising revenue, was still losing money. The *World's* enormous profit had been greatly reduced. The cost of reporting the war was staggering, with the two papers vying in purchasing dispatch boats and hiring correspondents. Another heavy expense was in putting out "extras," the *Journal* sometimes printing as many as forty editions a day and the *World* almost as many. Hearst alone spent $500,000 over ordinary expenses in the short conflict.[2] Pulitzer was unhappy about the war he had helped bring on, and never wanted another.

Hearst, on the other hand, gloried in the war that lost him money because it was a national triumph and because it gave him the circulation he wanted. He had a fixation about circulation. He believed that if he had masses of readers, the advertising would follow as surely as night follows day. He had spent the $7,500,000 he got from his mother and borrowed more.[3] Nevertheless, the vista of success ahead seemed bright. It was regrettable that the rush of events had kept him from carrying through the Decker expedition to liberate Captain Dreyfus; but now even the French seemed to admit that Dreyfus was innocent and it appeared that he would win his freedom. The *Journal*, having harried the *World* for six weeks about Colonel Thenuz, now assailed its treatment of the 71st New York Volunteers.

The *World* had hired Stephen Crane as a correspondent in Cuba. Crane had sent only one dispatch. This one proved a boomerang, for it told of the shaky conduct of the 71st at San Juan. It was true that the 71st had faltered in the battle and impeded other troops, among them the Rough Riders, which put Colonel Roosevelt in a fury. It was true but undiplomatic.

The *Journal* seized on this as a slander. "SLURS ON THE BRAVERY OF THE BOYS OF THE 71st," ran the headline. "The World Deliberately Accuses Them of Rank Cowardice at San Juan." The *World* had not gone nearly that far, but it might as well have. The *Journal* listed the 71st's casualties—

[15] Creelman, 178.
[2] *Pearson's Magazine*, Sept., 1906.
[1] N. Y. *Times*, July 7, 1898.
[3] *Collier's*, Sept. 22, 1906.

fourteen killed, fifty-nine wounded. "Eight per cent of the regiment," it said, "or one man in every twelve, was struck by a Spanish bullet." [4] When Hearst returned from Cuba, a headline read, "EDITOR OF THE JOURNAL'S PERSONAL EXPERIENCE OF THE SPLENDID HEROISM OF THE SEVENTY-FIRST." Under this was a short piece by Hearst (who had not been at San Juan), praising the regiment, corroborated by Edward Marshall (who had not been at San Juan either, having been wounded days earlier).[5] Crane *had* been there. But the *Journal* hammered on, distorting a measured military critique into a shameful insult of heroes.

The unhappy Pulitzer sought to escape the onus. The *World* started a fund for a battlefield memorial to the 71st and to the New York men of the Rough Riders. The *Journal* jeered at this repentance of a defamer. The men of the 71st, agreeing, refused to accept any memorial from Pulitzer, while the testy Roosevelt snapped that no Rough Rider could sleep in the same grave with the craven dead of the 71st. In the end, Pulitzer was forced to return the money that had been collected.[6]

Hearst's own memorial drive—that for the victims of the *Maine*—was attracting contributions from all over the country. But he was not without difficulties. After the Spanish surrender of Santiago, three unnamed *Journal* correspondents plastered the city with posters reading, "Remember the Maine!" with a legend at the bottom, "Buy the Journal." To General Shafter, the "Maine" cry seemed an invitation to vengeful Cubans to massacre Spanish prisoners. The general had the *Journal* men arrested and sent home.[7] This incursion on the freedom of the press drew instant pressure from the *Journal*. Its Washington staff got busy. The fear in which the newspaper was held by government officials was shown by the nervous protests Secretary of War Alger sent to Shafter.

"The New York *Journal* people are in great trouble," he cabled. "The *Journal* has been doing good work." Again, "The New York *Journal* is in terrible distress." [8]

Shafter refused to let the correspondents return, and thereafter he got the back of the *Journal*'s hand.

Simultaneously, the *Journal* was overwhelmed with admiration for the "First American paper in Cuba—*Journal*, of course." "PRESIDENT McKINLEY PRAISES THE CUBAN EDITION OF THE JOURNAL," it headlined, following this with further praise by General Garcia, Navy Secretary Long, Senator Cushman Davis and nine other officials.[9] It had a feeling that America could lick the world. When news came that Vice Admiral von Diederich, commanding a German fleet in Manila Bay, had gone out of his way to insult Admiral Dewey, it headlined, "WE'RE READY TO WHIP GERMANY—[She] Cannot Bully Us," declaring, "Having whipped Spain, we are ready to whip Germany if she desires a fight." [10] Remembering

[4] *Journal*, July 17, 1898.   [5] *Journal*, July 20.   [6] Seitz, 241.
[7] Holbrook, 292-93.   [8] Millis, 349.   [9] July 11, 12 and 15 issues, 1898.
[10] July 16 issue, 1898.

the large German population in New York, the *Journal* took pains to show that it meant no reflection on them. It ran a story on the sturdy patriotism of naturalized Germans under the head, "GERMANS LOVE THIS, THEIR LAND," another on the Bavarian ancestry of "Hero Schley" of Santiago, and a full-page biography of Bismarck.

The loss of Cervera's fleet and the surrender of Santiago, following the disaster in the Philippines, was enough to make Spain sue for peace. Although die-hard Cuban loyalists in Havana were hanging out women's clothing with signs, "To be worn by those willing to surrender," the fighting was over and the settlement remained for the conference table. One of the war's unsung sagas was the brilliant but futile effort of various *Journal* men to deliver Hearst's $2000 sword to General Gomez. Ralph Paine had carried the sword 5000 miles, joining several filibuster expeditions that failed to reach Cuba, before he gave up and handed the weapon to another *Journal* man, Granville Fortescue. Fortescue had likewise joined unsuccessful expeditions from Florida, finally becoming discouraged and passing the sword to other *Journal* men in Tampa.[11] Further efforts were made, but it was not until well after the war that the sword reached Gomez, who was reported to have shown a singular lack of appreciation.

"Those imbeciles in New York, with two thousand dollars to waste!" he said. "It would have bought shoes for my barefooted men, shirts for their naked backs, cartridges for their useless rifles. Take it away . . ."[12]

From a news standpoint, the war's quick ending was unfortunate. People who fought for fresh-from-the-press newspapers telling of stirring victories were indifferent about the listless ruminations of diplomats. The *Journal*'s circulation stuck briefly at its claimed (and doubtless exaggerated) 1,250,000, then began to drop off. Hearst knew this was inevitable, but he worked indefatigably to keep the drop at a minimum. The recipe was to find or invent new sensations.

"Your true yellow journalist," Hearstman Abbot observed, "can work himself into quite as fiery a fever of enthusiasm over a Christmas fund or a squalid murder, as over a war or a presidential campaign. He sees everything through magnifying glasses and can make a first-page sensation out of a story which a more sober paper would dismiss with a paragraph inside."[13]

The *Journal* stirred up a cyclone over the conviction of Martha Place, a murderess, gathering the opinions of many public figures as to whether it was proper to electrocute a woman, which fate Mrs. Place eventually met. It gave a full page to the execution of Martin Thorn, who had aided Mrs. Nack in butchering Willie Guldensuppe. While it warmly favored the Cuban republic, it demanded that the United States take all of the Philippines from prostrate Spain. It cast covetous eyes on other Spanish possessions including the Canary Islands, saying, "WHAT A SPLENDID COALING STATION THIS WOULD BE FOR US!"[14] It furnished a splendid exam-

---

[11] Granville Fortescue, *Front Line and Deadline*, 1–3.   [12] Paine, 175.
[13] Abbot, 207–8.   [14] *Journal*, Aug. 7, 1898.

ple of the something-out-of-nothing feature when for days it ran scare-heads on the tottering condition of the Brooklyn Bridge. Several main girders were buckling, it said, and officials were blind to the disaster that would occur should the whole structure topple into the East River. Yet, after city engineers inspected the bridge, found no girders buckling and pronounced it in perfect condition, the *Journal* headlined joyfully, "The Bridge is Absolutely Safe; Its Strength is not Impaired," with no apparent realization that this proved it a liar.[15]

In the strict sense, the Hearst papers were not newspapers at all. They were printed entertainment and excitement—the equivalent in newsprint of bombs exploding, bands blaring, firecrackers popping, victims screaming, flags waving, cannons roaring, houris dancing, and smoke rising from the singed flesh of executed criminals.

Hearst, whose early San Francisco *Examiner* had built a record of solid, though noisy, achievement, had sunk journalistically in New York. Some could not believe that this attractive, well-read, intelligent young man, with his perfect manners and his love of art, could possibly be responsible for the tasteless enormities of his newspapers. There was a suspicion that he was merely the owner, that his papers were really the work of Brisbane, Chamberlain and Goddard. The insiders knew that on the contrary, Hearst was the Chief in fact as well as name, and that his newspapers were the precise reflection of his wishes.

Some insiders wondered why, with his manners and his millions, he did not publish a paper priding itself on its taste and discernment in presenting the news. There were reasons. As a monumental spender, he was faced by the necessity of making money. Papers of highest news and literary quality had the lowest circulations and made the least money. Yet it is doubtful that even had money not been a factor he would have chosen to work for quality. He had a juvenile worship of size, noise and display. He wanted to be the biggest, the showiest. Quiet quality bored him. He aimed to reach the masses. The high responsibilities of the journalist toward truth and principle seldom affected him. A few keen observers reached a plausible conclusion: that through some accident of birth or upbringing, Hearst was devoid of certain attributes of character common in ordinary men, that he saw everything from a twisted, egocentric point of view, and that far from being a man of taste in his use of the news, his taste was execrable.[16]

IV. THE MAGNIFYING GLASSES

> Putting out a newspaper without promotion is like winking at a girl in the dark—well-intentioned but ineffective.
> —Hearst [1]

---

[15] Aug. 6, 1898, issue.   [16] *American Mercury*, Nov., 1930.
[1] W. R. Hearst Jr. to author, Dec. 8, 1959.

THE meeting between W. R. Hearst and Henry J. Pain has gone unrecorded, although in its way it was as historic as the meeting of Stanley and Livingstone and would produce a collaboration as persistent as that of Gilbert and Sullivan. There was such a strong natural affinity between Hearst and Pain that it was inevitable that they would come together. They were essentially in the same line of business, and could do much for each other. They saw the world from the same point of view. They had similar ideas about the entertainment and instruction of the masses. Strangely, there seems no record that Hearst and Pain ever met personally. Very likely they did not, since Hearst, being shy and busy, often delegated such conferences to lieutenants. Yet there can be no doubt that Hearst and Pain were as conscious of each other, and as sympathetic, as if they met daily over claret at their club, and it can safely be said that they met in spirit.

Physically, the two men had no resemblance, Hearst being tall and good-looking while Pain was middle-sized, homely and wore glasses. These differences were as nothing in view of their intellectual rapport. Starting from utterly different backgrounds, and making their way into manhood with educational opportunities in no way alike, they nevertheless had joined to complement each other, to work together in perfect accord for years.

Pain was known as the "Fireworks King" or "Pyrotechnist Pain." The art of displaying fireworks was as old as the ancient Chinese, but the man who brought it to its highest refinement in America was H. J. Pain. He owned scores of ponderous mortars for firing salutes. He employed crews of men skilled at operating them, and at shooting quintuple bombs that burst five times into flowers, stars, and silver or golden spray. He had a huge stock of flares and pinwheels in all sizes. But above all he was famous for shaping fire into the likeness of men, ships, waterfalls, or almost anything that came to mind.

Hearst had been a fireworks enthusiast in childhood and college. They remained almost an obsession with him—an item interesting to analysts who suspect some sexual motivation in an inordinate love for fire and fireworks. He also thought them unexcelled for attracting crowds. He had employed Pain's fireworks before, to celebrate circulation increases, the union of Greater New York and American war victories. But not until the end of the war did Pain and his men take the status of shock troops to be flung into the breach whenever some Hearst campaign needed crackling support.

By July, the *Journal* fund for a memorial to the *Maine* victims had grown to an impressive $102,000, collected from organizations and school children all over the country. Hearst was not satisfied. He saw in the fund an opportunity not only to glorify American arms but also to publicize his newspapers. At Manhattan Beach in Brooklyn, Pain had a 300-foot stage where he showed nightly two of his creations, "The Battle of Manila" and "The Blowing up of the *Maine*." Hearst hired him to take these representations on a nationwide tour in a special *Journal-Examiner* train that would visit San Franciso, Oakland, Los Angeles, Salt Lake City, Denver and Kansas City.

While the *"Maine"* spectacle was a triumph, it was exceeded by "The Battle of Manila," which showed twenty glowing battleships maneuvering on wheels as guns boomed.

"Experts who have seen Pain's fiery portrayal of the 'Battle of Manila,'" said the *Journal*, "declare it to be a perfect representation of the great naval fight. It is regarded as Pain's masterpiece." [2]

A portion of Pain's forces left New York under a subordinate, taking with them ammunition and equipment for a long campaign, in the Hearst-hired train which bore huge banners reading, "NEW YORK JOURNAL TRAIN —'MAINE' MONUMENT FUND." [3] Other Pain detachments remained in New York, where Hearst had work for them. On the night of August 9, after much drum-beating, the *Journal* gave a special program at Manhattan Beach for its *Maine* fund. Wounded soldiers from the Santiago campaign were the *Journal's* honored guests. The general public had to pay. They saw Pain's two *chefs d'oeuvre*, plus a special feature in fireworks that showed two soldiers on a pedestal, taking aim, and underneath them the fiery words, "Journal Monument Fund." Victor Herbert, who would later gain fame of a different sort, led his band in a rendition of "The Star-Spangled Banner" as this came into view, causing, said the *Journal*, "deafening" applause. [4]

In the midst of these doings, Hearst received an anticlimactic message from Washington. Now that the war was over, the Navy had got around to appointing him an ensign, its lowest commissioned rank, "and he will be ordered to active duty as soon as he accepts his commission." [5] This tardy work could hardly have been other than an intentional slight on the part of the McKinley administration, which had suffered from him and would suffer more.

Pain and his men were preparing for another *Journal* event, a "Carnival of Sports" to be held at Sulzer's Harlem River Park. This was also said to be for the monument fund, although newspaper rivals were sour enough to comment that in these affairs there was always less patriotism shown for the United States than for the *Journal*. Hearst was sowing seed for an even more momentous event, one in which Pain could not participate. Sampson's victorious fleet was sailing north and would steam up the Hudson on August 20. It was Hearst's idea to make this an unparalleled patriotic event and at the same time to maneuver the city authorities into a position that would give the impression that it was a *Journal* holiday and that the United States Navy was appearing under the auspices of the *Journal*. He sent a telegram to Mayor Robert Van Wyck:

> The *Journal* feels that the reception to the victorious American Navy on Saturday should come from the whole people of this city. May I suggest that you call upon the citizens of Greater New York to make of the day a complete holiday, abandoning all business save that of cheering the Navy

[2] *Journal*, July 29, 1898.   [3] *Journal*, Aug. 21.   [4] Aug. 10, 1898, issue.
[5] N. Y. *Tribune*, Aug. 7, 1898.

that has made America a bigger country and the American nation a bigger nation? —W. R. Hearst.[6]

Simultaneously the *Journal* loosed a front-page headline barrage: "MAKE SATURDAY A FULL HOLIDAY, SO ALL THE PEOPLE MAY SEE OUR VICTORIOUS FLEET." It urged all employers to close their stores and shops in a universal moratorium on business, continuing, "Give everybody, rich and poor, high and low, laborer and idler, a chance to properly greet the great fighting machines of our Navy as they steam up North River, showing their scars of battle to a proud people; a chance to get out and whoop and hurrah." [7]

These appeals were so enthusiastic and patriotic that anyone failing to heed them was placed in a position of apparent disloyalty. Mayor Van Wyck hastened to reply:

> My Dear Mr. Hearst: In reply to your wire, suggesting a full holiday on Saturday, I can only say that if I had the legal authority to proclaim such a holiday for this city I should do so at once.
> I will, in my official capacity, call upon the citizens of New York to give up business as fully as possible on the day of the great review and make Saturday a day of holiday rejoicing. . . .[8]

Journal emissaries visited places of business and got flattering cooperation. Macy's, Lord & Taylor's, Arnold, Constable and Company and other large establishments agreed to close down. Patriotic Thomas A. Edison said he would close his laboratory in Orange, New Jersey. The *Journal* published glowing statements about the *Journal's* patriotic enterprise from Governor Frank S. Black of New York, Governor Foster Voorhees of New Jersey, Senator Thomas C. Platt of New York and other officials, along with praise for the *Journal* by many business leaders. "JOURNAL'S PLAN FOR FULL HOLIDAY ADOPTED," it headlined. "ALL NEW YORK MAY GREET OUR HEROES." This was not quite true, since there were some business men so soulless as to refuse to shut down. Yet there was no doubt that the *Journal's* enterprise had liberated thousands of workers who otherwise would have missed the show.

To the deep annoyance of other newspapers, the *Journal* proceeded to appropriate the holiday and the fleet. It announced that it would send up a *Journal* balloon from Grant's Tomb, from which observers would keep the populace posted on the progress of the fleet. It published the "JOURNAL'S WAR BALLOON SIGNAL CODE." Showers of red confetti from the balloon would mean that the warships had left Staten Island. Showers of purple confetti would indicate its arrival opposite the Statue of Liberty. Green and then white confetti would show further stages of progress up the river, while "brilliant showers of red, white and blue, followed by all colors of the rainbow," would signal the fleet's arrival opposite Grant's Tomb. The *Journal* dispatch boat *Anita*, herself proud of her war record in carrying the

[6] *Journal*, Aug. 21, 1898.   [7] Aug. 17 issue.   [8] *Journal*, Aug. 19, 1898.

news from Cuba, would meet the fleet in New York Bay and escort it all the way up the river.[9]

"TAKE THIS PAGE OF THE JOURNAL WITH YOU TO THE PARADE TO-DAY," urged the *Journal* on a page covered with drawings showing identifying marks and enemy shell hits so that readers could pick out the *New York*, *Oregon*, *Iowa*, *Brooklyn*, *Indiana* and *Texas*. "WELCOME TO THE SEA KINGS!"[10]

When Admiral Sampson steamed up the Hudson on August 20, the river was dotted with tugs and other craft blowing whistles, and lined with spectators on both sides. Sampson may have been surprised to find the *Anita*, bedecked with *Journal* banners, leading the way for him. He may even have been surprised at a *Journal* headline, "ADMIRAL SAMPSON PRAISES THE JOURNAL," which appeared next day along with another story, "HOW THE JOURNAL SECURED THE HOLIDAY FOR THE PEOPLE." The *Journal* proposed a toast: "THE NAVY: May the record of glory begun by PAUL JONES, maintained by DECATUR, PERRY, HULL, PORTER and FARRAGUT, and renewed by SCHLEY, SAMPSON and DEWEY, be rightly rewarded by making our navy as strong in ships as it is in skilled hands and stout hearts." The *Journal* hurled defiance at England, Germany, and other naval powers who might underestimate United States strength, saying, "The Heroes Have Come Home, but the Ships Have Their War Paint on Yet. Europe, Please Take Notice." In the same issue, the *Journal* said it had 213,751 more daily circulation than its nearest contemporary in the world, the Paris *Petit Journal*, snubbing the *World* by ignoring it.[11]

Cynical representatives of the *World* and other rivals who felt that Hearst cared not a whit about the Navy so long as he could puff the *Journal,* were mistaken. He had a little-boy enthusiasm for military prowess. He had been sincerely thrilled by the Navy's triumphs. He would remain a friend of the Navy all his life, constantly urging more and bigger warships and better training for naval officers. Yet, with his peculiar mental astigmatism, he saw no reason why he should not combine a glorification of the Navy with a *Journal* circulation drive. Indeed, to have failed to do so would have shown a lack of vigorous American enterprise.

A salient feature of the Hearst genius was its negative quality. He was seldom enthusiastic about anything other than his own ideas—a trait in accord with his possessiveness and his Napoleonic complex. His strongest talent lay in attack, as it had in childhood when he played aggressive practical jokes, and in college when he found enjoyment in defying authority. Before the war he had assailed Cleveland, McKinley and Hanna with libelous disregard for party. Now that the war was over, he heaped special maledictions on the War Department for its treatment of the troops and its failure to get them back quickly and efficiently. Part of this was Hearst's own fault, since he had started the war in a country where yellow fever

---

[9] *Journal*, Aug. 20.   [10] Journal, Aug. 20, 1898.   [11] Aug. 21, 1898, issue.

was uncontrolled, for which the United States had to take the consequences. The War Department naturally was reluctant to withdraw troops until the situation in Cuba was in hand.

Nevertheless, it was true that the War Department, under aged Secretary Alger, was a model of mismanagement that had sent troops to the tropics in woollen winter clothing, given them inferior arms and fed them rotten beef. Now it was feeble in providing for the troops remaining in Cuba and unprepared to care properly for those who came back. The return of the *Journal's* Burr McIntosh, who had lost fifty-eight of his 250 pounds to yellow fever, and the death of another *Journal* writer, Sydney Tovey, of typhoid contracted in Tampa, doubtless made Hearst more aware of the dangers. Although the *Journal* ran an advertisement, "Soldiers Who Used Paine's Celery Compound Did Not Suffer From Fever," the fact remained that some soldiers were dying of disease. Besides, with the cessation of battle and the proved safety of the Brooklyn Bridge, other sensations had to be found.[12]

The *Journal* dug at General Shafter for sending troops home in the transport *Concho,* allegedly with bad water and supplies, causing the death of several soldiers en route. It began to call the army transports "pest ships," and headlined, "SHAFTER HELD TO ACCOUNT FOR MISERY IN ARMY." But the criticism of Shafter paled beside that leveled at Alger, whom the *Journal* frankly labeled a murderer. Conditions were indeed bad at the army reception center at Montauk Point, Long Island, where for a time there were not even tents to accommodate returnees. With a headline, "JOURNAL TO AID SICK HEROES," the *Journal* started a drive for contributions of food and clothing. At Montauk it erected three huge striped tents, flying pennons advertising the *Journal,* where the contributions were handed out. It sent Mrs. John A. Logan, the lady who had chaperoned Miss Cisneros, to investigate conditions at Montauk, which she found indescribable. A fortnight later it sent Mrs. Julian Hawthorne, wife of a *Journal* writer, who found matters even worse.[13] The water at Montauk was said to be poisonous. *Journal* headlines pictured scenes of stark horror among the soldiers:

"STARVING MEN AT MONTAUK POINT" . . . "SICK AND DEAD AT JACKSONVILLE" . . . "FEVER PLAGUE AT CAMP THOMAS" . . . "DYING HEROES SHIPPED TO HOSPITAL BY FREIGHT" . . . "STORY OF HORRORS HOURLY GROWS WORSE" . . . "FOOD ROTS ON TRANSPORTS WHILE SOLDIERS STARVE" . . . "IT IS MURDER THAT IS BEING DONE AT MONTAUK." A Davenport cartoon showed the figure of death hovering over a tombstone marked, "Killed by Spaniards, TWO HUNDRED; Killed by Official Negligence and Incompetence, TWO THOUSAND." [14]

Secretary Alger hurried to Montauk to investigate, said conditions there

[12] Gregory Mason, *Remember the Maine,* 287.   [13] *Journal,* Aug. 14 and 28, 1898.
[14] All from various Aug., 1898, issues.

were good, drank some Montauk water and declared it the best he had ever tasted. The *Journal* said Alger no sooner got back to Washington than he came down with dysentery from that same water.[15] The venom of its attacks were beyond belief. In an editorial headed "ALGER'S MURDER RATE," it named as his victims the 2,225 officers and men who died out of the total of 265,000 who had been enrolled.[16]

But the camps were improved, the men were mustered out, and the *Journal* turned to other sensations, among them the vindication of Captain Dreyfus and the New York gubernatorial race. The *Journal* favored the Democratic candidate, Judge Augustus Van Wyck, brother of the mayor, although the Republican candidate, Colonel Roosevelt, was made famous by Hearst. Had it not been for the war, Roosevelt might still have been an obscure Cabinet assistant. It was his enormous publicity as the intrepid leader of the Rough Riders—publicity which he shrewdly exploited—that formed the basis of his brilliant career in politics. Since Hearst brought on the war, it can be said that he also put Roosevelt in Albany as governor and in the White House as President. Roosevelt beat Van Wyck in a close race, and from then on his star rose swiftly.

Hearst, whose yacht *Buccaneer* had been returned by the Navy with thanks, was still impressed by his role in creating the war and by the power that lay in his hands as owner of the newspaper with "the largest circulation in the world." His reflections on this theme were embodied in a signed editorial, one of his earliest in the *Journal*, urging that other editors join with him in beneficent use of their influence:

> The force of the newspaper is the greatest force in civilization.
> Under republican government, newspapers form and express public opinion.
> They suggest and control legislation.
> They declare wars.
> They punish criminals, especially the powerful. They reward with approving publicity the good deeds of citizens everywhere.
> The newspapers control the nation because they REPRESENT THE PEOPLE.

Here Hearst suggested a union of newspapers in pushing good measures on which they could all agree, such as better schools, a cause in which he was sincerely interested. He even praised Pulitzer, Bennett and other editors he had formerly attacked, ending:

> I pledge the *Journal* to the support of all good measures proposed by other newspapers.
> I urge upon the men whose power gives them such great responsibilities the importance of formal editorial union—not for private profit but FOR THE PUBLIC GOOD. —W. R. HEARST.[17]

[15] Aug. 28, 1898.   [16] Sept. 30, 1898.   [17] *Journal*, Sept. 25, 1898.

Although nothing came of it, the editorial was an olive branch extended to editors who had assailed him as a publisher devoid of the finer instincts of journalism. While building his huge circulation, he had aroused not only the enmity but the actual disgust of almost all other editors in New York. For all his outward nonchalance, deep in his capricious heart Hearst sought to be admired. He did not entirely understand why he was so hated among his rivals of the Fourth Estate. He was hoping to climb out of the abyss of scorn that encompassed him because of what he felt was largely envy.

He was even beginning to sound like a candidate for office.

BOOK FOUR

THE CANDIDATE

1. Eye on the White House

THE tendency of men close to Hearst was to go through three stages of ratiocination: (1) to observe his activities with utter fascination; (2) to attempt to analyze and understand him; and (3) finally to throw up their hands and admit the impossibility of such understanding. This came about because he was a mass of contradictions, supremely inconsistent, ever in conflict with himself. General Weyler and the Brooklyn Bridge engineers could logically say that he was an unmitigated liar. Humble citizens of New York for whom he had fought and won a lower gas rate regarded him as the soul of virtue. Upper-crust New Yorkers who recoiled at his newspapers felt that he must be the most vulgar of men; yet people who met him personally were struck by his shy charm and genuine courtesy. Rival newspapermen regarded him as a monster of misrepresentation, but they had to admit that his own dispatches from Cuba were able and accurate.

President McKinley and Senator Hanna could truthfully charge Hearst with ruthless and cruel attacks. But to *Journal* reporter Bill Hart, an old *Examiner* man who came down with cancer after he moved to New York, and for whom Hearst sent to Paris for a Pasteur specialist, the Chief was an angel. This was also the opinion of a girl stenographer in Hearst's office, who suffered an attack of paralysis and was sent by the boss to a sanitarium, with all expenses paid. When she recovered and married a cripple she had met during her stay, Hearst gave her husband a job and fitted out an apartment for the pair.[1] All newspapermen in New York—even those on enemy sheets—were grateful to him for one boon. His bidding for able men had raised the whole scale of wages so that journalists, for the first time, were decently paid.

Hearst's enemies have made the common error of denuding him of virtue, seeing base motives behind all his kindly acts and building him into a specter of selfishness. Thus, he paid his men well because money meant nothing to him and it was his mother's money anyway; he fought for the common people simply to gain circulation; he was generous to employes only because this flattered his ego. These generalizations are all the more false because they are partly true. Hearst himself shares the blame for his low reputation because of his disregard for convention and his systematic employment of journalistic vulgarity. Those who knew him best understood that he was selfish and ruthless but that he was also moved by sincere generosity and human compassion.

[1] Carlson and Bates, 90.

The most balanced and competent witness for Hearst in this early-middle period is Willis Abbot, a Hearst editor for twenty years who later wrote a judicious appraisal. Abbot went through all three stages of ratiocination about Hearst, but emerged with some careful opinions.

". . . to those whom [Hearst] knew and whose work he liked, he was in those days an ideal 'boss,'" Abbot wrote. "A good piece of work always brought a word of congratulation over the 'phone and not infrequently more substantial recognition. Illness or trouble in the family of one of his workers always brought generous aid and practically illimitable leave with pay." ". . . he . . . never commits an act or speaks a word to those whom he knows that would be wounding." ". . . Hearst's charities to disabled or involved workers . . . are innumerable and never publicly proclaimed." ". . . I believe that Hearst . . . was, at the time I knew him best, entirely sincere in his sympathy for the masses. For the politicians who professed that sympathy in order to gain support, he had nothing but supreme contempt." [2]

These are words of rare praise, coming from an observer who detested some of Hearst's traits. They show him as gentle, considerate, generous without ostentation, a millionaire with a social conscience who sincerely wanted to help the oppressed.

At this time he had another engaging characteristic that later became almost submerged. He trusted his key lieutenants and allowed their talents considerable rein. He had grown fond of Arthur Brisbane because he was a resourceful editor and effective writer who worked like a drudge, devoting most of his waking hours to the *Evening Journal*. A hard worker himself, Hearst expected his top men to do likewise. When Brisbane joined him at a modest $150 weekly salary plus a circulation bonus, no one envisioned the Spanish war and what it would do to circulation. His bonus soared so fantastically with the war headlines that he became embarrassed and told Hearst that he would like to scrap the bonus agreement. Hearst generously declined, allowing the bonus to run its course and then putting Brisbane on a $50,000 annual salary, the biggest in newspaperdom at the time. Brisbane was on the job at 4:30 A.M., staying until late in the afternoon, cracking the whip over reporters and working with a zeal that carried over into his so-called leisure hours. [3]

In addition to hard work, Hearst, who could forgive horrendous news bungles, insisted on enthusiasm and enterprise. On one occasion he was talking with Brisbane, McEwen and Abbot about James Creelman, whom the three editors did not admire whole-heartedly because his vanity made him inject much about Creelman in anything he wrote. Hearst corrected them on this score.

"The beauty about Creelman," he said, "is the fact that whatever you give him to do instantly becomes in his mind the most important assignment

[2] Abbot, 142, 145, 150–51.   [3] Carlson, *Brisbane*, 111.

ever given any writer. Of course, it's a form of egotism. He thinks that the very fact of the job being given him means that it's a task of surpassing importance, else it would not have been given to so great a man as he."

Hearst pointed out the window to City Hall Park across the way.

"Now if I asked one of you fellows to go out and write a story about that fountain in the park, you'd either refuse or do it grudgingly, with the idea in the back of your head that I was crazy . . . But Creelman finds any assignment is dignified by being given to him. That's why he's so useful." [4]

With a Presidential campaign only a year off, a preposterous idea struck Hearst. He thought it would be nice to be second on the ticket with Bryan, who seemed the obvious Democratic standard bearer. Although he admired Bryan, he was not entirely satisfied with him as a Presidential candidate, and indeed had sent a *Journal* man halfway around the world to sound out Admiral Dewey as a possible candidate. But Dewey, great in battle, was hopeless as a politician. Bryan's silver mania, illogical even in 1896, was now a political liability, for the nation was riding into a wave of prosperity on the gold standard. In 1899, Bryan served notice that he still clung to the obsolete silver issue, saying, "I stand just where I stood three years ago"— a pronouncement that caused the Republican New York *Press* to suggest, "Sit down, Mr. Bryan. You must be awfully tired, too." [5] Yet no one could match Bryan's inspiring leadership. Hearst was prepared to support him despite his misgivings. Bryan had his own misgivings about Hearst.

Despite Hearst's great services to the party in 1896, not to mention his financial help, Democrats generally refused to take him seriously as a politician. One reason was his extreme shyness and inability to make a speech, certainly an insurmountable handicap for a vote-seeker. Another was his reputation as an amiable playboy and his habit of wearing gay plaid suits and dazzling neckties at a time when the uniform of any knowledgable politician was sober black. But Hearst had a wistful yearning for office, bolstered by his faith in the power of his newspapers to bring on war and to make and unmake statesmen. Being an incurable romantic with a liking for verse, he was also inspired by a poem that swept America that year.

At a party in San Francisco, a goateed Oakland school principal named Edwin Markham had read a poem he had written after viewing Millet's painting "The Man With the Hoe." One of the listening guests was Bailey Millard, Sunday editor of Hearst's *Examiner*. Millard was so impressed that he asked and received permission to publish it in the *Examiner*. Given the same title as the painting, it read in part:

> Bowed by the weight of centuries he leans
> Upon his hoe and gazes on the ground,
> The emptiness of ages in his face,
> And on his back the burden of the world.
> Who made him dead to rapture and despair,

[4] Abbot, 208.   [5] Quoted in Mark Sullivan, *Our Times*, I, 305–6.

> *A thing that grieves not and that never hopes,*
> *Stolid and stunned, a brother to the ox?*
> *Who loosened and let down this brutal jaw?*
> *Whose was the hand that slanted back this brow?*
> *Whose breath blew out the light within this brain?*

Succeeding verses identified the toiler as representing the exploited, underprivileged masses who were beginning to understand and resent the injustices done them. The poem ended menacingly:

> *O masters, lords and rulers in all lands,*
> *How will the Future reckon with this Man?*
> *How answer his brute question in that hour*
> *When whirlwinds and rebellion shake the world?*
> *How will it be with kingdoms and with kings—*
> *With those who shaped him to the thing he is—*
> *When this dumb Terror shall reply to God*
> *After the silence of the centuries?* [6]

The *Examiner* paid Markham forty dollars for the right to publish the poem, which he considered a handsome fee. Suddenly the *Examiner* found that it had a sensational scoop. The "Hoe Poem" caught the nation's fancy. It was quoted in other newspapers across the land. Lecturers discussed it. Preachers used it as a text. Conservatives assailed Markham as a prophet of revolution, while progressives hailed him as the spokesman for the underprivileged. Markham became famous. The nationwide furor arose from the plain people's feeling that the poem truly expressed the injustices perpetrated by the railroads and the trusts, which were uncontrolled and riding roughshod over the public interest. Collis P. Huntington, still in Washington fighting to save the Southern Pacific from paying its debt—and soon to lose the battle—was incensed by Markham's rebellious tone and doubtless also by the fact that the poem was published by his old enemy, the *Examiner*.

"Is America going to turn to Socialism over one poem?" he demanded. "Markham's Hoe Man has a hoe. Let him rejoice. The only man to commiserate is the man who has no hoe; the man who cannot help to enrich the world." [7]

Huntington offered a $750 prize for the poem best controverting Markham's heresy. Ambrose Bierce, still fighting Huntington in Washington, sourly remarked that the poem had "not the vitality of a sick fish."

Hearst, on the contrary, was delighted by the scoop and also by Markham's sentiments. He saw to it that Markham became the *Examiner*'s literary editor. He had long been a foe of the railroads and trusts, battling them in San Francisco and New York. Markham's feelings echoed his own. It would be surprising, however, if he were not struck by another fact that shone clearly through the furor—namely, the widespread public approval of the poem.

---

[6] San Francisco *Examiner*, Jan. 15, 1899.   [7] Lewis, *The Big Four*, 241.

As a man thinking of entering politics, Hearst would have been obtuse had he not seen that millions of people felt as he did, that he had a popular issue and a huge, ready-made following. Significantly, thereafter his attacks on the trusts became even more systematic and violent. As sponsor of the Yellow Fellow Bicycle Relay, he yet may have enjoyed one of the many parodies of Markham's poem, this one by a Boston bard and titled, "The Man With the Hump":

> *Bowed by the drooping handle-bars he leans*
> *Upon his bike and gazes at the ground;*
> *His back is humped and crooked and his face*
> *Is strained and agonizing in its look.*
> *Who made him sit upon a wheel like this?* [8]

But to Hearst, the Hoe Poem was a national rallying cry against the trusts. Shrewdly recognizing Bryan as the political spokesman of the injustices dramatized in the poem, he invited Bryan to write about it in the *Journal.* Bryan did so, pointing out that the poem was an artful expression of the evils afflicting America—the taxes on the poor, child labor and the rapacities of the trusts—writing in part:

> It is a sermon addressed to the human heart. It voices humanity's protest against inhuman greed . . . Wealth is being concentrated in the hands of a few . . .[9]

For twelve years Hearst had been satisfied with the journalist's role in politics—attacking politicians, supporting politicians, near the center of political power but not of it. Now he had that fatal, indescribable itch to hold public office himself. "The Man With the Hoe" did not start the rash, but it aggravated it. Ordinarily, when he wanted something he set out with purposeful energy to get it. Now, for the first time in his life, he wanted something he did not know how to get—indeed, had some doubt of his own capacity to get. Even a precinct leader had to have a few sparks of that vital flame known as leadership, the ability to speak to groups, attract men, make them eager to follow. Hearst knew his ghastly weakness in this respect. He must have known that here was an instance when his newspapers could not speak for him. To him an unfulfilled want was akin to physical pain. It is safe to say that as the itch progressed, so did his inner malaise.

He tried in a groping way to get into the political swim. On April 7, 1899, despite his scorn for the systematized corruption of Tammany, he attended a fund-raising meeting at Tammany Hall, on Union Square, at which boxes were auctioned for the coming Jefferson Dinner. Among those present were men with colorful reputations. Richard Croker, the leader of Tammany, had once been accused of murder. Edward S. Stokes had served time in Sing Sing for the murder of James Fisk, Jr. Fire Commissioner John J. Scannell had once slain a political enemy. Abraham H. Hummel, the city's foxiest

---

[8] Sullivan, *Our Times*, II, 246 fn.   [9] N. Y. *Journal*, Apr. 1, 1900.

divorce lawyer, would later go to prison for fraud. But there were also non-criminals in the crowd, among them Dock Commissioner Charles F. Murphy, who would later loom large in Hearst's horizon. Bidding for the boxes was brisk, the highest price being $240 paid for Box 1. Commissioner Murphy paid an even $100. Hearst, who appears not to have been in a lavish mood that night, paid a modest fifty-five dollars for Box 54.[10]

He attended the dinner a week later at Grand Central Palace. Bryan was the honored guest and chief speaker, but Hearst was merely a boxholder.[11] He was uncomfortable, ill at ease at such gatherings. He must have seen that he was regarded only as a useful Democratic publicist and donor who was well outside the inner council, and that there was no easily-found short-cut to the select circle. Those who sat with Bryan—among them John Clark Ridpath, James R. Brown and Eugene V. Brewster—were party stalwarts who had risen after years of loyal labor. Yet Hearst knew that he had something no one else there could offer—the largest newspaper circulation in the country. Bryan and the Democrats needed him. In this need he aimed to find the short-cut to political preferment that was barred to him under the conventional rules.

That fall, Hearst attended an auction more to his liking at his favorite theater, Weber & Fields' Music Hall at Broadway and Twenty-ninth Street. He had always enjoyed the broad humor of Joe Weber and Lew Fields, whose topical travesties had once included a take-off on the Hearst-Pulitzer battle for the Yellow Kid. This opening night of *Whirl-i-gig* was a special occasion, for the two comedians had lured into their troupe the opulent Lillian Russell. Another member of the cast, David Warfield, *né* Wohlfelt, was from San Francisco. Hearst, Stanford White and Abe Hummel were among those who paid "up to $750" for boxes, making it appear that Hearst set a higher value on Weber & Fields than on the Democratic party. The show opened with a sensation when the curtain rose to disclose Miss Russell in bed with a plug hat on her head and wearing what appeared to be a night-gown. Decency was saved when she emerged from the covers in a low-cut evening gown. One of the show's jokes came when Miss Russell and Warfield were addressing a waiter:

Miss Russell: "You might bring me a demi-tasse."

Warfield: "Bring me the same, and a cup of coffee." [12]

Hearst so enjoyed Weber & Fields that he often saw the same show again and again. He had no time for serious drama, opera or symphony. Music, indeed, had no appeal to him with one notable exception—the kind that had a swing or a laugh in it, the kind that went with vaudeville hoofing and the chorus line, or with Gilbert and Sullivan. For a time in San Francisco he had tried hard to master the banjo under the tutelage of Ashton Stevens, the *Examiner* dramatic critic, the banjo being the ally of the minstrel shows he admired. His taste for entertainment was frankly and enthusiastically low-

[10] N. Y. *Times*, Apr. 8, 1899.   [11] *Times*, Apr. 16, 1899.
[12] Felix Isman, *Weber and Fields*, 258.

brow. He went to the theater for amusement, not to have his brain exercised by subtle problems in character or situation, which bored him. He liked broad, farcical strokes of theater just as he liked black headlines, Davenport's uncompromising cartoons and the antics of the Katzenjammer Kids.

Shortly after the Weber & Fields extravaganza came an even bigger show —the biggest New York had ever seen. Admiral George Dewey arrived in New York from the Philippines with part of his squadron to be greeted with a two-day frenzy of adulation that quite upset Hearst's Madison Square. A dazzling white plaster "Dewey Arch" was built over Broadway at the south end of the square, through which a great parade passed while the admiral sat with officials in a reviewing stand at the Worth Monument banked with 20,000 pink roses. There was talk of renaming the square Dewey Square, and of replacing the plaster arch with one of enduring marble. But the flimsy plaster arch was fated to become a monument to public fickleness. Just as General Shafter had sunk in popular estimation, so Dewey lost his glamor when he went to Washington, seemed unenthusiastic about a house given him there by public subscription, and spoke of selling it. The newspapers which had idolized him now began to peck at him. It was the New York *Journal* that came gallantly to his defense.

"Admiral Dewey may undo the deed to the house presented him by a small portion of his fellow countrymen," said the *Journal*, "but he can never undo the deed of May 1, last year." [13]

Late in 1899, Hearst left for Europe, taking as his guests Millicent and Anita Willson and their parents, Mr. and Mrs. George Willson. Willson was a popular vaudeville performer, a buck-and-wing dancer and also a singer, known for his rendition of, *I Met Her by the Fountain in the Park*.[14] His daughters had followed the paternal tradition. When Hearst went abroad, he liked to take congenial companions for whom he would serve as planner and guide on sightseeing tours—in short, would take charge of all activities and would feel hurt if anyone had plans contrary to his own. Even on holiday, he liked to run things.

In February, 1900, Hearst and his party were cruising up the Nile when he chanced to read a week-old English newspaper. It told of the Hay-Pauncefote treaty by which England agreed to give the United States total control of a canal through Panama or Nicaragua. Hearst, who had developed a strong suspicion of English motives and saw no reason why England should have any authority over what he considered an exclusively American sphere, leaped from his chair at one sentence. The canal, the treaty stipulated, must be *unfortified*.

Along with his distrust of England, Hearst had an expanding vision of America's destiny of greatness. It would be an American canal, built by Americans with American money. How could Secretary of State Hay be so

[13] Quoted in Sullivan, *Our Times*, I, 342.
[14] Winkler, *Hearst—An American Phenomenon*, 184.

foolish as to let England tell him it must not be fortified? He dashed off an angry message to New York which a native rider carried seventy miles to the nearest cable office. The *Journal* got busy with attacks on Hay and the treaty. Creelman rushed to Washington to fight passage of the treaty. It was ultimately defeated. The canal, when it was later built, was fortified—a precaution that proved wise in World War I.[15]

All this may have come about without Hearst's Egyptian eruption. But it was manifest that he regarded himself as a guardian of American interests and that he did have strong opinions on matters more important than murder and scandal.

II. THE TWENTIETH CENTURY

IN the spring of 1900, Hearst returned with his party, loaded down with paintings and other objects of art. The Twentieth Century, dawning while he was abroad, found the United States prosperous enough so that to anyone but a Democrat, the chances of a Democrat beating McKinley seemed remote. The prosperity, however, was comparative, meaning for most citizens subsistence instead of want. Thoughtful men were concerned about the growing size, arrogance and ruthlessness of the trusts, something the amiable McKinley seldom worried about. Hearst did. For years his prime political weapon would be a campaign against the trusts.

In New York, the first horseless buses were running on Fifth Avenue—electrically operated twelve-passenger "jitneys" that caused pedestrians to stare. There was an automobile show at Madison Square Garden. A $35,000,-000 contract had been let for the city's first subway. Delmonico's had moved to a handsome new building at Fifth and Forty-fourth, a token of the uptown drift. Broadway was bustling, with some fifty theaters vying for the trade. The Tenderloin area swarmed with street-walkers and harbored many gambling halls. Under Mayor Van Wyck, Boss Croker's man, the lid was off and the byword was "to hell with reform." The Worth House, where Hearst had refurbished the third floor, was being razed. Doubtless he lived at a hotel for a brief period until he bought the four-story brownstone home at Lexington Avenue and Twenty-eighth Street once owned by President Chester Arthur.[1] Hearst moved in his bric-a-brac from the Worth House and his trophies from Europe. For the first time he became a New York householder, with George Thompson attending to his wants. It had long been a standing joke among his friends that any Hearst domicile was a place where one stumbled over statuary.

While he was away, an incident had occurred in Kentucky that would later have a violent effect on his fortunes. Governor-elect William Goebel had been shot dead in an election quarrel. Ambrose Bierce had written one

[15] Mrs. Fremont Older, *op. cit.,* 235–36; Leech, 504–11.
[1] Winkler, *Phenomenon,* 186.

of his less tasteful quatrains to mark the event, which was published in the New York *Journal:*

> *The bullet that pierced Goebel's breast*
> *Can not be found in all the West;*
> *Good reason, it is speeding here*
> *To stretch McKinley on his bier.*[2]

Phoebe Hearst had at last sold her Washington mansion and returned to California with her niece, Anne Drusilla, to live in a splendid, rambling, Spanish-inspired home she had built at Pleasanton and which she called the Hacienda. For greater convenience while shopping or visiting in San Francisco, she had a cozy five-room apartment built in an upper floor of the *Examiner* building at Third and Market Streets, insulated against the newspaper uproar going on all around her. Although she had not met Millicent Willson, her prejudice against "stage people" was fixed and she was hoping that her son would not marry her.[3] In Washington she had founded the National Cathedral School for Girls as well as kindergartens for white and Negro children. Now in California her incessant benevolences turned in the direction of higher education. She had sponsored an international competition of architects for the improvement of the University of California at Berkeley, offering $10,000 as the first prize. She gave funds to the university to send archeological expeditions to Mexico, Yucatan, South America, Egypt, Greece, Etruria and other places. She also proposed to give the university the largest girls' gymnasium in the country.[4]

Although Phoebe had "loaned" her son something probably nearing $10,000,000, her fortunes were still in gratifying shape for at least one good reason. The Homestake Mine in South Dakota, in which she was largest stockholder, had gone through expansion and was producing gold at a rate of about $6,000,000 a year.[5] The Cerro de Pasco copper mine in Peru, in which she had a large interest, was promising. It seems likely that despite the amount William Hearst had spent, the George Hearst estate was as big or bigger than when he died. Phoebe's father had died, but her mother was still living at the Apperson ranch in Santa Clara County. Aged Drusilla Apperson was fond of her grandson, William, who always visited her on his trips to California and declared her fried chicken unequaled.

In New York, Hearst was not yet ready to marry. He seems to have had few close friends. His old Harvard chum Cozy Noble was city editor of the *Journal,* but Noble was convivial while Hearst was abstemious and the camaraderie between them had flagged. Pancoast had married, ending the free-and-easy bachelor status with Hearst. Follansbee remained in Mexico all winter and spring. Orrin Peck was still in Munich. Hearst now invited Brisbane to live with him, and Brisbane moved into the commodious Lexington Avenue house.

[2] Feb. 4, 1900, issue.   [3] Mrs. J. M. Flint to author.
[4] *Berkeley—The First Seventy-five Years,* 68.   [5] Rickard, 220.

Offhand, Brisbane and Hearst seemed ideally matched as friends. Both men were bachelors, non-drinkers, non-smokers, and lovers of the stage. They were both hard workers at the same business. They sincerely admired each other's abilities. They even had similar sociological and political theories, for Brisbane had inherited some of the socialistic principles of his eccentric father, Albert Brisbane, and was indignant about the exploitation of the masses.[6] He was handsome, urbane, witty and learned, albeit somewhat shallow. Hearst had many friends during his long life, some of whom he genuinely prized, but they were successive or occasional rather than permanent. Never did he succeed in winning a friend who remained his friend in deepest mutual affection to the end, although Brisbane probably came closest. For all his kindly impulses, Hearst had his periods of aloofness. Also, he seemed incapable of the sustained reciprocity of concession that makes and cements true friendship. The kingly ego that lurked under his courteous exterior inevitably put any friend in the status of a subject. Hearst always had to govern the realm, gently but firmly. His friends eventually understood that the relationship was not really a two-way one, and experienced a feeling of subjection that was most easily solved by seceding delicately from the barony.

But Brisbane and Hearst got along well, and Hearst doubtless told him of his political aspirations. The Democratic party suddenly capitulated to Hearst. He traveled to Washington to attend a meeting of the National Association of Democratic Clubs on May 19, 1900. The biggest business of the meeting was the resignation of Governor Benton McMillin of Tennessee as president of the group, and the election of Hearst to the post.[7] Hearst was nominated by Senator James K. Jones, chairman of the Democratic National Committee. At the same time, Jones told Hearst that to elect a President, the Democrats needed a powerful organ in Chicago. Hearst agreed to publish a Chicago paper in a hurry if the Democrats would regard it as a direct contribution to the party. Obviously there was a bargain between Hearst and Jones, Hearst getting the presidency of the National Association of Democratic Clubs in return for his Chicago undertaking.[8]

It was Hearst's first entrance into organized politics. By his shrewd realization of his own power, he had entered not in any subaltern role but in a post of nationwide importance, hurdling the lower echelons in one leap. He must have been pleased when the Atlanta *Evening Journal* suggested him as the vice-presidential candidate, calling him "a firm Democrat."[9] In starting a Chicago newspaper, he was doing the Democrats less of a favor than they imagined. He had always intended to enter Chicago, and the deal with Senator Jones merely hastened him. In order for his Chicago paper to be of service in the campaign, it had to be in operation early in July, which gave him only about six weeks to launch a project that normally would take months.

[6] *Collier's*, Feb. 18, 1911.   [7] N. Y. *Tribune*, May 20, 1900.
[8] *Pearson's Magazine*, Sept., 1906.   [9] Quoted in N. Y. *Tribune*, May 31, 1900.

Probably no one but Hearst, with his immense drive and refusal to recognize the impossible, could have done it. He sent his business manager, satanic-bearded Solomon Carvalho, to Chicago to get the *Evening American* rolling. Carvalho worked like a maniac, soon joined by Hearst and others. They rented an old building at 216 West Madison Street, near Franklin. Owing to the shortage of freight cars, they shipped presses from New York by Pullman. They contracted for newsprint, ink, and above all for men to run the new machine. Hearst got them by offering good salaries. Chicago reporters were lucky to get thirty dollars a week until Hearst offered them fifty dollars or more.

"The newspaper man in Chicago who has not been offered 'steen hundred a week to work on Mr. Hearst's new paper is a freak," commented the New York *Tribune*.[10]

Brisbane hurried to Chicago, as did Homer Davenport, Jimmy Swinnerton and a horde of *Journal* headliners. Victor Lawson, wealthy publisher of the Chicago *Daily News,* viewed the invasion with apprehension, writing in the vein of a general before a battle, "All the people in our office are in good spirits . . ."[11] Lawson was irked when he found that Carvalho had snatched away the franchise for advertising on the city's street-corner trash cans, which long had borne *Daily News* placards. Henceforth they would read, "Buy the Chicago *American.*" After losing some of his men to Hearst, Lawson raised the salaries of some of those remaining.[12] As always, the arrival of Hearst meant a general boost in the wage scale.

The deadline was met with a touch of typical Hearst showmanship. On July 2, Bryan, who was in Indianapolis, pressed a key sending a "Start the presses" message, and the first issue of the Chicago *American* was in production.[13] Hearst and his men had performed a Herculean task for the party, but Bryan and the Democrats had likewise done well for Hearst. The *American* got off to a flying start as the official party organ in Chicago, blessed by Bryan himself, and thus assured of the readership of thousands of Chicago Democrats. Never had Hearst shown more adroitness in manipulating what seemed to be his own generous and sacrificial gesture into an operation that quickly proved profitable.

The Chicago *American* was distributed at the Democratic national convention which began in Kansas City on July 4, but Hearst was not a candidate. Bryan was nominated by acclamation, his running mate being elderly Adlai Stevenson of Illinois. In its three main planks, the party platform attacked Republican imperialism, advocated control of the trusts and demanded free silver. Hearst's mugwumpery was shown by his decided, though silent, disagreement with two of the three planks. He was opposed to free silver, and he was as strong an imperialist as Theodore Roosevelt, the Republican vice-presidential nominee. But he was as one with Bryan in enmity to the trusts,

[10] July 2, 1900.   [11] Lawson Papers, Newberry Library, letter dated July 7, 1900.
[12] Lawson Papers, letters of July 6, Aug. 2 and Aug. 14.
[13] Mrs. Fremont Older, *op. cit.*, 218.

which had become almost a monomania with him. It was this issue that the Hearst press dinned with an incessant barrage, running a line, "DESTRUC-TION OF THE CRIMINAL TRUSTS" on its editorial page and exposing the evils of the trusts on every front page.

Hearst took energetic steps to build up the influence of his new charge, the association of Democratic clubs.[14] Always one to work through subordi-nates whom he drove as unsparingly as he drove himself, he appointed curly-haired, plump Maximilian F. Ihmsen as his secretary in active charge of the clubs. Ihmsen, a veteran political reporter who had been on Hearst's Washington staff for several years, was the man who had sent the "interview" that Theodore Roosevelt repudiated. From a new office at 1370 Broadway, Ihmsen sent out a stream of publicity to Democratic clubs all over the country, urging zeal for the Bryan-Stevenson ticket.

Politically, Hearst was at last getting the recognition he wanted. When Bryan arrived in New York on October 16, and a banquet was given him in the Louis Quinze salon at the Hoffman House, Hearst sat at Table A with Bryan, Mayor Van Wyck, Boss Croker and others of the elect. The dinner was enlivened when ex-Governor W. J. Stone of Missouri turned up his nose at the wines being served.

"Waiter, I want some whisky," he said.

"Whisky is not on the menu, sir," the waiter replied.

"I told you I wanted some whisky, and bring it damn quick," Stone roared, and got his whisky.[15]

The liquor-hating Bryan, who must have looked askance at Governor Stone, was noticeably heavier and balder than he had been in the 1896 cam-paign, but still had his oratorical magic. When he spoke at Madison Square Garden after the dinner, Hearst sat on the stage with Croker, a man he despised as a political scoundrel, and heard Bryan attack the trusts and question the so-called "McKinley prosperity."

"They tell us we are prosperous," he said. "Who's we?"

"Croker," shouted a wag in the crowd, raising a laugh but bringing a frown to Bryan's face.[16] Hearst and Croker accompanied Bryan when he made later speeches at Tammany Hall and Cooper Union, then escorted him back to the Hoffman House, passing by the now dilapidated Dewey Arch, whose eroded plaster was covered with Democratic signs such as "All McKinley's Trusts We'll Bust."

Hearst's acquaintances must have seen that something momentous was happening to him. He was voluntarily submitting to needless tortures. During the campaign he even essayed something foreign to his nature and destructive to his digestion. He made speeches, or semi-speeches. He addressed a couple of New York Democratic clubs, writhing in agony as he delivered a few remarks before turning the meeting over to others.

[14] Carlson and Bates, 114.   [15] N. Y. *Times,* Oct. 17, 1900.   [16] The same.

Meanwhile, his newspapers were pounding at the trust issue with head-lines, editorials and some of the most provocative cartoons yet seen in print. Davenport was picturing "the trusts" in the shape of a grotesque, gorilla-like monster. A new *Journal* cartoonist, Frederick Burr Opper, had started a series called "Willie and his Papa," showing McKinley as a small boy, "Papa" as the dollar-sign-covered trusts, and a hulking nursemaid representing Hanna. McKinley, the cartoons clearly showed, was the obedient stripling of Papa Trusts and Nursemaid Hanna. In many of Opper's drawings the Repub-lican vice-presidential nominee, Roosevelt, was depicted as a show-off play-mate of McKinley's, riding a toy horse, brandishing a wooden sword, and so determined to steal the limelight that he made McKinley cry. The *Journal's* responsibility to report crime was not forgotten. For a time, Bryan had to share front-page billing with accounts of the murder of the aged millionaire, William Marsh Rice. But when Bryan arrived in New York a second time, he received a rousing welcome due in large part to the combined efforts of Hearst and Professor Henry Pain.

A hundred Yale Democratic collegians were Bryan's companions as he rolled in from New Haven. Hearst was at Grand Central Station to meet him, along with Max Ihmsen and James Creelman. There was some disorder as the boisterous Yale men, singing, "Here's to good old Yale, drink it down," good-naturedly tried to get some piece of Bryan's clothing as a souvenir. "They grabbed him from all sides," a reporter noted, "knocked his hat down over his eyes, pulled his necktie awry, and for a few moments the perpetual candidate acted as if he did not like it." [17] Hearst had some trouble rescuing Bryan and escorting him to a waiting carriage which took them, with Creel-man and Ihmsen, to the Hoffman House.

That evening, Mr. and Mrs. Bryan were Hearst's guests at an elaborate dinner, with covers for forty, in the Hoffman House's Green Parlor. Hearst, a few months earlier a political unknown, sat at the head of the table between the Presidential candidate and his wife, while among the guests were David B. Hill, the state Democratic leader, Boss Croker and Mayor Van Wyck, not to mention Mr. and Mrs. Creelman, Mr. and Mrs. Ihmsen and Hearst's old crony, the bachelor John Gilbert Follansbee. Hearst had spared no expense. An orchestra played softly as the diners enjoyed *huîtres, potage, Saucisson de Lyon, Ris de veau à l'Ecarlate,* and other delicacies. The room was "lavishly decorated with palms, ferns, white chrysanthemums and autumn leaves. The table was banked with roses, and the souvenirs were little silver baskets with candy in them." [18]

Hearst left the table at 7:30 with what must have been a palpitating heart and quaking knees. For the first time in his life he was to address a throng at Madison Square Garden, if only with a few words.

A great Democratic rally had been staged at the Garden, where Bryan

[17] N. Y. *Tribune,* Oct. 28, 1900.   [18] The same.

would speak later. As Hearst rode across Twenty-sixth Street, he could see the preliminary efforts of his collaborator, Pain. Rocket shells were screaming up from the square to burst into flowers and stars. The Garden tower was a mass of red light. A little later would come Pain's more ambitious creations —a portrait in fire of Bryan, a fiery representation of Old Glory, another fire picture showing an Opper "Willie and His Papa" cartoon, and still another, 600 square feet in size, bringing Davenport's cartoon of "the trusts" into flaming life.[19] Even in the hectic last stages of a Presidential campaign, Hearst found ways to advertise his *Journal*, and indeed it had to be said that he was paying for everything.

The huge Garden was packed with enthusiastic Democrats. Hearst, clad in evening dress, had to pound for order for ten minutes, the *Times* said, "laughing outright when some individual in the crowd yelled, 'Three cheers for Willie Hearst.'"[20] Then he simply announced that the meeting was in order and introduced Anson Phelps Stokes as permanent chairman. This brief moment of leadership was fated to enslave him like a drug. Later, when Bryan spoke, he began with warm praise for Hearst and led the crowd in three cheers for the president of the Association of Democratic Clubs. One good reason for the cheers: The clubs had raised $26,000 for the cause, which Hearst had matched with another $26,000 out of his own pocket.[21]

Hearst must have known that he was again backing a loser. Only one of the three Democratic planks—control of the trusts—was valid and popular. The others—free silver and anti-imperialism—would lose more votes than they would win. The *Journal* later announced that with Pain's help it would give celestial tidings of the election results, sending up twenty balloons which would emit "great showers of green stars" for a Bryan victory and golden stars if McKinley won. On election day, after the votes were in but not yet counted, a remarkably restrained *Journal* editorial admitted that McKinley's "moral character is irreproachable" and that the republic would be safe whoever won.[22]

Later, the twenty balloons sent up from the *Journal* building rained golden stars. Bryan went down to stunning defeat, losing even his own state of Nebraska. Hearst and his *Journal* knew why:

> The Democratic party has paid by two defeats for the adoption of an unpopular and discredited issue. Free silver was defensible in 1896, although even then its advocates had an uphill fight. But everything that has happened in the past four years has helped to bury it deeper in the graveyard of obsolete issues . . .[23]

[19] N. Y. *Evening Journal*, Oct. 27, 1900.   [20] *Times*, Oct. 28.
[21] *Evening Journal*, Nov. 6, 1900.   [22] The same.
[23] *Evening Journal*, Nov. 7, 1900.

III. LAYING MCKINLEY IN HIS BIER

FIELDS (to Weber): "I got nothing. You got nothing; he
got nothing. Let us form a trust."
Warfield: "Let us be thieves."
Fields: "It is the same."

IT IS a logical certainty that Hearst, from the moment he made his first
awkward efforts to get into the New York political swim, had his eye on the
White House. The ordinary routine of politics bored him. Mixing and handshaking with crowds of strange Democrats made him acutely uncomfortable.
Delivering a speech was a downright horror to him, and if it speaks volumes
for his courage that he was able through sheer determination to control his
stagefright, it is also eloquent of the ambitious end he had in view. Above all,
he loved his freedom to enjoy himself. In entering politics, he was deliberately sacrificing much of his freedom and shouldering a load of anguish.
He would not have done it for anything less than the Presidency, although
he would accept a lesser office or two as stepping stones. He thought always
in grandiloquent terms. As one of his associates said, "If you should put
Hearst in a monastery, he would become abbot or die." [1]

His outstanding talents were in the allied fields of promotion, propaganda,
advertising and showmanship. Since these talents had brought on war with
Spain, he had come to believe that if properly exercised they could accomplish anything. "The force of the newspaper is the greatest force in civilization," he had written. "[Newspapers] declare wars . . . They make and
unmake statesmen . . ." It was his intention to advertise himself into the
White House.

Hearst, who had formerly beat the drum for his newspapers while avoiding
personal publicity, now began to thrust his own name before the public.
"W. R. Hearst" appeared in sizeable type under the front-page titles of his
five newspapers, and under the mastheads. "Copyright by W. R. Hearst"
appeared over every news story of importance, and with cartoons and features. In every edition the name was imprinted from a dozen to twenty times
or more. Millions of readers in three major cities were exposed daily to his
name with the repetitive insistence that constitutes the basis of advertising
and would later be rivaled by short "commercials" dinned at frequent intervals over radio or television. He also intruded his name into the headlines,
a gaudy example coming at the time of the Galveston flood disaster of September 8, 1900, which cost 6000 lives and destroyed much of the city.

Although this occurred during the Bryan campaign, and the Hearst press
continued to support the candidate loyally, it also found many columns to
publicize itself and its owner. The New York *Journal*, the Chicago *American*
and the San Francisco *Examiner* all appealed for public contributions, each

[1] *Collier's*, Feb. 18, 1911.

of them sending a well-advertised relief train to Galveston bearing its name on great banners. The *Journal* turned it into a sort of sporting event, saying, "It will be a race to see which [of the three trains] gets its doctors, nurses and supplies to the scene of the disaster first." [2] Winifred Black, Hearst's favorite sob sister, was the first reporter from the outside world to enter the stricken city. She organized a relief unit to handle and dispense incoming supplies, founded an emergency hospital, and spent $60,000 Hearst sent her in cash from public contributions.[3]

In New York, Hearst drummed up a charity bazaar at the Waldorf and several theatrical benefits at which Weber & Fields, Lillian Russell, Tony Pastor and others donated their services. He called for more contributions. His own contribution of $1000 headed the list published in his papers, and was the largest single one. Day after day Hearst's name appeared at the top of the list along with the generous $1000. His name was printed in bold-faced type, whereas other contributors were listed in regular type. The *Journal* featured telegrams of praise and thanks sent to Hearst by Governor Joseph Sayers of Texas and Clara Barton of the Red Cross. Hearst's name was mentioned glowingly in news accounts of the relief work, and in one issue the name "Hearst" appeared in three headlines on the same page.[4]

For some, the good work the Hearst press did for Galveston was tarnished by the owner's use of the tragedy to publicize himself. It is safe to say that he saw nothing unworthy or tasteless in this course, his perception of such niceties being nonexistent. Hearst was imbued with a belief in his own towering abilities, never doubting that he had a destiny of greatness, convinced that his unique powers of leadership could benefit the nation as well as add to the glory of Hearst, and fated to be frustrated in his aims because he used the wrong methods, mistakenly thinking he could ride to the heights on headlines and skyrockets.

Bryan had failed in 1896 and 1900. Hearst, knowing where Bryan had made his mistakes, was aiming for 1904. In addition to his newspapers, he had a potent weapon in his presidency of the National Association of Democratic Clubs. To a large extent he had made them, as Creelman observed, "his personal property, supported and absolutely controlled by him." [5] The association now contained some 12,000 clubs all over the nation with almost 3,000,000 members, most of them vote-getters. Max Ihmsen, from his Broadway office, was sending out a stream of publicity to the clubs, rallying discouraged Democrats with talk of future successes and not forgetting to print the name of Hearst in large type. Hearst's enterprises were growing so complex that he dealt, like a potentate, through a series of ministers—Brisbane, Carvalho and others supervising the newspapers, Ihmsen in charge of the political secretariat, and Clarence J. Shearn serving as attorney general.

Attorney Shearn was thirty-one, an honor graduate of Cornell, a balding little man with a big voice. Hearst had retained him in his fight against the

[2] *Journal*, Sept. 11, 1900.
[4] *Journal*, Sept. 11, 1900, ff.
[3] Ross, *Ladies of the Press*, 63.
[5] *Pearson's Magazine*, Sept., 1906.

gas franchise grab—a successful effort that saved New York's millions precious dollars, but one that had to be constantly watched, with a Croker-led Tammany administration ever looking for spoils. Hearst, through Shearn, also had taken a hand in defeating the Ramapo scandal, another franchise deal whereby the Van Wyck administration aimed to saddle the city with a $5,000,000 water bill annually. With his usual vigor, Hearst had bought shares in the Ramapo company in order to bring a stockholder's suit handled by Shearn. In 1900, the Hearst-Shearn combination joined other newspapers in exposing an ice trust which had contrived to get exclusive use of docks where ice could be landed, in return for favors for politicians. The *Journal* disclosed that Mayor Van Wyck, Boss Croker, Dock Commissioner Charles Murphy and other officials owned large blocks of stock in the company, which proposed to double the price of ice. Shearn made an effort to impeach the mayor, which was unsuccessful, but the *Journal's* incessant portrayal of Van Wyck as the "Ice Man" finished him politically.[6]

Hearst, who loved to expose rascals, put serious thought as well as money into these and similar campaigns. Since he never went to bed until at least 2 and did his best thinking at night, he would often wake up Shearn in the wee hours to discuss legal action to prevent some civic injustice. Soon Shearn dropped his own practice and became Hearst's full-time attorney, sometimes running up to Albany to appear before the Assembly and often being aided by other attorneys. Hearst footed the bill, which came to some $25,000 a year.[7]

Having been brought up on California politics, Hearst had a nose for scenting crooked political deals. The club he held over corrupt officials and promoters was an effective one, beneficial to the people. His newspaper contemporaries, however, eyed him as a shallow posturer who played to the grandstand solely for headlines and circulation, and accused him of grabbing credit due others. This last was partly true, for it was the *World* that first attacked the Ramapo water deal before the *Journal* seized on it as if it were its very own, fought it with headlines and injunctions and claimed a "victory for the people" when it was defeated. The fact remained that the *Journal* was a powerful, though brazen, force for political decency, that Hearst gained valuable political experience through this back-door approach, and that many citizens began to regard him as a rich man with sympathy for the masses.

Busy as he was, Hearst was as confirmed a first-nighter as Diamond Jim Brady, and with the same taste for light entertainment. In the fall of 1900, Weber & Fields opened with *Fiddle-dee-dee*, with Lillian Russell again in the cast. Trust-attacker Hearst must have smiled at their likening of trusts and thieves. But Weber & Fields were suddenly overshadowed by a new show up Broadway at the Casino Theater, *Florodora*, in which a sextette of tall, gorgeous damsels, clad in pink walking costumes, black picture hats

[6] George B. McClellan, *The Gentleman and the Tiger*, 166.
[7] *Pearson's Magazine*, Sept., 1906.

and carrying frilly parasols, swished onto the stage and captivated New York for no other reason than that they were utterly stunning. *Florodora* became a craze that would run for hundreds of performances and tour the country. Each member of its original sextette married a millionaire. As a persistent theatergoer and diner-outer, Hearst lived in a gilded world inhabited by legend-making characters such as Diamond Jim, Jesse Lewisohn, Florenz Ziegfeld, J. P. Morgan, Stanford White and Wilson Mizner. Yet he was not of them. Silent, shy, he was insulated by his own reserve from the intimate circles of those who made the jokes, gossip and glamor of the Great White Way. He clung to Brisbane, to Follansbee, to those he knew.

The suave, languid Follansbee, still managing the Hearst Babicora ranch without soiling his hands at it, was a grandee in Mexico and one of New York's most engaging men-about-town. Spending the season from spring until late fall in New York, he joined Brisbane as a guest occupant of Hearst's handsome Lexington Avenue house, which Hearst with excessive coyness called "the shanty." He was Hearst's closest friend, bound to him by an intimacy reaching back to their college days. The two often attended the theater together. Follansbee was the gallant admirer and escort of many a footlight queen, never, however, allowing himself to become seriously involved. He had another passion in which Hearst had not the slightest interest, horse-racing. A member of the Jockey Club and owner of a string of horses which to him were the most fascinating of all creatures, he was often off to Sheepshead Bay, Saratoga or Chicago to watch them race. Occasionally he visited Paris to see the races at Longchamps. It may be that Hearst, with his predilection for supervising his friends, was mildly irked at Follansbee's possession of an independent existence beyond his control, but the pair got on famously when they were together although Follansbee enjoyed the flowing bowl.[8]

When Hearst had plunged into the Bryan 1900 campaign, for the first time taking an active personal role in politics, he had dragged what must have been a protesting Follansbee to the Hoffman House dinner for Bryan. Follansbee, who had no more interest in politics than Hearst did in racing, thought his friend was wasting his time in seeking office.[9] Hearst's inherent ineptitude for the uproarious game of politics was so obvious as to bring to mind a cripple who yearns to become a sprinter. He had none of the magnetism that draws people and wins their admiration. Perhaps his basic handicap was his total lack of the true politician's warm, gregarious liking for people, the spirit of greeting each new stranger as an adventure in comradeship and discovery. Every fiber of his cloistered being rebelled against easy familiarity, handshaking, backslapping, convivial story-telling. Much as he enjoyed vaudeville, and despite his own colorful background, he was offended by off-color stories.

His handshake told much about his instinctive retreat from intimacy. He

[8] N. Y. *Morning Telegraph*, Sept. 13, 1900, and June 21, 1903.
[9] N. Y. *Daily News*, Mar. 3, 1906.

disliked shaking hands. The hand this big, powerful man extended was limp, flaccid, and quickly withdrawn as if regretting the gesture.

With reason, Follansbee regarded Hearst's itch for office as an absurdity bound to end in disappointment. Hearst's own top executives advised him against the move, with the sole exception of Business Manager Carvalho, who felt that his entry into politics would increase the circulation of his newspapers.[10] It would have made no difference if they were unanimous in their disapproval. When the Chief made up his mind, he was adamant.

He made another trip to Europe, doubtless visiting with Orrin Peck, as he invariably did. Peck had come to view Hearst's visits with some apprehension, because Hearst would telegraph him from some point in Europe asking him to join him on tour, taking it for granted that Peck would drop whatever he was doing. This could be inconvenient, for Peck might be in the midst of sittings for a portrait. Yet he enjoyed Hearst's company and also felt a debt of gratitude because of Phoebe Hearst's kindness to him, with the result that he would join the publisher, accompany him for a time, then rush back to Munich to catch up with his work.[11]

Hearst returned in the spring of 1901 bearing more treasures from Europe's castles and galleries. It was said that his mother once remarked, "Every time Willie feels badly, he goes out and buys something."[12] This was more amusing than true. Hearst had a helpless craving for things he saw in shop windows, catalogues and auctions. He was at his happiest when he was buying them. He had this in mind when he acquired the Lexington Avenue house, for in its four floors were plenty of rooms for storing his strange assortment of possessions—suits of armor, mummies, figurines, bronzes, bibelots, a hundred other things.

All of his newspapers were carrying on a relentless campaign against President McKinley as a tool of the trusts. He was building for 1904. In McKinley's failure to attempt any control over the increasingly powerful and unscrupulous business combinations he had a legitimate issue that needed airing. The Hearst attack, however, was vicious and rabble-rousing. The Opper and Davenport cartoons were vengeful. Brisbane described McKinley as "the most hated creature on the American continent."[13] At one point Hearst repented the virulence of his assault enough to send Creelman to Washington to visit the President and "express his regret that his newspapers . . . had been led into excesses of personal attack . . ."[14] McKinley must have wondered about the sincerity of this "regret" when a subsequent editorial in the New York *Evening Journal* attacked him and added the inflammatory line, "If bad institutions and bad men can be got rid of only by killing, then the killing must be done."[15]

When this editorial, probably written by Brisbane, came to Hearst's atten-

[10] *Collier's,* Sept. 29, 1906.   [11] Mrs. J. M. Flint to author.
[12] Aline B. Saarinen, *The Proud Possessors,* 76.
[13] Quoted in *Collier's,* Feb. 18, 1911.   [14] *Pearson's Magazine,* Sept., 1906.
[15] Issue of Apr. 10, 1901.

tion, he had the presses stopped and the incitement to murder removed, so that it did not appear in later editions. But he had a myriad of enemies in Printing House Square who noted the offense and filed it away.

Although the United States in 1901 was said to be wonderfully prosperous, there was a disposition on the part of ordinary citizens to view the situation critically and wish for something better. The new century seemed to foster a more thoughtful attitude toward the nation and its capacity for spreading wealth down among the masses. The high-tariff McKinley administration held the belief that aid to industry would automatically shower benefits among workers and farmers as well. This was not entirely true, for many captains of industry believed that the Lord helped those who helped themselves. The destitution of the pre-war days was gone. Yet wages were low and sweatshop conditions common. Coal miners, for example, averaged only about $600 a year for dirty, dangerous work.

Corporation magnates found it easy to make monopolistic agreements with large competitors, freezing out small enterprises and hiking up prices. Railroads joined the parade, giving secret, favorable rates to large shippers that backed little business men against a wall. The Sherman Anti-Trust Act of 1890 had proved ineffective. The corporations found sharp legal ways to circumvent it, and the McKinley administration had taken no steps to plug the loopholes. In 1901 the nation's industries were moving into an era of bigger and bigger trusts. By the turn of the century, trusts were controlling the prices of hundreds of necessities, from basic materials such as steel, glass, copper, rubber and coal down to whisky, coffins and castor oil.[16] The trusts were a national menace. A groundswell of resentment was rising against them. Hearst, with his campaign against the trusts, was transforming the airy language of Markham's poem into a daily cannonade of headlines demanding reform. His campaign was needed, and would have found few serious critics had it observed some restraint.

McKinley himself that summer had been contemplating some cautious move against the trusts, knowing there would be strong opposition among the Senators of his own party. After a speechmaking tour in the West, he returned to give an address at the Pan-American Exposition at Buffalo on September 5. That night he saw a great fire portrait of himself, arranged by the ubiquitous Henry Pain. The next day he held a public reception in the Temple of Music, with characteristic geniality shaking the hands of hundreds of citizens who filed by. One of the citizens, twenty-eight-year-old Leon Czolgosz, had his right hand covered by a handkerchief. As he stepped up to the President, he whipped off the handkerchief, aimed a pistol and shot McKinley twice before he could be overpowered.

It was first thought that McKinley's wounds were fatal. Hearst was in Chicago, at the office of his *American*, when the news of the shooting came over the wire. Violent as he was editorially, he had an almost feminine revul-

---

[16] Sullivan, *Our Times*, II, 307–14.

sion against physical violence. He was shocked. He also regretted the bitterness of his attacks on McKinley.

"Things are going to be very bad," he said quietly to Charles Edward Russell, his publisher of the *American*.[17]

He worked furiously to soften the wrath he knew would fall on him. He sent policy telegrams to New York and San Francisco, counseling the proper attitude of sorrow and hope. Davenport, the artist assailing the trusts, executed a captionless drawing showing a tender-faced Uncle Sam holding the hand of the bedded McKinley. An editorial, appearing in all Hearst papers, read in part:

> The thoughts and hopes of every American mind are fixed upon the President battling courageously, patiently, for life. Earnestly he longs to live:
> First, and above all, that he may not leave his much loved wife alone behind him.
> Second, that he may devote his days and his strength to the program of national duty and national prosperity which his latest speech outlined. . . .[18]

Three days after the shooting, McKinley rallied and the doctors believed him out of danger. A man wandered into the *Journal* office in New York, saying that he had been at the exposition and had snapped a picture of the attempted assassination. Editors treated him with deference and bought his picture for five dollars. It was foggy, but it showed the gunman at the scene, and the *Journal* published it as a scoop.[19] The optimism of the physicians was proved unfounded when McKinley weakened rapidly and died September 14. Vice President Roosevelt, reached at a remote vacation spot in the Adirondacks, rushed to Buffalo to be sworn in as President.

"It shall be my aim to continue absolutely unbroken the policy of President McKinley," Roosevelt said.[20]

While this calmed the wavering stock market, the truth was that the new President was a man who could follow no policy but his own. Millions of Americans discovered with aching hearts that they had loved the kindly, unassuming McKinley. The journalistic enemies of Hearst, who comprised virtually all those not connected with his newspapers, had already begun an efficient hatchet job on him. They reprinted the *Journal* editorial about "killing must be done," which had appeared five months earlier, and the Bierce quatrain suggesting that the bullet which had killed Governor Goebel was "speeding here to lay McKinley in his bier," which had appeared twenty months earlier. They reprinted anti-McKinley cartoons and editorials featured in the Hearst press.

Going a step farther, they published reports that Czolgosz had in his pocket a copy of the New York *Journal* in which McKinley was assailed. This was a fabrication, but the killer was questioned closely as to whether he had been

---

[17] Mrs. Fremont Older, *op. cit.*, 238.
[19] Coleman, 49–50.
[18] Quoted in *Collier's*, Oct. 13, 1906.
[20] N. Y. *Tribune*, Sept. 16, 1901.

inspired in his deed by the Hearst attacks against McKinley. Czolgosz, a half-demented malcontent, disappointed his questioners by saying that what had provoked him was a lecture given by Emma Goldman, the anarchist.

The organized drive to blame Hearst was proof that he had scarcely a friend in the whole Fourth Estate. True, his anti-McKinley campaign had been inexcusably violent, but some of his newspaper enemies were motivated in part by malice and a desire to hurt a successful and hated competitor. In many cities Hearst was hanged in effigy, often along with Emma Goldman. The Grand Army of the Republic, meeting in Cleveland, passed a resolution "That every member . . . exclude from his household 'The New York Journal,' a teacher of anarchism and a vile sheet . . .'" There were threats against Hearst's life. He took to carrying a pistol, and refused to open packages that came in the mail. In New York, Chicago and San Francisco, crowds seized Hearst papers from newsboys and burned them. A boycott of his papers was started by many libraries and clubs. One of them was the Bohemian Club in San Francisco, which caused Edward Hamilton, Ashton Stevens, Jake Dressler and other *Examiner* men to quit the club in a body.[21] Hearst took the shower of abuse with dignity, but at length he was goaded to reply in an editorial reading in part:

> From coast to coast this newspaper has been attacked and is being attacked with savage ferocity by the incompetent, the failures of journalism, by the kept organs of plutocracy heading the mob. . .
>
> One of the Hearst papers' offenses is that they have fought for the people, and against privilege and class pride and class greed and class stupidity and class heartlessness with more daring weapons, with more force and talent and enthusiasm than any other newspapers in the country. . . .
>
> Note the thrift of the parasitic press . . . It would draw profit from the terrible deed of the wretch who shot down the President . . .[22]

Characteristically, Hearst punished neither Bierce nor anyone else. Bierce later explained that his quatrain had been meant not as an incitement against McKinley but as a warning that the President should be better guarded against possible assassins. Bierce went on:

> Hearst's newspapers . . . had been incredibly rancorous toward McKinley, but no doubt it was my luckless prophecy that cost him tens of thousands of dollars and a growing political prestige. . . . I have never mentioned the matter to him, nor—and this is what I have been coming to—has he ever mentioned it to me. I fancy there must be a human side to a man like that . . .[23]

[21] Coblentz, *Ambrose Bierce* (pamphlet).   [22] N. Y. *Journal,* Sept. 19, 1901.
[23] Neale, *The Life of Ambrose Bierce,* 93.

2. Hearst for Congress

1. GET EXCITED, EVERYBODY!

The papers must print murders as part of the news. Writers of plays and books are not under that compulsion but nevertheless they do "print murders". . . .

People are interested in the fundamentals, love, romance, adventure, tragedy, mystery. The world is not all sweetness and light—not all sunshine. There are storms and darkness. There is suffering and death. Whoever paints the world must paint the deep shadows as well as the bright lights. —Hearst [1]

IN his first message to Congress in December, 1901, President Roosevelt referred angrily to McKinley's assassin as one "inflamed by the teachings of professed anarchists, and probably also by the reckless utterances of those who, on the stump and in the public press, appeal to the dark and evil spirits of malice and greed, envy and sullen hatred. The wind is sowed by the men who preach such doctrines, and they cannot escape their share of responsibility for the whirlwind that is reaped." [2]

No one doubted that he meant Hearst. But the Yellow Kid, as some called him, could take punishment as well as give it. He never doubted his own patriotism—in fact, seemed to think it a shade better than anyone else's. He changed the name of his New York *Morning Journal* to the *American,* a title that became a favorite with him. He continued to attack the trusts, although McKinley's murder had a sobering influence causing the yellowness of his journals to pale a trifle.[3] Still, he was never satisfied with his newspapers unless they made the reader recoil in shock. One critic declared, "An ideal morning edition to [Hearst] would have been one in which the Prince of Wales had gone into vaudeville, Queen Victoria had married her cook, the Pope had issued an encyclical favoring free love, . . . France had declared war on Germany, the President of the United States had secured a divorce in order to marry the Dowager Empress of China . . . and the Sultan of Turkey had been converted to Christianity—all of these being 'scoops' in the form of 'signed statements.' " [4]

Shock was the goal. Hearst had a languid habit, when examining his newspapers, of putting them on the floor and turning the pages with his feet.

[1] From Hearst letter, undated 1933, to Mrs. W. J. Chalmers, Chicago Historical Society.
[2] N. Y. *Tribune,* Dec. 4, 1901. [3] *Collier's,* Oct. 6, 1906.
[4] *Collier's,* Sept. 29, 1906.

He was a speedy reader who missed nothing. If an issue did not have the requisite element of shock, he was unhappy. "This is like reading the telephone book," he often grumbled.[5]

The demand for shock was an endless daily pressure in all the Hearst plants. It came down through Brisbane, Chamberlain, McEwen and others and was felt by every editor, reporter and cub. Staff men were under continuous tension, seeking the angle, the slant, the gimmick that would transform ordinary news into something stupefying. On one occasion Chamberlain came out of his office and was offended because the city room did not have the vital atmosphere of madness.

"Get excited, everybody," he bellowed. "Everybody get excited!" [6]

Reporters nervously shouted for copy boys or hammered at typewriters, and he was satisfied. Delirium was expected in a Hearst shop and was usually present. Although there is no record that Hearst explicitly demanded embroidering of the facts, it was well known that he had few scruples about the sanctity of the news and would cheer a story containing manufactured shock and frown at one containing only dull fact. The pressure for shock caused writers to stretch fact to the bursting point, to stress some angle out of all semblance to its true significance, and often to bolster a commonplace story with delicate fabrication. Murder, adultery and scandal were sure front-page material, and newsmen on other sheets were cynically amused at the ability of the Hearst men to discover "secret diaries" and other astonishing sidelights in these cases which the most diligent search by competing reporters had failed to uncover. To be a Hearst reporter required talents unsought by sober journals—a lively imagination, a fictional sense that could touch up news stories with vivid glints, balanced by a subtle understanding of how far one could go without being accused of fakery. A Hearst headline writer was a specialist in condensed shock, seizing on the most fantastic facet in any story and compressing it into a capsule jolt. Hearst men worked hard, for in addition to their ordinary duties they had to boost the boss and turn a hand at his frequent parades, fireworks spectacles or balloon ascensions. In the Hearst press, Will Irwin observed, "the song of the spheres [became] a screech." [7]

The Hearst art departments likewise improved on fact. In the new century, photographic halftones were gradually replacing line drawings, but photographs were so often unobtainable at deadline time that drawings were still heavily used. It was a byword that the Chief held illustrations to be as important as the text. The *Journal's* art men kept handy a gallery of a few dozen drawings representing different male and female types. If there was no time to send out an artist to make an actual drawing, the newsman would telephone a rough description of the individual in the news—"buck teeth, black mustache, beetling eyebrows, half bald"—and an artist would make minor adjustments on the stock drawing that came nearest and send

[5] *Editor & Publisher*, Mar. 14, 1936.   [6] Lundberg, *Imperial Hearst*, 54.
[7] *Collier's*, Feb. 18, 1911.

it to the engraver. If the subject of a story bore some faint resemblance to a famous person such as John L. Sullivan or General Grant whose likenesses were already on hand, a retouch artist would make appropriate changes on Sullivan or Grant. One problem was to get suitable pictures of victims at the morgue, appearing somewhat as they did in life. Harry Coleman, a *Journal* photographer, always kept a shirtfront and bow tie at the morgue, which he would slip onto a corpse, snap the picture and leave it to a staff artist to retouch the closed eyes.[8]

Thus, regular readers of a Hearst paper would find other newspapers insipid, destitute of the racy detail to which they were accustomed. Conversely, a reader of the sedate New York *Times,* on turning to a Hearst sheet, would be apt to shudder at the discovery of a frantic world he had not dreamed existed.

In the Hearst Sunday supplements, Morrill Goddard was the master of sensation, supplying features about notorious criminals, adventuresses, the vagaries of the insane, odd creatures with two heads and fanciful flights into pseudo-science. Cartoons and comic strips were growing in number. Editorially, Brisbane was supreme because he managed to get something like shock into a department formerly regarded as sleep-producing. Until Brisbane came along, Hearst was dissatisfied with his editorials and often inclined to shrug them off as something expected in a newspaper but a dead weight circulation-wise. As an editorial writer, Abbot was too sensible and prosaic. McEwen was too brilliant and subtle, often going over his readers' heads. Brisbane, on the other hand, tossed astonishing statements at his readers which often were not quite true and yet had the ring of truth, and which were couched in simple, one-syllable words that had a battering-ram impact and could be understood by anyone with a rudimentary vocabulary. Although Hearst never said so, the effect he sought in his papers was the same as that produced by Pain's biggest bombshells, which made a deafening racket before they burst into fiery, fantastic shapes.

On the quieter side, his papers had features devoted to union labor and to feminine interests. The Hearst papers were invariably sympathetic with women, though their sins might be scarlet. The outpourings of Winifred Black were so successful that Hearst hired another sob sister, Dorothy Dix, whose real name was Mrs. Elizabeth Gilmer. Beatrice Fairfax (actually Marie Manning) solved the problems of young lovers with such success that a ditty was born:

> *Just write to Beatrice Fairfax*
> *Whenever you're in doubt;*
> *Just write to Beatrice Fairfax*
> *And she will help you out.*[9]

Hearst's brain sprouted ideas, always dramatic and often extravagant. His men discovered that it was not wise to suggest that any of his ideas were

[8] Coleman, 33, 34–35, 44.   [9] Ishbel Ross, 79.

impossible of achievement. He was apt to blame such an attitude on lack of enterprise or just plain laziness. He could point out that the defeat of the Southern Pacific, or the gas franchise, or the liberation of Evangelina Cisneros, had likewise seemed impossible, but that hard work and ingenuity had accomplished them all. If his men pursued any of his "impossible" ideas with sufficient vigor, and still failed, he was satisfied and would turn to something else equally improbable.

When Mt. Pelee erupted in May, 1902, destroying St. Pierre and killing some 30,000, the Hearst papers busied themselves with their customary relief work. But Hearst became more interested in another eruption nearer home—the strike of 145,000 anthracite miners in Pennsylvania. The miners' union, under swarthy, soft-spoken John Mitchell, had tried for months to negotiate with the coal operators. The operators, whose spokesman was George F. Baer, head of the Reading Railroad, refused to grant recognition to the union by parleying with its president. The operators, he said, would each deal with their own workers, not with the union, declaring, "There cannot be two masters in the management of business." [10]

The operators were unfortunate in their leader. Baer, a Philadelphia millionaire, was dogmatic and patronizing while the miners' President Mitchell was patient and reasonable. The miners were in the status of peons, although the companies had recently raised the price of coal. The hard-coal operators formed a tight little trust, most of them being railroad moguls who illegally had got control of the mines and thus controlled not only the product but its shipment.[11]

The *Journal* and *American* had warmly supported the miners long before the strike, blasting Baer as a "pious pirate" and running Davenport cartoons depicting the coal trust as a hairy Goliath. Hearst took over Madison Square Garden for a mass meeting addressed by Mitchell and Samuel Gompers, president of the American Federation of Labor. He was enthusiastically pro-labor. He was always enthusiastic about things he was *for*, violent about things he was *against*. He had the adolescent's capacity for seeing things in simplest terms—good or bad, beautiful or ugly—shunning the shadings, the modulations, the measured observation that can see two sides to a question. His legal department under Attorney Shearn was quietly collecting evidence of an illegal combination among railways and coal producers.

He was a busy man in 1902, for in addition to these activities he founded his sixth newspaper and became a candidate for office. Yet, like his late father, he never hurried, spoke slowly and had a habit of thrusting his hands in his pockets and lounging lazily in chairs, giving an impression of indolence. This was as unconsciously fraudulent as his outward shyness. The only visible sign of his immense internal drive was his incessant, nervous drumming of his fingers and swinging of his foot as he sat otherwise lax, and the almost fierce concentration he gave to anyone speaking to him.

[10] Sullivan, *Our Times*, II, 423.   [11] Peck, 689–90.

His Chicago *American* had prospered, with a circulation already nearing 300,000. In May he entered the Chicago morning field with the *Morning American,* sending another flying squadron of New York talent to get it started. A few months later, his candidacy for Congress came about in a peculiar manner. Although he was aiming for the Presidency in 1904, only two years off, and he must have realized the necessity for at least one lesser post before seeking the heights, he still shied from the horrors of personal campaigning. Possibly also he had some doubts as to whether he would be acceptable to Charles Francis Murphy, the former dock commissioner who had succeeded Croker as leader of Tammany. Could Murphy have forgotten that the *Journal* had published him as the owner of $40,000 in stock in the ice trust? It may have been a Hearst trial balloon when in September his good friend Arthur Brisbane asked to be nominated as candidate for Congressman in New York's Eleventh District. Murphy was agreeable.[12]

There was also a hint that Hearst was hoping for the Democratic nomination for governor. His newspapers had been tossing posies at William S. Devery, the flamboyant Tammany leader of the Ninth District, a jovial, rednecked mountebank whose term as head of the police under Mayor Van Wyck had seen vice and graft flourish. Devery, as keen a self-publicist as Hearst, kept scrapbooks of clippings about himself and maintained several bands for the purpose of playing his own tune, "Mr. Devery, every, every time." When the state Democratic convention opened at Saratoga late in September, there was a boomlet for Hearst. Brisbane, who was a delegate and rode up in a private car with Boss Murphy, may have had something to do with this, and Devery certainly did. He said of Hearst, "I ain't made no promises to nobody . . . But . . . if his name is mentioned in the convention yer can frame it up that I'll vote for him." [13] His band played a new variation on his unshrinking theme song:

> Mr. Devery, Mr. Devery,
>   At Saratoga he will be in line.
> That state convention
> Must pay attention
>   To Mr. Devery, every, every time.[14]

However, the state convention paid no attention, nominating Bird S. Coler, a Brooklyn broker who had made a good record as controller in New York City. It was immediately after this that Hearst asked Brisbane to step aside so that Hearst himself could be the Eleventh District candidate for Congress —a suggestion Brisbane acceded to as he would to any order from the Chief.[15]

While Hearst had only contempt for Murphy as a tarnished political boss, the support of Tammany was requisite for election. The stout, bespectacled Murphy, owner of a saloon at Second Avenue and Twentieth Street, had gained shrewdness by coming up slowly through the Tammany ranks. For

[12] *Collier's,* Oct. 6, 1906.
[14] N. Y. *Times,* Sept. 30, 1902.
[13] N. Y. *Tribune,* Sept. 30, 1902.
[15] *Collier's,* Oct. 6, 1906.

several years he had been leader of the Twelfth Assembly District, known as the Gas House District. Tough and unpolished, he yet had an organizational ability that would keep him on Tammany's throne for an unprecedented twenty-two years, during all of which time Hearst would be either an ally or a thorn in his side. Murphy in turn doubtless despised Hearst, but Tammany had come on lean times, with a Republican governor in Albany and a Republican President in Washington. Tammany badly needed the powerful support of the Hearst papers to elect its candidate for governor, Coler, and to give Hearst a Congressional seat would be a small price to pay.

Hearst was officially notified of his nomination in a private room in the Hoffman House on October 6. Although there were only a dozen present, he was noticeably uncomfortable as he accepted with thanks and spoke of the country's need for a "leaven of democracy." [16] His Republican opponent was Henry Birrell, a book company executive, but the district was so safely Democratic that Birrell was running only as a matter of principle.

Hearst, who could have won without campaigning, threw himself into the struggle as though he feared a close race. He sought the publicity that a big campaign brings. He wanted to win with a smashing majority that would mark him as a man with a popular following, a rising power among the Democrats who could not be overlooked in 1904. Not trusting Tammany to handle his campaign, he took charge of it himself. Lithographs of Hearst appeared on ashcans and billboards in the Eleventh District, and Democratic clubs in the area were on the *qui vive*.

Out in San Francisco, his *Examiner* the previous year had elected big, handsome Eugene E. Schmitz, a theater violinist and president of the musicians' union, as mayor. Schmitz, who owed Hearst his office, gladly traveled east to campaign for his sponsor. With him came former Governor James H. Budd of California, an old Hearst ally against the Southern Pacific. Schmitz and Budd arrived on the Twentieth Century Limited and put up in style at the Waldorf-Astoria. Other shock troops arrived from Chicago—Peter Dienhart, George J. Thompson and John Daly, Windy City union leaders who would speak for Hearst.[17] Boss Murphy, seeing all these reinforcements to help Hearst win a seat in Congress that was already assured, must have realized that he had a larger goal in mind than Congress.

II. DEATH IN MADISON SQUARE

WITH the coming of chill fall weather the coal strike assumed serious proportions. In New York City, the price of anthracite, normally five dollars a ton, rose steadily until it reached twenty dollars and was often unobtainable at that price. In the tenement districts, the poor were queuing at coal yards to buy it by the pail. There was fear of riots. The coal operators had trainloads of coal on sidings, keeping it out of the market on the theory that the shortage

[16] N. Y. *Times*, Oct. 7, 1902.   [17] N. Y. *Evening Journal*, Oct. 20, 21, 1902.

would bring pressure against the miners to end the strike. Hearst managed to get a few carloads of coal, which his men sold to the poor at the original rate.[1] His papers assailed the operators daily for their refusal to negotiate with the union. Shearn had gathered evidence of illegal monopoly among the mine owners and had filed a petition with Attorney General Philander Knox to take action against them. Hearst wrote personally to President Roosevelt on October 4 that the Shearn petition was all he needed to act on, saying, "I am IN POSSESSION OF DOCUMENTARY EVIDENCE establishing such [illegal] combination . . ."[2]

Roosevelt, who felt he needed a constitutional amendment to act against the trusts, was working to solve the crisis by using nothing more than the prestige of his office. He managed to get Baer and his fellow operators to meet with Mitchell in his presence. He slowly wore down Baer's arrogant refusals, got J. P. Morgan to exert his powerful financial influence, and eventually persuaded the operators to agree to arbitration.[3]

It was a victory for the miners and for Roosevelt. Hearst, who had worked energetically to defeat the operators by lawsuit only to have the President accomplish it by persuasion, was disgruntled. This was the first of many times that Roosevelt would steal a march on him. He nevertheless took credit for the settlement, publishing a facsimile of his letter to Roosevelt under the heading, "THE LETTER THAT BROUGHT THE COAL BARONS TO THEIR SENSES AND FORCED THE ENDING OF THE STRIKE."[4] He ran a Davenport cartoon showing the coal trust gorilla flattened and helpless, with a little girl, a miner's daughter, walking over his recumbent form carrying a full coal scuttle. He published facsimiles of letters from John Mitchell and other union leaders thanking him for the aid of his newspapers. He boomed the arrival of Schmitz, stressing that "Mayor Schmitz comes to tell the New York voters of the great debt which the organized workingmen of San Francisco owe to Mr. Hearst and the San Francisco *Examiner*."[5] Hearst indeed had worked for labor, and he wanted to be sure that this was understood. He wanted praise, recognition. He wanted to be President.

To Hearst, with his faith in bigness and noise as necessary ingredients in propaganda, nothing could compare with Madison Square Garden for a rousing political rally. He rented the great arena for the night of October 27 to stage a mass meeting for the Democratic candidates, thereby drawing the thanks of Boss Murphy for his generosity, Murphy's praise being duly noted in the *Journal*. Henry Pain's fireworks experts were called into service, bands were hired, banners painted, parades organized, and speakers detailed to address crowds in the square who could not get into the Garden.

As always, Hearst contrived to combine advertisements for his newspapers with political fanfare. As he and his Democratic colleagues entered the

[1] Mrs. Fremont Older, *op. cit.*, 247. [2] N. Y. *Evening Journal*, Oct. 14, 1902.
[3] Theodore Roosevelt, *Autobiography*, 532–35. [4] *Evening Journal*, Oct. 14, 1902
[5] The same, Oct. 20.

Garden at 8 P.M., the tower was covered by Davenport's and Opper's cartoons reproduced in electric lights, one of them showing the now famous "trust Goliath." Inside, over the speaker's platform, was an electric sign repeating the motto printed daily in the New York *American:* "Congress Must Control the Trusts." [6] Hearst's own man, Max Ihmsen, had trouble quieting the crowd so that he could introduce his boss, the first speaker. Even opposition newspapers admitted that Hearst drew an ovation. It must have warmed his heart to see and hear 10,000 people waving small American flags and cheering him, at the same time as his fear of crowds smote him and his knees shook at the prospect of addressing them. As a speaker, he was cursed by a soft voice that did not carry, but his short talk was carefully prepared and he made his points with emphasis and wit.

He was not so foolish, he said, as to believe every Republican a rascal and every Democrat a saint. But the Republicans had come to be the tools of the trusts.

> The trusts have received so many privileges from the Republican party, and the Republican party in turn has received so many favors from the trusts, that a bond has grown between them, uniting them like the Siamese twins, and you cannot stick a pin in the trusts without hearing a shriek from the Republican party; and you cannot stick a pin into the Republican party without hearing a roar from the trusts.[7]

The *Times* reported, "Mr. Hearst's voice is not of great penetrating quality and could not be heard by one-tenth of the vast assemblage, but the crowd was sympathetic and sat patiently, those in the rear and entirely out of earshot applauding vigorously whenever they saw those in front doing likewise. Considerable laughter was created by one foghorn voice bellowing, 'Oh, how I wish you had my voice.'" [8]

Among the other speakers were Coler, David B. Hill, former Vice President Adlai Stevenson, Budd and Schmitz. The last two did not forget their friend. Budd showered praise on Hearst for his fight against the trusts, and Schmitz extolled his support of organized labor.

"It has come to the attention of your brothers in the West," Schmitz said, "that their dear and always devoted friend, one who has stood by them in times of greatest need, is a candidate for Congress from the Eleventh District, and they therefore requested me to make this journey and ask their brother-workers in New York to stand by and support their friend and the friend of organized labor all over the United States, William Randolph Hearst." [9]

Outside, the Chicagoans, Dienhart and Daly, were addressing crowds in favor of the Democrats, particularly Hearst. A Hearst parade was snaking around the square, carrying transparencies, one reading, "IN THE MIDST OF PROSPERITY WE ARE COAL-LESS, PORKLESS AND PENNILESS." The demonstrations seemed to place more importance in the Congressional

---

[6] *Evening Journal,* Oct. 28, 1902.
[8] The same.

[7] N. Y. *Times,* Oct. 28, 1902.
[9] *Evening Journal,* Oct. 28, 1902.

candidate from the Eleventh District than in the candidate for governor or
any of the other Congressional or judicial candidates. The *Journal* next day
took the same line, giving Hearst's name unabashed prominence in headlines
and in occasional laudatory mention such as, "When the coal strike was mentioned the meeting was interrupted by salvos of cheering for John Mitchell
and William Randolph Hearst." [10]

Unfortunately for Hearst, Ronald Molineux, a social lion accused of a
particularly piquant murder, was on trial at the time. True to the inflexible
Hearst classification of story interest, Molineux got the front page and the
Hearst Garden demonstration was pushed back to Page 3, which it appropriated in toto. But in the final days before election, the *Journal* made up for this
with gratuitous puffs such as the following:

"I'M FOR A TRUE AMERICAN"

John W. Cochrane . . . an old G. A. R. man, caused a sensation this
afternoon by walking through the Fifth Avenue Hotel corridor [Republican
headquarters] with a picture of W. R. Hearst pinned alongside his army
badge.

"What's up?" queried one of his Republican friends; "you have a picture
of Mr. Hearst on your coat—do you know it?"

"You bet I do!" said Mr. Cochrane emphatically. "I am a Hearst man. He
has done more for the people than any other man in New York. I am for
W. R. Hearst in spite of everything, and I am proud of it." [11]

Some few were offended by the excesses of the Hearst publicity. One
speaker at a Republican rally sneered, "Fireworks and fancy cravats do not
make a statesman." [12] The *American* and *Journal* announced imperturbably
that there would be more Hearst fireworks in Madison Square on election
night and that "Professor" Leo Stevens would ascend in a balloon and announce the winners by "flashing colored lights."

Hearst won easily, as did most of the Democratic candidates. Coler lost
in a close race to the Republican incumbent, Governor Benjamin Odell. But
the crowd of some 40,000 who massed in Madison Square that night saw
something more than election results. Shortly before 10 P.M., a nine-inch
fireworks bomb ignited prematurely inside a cast-iron mortar. The mortar
burst, and a whole pile of bombs alongside exploded with a report like
heavy artillery. A band nearby stopped playing as the square rang with the
screams of the injured and dying. Broken glass rained down on sidewalks
from windows shattered by the blast. Stevens and his men in the balloon
were so unnerved that they brought their craft down. The square suddenly
looked like a scene of battle. A policeman named Shea had his head blown
off. Twelve persons were killed outright, six more died later, and newspaper
estimates of the number of injured ranged from fifty to 100.[13]

At the *American* and *Journal* offices, the worried editors played it safe,

[10] The same.   [11] *Evening Journal*, Nov. 1, 1902.   [12] N. Y. *Times*, Oct. 30, 1902.
[13] *Times, Herald*, Nov. 5, 6, 1902.

knowing that since it was a Hearst-sponsored celebration, some blame might attach to him. The early editions of the *American* made no mention of it at all. Not until Hearst himself arrived at the office was the story used, well back from the front page, with no indication of his connection with it. The *Evening Journal* described it as a "deplorable fireworks disaster" and said that John Craig, one of Pain's foremen, was being held in $10,000 bail.[14]

The other papers made no secret of Hearst's sponsorship but wisely forbore to blame him. "Neither the District Attorney nor the Coroner believes culpability attaches to any degree to those who paid for the fireworks display," the *Herald* commented.[15]

Yet it appeared that responsibility would have to be placed somewhere. District Attorney William Travers Jerome was puzzled, fearing that the onus might fall on the city itself. While Hearst was easily the biggest user of fireworks, the Republicans had used them as well. A permit had been granted for the demonstration that ended so tragically. There had been warnings that the city should be more stringent in its control of such spectacles, for within the past week there had been two fireworks accidents, once when a rocket started a blaze on the roof of a Broadway building, another when a mortar exploded and injured three persons, one of them losing an eye.

Hearst would be dogged for decades by lawsuits resulting from the disaster. It cast a pall over his triumph, and yet the triumph was undeniably there. He got almost three times the votes of his Republican opponent, his plurality being a record 15,800. He led the regular Democratic ticket by 3,500 votes, enough to make Boss Murphy take notice that the Hearst methods were successful. Hearst wrote a signed editorial headed, "Labor—Democracy's Natural Ally," saying that the election clearly showed that the Democrats must ally themselves more closely with the working people.[16] The *American* and the *Journal* and *Das Morgen Journal* found ways to get the Hearst name into headlines, such as "HEARST VOTE BANNER ONE OF CITY." Mayor Schmitz was quoted as giving Hearst credit for the many Democratic Congressional victories, adding something debatable:

"There is no question in anyone's mind," he said, "regarding the sincerity of Mr. Hearst." [17]

There were signs that Hearst was a little drunk with acclaim, with cheers, with victory—a shy man quaffing the heady rewards of an ordeal he had feared. To him, his flattering vote was a vindication of his campaign of personal publicity. The vision of the White House was clearer and closer. Governor Budd, on leaving for California, was quoted in the *Journal* as booming him for the Presidency.

"I say it was Hearst and Tammany," Budd said. "As former Vice President Stevenson said after personally witnessing the wild enthusiasm, 'Hearst is a name to conjure with.' Had the able and venerable Vice President witnessed the scene in that great labor meeting on Sunday night, when the name of

[14] Nov. 5 issue.   [15] Nov. 6 issue, 1902.   [16] *Evening Journal,* Nov. 6.
[17] The same, Nov. 7.

William Randolph Hearst was coupled with the Presidency, he would probably have added, 'and it is the only one.' " [18]

This was suggesting that Hearst was the only candidate in sight for 1904—a sweeping statement about a man who had just won his first election and had yet to prove himself in office.

No savant as yet has satisfactorily explained the complex mental and emotional upheaval taking place within a man seized by the desire to become President. The explaining would be harder and the symptoms graver with Hearst, who, when he wanted anything, wanted it badly and quickly. His yearning for the Presidency rose to a passion that colored almost everything he said and did for years. Now that he was a Congressman-elect, however, he had a whole year to wait before his first session even began.

Doubtless he was consumed by impatience. It is a safe assumption that Max Ihmsen was broadcasting literature telling the nation's Democratic clubs of the remarkable Hearst popularity, and at the same time sounding out party leaders about a Hearst-for-President boom. A crucial figure in this budding campaign was William Jennings Bryan. It was unlikely that Bryan, as a two-time loser, would be nominated in 1904. Yet he was the most powerful figure in the party, whose influence could be decisive. Hearst had supported him faithfully during his two campaigns, both with publicity and with funds, and now he needed his help. Two weeks after the New York election, Bryan sailed for Europe as a Hearst foreign writer. With him went the *Journal's* Charles Michelson, doubtless to help him with his writing. While abroad, Bryan wrote a series of articles for the Hearst press for which he was paid handsomely, and which might incline him to look with favor on Hearst in 1904.[19]

Attorney Shearn was kept hammering at the coal-railroad trust, seeking to get the state as well as the federal government to act. He appeared in Albany to give evidence of "an absolute monopoly" in the sale of anthracite.[20] Some time after the election, Hearst went to California to visit his mother and look after his *Examiner.* At Berkeley was rising a new mining building Mrs. Hearst gave to the university as a memorial to her late husband. She was so preoccupied with the university that she lived in Berkeley a part of the time, giving teas for students and professors, and she kept urging her son to make some handsome gift to the institution. He finally acceded, giving funds for an open-air Greek theater.

Hearst made his customary sentimental trip to Santa Clara County to visit his aged grandmother, who still called him "Willie." He told Drusilla Apperson something he had not yet told his mother—that he intended to marry Millicent Willson. He knew his mother would be seriously upset, and when he later gave her the news, she was.[21] Strong-willed Phoebe Hearst had still not given up hope of controlling her strong-willed son.

Returning to New York, the Congressman-elect was arrested for speeding

[18] The same.   [19] Long, *Bryan,* 162, 181.   [20] N. Y. *Tribune,* Jan. 27, 1903.
[21] Mrs. J. M. Flint to author.

on Riverside Drive. Policeman McAdam, who made the arrest, said, "Mr. Hearst ran his automobile from Ninety-eighth Street to Ninety-fifth Street in thirty seconds." According to a newspaper account, "Mr. Hearst said that he was not running his vehicle any faster than usual"—an unwise defense implying persistent violation.[22]

A traffic fine was of small moment with his marriage looming. He summoned Orrin Peck from Munich to be his best man, and also invited his friend, ex-Governor Budd of California. Although Hearst never went to church, he regarded himself as an Episcopalian. On April 28, 1903—the day before his fortieth birthday—he was married to Millicent Willson in the rose-bedecked chantry of Grace Church at Broadway and Tenth Street, Bishop Henry Codman Potter performing the ceremony. Anita Willson was her sister's bridesmaid. It was a small affair, with only some thirty present, among them Brisbane and Carvalho. Phoebe Hearst, who was said to be ill in California, sent the bride a "beautiful set of emeralds," while the bridegroom's gift was a rope of pearls. Journalist Hearst gave small cooperation to his own *American* and *Journal* photographers. He refused to let them into the church. They waited outside with cameras cocked, but the couple dashed out and entered their waiting carriage so quickly that only one blurred print was obtained.[23]

In the *American's* story of the event, tucked back on page 9, Hearst's age was not stated. That of his bride was given as twenty-one. No mention was made of the former Miss Willson's stage career, nor that of her father, who was described as "president of the American Advance Music Company." [24]

After a wedding breakfast at the Waldorf, the couple hurried to catch the 3 o'clock sailing of the *Kaiser Wilhelm II*. Even on his honeymoon Hearst liked to have companions. Governor Budd was also scheduled to sail with them and Hearst had reserved a stateroom for him, but Budd could not make the trip. By chance, lanky Fremont Older, editor of the San Francisco *Bulletin*, was on the liner with his young wife. They had a modestly priced stateroom near the stern that magnified the ship's roll so that on the second day out Cora Older was miserably seasick.

Older, who had worked briefly for the *Examiner*, met Hearst on deck. Although the two men had often hurled political brickbats at each other, they were on friendly terms. Learning of Mrs. Older's illness, Hearst insisted that the Olders take over Budd's luxurious suite—a move that swiftly cured her.[25]

As the *Kaiser Wilhelm* neared England, a telegraphic message was relayed to Hearst from the Lizard:

> The City of New York has been sued for $25,000 in the New York County Supreme Court by Solomon Landau, administrator, for damages for the death of George Landau, by your fireworks explosion in Madison Square on

[22] N. Y. *Tribune*, Mar. 31, 1903.   [23] Coleman, 60.
[24] N. Y. *American*, Apr. 29, 1903.   [25] Mrs. Older to author, Oct. 18, 1959.

election night, November 4 last, and notifies you to defend this action.
—George L. Rives, Corporation Counsel.[26]

It was only one of many lawsuits arising from the accident which Hearst would defend until he was an old man and in which the claims at one time were said to total $3,000,000. He and his bride visited Paris, bought an automobile and were off for a tour of northern Italy, one of his favorite sights being the gothic Cathedral at Milan.

For two years Hearst had contemplated entering the magazine publishing field. As an automobile enthusiast and probably the first Congressman to be arrested for speeding, he was interested in the British magazine *The Car* when he saw it in London. He cabled Carvalho in New York to start one like it at once, called *Motor*—the first of a long line of Hearst magazines.[27] An indefatigable traveler, he had hardly returned home with his bride when he took her to Mexico, no place for motoring. They rode in a private car to Mexico City, where they were received with honors by the aging President Porfirio Diaz, who had been a good friend of George Hearst and was now a good friend of Jack Follansbee.[28] They also visited Hearst's Babicora ranch, where 48,000 Hearst cattle roamed a million Hearst acres under the supervision of 150 Hearst vaqueros. The next stop was the Hacienda in California, where Phoebe Hearst, for the first time, met Mrs. William Randolph Hearst —a meeting that must have contained elements of unspoken drama.

Then Hearst was ready to return and save his country from the predators of great wealth.

[26] N. Y. *Tribune*, June 9, 1903.   [27] Mrs. Fremont Older, *op. cit.*, 255.
[28] Princess Pignatelli to author, Nov. 3, 1959.

3. Hearst for President

SOME observers ungallantly suggested that Hearst's marriage came about because his political advisers warned him that voters were suspicious of gay bachelors and much more prone to send respectable family men to the White House.[1] This was an injustice to the former Millicent Willson, a woman of great beauty and talent who would long be his helpmate. Yet, since he had kept company with Miss Willson for some years, it is not impossible that the marriage, contracted solely for love, was seen coincidentally to enhance his Presidential plans. The Hearst couple settled down in the Lexington Avenue house, which meant that Brisbane and Follansbee had to find other quarters. The indispensable George Thompson stayed on.

At forty, Hearst had gained a trifle in weight, but he was not flabby. He did not smoke, avoided spirits, and was a moderate eater. Tall, robust and healthy, with a clear, unlined complexion, he looked impressive if not downright handsome. The Presidential aspirant sartorially was a changed man. He gave ear to the gibes about his gay dress and thenceforth switched to black broadcloth and a broad-brimmed black hat, the sober garb of the statesman. "He used to wear checked suits and rather loud ties and avoid personal publicity," one reporter noted. "Now he craves it and wears a frock coat on the hottest days." [2]

He dropped the curt "W. R. Hearst" and thereafter called himself "William Randolph Hearst," which had more dignity. He wanted to erase any lingering trace of the man about town and build a firm public picture of grave concern about national issues. He traveled to California again in September, 1903, to speak in Berkeley at the dedication of the Greek theater he had given the university.[3] Some critics suggested that he would never have coughed up the money had he not believed it a publicity- and vote-getting gesture.

He started publication of Hearst Paper No. 7, the Los Angeles *Examiner,* and was anxious to acquire more for the dissemination of his theories. He made ready for action by hiring a private political secretary, quiet, bespectacled Lawrence J. O'Reilly, who had proved himself in similar posts under Brisbane and Carvalho. Ihmsen had been working hard, for when the New York Democratic State Committee met in Albany that fall, a group of boomers tried to get the committee to endorse Hearst for the Presidential nomination. State Leader Hill squelched any such early politicking, possibly con-

[1] Lundberg, 100.   [2] *Collier's,* Oct. 6, 1906.   [3] N. Y. *Tribune,* Sept. 25, 1903.

cealing surprise that an obscure Congressman-elect should have such exalted hopes.[4] The invaluable Ihmsen was busy forming William Randolph Hearst Clubs all over the country, recruiting many members from the Democratic clubs with which he was in constant contact.

In November, Hearst attended his first session of Congress. He had leased a handsome dwelling in Lafayette Square formerly occupied by Secretary of War Elihu Root, right across Pennsylvania Avenue from the White House. He would not have far to move if his hopes were realized. The Democratic party was crying for a leader to shepherd it out of the wilderness. The eyes of Congress and of scores of Washington correspondents were on this oddity from New York, this millionaire who pleaded the cause of the masses and was so little known outside of his own city. The impression he made on his Democratic colleagues and on the press was of first importance in the furtherance of his hopes. It was expected that he would conduct tactful missionary work to add to his friends and supporters. To everyone's surprise, he did almost everything wrong.

He badly wanted a place on the House Labor Committee. When the Democratic minority leader, John Sharp Williams of Mississippi, told him regretfully that the slate had already been made, Hearst seemed to accept it with good nature. But he sent telegrams to union leaders asking their support on the issue. Meetings were held and messages from union officials all over the country poured in on Williams and Speaker Joe Cannon asking that Hearst be named on the Labor Committee. Williams was annoyed at this backhand pressure. He stood firm, but one of his appointees gracefully withdrew from the committee in Hearst's favor. Hearst also wanted membership in the Ways and Means Committee, but did not get it. At the very start he had alienated Williams, one of the most powerful of Democrats, and soon they were at loggerheads.[5]

Hearst's enemies counted him a shallow demagogue, denying him any shred of sincerity. On the contrary, he sincerely felt that the country needed him, that he alone among the Democrats knew the answers to the nation's ills and could be elected in 1904. Far from having no deeply felt political aims, he had too many of them and pressed them too vehemently for a candidate who would have been expected to skirt risky, controversial issues. His broad political objectives, with few exceptions, were either sound or popular or both, some being well ahead of the times.

He was for control of the trusts, which badly needed controlling. He favored legislation to end the "secret rebate" evil among the railroads that was so prevalent and so destructive to free competition. He wanted the eight-hour work day, and government ownership of railroads, telegraphs and possibly mines. He believed in a graduated income tax. He sought the popular election of United States Senators, feeling that this would make them more responsible to the people and less subservient to "big business." A

[4] *Tribune*, Sept. 5, 1903.
[5] Charles Willis Thompson, *Party Leaders of the Time*, 239–40.

moderate imperialist, he favored the Nicaragua or Panama Canal, a big navy, and expansion of the academies at West Point and Annapolis. Like his mother, he was a fanatic on the subject of better public schools.[6]

Still dogged by shyness, Hearst made no speeches in the House and few in committee. He made his presence felt by proxy as the silent leader of a half-dozen sympathetic Representatives, one of them Edward Livernash of California, a brilliant eccentric who had gone into Congress from his previous post as political writer for Hearst's San Francisco *Examiner*. This group of men, who soon became known as the "Hearst Brigade," accepted him as their leader, took instructions from him and presented the resolutions he sponsored. In this oddly oblique way, he introduced a number of progressive measures, among them an amendment to the Sherman Anti-Trust Act to give it more teeth, an inquiry into the coal-railroad trust, and an amendment to give the Interstate Commerce Commission power to fix railroad rates.

He often had the help of his attorney, Shearn, in drawing up bills. Through his staff of Washington correspondents, he saw to it that they were publicized in his papers, although few were passed. Being bored with routine House meetings, he was a conspicuous absentee, answering rollcall only nine times in the first two sessions. Speaker Cannon joked that he did not know Hearst by sight.[7] It was the old story: Hearst, with his sense of possessiveness, was interested only in his own program. The New York *Times* Washington correspondent noted: "He never cared to attend except when something bearing on his own definite line of policy was involved. He was on hand when labor bills were up; any chance to advance his socialistic principles did not find him idle." [8] Behind the scenes, and through his control of the Hearst Brigade, he was a hard worker in his own sphere.

Another reason for his absences was his preoccupation with his Presidential campaign—a pursuit that made conservatives come near foaming at the mouth. Many large volumes could be filled with nothing but published attacks on Hearst over his long career, and they would cover an encyclopaedic gamut of bitter, libelous vituperation. It was his aspiration for the highest office that first brought nationwide invective down on his head. It ranged from the vulgarly vicious to the coldly intellectual. An example of the former appeared in the San Francisco *News-Letter* in a crude parody of Markham's poem called "The Man With the Dough":

> *Bowed by the weight of infamy he leans*
> *Upon his tub, and gazes at his gold,*
> *The emptiness of folly on his face,*
> *And on his back the brand of good men's hate.*
> *Who made him dead to decency and truth—*
> *A thing that feels not, and can never think,*
> *Stupid and dull, own brother to the ass?*
> *Who gave his face its vacuous, leering grin?*

[6] *Pearson's Magazine*, Sept., 1906.   [7] The same.   [8] Thompson, 234.

Whose was the hand that shaped those trembling lips,
Slobbering with weakness, tremulous with vice? . . . .[9]

The coldly intellectual appeared in Hearst's old enemy, the New York *Evening Post:*

> . . . It is not simply that we revolt at Hearst's huge vulgarity; at his front of bronze; at his shrieking unfitness mentally, for the office which he sets out to buy. All this goes without saying. There never has been a case of a man of such slender intellectual equipment, absolutely without experience in office, impudently flaunting his wealth before the eyes of the people and saying, "Make me President." This is folly. This is to degrade public life, but there is something darker and more fearful behind. It is well known that this man has a record which would make it impossible for him to live through a Presidential campaign—such gutters would be dragged, such sewers would be laid open . . . It is not a question of politics, but of character. An agitator we can endure; an honest radical we can respect; a fanatic we can tolerate; but a low voluptuary trying to sting his jaded senses to a fresh thrill by turning from private to public corruption is a new horror in American politics. To set the heel of contempt upon it must be the impulse of all honest men.[10]

A copy of this editorial, written by Rollo Ogden, was sent to every editor, clergyman and teacher in the Democratic South. This was libel in the grand manner, a virtual challenge to Hearst to sue if he dared. No record comes to light that he went to court for this or any other assault on his character. Doubtless he regretted the openness of his affair with Tessie Powers and possibly other lubricities which now came back to haunt him. His own careless past made him vulnerable, stripped him of the power to fight back. But he kept his eye on the White House, beginning a flirtation with Thomas E. Watson, the brilliant, half-mad Georgia Populist.

Watson, who had a large following in the South, in 1903 had written a biography of Thomas Jefferson—Hearst's political paragon—and had dedicated it to him: "Because he is to-day working with splendid ability along the same lines which Mr. Jefferson marked a hundred years ago, I dedicate this book to WILLIAM RANDOLPH HEARST." In March, 1904, Watson praised Hearst's candidacy in a public speech. Soon thereafter he received several letters from Arthur Brisbane begging him to accept a high post on the New York *American,* where he could aid the Hearst campaign.[11]

Watson, a 127-pound dynamo with wild prejudices, was a master orator and had a trenchant pen. Hearst, who needed support in the South, doubtless hoped that Watson would invest him with some of his Dixie popularity. Watson journeyed to New York and lunched with Brisbane at Delmonico's. One of Brisbane's odd beliefs was that blue eyes were the eyes of genius. Both Caesar and Napoleon, he said, had blue eyes. Mr. Hearst had blue eyes, and he was glad to see that Watson did also.

[9] San Francisco *News-Letter,* May 28, 1904.   [10] N. Y. *Evening Post,* Mar. 1, 1904.
[11] C. Vann Woodward, *Tom Watson, Agrarian Rebel,* 355–56.

"Suppose you take Mr. Hearst's morning *American* at $10,000 a year," Brisbane proposed. "You could come down to the office once a day, look over a few exchanges, dictate an editorial, and then have the remainder of your time for your more serious literary labors. If within one year you can make a success out of the *American,* you can practically name your own salary thereafter. Of course, if you don't make the *American* a success, Hearst will have no further use for you." [12]

The blue-eyed Watson decided that he would dislike living in New York, and the deal fell through. Hearst's luck was even poorer when he had a chat with Franklin K. Lane, a prominent California journalist and reform politician, whom he asked for his support. Lane was still burning because he had narrowly missed election as governor of California in 1902 and laid his defeat to the antagonism of Hearst's San Francisco *Examiner.* Hearst disclaimed blame for this, but the conversation, according to Lane, ended on a tart note.

"Mr. Lane," Hearst said, "if you ever wish anything that I can do, all you will have to do will be to send me a telegram asking, and it will be done."

"Mr. Hearst," Lane replied as he left, "if you ever get a telegram from me asking you to do anything, you can put the telegram down as a forgery." [13]

Hearst took a brief respite to hurry home to New York to become a father. On April 10, 1904, his first child was born, a son named George after the late Senator. Hearst saw his wife and child, sent a joyful message to his mother in California, and soon returned to Washington, where on April 22, for the first time, he opened his mouth in Congress.

This was not before the House but before the Judiciary Committee, where he asked for action on one of his pet bills, that calling for an investigation of the coal-railroad monopoly. Attorney Shearn had worked on this for two years and had succeeded in getting a report supporting his stand from the United States Attorney for the Southern District of New York. Hearst had spent more than $60,000 of his own money in the probe, but still Attorney General Knox was quiescent.

Six of the railroads carrying coal to tidewater from the Pennsylvania fields, Hearst said, not only had illegal agreements with coal operators but owned outright at least eleven mines. They had watered their stock at immense profit, then had raised the price of coal fifty cents a ton, netting themselves another $20,000,000 in annual profit.

"The Attorney General has been brooding over that evidence like an old hen on a doorknob for eighteen months," Hearst said. "He has not acted in any way, and won't let anyone take it away from him . . . What I want is to have this evidence come before Congress and if the Attorney General does not report it, as I am very sure he won't, as he has refused to do any-

[12] William W. Brewton, *The Life of Thomas E. Watson,* 299–300.
[13] Anne W. Lane and Louise Herrick Wall (editors), *The Letters of Franklin K. Lane,* 40.

thing of the kind, I then wish that a committee of seven Representatives be appointed with power to take the evidence. . . ." [14]

The Congressman tried hard, but failed. This was the very sort of legislation that Roosevelt himself had in mind. There can be little doubt that there was a conspiracy in Washington, overt or implied, to block anything Hearst wanted, even if it was something good. Hatred tied his hands in Congress. Roosevelt and others considered him partly responsible for the murder of McKinley. They were repelled by his noisy newspapers, his personal publicity, his presumptuous campaign for the Presidential nomination, and by the swelling cloud of rumor about his moral lapses. He might get votes from his constituents, but he would never get a helping hand in Congress. He was the House pariah. Even the regular Democrats disowned him. Inherently incapable of cooperating with others, he ran his own show regardless of how many party-line Democratic toes he stepped on. He was a political maverick, a reformer with his own program, determined to bulldoze it through or to blazon the infamy of those who balked him. He showed little interest in measures put forward by the regular Democrats. He sought to run Congress as he ran his New York *American* or *Journal*, a scheme veteran legislators resisted. For a freshman Congressman to read political lessons to graybeard Democrats was poor policy for one who needed to make friends. He soon quarreled with all the party leaders in the House, and came to be regarded with detestation by regular Democrats as a professional radical leading a small pack of obedient terriers whose constant snapping was demoralizing to party discipline.[15]

To old-line Democrats, the Hearst Presidential boom, now in full cry, was the joke of the new century. Yet no leader had come to the fore who seemed likely to give the puissant T. R. a semblance of a race. There was talk of dragging old ex-President Cleveland out of retirement for another try. Some preferred Judge Alton B. Parker of New York. There was a host of dark horses. The sneers at Hearst changed to concern when it was seen that he had strong support in many parts of the country. Platoons of Hearst agents were traveling from state to state in a surprisingly successful search for delegates at the coming convention, and there were charges that money was doing a large part of the persuading. Just when it was needed for the campaign, Hearst Paper No. 8, the Boston *American*, began publication. A Bay State supporter said, "Mr. Hearst's fight has been helped along greatly by the starting of his paper in Boston." [16] His candidacy affected his journalism somewhat. He ordered his editors to tone down on sensationalism and to refrain from using such words as "seduction," "rape," "abortion," "criminal assault" and "born out of wedlock." [17]

In a story headed, "HEARST OFFERS CASH," the Republican New York

[14] N. Y. *Tribune*, Apr. 23, 1904.   [15] Thompson, 236.
[16] N. Y. *Tribune*, Mar. 30, 1904.   [17] Moses Koenigsberg, *King News*, 385.

Tribune spread the money rumor, quoting an unnamed "Hearst supporter" as saying:

> The argument that is cutting most ice is that Hearst is the only candidate who is fighting the trusts fearlessly and who would use all the powers of government to disrupt them if he were elected. The Hearst men say that if Hearst is nominated, he and his immediate friends will contribute to the Democratic National Committee the sum of $1,500,000. This, it is urged, would relieve the national committee from the necessity of appealing to the trust magnates. The alternative to this is that if a conservative candidate is nominated the national committee will have to appeal to the trusts for their campaign funds, and in doing this will incur obligations which would make a Democratic victory absolutely fruitless. . . . the average Democratic politician, especially in the country districts, is hungry for the spoils of office. It has been a long time since he has seen any campaign money, and when the proposition is laid down to him as the friends of Mr. Hearst are laying it down these days he is quite likely to get aboard the Hearst bandwagon.[18]

If anything, the conservative Democrats were more opposed to Hearst than the Republicans. In his own state of New York, the two Democratic bellwethers, State Leader Hill and Tammany Boss Murphy, were saying nothing openly against Hearst but industriously boosting their own favorites, Murphy being for Cleveland and Hill for Parker. They had lost twice with the radical Bryan, and were having no part of Hearst, whom they considered more radical than Bryan. But his increasing strength in the West looked menacing. It caused Henry Watterson to sound a blast in his Louisville *Courier-Journal*:

> . . . Does any sane Democrat believe that Mr. Hearst, a person unknown even to his constituency and his colleagues, without a word or act in the public life of his country, past or present, that can be shown to be his to commend him, could by any possibility be elected President of the United States? But there is a Hearst barrel . . .[19]

More splenetic was Senator Edward Carmack of Tennessee, a Parker man. ". . . the nomination of Hearst would compass the ruin of the party," Carmack said. "It would be a disgrace, and, as I have already said to the people of Tennessee, if Hearst is nominated, we may as well pen a dispatch, and send it back from the field of battle: 'All is lost, including our honor.' "[20]

A lone pro-Hearst voice from New York City was that of William Devery, who had been expelled as a Tammany leader but still claimed strong influence in his own district. "I understand [Hearst] is a candidate for Presidential honors," Devery said without cracking a smile. "There's nothing like buildin' from the bottom up. If he's going to the St. Louis convention as a delegate we ought to know it. He's got a lot of friends, and he ought to come along and let us know if he wants our help."[21]

[18] *Tribune*, Mar. 23, 1904.
[20] N. Y. *Tribune*, Mar. 21, 1904.
[19] Quoted in N. Y. *Tribune*, Feb. 21, 1904.
[21] N. Y. *Tribune*, Feb. 24, 1904.

Hearst won the Iowa state convention, but ran into a bitter battle in Indiana before losing to Parker, drawing an angry statement from Indiana's John W. Kern:

> We are menaced for the first time in the history of the Republic by the open and unblushing effort of a multi-millionaire to purchase the Presidential nomination. Our state has been overrun with a gang of paid agents and retainers . . . As for the paid Hessians from other states, we are here to instruct the Indiana Democracy in their duty, I have nothing but contempt . . . The Hearst dollar mark is all over them . . .[22]

The talk of a Hearst "barrel" was increasing. Another Indiana observer later commented, "Perhaps we shall never know how much was spent [by Hearst], but if as much money was expended elsewhere as in Indiana a liberal fortune was squandered." [23]

In his fight for the Illinois and Indiana delegations, Hearst made several trips to Chicago to confer with Andrew Lawrence, the former San Francisco *Examiner* man who was now his Chicago kingpin, and once to meet with Bryan. On one visit he stopped at the office of the *American*, where he was known surreptitiously as "the Great White Chief," and for the first time met his managing editor, fat Moses Koenigsberg. Koenigsberg never did learn what Hearst wanted, for the latter shook hands and moved toward the door.

"Never mind, thank you," he said. "I must hurry to catch my train."

Another editor pointed despairingly at a bundle of letters that had accumulated for him, saying, "But Mr. Hearst, what shall I do with this correspondence?"

"I'll show you," Hearst replied, grinning. He took the stack of mail and tossed it into the waste basket. "Don't bother. Every letter answers itself in a couple of weeks." [24]

II. THE HEARST "BARREL"

HEARST hopped into a private railroad car with Max Ihmsen and made an arduous personal canvass for delegates in the western and southern states, always wearing a frock coat, listening intently to local politicians, and generally making a good impression. He laughed at a story that he planned to bolt the party if he was not nominated.

"I should, of course," he said, "like any other man, be honored and gratified should the Democrats see fit to nominate me. But I do not have to be bribed by office to be a Democrat. I have supported the Democratic party in the last five campaigns. I supported Cleveland three times and Bryan twice. I intend to support the nominee of the party at St. Louis, whoever he may be." [1]

The Hearst press followed the Chief's progress at the various state con-

[22] N. Y. *Tribune*, May 12, 1904.
[23] Claude G. Bowers, *The Life of John Worth Kern*, 139.
[24] Koenigsberg, 273.   [1] N. Y. *Tribune*, May 15, 1904.

ventions with its usual admiring attention, stressing the "enthusiasm" and "loyalty" he inspired. This was historic in its way, for it marked the first time an American Presidential aspirant had advertised his own virtues in his own string of newspapers spanning the land.

Yet his editors did not abandon their sense of story value. When Nan Patterson, a stunning and money-minded chorus girl who had appeared in a *Florodora* road show, rode down Broadway in a hansom cab with her married lover, Frank Young, she stopped the cab to disclose that Young had been shot dead, tearfully insisting that he had shot himself although experts said he could not have done so. The *American's* and *Journal's* front pages left no doubt that for the time being Miss Patterson was more important than Hearst. Likewise, when the excursion steamer *General Slocum* burned in the East River a few days later, bringing death to a thousand, Hearst's candidacy was pushed off the front page by a vast photograph of bodies on the beach.

The position of the Peerless Leader, Bryan, was the question of the hour. He was violently against the conservative Parker, but whom was he for? Late in June, with convention time nearing, he arrived in New York to speak against Parker. A reporter asked him what he thought of Hearst's chances.

"I do not wish to discuss Mr. Hearst at this time," Bryan said quickly. "I have nothing to say on that subject."[2]

Speculation buzzed when Bryan left town still uncommitted. "The impression prevails," said the *Tribune*, "that he effected some sort of combination with the Hearst managers . . . It is known that he dined twice with one of the Hearst men while here."[3]

One of the lighter political touches at this juncture was the nomination by the Prohibition party of Dr. Silas C. Swallow of Harrisburg for President.

Pundits of both major parties had underestimated Hearst, whose candidacy at first was viewed as amusing or absurd. Now it was clear that the only Democratic candidates with any sizeable preconvention strength were Parker and Hearst, and that unless something unforeseen occurred it would be a battle between the two. The Democrats were so torn by dissension that the Republicans watched the struggle with the good cheer of a general who sees his enemies fighting among themselves. The conservatives were rallying around Parker, the radicals shouting for Hearst.

Few Democrats felt dispassionate about Hearst. They either loved or hated him. The conservatives regarded him as not a genuine Democrat at all but a semi-socialistic hybrid whose movement was destructive to party ideals and party unity. His work for labor and his talk of government ownership of railroads, in their minds, stamped him as a dangerous radical. His quarrels with Democratic stalwarts in Congress, and his fostering of discord as a leader of dissidents, enraged the old-liners.[4] His independence of thought and action—his insistence on *running* things—was evident even in his drive

[2] N. Y. *Tribune*, June 20, 1904.   [3] N. Y. *Tribune*, June 23, 1904.
[4] Thompson, 236.

for the nomination, which was headed by Hearst and conducted by Hearst agents, many of them his own newspapermen. It was almost as if he were *competing* with the Democrats, not working with them. There was a feeling that he had made improper use of the National Association of Democratic Clubs to further his own candidacy. Some questioned the propriety of the owner of eight newspapers using them as organs of personal publicity. Rumors were circulated industriously depicting Hearst as an "unrivalled voluptuary," one of them even picturing him aboard a yacht on the Nile with a hundred Broadway beauties.[5]

On the other hand, Hearst's supporters boosted him with sincere and even fanatical loyalty. They included labor leaders all over the country, the more radical Democrats, and party men mostly in the West who remembered his all-out stand for Bryan and who fought domination by the Eastern "reactionary" wing. When the convention opened on July 6 at Convention Hall in St. Louis, observers estimated that of the 997 delegates, Parker had 302 and Hearst 215.[6]

Hearst opened elaborate headquarters at the Hotel Jefferson and was as free-handed as ever with bands, fireworks, flags and laudatory literature. But his hope for the nomination seems to have dwindled even before the balloting started. He needed Bryan, and Bryan was not with him. The Great Commoner was as silent as the Sphinx.

True, he could not entirely forget Hearst's services. It happened that Illinois, with its potent fifty-four votes, had sent contesting delegations, one committed to Hearst, the other in the hands of the anti-Hearst Chicago boss, Roger Sullivan. Bryan, who had a personal feud with Sullivan's Illinois machine, fought to seat the pro-Hearst Illinois delegates, but lost. This of itself was almost decisive.[7]

Hearst was nominated by Delphin M. Delmas, a San Francisco attorney who had been an ally of Senator George Hearst. Delmas spoke of Hearst's fidelity to the party, his aid to the poor and his popularity. Calling him "the foremost living advocate of the equality of man," Delmas sought to dispel the notion that Hearst would bolt if someone else was chosen.

"Though aspiring to this nomination," he said, "if your assembled wisdom shall deem another worthier, he will not be found a discontented grumbler, sulking in his tent." [8]

Clarence Darrow, the Chicago lawyer who had yet to attain fame as a defender of desperate causes, seconded the nomination. A six-foot portrait of Hearst was displayed on the platform, another in the gallery, while parading delegates hoisted smaller ones aloft on poles and a perspiring Hearst band played *America* and then *Dixie*. California led the way, carrying a large silken Hearst banner, followed by Arizona, Nevada, Iowa, South Dakota, Washington and Wyoming. The applause for Hearst was impressive, as even Republican newspapers admitted. His own papers still boomed the

[5] Koenigsberg, 277. [6] N. Y. *Tribune*, July 4, 1904. [7] Peck, 712.
[8] N. Y. *Tribune*, July 4, 1904.

Chief even though the cause seemed lost, the New York *American* head-lining, "HEARST IS CHEERED FOR 38 MINUTES," "Convention in Wild Tumult of Applause" (for Hearst), and "CHEERS FOR HEARST CAME FROM THE HEART, SAY DELEGATES." [9]

The Bryan mystery was finally solved when the Nebraskan rose to nom-inate Senator Francis Cockerell of Missouri, a man who had no chance. At the end of his address, Bryan, possibly feeling some pangs, made a left-handed gesture toward Hearst.

"If it is the choice or wish of this Convention that the standard shall be placed in the hands of the gentleman presented by California," Bryan said, "the man who, though he has money, pleads the cause of the poor; the man who is best beloved, I can safely say, among laboring men, of all the candi-dates proposed; the man who more than any other represents peace; make Hearst the candidate of this Convention and Nebraska will be with you." [10]

But the conservatives were in the saddle. Hearst got 194 votes on the first ballot, and later increased them to 263—the nearest he got to his life's high-est ambition. Alton Brooks Parker, the able but uninspiring chief judge of the New York Court of Appeals, secured the nomination late on July 8 with 658 votes. Henry G. Davis, a wealthy octogenarian from West Virginia, was named for Vice President in the hope that he would contribute liberally to the cause, which he did not. The disappointed Hearst boarded a train for New York even before the convention ended.

Here Judge Parker, who had remained in New York, tossed a bombshell into the convention's waning moments. The Democratic platform had skill-fully evaded any mention of the touchy gold-silver issue. Parker, a gold man, wired a henchman in St. Louis that he could not accept the nomination on any other than a gold-standard basis.

The telegram created an uproar. Hearst's lieutenants, Ihmsen and Law-rence, saw new hope for him. They wired him urgently to come back. Hearst, receiving the message when his train was flagged down in Indiana, returned to Chicago. But David B. Hill and other Parker men had managed to get their candidate accepted despite his stipulation, although Bryan fought them bitterly. It was an awkward contretemps further advertising Democratic disunity.

"The Democratic party can always be relied on to make a damn fool of itself at the critical time," Senator "Pitchfork Ben" Tillman of South Carolina said truly to Hill. [11]

The Hearst forces angrily called Bryan an ingrate for failing to support their candidate. Many observers felt that Hearst would have won the nom-ination had Bryan lent his whole-hearted aid from the start. [12] Since Bryan was sadly disappointed at the Parker nomination, and the only way he could have prevented it was to have thrown his influence to Hearst, he obviously disapproved of Hearst. Some suspected that Bryan, seeking to advance his

[9] N. Y. *American,* July 9, 1904.   [10] N. Y. *Evening Journal,* July 9, 1904.
[11] N. Y. *Tribune,* July 10, 1904.   [12] Abbot, 253.

chances for the nomination in 1908, feared Hearst as a possible rival and preferred to see a colorless candidate fail in 1904. But it seems more likely that Bryan, a godly man, had misgivings about Hearst as the nominee. In moral outlook there was a broad gulf between the two. The handicap of Hearst's inexperience was evident, but doubtless even more disturbing to Bryan was the buzz of rumor about Hearst's moral failings and his "purchase" of delegates.

With his convenient "end-justifies-the-means" philosophy, and his strong yearning for the Presidency, Hearst would hardly have been averse to making political use of money just as his father had done before him. Willis Abbot later wrote, "Many of his delegates at the St. Louis convention were obtained by purchase and perhaps more by intimidation through his newspapers."[13] The howl that came from Indiana suggested that Hearst money —or talk of it—was in evidence there, and there were similar complaints in Iowa. Andrew Lawrence, Hearst's Chicago publisher, was in charge of much of the politicking in the Illinois-Indiana-Iowa area. Lawrence, who had a reputation as an intriguer, was known as "Long Green Andy."

Yet James Creelman insisted that the money talk was grossly exaggerated. "It has been said that Mr. Hearst spent more than $2,000,000 in that attempt to be nominated for President," Creelman wrote. "The fact is, that, outside of the salaries and ordinary expenses of his regular employees, he paid out not more than $150,000—practically all for printing, fireworks, hall-hire, banners, badges, music and transportation. He had spent as much for Mr. Bryan." [14] Frederick Palmer, an observer critical of Hearst, declared that many of the delegates were resentful because Hearst did *not* scatter largesse. "His outlay went entirely to fireworks, bands, banners, and buttons, and hired adjutants," Palmer wrote. "The delegates who had voted for him went home thinking that he would have surely opened the barrel if he had been nominated, anyway. The sum he spent on his Presidential campaign was not more than his income for two months." [15]

The talk of the Hearst "barrel" was obviously exaggerated by his enemies. Perhaps the safest guess is that some delegates were bought and some swung into line by political leaders anxious to gain the favor of the Hearst papers, and that the rest of the money was just talk—cash that never got out of the barrel. It is not hard to imagine the busy adjutants, scouring the country for delegates, aiding their cause by loose talk about Hearst's great wealth and liberality.

III. REBEL IN THE RANKS

DOMESTICITY brought few changes to Hearst. He still got to bed in the neighborhood of 3 and rose sometime before noon. Proud of his lovely young wife, he took her to so many Broadway first-nights that she eventually tired of them. He never did. Often, after the show and a dinner at Martin's, he

[13] Abbot, 251.   [14] *Pearson's Magazine*, Sept., 1906.   [15] *Collier's*, Oct. 6, 1906.

would take her to the *American-Journal* offices, now in a larger building on William Street a block off Park Row, where she would wait while he pawed over forms or conferred with his editors. He adored his baby son and spoiled him dreadfully.[1] He seized every spare moment to shop for art among the galleries, sometimes taking Brisbane along to sandwich discussions of newspaper policy between conversations with dealers. His political secretary, L. J. O'Reilly, was himself a collector in a small way of copper and antiques. He often sent O'Reilly to bid for him at auctions.

Hearst was running a huge enterprise. He ran it himself, with an intimate knowledge of all its phases—circulation, advertising, typography, features, comics, pressroom routines. Minutes were precious to him. Yet he followed no set schedule, sometimes seeming guided by mere whim in his appearances at the office, but always working when he worked with the most intense concentration.

He detested going to parties, since he was comfortable only with his few well-worn companions. Being a guest of Hearst could be trying. Despite his elaborate courtesy, he was no conversationalist, generally depending on others to do the talking and sometimes delivering blunt judgments without regard for tact. His loss of the Presidential nomination had hurt him keenly. There was something about Hearst—his aloofness, his penetrating gaze, and his entirely unaffected feeling of superiority—that forbade familiarity even among those who knew him best. No one called him "Will" or "Bill" except his wife and his mother. Follansbee, Brisbane, Chamberlain and a very few others called him "W.R." Another small echelon of friends and employes slightly farther removed called him "Chief." To all others he was "Mr. Hearst," and he in turn addressed them as "Mister." Thus, in the Hearst organization, which everybody simply called "the Organization," one's rank or importance could be ascertained by his manner of addressing the owner. When an employe advanced from the "Mr. Hearst" to the "Chief" stage, it signified expanding prestige, and when he could say "W.R." he was in heaven.

Hearst was more distant than he had been in the joyous San Francisco days. There were two telephones in his home, but both were unlisted. Anyone wanting to see him had to get by George Thompson, and it took a very good reason to get by Thompson. The plump valet was also major-domo and something of a confidant, devoted to his master, always waiting up for him until the wee hours to attend to his wants.

One of the many things on Hearst's mind was New York real estate. Seeing the constant uptown drift, he knew he would have to follow it sooner or later. He looked around at Herald Square and Longacre Square (later called Times Square), but decided that both were too far downtown. Columbus Circle, at the south end of Central Park, he felt, was the coming area. He began buying property around the Circle which eventually would reach into the millions.[2]

[1] Mrs. William Randolph Hearst to author, May 15, 1959.
[2] M. F. Huberth to author, June 23, 1959.

A growing vein of toughness was evident in his attitude toward his employes. He was still benign and sometimes absurdly generous to those he knew personally, and was the most lavish of all publishers in giving credit to writers and artists in the form of bylines. He was especially gracious to women contributors. Mrs. John A. Logan, who worked for him for seven years, later mentioned his "most distinguished consideration." [3] His mechanical men were all unionized and received better pay than those on other New York papers with the exception of the *World* and the *Herald.*

But there were occasional shakeups in the city-room rank and file, and men were often fired without reason. Hearst picked up an old trick of Pulitzer's, occasionally putting two men on the same job and letting them fight it out on the theory that the best man would win. Now that the Organization was so big, the impersonal rules of competition set in. The old happy-family days when anything went, were gone. A man had to produce to hold his job. Security was unknown among the Hearst lower ranks, as it had long been unknown at other newspapers. [4]

In the upper brackets there was a silent war of intrigue and backbiting that was an inevitable result of Hearst's kingly manner of ruling his domain. Brisbane was jealous of Chamberlain. Carvalho was suspicious of Brisbane. This internal suspicion and envy went down the line among editors and writers. The way to rise in the Organization was to get the favorable attention of Hearst, either by some clever stroke or by cutting down a colleague. The pace was hard. In thirty-seven months there were twenty-seven city editors on the Chicago *American*. Edgar Sisson, who had three whirls at the job, each time wound up in the care of a nerve specialist. Men put in serious thought devising schemes to make the Chief take notice of them. Andrew Lawrence, an apt intriguer, said, "The quickest way to get ahead with W.R. is to have the other fellows 'knock' you to him. He'll figure that you must have something your colleagues are trying to kill off." [5]

A few thought that Hearst had a tinge of sadism—that it amused him to watch his men squirm, see them vie for his favor. If so, he was still tolerant of drunkards and thieves, if they were able or amusing. He looked on a man with an engaging personality as having earned a large part of his salary by the entertainment he supplied. He had a special fondness for Ike Allen, the genial tosspot who had sent him chowder in Egypt and was now back with the San Francisco *Examiner.* Hearst instructed Dent Robert, publisher of the *Examiner,* to steer Allen away from saloons. There were repeated instances when he found a man literally stealing company money. More often than not he would discharge the man, then hire him back in a position where stealing was less likely. "Hearst was more intolerant of employees who failed of enthusiasm for his policies," Abbot noted wonderingly, ". . . than of those who robbed his purse." [6]

Now, in 1904, Hearst was a changed man in one respect. Every Hearstman

[3] Mrs. John A. Logan, *Reminiscences of a Soldier's Wife,* 450.
[4] Barrett, *Pulitzer,* 97.   [5] Koenigsberg, 314.   [6] Abbot, 142–43.

from Boston to Los Angeles knew how badly the Chief had been bitten by the Presidential bug, and it subtracted something from their already limited integrity in reporting the news. Most of all it affected the Chief himself. Before politics seized him he had taken a fierce pride in his journalistic achievements, outlandish though they often were. Now, Politician Hearst subtracted something from Editor Hearst. While it would not be quite fair to say that he now considered his newspapers simply as a means to reach the White House, that would be an important part of their function.

After his convention defeat, he had decisions to make. How best to prepare for the race in 1908? What to do about Boss Murphy, who had scorned him at St. Louis? What to do about the horrendous candidate, Parker?

He was already moving away from the Democrats. They were not radical enough for his "Jeffersonian" democracy. They were too stupid to comprehend the wisdom of Hearst. Already in his mind was the idea of forming a third party, an ideal party because it would be a Hearst party, but he was not quite ready to cast the die. He would be up for reelection in the fall. He decided to be a Congressman for another term. He knew that with his popularity in the Eleventh District he could win even without Tammany support, and he was indifferent about Murphy's help. Murphy, on his side, had developed a strong aversion to the publisher who seemed to think that Tammany should dance to his tune. Murphy was for ditching Hearst. According to one political insider, Judge Parker, needing the support of the Hearst press, persuaded Murphy to swallow Hearst once more in the interest of "party harmony." [7] So Hearst again became the Tammany nominee for Congress, although he and Murphy were at loggerheads.

Before the convention, Hearst had promised to support the Democratic candidate, whoever he was. He kept his promise. However, he had not said how *enthusiastically* he would back him. His support of Parker was a study in tepidity. He later said, "I did, as a matter of fact, shut my eyes, hold my nose, and support Judge Parker . . ." [8] Parker indeed was a reactionary, friendly with Wall Street, so opposed to progressive measures that even Bryan admitted that it cost him a spiritual struggle to give the candidate his aid. Hearst's nose-holding was so evident that Parker doubtless regretted his "support."

The Hearst press, which could make a front-page, five-column-photograph, six-inch-headline hero of a man if it so desired, gave Parker its smallest type. The New York *American* headlined, "BRYAN ASSAILS PARKER BUT WILL SUPPORT HIM." The *American* warned Parker against the evil influence of financier August Belmont, whose New York subway was just beginning operation, clearly suggesting that Parker *was* under Belmont's influence. Hearst issued a proclamation to his National Association of Democratic Clubs (with a photograph of Hearst), appealing to the Democrats for "cooperation" without once mentioning Parker. [9]

[7] N. Y. *Tribune*, Dec. 6, 1904.   [8] Coblentz, *Hearst*, 37.
[9] N. Y. *American*, July 11, 13; N. Y. *Journal*, Oct. 15, 1904.

The Hearst press gave its front pages to the Russo-Japanese War, and to the Congressional candidacy of Hearst, extolling his services in the Spanish war, where "He was on the firing line repeatedly." As election day neared, each issue of the New York *Journal* contained an across-top-of-page quotation, in big type, from the speeches of William Randolph Hearst. The *Journal* also gave an amazing amount of space to Thomas E. Watson, the Georgian who had turned down a job on the *American* editorial staff. Watson had been nominated for President by the Populists, and obviously had no chance, but the Hearst papers treated him with marked deference, giving him at least four large articles and even quoting his attacks on Parker as a tool of the trusts. The Republican *Tribune* commented, "Mr. Hearst's editorial staff is reported to be almost solidly for Thomas E. Watson . . ." [10]

No one suggested that Hearst's flirtation might be aimed at getting the support of Watson, with his large Dixie following, for the Presidency in 1908.

The *American* and *Journal* had their usual fireworks and bulletins in Madison Square on election night, although it is safe to say that Pain was cautioned to be very careful with his mortars. Parker went down to humiliating defeat, carrying no state north of the Mason-Dixon line, but the *Journal* happily headlined, "HEARST REELECTED BY MAJORITY OF 11,397." [11] Again he had run ahead of his ticket, getting 1700 more votes than Parker in his district. He was more pleased than a good Democrat should have been at Parker's defeat.

Returning to Congress that winter, he cemented a friendship with Representative Champ Clark of Missouri that would continue for years, although Clark was never a member of the rebellious Hearst Brigade. Another member of that Congress was a beak-nosed young Texan, John Nance Garner. Hearst's following grew in size, sometimes numbering a dozen Representatives, and always drawing the contempt of the regular Democrats. He demonstrated a surprising grasp of parliamentary tricks in his effort to add an eight-hour law to a naval appropriations bill. A non-Hearst reporter wrote of Hearst, slouched at his desk with one knee in the air, never saying a word, yet keeping the House in a turmoil for forty-five minutes, continuing:

> He issued assignments to his followers as if he were issuing them to his reporters in his newspaper office, first to one and then to another; only instead of assignments to write "stories," they were assignments to offer amendments, make speeches or rise to parliamentary points.
>
> The old-line Democrats looked on silently at the curious scene. The members of the "Hearst brigade" would come over to their chief one after another and get their assignments. . . . the man assigned to the work would arise and throw a new bomb into the Republican side. All this time the chief never changed his position except once when he walked around to give an assignment personally to Mr. Livernash . . . Throughout the fight unversed and unsophisticated tourists in the galleries never suspected that the silent man

[10] N. Y. *Tribune*, Oct. 4, 1904.   [11] Nov. 9, 1904.

sitting crouched in his chair had anything to do with the fight; much less that he was the head centre of it.

He played on the House like a piano, and succeeded amply in his purpose —to put the Republicans on record against the eight-hour bill. . . .[12]

Hearst was still avoiding speeches, letting others do the talking for him, his ego doubtless tickled by this quiet but lordly pulling of strings. He introduced other bills, one of them to slap prison terms on railroad officials who indulged in secret rebates, another to empower the government to buy and operate the telegraph lines. They were defeated, as usual, causing his newspapers to begin an attack on Williams and the Democrats for failing to support him. Hearst had some sound ideas, but he failed dismally in the most vital Congressional function of all—the need to work patiently with his colleagues, win their friendship, appeal for their support, accept a reasonable amount of horse-trading. It was the old trouble—he wanted his own way. He sought rashly to cure the nation's ills in one session. His ability to offend the regular Democrats was unmatched. As Creelman, no longer a Hearst writer, noted, "So intense is the distrust of his Congressional colleagues that it is doubtful whether he could secure an indorsement of the Ten Commandments by the House." [13]

Hearst was also stirring up trouble among the Democrats in New York City. Formerly a supporter of Tammany's Mayor George B. McClellan, he now began to assail him. An *American* reporter put a sly question: "Mr. Mayor, Mr. Hearst wants to know if you have a corrupt motive in supporting the Remsen Gas Bill?" The angry mayor showed him the door, and saw a subhead in next day's *American:* "Mayor does not deny that he has a corrupt motive in supporting the Remsen Gas Bill." [14] Hearst, believing the gas bill unjust, fought it tooth and nail, got an injunction against it, and began calling the mayor the Gas Man.

Tammany Boss Murphy read the portents. He girded himself for battle with Hearst, suspecting that he intended to run for mayor in 1905 *against* Tammany.[15]

IV. THE NERO OF MODERN POLITICS

IN Congress a number of Democrats awaited their chance to humiliate Hearst. On February 13, 1905, the opportunity came to thirty-seven-year-old Representative John A. Sullivan of Massachusetts, precipitating what the New York *Herald* called "the most sensational scene in the House for years." Hearst's railroad rate bill of the previous year was reintroduced, causing Sullivan to complain in the House that Hearst was absent as usual instead of being on hand to explain his bill. The New York *American* snappishly commented that the "bald, red-nosed" Sullivan had "revealed his hitherto

[12] Thompson, 242–43.
[14] McClellan, 189.
[13] *Pearson's Magazine*, Sept., 1906.
[15] N. Y. *Tribune*, Dec. 6, 1904.

unsuspected presence in the House," and wondered about the "congenital incapacity" of a member who was not familiar with Hearst's bill after its many hearings. On February 13, Sullivan rose to reply, reading from a manuscript with the manner of one who has a score to settle. Among other things, he called Hearst cowardly, immoral and corrupt without once mentioning his name. He said in part:

> I presume my criticism that it might have been well for the gentleman from New York to have taken the floor and discussed his own bill seemed to him an infraction of his monarchical dignity, and he thereupon . . . [had] my name duly registered for slander in the political assassination of his newspaper. I trust the gentleman will have the decency to avail himself of the privilege of this floor after the fashion of a manly man, instead of hiding under the cover of further cowardly newspaper attacks.
> . . . "congenital incapacity to understand" is a term that covers a wide range of mental and moral deficiencies. It covers the case of the moral degenerate who insolently casts his eyes upon the noblest of women whose virtue places them beyond the contamination of his lust. . . . And it includes the man who, totally bereft of the sense of proportion, raises his profaning eyes toward the splendid temple of the people's highest gift—the Presidency of the United States—blissfully unconscious of the woeful contrast between the qualifications requisite for that high office and his own contemptible mental and moral equipment.

Two Hearst Brigaders appealed to Speaker Cannon to stop Sullivan, but the Republican Cannon, relishing this quarrel among Democrats, told him to proceed. Sullivan, mentioning his own good record of attendance, assailed Representatives who did not show up to support Democratic bills and who attended only when they pleased.

> Some of them come here solely because the position offers them an opportunity to exploit their candidacy for the Presidency of the United States. . . . There was a single precedent in their favor, for the Democratic Party had once nominated an editor; but they failed to remember that it had never nominated a mere check book. . . .
> The candidacy [Hearst's] which began in debauch ended in fiasco. While it lasted a campaign of corruption was waged that has no parallel in American history. Honest men who did not know him well supported him, but the main feature of that campaign was the use of the grossest forms of corruption that ever shocked the American conscience. Perhaps he has read the lesson of that failure. At all events he has framed a shrewd plan for the attainment of his ambitions. He has mapped out a scheme of wholesale political assassination, evidently with the idea that only by destroying the respectable elements of the party can his candidacy rise above the plane of farce comedy. . . .
> I know that prudential reasons warn against controversy with a newspaper of this character . . . But as long as I am in the House I will reply to unjust attacks in the gentleman's newspaper by sending to the Clerk's desk, to be read with the article complained of, an estimate of the character of

my traducer which was given upon this floor by a California member in 1897 as the judgment of those with whom the gentleman from New York then lived, and who knew him best.

Sullivan then inserted in the record the 1897 attack by Grove Johnson calling Hearst a liar, blackmailer, bribe-taker and diseased voluptuary.

> . . . If by my remarks I have checked the scheme of political assassination which has been marked out by a Nero of modern politics . . . I believe I have performed a service to the House and to the country. . . . [prolonged applause].[1]

Sullivan's attack, and the applause it drew, showed the pitch of the hatred among the regular Democrats for Hearst. But in reading the scurrilous, untrue charges of Grove Johnson into the record—and threatening to read them again every time a Hearst paper assailed him—he was hardly fair. Nor was Hearst quite fair when he rose to make his maiden speech in the House after more than two years of membership. He must have been raging, but he "spoke in a quiet, almost gentle voice, calmly facing a hostile minority and a critical majority."[2] He said:

> Mr. Speaker, it seems to me that the gentleman from Massachusetts has very largely exaggerated the article which appeared in my newspaper. He has altogether misstated the reasons for the publication of that article. Personally I did not inspire or suggest the publication of that article, but I am entirely willing to assume all responsibility for everything that appears in my newspapers, no matter whether I inspire or suggest them or not. . . .
>
> The gentleman from Massachusetts apparently criticizes my action, or lack of action, on the floor of this House. I wish to say in reply to that that I am proceeding here in the way that I think most effective to my constituents. I have heard incompetents speak on the floor of this House for hours for the mere purpose of getting their remarks in the Record; and I have heard the best speakers deliver the most admirable addresses on the floor of this House without influencing legislation in the slightest particular. [Applause.] I do not know any way in which a man can be less effective for his constituents and less useful to them than by emitting chewed wind on the floor of this House. [Laughter.] There is a certain class of gentlemen who are peculiarly sensitive to newspaper criticism, and have every reason to be. I was criticized on the floor of this House once before by a gentleman from California, Mr. Johnson. That gentleman had been attacked in my newspaper for subserviency to the Southern Pacific Railway. He had gone back to his constituency for vindication, and the district which had elected him by 5,000 Republican majority repudiated him and went 5,000 Democratic. It was the first time that district had gone Democratic, and it has never gone Democratic since that time, so it was obviously in order to reject the gentleman from California, Mr. Johnson. Mr. Johnson had been indicted for forgery—

A Republican member tried to have Hearst stopped, but Speaker Cannon told him to proceed.

[1] N. Y. *Times,* Feb. 14, 1905.   [2] N. Y. *Tribune,* Feb. 14, 1905.

Mr. Speaker, Mr. Johnson was indicted in New York State for forgery and fled to the West, where he changed his name, but not his character or habits. He was denounced not only by my paper, but by a Republican paper, the San Francisco *Chronicle*, for this indictment for forgery and for other faults or crimes that he had committed. It seemed to me just to the people of California, whom my paper represented, to tell the truth about Mr. Johnson, and I think the action of my constituents showed approval of the action of my newspaper.

I had no desire, really, to criticize the gentleman from Massachusetts, and if I had I should certainly not have done it in so puerile a way. When I was at Harvard College in 1885 a murder was committed in a low saloon in Cambridge. A man partly incapacitated from drink bought in that saloon on Sunday morning, when the saloon was open against the law, was assaulted by the two owners of that saloon and brutally kicked to death. The name of one of the owners of that saloon was John A. Sullivan, and these two men were arrested and indicted by the grand jury for manslaughter and tried and convicted. I would like to ask the gentleman from Massachusetts if he knows anything about that incident, and whether, if I desired to make a hostile criticism, I could not have referred to that crime?

There were shouts of protest. The House was in an uproar as Sullivan tried to speak. Speaker Cannon, enjoying the fight, told Hearst to continue.

Mr. Speaker, I really have nothing further to say except that I am proud to have incurred the hostility of that class of individual, and I shall make it my duty and my pride to continue to incur the hostility of that class of individual as long as I am in journalism or in politics. [Applause.] [3]

Hearst's account was technically correct. Sullivan was only seventeen when he and his father had the altercation with an abusive drinker, who died after falling and striking his head on a curb. Both were convicted, the father drawing a three-year sentence but being pardoned in eighteen months, the son being put on probation. Sullivan was applauded when he explained this to the House. Representative Gardner of Massachusetts, a Republican, rose to testify to his high character.[4] Anger had driven both Sullivan and Hearst to offensiveness. Hearst was convinced, probably correctly, that the regular Democrats had plotted with Sullivan to smear him.

"I need not say," he told reporters, "that I consider today's session of the House disagreeable to all, and absolutely disgraceful to those who deliberately planned such a scene and forced it upon myself and other unwilling members. . . . I am glad to be contrasted as an anarchist or a socialist, or under any other appellation with the 'respectable' elements of the Democratic party as represented by Mr. Sullivan . . ." [5]

Although Hearst had a remarkable memory, and had studied newspapers industriously at Harvard at the time of the Sullivan affair, one wonders whether he could have remembered the details so well, or whether he had brushed up on them later for possible use in an emergency.

[3] N. Y. *Times,* Feb. 15, 1905.   [4] The same.   [5] N. Y. *Tribune,* Feb. 14, 1905.

At this same time began a strange Hearst drama that would not be played out for eight years. The curtain rose in the luxurious office of John D. Archbold, vice president of the Standard Oil Company and a valued colleague of John D. Rockefeller, at 26 Broadway. Archbold, a Methodist deacon whose piety was elastic in business matters, lived in a mansion at suburban Tarrytown, where he had a trusted Negro butler, James Wilkins. Out of kindness, Archbold employed Wilkins' scapegrace twenty-four-year-old stepson, Willie Winfield, as office boy.

Willie, who had a weakness for playing the horses and needed cash, had read newspaper charges against the Standard Oil trust. He conceived the idea that Archbold's private letters might be worth money to the newspapers. He broached the proposition to nineteen-year-old Charles Stump, a white man who worked as a porter in the office. Stump, whose intelligence was near the moronic level but was not lacking in cunning, agreed. The two filched a telegram and a couple of letters from Archbold's desk, then got in touch with the New York *World*. A *World* man told them he was not interested. Stump then communicated with the New York *American*, where he dealt with an editor named Fred Eldridge. According to later testimony, Eldridge met the pair at the Little Savoy Restaurant on West Thirty-fifth Street. He said the messages they showed him were of no value. However, he would be interested in letters between Archbold and public officials such as Senators and Congressmen. He gave them a list of 200 men whose correspondence with Archbold he would like to see, if any existed.[6]

Thereafter, Stump and Winfield began a systematic rifling of Archbold's files. They took their loot to the *American* office of evenings, showing it to Eldridge and another editor, John L. Eddy. As they dickered on price with the two newsmen, the latter said on several occasions that they would have to "see Mr. Hearst." They would then retire for a time, to return and complete the negotiations. In one instance, Winfield and Stump, tiring of piecemeal theft, abstracted two whole letterbooks belonging to their employer. At the *American* office, the more interesting of the letters were photographed and the originals returned, to allay any suspicion on the part of Archbold.[7]

This breezy espionage began in December, 1904, and continued through January and February, 1905. Then Archbold had a feeling that something peculiar was happening to his correspondence files. Very likely he looked for some letters and could not find them, for at the time his suspicions were aroused his two employes had a large batch of them which they had not had time to return. Archbold accused Winfield and Stump of the theft. Although they denied any knowledge of it, he discharged them. They had been well paid for their work—later reports ranged from $12,000 to $34,000—and they opened a saloon at Seventh Avenue and 134th Street. They still had a group of letters which they hoped to sell for a fancy price.[8]

If the *American* men had any qualms about this crafty procedure, they

[6] N. Y. *Times*, Dec. 19, 1912.   [7] N. Y. *Times*, Jan. 15, 1913.
[8] The same.

were lulled by the astonishing disclosures in some of the letters. Archbold, it was clear, was Standard Oil's chief political wirepuller who spent much of his time "arranging" legislation favorable to the oil trust. He was on the warmest of terms with many public officials, to some of whom he made direct payments by check. Among the recipients of his letters were United States Senators and Representatives and state officials, both Republican and Democratic, whose careers might be damaged or ruined by their publication at the same time as Standard Oil itself would be placed in a most embarrassing light. Archbold must have been a worried man as he waited to see what would happen. He needed strong nerves, for he would have years to wait while Hearst bided his time, seeking the most propitious moment for making use of the letters.

4. Moiphy Voisus Hoist

THERE were clear signs that Hearst, in his drive for the Presidency in 1908, was aiming for the governorship of New York in 1906 as a stepping stone in preference to the mayoralty. Since his convention defeat in 1904 came about from his lack of support in the East, the governorship would give him strength where he needed it. Having quarreled with the Democrats in Congress and with the two leading Democrats in his own state, Boss Murphy and David B. Hill, he was now almost a man without a party. Yet he had great confidence in his personal popularity with "the people," in his own little political machine, and in his newspapers.

He had become gripped by an idea that would smite him off and on for years—the idea of a third party. His experiences in Congress, and the Democrats' rejection of him in favor of the reactionary Parker, had soured him on his own party. The Democrats, he felt, came little closer than the Republicans to representing the ordinary citizens for whom he considered himself the tribune. In his view, millions of plain people were disgusted with both parties. Given a leader who would show them the way, the voiceless masses would flock to his standard. He had no doubt about who the leader should be.

He and Mrs. Hearst went to Europe in the spring of 1905, returning late in the summer with the usual trove of treasures. For $400,000 he acquired *Cosmopolitan*, his second magazine, from John Brisben Walker, under whom it had languished.[1] Max Ihmsen was drilling the New York William Randolph Hearst League to the task of ousting Mayor McClellan in the fall. The problem was to find a suitable man to run against McClellan.

At this point, handsome, thirty-one-year-old Judge Samuel Seabury, a reform politician who, like Hearst, had grown disillusioned with the Democrats, entered the scene. Seabury favored public ownership of utilities, an idea Hearst long had espoused, and was head of a group called the Municipal Ownership League. Hearst issued a polite invitation that had become a kingly habit with him—he rarely called on anyone else—and Seabury visited him. Seabury was impressed by the millionaire progressive whose thinking was so much like his own. He also welcomed the aid of the Hearst money and newspapers. Hearst, on his part, saw in Seabury's municipal ownership organization a valuable adjunct to his own. The two men agreed

[1] Louis Filler, *Crusaders for American Liberalism*, 247.

230

to join forces in a campaign to clean up the city. Seabury did not know at the time that when one joined Hearst, he joined *under* him, not with him.[2]

The William Randolph Hearst League merged with the Municipal Ownership League under the latter name, and the hunt for a candidate began. An effort was made at fusion of the Hearst and Republican forces, with Arthur Brisbane trying to persuade the able but ill-tempered Judge William Gaynor to make the race. But the fusion effort failed, and Hearst urged Seabury to be the candidate under the lone M.O.L. standard. Seabury, knowing that Hearst would have to foot the bill for the campaign, was unwilling to incur such an obligation; he pressed Hearst to run for mayor himself, but he refused.[3] He wrote Seabury on October 3:

> I thank you for your kind letter and your good opinion, but I do not feel that it would be for the best interests of the independent movement to become its leader. . . .
>
> I have, as you say, good friends, and I am deeply grateful for their friendship; but I have also powerful and vindictive enemies that I have made through my endeavors to overthrow special privilege and corruption in high places.
>
> It does not seem to me that this fight for principle should be encumbered by the introduction of personal hostilities. I am proud of my friends . . . and I am almost equally proud of my enemies, for these belong to the rich, powerful and unscrupulous class that most people are afraid to have as enemies.
>
> I am NOT afraid of them. I glory in doing battle with them whenever I see their greedy hands outstretched for the public purse. But I AM afraid to array their power and wealth and unscrupulous methods in their most violent form against a movement which means so much for the welfare of the community. I think this movement can best be brought to success under some other man, and I will fight harder than I would for myself, and more effectively than I could for myself, for any upright man who will make an honest fight against the bosses and the forces of corruption. . . .[4]

The letter did not say "No." Seabury applied pressure, calling on Hearst at the *American* office with some Municipal Ownership colleagues to urge him to make the sacrifice. A group of representative Italians called on him with the same plea, as did a committee of German-Americans. Hearst, with his eye on the governorship, preferred not to run, but he found these appeals flattering. Next evening he entered Grand Central Palace, where the M.O.L. convention was in progress, and was cheered to the echo.

"When Mr. Hearst mounted the platform," the *Tribune* said, "for seven minutes the big crowd cheered and waved flags. Men, and even women, climbed upon their chairs and shouted. Through it all Mr. Hearst stood smiling, until he saw that no effort of his could stop the noise. Then he seated himself by the side of Chairman [James G. Phelps] Stokes and waited for the crowd to shout itself out." [5]

[2] Walter Chambers, *Samuel Seabury*, 97.   [3] Chambers, 101.
[4] N. Y. *Times*, Oct. 4, 1905.   [5] N. Y. *Tribune*, Oct. 5, 1905.

It was said that Max Ihmsen had a well-organized Hearst claque, but these cheers were spontaneous. The M.O.L. people had seen Hearst alienate himself from the Democrats by his aggressive radicalism in Congress. They applauded his fight against the trusts. They believed in him. "There was a time," Creelman commented, "when Mr. Hearst would tremble and grow pale at the bare thought of making a speech . . . His devices for avoiding speeches excited laughter and jeers." [6] Now, under the impetus of cheers that warmed his heart, he was actually beginning to enjoy speechmaking.

"You have your votes and the privilege of casting them," he told the crowd, "but for whom? For Mr. Murphy's puppet, or for Mr. Odell's puppet. [Benjamin Odell was governor and Republican state boss.] If you want gas that will burn and not merely poison, you can vote for Mr. Murphy's puppet and you won't get it. And if you want a reduction in your extortionate bills, you can vote for Mr. Odell's puppet and not get it. . . .

"I do not believe financial corporations are at fault. I do not believe that Mr. Murphy or Mr. Odell or Mr. Murphy's man or Mr. Odell's man is at fault—I am afraid that you are at fault. You are a sleeping majority. Wake up! Nominate honest and independent men like Judge Seabury or Senator Ford, who, I am sure, will lead you to victory and restore this city to a government of the people, by the people and for the people." [7]

The convention, taking this as a mere polite gesture toward Seabury and Ford, promptly nominated him for mayor. Even yet, Hearst, shooting for the governorship the following year, did not accept. That weekend he made an amazing move. Through a friend, he sent a message to Charles Evans Hughes, the Republican attorney who was even then scoring a sensation with his investigation of the corrupt political connections of large New York insurance companies and was much in the public eye. He urged Hughes to run for mayor on the Republican ticket. Hearst said he would support Hughes —would even run himself on a third ticket to split McClellan's vote and make certain Hughes' election. [8]

This was a gambit Machiavelli would have admired. If successful, it would have accomplished several objects desirable to Hearst.

It would have visited vengeance on Murphy and Tammany.

It would have assured the city of an able, honest mayor.

It would lessen the threat of Hughes as a candidate against Hearst for governor in 1906. It was unlikely that the conscientious Hughes would seek the governorship only a few months after taking office as mayor.

But—it would also have meant betraying the M.O.L., which Hearst had aided and encouraged. Would Hearst, wanting the governorship as badly as he did, have jettisoned the League—used it as a mere pawn in his own political chess game?

If this was his plan, the maneuver failed. Hughes, still immersed in his

[6] *Pearson's Magazine*, Sept., 1906.   [7] N. Y. *Tribune*, Oct. 5, 1905.
[8] Merlo J. Pusey, *Charles Evans Hughes*, I, 150. Hearst's intermediary was Erwin Wardman, editor of the N. Y. *Press*.

insurance probe, had already rejected Republican advances. He declined to run for mayor.

That left it squarely up to Hearst as the only man with a chance to oust McClellan. He apparently gave the matter deep thought. A few days later he wrote Seabury, accepting the nomination as a "duty," saying, "The situation in this city is so grave and the condition of the public in the face of organized bossism is apparently so helpless that no man has a right to consider anything else, least of all his private affairs or personal inclination . . ." [9]

II. A SHIVER OF APPREHENSION

CHARLES F. MURPHY, born and raised on New York's East Side, with a meager education, had learned to handle his fists as a shipyard worker, later became a street car conductor, and finally opened a saloon on Second Avenue where he served a schooner of beer and a bowl of soup for five cents. Workers at the shipyards and the nearby gas house were his patrons. Known as "Silent Charlie" or "Mr. Moiphy" by his cronies, he was a quiet, methodical politician, several cuts above his predecessor, the rapacious Croker, and was said to have remained reasonably honest until great power corrupted him. He had some wistful social yearnings. His good friend was J. Sergeant Cram, a Tammany anomaly, being a Harvard graduate listed in the Social Register. Cram had patiently taught Murphy how to eat peas with a fork, an accomplishment that aroused the scorn of red-necked Bill Devery. Devery said, "Since he has gotten in with J. Sergeant Cram he has got into a habit of tucking up his trousers at the bottom and wearing glasses, and instead of being a respectable gas house gentleman he goes on Fifth Avenue." [1]

Nor was his candidate, forty-year-old George B. McClellan Jr., a gas house gentleman. The son of the Civil War general, he was a Princeton graduate, well-tailored and boyish-looking. He had served in Congress, where he had known and liked Hearst. He had been personally honest as mayor even when incorrigible Tammany men staged shenanigans behind his back. He had believed the Remsen gas bill a good measure, and still believed so later when he was pained to learn that Murphy aimed to profit from it. [2] Hearst, the public's unofficial defender, was still fighting the bill, blocking it in the courts with an injunction.

At first, Murphy and McClellan were inclined to regard the Hearst candidacy as a joke. They concentrated their attack on the Republican candidate, William M. Ivins. What could Hearst do—a man without a party, with only his own small machine and the paltry Municipal Ownership League behind him? Soon they discovered that Hearst had a tremendous following. A reform sentiment had been growing among citizens weary of the everlasting peculations of Tammany and more than ever outraged by the revela-

[9] N. Y. *Tribune*, Oct. 11, 1905.   [1] N. Y. *Times*, Oct. 24, 1903.
[2] McClellan, 213.

tions of political corruption on the part of insurance companies which Hughes was then exposing. Hearst profited by the revulsion of the people against machines Democratic or Republican. He was surrounded by honest, idealistic men, among them Seabury, Ford and Stokes. He promised the voters down-to-earth things—cheaper government, lower utilities bills, better schools.

Murphy and McClellan forgot about Ivins and began to pour their fire at Hearst. The strategy was to label Hearst an anarchist. Banners were hung bearing an American flag under McClellan's likeness and a red flag under Hearst's, with the caption, "Under Which Flag Do You Vote?" [3] Others showed McKinley falling under Czolgosz' bullets, stressing Hearst's alleged connection with the crime. McClellan was a resourceful campaigner, a scholar who spoke German, Italian and French. He made speeches from a small open car, covering the foreign neighborhoods, always having a confederate in the crowd who would shout, "Speak to us in our own language." Thereupon McClellan, after seeming modest reluctance, would switch to German, French or Italian in a speech that appeared extemporaneous but was really carefully prepared, invariably scoring a hit among the foreign-born.[4]

Tammany orators made a field day of Hearst's "incitement" of the murder of McKinley. They also indulged in broad innuendo about his moral character. One of them, Bourke Cockran, touched all bases when he called Hearst a "promoter of assassination" and a "promoter of socialism," then made sly mention of Shaw's play, *Mrs. Warren's Profession,* which had recently been banned as indecent. "A municipality that would not tolerate the production of 'Mrs. Warren's Profession,'" Cockran said, "would hardly be expected to tolerate an account of Mr. Hearst's performances." [5]

But the surprise of the struggle was Hearst himself. The man who had scarcely spoken a word in Congress developed into a slashing platform spellbinder with a gift for ridicule and vituperation. He had trained his soft, high-pitched voice so that it would carry in large halls. Like a later and greater politician, he always began his speeches with "My friends." Unlike his newspapers, he spoke intelligently. It was said that at first he had an unfortunate habit of beginning all his sentences with "I," which his advisers persuaded him to change to "we." Even one of his critics admitted, "He had unquestionably a striking dignity and force about him—the dignity and force of the proprietor, of the man who is of and for himself, the leader by command . . . He threw energy into his words; he bent toward his audience insistently with each short sentence." [6]

Hearst, still bashful as a girl in private conversation with strangers, had conquered his fear of crowds by sheer courage and determination.

As always, he was running his own show, surrounding himself with his own men. His attorney, Clarence Shearn, was running on his ticket for

[3] N. Y. *Times,* Nov. 1, 1905.   [4] McClellan, 174.   [5] N. Y. *Times,* Nov. 2, 1905.
[6] *Collier's,* Oct. 13, 1906.

district attorney, promising faithful effort to put Boss Murphy in prison. His secretary, L. J. O'Reilly, was keeping his appointments straight. His political generalissimo, Max Ihmsen, was campaign manager. Arthur Brisbane was speaking for him, among other things assuring a gathering of clergymen that Hearst had been on good terms with McKinley and had nothing to do with his murder. Brisbane also mentioned that he had lived with Hearst for several years and could vouch for his moral character. Jack Follansbee, the convivial racing enthusiast, who at first thought Hearst was wasting his time in politics, was now treasurer of the Municipal Ownership League and amazed at the transformation in his formerly shrinking friend.[7] Hearst had his headquarters in a large block of rooms at his old stamping grounds, the Hoffman House, where Ihmsen rode herd over a regiment of workers, among them many Hearst newsmen, and called for more room. "The Hearst . . . headquarters continues to spread like a contagious disease," the hostile *Tribune* observed. "Another floor was added . . . yesterday." [8]

The *American* and *Journal* depicted Hearst as the answer to all New York's ills. They ran frequent pictures of Mrs. Hearst and baby George, to convey an image of the Chief as a solid family man. Every other newspaper was against him, most of them rabidly and vindictively against him—the *World, Times, Sun, Tribune, Herald, Post* and lesser organs. In the face of this mass "respectable" opposition, the Congressman made the battle of his life. Both sides used the familiar tactic of sending bullies to heckle and upset opposition meetings. It was no race for a weakling. Hearst prepared his speeches carefully, addressing eight or more meetings a night, but he also showed a talent for quick repartee. When one heckler shouted, "What's the matter with Murphy?" he replied, "My friend, we haven't time at this meeting to tell what's the matter with Murphy." When another demanded what had become of the fortune collected by the *Journal* for the *Maine* monument fund, Hearst said, ". . . if your money was as safe as the *Maine* monument fund you would be on Easy Street." [9] He addressed enthusiastic crowds who occasionally broke into a song some follower had devised to the tune of *Everybody Works but Father:*

> "*Everybody woiks but Moiphy;*
> *He only rakes in the dough . . ."*

By October's end, the "respectables" were in panic at the thought that the unspeakable Hearst might actually win. His campaign had taken on the aspect of a crusade for good government. His disciples were not only among the poor and ignorant but included a surprising number of middle-class people. Thoughtful anti-Hearst men realized that this test was crucial. If Hearst should win despite the enormous obstacles he faced, it would stamp him as a popular hero and put him on the highroad to the governorship and the Presidency—something that made conservatives shudder. The fear of

[7] N. Y. *Daily News*, Mar. 3, 1906.   [8] N. Y. *Tribune*, Oct. 25, 1905.
[9] N. Y. *Times*, Nov. 2, 4, 1905.

Hearst was even more pervasive than the fear of Bryan in 1896. Arthur Brisbane, speaking at a Y.M.C.A. meeting, made no secret of the Chief's ambitions.

"Mr. Hearst is the most misunderstood man in the country," he said. "He has been vilified and lied about more than any other man . . . Mr. Hearst is built for greater things even than the Mayoralty, and he's going to get them . . ." [10]

The liberal *Times* noted with alarm the sincere enthusiasm that Hearst inspired wherever he went. Once, his carriage was stopped by a crowd of East Side admirers who chanted their own queer praise:

> *"Hoist, Hoist,*
> *He is not the woist;*
> *We are for Hoist,*
> *Last and foist."* [11]

"Assaults upon the character of Mr. Hearst and denunciations of his newspaper methods cost him no votes," the *Times* editorialized. ". . . The vicious vote—and we suppose Mr. Hearst will poll absolutely the whole of it—likes him all the better for the qualities which his opponents denounce. The red flag foolishness and quotations of violent attacks upon President McKinley from Mr. Hearst's newspapers simply tend to make the Anarchist vote 'solid' for him." [12]

"Hearst may get 45,000 votes in all and he may not get as many," scoffed Charles Murphy, who was being depicted in the Hearst press as an arch-criminal. Murphy knew better. He was worried. If the "partyless candidate" could beat Tammany, Murphy was through. Hearst was campaigning for municipal ownership of the street railways and other utilities, careful to avoid any suggestion of confiscation or socialism, pointing out the efficiency of London's city-owned street railways. He promised an end to graft, fifty-five-cent gas, new schools and improvement in pay and working conditions for city employes. Repeatedly he promised, "I will make the further pledge now that if I find that I cannot keep my pledges I will resign." [13]

McClellan, said the Hearst papers in a bid for the Irish vote, was "the hireling of Great Britain," possibly because when he was in Congress he had often dined at the British embassy. When McClellan got word that the British North Atlantic Squadron, commanded by Prince Louis of Battenberg, would arrive for a courtesy visit in New York on the Saturday before election, he broke into a cold sweat. He would have to greet the British visitors. How the Hearst press would cartoon him as bowing, scraping and addressing the prince as "your highness"! McClellan hurriedly called the British ambassador in Washington, Sir Mortimer Durand, and begged him to delay the visit until after election. "He was not a very bright man," McClellan later wrote,

[10] N. Y. *Times,* Nov. 7, 1905.   [11] *Times,* Nov. 3, 1905.   [12] The same.
[13] N. Y. *Tribune,* Oct. 26, 1905.

"and it was difficult to make him see the point," but finally he seemed to catch on. He agreed, and McClellan was much relieved.[14]

On the Saturday night before election, Hearst, his voice growing hoarse, ended his campaign by giving twelve speeches in Brooklyn and Manhattan. "HEARST WIND-UP ONE LONG OVATION," the *Times* headlined warningly.[15] At Tenth Avenue and Forty-fifth Street he narrowly missed injury when a wagon filled with his supporters ran into his carriage, nearly overturning it. "A quick act of the candidate's saved a serious accident," the *Times* said. "He grabbed the bridle of the oncoming horse, gave it a hard pull and then forced the animal back."[16] He was not too tired the next night to attend a musicale sponsored by the Municipal Alliance at Madison Square Garden. This was supposed to be a strictly non-political public entertainment where partisanship was forbidden. Yet when Hearst entered his box with his wife after the program had started, he received a rousing ovation from a crowd of 12,000. In boxes near him sat Shearn and other fellow candidates. The musical program was disrupted as the audience began singing the anti-Tammany song:

> *"Everybody woiks but Moiphy;*
> *He only rakes in the dough."*

The musical director, Nathan Franko, bowed to public demand and the orchestra took up the tune. The "non-political" musicale turned into a Hearst rally. He was "persuaded" to make a brief address. After it was over, when the Hearst couple left, crowds "cheered and shouted 'Hearst! Hearst! Hearst!' continually."[17] Although by this time the city-wide enthusiasm for him was immense, one wonders whether the busy Max Ihmsen had not done some "arranging" at the Garden, packing it with the loyal.

The *Times*, suspecting no skulduggery, pointed to the Garden demonstration as proof of alarming Hearst strength.

"If he is elected Mayor tomorrow," the *Times* said fearfully, "of course he will try for the Governorship next year. Very likely he will get it, too."[18]

On election night, Hearst, brimming with the confidence of a man who has seen thousands cheer for him, was at the Hoffman House with Ihmsen and scores of workers. Tammany, with its back to the wall, was fighting with brass knuckles. Hearst election watchers came staggering in with bandaged heads and arms in slings. One of them "had a finger chewed off and his face cut."[19] It was all in vain. When the final count was in, Hearst had lost by an eyelash, getting 224,925 votes to McClellan's 228,397. Ivins, the Republican candidate, ran a poor third with 137,193.

There was talk that Tammany had employed "repeaters" and had dumped thousands of Hearst votes into the East River. Some contemporary commentators agreed that Hearst was defrauded and should rightly have been

[14] McClellan, 236.   [15] N. Y. *Times*, Nov. 5, 1905.   [16] The same.
[17] The same.   [18] The same.   [19] N. Y. *Times*, Nov. 8, 1905.

the next mayor.[20] Hearst himself had no doubt of it. It was said that he was "pale with anger" as he announced that he would contest the election.

"We have won the election," he said. "All Tammany's friends, all Tammany's corruption, all Tammany's intimidation and violence, all Tammany's false registration, illegal voting and dishonest count have not been able to overcome a great popular majority. The recount will show that we have won the election by many thousands of votes." [21]

The *Times*, speaking for all the New York "respectables," uttered a prayer of gratitude, saying, "the election of Mr. Hearst to be Mayor of New York would have sent a shiver of apprehension over the entire Union." [22]

[20] Charles Edward Russell, *Bare Hands and Stone Walls*, 140.
[21] N. Y. *Tribune*, Nov. 8, 1905.   [22] Nov. 8, 1905, issue.

1. George Hearst was seldom this neat.

2. Phoebe Hearst—sweet but resolute.

3. Willie Hearst—a terror at eight.

4. Willie wore a mustache at Harvard.

5. Hearst, on vessel off Santiago, snaps wrecked Spanish warship after the battle.

6. Annie Laurie, first of the sob sisters, was a loyal Hearst writer until she died.

7. Hearst (arm upraised) addresses outdoor crowd in New York City while seeking to unseat George B. McClellan as mayor in 1904. Hearst lost, claimed voting frauds.

CIVIC ALLIANCE

Remember Your Gas Rebates!

VOTE FOR HEARST

For MAYOR
Under Our New Emblem

Headquarters: Civic Alliance of Harlem, 2322 Eighth Ave. and 125th St.
OPEN EVERY EVENING [OVER]

8

9

THE WIZARD OF OOZE

TAMMANY

RECONCILED!

10

8. Hearst handbill. 9. Cartoon satirizes deal with Murphy. 10. Another shows Hearst dancing in mud—i.e., newspaper sensation.

11. Hearst, ballot in hand, casts vote in New York. As politician, he forsook his colorful "Broadway" attire, became addicted to the sober garb of the statesman.

12. Hearst and his beautiful bride, the former Millicent Willson, taken at time of their marriage in 1903.

13. The Hearst couple and their first three sons, photographed at their vast apartment on Riverside Drive.

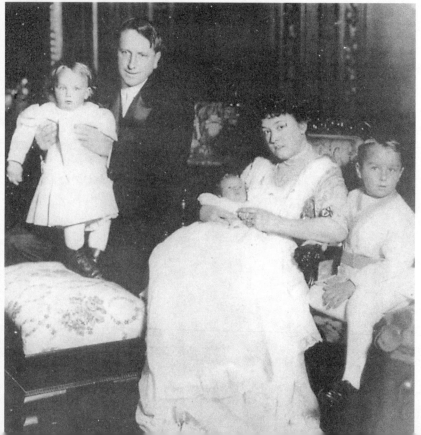

14. The Hearst family during World War I. Mrs. Hearst, a devoted war worker, is in uniform. Also uniformed are the five sons—possibly a Hearst touch to show his "sturdy Americanism" in the face of angry accusations of "pro-Germanism."

15. From left are Al Smith, Mayor Hylan, Hearst, Timothy Woodruff, and young FDR before his attack of paralysis. Hearst is the only one minus a silk topper.

Hylan Lauds Hearst Stand on All Issues

*M*AYOR *HYLAN* yesterday returned from a brief vaca-
tion, spent at his birthplace in the Catskill Mountains
At the City Hall he made public a letter written to William
Randolph Hearst. The Mayor's letter follows:

"**Dear Mr. Hearst:**

"I read with great interest your answers to the questions propounded by Cornelius Vanderbilt, Jr., in his interview published last Sunday. It was a masterly pres-
entation of your views of the subjects discussed. The
questions which you answered are uppermost in the minds
of the people of the nation

16. Headline from N. Y. *Journal* shows typical Hylan worship of Hearst.

21. From left: Hearst, Navy Secretary Claude A. Swanson, Louis B Mayer and Will Rogers. Mayer was long a close Hearst friend. Rogers less close, made Hearst pay dearly for a lot in Santa Monica.

17. Arthur Brisbane.

18. Richard E. Berlin.

19. Edmond D. Coblentz.

20. John Francis Neylan.

SIX HEARST CASTLES

22. San Simeon was his dream.

23. St. Donat's castle in Wales.

24. Beach house at Santa Monica.

25. Miss Davies' "bungalow."

26. Last home at Beverly Hills.

27. Hearst and dog at Wyntoon.

24

25

26

27

MARION DAVIES IN GREATEST ROLE OF CAREER

Historic Love Story Told on the Screen at Criterion Theatre in Elaborate Fashion, Setting New Standard for Photoplays

By ALAN DALE.

MARION DAVIES wiggled her bare toes at Henry VIII. of England, and English history gasped! If English history could possibly take cognizance of the magnificence of "When Knighthood Was in Flower," at the Criterion Theatre, it would gasp some more But as I said——

28. Headline from Hearst's *Journal* is typical of unblushing publicity he gave Miss Davies in such roles as *Janice Meredith* (29). She is seen (30) as a chorus-girl bathing beauty before she entered movies as Hearst dream girl.

31. Miss Davies poses in her beach palace between two of the life-size paintings Hearst had executed showing her in costume in the leading roles of her career.

32. William Jr., Hearst, John and George at San Simeon tennis court.

33. "Chief" huddles with Secretary Willicombe.

34. In great dining room at San Simeon Hearst is seen with guests and plain ketchup bottles.

35. Hearst, Miss Davies (on elbow) and guests at one of the caviar-and-champagne picnics near San Simeon.

36. Hearst, *à la* Tyrolean, "hams" with Ted Healy (left) and Harry Crocker.

37. Hearst and Miss Davies in a Dutch museum amid temptations that helped bring him close to disaster in 1937.

38. A trace of weariness and disillusionment shows as Hearst lolls in a garden chair at Wyntoon between "turns" at a game of croquet.

39. Hearst, hair awry, wears glasses to study editors' queries at San Simeon.

40. Always a splendid horseman, old Hearst masters a bucking carousel steed. This was part of his 80th birthday celebration—a milestone he did not precisely enjoy.

41. Hearst, aged 79, at Hollywood military ball with Miss Davies. As always, his jealously possessive eye was on her.

42. Hearst's dog Helena, snapped on bed the master died in two hours earlier.

5. The Do-It-Yourself Politician

ALTHOUGH Hearst lost, and a later recount availed him nothing since most of the alleged fraud was not in the count but in such things as corrupt voting lists and destroyed ballots, the loss did not dim his luster. On the contrary, he emerged with the highest political prestige he had ever enjoyed. Even his haters had to admit that his huge partyless vote in Tammany's own bailiwick was a stupendous feat. He loomed as a power in 1906. His newspapers, insisting that he won, called Boss Murphy a criminal, pictured him in stripes, and so insistently referred to McClellan as "the fraud mayor" and "the office thief" that he was strongly tempted to sue for libel.[1]

Long afterward, McClellan wrote, "Hearst was a hard-hitting, two-fisted fighter, who never pulled his punches, gave quarter, or asked for it . . . Years after the recount fight had been forgotten we met one day at the Union Club. We shook hands and lunched together, and I am glad to remember that we buried the hatchet and forgot our past differences." [2]

The fear and hatred of Hearst on the part of the conservatives went far beyond normal political opposition. His offensive journalism had particularly aroused his own newspaper contemporaries, who had powerful weapons of retaliation. Few of them doubted that when Hearst, with his admitted abilities, published such raffish sheets it was evidence *per se* that he was insincere, a demagogue of the shallowest sort. Actually, it was evidence only of his lack of taste and his amoral carelessness about truth in journalism. In Congress he was fulfilling his pledges by trying manfully, though in his own peculiar way, to put through the measures he had promised. His own Willis Abbot thought he would have made an efficient but unorthodox mayor, writing, "As with his papers, so would it have been with the city—the business would have been done, but in his own time, in his own way, and in such fashion as never to interfere with his own pleasure." [3]

Less known to the public, but damaging to Hearst among his political colleagues, was his insistence on bossing any group or movement with which he was connected. His enemy Franklin Lane wrote bitterly at this time:

> . . . [Hearst] knows public sentiment and how to develop it very well, and will be a danger in the United States, I am afraid, for many years to come. He has great capacity for disorganization of any movement that is not his own, and an equal capacity for organization of any movement that is his personal property. He feels with the people, but he has no conscience.

---

[1] McClellan, 229.   [2] McClellan, 230.   [3] Abbot, 152.

. . . He is willing to do whatever for the minute the people may want done and give them what they cry for, unrestrained by sense of justice, or of ultimate effect. He is the great American Pander.[4]

Imperturbably Hearst followed his star. His young wife saw that he was temperamentally unsuited for politics, but nothing could stop him.[5] He was having trouble in San Francisco, where his dear friend Schmitz, the "reform mayor," was accused of the most wholesale graft in the city's history and, among other things, of taking protection money from a string of brothels. Mt. Vesuvius erupted, and the New York *American* rushed to the rescue with a drive that gathered $35,000 for the victims—a move cynics ascribed to Hearst's concern for the large Italian vote in New York. Even before he got Italy straightened out, something worse than Schmitz hit San Francisco—the great earthquake and fire of April 18, 1906, which leveled 490 city blocks in twisted ruin with a loss of something like $500,000,000.

It was said that the Italians on Telegraph Hill saved their homes by drenching a wide strip with barrels of wine. The *Examiner* building—along with Phoebe's homey nook and valuable art collection—was gone. So was the *Call,* and the tall, steel-framed *Chronicle* building, where twenty tangled linotypes had fallen through burning floors to the cellar. Hearst was stunned. He could be thankful that his mother was in Paris at the time with Anne Drusilla, so that his loss was only in dollars, more than a million of them.

No pictures were immediately available, so the New York *American* characteristically used a fake, a retouched photograph of the great Baltimore fire of 1904 which other newspapers properly denounced as fraudulent.[6] Hearst, a master organizer, brought his talents into play. Well-publicized relief trains were sent from Los Angeles, Chicago and New York, while his newspapers went on a fund-raising spree featured by charity bazaars and theatrical benefits. He hurried to Washington to introduce a bill proposing an appropriation of $4,502,500 for the rebuilding of public structures in the gutted city, then was off to San Francisco like a general taking charge, carrying more than $200,000 his newspapers had raised.[7] This was one of the occasions when even his enemies must have wished that his greatness in action, in getting things done, was not marred by so many grievous flaws.

The *Examiner* had not skipped an issue, although its first one after the disaster had been combined with the *Call* and *Chronicle*. It was still being printed in Oakland. Manufacturers were unable to supply new presses on short notice. Hearst got one just shipped to a Salt Lake City newspaper by paying double for it. He visited the Hacienda to find that the damage was slight—only two toppled chimneys. In San Francisco, a city of tent-dwelling refugees, he established a relief camp and two emergency hospitals, which he could not forbear to exploit with Hearst signs. He temporarily raised the *Examiner* men's pay a dollar a day to compensate for the increased cost of

[4] Lane, 52.　　　[5] Mrs. William Randolph Hearst to author, May 15, 1959.
[6] Coleman, 131.　　　[7] Mrs. Fremont Older, *op. cit.,* 293.

living. The editorial office was now in a jerry-built shack on the waterfront, where the Chief himself took over in a slashing attack on the city administration for a proposed trolley franchise.[8] He was deeply moved by the ruin of the city of his childhood. Nothing less could have torn him from the aim that now obsessed him—the governorship of New York, which sent him back East early in August.

It had long since been decided that Hearst would be the candidate of the Municipal Ownership League in the fall. Because upstate conservatives shied at the "municipal ownership" tag, thinking it socialistic, the name of the organization was changed to the Independence League, with Seabury and his liberal group still serving as wheelhorses. Max Ihmsen had agents covering every corner of the state, persuading local politicians that Hearst was their man, and, it was said, handing out expense money with a reminder that Hearst was rich and generous, and there would be more.[9] He had opened no "barrel" in the city election, causing comments that he would have won if he had been more lavish. The barrel seemed in evidence now. A new Hearst paper, *Farm and Home,* was started to preach the gospel in the rural areas where his newspapers did not penetrate.

Ihmsen was also promoting Independence League organizations in Massachusetts, California and other states, drafting their membership from dissatisfied and radical Democrats, further enraging old-line Democrats who labeled Hearst a party-wrecker. Hearst was punishing the party for its failure to follow his leadership. He was putting his Independence League on a nationwide basis for use as a machine for the Presidency in 1908. In his own sphere, the man who fought the bosses would be the most unquestioned boss of all—an inconsistency that bothered him not in the least. Caesar could do no wrong. The means gave him little concern as long as the end was desirable. He was convinced that the country needed him.

At his Fourteenth Street wigwam, Boss Murphy was in a dilemma. With Hearst splitting the Democrats and drawing droves of independents, Murphy knew that no candidate he could put forward could match the vote-getting powers of Hearst or of any strong Republican candidate. Barring some legerdemain, the Democrats would run third. For all his detestation of the publisher who had pictured him in stripes, Murphy hated political humiliation even worse. Swallowing his pride, he began a cautious flirtation with Hearst, calculated to promote him as a fusion candidate of the Democrats and the Independence League.

"There is strong sentiment among the Democrats for Mr. Hearst," Murphy said publicly.[10]

If Hearst was listening, as he surely was, he must have exulted at his success in driving his enemy into a corner. His newspapers and Attorney Shearn meanwhile were attacking the "interests" in such efforts as battling the doubling of the nickel fare to Coney Island, and presenting evidence to the

---

[8] Walton Bean, 133.   [9] *Collier's,* Oct. 13, 1906.   [10] N. Y. *Times,* Aug. 1, 1906.

government of the sugar trust's illegal rebate deals with railroads. At vilification, the *American* and *Journal* were unsurpassed, dealing out invective impartially to the following distinguished men who were opposed to Hearst:

Joseph H. Choate, attorney for the sugar trust: "a servile lickspittle of corporations."

District Attorney William Travers Jerome: "the brass-buttoned bellboy of the trusts."

Richard Watson Gilder, the editor: a man with "no more manliness than an apple blossom."

Thomas Taggart, chairman of the Democratic National Committee: "a plague spot in the community spreading vileness."

Grover Cleveland: "a living, breathing crime in breeches."

Judge Alton Parker: "a political cockroach from under the sink."

President Roosevelt: one who "has sold himself to the devil and will live up to the bargain." [11]

These nosegays and many others represented the combative spirit of Hearst. But his taciturnity among strangers was the despair of his supporters. Brisbane, a sociable man, began what was to have been a series of dinners at which Hearst would meet state leaders and become better known to them. The first was with a group of judges, and it was the last. "Mr. Hearst and the judges met, and there was conversation," said a reporter, "but it was Mr. Brisbane who talked, he and the judges. Mr. Hearst sat mute, a silent listener." Brisbane gave up and canceled the remaining dinners.[12]

The New York *Herald*, published by the cynical expatriate, James Gordon Bennett, was assailing Hearst's moral and political character so effectively that he hit on an ingenious plan to strike back. The *Herald*, otherwise a well-edited newspaper favored by the elite, had long been so notorious for its "personals" columns in which prostitutes advertised in euphemistic phrases and assignations were arranged, that it was known by newsmen as "The Whores' Daily Guide and Handy Compendium." Hearst set Victor Watson, a tough young *American* reporter, to the job of tracing the more provocative advertisements, which were said to add some $200,000 to Bennett's annual income. Watson supplied Solomon Carvalho with enough evidence to go before the United States grand jury, which indicted Bennett for sending obscene matter through the mails. He later paid a $25,000 fine that hurt him much less than the humiliation.[13] Like the Lord High Executioner, Bennett had a little list—persons whom his editors were instructed never to mention except in a derogatory way. Hearst went to the top of the list and stayed.

II. A MOST ARTISTIC DEAL

Now that Hearst was in politics, his newspapers took a strong stand against sin. They attacked the racetracks as gambling hells. They supported the

[11] Quoted in N. Y. *Herald*, Nov. 2, 1906.   [12] *American Magazine*, Nov., 1906.
[13] Allen Churchill, *Park Row*, 164.

bluenosed Anthony Comstock's suppression of the magazine of the Art Students' League, which contained pictured nudes. They were sturdy in their opposition to salacious Broadway plays, managing to convey piquant slices of salacity in their attacks. Hearst artists were ordered to paint gym suits on pictures of semi-nude athletes. The Madison Square Roof Garden murder of Stanford White by Harry Thaw over the charms of Evelyn Nesbit received double-truck attention in the *American* and *Journal,* which viewed the slaying loftily as a lesson in morality while they gave explicit attention to the spicy aspects of the case.[1] These attitudes correctly reflected Hearst's inconsistency and his growing puritanism. He was against sin, smoking, drinking, gambling, off-color stories and immorality. His own colorful deviations from propriety made not the slightest difference in his high stand of what was proper for the public.

In August, Hearst and his wife traveled to Illinois, where he had purchased the sixty-two-acre farmstead of Abraham Lincoln. A huge crowd gathered in Springfield on August 17 to hear him speak glowingly of Lincoln as he presented the farmstead to the Illinois Chautauqua Association.[2] Cynics again felt that his public spirit was tinctured by his recollection of how narrowly he had lost the Illinois delegation in 1904 and his hope to win it in 1908.

Murphy continued his friendly overtures toward Hearst. Homer Davenport, who had quit the *Journal* and gone over to the *Mail,* cartooned Murphy on his knees in supplication before a horse-faced Hearst, who was surrounded by moneybags. Hearst gave the back of his hand to Murphy and to State Senator Patrick McCarren, the Brooklyn Democratic boss. McCarren was then being sued by Mary H. Dixon, who declared that she was his common-law wife and had had a child by him. It was noted that Mrs. Dixon's attorney was Manton Wyvell, a law partner of former Senator John Ford, who was a close ally of Hearst, giving rise to speculation that Hearst was taking the opportunity to add to McCarren's discomfiture. If so, McCarren triumphantly escaped by producing Mrs. Dixon's husband, whom she claimed she had believed dead.

Hearst was in the position of having the two bosses woo him while he assailed them.

"McCarren may be for me, as reported," he said, "but I am not for McCarren. I repeat now that I am absolutely . . . opposed to the Murphys and the McCarrens, the Sullivans, the McClellans, and to the kind of politics they represent. I am opposed to boss rule . . ."[3]

Buffalo was a Hearst stronghold, the newspapers there all supporting him. This came about, the *Times* charged, because Hearst held a club over their heads by threatening to start a newspaper of his own there which "would cut heavily into the circulation of the others."[4] Late in August, William Jennings Bryan reached New York after a world tour, to be greeted

[1] Coleman, 75; *Collier's,* Oct. 6, 1906.   [2] N. Y. *Tribune,* Aug. 18, 1906.
[3] N. Y. *Times,* Aug. 22, 1906.   [4] Issue of Aug. 11, 1906.

by Democrats who saw him as the 1908 candidate and to give a speech at Madison Square Garden. Hearst had cooled toward Bryan, but wanted his support in the gubernatorial race. He occupied a box in the Garden, wearing a frock coat despite the steaming heat, accompanied by his wife, his father-in-law, George Willson, and Jack Follansbee. He strolled over to the nearby box of Mrs. Bryan, congratulating her on her husband's reception although the heat was so oppressive and Bryan's speech so long that listeners left by the thousands.[5]

On September 27, at the Democratic state convention at Buffalo, Murphy managed by dint of some slippery work in excluding anti-Hearst delegates to get the Democratic nomination for governor for the man who had consigned him to Sing Sing. A chorus of catcalls arose from the anti-Hearst press. The bitter *Sun* resurrected McKinley's ghost, commenting, "In September, five years ago, the President of the United States was assassinated at Buffalo. At Buffalo this morning William R. Hearst was nominated . . . . let us hope that the party of assassination and the torch has done to mankind the only service of which it was capable and has extinguished itself forever." [6]

There were shouts of a Hearst-Murphy deal. Enemies made use of the song *Waltz Me Around Again, Willie,* as a theme for Hearst, the turncoat. The *Times* recalled how, only ten months earlier, Hearst had heaped Murphy with such epithets as "The Colossus of Graft," "Bill Sykes" and "The Black Hand." Edmund Wetmore burst into poetry, picturing Hearst as saying:

> So I lashed him and I thrashed him in my hot reforming zeal,
> Then I clasped him to my bosom in a most artistic deal.[7]

To be sure, there was a deal—an artistic one. Inconsistent as it was, there was nothing improper in Hearst's acceptance of the Democratic nomination if he did it without obligation to the man he had branded a thief. But there *was* obligation. In his use of the alliance he played the role of a political trickster rather than that of a candidate dealing frankly with the voters. He needed Murphy. In his assaults on the Boss he had burned his bridges behind him. He wriggled out of the dilemma by evasion, later saying it would have taken him twelve years to defeat Tammany, and he could not wait twelve years.[8] Outwardly he refused to make peace with Murphy, although his references to him were now less corrosive and he no longer mentioned Sing Sing. "Murphy may be for me," he said rather mildly, "but I'm not for Murphy, and never have been." [9] Bryan, now in the West, applauded the nomination and said Hearst would make a "good Governor." Hearst had the Democratic nomination while still clinging to the moral advantage of opposition to the bosses. He continued to make unkind but non-vituperative remarks about Murphy—a performance the opposition press labeled as bogus, as indeed it was. The Independence Leaguers had nominated a full slate of

[5] N. Y. *Times,* Aug. 31, 1906.
[6] N. Y. *Sun,* Sept. 27, 1906.
[7] Pusey, *Hughes,* I, 173.
[8] Martin Mooney to author, Oct. 28, 1959.
[9] N. Y. *Times,* Oct. 2, 1906.

candidates. In order to effect fusion with the Democrats it was necessary for some of them to withdraw in favor of Democratic candidates. Negotiation with Murphy was essential in this juggling, but it was said that Hearst refused to have personal dealings with him, letting Judge Seabury conduct all parleys.[10]

The Republican candidate was dignified Charles Evans Hughes, bearing the laurels of his victory over insurance-company connivance. The Hearst press, which had applauded his work at the time, now assailed it. As usual, all the important New York metropolitan newspapers except Hearst's own were fighting him savagely. Joseph Pulitzer, at Bar Harbor, telegraphed his editors to give Hearst fair treatment, saying in part:

> Treat Hearst without a particle of feeling of prejudice, if this is possible . . . while as a matter of conviction [I] sincerely detest most of his professions, principles, purposes and party, the same conviction compels an expression of respect for his courage in accepting a candidacy which cannot lead to his election and must appear as devotion to his principles. If he will give vigorous articulation . . . to the deep conviction among all intelligent Democrats that the . . . ancient Democratic party is used by unscrupulous bosses and politicians purely for money-making . . . he will render a public service whatever his motives.[11]

Pulitzer was wrong in thinking that Hearst was running out of "devotion to his principles." He was out to win. There was no blinking the fact that he had solid men with him, and that he had startling accomplishments to his credit. *The Outlook,* a magazine violently opposed to him, mentioned a few:

> It is due to Mr. Hearst, more than to any other one man, that the Central and Union Pacific Railroads paid the $120,000,000 they owed the government. Mr. Hearst secured a model Children's Hospital in San Francisco, and he built the Greek Theater of the University of California . . . Eight years ago, and again this year, his energetic campaigns did a large part of the work in keeping the Ice Trust within bounds in New York. His industrious Law Department put some fetters on the Coal Trust. He did much of the work in defeating the Ramapo plot, by which New York would have been saddled with a charge of $200,000,000 for water. To the industry and pertinacity of his lawyers New Yorkers owe their ability to get gas for eighty cents a thousand feet, as the law directs, instead of a dollar. In maintaining a legal department, which plunges into the limelight with injunctions and mandamuses when corporations are caught trying to sneak under or around a law, he has rendered a service that has been worth millions of dollars to the public.[12]

In fact, his achievements made the accomplishments of Hughes pale by comparison. The good that Hearst had done with his quick brain, his endless energy and his money added up to such a total that any other citizen boasting such a record could have had almost any office he desired. With Hearst, the

---

[10] Mrs. William Randolph Hearst to author, May 15, 1959.   [11] Seitz, 287.
[12] *The Outlook,* Oct. 6, 1906.

record was blighted by the mischief he had done, by his bad taste and self-praise, and by his ruthlessness of method that made thinking people regard his good works as a sham, a mere series of self-advertisements, a cunning means to an unscrupulous end. Always there was doubt of his sincerity. Probably he never suspected that there might be something horribly wrong in his approach to the public whose votes he needed. His own followers were fanatically loyal to him. His ego forbade any admission of error. Walled in as he was by his own imperial sense of righteousness, he sincerely believed that his enemies were ignoble in motive and subservient to "the interests."

As an imponderable new political force, Hearst suddenly drew the attention of magazines which had formerly ignored him. This was the muck-raking age, when writers for the first time were looking for truth rather than for polished pap. James Creelman, no longer in Hearst's employ, wrote a knowing appraisal of him for *Pearson's*. Frederick Palmer did a critical four-part summation for *Collier's*. The *North American Review*, loathing him, allowed Brisbane to sing his praises in its columns, saying among other things, "There is no doubt that Hearst will be elected President of the United States if he lives . . . He is the most popular individual in the United States today." [13] The *Review* countered in the same issue with an editorial calling Hearst dishonest, unscrupulous, reckless, brutal, and as a journalist "a burning disgrace to the craft."

By far the most searching effort was made by the keen Lincoln Steffens for *The American Magazine*.[14] Steffens accomplished a miracle. He penetrated —almost—the Hearst armor. He could never have done it had he not been ideally fitted for the job. He had spent his youth in California and attended the state university, continuing his education in Germany. He was a radical himself, and he possessed an innate sense of courtesy that could charm the crustiest—all qualities that gave him a common ground with Hearst. Even then he had his troubles.

Determined to solve the Hearst mystery, he interviewed him five times, once aboard a train between New York and Chicago. Steffens began as a profound disbeliever in Hearst. He soon discovered that the "respectables' " conception of him as a hollow shell of insincerity and mediocrity simply would not do. Without losing his critical faculty, he learned that the publisher had far more depth and substance than he was given credit for.

Hearst submitted in a docile manner, but Steffens found the job the most wearing in his experience because Hearst refused to *volunteer* anything. He answered all questions in a slow, gentle voice. When Steffens quoted published criticism and attacks, he reacted with silent indifference instead of coming to his own defense. He seemed immune to such shafts. Steffens had to pump him constantly. Interviewing him was like pulling teeth, but Steffens kept at it like a terrier and emerged with much that surprised him.

For one thing, he demolished what was left of the fiction that Hearst was

---

[13] *North American Review*, Sept. 21, 1906.   [14] Nov., 1906, issue.

a mere checkbook figurehead behind the brains of Brisbane. For another, Steffens was impressed by his earnestness. He wrote:

> He is a tall man who does not strike you as tall . . . He doesn't assert his strength either. Well built, and well groomed, he is strong physically, yet you get no sense of physical force. He never throws his chest out or his shoulders back. He uses his physical strength only for endurance. He is one of those tireless workers who work with the body at ease. . . . All is repose. Nothing is asserted, not even his authority. His orders to his editors go to them as suggestions and queries. . . .
>
> Everything about Mr. Hearst is elusive. His blonde hair is browning; his blue eyes are grayish; his clean-shaven face is smooth; his low voice speaks reluctantly and little, and then very slowly . . . you begin to notice that his straight, strong nose strikes straight down from his forehead; his straight mouth is thin-lipped and hard; and his eyes, cold, sharp and curiously close together, can look straight into yours. A smile blurs these features at first, a sober smile which disarms without winning you.
>
> But Mr. Hearst does not want to win you. He is not in the least magnetic or kind; he is generous, yes, but with his money and power, not with interest, confidences or affection. And he is most loyal to his own; but there is no warmth. And the reason there is no warmth seems to be that there is no sense of need of friends. Mr. Hearst is not only a silent, he is a lonely soul. But earnest. The strongest impression I carried away from my talks with him was that he was a man who was in deadly earnest . . . this man has a will. His very ability seems to be that of will, rather than of mind.

These were uncommon words about a man widely believed a charlatan. Steffens was struck by Hearst's aloofness and lack of warmth without quite identifying it for what it was—colossal egocentricity, with its accompanying feeling of superiority and removal. Hearst pointed out that making money had never been his primary aim in the newspaper business. "If money was what I was after," he said, "I could get that—now—more easily, surely, and with less trouble and less labor, in some other way." His aim in journalism had been leadership and accomplishment. While Steffens privately agreed that Hearst had achievements to his credit, he pressed him about his "sensational" journalism. Hearst demurred at that, preferring the term "striking." The interview was remarkable in that aspect alone, being the first and only time he ever allowed himself to be backed into a corner about the brutality of his newspapers. When Steffens taxed him about his handling of crime news, Hearst did not come off too well. He explained that he considered such news as the "tragedies and romance of life," but conceded that his papers sometimes failed to take this lofty tone.

"I must admit," he said, "that I haven't succeeded very often in getting crimes treated as tragedies, but I have given orders, and my orders are posted in all my newsrooms, forbidding even the word 'murder'. . . .

"I think that part of the fault for the failure is mine. If I had stuck to one newspaper, I might by personal direction in detail have made a newspaper to suit me exactly. But I went off starting papers in widely separated places, and, of course, I can supervise all of them only in a general way . . . I don't think my papers are so bad."

In publishing the interview, the magazine reproduced pages from a recent New York *Journal* in which, in headlines and captions, the words "MURDER" and "MURDERER" appeared four times and the words "HANG," "RANSOM," "KILL" and "KILLER" also stood out. Steffens, who was reflecting that if Hearst failed so signally in getting his own newsmen to follow his instructions he might have a deal of trouble in running the country as President, pressed him about his political aims. Hearst admitted an interest in Caesar, Alexander, Napoleon and Jefferson as leaders of "popular causes," and spoke with evident knowledge of history. He was a Jeffersonian Democrat, he said, and his program was a simple one—the restoration of real democracy.

"Jeffersonian democracy is not an empty phrase with me," he said. "It is full of meaning for me. I have studied Jefferson and Jackson and Lincoln; I have studied carefully the history of this country until I believe I know what it means to say 'equal rights for all and privileges for none.'"

Steffens emerged with an impression that Hearst was not a socialist—hardly even a radical; that his understanding of economic problems was thin, and that his tyrannical use of his terrible newspaper power was an ominous augury of what he might do should he ever hold high office. But outstanding in Steffens' mind was amazement at Hearst's "willful self-reliance":

> He didn't seem to care whether I believed his story or understood him; or whether I got the facts right or wrong. That was my business, not his. And it was business, all of it. There was no humor; no story-telling; no entertainment; no relief of any sort to that interview. Wearing as it was, however, it was interesting to reflect upon, for everything the man said went to bear out the impression that this indifference was nothing but self-reliance. Mr. Hearst doesn't count on anything that may be said about him, one way or the other, by those who are not his friends; he counts on himself and his own. Have your baseball nine; run your own publications; organize your own political party. That's the way to get done the things that you want to have done. Do it yourself.[15]

Steffens could congratulate himself, for never again during his long life did Hearst allow any interviewer to get inside his guard and probe so deeply. Self-reliant though he was, he had been caught on a touchy point, the offensiveness of his newspapers. Bearing in mind that he was running for office, he had forsworn his usual sturdy responsibility for them and had blamed his editors. This was an evasion. The tone of his newspapers was precisely

---

[15] The entire Steffens interview appeared in *The American Magazine*, Nov., 1906. Steffens commented twenty-five years later in his *Autobiography* (pp. 539 ff.), "I cannot describe the hate of those days for Hearst." His colleagues at the magazine expected the article to be an exposé, and Steffens was required to make it more anti-Hearst "to keep my job." He regretted this in 1931, writing of Hearst's "patience, his superb tolerance," and adding, "He is so far ahead of his staffs that they can hardly see him."

what he wanted it to be. More noxious than their handling of crime news was their constant incitement to envy and hate, their pitting of class against class. During the gubernatorial campaign, the New York *American* ran a typically rabble-rousing cartoon by Robert Carter to celebrate Labor Day. It showed a strong, clean-cut man, representing labor, shackled in harness and being driven by a bloated capitalist brandishing a whip. The caption, stark in its appeal to discontent, read: "The Harness Is Not Very Strong. The Big Man Is Getting a Little Tired of the Small Man's Horseplay. The Workmen are to have THEIR Say." [16]

This attitude was a Hearst attitude, the journalistic expression of his beliefs, the symptoms of something dark, lawless and violent in his nature. The mild voice and manner belied some of the instincts of the revolutionist. [17]

III. THE ROOSEVELT HATCHET

THE do-it-yourself candidate campaigned more luxuriously than his Republican opponent. He rode upstate in the private car *Reva* with his wife, little George and his personal entourage. Another private car, *Twilight*, carried a score of newsmen and photographers to publicize his appearances. He evidently regarded his lovely wife and chubby son as helpful adjuncts in impressing on voters a picture of Hearst, the family man, and combating the rumors about his moral character his enemies circulated. He was fond of George, fond of all children. "Mr. Hearst never let a baby in a mother's arms go by without shaking its hand and patting it on the back tenderly," said the *Times*.[1] He spoke at many county fairs, on town squares and at whistle stops, addressing six or eight crowds a day. A number of babies were named after him by admirers. He detailed his secretary to record the names of their parents so that they could be sent silver mugs. He paid several thousand dollars for silver mugs.[2]

Republican Congressman Michael Driscoll of Syracuse made capital of the luxury enjoyed by the candidate who was so solicitous for the underprivileged.

"Imagine, if you can," he said, "the Honorable William Randolph Hearst, my colleague in the House, riding through the country in a private car, with a private parlor, boudoir, bath, cuisine and chef, living in the most elegant and luxurious Parisian style, having any genuine sympathy for the ploughboy in the field. Think of this pampered creature . . . having any real fellow feeling with the man who shovels dirt or hoes corn." [3]

At Hearst's disposal were many private letters between John Archbold and divers Senators and Congressmen. Had he used them in his speeches he would have created an enormous sensation and brought in needed votes.

[16] Reprinted in *Collier's,* Oct. 6, 1906.
[17] Herbert Croly, *The Promise of American Life,* 164.
[1] N. Y. *Times,* Sept. 27, 1906.   [2] Mrs. Fremont Older, *op. cit.,* 307.
[3] N. Y. *Tribune,* Sept. 26, 1906.

He still kept silent. Confident of the governorship without them, he was saving them for his 1908 assault on the White House. His friend Follansbee, who was treasurer of the Independence League, was a devotee of the race-tracks which the New York *American* denounced as "low gambling resorts," and was a member of the Jockey Club, which Hearst characterized as "a robber trust dominated by August Belmont." A reporter asked Follansbee if it was not strange, if not insincere, for Mr. Hearst to have him as treasurer when he was so closely connected with these nefarious activities. Follansbee seemed nettled.

"Mr. Hearst is running for office and I am not," he said. "Mr. Hearst does many things that I do not agree with, but I do not question his right to do as he pleases any more than I allow him or anyone else to question my right to do as I please." [4]

Hearst in his speeches called for an eight-hour work day, a two-cent railroad fare, control of monopolies, teachers' pensions and "Americanism." He described the bearded Hughes as "an animated feather duster," an enemy of the unions. He promised that when elected he would remove Mayor McClellan and District Attorney Jerome for malfeasance. There were charges that what he had in mind were the many damage suits filed against him for the fireworks disaster of 1902, and that by installing a friendly mayor and corporation counsel he could shift all damages on the city. [5]

Eighty-five separate suits, totaling $3,000,000, had been brought against him and the city by the injured and the relatives of the dead. Pain and his fireworks men had been absolved of blame. It still remained to be settled whether Hearst or the city of New York were responsible. Hearst, while he deplored the tragedy, took the stand that he had merely hired the fireworks men, with the city's approval, so that he should not be held culpable. The city was working to saddle him with the damages. A lower court had found Hearst responsible, as had the Appellate Division. However, the Court of Appeals had reversed the decision, holding that since the board of aldermen had passed a resolution suspending the ordinance forbidding fireworks in the streets, the city was liable. Now, New York's Corporation Counsel John Delaney took a new tack. He contended that the aldermen had permitted only political demonstrations, and that the fatal display was not a political demonstration but "an advertising effort in aid of a private enterprise, the New York *American*." The McClellan men were saying that if Hearst was elected governor, a new corporation counsel would be appointed who would hand the city the bill for $3,000,000. [6]

Hughes declared that Hearst, the "enemy of corporations," was himself one of the state's biggest capitalists and had his newspaper and real estate holdings obscured under a bewildering maze of corporations so that he paid no taxes. The anti-Hearst press dredged up both fact and fiction in the fight. The *Tribune*, reminding voters of Hearst's attacks on the employment of

[4] N. Y. *Times*, Oct. 20, 1906.   [5] N. Y. *Tribune*, Sept. 11, 1906.
[6] N. Y. *Tribune*, Sept. 11, 1906.

cheap Chinese labor as endangering American labor standards, ran a picture purporting to show a gang of Chinese coolies working on the "Hearst estate" in California. Hearst owned no California estate, though his mother did. The *World* said that the pro-union, eight-hour Hearst made his 2700 workers at the Homestake Mine in South Dakota "slave" ten hours a day under open-shop conditions. Actually, Hearst had no financial interest in Homestake, although his mother was a heavy stockholder. The *Herald,* more vengeful than ever since Hearst secured Bennett's indictment, poured a running fire of abuse on him, renewing the old charge that he accepted a bribe from the Southern Pacific, accusing him of employing convict labor in California, and making sly references to his moral deficiencies.[7]

The *Sun, Post* and others joined the attack. The anti-Hearst press was replete with innuendo suggesting his moral unfitness for office. Hearst, knowing that his mother was deeply wounded, wrote her soothingly:

> These articles are outrageous, but don't read them. Any kind of success arouses envy and hatred. The best punishment is to succeed more. I shall try to do that. After a while when people understand what my papers are trying to accomplish everything will be all right. . . .[8]

Far from any turn-the-other-cheek attitude, he assailed his newspaper enemies with a flood of billingsgate in a Brooklyn speech in this manner:

> Joseph Pulitzer of the *World:* "a coward, a traitor and a sycophant."
> Oswald Garrison Villard of the *Evening Post:* ". . . was sued by his own sister, who alleged that he tried to rob her of her share in her father's estate."
> James Gordon Bennett of the *Herald:* "lately indicted . . . for printing obscene and indecent advertising."
> William Laffan of the *Sun:* "the mortgaged menial of Morgan." [9]

As election day approached, the Republicans lost their earlier confidence and blanched at the prospect of a possible Hearst triumph. Theodore Roosevelt, deeply concerned, unleashed a Presidential thunderbolt from Washington. He sent his Secretary of State, frosty Elihu Root, to save the state for Hughes. On November 1, Root delivered at speech at Utica unexcelled as a political hatchet job.

Coolly he flayed Hearst as a demagogue, a wily capitalist posing as the friend of labor, a tax-evader, an unscrupulous newspaper publisher specializing in the incitement of hatred, a Congressman absent at 160 of 185 rollcalls, a corruptionist "covered all over with the mark of Tammany." About his morals, Root suggested much by saying little:

> Of his private life I shall not speak further than to say that from no community in this state does there come concerning him that testimony of lifelong neighbors and acquaintances as to his private virtues, the excellence

---

[7] *Tribune,* Oct. 9, 26; *World,* Oct. 22; *Herald,* Oct. 3C, Nov. 2, 1906.
[8] Mrs. Fremont Older, *op. cit.,* 302.   [9] N. Y. *Tribune,* Oct. 28, 1906.

of his morals, and the correctness of his conduct which we should like to have concerning the man who is to be made the governor of our state. . . .

Most telling of all was Root's charge that Hearst was responsible for the murder of McKinley. He read incendiary passages from the *Journal*, including the famous Bierce quatrain. He quoted President Roosevelt's remarks about the "exploiter of sensationalism" who must share responsibility for the crime. He brought the full prestige of the President down on Hearst's head:

> I say, by the President's authority, that in penning these words, with the horror of President McKinley's murder fresh before him, he had Mr. Hearst specifically in mind.
> And I say, by his authority, that what he thought of Mr. Hearst then he thinks of Mr. Hearst now.[10]

Czolgosz had not read the *Journal*. He would have murdered McKinley had there been no such newspaper. Yet, since the Hearst press's appeal to hatred could conceivably have inspired such an act, perhaps the accusation was justified. Hearst's enemies, incensed at his own methods, did not draw a fine point of fairness to him. The speech was timed cleverly in the last days of the campaign so that there was no time to offset its devastating effect. The Republicans had a million and a half copies of it printed and distributed to factory laborers. The *Journal* replied in character with a front-page cartoon of "Root, the rat," nibbling at the people's rights.[11]

Hearst lost by some 58,000 votes out of almost 1,500,000 cast. McCarren had turned on him, whittling down the usual large Democratic plurality in Brooklyn. Boss Murphy had not done too well for him in the rest of the metropolis. But Hearst knew—and political commentators agreed—that he had been defeated by the President, working through Root.[12]

It was such a close race that Hearst would have emerged with some prestige but for one sad fact. He was the only Democrat who lost. All the rest of the candidates on his ticket had won, demonstrating that many voters had split their tickets to repudiate him.

After his sudden, amazing rise, his heyday as a politician was over. Clearly, people were beginning to disbelieve in him. One quails at the thought of the editor of the New York *Journal* in the White House. Possibly the nation owes an incalculable debt to Ambrose Bierce and his silly quatrain.

[10] N. Y. *Times*, Nov. 2, 1906.   [11] Philip C. Jessup, *Elihu Root*, II, 121.
[12] Sullivan, *Our Times*, III, 281.

6. Never Again a Candidate

I. THE BLOOD OF DESTROYED DEMOCRACY

WEARY, with his vocal chords raw from the effort of projecting his voice in a hundred speeches, Hearst left for Mexico in the private car *Constitution* with his wife, son and a "party of friends" that doubtless included Follansbee. Aloof though he was, he liked to make his trips into something resembling continuous, itinerant house parties, paying everybody's expenses. Before leaving, he filed a certificate showing that he had spent $253,370 on his campaign. Hughes' certificate showing personal expenses of $618.55 aroused sarcastic comment at the contrast which was unfair, since Hearst was his own moneybags and Hughes was not.[1] At a stopover in San Antonio, Hearst talked to reporters.

"I will never again be a candidate," he said. "I shall continue to live in New York and advocate and support the principles of reform which I have always stood for." [2]

From Ireland, where he had gone into wealthy retirement, came the warning voice of Richard Croker. Although Croker was hardly considered respectable, his sentiments echoed those of respectable Democrats when he said, "If Hearst had been elected Governor and had continued raising class distinctions, cursing those who made our country and vilifying everyone with a bank account, I am convinced he would have caused a class war. . . . His power to do this has not disappeared. . . . God help Democracy if Hearstism becomes its guiding principle." [3]

After a tour of his Mexican properties, Hearst and his family returned via California, where they visited his mother. Phoebe Hearst's long resistance to her son's fiancée had ended now that the marriage was a fact and she had a grandson. She had lost an intimate companion when her niece, Anne Drusilla Apperson, married Dr. Joseph Marshall Flint; the couple were now living in the East. At sixty-three, Phoebe was still the busy godmother of the University of California. She had started what became a tradition, inviting the graduating class, numbering some 500, to spend a day at the Hacienda. They would arrive by train at Pleasanton, to be met by a swarm of surreys, coaches and automobiles which would take them to the ranch, where they enjoyed a barbecue picnic and other entertainments as guests of the shy, smiling Mrs. Hearst.[4] Possibly Hearst inquired whether she employed any Chinese at the Hacienda or at San Simeon.

[1] N. Y. *Tribune*, Nov. 17, 1906.
[2] N. Y. *Tribune*, Nov. 19, 1906.
[3] N. Y. *Times*, Nov. 18, 1906.
[4] Randolph Apperson to author, Oct. 23, 1959.

To lose, in the space of a year, two close, hard-fought elections into which he had poured his whole soul, was a bitter pill for the man who so loved to win. The governorship of New York—the pathway to the White House—had slipped from his grasp, some said, because of a single speech by Elihu Root quoting an unfortunate quatrain by Ambrose Bierce. That quatrain had cost him dearly on three separate occasions. He might have been forgiven for holding some resentment toward Bierce.

On the contrary, the curmudgeon held resentment against *him*. Bierce, still in Washington after twenty years with Hearst, hated the Hearst press, which he labeled "frankly rotten," and held the fine craftsman's contempt for his employer's papers at the same time as he accepted his bounty. He constantly quarreled with Hearst's editors and with Hearst himself, occasionally resigning, only to be lured back. He wrote a friend, "My emancipation from Mr. Hearst's service was, alas, brief. He did not want it that way, and I can't resist him, for he has been, on the whole, mighty good to me." [5]

Bierce, who now did most of his writing for *Cosmopolitan,* delighted in sending rebellious letters to his employer. He was incensed at assignments given him, sometimes turning them down flatly, as when Hearst asked him to write a piece about Pulitzer. Bierce replied, "I don't like the job of chained bulldog to be let loose only to tear the panties off the boys who throw rocks at you." [6] He was irate about the "art layouts" the editors gave his articles. Hearst humored him, once writing him suggesting two possible art treatments for a Bierce piece, adding, "Do you like either of these, or would you prefer some sort of mystic cartoon . . . ? I suppose you would rather not have anything, but as we have got to spoil the article in some way, will you not indicate which would be the least objectionable?" [7]

Now and then Bierce would appear in New York to seek a personal interview, which Hearst dodged whenever possible. When he could not dodge, he would invite Bierce to lunch at his home, where there would be several ladies among the guests, reducing his opportunity for violent complaint, and he would be treated so royally that his anger would cool. [8] Hearst's unfailing consideration for Bierce in the face of frequent provocation was an earnest not only of the high value he placed on the writer's skill but also of his strong loyalty to "his own," particularly the men who had been with him in San Francisco.

Now, in 1907, "his own" also included a fledgling political party, the Independence League, which he bossed with an authority more complete than Murphy's over Tammany. Max Ihmsen was working to strengthen the League, drawing its membership largely from dissident Democrats, to the anger of Democratic leaders. Timothy Spellacy, chairman of the California Democratic committee, wired an eastern colleague, "In California, William R. Hearst denies justice. His papers malign our party here. He seeks to

[5] McWilliams, 295.   [6] The same.   [7] McWilliams, 300.   [8] Neale, 95.

nourish the Independence League with the blood of destroyed Democracy. . . ." [9]

Since Hearst had chosen to run for governor rather than seek another term in Congress, the session in the spring of 1907 was his last—his swan song, in fact, in public office. He introduced his final measure, one aimed at assuring honest elections, which was rejected like the others. Mrs. Hearst presented him with a second child, a boy who was named William Randolph Jr. The publisher, a fond husband and father, found that his Lexington Avenue house, already so overflowing with art accumulations that many pictures stood on the floor, was simply too small now that his family numbered four. He sought the counsel of his real estate expert, Martin F. Huberth, and rented the tenth, eleventh and twelfth (top) floors of the luxurious Clarendon apartment building at 137 Riverside Drive, at Eighty-sixth Street.[10] Here the Hearsts could spread out in more than thirty rooms, the biggest apartment on the West Side. Since the Clarendon measured 100 by 102 feet, they had three-quarters of an acre of living space not counting the roof garden. Although there was some danger that young George would get lost in his own home, there was room for his father's art treasures. After the place was redecorated and the Hearsts moved in, they gave a housewarming fancy dress party attended mostly by his executives. Mrs. Hearst was dressed as a milkmaid, while Hearst himself—perhaps significantly—appeared as Napoleon, in cocked hat and silk-faced uniform.[11] His newspapers, except for the Boston *American* and the Chicago *Morning American,* were making money at a merry clip. He spent it likewise, although he was occasionally forgetful about paying his bills. There were indications that he hoped to use his Independence League in national politics in 1908 as he had in New York in 1906 —as a powerful club to swing over the Democrats.

On April 13 he addressed a Jefferson birthday dinner of I.L. leaders at New York's Hotel Savoy. A reporter noticed his "diffidence" as he began speaking, and that it took him some time to recover his poise—this after the countless political speeches he had made. It was proof of his courage— proof also of the ambition that drove him, that forced him to speak when he was tempted to flee. He drew an ovation as he attacked President Roosevelt, saying that the I.L. would extend into every state in the union and would erect its political structure "tall and true upon the American foundation stones of liberty, equality, opportunity and independence." [12]

He went to Europe with Mrs. Hearst that summer, writing his mother from Paris, "I won't look at a paper, not even French papers. . . . I am not interested in the 'news.' I have the same aversion to news that I once had for stewed pears after having got sick from them." [13] The Hearst couple returned with tapestries and other decorations for the new Riverside Drive diggings.

[9] N. Y. *Herald,* Nov. 6, 1906.
[11] Mrs. Hearst to author, May 25, 1959.
[13] Mrs. Fremont Older, *op. cit.,* 317–18.

[10] Mr. Huberth to author, June 23, 1959.
[12] N. Y. *Times,* Apr. 14, 1907.

That fall, Hearst supported his political manager, Max Ihmsen, who ran for sheriff on a Republican-Fusion ticket against Tammany's "Big Tom" Foley. In a speech at Cooper Union he made gratuitous remarks showing how fixed had become his bias against the English.

"Before I retired from politics permanently, as I have done," he said, "I thought that if ever I were elected President of the United States I would send to the Court of St. James's an Irish-American. Now that I am out of politics I offer the suggestion to somebody else, with the ardent hope that it will be acted upon."

Criticizing American ambassadors who in England became "more snobbish than their English butlers," he added, "I have never seen the hand of England outstretched to this country unless there was some sort of brick in its clasp. We have been favored with two distinct types of these bricks— the ordinary barnyard variety of brick, and the gold brick." [14]

Ihmsen lost the election. It was an ominous portent when the once powerful Hearst could not elect a sheriff. In aligning with the Republicans he had again demonstrated that party regularity meant nothing to him, and doubtless had confused those of his followers who still remained with him. A politician could put his thumb down, but never know whether Hearst was under it or not. The idealistic Samuel Seabury, coming to the conclusion that Hearst was his own worst enemy, had urged him to curb his personal ambition and devote himself to the journalistic promotion of his principles—a suggestion he ignored. [15] His disappointing nibblings at the political board had only whetted his appetite. For all his talk of being "out of politics" he would keep reaching for the table as long as he lived.

Meanwhile, he undertook to revive his Boston *American*, a paper so troublesome that its publisher, Richard Farrelly, was hospitalized with ulcers. Shoe machinery manufacturers and other Boston tycoons, angered at Hearst's antitrust stand, refused to advertise in the *American*. The paper was a chronic loser. An added difficulty was that goateed Solomon Carvalho, Hearst's chief of staff on the business side, viewed it as hopeless, wanted to get rid of it, and was reluctant to extend it any aid. A penny-pincher, he received an enormous salary for his efforts to save money for his free-spending chief. He often clumped around the *Journal-American* offices on an artificial leg, turning off lights after careless employes.

Hearst could not bear to sell a newspaper, for three reasons. To do so was an admission of defeat; his unbounded optimism always persuaded him that he could turn a loser into a winner; and he regarded each of his papers as an indispensable adjunct to his political machine. He summoned Moses Koenigsberg from Chicago to inject life into the invalid. Koenigsberg arrived in New York to get his orders direct from the Chief, whom he found sprawled on the floor of his home examining comic pages, frequently chuckling over them. He greeted Koenigsberg graciously, then said nothing more to him, continuing to flip comic pages.

[14] N. Y. *Times,* Nov. 2, 1907.   [15] Chambers, 116.

"We sat for nearly a half-hour," Koenigsberg recalled, "he changing position from time to time like a carefree lad on a picnic ground while I commenced to fidget, at a loss whether to start a conversation or get down on all fours beside him." [16]

This was part of Hearst's imperial complex. He enjoyed his supreme authority over thousands of employes. He *liked* to make them fidget a bit. Finally he spoke, asking a series of questions which Koenigsberg realized were aimed at learning his attitude toward the Boston assignment. With his belief in optimism and enthusiasm, he wanted to make sure that Koenigsberg did not share Carvalho's defeatist attitude. Koenigsberg had to show every indication of confidence and anticipation.

Passing the test, Koenigsberg went on to Boston, where he found that the paper was deeply in debt and had other formidable problems. Working like a slave, and exercising measly economies—even saving string—he managed to reduce the *American's* deficit. Hearst wired him joyously: "Fine! Now please add a 'Metropolitan' and an 'Outing' section in colors." [17]

Two sections in color! Koenigsberg groaned. The expense would be ruinous. But Hearst had a fetish about giving readers value, especially in color, which would ultimately increase circulation and profits. Koenigsberg reluctantly obeyed. Soon he was in desperate financial straits. He owed a large sum to the Boston & Maine Railroad, among others. He was unable to use his own office because of the many bill collectors hounding him. The Boston & Maine finally issued an ultimatum: Unless it got $20,000 of its $70,000 debt by next morning, it refused to ship any Boston *Americans* on Sunday. Since the railroad shipped some 300,000 copies every Sunday—more than half its circulation—this would be fatal. Frantically Koenigsberg telephoned Carvalho, urging an immediate $50,000 loan from New York. Carvalho, thinking it best that the paper fail, snapped, "I can do nothing for you," and hung up.[18] At the last moment, Koenigsberg managed to raise a loan through a former Chicago friend. He was begging to be transferred from Boston, and ever afterward he recalled his stay there as a nightmare.

II. OPENING PANDORA'S BOX

HEARST well knew that his Independence League (now called the Independence Party) could not win in 1908. But he had a sincere feeling that both the Republicans and Democrats were betraying the masses, that the people were growing aware of this, and that a good third-party showing in 1908 might lead to victory in 1912. He also knew that his command of a strong independent group that could swing the balance between evenly matched Republicans and Democrats might win him concessions and office from one of the major parties. Certain of his mission to lead, he did not disdain the use of intimidation to gain power. To him, politics was a struggle for power won by the strongest man with the biggest club.

[16] Koenigsberg, 328.   [17] The same, 329.   [18] The same, 330.

258 THE CANDIDATE

Uppermost in his mind was his possession of the red-hot Archbold letters. In these letters he had a weapon that would put his name in headlines from coast to coast. It was a publicity coup he could not resist. It would give him an opportunity to vindicate his oft-repeated stand against the trusts, and to seize the limelight as the defender of the people against corporation-loving politicians of both major parties. He had an incurable weakness for the "big splash."

Archbold, after three years had passed, doubtless was breathing more easily. While he had done nothing criminal under existing laws, the oil trust had been under heavy fire in Miss Tarbell's book and Mr. Hearst's newspapers, among others. Public knowledge of his shady relations with legislators would arouse the nation and certainly bring what Standard Oil most feared—government regulation.

Hearst's course throughout the affair was discreditable. His sly method of obtaining the letters could be defended on the ground that other newspapers had occasionally paid informants for such material, and on the ground of public interest. But the undercover work was defensible only if conducted with the highest motives. Hearst's motives did not stand the test of purity. For him to withhold for three years information which the nation deserved to know at once, and to withhold it to suit his own political convenience, did not exemplify the "American patriotism" of which he was so proud. Probably there were several reasons why he had held the letters so long. For one, some of the legislators involved with Archbold were Democrats— perhaps even his own friends—and to embarrass them might have made it impossible for him to get the Democratic nomination for governor in 1906. For another, some of them were ardent enemies of President Roosevelt, as he was, and he disliked to spike their guns against Roosevelt until 1908 when his term as President was over in any case.

But his strongest reason must have been that 1908 was a Presidential year. He wanted to go before the country with a flaming issue—his very own issue, his private property, an "exclusive."

Late in July, 1908, he traveled to Chicago with Attorney Shearn to attend the Independence Party "national convention." While Hearst had made it plain that he was not a candidate, the convention, which opened at Orchestra Hall July 27, was, like the Archbold letters, his own property. It was guided by his men and would do his bidding. Judge Seabury, his colleague in two bitter campaigns, thinking this third-party effort foolhardy, went to Chicago hoping to dissuade him. When he got off the train he saw himself cartooned in a Hearst paper as a "tool of the trusts." He gave up his mission and returned to New York.[1]

There was a scattering of delegates from various parts of the country, many of them sincere reformers who saw in the Independent Party the only hope for political purification. But some states sent none at all. There were far from enough to pack the large hall with an impressive crowd. Here was

[1] Chambers, 116–17.

where Andrew Lawrence, Hearst's foxy vice-regent in Chicago, filled the breach by bringing in many employes of the Hearst Chicago papers as "delegates." [2] It was said that to fill the spectators' galleries, "several hundred free railroad tickets had been sent out to Gary, Ind., and other industrial centers." [3] The Republicans had already nominated the 320-pound William Howard Taft, while the despondent Democrats for the third time had nominated Bryan. Now the Independent Party would nominate the Hearst candidate.

The frock-coated Hearst drew an ovation, swelled by the voices of his own employes, when he addressed the convention as temporary chairman, assailed the Democrats and Republicans and said it was time for a new party to "take up the work of Jefferson, of Jackson, of Lincoln." [4] There were no men of national prominence present other than Hearst. No time was wasted. On the second day Thomas L. Hisgen of Massachusetts was nominated for President and John Temple Graves of Georgia for Vice President. The platform was all Hearst, asking for control of monopolies, the eight-hour day, federal operation of railroads, creation of a Department of Labor, popular election of United States Senators, and the building of a mighty Navy.[5]

Hearst picked his top candidate cannily, with the Archbold letters in mind. Fifty-year-old Thomas Hisgen was a business man of West Springfield, Massachusetts, who had been defeated for governor on the I.L. ticket in 1906. "Personally," he said, "I lost my faith in the Democratic Party when it failed to nominate Mr. Hearst four years ago at St. Louis." [6] With his three brothers he had fought a personal battle with Standard Oil. They operated a thriving axle grease enterprise, which Standard Oil had offered to buy out for a reputed $600,000. When the Hisgens refused, the company had used its time-tried method of trying to wreck them by price-cutting—a maneuver the Hisgens had met and survived, even managing to enlarge their sales.

John Temple Graves, a pint-sized newspaperman and former colleague of Thomas Watson in Georgia, was nominated in a bid for the Southern vote. The mercurial Watson had given up on Hearst, urging that "Jeffersonian Democracy" not be "gobbled up in the personal selfishness of Hearstism." [7]

In September, Hearst and Hisgen opened a speaking tour at Davenport, Iowa, in which the candidate was entirely overshadowed by his sponsor. Hearst denounced Bryan as "the world renowned loose skin man, who can reverse himself in his own integument, so that you cannot tell whether he is coming or going." [8] The attack made Hearst's enemies, recalling his many political shifts, say in effect, "Look who's talking." This was mistaken criticism, for Bryan had indeed altered his policies in an effort to suit the electorate, while Hearst, for all his party-jumping, had held doggedly to his principles, whatever their failings. The charge that Hearst was a "traitor" to

[2] Winkler, *Hearst—An American Phenomenon,* 224–25.
[3] N. Y. *Herald,* July 28, 1908.
[4] N. Y. *Times,* July 28, 1908.
[5] N. Y. *Times,* July 29, 1908.
[6] N. Y. *Times,* July 27, 1908.
[7] Woodward, 399.
[8] *World's Work,* Oct., 1922.

the Commoner was likewise unjust. He had aided Bryan far more than Bryan had aided him. If there was any debt it was Bryan who owed it.

Not until September 17, in a speech at Columbus, Ohio, did Hearst open his Pandora's box with an attack on the corruption of both Republicans and Democrats, continuing:

> I am not here with empty assertions, but with legal evidence and documentary proof.
>
> I am now going to read copies of letters written by Mr. John Archbold, chief agent of the Standard Oil, an intimate personal representative of Mr. Rockefeller and Mr. Rogers. These letters have been given me by a gentleman who has intimate association with this giant of corruption, the Standard Oil, but whose name I may not divulge lest he be subjected to the persecution of this monopoly.

He then read several letters from Archbold to Republican Senator Joseph Benson Foraker of Ohio, who had hardly had time to recover from his disappointment that his party had nominated Taft instead of him for President.

> March 9, 1900
>
> Dear Senator: I have your favor of last night with enclosure, which letter, with letter from Mr. Elliott commenting on same, I beg to send you herewith. Perhaps it would be better to make a demonstration against the whole bill, but certainly, the ninth clause to which Mr. Elliott refers should be stricken out, and the same is true of House Bill No. 500, also introduced by Mr. Price, in relation to foreign corporations, in which the same objectionable clause occurs.
>
> Am glad to hear that you think that the situation is fairly well in hand.
>
> March 26, 1900
>
> Dear Senator: In accordance with our understanding, I now beg to enclose you certificate of deposit to your favor for $15,000. Kindly acknowledge receipt, and oblige.
>
> February 16, 1900
>
> My Dear Senator: Here is still another very objectionable bill. It is so outrageous as to be ridiculous, but it needs to be looked after, and I hope there will be no difficulty in killing it.
>
> April 17, 1900
>
> My Dear Senator: I enclose you certificate of deposit to your favor for $15,000. . . . I need scarcely again express our great gratification over the favorable outcome of affairs.

Hearst then switched the attack to Republican Congressman Joseph C. Sibley of Pennsylvania, reading part of a letter from Sibley to Archbold which told of a talk Sibley had with President Roosevelt and ended:

> For the first time in my life I told the President some plain if unpalatable truths as to the situation politically, and that no man should win or deserve to win who depended upon the rabble rather than upon the conservative men of affairs. . . . Anything you may desire here in my power please advise.

Looking up from his manuscript, Hearst told the crowd, "You gentlemen, I, Mr. Hisgen—all of us are the rabble. Seekers after office cannot depend upon us; they need the conservative citizens, these magnates of the great criminal trusts." [9]

Ironically, the letters did not stir the Columbus audience to audible gasps because their purport did not entirely sink in. Reporters, however, recognized the sensation. The wires hummed. Hearst was so anxious for instantaneous national impact that he did not give his own papers a scoop but released the letters to all newspapers at once. Another reason was his story that the letters had been given to him in his Columbus hotel room shortly before the speech by a stranger to him. Had his newspapers been given advance publication, the "stranger" story would have held even less water than it later did. This fiction was fabricated to hide the fact that he had held the letters for years, awaiting this moment of revelation.

The Hearst speech made headlines all over the country. Senator Foraker, reading the papers, declared it was well known that he had represented Standard Oil years earlier, but "The employment had no reference whatever to anything pending in Congress." A spokesman for the unhappy Archbold also replied, saying his correspondence with Foraker was "entirely proper" and adding, "If Mr. Hearst had come to Mr. Archbold direct it probably would have cost him less to secure copies of Mr. Archbold's correspondence than for Mr. Hearst to have employed or dealt with thieves." [10]

By this time Hearst was in St. Louis making another speech, with Hisgen tagging along much like an employe. Here he read two more Archbold-to-Foraker letters, one asking the Senator's intercedence against an anti-monopoly bill, the other sending Foraker "$50,000, in accordance with our understanding." [11] A flock of reporters were now hanging on his words to learn whose political neck would next get the axe. Hearst also laced into Governor C. N. Haskell of Oklahoma, the Democratic treasurer, charging him with official acts favorable to Standard Oil. The next night he addressed a huge crowd at Memphis, where his chief victim was Democratic Senator Joseph Bailey of Texas. He read a letter to Archbold from Representative Sibley, whom he called "the miserable little Standard Oil spy in the House," in which Sibley suggested that Archbold have a talk with "Senator B., a Democrat," who would be a "tower of strength and safety." Hearst played cat-and-mouse with this, saying:

"Mr. Sibley does not say who Senator B. is. We'll have to do a little Sherlock Holmes work. Let us see. The vowels of the alphabet are a, e, o, i and u. It can't be Senator Bully as there is no Senator Bully. It can't be Bolly for the same reason. It can't be Senator Billy unless Mr. Sibley is calling some Senator by his first name. It can't be Senator Belly. Can it be Senator Ba—? Why, to be sure, there is a Senator Bailey and we have heard his name mentioned before in connection with Standard Oil. Another thing that makes me suspect

[9] N. Y. *Tribune*, Sept. 18, 1908.   [10] N. Y. *World*, Sept. 19, 1908.
[11] The same.

the Senator referred to may be Senator Bailey is this letter from Mr. Archbold asking Senator B. to come down to New York and step up to the captain's office quickly." Hearst quoted: " 'We are anxious to have a talk here at as early a date as possible with Senator Bailey of Texas.' " [12]

Hearst so enjoyed the sensation he was causing that he occasionally forgot that he was campaigning for Hisgen. His disclosures caused several reverberations. President Roosevelt found it necessary to issue a statement clarifying his interview with Representative Sibley. Taft, the Republican candidate, who had planned to speak from the same platform as Foraker, suddenly decided he had better dissociate himself firmly from Foraker. Bryan, the Democratic candidate, was so embarrassed by the linking of his treasurer, Governor Haskell, with Standard Oil that Haskell resigned as treasurer and talked of suing Hearst for libel.[13]

The Hearst readings also caused difficulty in the city room of the New York *Herald*. Bennett, the owner, had left orders that Hearst was not to be mentioned except in insult. The *Herald* editors, unable to ignore such a sensation, printed the letters without identifying the speaker except as one "regarded as a leader of the independents." Bennett was allowing his personal spleen to deprive his readers of legitimate news.

In later speeches at New York, Denver, El Paso and Los Angeles, Hearst continued his public readings from a seemingly inexhaustible flow of private letters. Among other things, they showed that Archbold had written Senator Mark Hanna, asking his aid in defeating a candidate for Ohio attorney general who was inimical to Standard Oil; that Archbold had manipulated judicial appointments in Pennsylvania, had sent large sums to Senators Boies Penrose and Matt Quay of Pennsylvania, had been on confidential terms with Senator John L. McLaurin of South Carolina, and that Standard Oil had contributed heavily to President Roosevelt's campaign in 1904. The Hearst press front-paged the exposures with headlines such as "W. R. HEARST PROVES THE RULE OF OIL TRUST IN POLITICS," and "Hearst Speeches Rout Old Parties." [14] President Roosevelt felt called upon to make another statement:

> Mr. Hearst has published much interesting and important correspondence of the Standard Oil people, especially that of Mr. Archbold with various public men. I have in times past criticized Mr. Hearst, but in this matter he has rendered a public service of high importance and I hope he will publish all the letters dealing with the matter which he has in his possession. If Mr. Hearst or anybody else has any letter from me dealing with Standard Oil affairs I shall be delighted to have it published.[15]

In San Francisco, with the almost unnoticed Hisgen still in tow, Hearst addressed a home-town meeting at the Central Theater, only a few blocks

[12] N. Y. *American*, Sept. 20, 1908.
[13] N. Y. *Herald*, Sept. 19; N. Y. *Tribune*, Sept. 26 and 30, 1908.
[14] San Francisco *Examiner*, Nov. 1, 1908.   [15] Carlson and Bates, 170–71.

from his tall new *Examiner* building. Admission was by invitation only, the intention being to pack the theater with Hearst supporters. Fremont Older, editor of the *Bulletin* and opposed to Hearst in local politics, had offered a daily five-dollar prize for the best "impertinent question" to ask Hearst when he spoke. Phoebe Hearst occupied a box—her first view of her son as a political spellbinder—and he aimed to keep out Older's hecklers. However, the Older men managed to buy up tickets. There was a considerable number of them in the house. After his speech, Hearst, thinking the audience securely his own, could not resist stepping forward and inquiring, "Are there any five-dollar questions in the house?" There was a storm of shouted queries from the hecklers, and some catcalling before order was restored—a demonstration that must have dismayed the proper Phoebe.[16]

The Hearst press made no pretense of hope for its ticket. It urged, "Vote for Hisgen, Graves and Principle," declaring, "The vote for principle is never thrown away. It is the only vote that isn't thrown away." [17]

The heedless electorate threw its votes away nevertheless in electing Taft over Bryan. The Hearst press used its smallest type in mentioning, "New Party Polls Substantial Vote," without giving figures. Thomas Hisgen had received only 86,628 votes, a third of them in New York City, a number whose humiliating smallness was shown by the number polled by Eugene Debs, the Socialist candidate—420,464. In New York, Massachusetts, Illinois and California the I.P. state candidates were also far back among the also-rans. One of the jokes of the day was "William Also-ran-dolph Hearst."

His disclosures ultimately drove Senator Foraker and Representative Sibley from public life. They did no lasting harm to Archbold, who later became president of Standard Oil of New Jersey, nor to Senators Hanna and Quay, who were dead, nor to Senator Penrose, who said the Archbold payment to him had been merely for campaign purposes. The letters hastened the movement for government control of Standard Oil and other trusts, and for laws requiring publication of campaign contributions. They even worried President Roosevelt a trifle, for he knew Archbold personally and the acquaintance might be misconstrued.[18] After the election, he invited Hearst to visit him at the White House, where the two men had a brief talk. The President was said to have asked whether Hearst had any gossip connecting him with Archbold, to which Hearst reassured him.[19] Certainly there was no suspicion of Roosevelt, who had fought Standard Oil steadily during his second term.

Meanwhile, *Collier's,* doubtless with Archbold's help, had published the story of the abstraction and copying of the letters. There was criticism of Hearst for publicizing private letters obtained in such an undercover way.

"There has been a good deal of hypocritical cant," Hearst replied, "chiefly from those whose rascality has been exposed, about the impropriety of publicly reading private letters. I do not consider that letters written to public

[16] Edgar Gleeson to author, Oct. 16, 1959.   [17] San Francisco *Examiner,* Nov. 2, 1908.
[18] Pringle, *Theodore Roosevelt,* 351.   [19] Carlson and Bates, 171.

men on matters affecting the public interest and threatening the public welfare are private letters." [20]

It was an effective answer—even convincing—but for the one fatal flaw. His three-year wait before producing the correspondence suggested that he was not so concerned with the public interest as with his own interest at election time. He had appropriated what should indeed have been a public issue to his own personal ends.

While he had enjoyed his day in the headlines, and had never expected to install Hisgen in the White House, his massive repudiation at the polls cut him deeply. In 1904, 1905 and 1906 his vote-getting power had struck fear among the mighty. Now he was a laughing-stock, apparently as dead politically as Senator Foraker. Eight years of planning, working, maneuvering, traveling, speech-making, all inspired by the bright dream of political leadership and the Presidency, had fallen in ruins about him. He had bolted the Democrats, condemned the Republicans, and failed dismally with his own hand-made third party, leaving him bereft of any place to go.

The do-it-yourself politician had found that political leadership was something he could not fashion for himself like a newspaper headline. Warm friends were needed, with belief in his principles and respect for his integrity. Of these he no longer had enough. Patience was needed, the ability to cooperate with others, to give and take, to compromise, to heed wise counsel. Of these qualities the great egoist had almost nothing. In any organization or movement he was connected with, he had to rule—absolutely.

[20] Later reprinted in *Hearst's Magazine*, May, 1912.

7. Once More a Democrat

To a man without Hearst's immense strength and fortitude, the 1908 shock of defeat and humiliation would have been crushing, leading even to melancholia and broken health. The redoubtable publisher, a born fighter, may have been bleeding but he was not *hors de combat*. True, it was said that he never quite recovered from the series of blows he had suffered. His agate gaze became a trifle more frosty. He appeared at his newspaper offices less frequently, and while there his camaraderie was not as of old. Yet, for a man with his silver-spoon upbringing and long habit of having all his wants fulfilled, he took defeat well. At forty-five he was toughened but not embittered. On the contrary, he was hopeful. One of the winning qualities of this enigmatic man was his eternal optimism and self-confidence. There were signs that, far from quitting politics in disgust, he still aimed for the Presidency, which perhaps was carrying optimism to the point of self-delusion.

His growing lordliness of manner was reflected in his way of doing business. He had a large room at the Clarendon fitted out as an office. He arranged for one of the building's elevators to be a private one, reserved for Hearst visitors. More and more his executives were summoned there, to wait in an anteroom until the roly-poly Thompson ushered them into the presence. "Waiting for the Chief" became a well-known ordeal among his lieutenants, one that always gave them the fidgets. For all his politeness, he was a master of devastating sarcasm. His gaze—intent, penetrating, cold—frightened hard-boiled editors who were themselves basilisks to their reporters. When Hearst looked at anyone talking with him, his brow and jaw and whole body seemed to join in an unblinking, concentrated stare, devoid of warmth, bent only on the matter at hand, that intimidated underlings and made them feel that they had better say what they had to say fast, and it had better be right. With his consummate grasp of all phases of publishing, he could sometimes give lessons to his specialists. He never forgot. He could recall discussions or letters of months or years previous with photographic clarity. He made quick judgments which were invariably admirable for his purpose, his purpose being circulation—always circulation.

His executives visited him as one visits an oracle, an attitude he did not discourage. His working hours, as always, were from about noon until 2 or 3 in the morning. Many a conference was held there long past midnight. Thompson was a veritable Cerberus who guarded his master against persons he did not wish to see and admitted the elect in a mystic order of precedence

265

no underling presumed to understand. Ambrose Bierce chose this time to resign again. Possibly it was a sign of Hearst's dwindling patience that now he took the testy writer at his word. Bierce expected to be humored as before. He told a friend that he would consent to return if Hearst would apologize, pay him for the time of his unemployment with six percent interest, and give him *carte blanche* in his writing for *Cosmopolitan*. But Hearst silently let him go. Bierce turned to other work, mistakenly blaming the trouble on Mrs. Hearst, who he felt disliked him.[1]

Before President Roosevelt left the White House, Hearst, never one to allow personalities to interfere with the interests of his newspapers, sent Morrill Goddard to Washington in a vain effort to coax Roosevelt to become a writer for the Hearst press.[2] He was also aiming to acquire more newspapers to help publicize his policies and blaze a new trail to the Presidency. He rescued Moses Koenigsberg from Boston and sent him on a tour of the nation's larger cities to appraise newspapers that could be bought. After returning from his annual trip abroad in the late summer of 1909, Hearst turned his attention to the New York municipal election.

He had no intention of running for mayor again. He merely wished to name the candidate and exert his power from behind the scenes. Feuding with Murphy and Tammany more vehemently than ever, he picked Judge William Gaynor as his candidate. Gaynor, whose signal abilities were marred by a sulphurous temper and a gift for vituperation fully equal to Hearst's, had been supported by the Hearst press for years. In turn, he had backed Hearst for governor. Gaynor called at the Clarendon, where Hearst promised him his support and that of the Independence Party. What Hearst sought was a fusion of his own forces with the Republicans against Tammany.[3]

Again he was dogged by his impulse to dictate the terms. Boss Murphy, eyeing the political horizon, announced that *he* was considering Gaynor for the Tammany nomination. This cunning move—stealing his candidate from under his nose—enraged Hearst. At once he demanded that Gaynor refuse Tammany support if given, something the judge was not ready to do. Samuel Seabury, willing to see a good man elected even with Tammany support, and out of patience with the publisher's dictatorial methods, neatly demonstrated the inconsistency of his stand:

> Mr. Hearst through his newspapers has repeatedly praised Justice Gaynor and pointed out that he was an ideal candidate for mayor. He is now unwilling that Justice Gaynor should succeed where he himself has failed. . . . he will support Justice Gaynor only upon the condition that Justice Gaynor will attempt to insure his own defeat. . . .
>
> It is not so long ago that Mr. Hearst saw no impropriety in accepting a Democratic indorsement. But now, when he himself is not a candiate, he will tolerate no indorsement.[4]

[1] Neale, 97.   [2] Koenigsberg, 446.   [3] Louis H. Pink, *Gaynor*, 129-131.
[4] Chambers, 125.

Gaynor, still hoping for Hearst's backing, said, "I value Mr. Hearst's support more highly than I can express. . . . He has done great good in this community and it will never be lost." [5]

But when Gaynor accepted the Tammany nomination, Hearst turned on him and the two became the bitterest of enemies. Hearst sulked in his tent for days. A Republican-Fusion element nominated Otto Bannard for mayor along with a complete ticket. Finally, on October 6, Hearst held a convention of his own party and had himself nominated for mayor on a third ticket. Determined to beat Gaynor and Tammany, he endorsed all the Republican-Fusion candidates except for Bannard and tried strenuously to have Bannard dropped in his favor, which the fusionists refused to do.[6] The campaign that followed was notable for the vilification between Hearst and Gaynor, with Hearst for once meeting his match.

Gaynor assailed him as a liar who had solemnly promised him support, then withdrawn it. Pulitzer's *World* was strongly behind the judge. Brisbane, always a loyal worker for the Chief, persuaded the *World* to throw its columns open to Hearst and Bannard as well. Brisbane thereupon wrote for the *World* a savage denunciation of Gaynor, so incensing the judge that he sued the *World* for libel—an odd development, since the paper was his most potent backer.[7] Gaynor painted Hearst as utterly odious, blaming him for "the awful holocaust in one of the squares of the city, where people were killed and maimed by the explosion of his bombs and Greek fire and rockets, without which he can do nothing, because he thinks everybody to be a fool only to be deceived by his fury and noise . . ." The judge made sly reference to a point most listeners now understood as bearing on Hearst's moral character, saying he had come to New York from California "for reasons well known to a great many people." [8]

Some Gaynor supporters published a scurrilous, forty-eight-page pamphlet depicting Hearst as a debauchee, featuring cartoons with meaning references to "Sausalito Scandal," "My Trip to Egypt," "Orgies in a Yacht," "Trixie Scandal," and others, and an unsubtle "Fable of the Yellow Peril," reading in part:

> From earliest youth the Yellow Peril had been invincible with the Female Sex, and he left behind him Foot-prints on the Sands of Vice. His Game was from the Servants of the Rich to the Daughters of the Wealthy. . . . Having debauched his Life, he now conceived the Idea of Debauching the Democratic Party.[9]

For the first fortnight of the campaign, Hearst seemed resigned to the hopelessness of his own candidacy. He made few speeches, and in them concentrated on pleading for the election of the other Fusion candidates. But he loved a fight, and the acid Gaynor attacks aroused him. Only a week

[5] Pink, 133.   [6] Chambers, 126–27.   [7] Seitz, 390.   [8] Pink, 135.
[9] *Life of William Randolph Hearst*, anonymous.

before the election, he began a heavy speechmaking tour by auto, saying, "I am going after the election." He tried to differentiate between his accept-ance of Tammany support in 1906 and Gaynor's, pointing out that he had refused to speak at Tammany Hall and had defied McCarren. "When Judge Gaynor does as much," he said, "let him speak of my surrender to Tammany Hall." [10]

It was still hopeless. Gaynor won with 250,387 votes. Bannard came second with 177,304, Hearst trailing with 154,187. However, all of the Hearst-Bannard running mates were elected, so that Tammany won only the mayoralty. Hearst could lay claim to a partial victory over Murphy and Gaynor. It seemed likely that Bannard would have beaten Gaynor but for Hearst's splitting of the anti-Tammany vote.

A few months earlier, the Hearst couple had become parents of their third child, a boy whom they named John Randolph. Phoebe, who had been hop-ing for a granddaughter, took the reverse with good grace. She announced that the Hearst children must spend their summers at the Hacienda. She ordered construction of the "Boys' House" on the property, an elaborate affair fussed over by architects, emerging as a splendid two-story building with large playrooms downstairs, including one big enough to permit bicycle riding, and thirteen rooms upstairs for the boys, their governesses and friends.[11]

While Hearst's enemies were uncounted, his feeling toward Gaynor was marked by a special vindictiveness. Because he had supported the judge for years, he felt that his alignment with Murphy was deepest treason. This was compounded by Gaynor's forked-tongue invective and his utter absence of fear of the Hearst press, which he referred to contemptuously as "ragbag newspapers."

Six weeks after the election, the New York *Journal* mysteriously obtained and printed some confidential letters that had passed between Boss Murphy and his lieutenants while Murphy was vacationing at a resort at Mt. Clemens, Michigan. They concerned the matter of finding city jobs for the Tammany faithful under Gaynor, and showed that Gaynor and Murphy were in har-mony—hardly a shock to political realists but treated by the *Journal* in exposé fashion as proof of Gaynor's surrender to all the horrors of bossism.[12] How had the *Journal* obtained the letters? Murphy said angrily that a Hearst spy had followed him to Mt. Clemens and bribed a maid to hand over the con-tents of his wastebasket. "It is pretty low down," Murphy said, "for a man who has run once for the nomination for President of the United States, once for Mayor of New York and once for Governor to hire an agent to enter a man's room and steal his correspondence." [13]

Hearst's magical way of producing embarrassing letters brought tighter security measures among politicians within his reach.

On December 31, 1909, the last day of Mayor McClellan's tenure, Daniel

[10] N. Y. *Tribune,* Oct. 19, 1909.   [11] Mrs. Fremont Older, *op. cit.,* 336.
[12] N. Y. *Journal,* Dec. 15, 1909.   [13] N. Y. *Tribune,* Dec. 16, 1909.

F. Cohalan, a powerful Tammany sachem who had done some franchise tax work for the city, presented a bill for $48,000 for his services. The bill was paid after Gaynor took office, and the huge payment to a Tammany chieftain blew up a scandal. McClellan sidestepped blame, saying it was Gaynor's responsibility. Gaynor testily laid the onus on McClellan. The fact remained that Gaynor made no effort to stop payment. Hearst promptly charged that Gaynor had "paid off" Tammany for the mayoralty out of public funds. Through a dummy, he sued Gaynor, Cohalan and the city chamberlain to recover the money.[14]

The *American* and *Journal* made a yellow holiday of it, questioning the mayor's honesty and running a front-page reproduction of Cohalan's bill. However, in the newspaper reproduction, the date the bill was submitted— December 31, 1909—had strangely disappeared. The only date visible was that of payment, showing that it had been paid after Gaynor took office. The omission made the mayor livid. Hearst later explained it as a technical failure, saying that the ink did not photograph—a story Gaynor did not believe for a minute.[15]

On April 28, 1910, Mayor Gaynor addressed members of the Associated Press at the Waldorf on the relations of the press and public officials. Among the 700 guests were Woodrow Wilson, president of Princeton University and the leading newspapermen of the country, including many Hearst editors and executives. To everybody's surprise, the peppery little mayor used the opportunity to excoriate Hearst for his handling of the Cohalan matter and the disappearance of the date on the bill.

"In no nook or corner of his head or heart," Gaynor shouted, "is there the slightest sense of truth or justice. . . . In plain words, two state prison felonies, namely forgery and falsification of a public document, were committed in the eagerness of this publisher to wrong the Mayor of the city of New York. . . .

"And just think of a man who is capable of doing things like this being possessed of the notion that he is fit to hold any office, from Mayor to President of the United States! Morally speaking, his mind must be a howling wilderness." [16]

Thomas T. Williams, who had been transferred from San Francisco to become business manager of the New York *Journal*, pushed to the speakers' table in a rage and shook his fist at the mayor.

"Mr. Hearst is not here," he yelled, "and I am a member of this body, and I claim the right to say a few words."

Many of the diners cheered Gaynor, while a few asked that Williams be heard, causing a twenty-minute uproar that did not end until Williams left the room.[17]

The scene did not make the Hearst attacks on Gaynor abate. Four months later, shortly after boarding a vessel bound for Europe, the mayor was shot

[14] Pink, 157.   [15] Pink, 159.   [16] N. Y. *Tribune*, Apr. 29, 1910.
[17] The same.

and wounded by a disgruntled dock department employee, James Gallagher. Herbert Bayard Swope, then a *World* reporter, had not forgotten the Mc-Kinley assassination. He rushed to Gallagher's jail cell in Hoboken and fired questions at the assailant. He read the Hearst papers, didn't he? That was what inspired him, wasn't it? Henry Stansbury, a reporter for the *American,* arrived in time to see Gallagher shake his head. No, he said, he read the *Times.* Gallagher was puzzled to see both newsmen burst into uncontrollable laughter.[18]

Later that year, although Hearst's papers had been jocular about early experimental flying efforts, his Los Angeles *Examiner* sponsored the first international aviation meet. At Los Angeles, Hearst squeezed his 200-pound frame into a shaky-looking Bleriot monoplane with Aviator Louis Paulhan and went for a flight at a time when flying was generally regarded as suicidal.[19] The man whose first crossing of the nation by train in ten days in 1873 had been considered a revelation in speed, had the imagination to recognize the potentialities of air travel. He was thereafter an enthusiastic convert to flight. At the same time, his political hopes, so long airborne, came to a crash landing. He made plans to run on his Independence Party ticket for lieutenant governor of New York, but abandoned the idea before election. His party, he realized, had largely disintegrated.[20]

This was true although in its principles it represented a progressive-movement protest against Republican-Democratic conservatism that was gaining ground all over the country. This was precisely what Hearst had foreseen. But the progressives no longer flocked to his standard even though he wanted largely what they wanted. He had thrown away his leadership and lost his following by political ineptitude.

He kept hoping. Koenigsberg was still touring the country, looking for newspapers the Chief might want to buy. "It revolved around an obsession," Koenigsberg later wrote, "—a yearning for the ownership of a newspaper in every advantageous center in America. By gratifying that ambition, he could command the performance of any program he favored, including his installation in the White House." [21] For some time Hearst failed to add to his string, possibly because he was pinched for funds. Koenigsberg, during his travels, also sold the Hearst syndicated features—comics, columns and the like. When he entered a city and talked with a local newspaper owner, the proprietor was invariably paralyzed with fear that Hearst meant to start a paper there, upset all the local standards and run him out of business. Often he would buy the Hearst features in the belief that this was the best way to keep Hearst out, so Koenigsberg found his tours highly profitable.[22]

Meanwhile, in Chicago, the efforts of "Long Green Andy" Lawrence to gain circulation were punctuated by the sound of bullets. Until 1910, the *Examiner* (the new name of the morning *American*) was the city's only morning paper selling for a cent. That year, Medill McCormick's Chicago

[18] Winkler, *Hearst—An American Phenomenon,* 241.   [19] Mrs. Older, *op. cit.,* 338.
[20] Carlson and Bates, 161.   [21] Koenigsberg, 336.   [22] Koenigsberg, 343–44.

Tribune posed a threat by dropping to a cent, then added to the injury by hiring away Lawrence's two circulation managers, Max and Moe Annenberg. The Annenbergs had employed a group of hard-fisted customers whose duty it was to persuade newsdealers to take and sell more Hearst papers and fewer opposition papers or to suffer the consequences, which generally consisted of beatings. When the Annenbergs moved over to the *Tribune*, they took with them some of these gentry, including "Mossy" Enright, Red Connors, Walter Stevens and others who later became prominent in Chicago gang wars.[23] Lawrence, a dapper, unscrupulous man who always maneuvered for political "connections," replied in kind. He hired a gang of gunmen, among them the three Gentleman brothers, Gus, Dutch and Pete, Vincent Altman and Frankie McErlane. Chicago saw a new kind of circulation war as armed thugs roamed the streets, wrecking opposition newspaper delivery trucks, dumping papers into the river and slugging newsdealers who refused to take more papers than they could sell. This warfare reached its natural climax when gunmen on the opposing sides began shooting at each other.[24]

Hearst stood aloof from this gunplay. It was said that he had begun a policy, advised by his lawyers, of refusing to inquire into his underlings' methods on the theory that non-involvement was safer should there be legal repercussions.[25] But to think that he—any more than the owners of the *Tribune*—was ignorant of what was going on, would be to underestimate his keen knowledge of affairs. He had his eye on the Presidency in 1912—or, barring that, at least a high post such as a seat in the Cabinet—at the same time as he was employing gunmen in a Chicago gang war.

II. THE .38 CALIBER CIRCULATION DRIVE

> Mr. Hearst was the kindliest man I ever knew. I remember one time Jack Follansbee and I were walking down Broadway with him. We got to Herald Square, where there was a big water trough for horses. A teamster had taken his horses over to the trough, but he had trouble with one of them and he started to hit the beast on the muzzle with his fist. Mr. Hearst was upset. He went over to the man, and in a nice way he said, "Please don't do that. You'll get better cooperation from him if you use a little patience." The man stared at him as if he were crazy, but he stopped hitting the horse.
> —Martin F. Huberth [1]

It became a habit of the Hearst family to vacation each year in California, where the children took over the Boys' House at the Hacienda. Phoebe, who had always wanted more children, found this yearning fulfilled in her grandsons, whom she spoiled almost as fondly as did their father. While Phoebe

[23] Lundberg, 153.
[25] Silas Bent, *Strange Bedfellows*, 221.
[24] Burton Rascoe, *Before I Forget*, 270.
[1] To author, June 23, 1959.

had forgiven Millicent Willson for marrying her son, her feeling toward her daughter-in-law was said to be hospitable but not truly warm.[2] Hearst, on his part, was genuinely devoted to his mother and proud of her accomplishments. Yet there were occasional disagreements between these two strong-willed persons.

Hearst did not have the same fondness for the placid country around the Hacienda as he did for the rugged ranch at San Simeon. San Simeon drew him like a magnet. Over his mother's protest, he would take his wife and sometimes the children there during the busy ranching season, order horses and tents, summon cowboys from their work, and generally demoralize the establishment. Phoebe, an orderly person, was exasperated, and this became a point of friction between them, but her son went his way.[3]

Hearst had his eye on a commanding hill set back and above the high tract where his father had built the original ranch house. Although almost barren of trees, it had a spectacular view of the Pacific and, to the landward, of the craggy Santa Lucia Mountains. It was an ideal spot for a castle. Hearst, who had an interest in castles unusual in one so devoted to the underdog, planned to build one there. It had been in his mind since 1905, possibly earlier. He loved California better than any place on earth, and this was a dream he had nurtured for years with never any doubt that he would fulfill it when his other affairs were more settled and he had the money. With his passionate sense of property, of ownership, he could never get enthusiastic about the Hacienda, which his mother had taken away from him in 1894 and which was hers, not his.

The rich member of the family was Phoebe, not Hearst. She gave away millions, but in her careful scheme of operations the income was never too far from the outgo. She had none of her son's outlandish extravagance. *That* came from his father. True, she enjoyed luxury and owned a castle of her own. In 1903 she had built a five-story medieval manor house called Wyntoon on the rushing McCloud River in northern California. It was designed by Bernard Maybeck, the University of California architect who also designed the Hearst mining building on the campus.[4] Since the Hacienda was also palatial in size and grandeur, it would seem that Hearst came by his castle-building propensities honestly.

But unlike his mother he was fiscally anarchic. Occasionally he discovered to his surprise that he, the owner of millions in newspapers and real estate, had only small change. It was not uncommon for him, while passing through Chicago, to visit his newspaper office there and take all the money from the safe. At times he was in arrears in paying his bills. It was said that the milkman once stopped delivery of milk to the Clarendon because he had not been paid. Hearst was sued for a paltry $168 owed to an auto rental agency.[5] He was often slow in paying for art objects he bought.

The force of his wants, and his unquenchable optimism, made him aban-

---

[2] Mrs. J. M. Flint to author, Feb. 20, 1960.   [3] Mrs. Flint.
[4] *Siskiyou Pioneer*, Vol. III, No. 1, 1958.   [5] N. Y. *Tribune*, Nov. 15, 1906.

don financial prudence. Debts bothered him no more than important appointments, which he sometimes ignored. He continued to invest heavily in real estate, and the amount he spent on art and antiques was staggering. He had long since become a familiar and welcome figure to New York and European art dealers, who knew that Mr. Hearst wanted almost everything precious he set eyes on and was willing to pay handsomely. The thing that puzzled dealers was the promiscuity of his buying. Most collectors specialized, but he was interested in everything from howdahs to reliquaries, and he seemed gripped by an uncontrollable urge to buy, buy, buy. Moreover, when he wanted something he wanted it fast. Late one Saturday night, seeing an antique he wanted in a New York shop window, he aroused the proprietor at his home by telephone and got him to come to the shop and close the deal at once.[6] Doubtless dealers wondered if he were not a trifle insane. One of the things that drove him was his dream castle at San Simeon. He could not yet build his castle, a delay that gnawed at him, so the next best thing was to buy the decorations that would make it what he intended it to be, the most beautiful place in the world.

When he was pinched, he got occasional financial help from his mother. The new San Francisco *Examiner* building—part of the proud new city that rose from the ashes—was built with Phoebe's money and was her property. There were signs of economy in his newspaper organization. Rube Goldberg, a young cartoonist from San Francisco, had come to New York and got a job with the *Mail* at fifty dollars a week. One day Brisbane summoned him to the *Journal* office, a call that excited him because it was the hope of every cartoonist to work for Hearst, who valued cartoons and paid handsomely. Goldberg was crestfallen when Brisbane offered him fifty dollars a week, pointing out that the *Mail* might "fold" at any time. Goldberg replied that if the *Mail* could pay him fifty dollars a week while on the verge of collapse it would seem that Hearst could do better.

"Take it or leave it," Brisbane snapped.[7]

Goldberg left it, staying with the *Mail*. Brisbane, in his efforts to hold down cartoonists' salaries, used a dodge that became familiar. When Tad Dorgan's contract was ready for renewal, Brisbane appeared arm in arm at the *Journal* office with Robert Edgren, who drew similar material for the *World*. Dorgan understood perfectly that this was a warning that unless he was docile about salary, Edgren might take his place.[8] There was a feeling at the office that Brisbane was cutting costs merely to impress Hearst, but it seems more likely that there was pressure from above. Hearst still paid fantastic salaries for "stars," but the rank and file were now on the same pay rate as at other newspapers.

Despite his attacks on the "money power," it was at work right in his own offices. According to the crusading *Collier's*, the New York *Journal*, which had always been weak in theatrical advertising, gained revenue in

[6] Harry Hershfield to author, Sept. 10, 1959.
[7] Rube Goldberg to author, Feb. 11, 1960.   [8] Harry Hershfield to author.

this field by "selling" favorable Brisbane reviews. By now, Brisbane's pile-driver editorials wielded great influence. "Every [theater] manager knew that the *Journal* offered a page advertisement and a Brisbane editorial for a thousand dollars," said *Collier's*. "It was remarked that Brisbane would not 'boost' under this arrangement any play which he did not like—but his tastes are catholic." [9]

In Chicago, the .38 caliber method of selling newspapers reached its peak in 1912. Dutch Gentleman, a Hearst gunman, was enjoying whisky at a saloon when a *Tribune* thug walked in and shot him dead. Vincent Altman, another Hearst hoodlum, likewise found liquor perilous. He was quaffing at the bar of the Briggs House when competing journalists shot him fatally. Many newsstands were wrecked. While riding a street car, a Hearst slugger became enraged because the passengers were not reading Hearst papers. He fired repeatedly into the ceiling to warn them to mend their ways. By general agreement, the newspapers printed almost nothing about all this violence, and it was said that law-enforcement officials looked the other way because of the political connections of both the *Examiner* and the *Tribune*.[10] The *Tribune* strong-arm squad seemed the more efficient, for *Tribune* circulation went up and *Examiner* sales went down. By the time comparative peace came, twenty-seven newsdealers had been killed and many others injured.[11] Observers have since pointed out that this was the beginning of organized gangsterism and racketeering in Chicago.

III. HEARST AS PRESIDENT-MAKER

IN maneuvering to swing what influence he could in the 1912 national election, Hearst made constant use of his newspapers and magazines. In 1911 his Chicago papers supported the progressive Carter Harrison, Jr., for mayor. On Harrison's victory, Hearst wrote him to say how "delighted" he was, adding:

> What a satisfaction it must be to you to have won out so handsomely without the "bosses," without the public service corporations, without obligations of any kind except to the citizens themselves. If ever I am elected to any office I hope it will be only under such unhampered conditions, and I congratulate you most heartily on the opportunities that lie before you.[1]

This beautiful idealism was lost on Harrison, who had not forgotten that before supporting him, Hearst had tried to get his help for the Democratic Presidential nomination in 1912. "Hearst support apparently only went with some sort of a pledge," Harrison later wrote. ". . . Andrew M. Lawrence bore down on me for a pledge." [2] Harrison, not devoid of Presidential

[9] *Collier's*, June 3, 1911.   [10] Lundberg, 154, 161.
[11] Wayne Andrews, *Battle for Chicago*, 323.
[1] Carter Harrison Papers, Apr. 12, 1911.   [2] Carter Harrison, *Stormy Years*, 268.

ambitions of his own, and unimpressed by Hearst's qualifications, refused to tie his hands. Hearst supported him anyway, and Harrison had to admit that it was this newspaper backing that elected him.

That Hearst, after his excoriation of the Democrats and his political collapse in 1908, could think of himself as a Presidential candidate was a joke to everyone but him. Realistic enough to know that the chances were slim, he nursed the hope nevertheless, never forgetting the power of his circulation. In 1912 his own Independence Party was dead nationally, although still active in New York. He had nowhere to go but to the Democrats. Thither he went. He busily groomed the candidacy of Champ Clark of Missouri, the Speaker of the House he had known as a Congressman, meanwhile working to place himself in the field as a dark horse.

The Democrats' willingness to take him back was not for love but out of intimidation. In 1912 he acquired his ninth newspaper, the Atlanta *Georgian.* The millions he reached represented millions of votes. Hearst, aware of this, did not rejoin the party with his hat in his hand, but almost on his own terms, as a power to be reckoned with. Democratic leaders admitted privately that he was a problem, unpredictable and capricious, but the party that had been beaten in every Presidential election since 1892 would rather have him as a friend than an enemy. There could have been no better sign of Democratic capitulation to Hearst than that he was invited to speak at the Jackson Day dinner held at the Raleigh Hotel in Washington on January 8, 1912. His was not the major speech—Clark and Governor Woodrow Wilson were the chief speakers—but he *spoke.* Cannily, he assailed Theodore Roosevelt, who loomed as leader of a new progressive movement. Without precisely saying so, he suggested himself as a progressive leader with votes in his pocket, saying, "This coming election, and many elections to follow, will be decided by the independent progressive voters. . . ."[3] Among his listeners were William Jennings Bryan and Judge Alton B. Parker.

He returned to New York, where the Woolworth Building was rising to an incredible fifty-five stories, to join a sentimental pilgrimage. Weber & Fields, who had quarreled and been estranged for seven years, had reunited. On February 8, at the Broadway Theater, they appeared with Lillian Russell, David Warfield and others of the misty old cast in *Jubilee.* It was an occasion that drew hundreds of admirers who had mourned the separation of the two desecrators of syntax, many of whom wept unashamedly. Hearst was there with his wife, older sons and Brisbane, in an audience that included Caruso, David Belasco, Diamond Jim Brady and Charles Dana Gibson.[4] Two months later there was weeping of a different kind when the *Titanic* went down and the metropolis went into mourning.

That winter, the Hearst couple vacationed at Palm Beach, Florida. C. J. "Joe" Hubbell, a New York portrait photographer who had opened a studio in Palm Beach for the winter, was surprised to see a big man enter whom

[3] N. Y. *Times,* Jan. 9, 1912.   [4] Isman, 309–12.

he recognized from photographs as Hearst. The publisher was fascinated by photography. After some talk, he said, "Why don't you come out on the boardwalk with me?" Hubbell closed his shop and the two men rode together in a beach chair—a chat that ended when Hearst said, "I want you to work for me. You see Ed Hatrick when you get back to New York." Hubbel did so, and began an employment with the Organization that would stretch out to nearly a half century.[5]

In California, Hearst supporters were working to win that state's delegation for him, although there was strong sentiment for Clark. Clark graciously offered to bow out in favor of Hearst as a native son, writing, "He and I have worked together for many reforms. We have been personal friends for years. He has done me many kindnesses and I do not forget such things."[6]

Hearst countered with a telegram to his old Democratic friend in San Francisco, M. F. Tarpey, calling Clark's stand "generous" but saying he was the "ideal candidate," and "I am more than ever determined to support Mr. Clark and to urge every friend I have in California to support him."[7] Anti-Hearstians sneered that the only reason he stepped aside for Clark was because he realized that he could not win the delegation for himself.[8]

A few weeks later, Arthur Brisbane appeared at a dinner in New York sponsored by society women who favored Woodrow Wilson, astonishing them with "an impassioned appeal for the nomination of Hearst."[9] He would never have done this without the Chief's approval. Hearst saw Clark as the likely candidate, but at the same time he made every effort to enhance his own prestige and place himself at least in a strong position to bargain for a share of the spoils.

Clark's sternest rival seemed to be the cold, pince-nezed Wilson. Hearst claimed to doubt Wilson's progressiveness, but prejudice was not unknown to him. His dislike arose also from three sins committed by the New Jersey governor: he had refused an invitation to dine with Hearst; in his writings he had expressed admiration for the English parliamentary system; and he represented a threat to Hearst's own candidate, Clark.

The Hearst propaganda machine began to operate on Wilson. There was a sledgehammer unsubtlety about this great, noisy, nationwide engine of persuasion, but all of its many parts were well oiled, showing the attention of the master mechanic who pulled the levers. Without vilifying Wilson, the Hearst press portrayed him as merely contemptible. Hearst had hired his 1908 Vice Presidential candidate, John Temple Graves, as a writer. Graves was in Washington, busily stirring up sentiment against Wilson.[10] Hearst also called on the talents of his most practiced master of the slur, the veteran Alfred Henry Lewis, whose hatchet work had so disfigured Mark Hanna. In 1911 Hearst had picked up for $25,000 a magazine called *World To-Day*, which, with his indomitable refusal to shrink from publicity, he

[5] Mr. Hubbell to author, Nov. 1, 1959.   [6] San Francisco *Chronicle*, Feb. 22, 1912.
[7] The same.   [8] S. F. *Chronicle*, Mar. 19, 1912.   [9] McClellan, 323.
[10] Ray Stannard Baker, *Woodrow Wilson*, III, 260.

renamed *Hearst's Magazine*. In this publication, timed just before the Democratic convention, Lewis essayed to smear Wilson. His effort glowed with
the obedient endeavor of the underling taking orders. In Wilson's quiet,
academic background, Lewis could not find the enormities he had so joyfully enlarged on in Hanna's. Throughout his article ran the plaintive dis-
satisfaction of the muckraker who finds no muck. The pipsqueak bolts he
hurled were these:

Wilson's father, a Southerner, betrayed the Confederacy by refusing to
trust its currency, converting it all into tobacco.

A snob at college, Wilson read a snob publication, *Gentleman's Magazine*,
published in England.

He had graduated only forty-first in a class of 122.

He had remained a teacher just twenty-five years—exactly enough to draw
a Carnegie pension, paid by a capitalistic exploiter of the people.

He was a Hamiltonian, not a "Jeffersonian Democrat."

He was "as affected as any Sir Henry Irving."

He had written a pro-English thesis, *Congressional Government*.[11]

Hearst, with his memories of Harvard, should not have quarreled with
Wilson's scholarship. *Hearst's Magazine* gave Champ Clark a full-page photographic portrait with the phrases "universally popular," "a man's man,"
"rugged personality," and "masterful sincerity." [12]

In the same magazine, Hearst dusted off the Archbold letters again, waiting as before for a Presidential year to give them maximum political importance. In a foreword, Hearst told how "a gentleman," identified only as
"J. E.," gave him the letters in a Columbus hotel room in 1908. "J. E." carried on from there with an elaborate commentary on the political implications of the letters, some of which were reproduced photographically.[13] In
this series, which ran for seven months, more than a hundred of Archbold's
letters were printed and discussed, some of which had never been published
before. By now the most recent of them were seven years old, the others
ranging up to fourteen years old. Despite the mildew on them, they still
conveyed an air of keyhole-peeping into the machinations of the mighty.
They were running full blast when the Democratic national convention
opened in Baltimore.

On June 23, Mayor Harrison of Chicago, a Clark man, arrived in New
York to be met at the station by Hearst's Andrew Lawrence, who had arrived from Chicago before him. Lawrence took him by limousine to the
Clarendon for a conference with the publisher.[14] Hearst, who had not given
up an off-chance hope for his own candidacy, may have won an agreement
from Harrison (who owed his election to Hearst) for help if the wheel of
fortune should turn his way. The three men left together for Baltimore.
Hearst attended the convention as a private citizen, the real power behind
Clark, who was easily the favorite on the basis of state primaries. The pub-

[11] *Hearst's Magazine*, May, 1912.   [12] Sept., 1911 issue.
[13] *Hearst's Magazine*, May, 1912.   [14] N. Y. *Tribune*, June 24, 1912.

lisher must have been buoyed by high hopes. After years in the political wilderness, he had maneuvered himself into the position of chief backer for the man most likely to become the next President.

The convention was pervaded by a spirit new to the Democrats, for they could scent victory after two decades of defeat. The Republicans had already named Taft, and Taft's historic feud with Roosevelt had split the party hopelessly. The Hearst feud with Boss Murphy, less world-shaking, still persisted. It was said that Murphy, at the head of New York's potent ninety-vote delegation, was "bitterly opposed" to Clark, fearing that Clark's election would elevate Hearst to such Democratic eminence in New York that Murphy would be deposed.[15] By the unit rule, New York's votes would be cast unanimously for Governor Judson Harmon of Ohio. Bryan, the Peerless Leader now sometimes called the "peerless loser," was with the Nebraska delegation, no longer a friend of Hearst.

From the start there was worry about the potency of Hearst. There were rumors that if Clark won, his influence would make Hearst the next Democratic candidate for governor of New York. It was said that the Murphy men, ready to make a deal with Hearst rather than lose all, were asking what Hearst would demand if Clark won. Other gossip had it that Hearst was looking for bigger game than the governorship and would expect either a place in the Cabinet or an ambassadorship.[16]

The tale also was prevalent that Hearst was eager to make a deal with Murphy if Murphy would swing New York's votes to Clark at the climactic moment. In return for this, it was said, Hearst would lend his Independence League's support to Murphy's local ticket in New York in the fall—a deal that would almost surely give Murphy control of the New York legislature, which he badly wanted.[17]

Clark started out strongly. When Murphy swung his ninety votes to the Missourian on the tenth ballot, it was intended to start a Clark stampede. It was also interpreted as a sure sign of a Hearst-Murphy deal. Strangely, the stampede failed to materialize. The reason was Bryan. Still influential, he began a last-ditch fight for Wilson and called Murphy a tool of the interests. To counter this, Hearst's New York *American* ran a large picture showing Bryan, at an earlier date, shaking hands with Murphy. Bryan admitted this. "I have even shaken hands with Mr. Hearst," he said, in one of the convention's neatest ripostes. "In fact, a man who is in politics is required to shake hands with almost everybody without requiring a certificate of character." [18]

Bryan was hurting Clark. For ballot after ballot, Clark still led but could not get the required two-thirds majority. The tension grew. Hearst went to plead with Bryan, but Bryan "would have no dealings of any kind with William R. Hearst." [19] Speaker Clark hurried from Washington at midnight

[15] N. Y. *Times,* June 27, 1912.
[17] N. Y. *Tribune,* June 27, 1912.
[19] N. Y. *Times,* June 30, 1912.
[16] *Times,* June 28, 1912.
[18] N. Y. *Tribune,* July 2, 1912.

to confer with his managers and with Hearst. But Bryan, who could never win himself, was backing a man who could. Wilson passed Clark on the thirtieth ballot and was nominated on the forty-sixth. Murphy, happy in the knowledge that this divested Hearst of any importance in the party, praised the choice of the convention.

Hearst was one of the few who did not wire congratulations to Wilson. Bryan's snub still rankled.

"Mr. Bryan must be mistaken about me having shaken hands with him," he said. "I am rather particular about the people whom I shake hands with. The only time I have noticed Mr. Bryan's hand was when it was extended for campaign contributions." But he added in more practical vein, "We have made a good fight and lost. I will support the ticket nominated, and expect to see it win. I intend to die game in this fight. I am now for Wilson." [20]

Hearst was as unlucky in politics as his father had been lucky in mining. The convention had suddenly shorn him of power. For the third time he had been in sight of the political victory his heart craved, only to have it snatched away by a turn of fate no one could have foreseen.

Hard on this came an assault from *Collier's*, edited by Norman Hapgood, who had long warred on Hearst. Hapgood was interested enough in Hearst's latest publication of the Archbold letters to commission writer Arthur Gleason to investigate. Gleason took facsimiles of the letters to L. C. Smith & Brothers, typewriter manufacturers at Syracuse, New York. With the aid of type experts and other specialists, Gleason discovered the following:

Five of the letters, allegedly written to Senators Quay, Hanna and Penrose and to Congressman Charles Grosvenor, bearing dates from 1898 to 1904, had been written on a Smith machine with elite type. The company had not manufactured machines with elite type until 1906, so these letters were obvious forgeries.

Type imperfections showed that a letter allegedly written by Congressman Grosvenor in Ohio, and another written by Archbold in New York, had been typed on the same machine.

Eight of the "Jno. D. Archbold" signatures were so identical in every measurement that they could not have been hand-written but must have been stamped from an engraver's block.

An unwary reference made by Hearst in his foreword to "J. E.'s" articles, coupled with a similar reference by "J. E.," indicated that Hearst himself was "J. E.," the writer of the entire series.

"Mr. Hearst has many genuine facsimiles in his possession," Gleason wrote. "Photographs were made in his *American* office of genuine original documents. Why is he using forgeries?" [21]

---

[20] N. Y. *Tribune*, July 3, 1912.　　　　[21] *Collier's*, Oct. 5, 1912.

IV. THE COLUMBUS HOTEL MYSTERY

> [Hearst is an] unspeakable blackguard [who combines]
> with exquisite nicety all the worst faults of the conscience-
> less, corrupt and dissolute monied man, and of the con-
> scienceless, corrupt and dissolute demagogue . . .
> —Theodore Roosevelt [1]

Ex-SENATOR Joseph B. Foraker of Cincinnati, four years out of politics, had not forgiven the man who read him out of public life nor was he happy about the republication of the letters in 1912. The letters had correctly pictured him as receiving a total of almost $100,000 from Archbold. Of that sum, $50,000 was a loan from Archbold to Foraker and a group of associates for the purpose of buying a newspaper in Ohio. The deal had fallen through, and Foraker had returned the $50,000. However, in the letters published by Hearst the one showing the return of the $50,000 was not included. Foraker thought this omission intentional. Still trying to clear his name, he saw in the *Collier's* exposure a weapon to aid him and to strike back at Hearst. An able lawyer, he wanted proof that *Collier's* tale was correct. Traveling to New York, he had a meeting with Gilchrist Stewart, a Negro law clerk who had served as deputy clerk of the New York Assembly. Stewart agreed to serve as Foraker's private investigator. He was to locate Willie Winfield and Charles Stump, take statements from them and verify the account of the theft of the letters.[1-A]

Stewart found that Stump had died in 1909. However, he located Winfield in Chicago, where he lived on Wabash Avenue between runs as a Pullman porter. Winfield corroborated the basic details of the theft. Strangely, after seven years he still had some Standard Oil letters and was said to be negotiating to sell them.[2]

At this time the Clapp Committee of the Senate was investigating political campaign contributions. Part of Foraker's strategy was to arrange for Hearst's appearance before the committee and to be ready with ammunition that would shoot his testimony full of holes. Since some of the Archbold letters concerned political contributions, they came within the committee's scope. Archbold, Foraker and Hearst were among those called to testify.

Hearst testified in Washington on December 17, 1912. He seemed ill at ease. "Mr. Hearst was not a fluent witness," the *Times* commented. "To the most trivial questions he gave prolonged thought before answering and seemed reluctant to discuss in any way how the correspondence had come into his possession." [3] He was under oath, and he knew the penalty of untruth. His memory, usually infallible, seemed to fail him. He prefaced many

---

[1] Robert G. Cleland, *California in Our Time*, 55.
[1-A] Charles H. Walters, *Joseph Benson Foraker*, 286.
[2] N. Y. *Tribune*, Dec. 19, 1912.   [3] N. Y. *Times*, Dec. 18, 1912.

answers with "I think," "I don't think," or "I am quite sure." Indeed, he seemed evasive, much like a man who has paid for stolen letters but cannot own up to it since this would harm his reputation and might actually get him into legal trouble. When Senator Clapp, chairman of the committee, asked him point-blank how he had got the letters, he hesitated.

Mr. Hearst: Now, Senator, I am anxious to testify very fully to everything that I am personally concerned in, and to everything that is necessary to the purpose of this inquiry. Do you feel that is essential to the objects of the inquiry?

Senator Clapp: . . . I am rather inclined to think that as determining the genuineness of them, the committee would be not only empowered but expected to get the evidence of the men who photographed them. . . .

Mr. Hearst: Have not most of the letters already been pronounced genuine by the people to whom they referred, and by the gentlemen by whom they were written?

Senator Clapp: Some; very few. In most cases, as far as the witness [Archbold] would go, as I recall it, was that he had no reason to suppose that they were not genuine. Others, as I believe, were challenged as to their genuineness. . . .

Mr. Hearst: Of course, as I say, I am more than willing—anxious, in fact —to testify, and to bring out all the facts in connection with these letters. I think I have shown that by bringing the letters out, but I am not anxious to contribute any information merely to satisfy the curiosity of Mr. Archbold. So that whatever the committee desires, I will go ahead and testify to.

Senator Clapp: It seems to be the sense of the committee, and I feel myself that we should go to the bottom of it . . .

Mr. Hearst: Very well. Your question was?

Senator Clapp: From whom you obtained these photographic facsimiles of the letters that are published in the *Hearst Magazine* . . .

Mr. Hearst: From the gentleman who wrote the first four articles in this series in *Hearst's Magazine,* Mr. John Eddy.

Senator Clapp: And what is his address?

Mr. Hearst: His present address?

Senator Clapp: Yes, sir.

Mr. Hearst: It is in London. I do not know his detailed address.

Senator Paynter: How long has he been living in London?

Mr. Hearst: I think about two years.

Senator Clapp: Did he purport to have made these copies?

Mr. Hearst: No; I do not think so.

Senator Clapp: Do you know of whom he obtained the originals?

Mr. Hearst: No, sir.

Senator Clapp: Well, have you ever heard him state of whom he obtained the originals?

Mr. Hearst: No, sir.

Senator Clapp: Do you know who made the photographic copies?

Mr. Hearst: No, sir.

Senator Clapp: Do you know of any fact or circumstance that would throw light upon the subject as to who made them?

Mr. Hearst: I do not think I do.[4]

The thought of Hearst, preparing his speech in his Columbus hotel room, seeing Eddy enter with letters of a most explosive nature, ruinous to men in high office, and not even asking him where or how he got them but accepting them as valid without question, struck the Senators as odd. They returned to the subject.

Senator Oliver: Mr. Hearst, I understand you to say that Mr. Eddy is now abroad.

Mr. Hearst: Yes, sir.

Senator Oliver: Is he in your employ?

Mr. Hearst: No; he is in the employ of a London publication.

Senator Oliver: One of your publications?

Mr. Hearst: No. I will not say I have not any interest in it; I have a slight interest in it.

Senator Oliver: I would infer so from what you say. When was the correspondence first handed to you, Mr. Hearst?

Mr. Hearst: In Columbus.

Senator Oliver: Mr. Eddy was employed by you at that time, was he not?

Mr. Hearst: I think he was; but I am not quite positive, as he left my employ for some time and went into the ranching business out West. . . . but I think he was in my employ.

Senator Oliver: Did he not obtain this correspondence substantially as your agent?

Mr. Hearst: No; not at all as my agent.

Senator Oliver: Do you know from whom he obtained it?

Mr. Hearst: No.

Senator Oliver: Did you, Mr. Hearst, or any person acting in your behalf, pay or agree to pay any money for these letters?

Mr. Hearst: I did not pay any.

Senator Oliver: Well—

Mr. Hearst: Nor no one acting in my behalf; no, sir.[5]

The Senators returned repeatedly to the scene in the Columbus hotel room. Hearst continued to insist that he had taken the letters from Eddy without inquiring as to their origin, and that so far as he knew Eddy was the only person who would know where they came from.

[4] U. S. Privileges and Elections Committee—Campaign Contributions (Senate). 62nd Congress, 3d Session, Vol. I, 1253–55.

[5] The same, 1260–61.

Senator Pomerene: Do you know whether he [Eddy] is staying out of the country to avoid testifying in this matter?

Mr. Hearst: I am almost positive that he is not; as positive as one can be of another man's motives.[6]

The Senators turned to the charge that some of the letters had been forged.

Senator Pomerene: . . . After you had published some of the letters there was some statement in *Collier's* . . . in which the writer attempted to demonstrate the fact that some of these copies of letters and telegrams printed in your magazine were in fact forgeries. What, if any, explanation have you to make of that?

Mr. Hearst: Well, I haven't any explanation to make. I believe that some explanation was made at the time. I didn't have anything to do with that. I was abroad at the time. . . . I believe it was said that in a letter like that, where the text is so obscure as to make photographic reproduction in a magazine impossible, that the text was written out in typewriting.

Senator Pomerene: For the purpose of—

Mr. Hearst (interrupting): Making it clear.[7]

This was Hearst's only explanation of the so-called forgeries. It seems convincing. Had there been downright forgeries, there would have been protests and lawsuits from those injured. The retyping of letters which were not sufficiently clear would explain the use of a 1906 typewriter on letters written years earlier. It also seems likely that in the retyping, the names of persons mentioned innocently and in passing, and who might sue if their names were published in connection with the exposures, had been eliminated. The retyping also involved some faking in the photography—placing the retyped material under the proper letterhead and over the proper signature—altogether a dubious business. All this must have been evident to the Senators, as well as Hearst's own statement that he abandoned the most elementary sense of responsibility in taking the letters from Eddy without question, without any effort at verification, to read them and publish them before the world. The Senators were strangely kind to Hearst, for they made no mention of these things. They did try to coax Hearst to hand *all* of the correspondence over to the committee for examination instead of only a part of it. Strictly speaking, the committee was empowered to look into campaign expenditures only since 1900, which Hearst knew. Some of the letters bore dates earlier than 1900.

Mr. Hearst: Well, I have produced all the letters that I think come under the scope of this inquiry. . . .

Senator Oliver: But you must be aware, Mr. Hearst, that in producing and making public some correspondence which perhaps does not come

[6] The same, 1267.   [7] The same, 1262.

strictly within the scope of the investigation, in justice to the parties named as well as yourself, it seems to me that the committee ought at least to have the chance of seeing the whole correspondence.

Senator Clapp: I think, Mr. Hearst, that is so.

Mr. Hearst: I do not agree with you, Senator.[8]

Thus Hearst defied the committee and got away with it. The Senators did not press him any farther. He left the stand after having made only one basic declaration—that he had taken the letters from Eddy and used them without any knowledge of their source.

Foraker, who took the stand next day, was sarcastic. "Mr. Hearst said yesterday that he did not know how the letters were procured," he said. "Such a preposterous story you might tell to the marines, but to no one else." [9]

He had the *Collier's* articles about the theft of the letters and their sale to the New York *American,* and the alleged forgery of some letters, put into the record. He told of a report he had received from his investigator, Gilchrist Stewart, verifying the story of Winfield's and Stump's theft and sale of the letters. According to the report, Winfield and Stump never saw Hearst but were told by the *American* men that Hearst had said they "were performing a great public duty." Foraker suggested that the committee question Stewart and Winfield.[10]

In Chicago, according to Stewart's later testimony, strange things happened to Stewart and Winfield. Late on the night of December 21, Stewart was waiting in Gumb's cafe on South State Street for Winfield, due in from a railroad run. A half-dozen men entered, represented themselves as detectives, produced a warrant and arrested Stewart. Suspicious, he questioned their warrant until they dragged him forcibly outside and shoved him into a taxicab, saying they were taking him to "headquarters." Stewart felt that they had "the look of gangsters on their faces." They stopped at his lodgings on Rhoades Street and took him inside while they searched his room for papers. While there, Stewart managed to telephone a lawyer friend, asking him to get a bondsman and come to the police station to get him out of jail.

The men then took Stewart to a Loop building which to him had the appearance of an office building, not a police station. He was escorted via elevator to an upper-floor office. "As I crossed the threshold," he said later, "I noticed a rubber doormat on the floor with the name 'Hearst' on it. Then I knew where I was and what was up."

A man seated at a desk said sternly, "Officers, have you searched the prisoner?" Stewart recognized him as Andrew Lawrence. He began questioning Stewart about his relations with Winfield. Stewart said, "Now, Mr. Lawrence, you ought to know that I know . . . that I do not have to answer any questions that you desire to ask, and that it is ridiculous to attempt to hold a mock court for me in the editorial rooms of the Hearst Building." [11]

[8] The same, 1259.   [9] N. Y. *Tribune,* Dec. 19, 1912.
[10] Privileges and Elections Committee, *op. cit.,* 1275 ff.   [11] The same, 1354 ff.

Another of the questioners, Stewart said, was Victor H. Polachek, also a Hearst executive. Stewart threatened suit for kidnaping, at which Lawrence and Polachek exchanged jocular remarks about his chances of success against their political influence, Lawrence saying, "Nobody in Chicago would issue a warrant against me." [12] At length Stewart was released. He made efforts to bring charges against Lawrence and Polachek, apparently without success.

Willie Winfield, who also testified before the Clapp Committee, declared that when he arrived at Gumb's cafe to meet Stewart, five "detectives" arrested him, took him to his home and searched the place for letters or papers. He thought at the time that his captors were Standard Oil agents, trying to recover letters he had stolen, or to arrest him for larceny.[13]

In producing this evidence before the committee, Foraker seemed intent on proving that Hearst had perjured himself in saying that he did not know how the letters had been obtained, and that they had not been paid for. The story of Stewart's "kidnaping" and Winfield's "arrest" came only from their own testimony. When they testified, there were minor discrepancies in their accounts. An address proved erroneous. Stewart's statement that Stump and Winfield had received $34,000 for the letters was contradicted by Winfield, who claimed he had received only $2500 as his share, though he believed that Stump had "held out" on him. Winfield was nervous on the stand, being in the unhappy position of admitting stealing the letters. He tried to make his own part in the theft a minor one, laying the blame on the late Charles Stump.[14]

On the basic fact of the theft of the letters and their sale to the *American*, however, Winfield corroborated the earlier *Collier's* account, which had been written on information supplied by Stump. This account had never been challenged and was obviously true.

The Senate committee went no further. Although Hearst's evasive testimony had been impugned, he was not recalled for explanation. The committee did not summon Eddy from London, nor Fred Eldridge, the other Hearst editor who had dealt with Winfield and Stump, who was now in San Francisco. Nor did it question Lawrence and Polachek about the Chicago "kidnapings." Although Chairman Clapp had vowed to "go to the bottom" of the matter, he stopped very close to the top. The committee acted like a group of men avoiding a showdown that would have aroused the ire of Hearst and his press.

Careful readers of other newspapers must have wondered why the inquiry was so abruptly ended. Readers of the Hearst papers, however, found Hearst pictured as the heroic assailant of the oil trust. Stewart was depicted as a liar, a "Standard Oil agent," and Winfield as entirely discredited. By avoiding "Q. and A." reporting, the Hearst editors skipped the testimony

[12] N. Y. *Tribune*, Jan. 14, 1913.
[13] Privileges and Elections Committee, *op. cit.*, 1392 ff.
[14] N. Y. *Tribune*, Jan. 15, 1913.

about the sale of the stolen letters to the *American.* They likewise skipped the testimony that Stewart had been kidnaped by Hearst agents in Chicago, representing him as having been arrested by "the police." [15] When it was all over, Hearst could truly reflect that he had defeated the United States Senate.

While the tortuous history of his manipulation of the Standard Oil letters was too complicated to be understood by most of the public, it was not lost on the intelligent citizenry or on politicians and public officials. It exposed his weakness, his willingness to stoop to almost any device to gain an end. It enveloped him in an atmosphere of the sinister. It caused critics to forget his good works, question all his motives. Thereafter, he would have been cast into political limbo but for one thing: the great and growing power of his newspaper chain, which he used with such strategic cunning that even national leaders who loathed him could not afford to disregard his millions of readers and voters.

[15] N. Y. *American,* Dec. 8, 1912; Jan. 11–17, 1913.

8. Bathtubs and Printing Presses

I. LOVED ONLY BY GOD

WHEN Joseph W. Bailey of Texas resigned from the Senate in 1913, he was still furious at Hearst's charges that he had been unduly friendly with the Standard Oil Company. In a bitter valedictory he denounced Hearst's role in the affair, calling him "a moral pervert, a political degenerate, a physical coward." Senator Henry Ashurst of Arizona spoke up to defend Hearst, describing him as "a firm friend, a loving husband, and a faithful father." [1]

These two descriptions reflected the disparity of opinion between those who had suffered from Hearst's enmity and those who knew only his charm. In listening to an appraisal of Hearst given by an enemy, and one given by a friend, one would think they were talking of two different persons. Although confusing, this was entirely correct, for he *was* two persons. Of all public figures, Hearst carried the split personality to its widest cleavage. His kindliness and his ruthlessness were both carried to excess. He either delighted people or he outraged them. Ambrose Bierce, who had known him well for years, laid his trouble to extreme selfishness. Bierce intended to write a careful appraisal of Hearst whose tenor can be divined from the fact that Bierce refused to publish it during the life of Phoebe Hearst, whom he held in high regard. He never got around to it, but he did compose a devastating paragraph:

> With many amiable and alluring qualities, among which is, or used to be, a personal modesty amounting to bashfulness, the man has not a friend in the world. Nor does he merit one, for, either congenitally or by induced perversity, he is inaccessible to the conception of an unselfish attachment or a disinterested motive. Silent and smiling, he moves among men, the loneliest man. Nobody but God loves him and he knows it; and God's love he values only in so far as he fancies that it may promote his amusing ambition to darken the door of the White House. As to that, I think that he would be about the kind of President that the country . . . is beginning to deserve. [2]

This was ungrateful, coming from a man who had received many kindnesses from Hearst—the man who had written the disastrous quatrain for which any other publisher would have fired him instantly. Nor was it entirely true, since Hearst, although he had few close friends, had his quota of admirers, and most of his executives were fierce in their loyalty to him. Tom Williams' spirited objection to Mayor Gaynor's remarks was symbolic. Yet

[1] N. Y. *Times,* Jan. 3, 1913.   [2] Bierce, *Collected Works,* XII, 305.

there was some truth in what Bierce said. Some forty years earlier, Hearst's father had spotted a basic trait when he said, "There's one thing sure about my boy Bill . . . I notice that when he wants cake, he wants cake; and he wants it now."

This characteristic of wanting things badly and wanting them fast was what made Hearst the astonishing eccentric he was. It was what caused him to awaken a dealer in the middle of the night: he wanted an antique, fast. It was responsible for his newspaper sensationalism: he wanted big circulation, fast. It drove him to violence in politics: he wanted success, fast.

The overmastering want of his entire lifetime was the Presidency. That ambition was common to many politicians. In Hearst it was different in its degree of intensity—the difference between a slight headache and a raging fever. The hunger was so powerful that it upset his balance, impaired his self-control and caused him to lose his perspective in lesser matters. He wanted it so desperately that he was not considerate of those standing in his way, nor did he exercise high-minded discrimination in his methods. He schemed, maneuvered, pulled strings, used the power of his newspapers as a bludgeon, and was guilty at times of grimy expedients. Certainly, in his own mind there was no doubt that he would make the greatest of Presidents.

In 1913, he was only fifty, and there was yet time. Now he aimed to climb to the pinnacle via the Senate. He had formed an alliance with New York's Governor William Sulzer, whom he had supported with funds and publicity. It was said that Hearst was working with Sulzer to depose Boss Murphy as state Democratic leader and take over the leadership themselves—meaning, of course, that Hearst would take it—and that Hearst would run for the Senate in 1914.[3]

After supporting Wilson feebly during the election, Hearst attacked the new President the first time he opened his mouth. His maiden speech to Congress, said Hearst, was pro-English. Wilson read it personally instead of sending it in written form—an English Parliamentary practice and un-American. He quoted the London *Times*. He espoused a reduction of the tariff that smacked of English free trade.[4]

Pro-British or not, Wilson at his inauguration was photographed by several Hearst photographers using heavy, hand-cranked movie cameras. The successful showing of these films made Hearst enter seriously a field that soon fascinated him—motion pictures.[5]

On April 28—the day before Hearst's fiftieth birthday—he and Mrs. Hearst celebrated their "tin wedding" with a dinner and dance for some fifty guests at the Clarendon. "The menus were engraved on a thin scroll of tin with a photograph of Mr. and Mrs. Hearst at the top," [6] the *Times* noted. Jack Follansbee was there, beginning to show the wear of a life of bachelor conviviality. Also present were Judge Elbert H. Gary and Joseph Duveen. Gary was head of the United States Steel Corporation, the sort of man Hearst was wont

[3] N. Y. *Times*, Apr. 10, July 2, 1913.   [4] N. Y. *American*, Apr. 14, 1913.
[5] C. J. Hubbell to author.   [6] N. Y. *Times*, Apr. 29, 1913.

to lump with the "robbers of the people." Duveen was the cunning, aggressive British art dealer who had opened a gallery in New York because that was where the millionaires were. Hearst and Gary, both being victims of Duveen, had become fast friends. Neither could resist the sly artifices practiced by the dealer to make them disgorge huge sums for works of art. Duveen, who could always spot the covetous gleam in a client's eye, was expert at feigning reluctance to sell, or at suggesting the interest of other buyers, so that the price would skyrocket. Hearst was putty in his hands.

Phoebe Hearst's remark that her son Will, when he felt badly, would "go out and buy something," will be recalled. On one occasion Hearst and his wife had a minor difference that nevertheless upset him, with the result that he turned up at Duveen's Fifth Avenue gallery. Duveen was just leaving with Van Dyck's portrait of Queen Henrietta Maria, which he had promised to Mrs. Duveen. He gave Hearst a look at it. Hearst wanted it immediately. Duveen, who this time had a real reluctance, explained the situation. Hearst thereupon *had* to have it. The debate went on until he finally won it with a fantastic bid the dealer could not refuse—$375,000.[7]

By now his three-floor apartment at the Clarendon, although one of the city's biggest, was inadequate. Guests picked their way through statuary and armor. More wall space was needed to accommodate tapestries and large paintings. Hearst delighted in planning and design. With the nominal help of an architect, he drew plans for the revolutionizing of the upper part of the building. It involved evicting the tenants of the eighth and ninth floors, which the Hearsts would take over, and tearing out two floors to make a vast, three-story room fronting on the Hudson with walls some thirty-five feet high. The owner refused to permit such drastic alterations, so Hearst bought the building for "about a million dollars" and did what he wanted.[8] When this was finished, there was no doubt that he had not only the biggest apartment in New York but the biggest in the world.

A big man, he had been annoyed by the smallness of the apartment's bathtubs, which bruised his elbows. It happened that the 320-pound President Taft had installed in the White House a bathtub of Parian marble, of heroic proportions, which was being removed under the Wilson administration. Hearst agents snapped it up and it was installed at the Clarendon.[9]

Hearst was still fighting fireworks suits after eleven years. But he did finally get around to expending public moneys he had held in trust for some fourteen years—the *Maine* monument fund, about which some critics were making unpleasant remarks.

He handled this with typical showmanship, beginning with a dinner at his home for Secretary of War Lindley Garrison, Secretary of the Navy Josephus Daniels, Rear Admiral Sigsbee, and the commanding officers of

---

[7] S. N. Behrman, *Duveen*, 56. [8] N. Y. *Times*, July 6, 1913.
[9] Private source.

the Atlantic Fleet, which was anchored in the Hudson for the occasion. In Hearst, all these guests knew they had a staunch friend and advocate of a strong army and navy. The next day—Memorial Day—the affair began with a great parade and ended with a ceremony at Columbus Circle. By now, Hearst owned half the real estate around the Circle. The monument, the work of Sculptor Attilio Piccirilli, was placed right there, at the entrance to Central Park, where it would enhance his property. Nine-year-old George Hearst, wearing a white Navy uniform, pulled a cord unveiling the monument as a band played *The Star-Spangled Banner* and the warships in the Hudson fired twenty-one-gun salutes while some 70,000 spectators cheered. Ex-President Taft was the orator of the day, followed by many others, with Hearst himself having the last word.[10] Lunching with Taft later, Hearst doubtless had an opportunity to compliment him on his choice of bathtubs.

In politics, Hearst had hurt himself because it was believed, with some truth, that he would sell his immortal soul to get into the Senate. His alliance with Governor Sulzer collapsed when Boss Murphy, seeing Sulzer as a rival, managed to get him impeached. Hearst then began overtures for a truce with Murphy. This so incensed his own enfeebled Independence League that several of the leaders denounced him and quit in disgust.[11] He flirted with Theodore Roosevelt, with whom he shared a detestation for Woodrow Wilson. When he made a statement intimating that he might be willing to run on the Progressive ticket for the Senate while Roosevelt ran for governor, it was generally interpreted as a threat for Murphy's benefit —to frighten Murphy into making Hearst the Democratic candidate rather than to encourage such strong Progressive opposition.[12] If so, Murphy recoiled at the publisher's busy maneuvers, decided he was more of a liability than an asset, and ditched him for another candidate. Once again Hearst had lost out by overplaying his hand.[13]

In 1914, New York suddenly went dance-mad, with stenographers tangoing and bunny-hugging at lunch. Hearst and his wife attended Louis Martin's supper club on Forty-second Street one evening, where a stunning young couple, Irene and Vernon Castle, were dancing with a fluid grace that would soon make them nationally famous. When their program was over, the Castles found a huge bouquet and a note from Hearst. Would they be so kind as to see him? They did. "He was shy and charming," Mrs. Castle recalled forty-five years later. "He asked if Vernon and I would teach him and Mrs. Hearst the latest steps." [14]

For weeks thereafter, the Castles were picked up at the club by a Hearst limousine and whisked to the Clarendon. They noticed that the Hearst chauffeur and all the other servants were not uniformed but wore ordinary business clothing. It was explained that Mr. Hearst's theory of equality forbade him from distinguishing his servants with uniforms. A butler rolled

[10] N. Y. *Times,* May 30, 31, 1913.   [11] N. Y. *Times,* Sept. 25, 1913.

[12] N. Y. *Times,* June 9, 10, 1914.   [13] San Francisco *Chronicle,* July 8, 1914.

[14] Mrs. Castle to author, Nov. 11, 1959.

back the rug in a huge drawing room, turned on the phonograph, and Mrs. Castle danced with Hearst while Millicent Hearst glided off with Vernon Castle. Mrs. Hearst, a dancer herself, was as light as a feather. Hearst, for all his 220 pounds, had not forgotten his youthful imitations of vaudevillians and his Hasty Pudding capers. He was surprisingly graceful. "He had a good sense of rhythm and a nice bounce to the knee," Mrs. Castle recalled. "He didn't really need us, except to learn the new steps." [15]

Jack Follansbee, who for years had been the Waldorf's suavest guest while in New York, died in a New Jersey sanitarium December 15, 1914, after months of declining health. It was a blow to Hearst. Follansbee had been his warm friend for more than thirty years—his companion in the wild Harvard days, in Cuba during the war, in Mexico, and his supporter in several New York elections. Except for Orrin Peck, still in Europe, Follansbee was his last remaining boyhood friend of any intimacy. Although he disliked funerals, he was one of Follansbee's pallbearers.[16]

Another old colleague, James Creelman, had returned to the fold. After holding several editorial and municipal posts, Creelman rejoined the New York *American* with one desire in his adventurous heart—to get to the scene of the war now raging in Europe. Hearst showed the limit of forbearance, forgiving Creelman for accepting the direction of the Civil Service Commission under Mayor Gaynor, and actually having been friendly with Gaynor. Creelman dashed off to Berlin in January, 1915, only to come down with a kidney ailment and succumb February 12. When his funeral was held later in New York, Hearst did not attend but sent flowers.[17]

II. MEET ME AT THE FAIR

BEFORE the Panama-Pacific Exposition of 1915 opened in San Francisco, Hearst visited the site with his crony of the early days, George Pancoast, now mechanical director of all Hearst papers. He was chagrined to discover that his *Examiner* planned to have a modest exhibit at the fair similar to those of other local papers. This could not be. Rapidly he outlined a plan to make the *Examiner* scintillate. He wanted the Hoe Company to build a special twelve-cylinder color press that would spew out copies of the *Examiner* magazine and comic sections before the eyes of visitors at the exposition. Was there time?

Pancoast did not think so. The fair would open in four and a half months, and the construction of such an elaborate press normally took much longer. But he knew that when the Chief wanted something, he wanted it badly. He hurried back to New York, impressed the Hoe experts with a sense of crisis, and succeeded in getting the new press to San Francisco in the form of six carloads of jumbled machinery fourteen days before the fair opened. Pancoast and a crew of mechanics worked night and day to assemble the

[15] Mrs. Castle to author.   [16] N. Y. *American*, Dec. 16, 19, 1914.
[17] N. Y. *Times*, Feb. 13, Mar. 27, 1915.

parts. They made the deadline at the same time that Pancoast collapsed from overwork.[1]

Hearst, who had no compunctions about driving his men to exhaustion for what he considered a good cause, enjoyed the exposition because his *Examiner* exhibit was an acknowledged highlight. The city of his birth showed few signs of the holocaust that had leveled it nine years earlier. Still an avid photographer, he wandered around the exposition grounds with his newsreel cameraman, Joe Hubbell, taking both still and motion pictures. Behind them, carrying extra cameras, trotted the chubby valet Thompson, without whom Hearst seldom went anywhere. Hubbell was struck by the Chief's kindliness, and also by the boyish delight he took in snapping pictures he thought his papers might use. When he spotted a bathing beauty show on the Midway, he decided that the shapely bathers would make a good layout for his Sunday magazine.

"Mr. Hearst," Hubbell demurred, "you know, this show hasn't a very good reputation."

"The pictures won't show that," Hearst grinned, setting up his camera.[2]

Hearst pushed his mother around the exposition in a rolling chair, taking particular pride in showing her the *Examiner* exhibit. Later, he called Hubbell out to the Hacienda to take motion pictures of his mother and his sons. Hubbell set up his heavy camera to "shoot" Phoebe Hearst, who was seated in an outdoor rocker.

"Not quite so close, please, Mr. Hubbell," she said. "Remember, I'm an old lady."

Hubbell dutifully moved back, but he tricked her. He used a telescopic lens.[3]

In Washington, William Jennings Bryan was not allowed to forget that he had betrayed Hearst by making Wilson President. Bryan had accepted the Secretaryship of State on condition that he would not be required to serve liquor at official functions. When this became known among the diplomatic corps, some of them made a habit of "loading up" beforehand, arriving at Bryan's gatherings in a condition less respectable than if he had served wines at his own table. The Hearst Washington correspondents never failed to ask him embarrassing questions about these and other events.

Bryan had insisted on continuing his profitable weekly lectures on the Chautauqua circuit—an undignified procedure for the highest Cabinet member. The Hearst men delighted in asking him where his next "performance" would be, and whether he came before or after the Japanese tumblers and the Swiss bell-ringers. They drove him to distraction with their sly queries. "Mr. Bryan," recalled Oswald Garrison Villard, who was there, "reminded me of a clumsy old buffalo trying to ward off attacks by a pack of young and agile hounds."[4]

In 1915, Sophie Treadwell returned from Europe, where she had been

[1] *Editor & Publisher*, Mar. 18, 1939.   [2] C. J. Hubbell to author, Nov. 1, 1959.
[3] Mr. Hubbell to author.   [4] Villard, *Fighting Years*, 266.

a correspondent for the San Francisco *Bulletin*. Hearst, who had never met Miss Treadwell but had admired her work on the *Bulletin*, was in California at the time. He telegraphed New York demanding that she be hired. Before she knew it, she was on the staff of the *American*. "He was the most generous and appreciative of employers," she later recalled.[5]

She was struck by an instance of the noncensoriousness of his sympathy. A young woman reporter on the *American* was well known to be so infatuated with her older lover that she supported him on her salary while he enjoyed luxurious idleness. One day she was run down by a taxicab and badly injured. Although she was an expendable reporter, Hearst insisted that all her bills be paid until she recovered, knowing that he was also supporting her ne'er-do-well lover.[6]

[5] Miss Treadwell to author, Sept. 27, 1959.   [6] Miss Treadwell to author.

9. The Most Hated Man
in the Country

I. HE WANTS WAR, HE WANTS PEACE

In what was then known as the Great War, Hearst, who yearned for high office and public acclaim, deliberately made himself the most hated man in the country. He fought for American neutrality at a time when neutrality was considered little short of treason. He defended the Germans. He assailed the British. He was called pro-German and anti-English. His relatives and his executives still living deny that he was either. "He was simply pro-American," his son, W. R. Hearst, Jr., said.[1]

Hearst sincerely believed that the United States should stay out of the war. Years after the conflict, many who had attacked his anti-war stand came to regard him as right and to admire the stubborn courage with which he held his ground in the face of nationwide opprobrium. Yet the record shows that he *was* anti-British, although pro-Germanism would be harder to prove.

What did Hearst, whose ancestry was English, have against England? In the earlier days, apparently nothing more than the fairly common feeling then that England's subtle diplomats outwitted us at every bargain. In 1896 the Hearst press was notably anti-British in its reporting of the Venezuela-British Guiana boundary treaty which President Cleveland brought about after considerable difficulty with the English. Subsequently there were occasional slighting comments about the British in his papers. His rage when he learned of the first Hay-Pauncefote treaty forbidding fortification of the Panama Canal was typical. England had cheated us again.

He married a woman of Irish antecedents. He was always benevolently inclined toward peoples fighting for freedom, and his sympathies were with Ireland in her struggle with England. He liked Irishmen—had many in his employ. He had spoken publicly of the "gold bricks" England habitually sold the United States. He had advocated sending an Irishman as ambassador to England. But his animus toward England did not come to full flower until Wilson became President. Probably Wilson had something to do with it. For the President, Hearst developed a hatred as bitter as his feeling toward Gaynor. Whatever Wilson did, Hearst instinctively felt that it was wrong. Wilson admired the English. Wilson quoted the London *Times.* Wilson, as the war in Europe grew deadly, tried to maintain a

[1] To author, Dec. 8, 1959.

294

neutral attitude but was at heart in favor of the Allies. In trying to keep America out of the war, he was in basic agreement with Hearst, the difference being that Hearst felt that Wilson was not doing *enough* to keep us out of war, that his policies favored the Allies, as indeed they did.

There were other reasons. American bankers, including the Morgan interests, gave loans to the Allies which in effect was betting on their victory. Hearst loathed the bankers. England had Japan as an ally, and Hearst was ever fearful of the "yellow peril." It was said—possibly mere rumor—that he had been snubbed by British society.[2] In 1914 he was sued by the British art firm of Charles of London for $18,155 still due them on his purchase of $46,205 worth of antique furnishings. He in turn sued the firm for $3000, saying they had palmed off on him an "Elizabethan" chimney piece that proved to be a fraud.[3] However, this seemed to leave no lasting resentment, for he continued to buy English antiques and only eight months later bought the entire "Julius Caesar room" from the Rotherwas mansion in Hereford through the same Charles of London.[4]

As to his alleged pro-Germanism, there is little evidence. During the Spanish war he had talked of going to war with Germany when the Kaiser's admiral in Manila Bay insulted Admiral Dewey. He owned a German newspaper, now called the *Deutsches Journal*, but was hardly aware of it. It is true that he liked Germany—enjoyed the scenery, the people, the Rhine castles, the art galleries, and German beer. It had long been his habit on trips to Europe to stop at Bad Nauheim and take the month-long medical treatment along with the carbon dioxide baths at the world-famous health resort. He had developed a minor heart murmur—virtually the only chink in his armor of rugged health—and Bad Nauheim's physicians were preeminent in treating heart conditions. Who knows whether this strange, lonely man, so susceptible to prejudice, had met some German who happened to charm him, who spoke of the sins of the British and influenced his thinking? But this is speculation, for so far as is known, his only close friend in Germany was Orrin Peck. Peck, no Germanophile, had fled to London, then finally back to San Francisco, denouncing the German invasion.[5]

Another factor that undoubtedly influenced Hearst was the effective propaganda spread in the United States by the Allies, notably the British, who controlled the cables to America. This propaganda was so successful that within a few months most American political leaders and educators were pro-Ally. The story that the Germans systematically cut the hands off Belgian children was so firmly believed that those who doubted were regarded with suspicion as pro-German. People with Teutonic names were subjected to insult. Dachshunds were kicked in the streets. Hearst loved dachshunds. But above all, as a master propagandist he saw that a propaganda counter to his own thinking was gaining ground. It challenged him. He liked to run things, including the country. A born noncomformist, he had an instinct for

[2] Carlson and Bates, 192.
[4] N. Y. *Times,* June 8, 1915.
[3] N. Y. *Times,* Nov. 7, 1914.
[5] Mrs. J. M. Flint to author, Feb. 20, 1960.

independence that made him suspect automatically the attitudes of the so-called respectable element. He enjoyed a good fight, especially against the respectables. The claim that he favored the Germans in order to win circulation among German and Irish readers is unfounded. On the contrary, he lost circulation, advertising, money, friends and prestige by the stand he took, and he must be acquitted of any profit motive.

So Hearst, who had pushed the nation into war with Spain, had reasons for pushing it away from war in Europe. Underlying them all was his worship of Washington's advice against "foreign entanglements." But his activities seemed improvised from such a confusing multiplicity of motives and prejudices that it is hard to tell how far he was with the angels. And, as always, he could pursue a sincere aim with methods most deplorable.

He began by waving the yellow peril in the face of America, warning that the Japanese would stab us in the back the moment we became involved in Europe. The New York *American* featured under the heading, "Japan's Plans to Invade and Conquer the United States," a "translation" of a book published in Japan, titled *The War Between Japan and America*. It was declared to have been sponsored by high Japanese officials and to have sold more than a million copies.[6] It told how Japan would ally with Mexico in an invasion that would also include the destruction of the Panama Canal.

The Japanese consul-general, who had never heard of the book, cabled home for information. He learned that the original book had been written by a Japanese newspaperman to exploit the measures against Japanese in California. It was a flimsy effort that sold only a few thousand copies, had no official support and was ignored by the intelligent public. Its true title was *The Dream Story of the War Between Japan and the United States*. In it there was no mention whatever of the Panama Canal. The "translation" for the Hearst press was no translation at all but included many inventions calculated to inspire fear. It was, in short, a fake.[7]

Japan and Mexico were much in Hearst's mind. One reason was his and his mother's holdings of ranch, oil, mining, timber and chicle property in Mexico which he later valued at $4,000,000 but was probably worth more. Under the iron regime of his good friend Porfirio Diaz, this property had been protected, but since the exile of Diaz in 1911 governmental authority had crumbled and the country was in chaos for many years. There were threats among the revolutionists to drive out the Yankee imperialists who had taken so much of the land and its resources. Hearst began to portray Mexico as a potential enemy, an ally of Japan against the United States. In his newspapers he called for a strong American stand in Mexico.

In his expanding motion picture interests he saw an opportunity to beat the same tocsin. In 1915 his International Film Service began work on a fifteen-part "patriotic" serial, titled *Patria*. Irene Castle, who had become a good friend of the Hearst family since the dancing lessons, was engaged as

[6] N. Y. *American*, Sept. 26, Oct. 3, 1915.   [7] Carlson and Bates, 184–85.

the star. Hearst became deeply absorbed in the serial. Work dragged on so long that Miss Castle demanded a $5000 bonus for overtime, which was not forthcoming. She tried to see Hearst but could not get past his outer pickets, so she complained to Brisbane and was finally forced to settle for $2500.[8] *Patria* turned out to be a thriller concerning a Japanese-Mexican plot to overpower the United States, with Warner Oland portraying a sinister Japanese baron. It was a sensation, playing to packed houses but gravely offending Japanese Ambassador Hanrihara. International Films received a note from President Wilson, reading in part:

> May I not say to you that the character of the story disturbed me very much. It is extremely unfair to the Japanese and I fear that it is calculated to stir up a great deal of hostility which will be . . . extremely hurtful. I take the liberty, therefore, of asking whether the Company would not be willing to withdraw it.[9]

Patria was called in for alterations and the more offensive scenes were changed. Meanwhile, the disorder in Mexico increased. Hearst's Babicora ranch in Chihuahua was caught in a whipsaw and cruelly treated. It was taken over and looted by the irregulars of Pancho Villa, one employe being reported killed and four held prisoner. Villa, it was said, stole 60,000 of Hearst's cattle. Later the ranch was occupied for a time by the Carranza forces. John C. Hayes, Hearst's manager who had succeeded Follansbee, felt it advisable to flee to El Paso.

Title to the ranch, which had been given by the late Senator to Hearst, had been taken over by Phoebe in return for the many loans she had given her son. Phoebe complained to the Secretary of State about the lawlessness. Babicora vaqueros at length formed their own 100-man "army" and were reported to have killed more than twenty bandits in one pitched battle.[10]

Hearst had such a possessive sense toward his or family property that any encroachment filled him with an anger like that of a monk who sees a shrine desecrated. Feeling it the duty of the United States government to restore order in Mexico, he stepped up his propaganda campaign. His newspapers sprouted inflammatory headlines: "BANDITS JOIN CARRANZA TO FIGHT U.S." and "MEXICANS PREPARE FOR WAR WITH U.S." They belittled American half-measures and called for large-scale invasion: "Is it not time for the soldiers of the United States to do something PERMANENT? . . . . Nothing worth while will be accomplished by occasional 'punitive expeditions'. . . . The way to IMPRESS the Mexicans is to REPRESS the Mexicans. The way to begin is to say to them:

". . . We are no longer planning to catch this bandit or that. We are GOING INTO MEXICO. And as far as we GO, *we'll stay.*" [11]

His two-way posture as a jingo looking south and a man of peace toward Europe caused comments that war did not offend him if it was carried on to

[8] Irene Castle, *Castles in the Air*, 149, 155–56.
[10] San Francisco *Examiner*, May 21, 1916.
[9] N. Y. *Times*, Dec. 14, 1918.
[11] N. Y. *Journal*, June 19, 1916.

protect his own interests. Hearst, who was in New York's Presbyterian Hospital recovering from an appendectomy, replied:

> I have noticed the attacks of the small Americans and the statement that the attitude of the Hearst newspapers on the Mexican situation is due to the fact that there are Hearst property interests in Mexico.
>
> . . . the attitude which is maintained by the Hearst publications . . . is the exact attitude which the Hearst publications maintained with reference to the Cuban situation, and there are no Hearst interests in Cuba . . .
>
> [My view] is merely that the United States Government exercise the fundamental functions of all governments and protect its citizens; that it prevent the Mexicans from murdering any more of our citizens and that it punish Mexico for the murders and outrages already committed upon our citizens and our soldiers.
>
> This is not an extreme attitude. . . .
>
> It would seem to me that any one who was not an incurable idiot would see at a glance that I am incurring the greatest possible risk to any properties I or my family might have in Mexico by taking this stand, so objectionable to the powers in Mexico; and that nothing but a strong sense of patriotic duty would impel a man to take a stand so offensive to a vicious and vindictive Mexican government when there were properties in which he was directly or indirectly interested at the mercy of that government . . .[12]

The picture was hardly that simple. Surely Hearst knew that if American troops moved en masse into Mexico, they would not be likely to leave until American interests had been safeguarded.

But it was his crusade for strict neutrality toward Europe that piled greater wrath on his head. In retrospect, the spectacle of Hearst bearing olive branches and counseling against national impulsiveness is refreshing. His slogans, "America first" and "no entangling alliances," were not indefensible and were shared by an intelligent minority. Indeed, the great majority of Americans were as one with him in hoping to stay out of the war. But although opposed to sending their sons to European trenches, they were not neutral. They became increasingly pro-Ally and anti-German. They favored aiding the Allies with loans and arms and all other means short of war. Hearst, in his insistence on absolute, hands-off neutrality, and in his Anglophobia, struck them as pro-German. Even most of the intellectual pacifists, whose principles were similar to his and who might have been expected to hail him as a spokesman and leader, saw him as discredited, suspected his motives and refused to accept him to membership.

II. RUN LITTLE AMERICAN FLAGS

WHEN the *Lusitania* was sunk in 1915, sending to the bottom sixty-three infants and children among the 1198 victims, the Hearst press called it "a deed of wholesale murder" by the Germans.[1] Later, when public horror had

---

[12] S. F. *Examiner*, July 8, 1916.   [1] N. Y. *American*, May 8, 1915.

subsided a trifle, it pronounced the sinking justified "under the accepted rules of civilized warfare," saying, "The *Lusitania* incident is, of course, no cause for a declaration of war." [2] Secretary of State Bryan, who felt that the President and Cabinet favored the Allies, balked at a Wilson note to Germany as too stern and resigned. The Hearst press, which until then had been contemptuous of Bryan, became his friend.

The United States, Hearst wrote over his own signature, had no right to demand that Germany stop its submarine warfare.[3] He opposed loans and shipments of munitions to England and France, and the arming of United States merchantmen. He hired a former New York *Times* correspondent, William Bayard Hale, and sent him to Germany. Hale was later found to be in the pay of the Germans, which was unknown to Hearst, although his pro-German bias was not.

The respectables were sniping at Hearst in the summer of 1915. Mrs. Hearst was then pregnant. The Hearsts, already having three sons, confidently expected a girl. Phoebe, who had always longed for a daughter of her own, hoped for a granddaughter who would be named after her. At the Hacienda she had as her guest and companion the pretty young Conchita Sepulveda, daughter of Judge Ygnacio Sepulveda, who had been an adviser of the Senator and an overseer of his Mexican interests.

The New York press was unanimously inimical to Hearst, whose errors they delighted in magnifying while soft-pedaling his achievements. *Harper's Weekly* grew suspicious of stirring dispatches sent to the Hearst press by Hearst's International News Service correspondents Frederick Werner in Berlin, Franklin P. Merrick in Paris, John C. Foster and Lawrence Elston in London, Brixton D. Allaire in Rome, and Herbert Temple, European news manager of I.N.S. *Harper's* tried to locate these men by mail, then via queries to other newsmen in those cities. It could not reach any of them, and was informed that the gentlemen did not exist. The Hearst service, *Harper's* charged, in order to make its foreign news service look impressive while at the same time saving money, was having hacks in London or New York pound out copy under the bylines of mythical correspondents.

Like the other five, *Harper's* said, "Brixton D. Allaire, dear reader, is not a romantic figure in khaki, braving untold dangers in the field of battle, but simply a common, ordinary, contemptible Hearst fake." [4]

Early in December, Mrs. Hearst confounded the family plans by giving birth not to one boy but twin boys. Hearst, after his first astonishment, sent his mother a teasing telegram: "Dear Mother: I regret that we cannot name them Phoebe." [5] The boys were named Elbert Willson and Randolph Apperson Hearst.

In February, 1916, an olive-skinned Levantine financier and newspaper publisher of Paris, Paul Bolo Pasha, arrived in New York and had several mysterious meetings with Count von Bernstorff, the German ambassador,

[2] N. Y. *American*, June 6, 1915.   [3] The same.   [4] *Harper's Weekly*, Oct. 9, 1915.
[5] Princess Pignatelli to author, Nov. 3, 1959.

there and in Washington. Bolo was a French traitor in the pay of the Germans, although this was not known at the time. He lived handsomely during his visit, staying at the Plaza Hotel and giving a dinner at Sherry's at which the guests included the Hearst couple, Carr Van Anda, managing editor of the New York *Times,* and others, the whole party topping off the evening by going to the theater. Hearst returned the favor by inviting Bolo to the Clarendon, an incident he would hear of later.[6]

When the 1916 national conventions rolled around, it marked the first time since 1896 that Hearst had not taken a prominent part in the quadrennial affairs. Now he seemed to be persona non grata everywhere. When the Democrats went through the formality of nominating Wilson for another term, he saw ruin ahead despite the fact that Wilson, thus far, had kept the nation out of war. He was ready to bolt the party if the Republicans would nominate a "progressive" candidate. He startled many Republicans by attending that party's convention in Chicago as an observer and also to help the Republicans to straighten out their political thinking. He met Alice Roosevelt Longworth in the hall and asked her to urge her father to board the next train to Chicago. He distinctly did not want Roosevelt to be the Republican candidate—the former President was all for fighting Germany at once—but he felt that Roosevelt's magnetic presence at the convention would turn the Republicans away from reaction and toward progressivism. To Roosevelt at Oyster Bay he addressed a newspaper appeal interesting in its combination of flattery and logic:

> I urge you to come to Chicago to use your splendid ability and mighty influence . . . to establish a permanent, patriotic, radical party. . . . Stop wasting your wonderful opportunity and your magnificent energy in an effort to secure the Presidential nomination of the old discredited and discarded Republican Party. . . . If you secure the Republican nomination, you will be defeated because the ultra conservatives would resent you and the radicals would distrust you, and both would vote for Wilson rather than you. Come to Chicago by all means, Mr. Roosevelt, but come to do your real duty, to embrace your true opportunity. . . . Here is the occasion for another Alexander.[7]

Roosevelt, denying Hearst any standing as a Republican soothsayer, turned his back and stayed at Oyster Bay. The Republicans turned their backs on him too, nominating Charles Evans Hughes, the "animated feather duster" whose integrity Hearst respected but whom he considered far too conservative. He had come full circle again to what for him was a profound truth: The only party that could really be trusted to steer the nation's course was a Hearst party, led by Hearst and espousing Hearst principles.

The Hearst press "supported" Wilson in the election, if nominal approval coupled with violent attack could be called support. In its enmity it gathered dubious friends. It even took up the cudgels for the wild-eyed Jeremiah

O'Leary, head of the "American Truth Society," a frankly pro-German organization of Irish and Germans in America. When O'Leary sent an insulting telegram to Wilson, to which Wilson made an equally discourteous reply, the New York *American* came to O'Leary's defense as "an American citizen" and assailed "President Wilson's policies of submitting to British aggression . . ."[8]

The Hearst anti-British line, including his warm defense of Sir Roger Casement, the Irish patriot executed for holding secret parleys with the Germans, did not go unnoticed in England. Sir Cecil Spring-Rice, the British ambassador in Washington, sent worried messages to London about the baneful influence of the Hearst press. On October 11, 1916, the British government retaliated with a stringent and unwarranted measure. It banned the Hearst press from the use of the cables and mails. The French government followed suit on October 29, while on November 8 the Hearst papers were banned in Canada.[9] Thereafter, a Canadian caught reading Brisbane or the Katzenjammer Kids was subject to a $5000 fine or up to five years in prison.

The British would hardly have made such an autocratic move had they not known that Hearst was in bad odor with the Wilson administration and with the respectables in general, who were unworried at the prospect of Brixton Allaire and his ghostly mates being thrown out of work. The ban enraged Hearst. It gave him an opportunity to publish a series of hard-hitting editorials throwing doubt on all news that came from England. Actually, he was not slavishly pro-German, as a memorandum from Dr. Albert Fuehr, German propaganda director in the United States, to the German government indicated:

> It must be emphasized that the Hearst papers are . . . not to be classified as blind champions of the German cause, since they print many things which could scarcely be to our taste. For example, occasional articles about the 'German danger,' an idea which has received fresh impetus as a result of the exploits of the *Deutschland* and particularly of the *U-53*, and which is being used as an argument for the expansion of the army and navy. The fact is that the [Hearst] newspapers . . . stand upon the ground of a sound American policy, but with their sharply anti-English tendencies are much more effective in support of our cause than newspapers with pronounced German orientation could be.[10]

Hearst editors themselves became concerned over the Chief's anti-British line. Willis Abbot quit in disgust after almost twenty years with Hearst and went over to the *Sun*.[11] S. S. Carvalho was growing nervous. A Hearst favorite was squat, swarthy Philip Francis, who wrote editorials for his morning papers, usually with a strong German line, such as the following excerpt:

[8] N. Y. *American*, Sept. 29, 1916.   [9] N. Y. *Times*, Nov. 9, 1916.
[10] U. S. Judiciary Committee (Senate), *Report and Hearings, 66th Congress, 1st Session, 1919; Brewing and Liquor Interests and German and Bolshevik Propaganda*, Vol. II, 1616.
[11] Abbot, 304.

The Teutonic powers are winning the war. The genius of Hindenburg has triumphed. That wonderful old man, who now looms up as the greatest of living soldiers, among the greatest of soldiers living or dead, has altered the whole face of the war in eight short weeks. The Allies are beaten.[12]

This was the sort of thing, along with the pro-German dispatches of William Bayard Hale, that made the Hearst editors uneasy. Moses Koenigsberg, now head of Hearst's King Features Service, was one of them. A few days later, Koenigsberg went to the Clarendon for an appointment with Hearst, and found Francis there. The German authorities had had the editorial translated into forty-odd languages for distribution by the millions as propaganda. Koenigsberg took Francis to task for it. As the two men argued, Hearst entered, put his arm affectionately over Francis' shoulder, and led him away. The frog-eyed valet, Thompson, who seemed to have a clairvoyant knowledge of his master's wishes, was watching from a balcony above. A moment later he said to Koenigsberg, "Your appointment has been cancelled," leaving no doubt in Koenigsberg's mind of Hearst's fondness for Francis.[13]

Hearst clearly saw and understood the massive Allied propaganda effort to drag the United States into the war. His stubborn resistance took courage. It was not surprising that he whipped his newspapers into organs of counter-propaganda. He firmly believed that the Allies were on the verge of defeat and that America should shun a losing cause. Many who knew him best, even though they might disagree with his opinions or methods, never doubted his fundamental patriotism.

Phoebe Hearst, on a trip to New York to visit her son and his family, was shocked at the bitter criticism of his "pro-German" policy. On a side journey to see the Joseph Marshall Flints in New Haven, she brought up the subject. Dr. Flint, a professor of surgery at Yale who would later form and command the Yale medical unit in France, told her that Hearst's line was dangerous. At Phoebe's suggestion, the Flints went to New York to dine with her at the Hearst apartment. Hearst had great respect for Dr. Flint, but when both he and Phoebe urged him to temper his editorial attitude, he insisted on the justice of his views. A few days later, the Flints again dined at the Clarendon. On this occasion Hearst showed them copies of that day's *American* and *Journal*. Each bore the American flag in color on the front page.

"Look at this," he said impatiently. "I hope that suits you." [14]

That winter, Hearst and his wife took a Florida vacation, staying at The Breakers in Palm Beach. These were historic days, for on January 31, 1917, Von Bernstorff delivered the fatal announcement that Germany would resume unrestricted submarine warfare. The United States severed diplomatic relations. Bernstorff sailed with his entourage. It appeared that we would soon be at war with Germany, but Hearst was still trying to stem the tide.

[12] N. Y. *American*, Nov. 23, 1916.   [13] Koenigsberg, 413–14.
[14] Mrs. Flint to author, Feb. 20, 1960.

From Palm Beach he ordered his newspapers to run their titles in red, white and blue and to print stanzas of *The Star-Spangled Banner* atop the editorial pages. On February 25 he telegraphed Francis:

> Please make editorial . . . amplifying and improving following suggestions: "America is not only being starved for the benefit of Europe but it is being plundered of its wealth as well. We are sending abroad genuine wealth . . . We are receiving in return counters, media of exchange, which may never be redeemed. Of what use are the I.O.U.'s of a bankrupt?
>
> "Uncle Sam is being gold-bricked. He is being sold a satchel full of green goods in return for his genuine and hard-earned property. We are revelling in mock prosperity and will all wake up some fine morning and find the Sheriff at our doors. . . .
>
> ". . . Let us end these shipments of food and ammunition and money to the warring nations of Europe for their sakes and for ours. Let us preserve our property and our self-respect. Let us end the war and the wastage of war and the woe which the war is wreaking. Let us feed our own people, build up our own country, conserve our own resources. America first and for ever." [15]

The German action had brought a wave of indignation in the United States. The worry of Caleb Van Hamm, managing editor of the New York *American,* over the unpopular stand Hearst was taking was implicit in the telegram he sent his chief the next day:

> Earnestly urge immediate action to check or stop Hale despatches. They come by wireless and are surely picked up. Despite your well-known attitude of neutrality, these despatches are so worded as to permit the inference that Berlin is dictating our policy. I find we are drifting into a situation akin to the false McKinley one, only accentuated manyfold. I urge we check Hale and all agencies that tend to throw discredit upon our declared attitude of sturdy Americanism.[16]

Hearst's own concern was shown in a suggestion sent that same day to Carvalho:

> Why not run the red, white and blue title that we had for last edition through all editions for a few days during these troublous times? I think it will meet popular sentiment. Also please run little American flags to right and left of date lines on inside pages. . . . Our editorials should be patriotic without slightest criticism of administration. I guess Germany is going to sink every ship that tries to run the submarine blockade and this means three things—first, that we will get into the war; second, that England will be starved into submission in less than six months; third, that Germany will then have time to devote to us, and this country will soon be in a condition similar to warring European countries. We must prepare in every way. Can we say these things editorially? [17]

[15] U. S. Judiciary Committee (Senate), *op. cit.,* II, 1608–9.
[16] The same, 1609. [17] The same, 1610.

Two days later, the administration disclosed the interception of the famous Zimmermann note, in which Germany offered Mexico the return of her lost territories in Texas, New Mexico and Arizona, if Mexico would attack the United States in the event of a United States declaration of war against Germany. The offer was so fantastic that even the administration doubted the authenticity of the note until it was verified beyond question. It was not surprising that Hearst was skeptical. His editorialist, Philip Francis, wired him that the note was fraudulent. Francis' real name, when he later became involved in a dubious stock promotion, turned out to be Diefendorf, which might account for his bias.[18] Hearst replied on March 2 to Carvalho:

> Agree with Francis Zimmermann note all probability absolute fake and forgery, prepared by a very unscrupulous Attorney General's very unscrupulous department. [Thomas W. Gregory was Wilson's Attorney General.] Everybody knows that the secret police are the most conscienceless manufacturers of forged evidence in the world. . . .
> The object of the Zimmermann forgery was to frighten Congress into giving the President the powers that he demanded. . . .
> I believe in war if the people want war. They have to do the fighting. They ought to do the deciding. I believe in, first, a referendum to the people; and, second, failing that, a decision by the people's representatives in Congress assembled. We are getting very far away from democracy. . . .[19]

But it quickly became plain that the Zimmermann note was not a forgery. The Hearst press did not impugn Attorney General Gregory. Two days later, Hearst returned to his "yellow peril" theme in a telegram illustrating his showman's facility at putting across a stark idea via his cartoonist, Winsor McCay:

> McCay could make strong eight-column cartoon, occupying in depth two-thirds editorial page, showing smaller figures Uncle Sam and Germany shaking their fists at each other on left side page and on right side big head and shoulders of Japan, with knife in hand, leaning over into picture and evidently watching chance to strike Uncle Sam in back. Title of picture to be, "Watchful Waiting." "Look out, Uncle Sam, your neighbor, Japan, is eagerly waiting an opportunity to strike you in the back." [20]

On April 6, for all Hearst could do, the country was at war.

III. MISS DAVIES

SENATOR ASHURST's description of Hearst as "a firm friend, a loving husband, and a faithful father" was true in a sense but scarcely definitive. Hearst had an uncommon capacity for championing bourgeois conceptions which he did not recognize as applying to himself. He was against sin in the abstract.

[18] Koenigsberg, 431–32. [19] U. S. Judiciary Committee (Senate), op. cit., II, 1612.
[20] The same, 1613–14.

He favored fidelity in the abstract. Yet he was always able to regard himself as beyond the jurisdiction of rules applying to the herd. To dismiss him as a lecher would be mistaken. He had an enormous zest for life, an almost pagan worship of youth, energy, activity, sensation. He was in his fifties, and time was rushing inexorably on. The youth he prized was slipping away from him.

He had become interested in a number of women—affairs of the moment that for one reason or another did not satisfy him.[1] He was incurably romantic in a child-like, story-book way. He was, without over-stretching the imagination, a king with his own vast domain of newspapers, real estate, ranches, mines, paper mills, and thousands of employes over whom he had absolute authority. His castle would come later. Perhaps without knowing it, he was looking for a queen—or, more accurately, a princess who would glorify his castle and shed glory on himself. Marion Cecilia Davies was his princess.

Miss Davies, *née* Douras, was the blonde daughter of a minor New York politician, Bernard J. Douras. Born in Brooklyn, educated at a convent at Hastings, New York, she left school for the stage while still hardly more than a girl. After lesser engagements, she appeared in the chorus in *Chu Chin Chow*, then in *Oh, Boy!*, when the miracle dreamed of by all chorus girls came to pass. Florenz Ziegfeld discovered her, and put her in the chorus of his *Follies of 1917*.[2] Apparently it was here that Hearst met her, although there is conflict on this point.

The 1917 edition of the Follies was a memorable one, still remembered with misty eyes by old-timers. It had a couple of new and little-known comedians, Will Rogers and Eddie Cantor. It had dreamy sets by Joseph Urban. It had a particularly glamorous parade of beauties, including Billie Dove, Mae Murray, Dorothy Mackaill and Justine Johnstone. With war in the air, Miss Johnstone, known as "America's loveliest woman," was called upon to ring down the curtain with a tableau in which she appeared as Columbia, wrapped in an American flag.[3]

The latter production may have left the anti-war Hearst cold, but Miss Davies did not. It was said that he always got two seats for the *Follies*, one for himself and one for his hat. It was also said—probably an exaggeration—that he attended the *Follies* every night for eight weeks just to gaze at her. Miss Davies was born either in 1897 or 1900, depending on the authority, so he was either thirty-four or thirty-seven years older than she. Her friends, then and now, are unanimous in judging her an incredibly warm and winning personality—fun-loving, joyous, a born comedienne, wildly sentimental and generous.

She stuttered delightfully, sometimes getting stuck on a word. While Hearst was not oblivious to her beauty, he was smitten likewise by her

[1] Private source.   [2] Eddie Cantor, *Ziegfeld, the Great Glorifier*, 57.
[3] Marjorie Farnsworth, *The Ziegfeld Follies*, 131, 140.

bubbling vitality, her appreciation of the ridiculous. There were no dull moments when Miss Davies was around. She was gorgeous to look upon, and she made him laugh, two things he prized.

The meeting of these two began a drama that would unfold for more than three decades and which, with its implausible overtones of unconventionality and extravagance, would make one of the arresting love stories of the century.

IV. THE "SPOKESMAN OF THE KAISER"

To be a pacifist while the United States was yet uncommitted was safe, if unpopular. To be a pacifist after the nation was at war was both unpopular and unsafe. At first the Hearst press bristled with a panoply of "little flags" and patriotic slogans. Hearst heartily favored conscription and Liberty Bonds. But soon it developed that the kind of war he had in mind was not Wilson's kind at all. With his fixed conviction that Germany was winning, he felt that to transport an army overseas through swarms of U-boats meant sending a large part of it to the bottom, while the rest of it would be lost in the European debacle. Besides, it meant helping England. This was inconsistent, since he believed England beyond saving, but one could never expect consistency in him. He was unexcelled at using mutually contradictory arguments to bolster an untenable position. "The painful truth," said the New York *American*, "is that we are being practically used as a mere reinforcement of England's warfare and England's future aggrandizement." The thing to do, Hearst said, was to arm to the teeth but stay right here and let Germany "come to us." Otherwise we would only be sending our men to "bloody sacrifice." [1]

There were rumbles of anger. The respectables' opinion of the Hearst press, always low, had hit bottom when Hearst's International News Service was found guilty by a federal judge of stealing news from the Associated Press and was enjoined from so doing.[2] In most Hearst-paper cities, circulation skidded. Yet in New York City, with its heavy Irish and German population, Hearst had a large following among the masses. The Irish Boss Murphy was even considering running him for mayor because of "his strength among the pro-German element." In any case it was agreed that Hearst would have "considerable to say" in the selection of candidates.[3] All this heralded a healing of the long breach between him and Boss Murphy.

The Hearst family went to California that summer, one of the penalties of the war being that it forbade trips to Europe. As always, they spent much of the time at Hearst's Shangri-La, San Simeon. This had become an annual event of some magnitude, requiring the help of the ranch hands in erecting a flock of large tents and a demountable wooden house for the Hearsts on

[1] N. Y. *American*, Apr. 24, May 17, July 27, 1917.   [2] N. Y. *Times*, June 22, 1917.
[3] N. Y. *Times*, Mar. 5, June 30, 1917.

the very top of Camp Hill, the spot where his castle had already arisen in his mind's eye. He made a Roman holiday of it, inviting friends from California and executives from his various newspapers, so that there would be as many as fifty inhabiting the hilltop village of tent-houses. Hearst, as vigorous as a man half his age, led the way in a round of entertainments—riding, dancing, picnics, amateur movies. He was a splendid rider, so big a man that a spare horse was always kept ready for him. He doted on picnics, far off in the mountains or down on the beach near the village. He took great pains with his movies, picking the cast from his guests, getting his camera-man Joe Hubbell to help, writing the scenarios himself, giving the guests careful instructions in acting their parts. In one of them, *Romance of the Rancho*, Mrs. Hearst played the role of a heroine kidnaped by bandits, Hearst himself dashing into the scene with a six-shooter to rescue her, while most of the San Simeon cowhands were impressed into service as bandits.[4] Hearst, to whom doggerel came easy, wrote the subtitles in amusing rhymes. He ran the show, gave the orders—most pleasantly but with authority.

Conchita Sepulveda, who was one of the guests, later recalled how Hearst came out to the group with the air of one giving an important announcement. He bore a bulky object. "I have something to show you all," he said. He held it aloft. "This is the house I will build right at this very spot."[5] It was a scale model of a double-towered castle, beautifully worked out in plaster by Julia Morgan, a young woman architect who had done much of the work at the Hacienda.

In New York, the rumor that Boss Murphy was considering Hearst as the 1917 mayoralty candidate split the Wigwam. Thomas F. "Big Tom" Foley, the powerful lower Manhattan Tammany leader who had defeated Max Ihmsen for sheriff ten years earlier, led the anti-Hearst forces, saying that if Hearst was nominated he would "not get a vote below Fourteenth Street."[6] Alfred Emanuel Smith, a young political protégé of Foley who had served in the state Assembly and was now sheriff of New York County, joined Foley in the drive against Hearst. The opposition was so strong that Hearst ultimately withdrew and agreed to support Tammany in the candidacy of Brooklyn County Judge John F. Hylan, a politician of such meager talents that his designation caused impolite laughter in the anti-Tammany fold.[7] There was a belief that Hearst was not really interested in the mayoralty, having his eye on the Presidential nomination in 1920, and that Hylan was his hand-picked candidate. He was thirsting to defeat the incumbent, Mayor John Purroy Mitchel, whom he felt had neglected the city schools. Furthermore, Tammany and Hylan were now committed to municipal ownership of public utilities, the old Hearst ideal which he had upheld for almost thirty years in San Francisco and New York and for which he deserved credit for stubborn consistency.

[4] C. J. Hubbell to author.
[6] N. Y. *Times*, Aug. 25, 1917.
[5] Miss Sepulveda (Princess Pignatelli) to author.
[7] N. Y. *Times*, Sept. 1, 1917.

The campaign, as was true of any involving Hearst, was bitter. Mayor Mitchel, running as an independent, assailed "Hearst, Hylan and the Hohenzollerns." [8] Hylan was depicted as a straw man, the puppet of Hearst, so insignificant that his speeches had to be written for him in words of one syllable. It was recalled that the Germans had praised Hearst in the Berlin *Vossische Zeitung,* saying, "he has exposed the selfishness of England and her campaign of abuse against Germany, and has preached justice for the Central Powers. Since Wilson became a potentate he has untiringly fought to keep the people from following Wilson." [9] There were hints that he was a crony of German spies.

This came about because of his meetings with Paul Bolo Pasha. Bolo had since been court-martialed in France as a traitor when it was learned that he had received $1,700,000 in this country from Count von Bernstorff to finance his subversive work in France. Investigations on this side of the water had brought to light Hearst's relations with Bolo. Witch-burning was in vogue, particularly when Hearst was the witch. Although Bolo's traitorous intentions were unknown when he was in the United States, and no reasonable fault could be found with dining with him in a public room at Sherry's, dark implications were read in the fact that Bolo had also been a guest at the Clarendon. It was charged that Captain Fritz von Papen and Captain Karl Boy-Ed, the German military and naval attachés who had later been expelled for espionage, were among the guests at Sherry's.[10] Naturally the Germans, pleased at Hearst's anti-British line, would have felt grateful to him. Since the German ambassador's staff were all emissaries of a technically friendly nation until they were dismissed, taking tea with them should not have been regarded as treason. Yet Hearst found it necessary to issue a statement that he had seen Bolo only once, that Bolo had merely asked his help in getting newsprint, almost unobtainable in Paris, and that "I have never met von Papen or Captain Boy-Ed in my life." [11]

Candidate Hylan was virtually forgotten in the onslaught on Hylan's master, Hearst, "the spokesman of the Kaiser." James M. Beck, later to become Solicitor General, addressed a meeting at Carnegie Hall sponsored by the American Defense Society, assailing Hearst as the "fountain head" of pro-Germanism in the United States whose "power for evil is immeasurable." [12] Theodore Roosevelt took the stump for Mitchel, branding Hearst as "one of the efficient allies of Germany on this side of the water," and declaring that "Huns within" were more dangerous than "Huns without." [13] One of the bitterest denunciations came from an old friend, Judge Samuel Seabury, who had once revered Hearst as the great hope of the liberals. Seabury spoke not only of Hearst's politics but also of his private life when he said:

[8] N. Y. *Tribune,* Oct. 2, 1917.
[10] N. Y. *Times,* Oct. 4, 5, 1917.
[12] N. Y. *Tribune,* Nov. 3, 1917.
[9] N. Y. *Times,* Aug. 14, 1917.
[11] N. Y. *Times,* Oct. 5, 1917.
[13] N. Y. *Tribune,* Oct. 30, Nov. 2, 1917.

By virtue of what right does Hearst assume to dictate Democratic candidates? For the last six years he has consistently and persistently black-guarded the President of the United States. Today he stands as the most pronounced advocate of the pro-German cause who is still at large in the United States. I esteem him false not only to his own country but to every ideal of decency.[14]

But Hearst had his revenge. Judge Hylan won with an overwhelming plurality of 147,000 votes.

[14] N. Y. *Times,* Oct. 4, 1917.

10. How to Make Enemies

I. THE JELLYFISH AND THE TOAD

JOHN F. HYLAN, known slightingly as "Red Mike," was a forty-nine-year-old political curiosity unheralded outside of Brooklyn, where he was famous for his naïveté. A hefty, red-headed six-footer who neither drank nor smoked, he was a self-made man, which his detractors said was cause for blame, not praise. Born on an upstate farm, he had come to the city, worked as a fireman and engineer on the "elevated," studied law nights, and passed the bar just in the nick of time, for he was fired by the railroad for "rounding a curve too quickly." [1] When he rounded the quick curve into the mayor's chair, critics wondered whether the city could survive his ministrations. The *Times* called him a man of "marvelous mental density." [2] Hylan, even more than Seabury had a dozen years earlier, looked on Hearst as a blessing to honest, progressive politics. One of the first things he did was to appoint Mrs. Hearst chairman of the women's division of the Mayor's Committee on National Defense.

Mrs. Hearst selected a committee to instruct housewives in such war-economy measures as how to maintain furnace fires with minimum wastage of coal. Her husband set a poor example in conservation. One night, very late, he arrived at the Clarendon with Albert Kobler, who had made a prodigious success of promoting advertising sales in Hearst's *American Weekly*. Wanting to have some cold beer with Kobler, he found that the servants had retired and that the lock on the huge refrigerator door had jammed. He found an axe and chopped the door open, discussing advertising as the chips flew. [3]

In his affair with Miss Davies, Hearst adopted a new policy of caution. As a Presidential or gubernatorial aspirant, he had to maintain an image of middle-aged circumspection in the public eye. Also, if his mother learned of his dereliction it would be a shock that might even shorten her life. Some of his lieutenants knew of it and kept quiet.

At this juncture, portly Orrin Peck arrived from San Francisco to be entertained by the Hearsts. Although Peck denounced the German aggressions, Hearst did not allow a difference of opinion to mar an old friendship. Later that winter, while Mrs. Hearst remained in New York at her war work, Hearst left for Palm Beach. Miss Davies was with him, although this was unpublicized. Also with him was Orrin Peck, who must have felt that he was fated to cross the paths of the women in Hearst's life. He had soothed

[1] N. Y. *Times*, Nov. 7, 1917.   [2] Issue of Nov. 4, 1917.
[3] John Kobler to author, Dec. 19, 1959.

Hearst on losing Tessie in 1894. He had been best man at his wedding ten years later. Now there was Miss Davies. In Palm Beach, she was kept in handy concealment while Hearst partook in activities aimed at improving his prospects as a candidate.

Palm Beach was also Mayor Hylan's favorite winter resort. He arrived with his family in February, 1918, while Hearst was there, and soon was trotting proudly around with his powerful patron. Hearst and the mayor both served as volunteer auctioneers at a society benefit for the Red Cross, Hearst making a "vigorous speech eulogizing the Red Cross" before he called for bids on a young bulldog. One suspects that Hearst, sometimes the victim of "booster" bids at art sales, passed a preliminary word to Orrin Peck, for Peck kept bidding for the dog until the price reached $575, when he retired and let Mr. Atwater Kent of Philadelphia take it for $600.[4] A few nights later, Hearst, gravely denying any thought of politics, gave a dinner for the mayor at the Palm Beach Country Club. One of the guests was William Jennings Bryan, now a resident of Florida and certainly unaware that Miss Davies was in the offing.[5] It was a dramatic meeting between the two political war-horses, friends in 1896, 1900 and 1904, then enemies from 1908 until 1915, when Bryan won his way back into Hearst's good graces by quitting Wilson's Cabinet. Bryan had yearned for the Presidency, fought for it three times and lost. He still had hopes, although he now professed to be interested chiefly in urging the adoption of the Prohibition Amendment. Hearst had yearned for the Presidency with an even greater intensity, had never come as close, and was even farther from giving up. He was for Prohibition, too, and he knew that a friendly Bryan could still do him some political good. When he spoke next day before the Florida state educational convention, he did not bother to correct a previous speaker who predicted that he would run for President in 1920 "and would be elected." Political observers, who had long marveled at his passion for office and bizarre maneuvers to gain support, now felt he was trying to line up a new combination of blocs behind him—dissident Democrats, socialists, and the dry and suffragist forces.[6]

Mayor Hylan fell in enthusiastically with his patron's desire for publicity. He wrote a long "personal letter" to a friend in New York, a veritable hosanna for Hearst, which was promptly published in the papers. "One thing I like about Mr. Hearst," he wrote among other things, "is that he never asks me for anything." Hearst grinned when reporters asked him about the Hylan eulogy, saying the mayor was too kind. "My clothes no longer fit me, and my hat is bursting," he said.[7]

Hylan worked hard to correct any mistaken ideas the public might have of Hearst. "I might say that I had an entirely different impression of him," he said, "until I knew him personally. This will give you an idea what I mean: we were on the beach yesterday and a jellyfish had closed about a little toad.

[4] N. Y. *Times*, Feb. 20, 1918.   [5] N. Y. *Times*, Feb. 23, 1918.
[6] N. Y. *Times*, Feb. 24. 1918.   [7] N. Y. *Times*, Mar. 5, 1918.

Hearst flicked it away with the end of his cane and said, 'Why let the poor little thing suffer?' I think that typifies what I like in Hearst." [8]

After Peck returned from Palm Beach, he had a reunion with Mrs. Flint, the former Anne Drusilla Apperson. They shared the confidences of those who have been friends since childhood. The painter naturally had an interest in Hearst's romances, since he had been involved in them in one way or another for twenty-four years. He told Mrs. Flint of Hearst's infatuation with Miss Davies, and of the stipulation that it must be kept confidential.

"Why, Anne," he exclaimed, "he's in love with her! I've never seen him this way before. She can do anything with him." [9]

The case of the jellyfish and toad appealed to many New Yorkers as symbolic of the Hearst-Hylan entente. City Hall reporters had a gay shindig at the Astor Hotel, featuring a centerpiece with a likeness of a jellyfish and toad alongside of a cane. To newsmen, Hylan was the most amusing unconscious comedian ever seen in City Hall, and even Hearst had his comic aspects. The comedy was submerged, however, when Hearst launched his drive for the 1918 gubernatorial nomination—a drive preliminary to another assault on the White House in 1920—while his papers continued their anti-English line. With Americans in the trenches, every other New York newspaper, along with many throughout the country, joined in a mass attack on Hearst. By now, the New York opposition papers had entered into a silent agreement to hurt Hearst whenever and however possible.

The *Tribune* opened with a bitter weekly series titled *Coiled in the Flag—Hears-s-s-s-t,* likening him to a snake, citing his "pro-Germanism," quoting his editorials, accusing him of "sowing distrust of the Allies." The *Tribune* had these attacks bound into pamphlet form and spread broadcast. Roosevelt joined the parade, denouncing Wilson for not suppressing the Hearst press. In an address in San Francisco, the Rev. Henry Frank demanded "instant investigation" of Hearst. The Kaiser was quoted as saying to an American before the United States entered the war, "Mr. Hearst . . . has helped our cause very much in your country." Citizens in Poughkeepsie burned bundles of the New York *American*. Hearst newsboys, being in danger of rough handling, were given American flags to wear as evidence of patriotism. Clubs in Los Angeles banned the Hearst papers. "One had need of great fortitude even to serve [Hearst]," recalled the *American* reporter, Nat Ferber. "His delivery men were greeted by bonfires made of the papers they were attempting to distribute. As for the Hearst reporter, few were the assignments on which his ears didn't ring with the abuse heaped on him." [10]

The journalistic conspiracy against Hearst was tacit but nonetheless effective. As the campaign against him spread, he became easily the most detested public figure in the country. His effigy was burned in many cities.

[8] The same.   [9] Mrs. Flint to author, Feb. 20, 1960.
[10] Nat J. Ferber, *I Found Out,* 63.

Many advertisers had already withdrawn from his papers. Now they deserted in droves, causing a heavy loss of revenue. Carvalho, his right-hand man for twenty-three years, resigned because he would not change his policies, returning to the fold later when the hubbub subsided. Snubbed by friends, Hearst wrote the *Social Register* asking that his name be withdrawn. In a New York restaurant, a woman hissed at him, *"Boche!"* Hearst bowed and replied, "You're right, madam. It is all bosh." [11]

The Attorney General's office scanned the Hearst papers for sedition. The Department of Justice put him under surveillance. A new butler in his household was found to be a federal agent.[12] His editors, frightened, pleaded vainly with him to "ease up." "I just love to be investigated," Hearst said jovially to Moe Koenigsberg.[13]

Perhaps it did tickle his kingly complex to be the center of a nationwide uproar, the lone defender of the right. In view of his craving for office and the plain fact that he was damaging his own chances by his stand, even some of his enemies later gave him grudging credit for standing fast. Even if he was moved more by bull-headed prejudice than principle, he was fighting prejudice on the other side and was one of the few who helped preserve a flicker of journalistic independence. He felt that he was speaking for a large but inarticulate segment of the population. His landslide success in electing Hylan despite the "Hearst-and-Hohenzollern" attacks was fresh in his mind, proof that many voters were on his side.

But the anti-Hearst fury, in addition to cutting his profits, was hurting his chances for the governorship. He took to counter-propaganda. A pamphlet spread by the millions depicted him as a true patriot bedeviled by newspaper enemies who sought to cripple him as a competitor. His political agents worked hard upstate to fight the "pro-German" taunts.[14] His newspapers linked Standard Oil with the Hearst enemies, and with cool effrontery reprinted more of the old, old Archbold letters.[15] He ran advertisements in other newspapers headed "WHAT THE HEARST PAPERS HAVE DONE TO HELP WIN THE WAR," stressing his support of conscription and preparedness and ending, "the Hearst papers will continue while the war shall last to put forth all their efforts toward securing the great victory which shall forever crush the Teuton menace to the peace of the world." [16] To speak of the "Teuton menace" was a new note for Hearst, as was the occasional praise for President Wilson that began appearing in his papers. It was charged that he even sought to capitalize on his wife's war work. The name of Mrs. William Randolph Hearst was blazoned in such large letters on a sign over the entrance to a service men's canteen at Fifth Avenue and Fortieth Street that a woman identified only as "Mrs. Russell" was said to have protested. "Mrs. Hearst is known to be pro-German," she was quoted

[11] Mrs. Fremont Older, *op. cit.*, 403.
[13] Koenigsberg, 428.
[15] N. Y. *American,* Apr. 14, 1918.
[12] The same, 407.
[14] N. Y. *Times,* Apr. 15, 1918.
[16] N. Y. *Times,* June 1, 1918.

as saying, "and her name keeps many soldiers and sailors from coming here." [17] Mrs. Hearst, an earnest patriot, sued three newspapers for $100,000 each for printing the libel.

II. A POLITICAL TYPHOID CARRIER

HEARST's greatest effort to dramatize his patriotism came at the end of June. Senators and Congressmen in Washington were startled when they were approached by Hearst capital newspapermen and invited to travel to New York for a huge July 4 loyalty celebration, complete with parade, meals and theater tickets, all at Mr. Hearst's expense.[1] The invitations were issued to 250 legislators. There was some consternation in Washington. Many of those invited were not averse to such a free-loading festival but feared that accepting the Hearst bounty might hurt them politically. In the end, only some thirty-four Senators and Congressmen accepted, with their families. They rode to New York in special Pullmans provided by Hearst. The response was so disappointing that reporters who tried to get a list of the guests from Hearst retainers were unsuccessful.

The visitors, with their wives and children, were accommodated in a reviewing stand in Madison Square, where they witnessed the parade, then were transported to the Holland House on Fifth Avenue for luncheon. Mayor Hylan, always reverential toward his sponsor, greeted them at luncheon, saying modestly, "Of course, I am not a public speaker such as Mr. Hearst." Hearst himself proposed an astonishing toast, with his usual glass of water.

"May our first toast," he said, beaming on the legislators and their families, "be to the President of the United States."[2]

Perhaps this did not sit well with one of his listeners, Senator James Reed of Missouri, who had long assailed Wilson. The free dinner that evening, complete with wines and favors, was at the splendid Astor Hotel. Madame Schumann-Heink sang. Speaker of the House Champ Clark, who had so narrowly missed the Presidency, addressed the group in praise of their host.

"He is the biggest publisher that has ever lived on the face of the earth," Clark said, "or ever will live. I will let you into a secret and tell you that I have been writing my autobiography and in it I put off saying anything about Mr. Hearst until the last chapter. It will be published in Mr. Hearst's magazine. In the last chapter I say that not a measure has been proposed for the alleviation of human beings in the last quarter of a century that he did not originate or advocate."[3]

Hearst also gave a short speech, as did Senator Reed, who pronounced those who questioned Hearst's loyalty as "contemptible." After dinner, the party enjoyed the Ziegfeld *Follies* and the Cocoanut Grove, with the compliments of Mr. Hearst.

[17] N. Y. *Tribune,* June 14, 1918.
[2] N. Y. *Times,* July 5, 1918.
[1] N. Y. *Times,* July 1, 1918.
[3] The same.

The bill for all this must have been considerable, but it did not stem the tide. Louis Master, a Flushing realtor, put out a six-foot sign in front of his office reading "Do not read the Hearst newspapers." He was arrested by a Hylan policeman for "creating a disturbance." An upstate Democrat said, "Hearst is a political typhoid carrier . . . Install [him] as leader and the Democratic Party will go into indefinite quarantine." [4] Hearst, determined on a strong bid for the gubernatorial nomination, reserved twenty-seven rooms at the Grand Union Hotel in Saratoga for his followers. Samuel Seabury, who had appointed himself chief warner-against-Hearst, said sarcastically that Hearst, after heaping abuse on Wilson for years, was now praising only "enough to win the nomination." [5]

When the Democratic convention met at Saratoga late in July, Seabury was ready. He introduced a resolution to "repudiate every truckler with our country's enemies who strives . . . to extenuate or excuse such crimes against humanity as the rape of Belgium, the sinking of the *Lusitania,* and the German policy of assassination by submarine." [6] The delegates, in no doubt as to whom Seabury meant, passed the resolution, eliminating Hearst from consideration. Hearst then tried vainly to get the nomination for his friend, James W. Gerard, former ambassador to Germany. The convention chose Al Smith.

One can imagine Phoebe Hearst's distress when she read the daily assaults on her son, read of the banning of his papers from San Francisco clubs, of the several hundred citizens of Eugene, Oregon, who seized all Hearst papers and magazines from a newsstand and set them ablaze as they sang *Keep the Home Fires Burning.* In cinema houses showing the Hearst-Pathé News, the hissing was so tumultuous that the company felt obliged to shorten the name to "Pathé News." [7]

Hearst became the whipping boy of all factions. At this juncture Arthur Brisbane paid a visit to Republican Governor Charles S. Whitman. Attorney General Merton Lewis, who was opposing Whitman for the Republican nomination, leaped to the conclusion that Hearst, scorned by the Democrats, was now backing Whitman. Lewis, aiming to blacken Whitman by association with Hearst, did some undercover work. He got affidavits from several taxicab drivers and from a doorman, an elevator operator and a former superintendent of the Clarendon apartments. The affidavits stated:

That Bolo Pasha, whom Hearst said he had met only once, and who since had been executed in France for treason, had actually seen Hearst at least three times.

That Count von Bernstorff, the German ambassador, had been a frequent visitor at the Hearst apartment before the United States entered the war.

That on one occasion Bolo and Bernstorff arrived together.

[4] N. Y. *Times,* July 10, 1918.   [5] N. Y. *Tribune,* July 15, 1918.
[6] N. Y. *Times,* July 24, 1918.
[7] San Francisco *Chronicle,* Aug. 13, Sept. 17, Oct. 15, 1918.

That Bolo and Bernstorff became so familiar to the Clarendon staff that they invented nicknames for them, Bernstorff being called "the Duke de la Brew" and Bolo "the Duke de la Car."

That Hearst had had an iron bridge built from the roof of the Clarendon to the adjoining apartment roof. This he was said to use to "avoid process servers," but there was also speculation that it was a handy passage for German spies.[8]

Since none of this had any direct bearing on Lewis' campaign, one must assume that he exploited it simply as a sensation, to gain publicity, and because assailing Hearst had become a popular pastime. Yes, Hearst said in a public statement, Bolo had called on him to ask his help in getting newsprint, unobtainable in France.

"I did not know that Bolo Pasha would turn out to be a spy," he went on. "His own Government did not know it." As for Bernstorff—"I will help the Attorney General out there, too. I had met von Bernstorff several times, and I had also met Jusserand, and Spring-Rice, the French and British Ambassadors . . . There was no secrecy about any of this matter, as Mr. Lewis' own affidavits prove . . ."[9]

Hearst had some reservations about Alfred E. Smith on the municipal ownership issue. But he persuaded Smith to issue a statement favoring municipal ownership, and he supported the man with the brown derby against the eventual Republican candidate, Governor Whitman. Smith won by a mere 14,000 votes. Obviously he would have lost had not the Hearst press backed him, and it was an easy step for Hearst to reflect that *he* had elected the governor.

Shortly thereafter, Hearst went to the opera with his wife. It must have been a benefit he could not avoid, for he loathed opera. During the intermission, he left his box to find a chunky man in a dress suit waiting for him.

"Mr. Hearst," the man said, "I am Julius Klein, a reporter on your Chicago *Examiner*. That is, I was until Mr. Ranck fired me because of a misunderstanding. I wanted to explain it to you and see if you would take me back."

"How did you find me here?" Hearst inquired.

"I got into town and telephoned your home. They said you were at the opera, so I rented a dress suit and bought a ticket."

The idea of a reporter coming from Chicago and renting a dress suit to get his job back tickled Hearst. "I'm going to Chicago tomorrow," he said. "You can ride with me and tell me about it on the way."

The two men rode to Chicago in Hearst's private car. Klein explained that he was fired because he had been beaten on a story, but that he was not responsible. It is doubtful that Hearst was so impressed with this as he was with Klein's determination in making the trip from Chicago and invading the Metropolitan Opera House. When they arrived in Chicago, they were met at the station by Thanatopsis V. Ranck, the editor who had discharged Klein.

[8] N. Y. *Tribune*, Aug. 12, 1918.   [9] N. Y. *American*, Aug. 12, 1918.

Ranck's jaw sagged when he saw Klein emerge from the car with Hearst.

"Mr. Ranck," Hearst said, "I think we'd better take Mr. Klein back into the family. He has a persistence I like in reporters." [10]

III. GREETER HEARST

WHEN the war ended, and preparations were made for shipping doughboys home, Mayor Hylan committed a civic outrage. He appointed Hearst chairman of a committee in charge of welcoming returning soldiers.[1] Surely the mayor, for all his *gaucherie*, knew that this was colossal impudence. Hearst obviously sought the appointment, for the mayor was in his vest pocket. It gives a revealing glimpse into his enigmatic character—a glimpse of a man long pilloried by the respectables, deliberately taking a step that would enrage them and enjoying his power to do so. This was subtle Hearstian revenge.

Hylan, who said, "Mr. Hearst never asks me for anything," was nevertheless doing things for Hearst. Three days later appeared a modest news item that attracted no attention at all: "Mayor Hylan announced yesterday the appointment of Bernard J. Douras of 529 Cortlandt Avenue, the Bronx, as a City Magistrate. . . . The salary is $7000 a year." [2] The new magistrate was the father of Marion Davies.

Editorialists sizzled over the spectacle of Hearst, the apologist for the Kaiser, shaming the city as its official soldier-greeter. Ironically, at this same time began a drama in Washington that—if such a thing were possible—heightened the wrath of the "patriots." A Senate judiciary committee held hearings on German and Bolshevik propaganda during the war. It soon became evident that federal agents had been snooping into Hearst's wartime activities.

A. Bruce Bielaski, head of the Department of Justice's bureau of investigation, pointed to Hearst's opposition to sending troops to Europe, saying, "There was no other man whose attitude was so friendly to Germany during the war." [3] Somehow the investigators had got hold of Hearst's private communications from Palm Beach shortly before the United States entered the war. They were spread out in the newspapers to be pondered by a nation still inflamed against Germany. Millions of readers all over the country were treated to Editor Van Hamm's plea that Hearst put a stop to William Bayard Hale's pro-German dispatches; to a telegram sent Hearst by George Sylvester Viereck, a leading German propagandist in New York, saying that the Zimmermann note was "a brazen forgery"; to Hearst's message to Carvalho agreeing that it was in "all probability absolute fake"; to Hearst's orders to his editors to use "little flags" on his newspapers to convey a tone of patriotism.

Readers learned that Hale, who was paid $300 weekly by Hearst until the

[10] John W. Dienhart to author, Nov. 12, 1959.   [1] N. Y. *World*, Dec. 3, 1918.
[2] N. Y. *Times*, Dec. 6, 1918.   [3] San Francisco *Chronicle*, Dec. 10, 1918.

United States declared war, also received $15,000 a year from the German government as a paid propagandist. They learned that Ambassador von Bernstorff had asked his government to give Hale preference over other correspondents because the Hearst papers had "placed themselves on the German side." [4] Hearst was in the embarrassing position of having employed, before the war, a man also employed by the Kaiser.

Bradford Merrill, a New York Hearst executive, declared that Hale, although unknown to be a German propagandist, had been deliberately hired to give the Hearst press the official German version of the news, just as other correspondents in Paris and London were expected to transmit the French and British versions. [5] Another Hearst statement said, "The New York *American* never knew or suspected, or had any reason to suspect, that Mr. William Bayard Hale had any relations whatsoever with the German Government or with the German Ambassador." [6]

This was true, for one of Bernstorff's messages to the German Foreign Office said, "Hearst is not aware that Hale is our agent, but knows him only as a Germanophile journalist . . ." [7] The evidence showed nothing more than was already well known—that Hearst had sought to present the German side of the quarrel, which in all truth was little heard in this country. But to citizens who recalled that Bernstorff had been known to Clarendon employes as "la Duke de la Brew," and who had difficulty in distinguishing prewar from wartime activities, and in differentiating between propagandists and downright spies, the implication of disloyalty was strong.

The Senators went into another matter—the purchase by Arthur Brisbane of the Washington *Times* in 1917, shortly after America went to war. Brisbane admitted that he had been "loaned" $375,000 by thirteen wealthy German-American brewers headed by Christian Feigenspan so that he could buy the newspaper. He insisted that the brewers' generosity was not caused by any pro-German sentiment in his editorials, which sentiment he denied, but thought it arose from his favorable attitude toward light wines and beers as opposed to spirits. The brewers, fearful of prohibition, were lobbying energetically to keep beer from being banned. The Senators thought it had the earmarks of a gift rather than a loan.

"It is absolutely a loan, Senator," Brisbane said firmly. [8]

But he had to admit that the loan was not bound by any written agreement. The Senators also wondered if Brisbane had not acted as a dummy for Hearst, the real buyer. It was pointed out that Brisbane was still being paid $104,000 a year by Hearst at the same time as he skipped off to Washington to buy his own paper. Brisbane said that Hearst had been worried but had accepted his assurance that the arrangement would not impair his value to

---

[4] N. Y. *World*, Dec. 7, 11, 1918.
[5] U. S. Judiciary Committee (Senate), *op. cit.*, II, pp. 1910–12.
[6] N. Y. *American*, Dec. 7, 1918.   [7] San Francisco *Chronicle*, Dec. 7, 1918.
[8] U. S. Judiciary Committee (Senate), *op. cit.*, II, 741.

the Hearst press. Indeed, the Chief had even been so magnanimous as to agree to buy the paper from Brisbane if the financial burden proved more than the latter could bear. When a Senator asked Brisbane if Hearst gave him a free hand to write as he pleased, the editor replied with a revealing vignette:

"No," he said. "My understanding is that I write what I please and he publishes it if he pleases; but if Mr. Hearst has a campaign, for instance, I do not write what I do not please . . . Mr. Hearst does not wish to be told anybody's views—at least not mine. He rules his papers absolutely, and trusts to me (as I know about what his line of thought is) not to go outside of that. . . . Occasionally, if he sees something in the paper that he does not like, he throws it out, naturally. The papers are his property."

What the Senators inferred, without putting it so bluntly, was that it looked fishy for Brisbane (or Hearst, through Brisbane) to acquire an expensive newspaper via a loan granted by German-American brewers who had no security whatever for the loan. Clippings from the Washington *Times* were produced to show that under Brisbane it followed the Hearst line, sympathetic with Germany, stressing the horrors of war and opposing the shipment of American soldiers overseas. In short, the Senators suggested that Brisbane (or Hearst) had accepted a subsidy from German-Americans and had then followed an editorial policy favorable to them. The brewers themselves, however, insisted that the money had been gathered to "save their business" from the growing Volstead sentiment. Senator James Reed, who saw eye to eye with Hearst in many matters and had enjoyed the *Follies* as his guest, appeared before the committee in defense of the publisher. Hearst was not asked to testify. Brisbane's explanation of the brewers' contribution remained technically unshaken. The probe ended on an inconclusive note—even more so than the Senate investigation into Hearst's manipulation of the Archbold letters had in 1913.[9]

IV. A GREAT LADY PASSES

WHILE nothing was established against Hearst in Washington, the news of the hearings solidified the feeling of many New Yorkers that to send him as the city's official welcomer of homecoming soldiers was a civic scandal. The case of Greeter Hearst became a burning issue which the anti-Hearst press whipped up joyfully.

Colonel Henry L. Stimson started a parade when he wrote Mayor Hylan that he could not serve on a committee blemished by Hearst's presence. Charles Evans Hughes let it be known that he felt the same way. The mayor had appointed some 5000 citizens to various committees charged with the reception and entertainment of soldiers, but the forces of attrition were at

[9] Judiciary Committee, *op. cit.*, Brisbane testimony, 732–59.

work as the resignations poured in. One resigner wrote, "Our boys deserve a red, white and blue welcome, untinged with yellow." Scores of city leaders signed a petition urging the mayor to ask Hearst to retire.[1]

Hylan, whose own syntax was shaky, added fuel to the fire by having his literate secretary, Grover Whalen, write a fawning letter to Hearst which he immediately released for publication. In it the mayor told Hearst in part, "The attack on you and your papers by the profiteers, the privilege seeking and predatory interests . . . will fail because the great mass of people know that you are their constant and vigilant defender."[2]

Hearst could—and should—have solved the situation neatly by a graceful resignation. This he would not do. He was enjoying the discomfiture of his enemies.

Phoebe Hearst, still an indefatigable traveler at seventy-six, arrived to spend the holidays with her son's family. The bitterness of public feeling against her Willie had hurt her. Ever since he had been expelled from Harvard she had been torn between pride in his abilities and sadness at his shortcomings. Now she found him the center of another controversy, the target of general abuse.

Since neither Hearst nor Hylan would give way, a group of citizens formed their own independent committee to greet the soldiers, with Theodore Roosevelt accepting the chairmanship. The great Rough Rider, however, died at Oyster Bay before he could act on it. The dispute gained national prominence. The South Dakota legislature, regretting that there was no seaport in their state, passed a resolution asking that returning soldiers escape the Hearst blight by landing at another port—any other port—than New York. The Ohio state senate did likewise.[3] The Hearst press countered with a petition signed by many wounded soldiers already in New York asking that Hearst be retained as greeter. The opposition press charged that New York *Journal* emissaries went to wounded soldiers at the Debarkation Hospital and deceived them by saying they were signing a petition to obtain six months' pay after discharge.[4] Since Hearst was campaigning for six months' additional pay, it is not impossible that the *Journal* men strained a point in that direction. The lines were now clearly drawn. It was Hearst against all the respectables in town.

When the *Mauretania* came in with a boatload of soldiers, Hearst insisted on going out into the harbor in person. It was a mission he might well have feared, but cowardice was not among his failings. He was embarrassed, however, because no one but his own newsmen and some of Hylan's lieutenants would consent to be seen with him. At the last moment, Victor Watson, now city editor of the New York *American,* managed to coax a few theater notables to augment the group. Watson also arranged to have thousands of free copies of the *American* with front-page headlines telling of Hearst's

[1] N. Y. *Times,* Jan. 14, 1919; N. Y. *World,* Dec. 30, 1918.
[2] N. Y. *Times,* Dec. 24, 1918.   [3] N. Y. *Times,* Jan. 15, 24, 1919.
[4] N. Y. *Times,* Jan. 15, 1919.

presence in the flesh as greeter, placed aboard the *Mauretania* at Quarantine.

Hearst and his troupe sailed out in a city launch, complete with band, Hearst clad in overcoat and winter cap. The band was playing *Home Sweet Home* as the launch approached the liner. There was trepidation among the greeters as to whether they might be showered by brickbats hurled by soldiers itching to settle a score with the "pro-German" publisher. Instead, the doughboys, too glad to be home to draw fine points about who met them, cheered lustily. Reporter Ferber later recalled his jubilation:

> Placing one arm about Gene Fowler, a fellow reporter, and the other around me, he skipped with us, schoolboy fashion, down the deck, the ear-laps of his "Sherlock Holmes" cap flapping in the wind.[5]

The anti-Hearst forces organized a mass meeting at Madison Square Garden to protest against the appointment. Hearst's political secretary, O'Reilly, passed the word to City Editor Watson to heckle the meeting into ridicule. Watson, furnished with an unlimited expense account, sent *American* reporters to use bribes and cajolery to fill a large part of the Garden floor with returned soldiers, instructed to resist any derogation of the Chief.[6] The remarks of the principal speakers, the Rev. Dr. William Manning, rector of Trinity Church, and Lawyer James Beck, were exclusively in derogation. As indignant society matrons in the boxes flashed their lorgnettes, the soldiers created an uproar that threw the meeting into confusion, then marched out in a body.[7] The Hearst press hailed this as a vindication of Hearst and a repudiation of the selfish interests opposing him, delivered by the men in khaki themselves. The chances are that Watson drew a fat bonus for his sabotage.

Nevertheless, Phoebe Hearst, during her stay in New York, was constantly reminded that her son was a pariah among civic and social leaders of the kind with whom she associated. It was regrettable that her last visit should have been so beclouded. She came down with influenza, the wartime scourge. Recovering, she returned home to the Hacienda, where she suffered a relapse. Hearst and his wife hurried out to be with her. Mrs. Flint, the niece who had been Phoebe's confidante during the years in Washington and on many trips to Europe, joined them at the Hacienda.[8]

Phoebe lingered for more than a fortnight. Hearst spent part of the time in San Francisco with Miss Morgan, the architect, working on plans for the castle at San Simeon. When Phoebe died on April 13, 1919, it was the passing of California's greatest lady and one of the nation's most remarkable women. She was buried beside the late Senator. During her lifetime she had given some $21,000,000 to educational and philanthropic causes. She left an estate of $11,000,000, her son being the chief legatee. She left the Hacienda and the *Examiner* building in San Francisco to her five grandsons, and legacies ranging from $1000 to $250,000 to members of the family and friends.[9]

---

[5] Ferber, *I Found Out*, 80–81. [6] Ferber, 82–86. [7] N. Y. *World*, Jan. 18, 1919.
[8] Mrs. Flint to author. [9] N. Y. *Times*, Apr. 18, 1919.

The sentimental Hearst insisted that no one but Winifred Black Bonfils, the ubiquitous Annie Laurie, should write his mother's obituary for the *Examiner*. Later he was guilty of appalling thoughtlessness. He asked Annie to write a full-length biography of Phoebe. Annie, under the impression that it was to be in pamphlet form, dashed off 54,000 words in twelve days. Instead Hearst had it hand-set and bound in vellum in Germany in a lavish edition published for him by John Henry Nash at a cost of thirty-five dollars a copy.[10] He presented them to his friends. Phoebe Hearst, whose career deserved the attention of a conscientious biographer, was instead commemorated by a handsome volume written in gushy prose, replete with errors—the work of a sob sister in a hurry.

[10] Ishbel Ross, 66.

11. The Man with the Brown Derby

1. THE BEST IS NONE TOO GOOD

The possession of his mother's fortune accelerated Hearst's already enormous activities in several directions. He began building his castle at San Simeon. He increased his buying of art objects and antiques, many of which he never saw. He bought more New York real estate, always with high mortgages, almost all of it in the upper Fifties. It was said that he was convinced a bridge would be built across the Hudson around Fifty-seventh Street which would make his Columbus Circle properties the hub of a great new traffic artery, the center of the expanding city.

He placed Moses Koenigsberg in charge of the International News Service, which, with its mythical writers, its "pro-Germanism" and its pilfering of news had sunk to such depths of discredit and unreliability that even the Hearst editors, who had to use it, were fearful to do so. It had lost $388,000 the previous year. Koenigsberg's job was to bring it to life.[1] The low estate of I.N.S. was a direct result of the policies of Hearst, to whom truth in the news was never of great importance and who was essentially a showman and propagandist, not a newsman.

Hearst's most dramatic 1919 move was his headlong plunge into the movies. Previously he had given his motion picture properties only sporadic attention, leaving them in charge of his picture chief, the smiling young Edgar Hatrick. Now he made it plain that they were no longer a side-issue but a primary interest. He bought Sulzer's Harlem River Park Casino, a former amusement center at Second Avenue and 127th Street, as a movie studio. He supplied Miss Davies, whose education had been limited but whose mind was quick, with tutors in poise, expression and stagecraft. She had a comfortable studio apartment in the Beaux Arts Building on Sixth Avenue. A telephone girl at the Hearst office was entrusted with the duty of knowing always where Miss Davies was, and where Hearst was, so the two could keep in touch.[2] It was Hearst's considered intention to make Miss Davies the greatest screen star in the nation. It was also his aim to make himself, working with Miss Davies as star, the top mogul of all cinema impresarios.[3]

These were not mere whims. They were ends Hearst wanted with the implacable force that he wanted everything he wanted. One of the keys to his locked-in character lay in the violence with which he wanted things. This was a force apparently beyond his control. In its intensity, Hearst was abnormal. Certainly it contained among its ingredients the acme of egoism—a

[1] Koenigsberg, 454. [2] Private source.
[3] Frances Marion to author, June 9, 1960.

323

heritage of his silver-spoon childhood and of an iron will transmitted through both maternal and paternal genes. There is an oversimplified theory that if he had been spanked regularly as a boy, he might have become both great and good, instead of more great than good. The pressure of his wants, never curbed or disciplined, drove him incessantly. It explained the contemptible things he did, and the admirable. It explained the immense energy he threw into all his pursuits. It explained his capacity for work—he who could have spent his years in luxurious idleness.

His ego revolted at any subsidiary capacity in any endeavor in which he was engaged. To take orders from anyone, even the Almighty, was not in him. Now, in addition to the White House, his dream of power encompassed himself and his princess, Miss Davies, occupying a castle in California and ruling a domain of newspapers and motion pictures.

Although both Hearst and the young lady herself knew that she had things to learn about acting, he had no doubt about his ability to transform her into a vibrant Galatea. She had beauty and talent. He would supply the instructors, the writers and directors to bring it out, and the publicity to exploit it. His creative instinct, so entangled with jimcrack tricks to beguile the public, was excited. He was possessive about everything he owned. Miss Davies was his most prized possession whom he would train, groom, push and publicize until she reached the heights, eclipsing the reigning Mary Pickford.

The only talent he would consider was the best, the most expensive. He hired Joseph Urban, the temperamental Viennese whose sets had glorified the *Follies*. He lured from California the top scenarist of the day, Frances Marion, who had written several of Mary Pickford's vehicles, paying her $2000 a week—the same as he paid the trusty Brisbane. He brought in famous directors. He hired expert publicity men—a department he never overlooked. Miss Davies was not his only star, for Gloria Swanson, Seena Owen, Ramon Novarro, Lionel Barrymore, Alma Rubens and others performed at his Harlem River lot, but they discovered that Hearst's interest in them was superficial. Miss Davies was the hub around which the whole operation revolved. "W. R. was fascinated by the movies," Miss Marion later recalled. "He concentrated his attention on Miss Davies, certain that there were no limits to her future." [4]

He was a crank on authenticity in costumes and sets. In one of Miss Davies' scenes appeared a Colonial fireplace that he ruled out as soon as he saw it.

"That's a cheap copy," he said. "I bought a real one some years ago. Find it and we'll use it." [5]

This was not easy, for he had two warehouses in the Bronx crammed with art objects and antiques. Production halted while a search was begun. Costs mounted as days passed while men combed dusty warrens, but Hearst was adamant and his long memory was vindicated when the fireplace was found.

[4] Miss Marion to author.   [5] Private source.

II. PUBLICITY CAN DO ANYTHING

MISS DAVIES' first starring vehicle, a domestic drama called *Cecilia of the Pink Roses*, had its New York première in June, 1918. Motion pictures were not then regarded seriously as an art form. The New York *Times* and other newspapers gave them casual treatment—a paragraph or so devoted to each new film. The Hearst press itself had never shown real interest even in the ambitious efforts of Miss Pickford.

But the Hearst newspapers recognized immediately in *Cecilia* a cinema landmark, a work of stirring art, and above all a glittering new star in the film firmament. "Marion Davies Wins Triumph in 'Cecilia of the Pink Roses,'" said the *American*'s three-column headline. According to an unnamed reviewer, "There were few dry eyes at the Rivoli Theater yesterday when the vision of Marion Davies faded on the screen." The review went on with praise that included the phrases, "vision of loveliness," "bewitching beauty," "triumph for Miss Davies," "masterpiece," and "brought tears to eyes to which they had long been strangers." There were two large photographs of Miss Davies in scenes from the picture. It was mentioned that there were bushels of real pink roses on either side of the screen, surely a Hearst idea, and "the delicate scent of the roses was wafted over the audience by the theater's ventilating system." So outstanding was the picture that a second review by Max Smith was given, beginning, "Only a marble heart could have withstood the charms of Marion Davies." [1]

But the *American*'s reaction was conservative compared with that of the *Journal*, which gave "CECILIA OF THE PINK ROSES" a frank eight-column headline in capitals—a display rivaling the war screamers—and a three-column photograph of Miss Davies allowing handsome Harry Benham to kiss her hand. The *Journal* was impressed enough to run *Cecilia* as a continued story and to print an enthusiastic free blurb: "See Marion Davies in 'Cecilia.' Marion Davies by her beauty and talent has made a great success of 'Cecilia of the Pink Roses,' the appealing motion picture drama now being shown at the best theaters here. Having read the serial here, be sure to see the film today." A glowing review was headed, "It Will Delight Millions All Over the Country." The *Journal* continued the praise the next day, and the next, with more *Cecilia* headlines and a huge drawing by Nell Brinkley featuring Miss Davies, large in the center, with other members of the cast suitably smaller and clustered around her. A Hearst columnist, Mrs. Wilson Woodrow, did her stint under the headline, "Mrs. Woodrow Captivated By 'Cecilia,'" beginning, "I went last night to see 'Cecilia of the Pink Roses' and fervently thanked my stars that I had done so." Mrs. Woodrow launched into a torrential panegyric, saying among other things that Miss Davies was "a pink rose of a girl." [2]

[1] N. Y. *American*, June 3, 1918.   [2] N. Y. *Journal*, June 3, 4, 5, 6, 1918.

Said the dour New York *Times:*

> There is no objection to Miss Davies. She is by no means a sensational actress . . . [but] the trouble is with the play . . .
>
> Take one lovable girl, one poor but honest Irish father, one weepy mother about to die . . . and plenty of platitudinous sentiments; mix all thoroughly in a simple and obvious plot that will tax no one's intelligence . . . result: "Cecilia of the Pink Roses." [3]

III. A PESTILENCE THAT WALKS IN THE DARK

HOWEVER he expanded, Hearst would never admit that he was spreading himself too thin. In 1917 he had bought the Boston *Advertiser,* and in 1918 the Chicago *Herald,* which he combined with his morning *Examiner.* In 1919 he bought the San Francisco *Call* and also fulfilled the peculiar deal with Brisbane, buying the Washington *Times* and the Milwaukee *Wisconsin News.* He now owned thirteen newspapers spread over the country. He owned six magazines: *Cosmopolitan, Hearst's International, Motor, Motor Boating* and *Harper's Bazaar* in the United States, and *Nash's Magazine* in London. He owned such semi-independent agencies as the ailing I.N.S., the immensely profitable King Features Service, the rich *American Weekly,* and others. He owned ranches, mines, millions in New York real estate, and the mayor of New York. He was building a castle in California and giving close attention to art sales on both sides of the Atlantic. He was augmenting his motion picture enterprises. Entirely aside from the fact that he had a wife and five sons, he had too much for one man to attend to. Yet, although he employed highly paid executives to head his various interests, he did not delegate full authority. He was the super-executive over them all. They knew that he was watching, that he might call them at any hour to the Clarendon, and that he had a remarkable knowledge of what was going on. It is a measure of his megalomania that he thought he could do all of these things at the same time that he was involved with Miss Davies and Colonial fireplaces, and the surprise is not that he did not always do them well but that he could do them at all.

His idea was expansion, never retrenchment. His magazine *Motor Boating* had suffered from the war's suppression of such luxuries as yachting. Advertising was down. The editor, Charles F. Chapman, heard a rumor that the Chief wanted to sell the publication. If so, Chapman, confident in its future, wanted to buy it and told this to Carvalho. Carvalho sent him on to Hearst at the Clarendon. Hearst said, "Mr. Chapman, if you owned the magazine, what would you do with it?"

Chapman outlined a program he had in mind. Hearst, the optimist, always impressed by optimism in his editors, beamed.

"Mr. Chapman," he said, "it's a splendid program. You go ahead and do these things for me and I won't bother you." [1]

---

[3] N. Y. *Times,* June 3, 1918.   [1] Mr. Chapman to author, Sept. 20, 1960.

On top of all this, he was shooting for office in 1920, if not the Presidency, the governorship. And at this time he began a tactic that proved disastrous —an assault on Governor Smith.

The Hearst-Smith quarrel was one of those phenomena fit to make philosophers ponder the consequences of human prejudice. It was fated to make history. Mushrooming from small beginnings, it became an implacable feud that affected profoundly the careers of them both, but it did a good deal more than that. It would reach out over the years to give an incidental boost to a younger New York politician, Franklin Delano Roosevelt, and elevate him to the post both Hearst and Smith longed for and failed to achieve—the Presidency.

Hearst's differences with Smith went far back. Smith's political godfather was Saloonkeeper "Big Tom" Foley, the Tammany district leader. Smith revered Foley. In 1907, when Hearst tried to elect Max Ihmsen sheriff, his papers used their customary personal invective against Foley, the opposing candidate. Although Foley easily won, he never forgave Hearst. In 1917, when Hearst sought to be mayor, both Foley and Smith fought him, so that Hylan became the candidate. In 1918, when Hearst sought to be governor, it was Smith who took the nomination. Hearst then supported him, and doubtless took credit for his narrow victory. He often had an engaging ability to forget past differences. This seemed to be the case with Smith, for the Smith children were occasionally invited to Riverside Drive to play with the Hearst youngsters.[2]

Smith took office January 1, 1919, and for four months the *Journal* and the *American* found no fault with him. On May 7, the governor appointed Robert L. Luce to fill a vacancy in the Supreme Court. On May 8, the Hearst papers assailed him for the appointment, describing Luce as a "tool of the interests" who had served as attorney for the New York Central Railroad. It was the first break between Hearst and Smith. It was said that Hearst, through an intermediary, had asked Smith to appoint William De Ford, long Hearst's attorney, and was angered because his suggestion had been ignored.[3] Hearst denied this.

"I have been particularly careful," he said, "never to ask any appointment or any other political favor of Governor Smith, for I have never been quite convinced of the sincerity of his professions of progressive principles. He has always been too close to Tammany, and too close to certain public service corporations to make him an ideal public official from my point of view. . . ."[4]

The complaint that Smith was "too close to Tammany" when the Tammany mayor, Hylan, was Hearst's own errand boy, drew snickers. However, Hearst, even when he was allied with Tammany, felt himself above and beyond it. One of his most unremitting crusades was seeing fruition in the construction of a municipally owned New York subway. Municipal owner-

[2] Henry F. Pringle, *Alfred E. Smith*, 23 ff.   [3] N. Y. *Times*, May 9, 1919.
[4] N. Y. *Times*, May 10, 1919.

ship was a Hearst fetish. When he had supported Smith, he had done so with the proviso that Smith push legislation enabling municipal ownership of public utilities in cities throughout the state.[5] He felt that Smith had not been energetic enough in this respect, from which it was an easy step for him to charge that the governor was "too close" to public service corporations. There is also a possibility that Hearst saw in Smith's growing popularity a threat to his own ascendancy in Democratic politics and a potential rival in 1920.

The *American* and *Journal* began a sustained attack on the governor. It happened that a milk producers' strike had diminished the flow of milk to the metropolis, and that even after the strike was settled the price remained at eighteen cents a quart. After assailing Smith on other issues, the Hearst press settled on the "milk scandal." The governor had no jurisdiction over the price of milk, but he tried to bring relief by the appointment of a Fair Price Milk Committee. The attacks continued all summer and into the fall, reaching a pitch of virulence seldom attained even by Hearst. New York children, said the *Journal,* were "starving to death," and the governor was to blame.[6] Hearst was in California most of the summer, supervising the construction of his castle, but it was well understood that he was behind the onslaught. While he had other quarrels with Smith, one suspects that he seized on the milk issue because it was a simple propaganda line that the poor and uneducated could understand and resent.

Smith, although represented as being "in league with the Milk Trust," held his peace for months. Undoubtedly he feared the publisher's power. The *Journal* and *American* began running cartoons of children emaciated for lack of milk, inferentially accusing the governor of causing the deaths of slum children. Smith's widowed mother, ill at the time, heard of the charges and was said to have murmured in delirium, "My son did not kill the babies."[7]

Smith, the product of the East Side, was fond of children. His temper finally snapped. In an angry speech before a women's group he denounced Hearst as "a mean man, a particularly low type of man," and challenged him to a public debate on the milk issue.

"My friends will hire the hall," he said. "He [Hearst] will get half the tickets. . . . He can get up on the platform and he can ask me any question he likes about my public or about my private life, if he will let me do the same."[8]

New Yorkers goggled at this sudden crisis between two of the most powerful Democrats in the state. It looked like a fight to a finish, with Smith taking his political life in his hands unless he had strength enough to win. If Smith had second thoughts about his own temerity, they may have been lulled by some 5000 letters he received from citizens applauding his stand. His fol-

[5] N. Y. *American,* Aug. 2, 1918.
[7] Henry Moskowitz, *Alfred E. Smith,* 288.
[6] N. Y. *Journal,* Oct. 1, 1919.
[8] N. Y. *Times,* Oct. 19, 1919.

lowers hired Carnegie Hall for the night of October 29, and an official invitation was sent Hearst, who had returned from California. Hearst must have pondered the challenge. Skillful though he was as a public speaker, he was hardly a match for Smith at rough-and-tumble debate. Also, he must have realized that he had no grounds for his attack on the governor on the milk issue, and he may have wondered if Smith's mention of questions about his "private life" was a veiled threat that he meant to carry out. Hearst replied in his best vituperative style:

> . . . I have no intention of meeting Governor Smith publicly or privately, politically or socially.
>
> I do not have to meet him, as I am not running for office, and I certainly do not want to meet him for the pleasure of association, as I find no satisfaction in the company of crooked politicians.
>
> Neither have I time or inclination to debate with every public plunderer or faithless public servant whom my papers have exposed, for the reason that every pilloried rascal in every city where my papers are published always tries to divert attention from the real issue of his political crookedness by making some sort of blatherskite onslaught upon me.
>
> I have no explanations to make for attacking the Milk Trust and the Traction Trust and the politicians who have surrendered to these rich and powerful plundering corporations and are committed to twenty-cent milk and ten-cent street car fares. . . .
>
> The only apology I would have to make would be for having supported Governor Smith, and that I did because of the perjured pledge of that individual made publicly in my papers on Aug. 2, 1918.
>
> I had no confidence in the progressive sentiments of Candidate Smith, and in reply to his request for support I asked for a public pledge, as the private assurances of men of his type have no weight with me whatever.

Hearst here quoted the Smith statement commending municipal ownership and predicting its early adoption. He finished:

> And, in conclusion, let me say that if you . . . are going to hire Carnegie Hall every time my papers expose rascally politicians, you would better take a long-term lease on the property.—Yours very truly, William Randolph Hearst.[9]

Hearst's letter evaded detailed mention of the milk issue, in which he must have felt his weakness, and shifted the emphasis to the municipal ownership issue. Al Smith, angrier than he ever had been, appeared alone on the stage at Carnegie Hall. He was carrying his fight against Hearst to the newspapers and the people. Born poor, with a meager education, but gifted with acumen and the common touch, he resented everything about the lordly millionaire. Contempt oozed from him. His face was red as he began a measured indictment, never polished, often grammatically chaotic, but effective. In his attitude and intonation, he came near being as brutal as Hearst.

[9] N. Y. *Times,* Oct. 28, 1919.

"I am going to ask," he said, "for your absolute silence and attention. I feel that I am here tonight upon a mission as important not only to myself, but to this city, to this State and to this country, as I could possibly perform. Of course, I am alone. . . . I know the man to whom I issued the challenge, and I know that he has not got a drop of good, clean, pure red blood in his whole body. And I know the color of his liver, and it is whiter, if that could be, than the driven snow.

". . . Why, the man is entirely lacking in any understanding of the situation. He doesn't spend any time in New York, to know what is going on here; he is in Palm Beach all winter, and in California all summer."

Smith made only passing mention of the municipal ownership issue, on which *he* doubtless felt less sure of himself, and concentrated on the question of the babies he had slain by depriving them of milk. He demonstrated that his authority was limited and that he had done what he could. He charged that Hearst's animus arose from his failure to dictate to the governor. He charged that Hearst had asked through intermediaries for two appointments (which Hearst denied) and that the newspaper attacks began when he failed to honor the requests. "I cannot think," he said, "of a more contemptible man . . . than the man that exploits the poor." Hearst, he said, was a professional falsifier and character assassin.

"Follow back the history of this man's newspapers since he came to this part of the country, and you will have to read out of his newspapers this remarkable fact: That in this great democracy . . . there has never been a man elected to office yet that has not been tainted in some way. . . . no public man in this State, from Grover Cleveland right down to today has ever escaped this fellow. We all know that. The children on the street know it."

Smith read to the audience a scurrilous, anonymous letter he had received from a Hearst defender, assailing him and "Judas Wilson."

> Now, I would not have paid much attention to that letter, were it not for the fact that . . . I find that it contains almost verbatim a number of headlines from the Hearst papers. Now, that is where that man got his idea . . . and that is his idea of this country and his treatment for the President or any other public official. . . .
>
> Nobody that ever went to the Governor's office went there with a graver sense of the responsibility of that office than I did. What could there possibly be about me that I should be assailed in this reckless manner by this man? I have more reason probably than any man I will meet tonight to have a strong love . . . for this country, for this State and for this city. Look at what I have received at its hands: I left school and went to work before I was fifteen years of age. I worked hard, night and day; I worked honestly and conscientiously at every job that I was ever put at, until I went to the Governor's chair in Albany. What can it be? It has got to be jealousy, it has got to be envy, it has got to be hatred or it has to be something that nobody understands, that makes me come down here . . . before this audience, and urge them to organize in this city to stay the danger

that comes from these papers, to the end that . . . we may get rid of this pestilence that walks in the darkness.[10]

What can it be? Smith asked, and admitted that the Hearst wellsprings were not within his ken. In so saying, he echoed the sentiments of many other public figures. Hearst was a puzzle to more than Smith—in fact, was on a fair way to becoming the Great American Enigma.

Even if Hearst's motives were honest, in this quarrel the bulk of virtue was surely on the side of Smith. The newspaper attacks on Smith exhibited the publisher's least lovely trait—cruelty combined with untruth in appealing to the ignorance and hatred of his readers.

The attack misfired. Governor Smith emerged the winner. When he defied Hearst in Carnegie Hall, he won widespread admiration and achieved a new political stature. For the first time, party men began to look on him as Presidential timber.[11]

[10] N. Y. *Times,* Oct. 30, 1919.   [11] Pringle, *Alfred E. Smith,* 20.

12. Hope Springs Eternal

I. THE MUD-GUTTER GAZETTE

> Of all the people I've met in my life, Hearst and President Wilson have been the most difficult for me to fathom. I must say that I admire Hearst for his sincere and vociferous Americanism even though from time to time I have disagreed with his policies. —James W. Gerard [1]

FORMER AMBASSADOR GERARD, a solid Democrat and often a guest at the Hearst apartment, enjoyed the publisher's keen appreciation of the ridiculous. Once Gerard told Hearst how he had made a speech, then later heard a couple of his auditors speak disparagingly of his oratorical ability.

"Don't mind that," Hearst said. "I heard two girls talking about me after one of my speeches. One said, 'What do you think of him as a speaker?' and the other said, 'Well, I don't know, but his trousers bag at the knees just like William Jennings Bryan's.'" [2]

Early in 1920, Bryan arrived in New York to make a speech which he hoped would move him toward his quadrennial Promised Land, the Democratic nomination. Gerard told him Hearst's story. Bryan was nettled.

"I don't think that's funny," he said coldly; "not funny at all. I often have my trousers pressed." [3]

When Gerard said Hearst was "difficult to fathom," he was in agreement with Smith, Boss Murphy, Bryan and other politicians who thought along reasonably balanced lines. Hearst was not balanced, his keen brain being at the mercy of his emotions. His thinking was colored by frustration at his repeated failure to gain office, his hope yet to succeed, and his anger at politicians who did not do as he wished. The Hearst pattern had become almost predictable. He would support a candidate, go along with him for a time after his election, and then begin to assail him. This tendency to turn on former friends was due in part to his sincere feeling that they had shirked their duty, and in part to his certainty that he was, after all, the man who could have handled the job perfectly.

There was an exception. He got along beautifully with the bumbling Hylan. Hylan was the perfect mayor because he followed the Hearst policies, including municipal ownership. If cynics would say that Hearst was not so interested in placing able men in office as he was in electing men who would do his bidding, it should be noted to Hearst's credit that Hylan was honest.

[1] James W. Gerard, *My First Eighty-three Years in America*, 288. [2] Gerard, 272.
[3] The same.

332

For all his many *faux pas*, he steered a straight course and never became involved in scandal.

Governor Smith, perhaps surprised at the success of his attack on Hearst, was keeping it up. He described Hearst as "a cuttlefish who emits this black vapor of ink," and took to calling the New York *American* the "Mud-Gutter Gazette." Hearst replied in kind and also continued his one-man war against England. When the government proposed to auction off to the British twenty-nine German vessels which had been seized in United States ports when the war began, he retained attorneys in Washington and secured an injunction against the sale.[4]

But in 1920 he was chiefly interested in the Presidential conventions. Although he did not discount his own chances, he mended fences in all directions so that his influence would at least be an important factor. A third-party group in Brooklyn was booming him for President. At the same time, he was backing Senator Hiram Johnson of California for the Republican nomination, and urging that Johnson should take the third-party nomination if the Republicans failed to select him. Harry Chandler, publisher of the Los Angeles *Times* and an enemy of Hearst and Johnson, viewed the portents uneasily, fearing that if Johnson won out he would be Hearst's "man."

". . . people out in my State," he said, "are worrying for fear [Hearst] is gunning now for the Presidency by proxy. . . . They are keenly aware that he virtually made himself Mayor of New York by electing his own creature, Hylan, whom he could control." [5]

In June, Hearst and Brisbane went as newspapermen to the Republican convention in Chicago, where Hearst pulled for Johnson while Brisbane sat in the press box and recorded his observations for some 3,000,000 readers. He dictated ceaselessly to a secretary beside him, in what Edna Ferber, who sat just ahead, decided was not writing but "a sort of verbal dysentery." Brisbane leaned forward.

"Are your pearls real?" he asked Miss Ferber.

"Certainly," she replied. "I paid five dollars for them at Mandel's."

Brisbane droned to his secretary, "Edna Ferber has just come into the press section she is wearing a blue dress with a scarlet hat and pearls the pearls look real but she says they cost five dollars . . ." [6]

"If Senator Johnson is nominated," Hearst kept saying, "he will be elected." [7] The heedless Republicans nominated Warren G. Harding. Hearst had a chat with Harding, himself a former editor. Harding asked him to convey to Johnson an invitation to be the Republican running mate. Hearst did so, but Johnson declined, and Calvin Coolidge was the ultimate choice.[8]

Again fate cheated Hearst—and Johnson—of leadership. If Johnson had accepted, he would have been President by 1923. A few days later, Hearst

[4] N. Y. *American*, Feb. 11, 1920; N. Y. *Times*, Apr. 18, 1920.
[5] N. Y. *Times*, Apr. 24, 1920.   [6] Edna Ferber, *A Peculiar Treasure*, 251.
[7] N. Y. *Times*, June 11, 1920.   [8] Mrs. Fremont Older, *op. cit.*, 429.

angrily said the Republican platform "straddled on almost everything" and sent out a call through his newspapers for a third party which should nominate Johnson, a "safe and sane progressive to whom no reasonable or honest business interest could properly object." [9] His next stop was the Democratic convention at San Francisco, where Al Smith also had a Presidential gleam in his eye. Hearst could scarcely have failed to reflect that if he had been governor of New York instead of Smith, he could have made a strong bid for the nomination. As it was, he got exactly one vote on the first ballot [10]—the first time he had received a vote in a Democratic convention since 1904, when he got 263. James M. Cox, another Ohio editor, became the nominee, and Hearst again had a four-year wait, this time until 1924.

He did his best to solidify his position for 1924. It was said that after the convention he entertained a number of friends at the Hacienda, among them Congressman George White, a member of the Ohio delegation and a close friend of Nominee Cox. Hearst took White aside and said he would give Cox the support of his newspapers if Cox, in the event of election, would pledge to make Hearst Secretary of the Navy. White was noncommittal, and Cox never made the pledge.[11]

Hearst also visited San Simeon, where a road had been built at great expense up the mountainside, steel and cement were arriving by coastal steamer, and foundations for three guest houses were under way. Julia Morgan, the architect, a tiny woman who wore old-fashioned hats and horn-rimmed glasses, was supervising the beginnings of an American structural phenomenon. Orrin Peck was there too, using his artist's sense in designing the landscaping around the group of buildings. Peck, who had done portraits of Senator Hearst, Phoebe, and Hearst himself as a young man, had later gained a solid reputation in San Francisco, but he was careless about money and doubtless his employment at San Simeon was not unwelcome.[12]

Hearst hurried back to Chicago, where a convention of third-party groups partly sponsored by his own newspapers was in progress. It was his third convention within a month. Observers who tried to classify his political affiliations must have been dazed. The more knowing ones realized that Hearst was not essentially a Republican, a Democrat or a third-party man, but was an independent thinker who was for whatever party would embrace the Hearst program and give him the office or influence he felt his due. There was some talk of Hearst himself as the third-party nominee, but he coyly side-stepped. He proposed Senator Reed of Missouri as the standard bearer, for Reed was as one with him in isolationism and hatred of Wilsonian policies. But Reed, despite his dinner at the Astor and evening at the *Follies*, could not see that a third party would get him anywhere. Hiram Johnson

[9] Chicago *Herald-Examiner*, June 20, 1920.
[10] James M. Cox, *Journey Through My Years*, 230.
[11] Nicholas Murray Butler, *Across the Busy Years*, II, 327.
[12] San Francisco *Examiner*, Jan. 21, 1921.

had already shown similar skepticism, so Hearst made overtures to Senator Robert La Follette.[13] Apparently even Hearst grew discouraged about third-party prospects, for he left Chicago before the convention was over and returned to California. He had newspapers to worry about in San Francisco and Los Angeles, but his real passion was San Simeon and his castle, his dream, his monument.

From Los Angeles he sent several telegrams to his New York *American* regarding the looming New York gubernatorial election. Smith was running for reelection, with Judge Nathan Miller the Republican candidate and Dudley Field Malone on a Farmer-Labor ticket. "Please directly urge all progressives to vote for Malone," Hearst telegraphed. "He is honest, clean, courageous, progressive. He was a distinguished young Democrat until Wilson suppressed the Democratic Party and drove Malone out of the Wilson party." [14]

But there were signs of a rapprochement between Hearst and Smith, who had so recently insulted each other. A later instruction the *American* got from the Chief, which was published as he intended it to be, showed bewildering vacillation:

> Miller's definite declarations against municipal ownership and direct primaries make it necessary for me to attack him vigorously. I am concerned for my progressive policies and principles and I don't care whether Smith is elected or not. He is better than Miller.
>
> I want to support Malone as a progressive and genuine Democrat, and if I could get Smith sincerely to pledge himself to progressive legislation I would not oppose him.
>
> His personal attacks upon me are wholly unimportant. I don't consider them at all.
>
> The objection to Smith is that he isn't sincere and isn't truthful and probably will not do what he says he will do . . .[15]

Smith, for all his contempt for Hearst and the Mud-Gutter Gazette, knew he was in for a hard battle against Judge Miller. Without the support of the Hearst press he would almost certainly lose, as Boss Murphy must have reminded him. He needed Hearst. That same day, Smith came out with a strong statement in favor of municipal ownership. The chances are that this was exacted from him by Hearst, with whatever other demands one can only guess. The two enemies climbed into the same expedient bed. The *American* promptly dropped Malone and came out for Smith with a platitudinous refrain:

> Every one who wants the power of corrupt corporations curbed and the domination of political bosses restricted in New York State must vote for Al Smith and against Judge Miller.[16]

[13] N. Y. *American,* June 30; Chicago *American,* July 12, 1920.
[14] Quoted in N. Y. *Times,* Oct. 26, 1920.   [15] The same.
[16] N. Y. *American,* Oct. 28, 1920.

Hearst returned to New York with a problem on his mind. Arthur Brisbane, whose editorials were widely heralded and whose daily column *To-day* was a great popular success, had shown some indication of feeling underpaid. In Brisbane, Hearst had found his ideal aide-de-camp, a skilled workhorse to whom the Chief's word was law. He had no intention of losing Brisbane, but he did not feel him underpaid. He called Moses Koenigsberg to the Clarendon.

"Brisbane's contract is about to expire," he said. "He's acting up. Whom can we get—someone that Artie will consider a possible successor?" [17]

Koenigsberg had just the man—Herbert Kaufman, who was writing an editorial feature for the Hearst press. Hearst used against Brisbane the same device Brisbane had used against his cartoonists. He waggled Kaufman in Brisbane's face to keep the editor from holding him up.

The cartoonist Rube Goldberg, now syndicated by Hearst, was also summoned to the Clarendon, but he had no money troubles with the Chief in renewing his contract. "How are you?" Hearst asked Goldberg. "How is everything going?" Goldberg said things were going fine, after which the talk languished and Goldberg became embarrassed because Hearst was obviously ill at ease.[18]

Hearst's political activities alone in 1920, to take no account of his many other enterprises, were such as would have exhausted most younger men. He had traveled back and forth across the country, lived at hotels, partaken in three conventions, conferred in smoke-filled rooms, made moves and counter-moves, all with the same result—utter failure. Politicians had generally grown suspicious of him. His were the frantic stratagems of the eager power-seeker who sees his youth slipping away and races against time to gain his goal. Party-line men must have shaken their heads when they totaled his maneuvers:

He had tried to get the Republicans to nominate Senator Johnson, failed, and had denounced the Republican platform.

He had sought the Navy post from the Democratic candidate, and failed.

He had tried to launch a third party, and failed.

Whom was Hearst for, other than Hearst? An even more engrossing question was, whom would he support in the fall?

He supported Governor Smith, of course. And he supported the Republican Harding, whose platform he deplored. Harding won in a Republican landslide. Al Smith was swept out of office in that same landslide. Hearst was happy at any rate for one thing: Wilson and the League of Nations had been repudiated.

"Mr. Wilson wanted a referendum on the League of Nations," he wrote, "and he has had it." [19]

Early in 1921, Orrin Peck took a respite from his work at San Simeon and visited a friend in Los Angeles, where he died suddenly of a heart

---

[17] Koenigsberg, 409.   [18] Rube Goldberg to author, Feb. 11, 1960.
[19] Mrs. Fremont Older, *op. cit.*, 430.

attack.[20] Hearst had known Peck as a boy in San Francisco, had known him in Munich, had traversed Europe with him, had entertained him in New York, Florida and California, and had taken him into his confidence about his affections for three different women over a period of three decades. Hearst, who had so few real friends, had lost his closest one, one of the last remaining links with his childhood. He could not bear to go across the country to the funeral.

Besides, Miss Davies was working on *The Young Diana,* and everything had to be just so. For a scene representing St. Moritz, an artificial skating rink was installed at the lot, on which Miss Davies was to perform intricate maneuvers. She could not stand up on skates, so the champion figure skater Bobby McLean was hired to double for her. McLean had a big, unladylike nose. He stayed at a distance from the camera as, clad in a trig, fur-trimmed costume like Miss Davies', he performed superb pirouettes on the ice. For the close-ups, Miss Davies was propped upright by two stagehands.

All this was expensive and time-consuming, but when it was finished Hearst was dissatisfied with it. He junked it and decided that a snow scene would be better. At further expense, another studio was hired in the Bronx, filled with artificial snow, and the whole sequence was started again from scratch.[21]

II. SOUTH OF THE BORDER

WHILE Hearst's chief efforts in reform were in the field of politics, he also felt it his duty to redeem the clergy from error. When in 1921 Dr. Manning was the leading candidate for Episcopal Bishop of New York, Hearst perhaps recalled how Manning had mounted the rostrum at Madison Square Garden to denounce his appointment as soldier-greeter. The New York *American* ran an editorial attack on him which was sent to all voting Episcopal clergymen in the diocese in the form of telegrams.[1] The editorial was denounced at the conclave of clerics, who promptly elected Dr. Manning their bishop.[2]

Although Hearst's record was replete with such failures, this was largely because he tried to do everything. He was still one of the nation's most powerful political bosses, for all his hatred of bosses. With his three great newspapers in California, he virtually controlled the state. He was potent in Chicago, where his friend Mayor William Hale Thompson challenged King George, and was a strong factor in the state of Illinois. His judgment was respected by politicians of such importance as Hiram Johnson and James Reed. He controlled New York's City Hall and was a force Boss Murphy and Al Smith had to consider. It should not be forgotten that New York City, in population, expenditures and patronage was a more important entity than any of the nation's states and represented double the rest of the Empire State. The mayor's salary was $25,000 a year. The governor's was

[20] San Francisco *Examiner,* Jan. 21, 1921.
[1] N. Y. *American,* Jan. 26, 1921.
[21] *The New Yorker,* Sept. 14, 1940.
[2] N. Y. *Times,* Jan. 27, 1921.

$10,000 a year—the same as that of the mayor's secretary. Hearst, with his grip on Mayor Hylan, posed a constant threat to Murphy, whose chief weapon was patronage.

For nineteen years Murphy had been forced to fight Hearst or to collaborate with him. He may have been hard put to tell which was worse. He personally detested the publisher, but he could never ignore him. In normal city politics, the Tammany leader had patronage claims which no dutiful Tammany mayor could refuse to honor. With Hylan it was different. The mayor, who had grown annoyingly vain because of his friendship with the publisher, did not show the deference due Murphy as boss. It was no secret that Hearst was far more Hylan's boss than Murphy was, and this was a humiliating situation which Murphy was powerless to solve. So far, Hylan, who had nominal control of city jobs and patronage, had appointed most of the men Murphy wanted. But this was done with the understanding that it was with the approval of Hearst. This placed Murphy in the position of asking Hearst for favors which he should normally have demanded of the mayor as his due.[3] It also gave Hearst a ready weapon, for if Murphy displeased him in any way, he could strike back at the boss through Hylan.

This was entirely apart from Hearst's financial help, always important in an election, and the power of his press. Murphy was no more than a sub-boss, and when he and Hearst elected Hylan for a second term in 1921, it seemed that Murphy was in for four more years of sub-bossism.

Meanwhile, the Hearst press resumed its complaints about the continuing revolution and disorder in Mexico and was clamoring for armed United States intervention. One of the indices to Hearst's egomania was his recurrent demand that the United States protect his property in Mexico. It was true that he had suffered financial loss in the endless struggle there, and that a few pieces of his Babicora ranch had been expropriated. It was also true that his father had originally got his millions of Mexican acres from the dictatorial Porfirio Diaz for a song, and that Diaz's careless sale of land and resources had resulted in a flock of Yankee capitalists fattening in Mexico while peons were in the most abject poverty.

In October, 1921, Hearst took Miss Davies, Joseph Urban, and a group of his cinema people and other friends for an evening cruise in his steam yacht, *Oneida*, where they looked at rushes from the latest Cosmopolitan movie as the boat churned out of New York harbor. Among the guests were Miss Davies' mother, Mrs. Rose Douras, and sister, Ethel Douras, Director William LeBaron and Luther Reed, a script writer.

Hearst, apparently inspired by the beautiful night, had a sudden idea. They would not return to New York, he said. If everyone was willing, they would continue on to Mexico, where he had business anyway. This was

<hr />

[3] Pringle, *Alfred E. Smith*, 43.

fairly startling even for Hearst, but his guests were agreeable, since he would pay all expenses.

Urban's young daughter Gretl was one of the party. Hearst, who had always wanted a daughter, was fond of her, winning her admiration because of his overwhelming kindness and his habit of talking with her entirely without condescension, as if she were an adult. She knew him as a man who did surprising things, and yet she was astonished by this evening cruise that had turned into a six-week tour of Mexico. "None of us were equipped for such an extended journey," she later wrote, "so Mr. Hearst dispensed cash largesse to one and all for necessary supplements of clothing, etc." [4] They put in at Baltimore to buy the clothing and also to pick up a few more guests. In Mexico, they continued the journey in a private train Hearst hired. Miss Urban noticed that he worked for hours on the train, surrounded by newspapers, while the others were enjoying themselves. "He adored Mexico," she recalled, "and would get off the train early in the morning to bring fresh fruit and tamales for his guests' breakfast."

Miss Urban observed on this and many other occasions that Hearst, as a host, was the very soul of benevolence—nothing like the wicked and selfish man pictured by his enemies. "I shall cherish his wonderful kindness forever," she wrote.[5]

Hearst inspected his properties in Chihuahua and Campeche. In Mexico City, government officials took his guests to a bullfight—a spectacle he loathed and refused to attend, regarding it as cruel. He and Miss Davies had a long visit with the new president, Alvaro Obregon. Obregon must have given him satisfying reassurances, for he returned to the United States singing a new tune. "[My] properties were in continual trouble and turmoil during the several preceding administrations," he said, "but have been in complete peace and security during the administration of Pres. Obregon." [6]

Shortly after his return, Hearst, this time with his wife, had lunch with another President, Warren Harding, in the White House.[7]

[4] Gretl Urban to author, Sept. 6, 1960. [5] Miss Urban to author.
[6] San Francisco *Examiner*, Nov. 13, 1921.   [7] N. Y. *Times*, Dec. 28, 1921.

13. The Coup de Grâce

I. PROBLEMS POLITICAL AND MARITAL

ALTHOUGH capable of holding a grudge, Hearst often showed an admirable ability to let bygones be bygones. When Fremont Older, long editor of the San Francisco *Bulletin,* had a finish fight with his publisher over his crusade for Tom Mooney, Hearst offered him a job. "Come to the *Call,*" he wired, "and bring the Mooney case with you." [1] Older, who had on occasion fought Hearst bitterly, became editor of the *Call* and a Hearst admirer until his death. After much angling, Hearst also snagged Norman Hapgood as a Washington writer—Hapgood, who as editor of *Collier's* had assailed and exposed Hearst repeatedly, and who thereafter became another Hearst admirer.[2] Hearst had likewise almost forgiven Al Smith's pungent remarks about the color of his blood and liver.

Smith, however, had never forgiven Hearst or his Mud-Gutter Gazette and its baby-murder charges. That winter, Hearst agents were drumming up a boom in upstate counties for the publisher, who wanted either the gubernatorial or Senatorial nomination in 1922.[3] Smith, prosperously employed during the interim as a trucking executive, watched this grimly. He knew that he could have the gubernatorial nomination for the asking. He knew, too, that he would not take it if he had to take Hearst along with it.

As a poor man who for twenty years had fought his way from precinct politics to the governor's chair, Smith had reservations about a millionaire's concern for "the people." As a born-and-bred New Yorker, he was skeptical about a transplanted Westerner who spent so much time in Florida and was building a castle in California. As a Catholic, a family man, he was repelled by the talk of Hearst's moral shortcomings. As a firm Democrat, he resented Hearst's assaults on Wilson and his support of Harding.

But most of all, Smith, who had been largely exposed to Hearst's satanic side, considered him the essence of journalistic and political evil, a ruthless opportunist, a threat to the New York Democracy. His newspapers *lied.* Smith knew that Murphy was afraid of Hearst, his millions, his newspapers, his hold over Hylan and the city patronage. Murphy was willing to compromise with Hearst. Smith, viewing the situation from his new status of independence as a $30,000-a-year executive, was not. The lines were drawn for battle.[4]

Samuel Seabury, the perennial defender-of-the-public-against-Hearst, was

---

[1] Evelyn Wells, *Fremont Older,* 310. [2] Norman Hapgood, *The Changing Years,* 260.
[3] N. Y. *World,* Jan. 22, 1922. [4] Pringle, *Alfred E. Smith,* 43–45.

warning that the menace was abroad again. Mayor Hylan, the one-man claque, was lauding Hearst's capacity for office. Murphy, cagey as always, was saying little, taking his time-tried stand that the convention would pick the candidates. Smith kept silent. Hearst aroused laughter by announcing that he was not a candidate.[5] The laughter grew when he bought two more newspapers, the Syracuse *Evening Telegram* and the Rochester *Evening Journal.*[6] These papers, located in upstate centers where the Democrats were traditionally weak, were just what the publisher needed to get him influence and votes.

Hearst carried on his activities as usual although he was faced by a personal crisis.

Miss Davies was not merely another of his passing fancies. He wanted to marry her. She wanted to marry him. Mrs. Hearst, however, refused to give him a divorce. One of her good friends was Elsa Maxwell, whom she had met in war work and with whom she remained on close terms for many years. Miss Maxwell later wrote indignantly of the blow suffered by Millicent Hearst, the mother of Hearst's five sons, when she was asked to step aside in favor of a young actress. She was still a beautiful and accomplished matron, the object of admiring glances wherever she went. She had her own firm principles. According to Miss Maxwell, Mrs. Hearst showed only one flash of anger, indulging it by going to Tiffany's, buying a pearl necklace priced in "six figures," and saying, "Send the bill to my husband's office."[7]

Since Hearst hated to have even small wishes thwarted, and this was a big one, one suspects that he did not take the refusal with equanimity. Yet he came around in time to the realization that the fault, if any, was his. It would be surprising if Mrs. Hearst did not entertain the hope that he would recover from his infatuation. She had their five sons to think about. Eventually they reached an understanding. They would remain officially man and wife even though the relationship had ended. Each continued to reside at the Clarendon and to act as a parent of the boys. Mrs. Hearst continued to appear with her husband at occasional social and political functions. Her balls and charities, including her annual Milk Fund drive, were well publicized in the Hearst press. For a time, Hearst continued his futile efforts to reach a divorce agreement. The marriage had become a pretense, but the couple remained on friendly terms and Mrs. Hearst won admiration for the tact and dignity of her efforts to hold her family together.

Almost four decades later, she told this writer, "W. R. was a great man. Those who thought otherwise just didn't know him."[8]

II. PRESIDENTIAL TIMBER

HEARST was exhibiting his usual kindness not only toward Miss Davies but also her relatives. Her father, Magistrate Douras, was so pleased at his new

[5] N. Y. *Times,* Jan. 15, 1922.   [6] Frederic L. Paxson, *Postwar Years: Normalcy,* 287.
[7] Elsa Maxwell, *R.S.V.P.,* 128–29.   [8] Mrs. Hearst to author, May 15, 1959.

eminence that he left the plebeian Bronx and moved to Hearst's fashionable Riverside Drive (No. 336), where he vainly sued a tailor to whom he sent a pair of pants containing twenty dollars, getting the trousers back well pressed but minus the twenty dollars.[1] Her brother-in-law, George Van Cleve, was an executive in the Hearst film corporation. He likewise moved to Riverside Drive (No. 331). Her sister, Reine Douras, was a well-paid supporting actress at the Hearst movie lot.

For a man seeking the governorship in the fall, Hearst did a lot of flitting while others carried on for him. He went to San Simeon in the spring, wiring a Brooklyn newspaperman who asked about his political plans: "I am a rancher enjoying life in the high hills overlooking the broad Pacific. If you want to talk about Herefords, I will talk to you—but not about politics." [2] He returned in mid-May, by which time his old Buffalo friend, William J. "Fingy" Connors, was beating the drum for him. Connors, who had helped him in his 1906 gubernatorial campaign, said warmly:

"Hearst is the biggest man in the country. He is Presidential timber. . . . The people of New York will demand him for Governor. . . . Without doubt, he will be the next President." [3]

This talk gave national Democratic leaders the shakes. "They realize," said the *Times*, "that should Hearst be elected Governor he would become an exceedingly troublesome factor as an aspirant for the Presidential nomination in 1924." [4] Hearst let others do the talking. In his incessant activity he had had small time to give to his sons, which he now corrected. With Mrs. Hearst and their three eldest sons, he boarded the *Aquitania* for Europe—his first trip abroad in ten years—taking Mr. and Mrs. Guy Barham of Los Angeles with them. Barham, a good friend, was publisher of Hearst's recently-acquired Los Angeles *Herald*. Lady Nancy Astor, on the same liner, spied Hearst and said archly, "When I am running for office, I don't run away." [5] Hearst cheerfully posed with his family for newsphotographers before the ship sailed, laughing heartily at one newsman's suggestion that he might be presented at the Court of St. James's.

"This is the first time I have heard of it," he said, "and I doubt if the Court has heard of it." [6]

By what may have been coincidence, Miss Davies also visited Europe at this time. Hearst's European tour was cut short when Barham died June 9 in London after an operation. He left his wife to continue with the boys while he returned home aboard the *Olympic* with the widow and Barham's body. Miss Davies also returned from Europe, although it is unknown whether she was on the same ship.[7] By this time Fingy Connors had opened Hearst headquarters at the McAlpin Hotel, saying devoutly, "If I am spared, Mr. Hearst will be nominated for President before I quit this job." [8]

[1] N. Y. *Times*, July 24, 1920.
[2] N. Y. *Times*, May 4, 1922.
[3] N. Y. *Times*, June 10, 1922.
[4] Issue of June 18, 1922.
[5] N. Y. *Times*, May 24, 1922.
[6] The same.
[7] N. Y. *Times*, June 10, 15, 1922.
[8] N. Y. *Times*, June 18, 1922.

Saying nothing of this, Hearst seemed more preoccupied with Miss Davies, who was working on her *magnum opus,* the Tudor romance, *When Knighthood Was in Flower.* In this picture the Hearst Cosmopolitan studio pulled out all the financial and artistic stops. The temperamental Urban designed the sets, tearing his hair when Hearst proved dissatisfied with one of them and had it redone.[9] Robert Vignola was the director (under Hearst). Victor Herbert was employed to write two special songs, one of them *The Marion Davies March.* Vast sums were spent. Hearst was determined that this production should catapult the young actress into first-rank fame.

At this time, while he was worrying about the governorship, the Presidency, and *Knighthood,* occurred a disturbing mishap.

Reine Douras, Miss Davies' sister, had a suburban cottage in Freeport, a town then favored by artists and actors. On the night of June 25 she gave a lawn party, attended by some forty guests including the Leo Carillos, the Victor Moores and the Harry von Tilzers. Prohibition, which Hearst had hailed as America's victory over the hangover, was in force, but gin, whisky and "home brew" were in evidence. It was rumored that the party was meant to honor Miss Davies on her return from Europe. Her father, the magistrate, was certainly there. However, the stars of this production were two previous unknowns, Mr. and Mrs. Oscar A. Hirsh. Hirsh became what was later described as "stewed to the eyes." Around midnight, he and his wife wandered off into the back yard and became involved in a struggle over a pistol that ended when Hirsh was shot and wounded in the neck.

The wound was not fatal, but the police came and quite a little scandal blew up. The Hearst press covered the shooting with never a mention of Miss Douras and her party. Other papers were less circumspect. "Freeport gossip," said the *Herald,* "had it that Marion's return from Europe had been the inspiration for the merrymaking." [10] There were the inevitable rumors— that Hirsh had been paying attentions to "a certain well known woman of the stage," arousing his wife's anger. The Hirshes denied this, though admitting that they could remember little of what happened. One suspects that Hearst sprang into the breach. Miss Davies' attorney immediately telephoned the newspapers to say that she was not at the party.[11]

The reason for the importance in establishing that Miss Davies was not present probably arose from a growing public feeling that film people led dissolute lives. The previous fall, Comedian Fatty Arbuckle's involvement in the wild party in San Francisco that resulted in the death of a minor actress had been splashed in the Hearst press with headlines that helped ruin Arbuckle's career. That scandal proved the climax of a series of lesser ones which the newspapers had seized on so avidly that clergymen began to denounce the "liquor-and-sex orgies" of screen actors and to campaign for a boycott. The movement grew. The cinema industry, frightened, had appointed Will H. Hays "czar" of the movies with instructions to keep a

[9] Frances Marion to author.   [10] N. Y. *Herald,* June 26, 1922.
[11] N. Y. *Herald,* June 27, 1922.

stern eye on photoplays and the people who made them. Film folk were warned to be on their good behavior or to suffer the consequences.

With this background, the Hirsh shooting could have had an adverse effect on Miss Davies' career. She brought suit against the *Herald,* the *Daily News* and the *Telegram* for suggesting that she might have been at the party.[12]

III. PUBLICITY CAN DO ANYTHING

IN September, New York saw the opening of *When Knighthood Was in Flower,* which Hearst launched with large advertisements in competing newspapers describing it as "the greatest, most costly and most beautiful photoplay ever produced, from the sweetest story ever told." [1] Although the Criterion Theater, where it opened, was not his property, he refurbished the place as if it were. Joseph Urban redesigned the theater, with twelve new loges modeled after the royal boxes in the tournament scenes in the film. The orchestra pit was enlarged to accommodate both a symphony orchestra and twenty picked singers who would render an operatic accompaniment. The lobby was turned into an art gallery, festooned with original posters by Howard Chandler Christy, F. X. Leyendecker, W. T. Benda and other artists showing Miss Davies in an array of Tudor costumes. An advance set of films had been sent to London for a private showing before the Prince of Wales, who, although not a Tudor, was believed well versed in that era.

While Miss Davies' previous efforts had been colossal, the Hearst press was quick to see that this one eclipsed them all. In the *American,* under the headline, "Marion Davies in Greatest Role of Career," the delighted critic Alan Dale wrote at length in a vein suggested by some of his phrases: "Marion Davies soars to new heights. . . . Miss Davies certainly rose to the capital occasion . . . . sets a new pace for pictures . . . . this priceless film." Society Writer Cholly Knickerbocker pointed out that the elite of society were there. A large photograph of young Prince Edward appeared under the headline, " 'When Knighthood Was in Flower' Wonderful, Says Prince of Wales." [2] In the *Journal,* Critic Margery Rex saw in Miss Davies an actress without a peer: "Nothing previously done in motion pictures can compare with this perfect photoplay . . . . sets a new photoplay standard . . . . superlative performance of the talented star. . . . Bewildering in its magnificence . . . . best of all, fortunate in its lovely star, Marion Davies." Under still another of the many headlines devoted to the event, "Mayor Overwhelmed by Beauty and Story of 'Knighthood' Film," Mayor Hylan admitted that his wonderment left him almost speechless:

> "When Knighthood Was in Flower" is unquestionably the greatest picture I have ever seen. . . . I am overwhelmed. . . . The acting of Miss Davies in the role of Princess Mary Tudor is marvellous. . . . Her sword play is

[12] N. Y. *Times,* July 2, 6, 25, 1922.   [1] N. Y. *Tribune,* Sept. 12, 1922.
[2] N. Y. *American,* Sept. 14, 15, 1922.

exquisite. . . . The settings are the most superb I have ever had the pleasure to see. The costumes are gorgeous. . . . No person can afford to miss this great screen masterpiece.[3]

While other newspapers were more restrained, they were generally approving. The *Times* praised Vignola's direction, saying, "As a spectacle it is dazzling to the eye. . . . Marion Davies as the Princess Mary is surprising. . . . There are scenes in which she really seems to have caught the spirit of the role, even if, at times, she gives the impression that she is well-drilled in the part, rather than spontaneous." [4]

A young woman named Louella O. Parsons was covering the movies for the New York *Telegraph* at $110 a week. Miss Parsons, enchanted by the film, wrote a piece taking Hearst to task for boasting of its great cost and lavish costumes rather than boosting Miss Davies as the star. This was strange, since Miss Davies' likeness was appearing everywhere in posters and in half-page newspaper advertisements, and her name was mentioned, always approvingly and often in big-type headlines, no less than seventy-three times in two days of the *American* and *Journal*. Yet Hearst, when he read Miss Parsons' column, was struck by a suspicion that he and his staffs had somehow been delinquent in publicizing Miss Davies. If Miss Parsons could point out their shortcomings, she was indispensable.

"We must hire that woman," he said.[5]

Shortly thereafter, Miss Parsons went to work for Hearst at $250 a week. So far, Miss Davies' pictures had lost heavily, largely because he spent too much on them. *Knighthood* was said to have cost more than $1,500,000—a staggering sum in that era when a pretentious film could be made for $100,000 and a quickie for half that. Deficits meant nothing to Hearst, with glory looming ahead. When a friend said to him, "There's money in the movies," Hearst's eyes twinkled.

"Yes," he agreed. "Mine." [6]

IV. POLITICAL MURDER

To pin the governorship on his lapel along with the Davies laurels was a coup Hearst firmly expected to execute, and its consummation would have made him the happiest of millionaires. In New York he had played his cards skillfully enough so that after years in the political shade he seemed destined to emerge into the bright sunlight of office. He was making placating gestures toward the angry Smith. He felt sure of Murphy. Hylan was his property. He played the role of dutiful husband, being the first to greet Mrs. Hearst when she returned with her sons on the *Mauretania*, to be greeted also by the Police Band, the Street Cleaners' Band and a deputation of thirty-

[3] N. Y. *Journal*, Sept. 15, 1922.   [4] N. Y. *Times*, Sept. 12, 1922.
[5] Frances Marion to author, Aug. 24, 1960.
[6] Harry Hershfield to author, Sept. 16, 1959.

three women appointed by Mayor Hylan to welcome distinguished guests.[1]

A sign of the Hearst power came when George A. Colgan, the city Commissioner of Markets, was dismissed by Hylan. Colgan was a strong Smith man and an exalted Elk. He complained that the reason for his discharge was his refusal to make a tour of all Elk lodges in the state and urge the brethren to vote for Hearst. Colgan said the same request had been made of city employes who were prominent Masons, Knights of Columbus and Moose.[2] The dismissal of Colgan could be interpreted as a warning by Hearst, through Hylan, that Murphy and Smith had better keep in line or more of Tammany's faithful would lose their jobs.

The Democratic state convention opened in Syracuse on September 28. Hearst was not there, but was well represented by his alter ego, Mayor Hylan, his personal attorney, William De Ford, the White House-bound Fingy Connors, and others. His veteran political secretary, O'Reilly, had recently died. White-haired John H. McCooey, the Brooklyn Democratic boss, joined the group friendly to Hearst. McCooey could scarcely have forgotten that during the war, Mrs. Hearst selected Mrs. McCooey as a member of her celebrity-studded war-work committee. The maneuvering of the chieftains that composed the real work of the convention took place in the splendid Onondaga Hotel, where Murphy had a second-floor suite. Smith, immobilized by a rheumatic foot, chewed on a cigar in his sixth-floor diggings. The Hearst men were saying that although their chief preferred the governorship, he would willingly give that to Smith and take the Senatorial nomination. A Tammany emissary went to Smith with this offer. Smith removed his cigar and used the cuspidor.

"I'm damned if I will," he snapped.[3]

He let it be known that he refused to appear on a ticket that also contained Hearst.

There was consternation in the Tammany ranks. Smith's loathing for Hearst was well known, but it had been taken for granted that he would bend to the Tammany code. The Smith-Hearst ticket offered a well-oiled machine, with plenty of money and headlines, that was almost certain to roll to victory. Alienating Hearst might court defeat.

McCooey went to plead with Smith. Norman Mack, the Buffalo leader, reasoned with him. Several others tried. Smith would not be budged.

"Nothing doing," he growled. "Say, do you think I haven't any self-respect? You can tell Murphy I won't run with Hearst on the ticket and that goes!" [4]

Big Tom Foley was squarely behind Smith.[5] Smith later said that unless he had put his foot down, Hearst would inevitably have become the state Democratic leader, with Tammany in his pocket, and what could have been worse? Murphy, despite his dislike for Hearst, was worried. Although there was some resentment at Smith's bull-headedness, it was apparent that the

[1] N. Y. Times, July 15, 1922.
[2] Pringle, Alfred E. Smith, 52.
[5] Alfred E. Smith, Up To Now, 233.
[3] N. Y. Times, Aug. 2, 1922.
[4] The same, 53.

delegates, if they had to choose, would pick the popular Smith and ditch Hearst. Murphy, in his heart, felt the same way.

Hylan was in anguish. The Hearst men, seeing the trend clearly against them, telegraphed their chief in New York for instructions.

Hearst, until then certain of the nomination he so dearly sought, saw his hopes shattered through the agency of one man, Smith. He decided against making a fight which he would surely lose. He wired De Ford:

> Please be sure not to allow my name to go before the convention. I certainly would not go on any ticket which, being reactionary, would stultify my record and declaration of principles and which would be a betrayal of genuine Democracy.
>
> My nomination for public office is not important, but it is important that the party declare for progressive principles and show the sincerity of that declaration by nominating men who can be trusted to make it effective.[6]

He had been politically murdered by a maneuver the like of which Tammany never saw before. He had virtually been read out of the party, while Smith, in a test of personal power, had shown himself stronger than Hearst, stronger than Murphy, and emerged as a real Presidential prospect. The convention went on happily to nominate Smith for governor. A bone was tossed to Hearst in the nomination for Senator of his good friend Dr. Royal S. Copeland, the New York City Health Commissioner.[7]

Old-time politicians searched their memories in vain for an instance when a power in the party had been so humiliated and shattered in one stroke by a single, determined enemy.

Occasionally, when thwarted, Hearst would go into a private rage, stamping around, screeching in his high-pitched voice and breaking chairs and other objects that came within reach.[8] It would be surprising if he did not indulge such a rage at this time.

From then on, he hated Smith with unalloyed hatred. Yet he supported both Smith and Copeland in the election, which both—to add to his sense of loss—won by huge majorities. One doubts that his support of Smith was motivated only by staunch Democratic principle. Hearst, a man with an obsession, still had a wistful hope that he might be a Presidential candidate in 1924, and he needed friends more than he needed anything else.

[6] N. Y. *World*, Sept. 30, 1922.   [7] Edward J. Flynn, *You're The Boss*, 36.
[8] Private source.

BOOK FIVE

THE MEDIEVALIST

1. The Great American Enigma

1. ATTRACTING THE CHIEF'S ATTENTION

In 1923, Hearst, who disliked to grow old, reached sixty. In point of energy expended and scope of activities, he had already outstripped a score of average lifetimes. In his mastery of journalistic techniques he was unrivaled. In his observance of the best standards of journalism, he was precisely what the *North American Review* had called him years earlier, "a blazing disgrace to the craft."

Al Smith had touched the root of the evil when he said of the *Journal*, "you cannot look for truth in this paper." Others had tried in their own way to describe the peculiar delinquencies of the Hearst press. Will Irwin had said that in it "the music of the spheres became a screech." R. L. Duffus said it "reduced everything to the common denominator of two or three instincts and passions." [1] Arthur James Pegler, a Hearst writer and the father of Westbrook Pegler, remarked, "A Hearst newspaper is like a screaming woman running down the street with her throat cut." [2] Oswald Garrison Villard described Hearst journalism as "gathering garbage from the gutters of life." [3]

The trouble with Hearst's newspapers was to be found in the deep-seated flaws in his own character—his instability, his hunger for power, his insatiable need for money, his vein of cruelty.

His papers were seldom indecent. He forbade indecency. They merely "plugged" crime and scandal for circulation. It had to be said that from Ambrose Bierce and Mark Twain to Kipling and Shaw, they printed an enormous amount of quality material. They had fought many good fights. They were preeminent in features, in their ownership of Barney Google, Jiggs and other cartoon characters loved by the millions. They were deficient in the newspaper's first requisite—news. The faking of news stories and photographs was brought to a high art by the romancers of the Hearst press. Truth, the touchstone of news value, was unimportant to Hearst because circulation, money and power were his goals. He had—always with startling exceptions—sold out his own newspapers to his own weaknesses.

For years they had been used unblushingly as personal publicity organs for Hearst. Now they were employed, with equal impudence, to advance the career of Miss Davies.

But the fearsome thing about this big, soft-voiced man who liked nothing better than a good joke, was his occasional hatreds. He specialized in attack, and in attack he was pitiless. He loved political cartoonists who could inspire hatred. He had preached hatred of Huntington, Mark Hanna, Mc-

[1] *World's Work*, Oct., 1922.
[3] *Villard, Prophets, True and False*, 302.
[2] Ben Hecht, *A Child of the Century*, 144.

Kinley, Boss Murphy, Archbold and Standard Oil, Wilson, England, and Al Smith, to name only a few. The insinuating, venomous quality of his appeals to hatred were unmatched. There was a diabolic strain of abnormality in the man who could accuse Wilson, who wrecked his own health in a trip to Europe to fight for his cherished League, of going there merely to receive honors and gifts; and in the man who could suggest that Al Smith was the murderer of tenement babies.

Hearst's streak of sadism warred constantly with his kindly impulses and sometimes won out. It generally was brought to bear on enemies, but occasionally it impaled employes. There were times when he seemed to enjoy the squirmings of two of his executives who were placed in an irreconcilable position that a word from him would have dissipated.[4] The business of putting two men on the same job also occurred frequently, and some felt the reason was not so much to determine the best man as to afford the Chief a malicious amusement. One of the marvels of the whole Fourth Estate was the fantastic salaries he paid his executives. Some of them such as Brisbane, Goddard, Merrill, Carvalho and Kobler became wealthy men or millionaires in their own right. A much larger and lower echelon were, if not quite rich, far more prosperous than they had ever dreamed of being. Walter Howey, for example, was making $8000 a year as city editor of the Chicago *Tribune* when he was lured away by a Hearst offer of $35,000.[5] The big-pay Hearst men knew that they could get no such salaries elsewhere, and they knew that Hearst knew they knew it. While they respected him, admired him, and in some cases came close to loving him, they were also in terror of him, for on any whim he could cast them into darkness. This inevitably inculcated a kind of groveling which Hearst, always the king, seemed to enjoy. Executive messages to him were usually couched in flattering and cautious terms, replete with phrases such as "with the greatest respect," and "if I may be so bold as to suggest." As the first buildings of his *palazzo* complex were completed, he began holding occasional conferences of executives at San Simeon. It became *de rigueur* for each of them to take him some gift, knowing they would be entertained royally during their stay.

The question of what gift to select was known to give Hearst men gray hairs. It had to be costly, rare or distinctive. But what could one give Hearst, who had everything? Albert Kobler, like his chief, had become a collector of letters and autographs, owning a fine collection of Napoleon letters which he had promised his son. Kobler solved one of the what-to-give-Hearst problems by presenting him with a real rarity, a letter Napoleon wrote from Moscow—a gift his son still regrets.[6]

The absolute, dynastic power Hearst reserved for himself, and his refusal to delegate real authority to his subordinates, placed them in the position of courtiers vying for his favor. This sometimes had the effect of elevating those who were the more skilled courtiers and of downgrading able men

[4] Winkler, *Hearst—An American Phenomenon*, 258.
[5] Burton Rascoe, *Before I Forget*, 244.   [6] John Kobler to author, Dec. 19, 1959.

who refused to curry favor. Great scorn was exhibited in the Organization for men who worked to "attract the attention of Mr. Hearst," although most of the executives were guilty of that very thing to some degree. This created one of the most appalling jungles of office politics ever seen. There was jealousy, suspicion, intrigue. There was a constant jockeying for position, with editors in Atlanta, Rochester or Los Angeles lying awake nights to perfect schemes for gaining elevation in the hierarchy, sometimes at the expense of a colleague. The stakes were high, with salaries of $100,000, $200,-000 or more waiting those who climbed. Hearst undoubtedly encouraged this feeling of competition, knowing that it stimulated his men to strain every nerve for circulation and revenue. It also inspired them in some cases to resort to dubious methods of gaining circulation or advertising. A number of executives became known as favorites of the Chief, among them Brisbane, Carvalho, Bradford Merrill, the irrepressible Walter Howey, and Clarence Lindner in San Francisco. Some of them wielded enormous influence, and there were those less favored who were pulling strings to displace them. In the Organization, an executive had to watch his step and watch his colleagues.

Running contrary to Hearst's subtle cruelty was his unswerving loyalty to his employes if they were assailed from some outside source, or if they were victims of ill luck. His sentimentality was as overwhelming as his brutality. "Tell him a sad story," Frances Marion recalls, "and tears would roll down his face." [7] The instances of his sudden kindnesses, entirely on impulse and without plan, will never be counted. He was one of the most delinquent of millionaires in contributing to organized charity, and one of the most generous when hardship came to his personal attention. He happened to read a pathetic story in his Chicago *Herald-Examiner* of a family whose father was unemployed, the children in rags. They lived in an attic flat and were about to be evicted. Hearst sent a telegram to his Chicago editor ending, "Please give them $10,000 and furnish them with a home." [8] The Chicago staff saved money by finding a good flat and getting the father a job. When Cartoonist Swinnerton came down with tuberculosis, Hearst sent him to Arizona on full salary. When Henri Pene Du Bois, art critic for the New York *American,* developed a heart condition that numbered his days, he wanted to die in Italy. Hearst sent him to write a series about Italian art galleries, and Du Bois' melancholy wish was granted. Numbers of old Hearst employes drew "advances" which they never bothered to repay. In many instances, men facing financial crisis because of wild speculation or gambling, had their debts paid by order of the Chief. In San Francisco, a veteran *Examiner* stereotyping foreman was found to have swindled the company for a long period by padding the payroll and stealing type metal for resale. Hearst let him go but put him on a substantial pension. [9]

Hearst not infrequently defended his employes against arbitrary acts of

[7] Miss Marion to author, June 9, 1960.   [8] John Dienhart to author, Nov. 12, 1959.
[9] Charles Mayer to author, Oct. 15, 1959.

his own executives. On one occasion, Arthur Brisbane decided to remove all bylines from cartoons and strips—a move calculated to keep the owner-ship of the cartoon copyright even if the artist should leave the Organization. The angry cartoonists appointed Harry Hershfield, creator of *Abie the Agent*, to present their case to Hearst at the Clarendon. Hearst listened to Hershfield intently. "I didn't know Artie was doing that," he said. "Don't worry. I'll see that you not only get back your signature bylines but that you also get printed bylines." He did.[10]

A showman to the core, Hearst favored men who scored newsbeats by exhibitions of nerve and ingenuity, by striking methods such as climbing fire escapes or donning disguises, or who handled run-of-the-mill stories with a flair that gave them distinction. Many an obscure reporter was de-lighted to get a bonus of fifty dollars or more along with the Chief's ac-colade for such a feat.[11] The men in the Organization had the satisfaction of knowing that their boss, however unpredictable, was no rich dilettante but one of the most skilled professionals in the business, a man who could write rings around his best editorialists and was likewise accomplished at all other facets of the game.

When he made one of his rare errors in judgment, it could be a big one, as in his original skepticism about the future of tabloids. Once the innovator, he was badly beaten by the tabloid New York *Daily News*. He grew con-cerned when the *News* neared a half-million circulation, passing his own *American* and threatening his *Journal*. The *American*, his favorite, was slip-ping, and Editor Victor Watson got orders to do battle. The *American* announced a circulation-promoting lottery with a grand prize of $1000 and many lesser ones. Next day the *News* launched its own lottery, with a daily prize of $2500. The *American* doubled it to $5000, the *News* countering by going to $10,000. Joseph Patterson, publisher of the *News*, was almost as rich as Hearst and fully as determined. The contest was operated by sending out trucks loaded with coupons, which were distributed to frenzied crowds in such places as Times Square, Columbus Circle and the Battery. Prizes were awarded to lucky persons holding numbers corresponding with those published in the newspaper. The details of the lottery so absorbed the staffs of both papers that the news got little attention. Watson, it was said, col-lapsed when the *Daily News* raised its grand prize to $25,000 and promised to double any rival. By now the contest was so expensive that both publishers were glad to call it quits, losing most of the circulation gain they had won.[12]

Another paper that passed the *American* was the full-sized *Times*, which had been dying when Hearst entered New York and which he had sometimes scoffed at for its sobriety. It had registered steady gains under Adolph Ochs, who shunned stunts and set a new standard in careful news reporting. Ochs was the tortoise and Hearst the hare. Ochs had been satisfied to build slowly,

[10] Harry Hershfield to author, Sept. 10, 1959.
[11] Martin Mooney to author, Oct. 28, 1959.
[12] Simon Michael Bessie, *Jazz Journalism*, 96–98.

with a passion for accuracy and fairness. The impatient Hearst wanted circulation fast. Surrounding the title of his *American* were the words, "Character, Quality, Enterprise, Accuracy." Its character was dubious, its quality poor, its accuracy notoriously shaky, and its enterprise, while undeniably vigorous, was prone to exhaust itself in schemes for getting the best pictures in the latest love slaying. Being himself theatrical, exotic and violent, Hearst expected his papers to be that way. A champion rationalizer, he could send out these instructions to his editors:

> Make a paper for the nicest kind of people—for the great middle class. . . .
> Omit things that will offend nice people. Avoid coarseness and slang and a low tone. The most sensational news can be told if it is written properly . . .
> Do not exaggerate.
> Make the paper helpful and kindly. Don't scold and forever complain and attack in your news columns. Leave that to the editorial page.
> Be fair and impartial . . . Make a paper for all the people and give unbiased news of all creeds and parties. . . .[13]

Undoubtedly he believed these precepts and would have resented any suggestion that his newspapers did not live up to them. The great egoist was able to manufacture his own logic. Not surprisingly, some thousands of Hearst city-room underlings, faced by the realities of their jobs, wondered cynically whether the Chief was a mite crazy or just a plain liar. The evidence suggests that Hearst was not an intentional or conscious liar, although the truth was an elastic substance in his hands. He easily believed what he wanted to believe, so much so that his ratiocination sometimes soared into a dream world. Yet when he came down from the clouds, he could be wonderfully practical and even eloquent. When he hired Fremont Older to take charge of the San Francisco *Call,* he knew that Older had felt impelled to leave his cherished *Bulletin* because the publisher had ordered him to stop his campaign for Tom Mooney. The separation had almost broken Older's heart. He was a crusader of great gifts, and Hearst, obviously fearful that Older might go overboard on Mooney to the detriment of other news, wrote him delicate instructions which also illuminate his drift toward conservatism and away from the radicalism of his youth:

> My Dear Mr. Older: I have your letter about the Mooney case. Of course I understand, as you say, that the labor people are not always grateful for the work done for them. Neither is any other class of the community. But our object is not so much to secure the gratitude of this or that element as to do what in our opinion is essentially just and right, and secure the approval of our own conscience.
> The one thing, however, that I want to warn you against becoming in the *Call* is a class newspaper, a newspaper with the limited viewpoint of any faction in the community.

[13] Carlson and Bates, 174.

This is not only undesirable because of its inevitable limitation of our objects and ideals, but it is undesirable because of the distinct limitation of our influence and our opportunity to accomplish our objects and ideals.

A newspaper, in order to do great good, in order to convince all the people and secure the general support of the public, must be a paper of all the people, and not of one faction arrayed against the other factions in the community.

A newspaper only gets an open minded hearing when it is generally believed to be a broad minded newspaper, when its policies are liberal and tolerant, when it sees the good in all classes, and the actual need of various factors in our civilization.

Radicalism has its value, but an excessive radicalism is dangerous. Conservatism has its uses. It is only the hide bound conservatism that can see no benefit in new ideas that is a brake on progress. . . .[14]

Out of his long experience in journalism, government and politics, Hearst had formulated a moderate and practical philosophy, however he failed to live up to it.

But Hearst at sixty had lost most of his public following because he so often compromised his own ideals for expediency. Samuel Seabury was the vocal symbol of a public trend. Liberals who once hailed him had lost faith in him. His bewildering political shifts had alienated the steadfast. People were offended by talk of his private life. Many readers of the Hearst papers had come to view Hearst's editorials and crusades as nonsense. They bought the papers for Happy Hooligan, Krazy Kat, and extensive coverage of the Hall-Mills scandal. They decided that Hearst was, after all, a millionaire building a castle in California and that his concern for "the people" was a sham. He had become a political monstrosity. And yet, because he spoke to millions, he remained a powerful voice from the wings.

II. THE ODDITIES OF GENIUS

HEARST's journalistic recklessness, political unintelligibility and personal eccentricities had long since made him a national conversation piece. Over bars, teacups and dinner tables he was an object of discussion, often heated, aimed at disassembling him and isolating that part which was faulty. He provoked a frustration like that caused by a Chinese puzzle that refuses to be solved.

What *was* wrong with Hearst? Certainly there was something wrong with him, as there is something wrong with everyone, but in him the physical or psychological imperfections, joined as they were with genius, produced a combination never seen before in mortal man. Whatever was wrong with him was wrong in a greater degree than customary, or in an uncommon blend of defect. Journalists from Willis Abbot to Oswald Garrison Villard, and politicians from Bryan to Al Smith, had tried and failed to understand him.

[14] Fremont Older Papers, letter of Jan. 2, 1919.

Those closest to him could agree only on one trait that was itself confusing—his duality, his inconsistency, his unpredictability. He seemed two men rather than one.

It is a truism that every normal person veers somewhat from his average behavior, with moments of selfishness balanced by surges of idealism—a duality Stevenson dramatized in his *Dr. Jekyll and Mr. Hyde*. Dr. Jekyll was a saintly physician until he drank a potion that turned him into Mr. Hyde, suppressing his virtues and unleashing his evil. Hearst was Jekyll and he was Hyde, with no need for chemical draughts. As Jekyll he could rescue an imperiled toad, overwhelm his friends with generosity, fight for "the people." As Hyde he could descend to lies, chicanery and cruelty.

Hearst *was* two men, to such an extent that he rightly should have been equipped with two bodies. In him, the minor deflection of personality seen in ordinary persons became a wild, schizoid plunge from the heights to the depths. If the average swing of the personality pendulum is a modest twenty degrees, Hearst's could swoop a fearful 180. He lacked the psychic brakes that hold normal persons within reasonable limits of behavior so that they can be identified and understood by their unchanging or little-changing traits. He was like an intricate jeweled mechanism, lacking one vital part so that it sometimes whirled out of control.

Any effort to analyze this inscrutable Sphinx has its dangers, but when one sees elements of comedy as well as tragedy in him, the blurred image gains some approach to focus. Hearst was an incurable adolescent. Maturity in normal persons implies the disenchanting realization that many of the desires and fantasies of childhood must be postponed, must be labored for, and that many others can never be achieved even after infinite labor. Maturity, the gradual adjustment to reality, the stoic acceptance of disappointment, never became a part of the Hearst ego. He refused to let it enter. He operated on the pleasure principle. He would admit of no doubt that he could do what he wanted to do, have what he wanted to have. Had he not been gifted with an ability and a drive that enabled him to satisfy most of his wants, he would in all probability have gone insane.

On those occasions when he failed to achieve his aims, as in politics, the blow was so wounding that he would do precisely what a thwarted child would do. He would go into a rage.

As an exhibitionist, he had few peers. Painfully shy, he had to prove his leadership to himself and the world. This need found expression from childhood on in his bent for impact and sensationalism. He would make his presence felt if he had to break windows, corrupt an alligator, touch off rockets, start a war, buy stolen letters, or defame Al Smith to do it. He would gain leadership even at the cost of the personal torture public speaking visited on him. Since early in the century, his desire to be President had led him into so many comic or desperate byways that it had come to be a joke, first to other politicians, then to a growing segment of the public. In his hunger for office, his newspapers, at first his most sacred possessions, had become chiefly weapons, a means to gain power to satisfy his wants.

His childhood was abnormal in the closeness and long duration of his communion with his mother, coupled with his father's absences. His reverence for his mother seemed to color his adult relationships. He had been almost equally devoted to his grandmother. Annie Laurie, Mrs. Logan and Louella Parsons were only three in a long line of Hearst women employes who considered him the personification of kindliness. Women occupied a special niche in his regard. When Miss Davies entered his life, she became the fulfillment of his childish, romantic dream of womanly perfection. Whatever minor flaws she might have, he would correct with the best of tutors. With affectionate selfishness, he would mold her to fit his dream. He loved her in romantic roles, in rich period costumes, with a background of portcullises, tapestries or other symbols of queenliness and luxury. He would not permit her to take any role that even verged on realism or sordidness. Miss Davies, who could rule him in almost every other way, had no authority over her own screen activities. Artistically she was his property.[1]

In his childhood he had been paraded through castles and art galleries until his busy imagination was fired by visions of medieval and Renaissance magnificence which he never lost. Certainly he pictured himself as a Tudor, a Bourbon, a Hapsburg, a prince of absolute power, surrounded by beauty and luxury. To him, maturity did not mean the surrender of this roseate dream, but merely a skillful adaptation so that the dream could be achieved within the realities of twentieth-century life. An atavist, a medieval character transplanted out of his time, he was determined to cling to the imperial ideal even if it had to be done on Riverside Drive, at Palm Beach and San Simeon, determined to gain power even if it had to be done in the unsatisfactory way of asking people for their votes instead of taking power by succession. If he never quite succeeded in reconciling his medievalism to the twentieth century, he never stopped trying and he came closer than anyone else ever got or ever will get. At sixty, Hearst was the nearest approach to a Lancaster or a Burgundy in the democratic United States. He was kingly in his power, in his possessions, in the way he did, with few limitations, what he wanted to do. But he was beginning to encounter certain democratic curbs on his kingliness that would plague him for the rest of his life.

Emotionally, he was a jumble of contradictions, afflicted by the polarity that often accompanies genius. Some of his whims and postures were too fantastic for normal understanding. He lived in a dream world which he turned into near reality through sheer force of will, ability and energy. It is significant that he became fascinated by the stage and then by the screen, where his fantasies could be acted out just as he wished them to be and he could avoid the hurtful jolts of reality. He forever hopefully regarded the real world as one vast stage where he would write the script, serve as producer and director, shift the scenes, manipulate the actors and produce a cosmic

[1] Frances Marion to author.

drama utterly enchanting because he created it to suit himself. He failed in this because of his own political ineptitude. But he did not fail in his cut-down version of the dream—iron control over a great chain of newspapers and thousands of employes, and possession of his own duchy in the West, complete with castle and lovely duchess.

As a husband and father, he was kindly but delinquent because he was too preoccupied with his ambitions to give himself to his family. He was devoted to his sons, but they seldom saw him. When he felt remorse about this, he tried to rectify it by giving the boys lavish gifts of money or motorcars.

For all his kindness, he lacked the essence of friendship, the ability to un-bend, to confide, to reveal himself. He must have been aware of deep flaws of personality, for he concealed them from outsiders.

His inconsistency, which so puzzled observers, was in reality a key to his personality. He could vary from day to day and from hour to hour. His closest colleagues never were sure how he would react to a situation. He took pride in this as proof that he was not hidebound in opinion. He was fond of paraphrasing Emerson by saying, "Consistency is the hobgoblin of little minds." This was an evasion. When a problem arose, he judged it not from any immovable standards or moral values, since he had few of these, but from the impulse or advantage of the moment. He could, and did, argue on both sides of a question with equal facility and apparent conviction, depend-ing on which of his two selves was in charge. He was forever taking positive stands on public questions, grounding his arguments on "principle," which he doubtless believed at the time. It was his capacity to shift diametrically in opinion, sometimes apparently for his own advantage, that caused critics to damn him for insincerity, cynicism and downright demagoguery. He had brilliant powers of reasoning and persuasion without any solid inner ground to anchor them on.

Traditionally, great men are remembered in part for their principles but more for the manner in which they fought for them. History lays down basic rules of fair play which public men are expected to observe in fighting for their principles. While Hearst for decades had a sympathy for "the people" and for progressive measures beneficial to them, he so often violated the amenities of the game that the referees—the politicians and eventually the public—threw him out bodily. His ideas were often wonderful. His methods were often deplorable. The mistaken suspicion grew that he was utterly selfish and would sacrifice any principle to gain power and office.

In the end, it is futile to attempt to analyze him as one man, since he was two. General conclusions about him must always be qualified as referring to Hearst in his Jekyll aspect or to Hearst as Hyde. The true story of Hearst must be what Hearst was himself—a riot of incongruity. He could only be described in contradictions. He was true, and he was false. He was a puritan, and he was a libertine. He was democratic, and he was kingly. He was im-movable, and he was fickle. He was kindly, and he was cruel. He was great, and he was contemptible.

2. Fiscal Anarchy

In 1923, employes at Johnson & Faulkner's deluxe dry-goods establishment near Union Square sprang to attention when a big, impressive-looking man entered with a blonde beauty on his arm. The man was Hearst, the young lady Miss Davies. "They seemed like a father and a lovely daughter," one of the salesmen recalled.[1] They were planning a grand première of Miss Davies' latest picture, *Little Old New York,* at the Cosmopolitan Theater on Columbus Circle, which Hearst had recently bought. Under Urban's supervision, the theater was being rebuilt and renovated for the event at a cost of $225,000. Miss Davies was stunning in a sky-blue crepe dress that set off the vivid blue of her eyes. She and Hearst picked heavy, rich upholstery and drapery fabrics for the theater—cost no object. They were fussy about it, with Hearst, the connoisseur of tapestries, taking an active hand in the selection.

He was growing careless about keeping his interest in the actress sub rosa. Later, when he and Miss Davies returned to buy fabrics of a more homey kind, the gossip at Johnson & Faulkner's had it that it was intended for a home the publisher had given her across the river in Astoria.

He gave her new picture the usual hang-the-expense launching. For the première an elaborate printed program was designed for which he and Miss Davies selected gilt decorations on the outside cover. Victor Herbert's orchestra played to an audience studded with society folk and city officials. Women spectators discovered too late that the gilt on the programs rubbed off to soil their gowns. It was announced from the stage that the management (i.e., Hearst) would pay the cleaning bills.[2]

The Hearst press, deciding there was no point in waiting for the showing, boomed the picture in advance. The *American* gave it a banner headline calling it "A SUPER-SCREEN PLAY," and another warning that "MARION DAVIES' GREATEST FILM OPENS TONIGHT," along with a four-column picture of Miss Davies. Next day, Reviewer Joseph Mulvaney started out like a man who had been cautioned not to shilly-shally:

> Let us get the dominant fact clear at the outset.
> The finest thing about "Little Old New York"—and there are many fine things about that picture—
> Is the acting of Marion Davies!

[1] James O'Shea to author, Feb. 22, 1960.   [2] Private source.

He went on, "Marion Davies simply skipped away with 'Little Old New York' . . . . Marion Davies ascends to her utmost as an actress . . . . Miss Davies' career on the screen has been an unbroken advancement . . . . she has soared into this film." [3]

Miss Parsons' advice that Miss Davies had not been sufficiently mentioned had been heeded. The *Journal* contributed headlines such as "Marion Davies Scores Her Greatest Triumph," and "Great Metropolitan Audience Marvels at Wonder Play and at the Beautiful New Cosmopolitan Theatre." Critic Julia West said in small part, "In the difficult role of Patricia O'Day, Miss Davies triumphs . . . . gently appealing . . . . poignant . . . . an exquisitely wrought reproduction of the period it portrays." Stress was placed on the number of social leaders present, among them Vincent Astor, Reginald C. Vanderbilt and Mrs. Harry Payne Whitney, as well as high-ranking city officials including Mayor Hylan and Commissioner of Plant and Structures Grover Whalen. Policemen, the *Journal* suggested, were needed to restrain the eager crowds: "Captain Thomas Mullarkey and Sergeant William Webber had thirty patrolmen to keep the passageway clear."

That veteran first-nighter and patron of the arts, Mayor Hylan, who had recently reappointed Magistrate Douras, boosting him to $8000 a year, was called on for his candid opinion of the film. Hylan, never facile with words, could count on a Hearst writer to help sort out his thoughts. He was quoted:

> This production is unquestionably the greatest screen epic I have ever looked upon, and Marion Davies is the most versatile screen star ever cast in any part. She displayed her superb ability at its best . . . the wide range of her stellar acting is something to marvel at.
>
> Every man, woman and child in New York City ought to see this splendid picture. . . . I must pay my tribute to the geniuses in all lines who created such a masterpiece.[4]

While *Little Old New York* did not reach epic proportions, it was an impressive picture for its day. The *Times* called it "one of the most exquisite productions ever thrown upon a screen," while the *Herald* cheered Director Sidney Olcott because "he has actually induced Marion Davies to act like a human being." [5]

II. THE GLORIOUS SPENDER

It was noticed in the Organization that the Chief disliked to attend funerals. When some old employe died, he would send solicitous condolences and magnificent wreaths, but was reluctant to attend the services in person.[1] He loved life, and his remarkable energies showed no sign of flagging. Yet, as a sexagenarian he hated to be reminded that his youth was gone and that his

[3] N. Y. *American*, Aug. 1, 2, 1923.   [4] N. Y. *Journal*, Aug. 2, 1923.
[5] N. Y. *Times*, Aug. 2; N. Y. *Herald*, Aug. 2, 1923.
[1] Winkler, *Hearst—An American Phenomenon*, 313.

years were growing numbered. He had, however, been present at the funeral of his political secretary, L. J. O'Reilly, to whom he had been close for almost two decades. Several years earlier he had taken strapping Joseph Willicombe, a Hearst reporter since 1905, as his secretary on the newspaper side. On O'Reilly's death, Willicombe was elevated to the top secretarial spot. A former New York *American* man, accomplished at shorthand, he was required to mold his life to that of his employer, adopt the Hearst noon-to-3 A.M. schedule, and often to accompany him on his journeys.

In Hearst, the Presidential hope died hard. In the fall of 1922, when Mayor Hylan and Commissioner Whalen went to Chicago to confer with Mayor Thompson, the story was that they were planning a Hearst-Hylan-Thompson third party to support Hearst for President in 1924.[2] The Independence League, dormant for years, made a feeble effort to reorganize in New York and boom Hearst.

A more realistic honor came when Mayor Hylan decided to name a new Staten Island ferryboat the *William Randolph Hearst*. It was the first electrically-propelled ferry in New York, designed to carry automobiles on its lower deck. It could have been named after almost anyone else without complaint, but the Municipal Art Society assailed the honor to Hearst. This objection was ignored as Hearst and his wife went with Whalen, McCooey and others to Staten Island, where Mrs. Hearst smashed a bottle of champagne against the prow and the Street Cleaning Department band played as the ship slid down the ways.[3]

But when the Hearst couple held their twentieth anniversary party at the Clarendon on April 28, 1923, on the eve of Hearst's sixtieth birthday, they eschewed the Tammany crowd. Two orchestras played for a group of guests including some who sounded anomalous at the home of the defender of "the people"—Prince and Princess Rospigliosi, the Duke and Duchess de Richelieu, Count and Countess Thaon di Revel, and Sir Joseph and Lady Duveen. The Hearsts' eldest son, George, eighteen, who had been studying at the University of California until he eloped with a coed from Idaho, was present with his bride. Mayor Hylan, whose foot had a habit of getting into his mouth, was not.[4]

One reason some progressives became disaffected with Hearst was their feeling that he had more in common with the Duke de Richelieu than with "the people." He was growing conservative. He had taken a strong stand against the Boston police strike, and was likewise opposed to the unionization of editorial workers. Worse yet, he was a pioneer proponent of the graduated income tax, had seen it come to pass, and now that he had it he hated it. His newspapers, right along with the *Wall Street Journal*, had supported a Congressional sales-tax measure, always anathema to progressives. He had taken several dozen Congressmen in a special train to Canada in an effort to show them how well the sales tax worked there.[5]

[2] N. Y. *Times*, Nov. 22, 1922.   [3] N. Y. *World*, Mar. 18, 1923.
[4] N. Y. *Times*, Apr. 29, 1923.   [5] Paxson, 261.

Although he had one of the world's top incomes, he was in some financial discomfort. His newspapers alone were estimated to have earned $100,000,000 in 1922, of which $12,000,000 was accounted net profit.[6] His magazine, mine and ranch properties must have added millions more. But he never saved a dime. He actually lived from hand to mouth. It was the duty of the publisher of the New York *Journal,* one of his most profitable papers, to send him $25,000 each week. Other newspapers sent him lesser but still substantial sums weekly.[7] He spent the money immediately, and used credit to the bursting point. Often pressed for cash, he would raid the till of the newspaper nearest him. If their cash reserve was too small, he would make them borrow for him. Once he arrived in Chicago in his private car, found $30,000 in the *American's* till, and demanded it. The business manager explained nervously that Mr. Carvalho had ordered him to send him $25,000. "What a joke on Carvalho!" Hearst chuckled, and pocketed the $30,000.[8] He never bothered to refund such "loans," which were of course his own money. Sometimes on payday the employes at Cosmopolitan Productions were warned not to cash their checks for a day or two, as they were not good at the moment.[9] Occasionally creditors had to wait inconveniently long for Hearst to pay his bills.

He was easily the nation's biggest spender. If he wanted something, which he always did, he bought it with no regard for cost. He spent an average of $1,000,000 a year on art and antiques alone. It was said that his total personal expenses ran to $15,000,000 a year.[10] This can be nothing more than an estimate, and is probably inflated, but his expenditures personal and otherwise were staggering. He was pouring vast sums into San Simeon. He constantly added to his New York real estate, buying property every month or two, always with heavy mortgages. He had added newspapers at a fast clip. His huge apartment at the Clarendon had taken on the aspect of an overstuffed museum. To make more room, workmen added an expensive penthouse on the roof.

He was wounded to discover that he had to pay $949,101 in inheritance taxes on his mother's estate.[11] His advisers, affrighted at his expenditures, pleaded with him vainly to slow down. He spent a fortune on his 220-foot steam yacht *Oneida,* which was kept staffed on the Hudson while he was in New York and was taken around via the Panama Canal to be ready for him when he was in California. When he was away, he often left the boat for the use of Florenz Ziegfeld or other friends. Although he used the *Oneida* only occasionally, he took a fancy to a yacht of equal size, the *Hirondelle,* which the Prince of Monaco offered for sale, and bought it. The prince had used it for oceanography. When a button was pressed, the floor would slide away to disclose a glass bottom. Another push-button arrangement made a pipe-organ emerge from a niche in the saloon wall. Hearst was as fas-

[6] *World's Work,* Oct., 1922.
[8] Villard, *Prophets True and False,* 309.
[10] Villard, *Prophets True and False,* 311.
[7] *Saturday Evening Post,* Aug. 27, 1938.
[9] *New Yorker,* Sept. 14, 1940.
[11] N. Y. *Times,* Aug. 6, 1923.

cinated as a boy by these features, but after the yacht was purchased it was moored at Tebo's yacht basin in Brooklyn and never used, although it was kept in constant repair.[12]

For a time, Hearst went boat-happy. One day he telephoned Charles Chapman, editor of *Motor Boating*. "Mr. Chapman," he said, "would you please meet me in front of your office in ten minutes? Two of my sons want motorboats, and I'd appreciate your advice."

Chapman accompanied him and the boys to a boat dealer in the Fifties. On the floor was a glistening fifty-seven-foot A.C.F. motor cruiser.

"What's that?" Hearst inquired.

Chapman explained that it was the largest stock boat built. Hearst went aboard, ascended to the bridge and surveyed the craft admiringly. "How much is it?"

"Fifty thousand dollars, Mr. Hearst," the salesman said.

"Could you ship it to California for me?"

"Yes, we'd be glad to."

"I'll take it."

This was for himself, although he had no original intention of buying another boat for his own use. With Chapman's help he went on to buy two smaller boats for the boys, spending a total of some $75,000 within an hour.[13]

A confirmed window shopper, Hearst could not resist pretty things he saw on display. Once, passing W. & J. Sloane's store on Fifth Avenue, he spied a huge Oriental rug in the window, labeled as the most expensive rug in the world. He went inside, bought it for $40,000 and had it sent to his Bronx warehouse, where it lay in storage for years. Again, he saw a dollar shirt in a Broadway haberdasher's window, walked inside and ordered a hundred of them. He regarded his huge income as spending money, and in this sense he was not a capitalist. He saw no need for rigid bookkeeping, for maintaining a capital reserve, because in his unquenchable optimism he felt that there would always be more money coming in, not less.

One of his biggest single losers was his motion pictures, largely because of his love of spectacle and his insistence on surrounding Miss Davies with perfection in every detail. She was now at work on *Janice Meredith*, a drama of the American Revolution, which had scenes showing Paul Revere's ride, the Boston Tea Party, Washington at Valley Forge and Washington crossing the Delaware. Some 7500 players took part in it. More than 2000 uniforms were used to depict redcoats, Hessians and Colonials. Miss Davies herself appeared in twenty different gowns. Some of Hearst's priceless antiques were used in the settings. Scenes were shot in a half-dozen different locations. The whole company moved up to Plattsburg, New York, where there was plenty of snow and water to serve as background for the crossing of the Delaware, and where forty-six houses were constructed to

[12] Private source.   [13] Mr. Chapman to author, Sept. 20, 1960.

represent the town of Trenton. It was discovered that falling snow did not photograph properly, so the director, E. Mason Hopper, employed a dozen men to hurl a total of 4000 bags of confetti in front of whirling airplane propellers to give the desired effect of driven snow. An unseasonable thaw removed the real snow from the ground just as they were ready to enact the Valley Forge scenes, so the whole company was moved at great expense to Lake Placid, where there was no lack of snow.[14]

Hearst was in his element as a cinema impresario, a field where fiction had full sway and there was no annoying necessity to observe fact as there should have been in journalism. His insistence on verisimilitude was admirable, but he was ahead of his time in the production of super-spectacles. The public was not yet ready to pay a premium for excellence in motion pictures. His losses brought gray hairs to Carvalho and to his treasurer, Joseph A. Moore.

III. A DIPSOMANIAC WITH A BOTTLE

It was no wonder that political progressives who became aware of Hearst's orgy of spending had little sympathy for his complaints about taxes and decided that he was not one of "the people" at all but the very thing he had so often pilloried—a captain of industry, looking out for his own interests. He had employed as his personal attorney John Francis Neylan, a San Franciscan who had been a crack reporter on the *Bulletin* before taking up the law and becoming associated politically with Senator Hiram Johnson. Neylan, a tall, Lincolnesque figure and a Republican, at first had strong reservations about Hearst's character and sincerity. As he came to know the publisher, he decided that he was simply a man of titanic independence, sincere even when he was misguided.

Neylan speedily became Hearst's right-hand man, a trusted adviser who came as close to warm personal friendship as it was possible with Hearst. One of his jobs was to bring order into the fiscal anarchy prevailing in the Organization, which meant scaling down the Chief's fantastic expenditures. Among other things, Neylan urged him to cut his buying of art, which had reached ridiculous proportions, with several warehouses jammed with more treasures than a dozen men could ever use. Hearst shook his head sadly.

"I'm afraid I'm like a dipsomaniac with a bottle," he said. "They keep sending me these art catalogues and I can't resist them."[1]

Hearst had been cautious about getting into the tabloid field, believing it a fad, but the enormous success of Patterson's *Daily News* proved him wrong. By 1923 he was busy with plans for his own tabloid New York *Mirror*, aimed at challenging the *News*. That same summer, twenty-five-year-old Cornelius Vanderbilt, scion of the wealthy New York family, was in Los Angeles starting his own tabloid there. He was unable to get presses delivered in time. He went to Hearst, then staying at the Ambassador Hotel,

[14] N. Y. *Times*, Aug. 10 and 24, 1924.   [1] Mr. Neylan to author, Oct. 13, 1959.

and asked if he could use his presses temporarily. Hearst was in his omnipotent mood.

"Los Angeles is not the place for you," he said. "Here's what I want you to do. I am about to start a tabloid in New York. I will hire you as editor. You know nothing about editing a newspaper but your name is worth thirty thousand dollars a year to me. You will leave tonight for New York and report to Arthur Brisbane. My secretary will attend to your transportation. Good-by and good luck."

The bewildered Vanderbilt was ushered out of the room without a chance to explain that he could not accept the offer, that he was starting his own paper regardless.[2]

That fall, Hearst renounced his brief truce with Murphy and Smith, declaring war once more by opposing the Tammany slate for the judiciary and entering a ticket of his own. To the Boss and the governor, this was the last straw. Smith denounced Hearst as "the leading agent for the dissemination of political bunk." An anonymous pamphlet appeared, "Hearst's Life—A Record of Shame," touching on his private derelictions.[3] The Democrats denied its authorship, although Smith several times had made ominous hints about Hearst's personal irregularities. In the election, Tammany was triumphant and the Hearst candidates were trounced. Murphy, who for years had refused to condemn Hearst publicly even when convulsed with private rage, now permitted himself the luxury of saying what he thought.

". . . it is to be hoped," he said, "that our decent, clean-thinking men and women will not hereafter tolerate in their homes the lying, filthy newspapers under the Hearst management. . . . I start to exclude them from my home tomorrow."[4]

It was the manifesto of a liberated man. Murphy and Smith were already embarked on a plan to strip Hearst of his last vestige of influence in New York politics by getting rid of his obedient Mayor Hylan in the next election. A fortnight later, Murphy vacationed at French Lick, Indiana, with his anti-Hearst sachem, Big Tom Foley, where they talked with the Democratic leaders of Illinois and Indiana, George Brennan and Thomas Taggart. Murphy demanded that Brennan and Taggart join him in formally excommunicating Hearst from the party. The two Midwestern leaders, however, were more cautious. They had seen Hearst emerge from the political junk heap before, they feared his newspapers, and, as one correspondent put it, "they do not consider it certain he will stay dead."[5]

Hearst, after a stay in Palm Beach, joined his wife in a White House call on President Coolidge, assuring Coolidge of his delight at Treasury Secretary Andrew Mellon's tax-reduction proposals. Emerging, he gave reporters his thoughts on taxes.

"I think all taxes are a burden upon the community," he said, "no matter where the taxes are imposed. If you put water on top of a mountain it is

[2] Cornelius Vanderbilt, *Farewell to Fifth Avenue*, 59.   [3] N. Y. *Times*, Nov. 3, 1923.
[4] N. Y. *Times*, Nov. 8, 1923.   [5] N. Y. *Times*, Nov. 21, 1923.

sure to flow down into the valley—and if you put taxes on the richer classes, those taxes will eventually descend down to the purchasing public. . . . Secretary Mellon's able conduct of the Treasury Department is an example of the wisdom of putting experts in charge of the various departments . . ." [6]

Hearst, the indefatigable, driven by more wants than he could ever fulfill, continued a round of activities so ceaseless that it would have exhausted an ordinary man merely to follow him around. He applied for a commission as colonel in the Army Reserve Corps—a move which, when it became known, caused the New York chapter of the Military Order of the World War to meet in indignation and send more than fifty telegrams to Washington protesting any commission to a man with such a war record.[7] He saw Max Reinhardt's great spectacle, *The Miracle,* and was so impressed that he immediately began negotiations with the German director. It was announced that Reinhardt had been signed to direct Miss Davies in a series of pictures for five years at "one of the largest [salaries] ever paid to a film director." [8] Some hitch developed, for Reinhardt soon thereafter returned to Germany. Hearst, through his trusted realtor Martin Huberth, bought a large lot at Eighth Avenue and Fifty-seventh Street and planned to erect there an impressive building exclusively for his magazines.[9]

Early in 1924 he was in Palm Beach again. Since the newspapers did not mention Mrs. Hearst's presence with him, it is likely that Miss Davies was his companion. Here he encountered Addison Mizner, the huge, eccentric San Franciscan who had taken up architecture without benefit of formal education and had cut a swath in the society playground as a master of what came to be called the "Bastard-Spanish-Moorish-Romanesque-Gothic-Renaissance-Bull Market-Damn-the-Expense" style of architecture. It was reported that Hearst set Mizner to planning the most elaborate residence in Palm Beach for him, one that would surpass Edward Stotesbury's El Mirasol, which even had a reception room for guests' chauffeurs.[10] This plan, like the one involving Reinhardt, did not materialize, and it is possible that Hearst's agitated advisers talked him out of it. Perhaps it was just as well, both financially and architecturally, since Mizner had built a palace for a millionaire grocer and forgotten to include a staircase.[11] On his way back north, Hearst stopped for another friendly chat with Coolidge. He added the San Antonio *Light* to his newspaper chain. There were continuing rumors that he was angling for the Democratic nomination for President.[12]

Soon after he returned to New York, Boss Murphy died suddenly at the age of sixty-six at his Seventeenth Street home. His death removed a powerful enemy, but Governor Smith had no doubt about his ability to handle Hearst himself.

[6] N. Y. *Times,* Dec. 2, 1923.   [7] N. Y. *World,* Jan. 12, 1924.
[8] N. Y. *Times,* Jan. 18, 1924.   [9] N. Y. *Tribune,* Feb. 6, 1924.
[10] N. Y. *Times,* Mar. 16, 1924.   [11] Alva Johnston, *The Legendary Mizners,* 25, 33.
[12] N. Y. *Times,* Mar. 25, 1924.

3. Unpleasantness

In 1923, Hearst presented an outward picture of glittering journalistic success. He owned twenty-two daily papers with a total claimed circulation of 3,028,437, and fifteen Sunday papers with a total claimed circulation of 3,587,871. He owned seven magazines in the United States and two in England, with a total circulation of 2,773,784. They included his big-selling *Cosmopolitan, Good Housekeeping, Hearst's International* and *Harper's Bazaar,* and the lesser *Orchard & Farm, Motor,* and *Motor Boating.* His advertising was booming. It cost him over $90,000,000 a year to produce all his publications. His publicists claimed, probably with some exaggeration, that 6,972,512 families, or one out of every four in the United States, read a Hearst publication. He was the biggest user of paper in the world. It took thirty-two tons of paper to produce only a single page of his daily newspapers. He had 38,000 people on the payroll of his publications, not counting woodchoppers and paper mill workers.[1] His profits were enormous, but they were not enough for him. What worried him more was his political decline in New York.

For this he had three men to blame—Boss Murphy, Governor Smith and Big Tom Foley. Murphy was beyond his vengeance, but he was not above settling the score with Smith and Foley. A year earlier, he had sent a flood of telegrams from California to Victor Watson of the *American,* urging Watson to get his best men busy and expose the bucket shops operating in New York and the political influences protecting them.[2] He had a hunch that Foley was involved in it.

The bucket shop operators were simply crooked brokers who pretended to buy stock for clients on margin, requiring them to pay only about ten percent in cash and charging them six percent interest on the remainder. They then did not bother to buy the stock at all, or merely bought it and sold it immediately just for the record, collecting their clients' interest in a subtle form of robbery. It was an extensive racket in the Twenties, fleecing victims of millions. What particularly aroused Hearst was that two palpable bucketeers, Edward Fuller and William F. McGee, operating under the name of Fuller & Company, had been caught virtually red-handed, and yet three juries sitting in judgment on them had all mysteriously disagreed. Who, Hearst demanded, was protecting Fuller and McGee?[3]

[1] Villard, *Some Newspapers and Newspapermen,* 17–20.
[2] Ferber, *I Found Out,* 119. [3] Gene Fowler, *The Great Mouthpiece,* 328.

Watson, a burly firebrand who lived for headlines, put Nat Ferber and a squad of reporters on the assignment. They uncovered several bucket-shop scandals which furnished the *American* with daily sensations and made a good start at cleaning up the racket. It was Ferber who pawed through the records in the United States District Court and found a canceled check for $10,000 made out by Fuller & McGee to Foley. This was the first concrete indication that Big Tom might have any connection with the criminals, and it inspired Watson and his staff to greater efforts. Watson put more men on the story regardless of cost. Soon the *American* was one jump ahead of the police in its investigation of the swindle. Hearst, who loved a crusade all the more when it might accidentally scuttle an enemy who was a close friend of Al Smith, congratulated Watson and egged him on. Watson even went to the length of having a Hearst representative in Paris seek out Mrs. Nellie McGee Herrick, former wife of McGee, who was in the French capital, and offer to pay her passage home. It was felt that she might know something about her ex-husband's affairs, and it was also known that she came from Foley's neighborhood and that he had been kind to her.[4]

The Hearst papers began a savage attack on Foley, suggesting that he was the "power" behind the bucket shops. Foley was placed in a painful position, but when he was called on to explain the money he had received from the Fuller-McGee firm, he declared it was in payment of a loan he had earlier given McGee. He was actuated, he said, by friendship for the then Mrs. McGee, whom he had known as a little girl in his district.[5] Although there were jeers at this, it was nevertheless true that Foley was a saloon-keeper-philanthropist who left a mere $15,000 estate when he died a few years later. His story was not shaken, and the Hearst effort to put Foley behind bars failed.

But Watson went ahead full cry with his exposures. The attorney for Fuller and McGee had been thirty-eight-year-old William J. Fallon, a friend of Foley's, an irrepressible Broadway playboy with dramatic courtroom gifts which included a gift for framing evidence. Watson's journalistic sleuths got next to Fallon's right-hand man, fat Ernest Eidlitz. Eidlitz declared that Fallon had bribed a juror named Charles Rendigs to hold out for an acquittal of Fuller and McGee. Rendigs soon confessed taking the bribe, and drew a prison term. Attorney Fallon was then indicted, whereupon he disappeared. He was found days later in the apartment of his mistress by detectives and a covey of Hearst reporters. Thus the newspaper barrage which had been aimed at Foley had misfired and now was turned on Fallon. Watson, an inveterate headline-hunter, turned his front pages over to the misdeeds of Fallon, never knowing that he was stirring up a hornet's nest.[6]

While all this was going on, Hearst kept a close eye on the Democrats, who would hold their national convention at Madison Square Garden that summer. He took a severe loss when his movie studio on the Harlem River

[4] N. Y. *Times*, July 27, 1923.   [5] The same.
[6] Fowler, *The Great Mouthpiece*, 335.

burned in a spectacular fire. Some of his fine antiques were destroyed, but, with his typical thoughtfulness, he seemed more concerned about Joseph Urban's library, which had been damaged in the flames.[7]

He had intended to move his film operations to California anyway. Frances Marion, his scenarist, left for the West Coast by train with a company of Cosmopolitan actors in tow. Miss Marion had tried to reach Hearst by telephone, but he was not to be reached as was often the case, so she departed without speaking to him. When the troupe reached Chicago, Miss Marion heard herself being paged in the station. Mr. Hearst wanted her, and she was to call the local *American* office. She did so, and was told by one of the editors that Hearst was anxious to talk to her on "a most important matter." She was in despair, having missed her train connection. There was some trouble getting through to Hearst in New York, but finally the connection was made.

"Frances," Hearst said in hurt tones, "are you angry at me? You left without saying a word."

Miss Marion explained. "Is that all you wanted?" she demanded in annoyance. "Now you've made us all miss our Santa Fe train."

"No, no," Hearst assured her. "I've had them hold the train. It's waiting for you."

It was. The troupe got aboard, with Miss Marion pondering the whims of Hearst, who so enjoyed his power that he would hold up the Santa Fe for twenty-five minutes to ask if she was angry.[8]

Hearst's own Presidential boom had fizzled, but his retention of some dark-horse hope was indicated by a quiet "non-political" luncheon he had with George Brennan, leader of the Illinois delegation, before the convention began at the Garden.[9] Governor Smith had strong yearnings for the White House, but if he got there it would be over Hearst's dead body. Hearst printed a signed blast across the front page of the *American* saying that "the Hearst papers have always been opposed to the 'booze and boodle' element of the party, and will conscientiously oppose any candidate representing 'booze and boodle.' " [10] It took no divination to interpret this as a shaft at the anti-Prohibition Smith.

Hearst also kept his name before the Democrats by giving a Lucullan dancing party for more than 600 delegates and their wives. The entire first floor of the Ritz-Carlton Hotel was transformed for the occasion into a conservatory with "towering palms, orange trees, rambler roses and ferns." Mrs. Hearst, gorgeous in white chiffon, a rope of pearls and a pearl-and-diamond tiara, stood with her husband in the Palm Court to greet the guests. Among those invited were William Jennings Bryan, William McAdoo, the George Brennans, the Franklin Delano Roosevelts, the Hylans, the Bernard Baruches, the James A. Farleys and the Brisbanes. Governor and Mrs. Smith were no-

[7] Gretl Urban to author.
[9] N. Y. *Times*, Apr. 30, 1924.
[8] Frances Marion to author.
[10] N. Y. *American*, June 21, 1924.

where to be seen. Paul Whiteman's band played for the dancers, spelled by Eddie Elkins' orchestra. At midnight the host presented a divertissement starring such headliners as Will Rogers, Clifton Webb, Jimmy Savo and Mistinguett.[11] Some of the delegates must have left with mixed emotions about Hearst's tax troubles.

Hearst went unmentioned at the convention. When it went into a long deadlock between Governor Smith and McAdoo, Hearst let his feelings be known by denouncing the "boozing, bootlegging and bartending faction of Tammany" (meaning Smith) and urging the delegates to compromise on Senator Thomas J. Walsh of Montana. The convention paid no heed, finally nominating John W. Davis. Hearst promptly blasted Davis as a "Morgan attorney" and said the "proud old Democratic Party" had "committed suicide." [12] Suicide or not, it was said that Hearst later made overtures to allies of Davis, asking, in return for his support, that he be made Secretary of the Navy in case of Democratic victory.[13]

Hearst left for California two days later on the Twentieth Century Limited with his wife and Mayor and Mrs. Hylan, bound for San Simeon. In all consistency he should have supported Senator La Follette, the Progressive candidate, but his growing conservatism was evident as well as a possible feeling that La Follette might not have a properly sympathetic attitude toward the tax burden of the wealthy. During a stopover in Chicago he told a reporter that both Coolidge and Davis, although "fine gentlemen," were too conservative. "Mr. La Follette," he added, "is a little too radical." [14]

II. HEARST BY HIS OWN PETARD

It was as well that the Hearsts left town, for ten days later Fallon's trial began in New York on an ominous note. Two of the questions Fallon's attorney asked prospective jurors were, "Are you acquainted with William Randolph Hearst?" and "Are you acquainted with Marion Davies?" [1]

There was consternation at the *American* office. This was the first time any mention of the Hearst-Davies acquaintance had been made in a courtroom or in the newspapers. What was Fallon driving at? Reporter Ferber hurried to talk with him. Fallon, always histrionic, told Ferber that his defense would be that Hearst was hounding him because Fallon had birth certificates to show that Hearst was the father of twins born out of wedlock. Ferber took the news to Watson, who was appalled. Just what connection Hearst's private life had with Fallon's bribing of a juror was obscure, but Fallon faced the ruin of his career. He was reckless and unscrupulous enough to try any means to becloud the issue before the jury. His mention of the Hearst-Davies affair in court would mean that it would be printed in all the

[11] N. Y. *Times*, June 26, 1924.
[13] Nicholas Murray Butler, II, 327.
[1] N. Y. *World*, July 23, 1924.

[12] N. Y. *American*, July 8, 10, 1924.
[14] N. Y. *Times*, July 13, 1924.

non-Hearst papers. Watson, with the sick feeling of an editor who sees a story blow up in his face, telephoned San Simeon and was connected with the Chief. He told him what was in the offing.

"You won't have to worry about your first-page line tomorrow, Victor," Hearst commented.

"You mean we carry it?" Watson quavered.

"You'll have to, if the other papers do, won't you, Victor? You don't want to be scooped on your own story."

Watson hung up, muttering, "Well, I'll be God-damned!" [2]

This was Ferber's recollection of the conversation as told him by Watson. It was verified by Gene Fowler, another *American* editor.[3] Subsequent events, however, indicated that Hearst was not unruffled at the prospect and that he may have had a few suggestions as to treatment. A fortnight passed while jurors were picked and the trial got under way, an interval during which nerves in the *American* city room were strung ever tighter.

In the interim *Janice Meredith* had its première at Hearst's Cosmopolitan Theater. The Hearst press gave this its usual all-out attention. Louella Parsons, in her review, unveiled a line of propaganda containing a new element of cunning. It was to praise the picture as something unmatched, but to make very clear the point that in spite of the transcendent qualities of the film, even these were overshadowed by the acting of Miss Davies. Miss Parsons highlighted a two-column encomium by writing, "Marion Davies is at her best as Janice . . . . she astonished me by her versatility and by her ability to get across subtleties that would have fallen flat in less skilled hands . . . . Miss Davies' artistry . . . is the outstanding feature of the film and to which all else must be secondary." [4]

There has been an unkind impression that only the Hearst press ever praised Miss Davies' pictures. This is untrue, a more accurate appraisal being that only the Hearst press did nothing else but praise her and scored publicity breakthroughs both in quantity and ingenuity of praise. The *Times* was enthusiastic about *Janice*, saying, "No more brilliant achievement in ambitious motion pictures dealing with historical romances has ever been exhibited." [5] The *Tribune* and other non-biased papers had kind words for it. It was mentioned that Miss Davies herself was not at the première, being in California—a soft obbligato to the threats of Fallon. The Hylans had returned to New York, and Mrs. Hearst had also left California for a trip to Europe, so Miss Davies had joined Hearst at the new film location. Meanwhile, *American* emissaries talked earnestly with the judge and the prosecutor in the Fallon case, representing to them that Mr. Hearst's private life had nothing to do with the question of Fallon's guilt and urging them to silence the defendant whenever he strayed from the points at issue.[6]

This was not easy with the handsome, dissipated Fallon, a confirmed

[2] Nat Ferber, *I Found Out*, 221.   [3] Fowler, *The Great Mouthpiece*, 374.
[4] N. Y. *American*, Aug. 6, 1924.   [5] N. Y. *Times*, Aug. 6, 1924.
[6] Nat Ferber, 222.

strayer. At the trial, he soon developed his theme that he was an innocent man, the victim of a plot engineered by Hearst and his newspapers. He easily discredited his former associate, Eidlitz, who was a witness against him. Eidlitz, he said, had later repented his tale-telling to the Hearst men and had admitted it to Fallon. Fallon, who had a theatrical habit of referring to himself by name, went on:

"He [Eidlitz] said he told Victor Watson that Fallon had the birth certificates of children born of a certain prominent motion picture actress. He told me also that he had told Watson that I had learned that Hearst had sent a certain woman, supposed to be a Countess, to Florida to get evidence against Mrs. Hearst. He said he told Watson I knew all the details of a trip of Hearst and this party, the actress, to Mexico. He said he told Watson he believed I was going to use this information to blackmail Hearst."

There was an uproar in the courtroom, with the prosecutor trying to object, but Fallon shouted, "Eidlitz said Watson a few days later told him he had communicated with Hearst and that Hearst said, 'We must destroy Fallon at any cost.'"[7]

Fallon kept building the spectacle of a Hearst plot to ruin him. Two days later he said again, "Do you think he [Hearst] wanted it to come to public attention that Fallon had the birth certificates of certain illegitimate children?"[8]

All this was the cunning fiction of an accomplished liar. Hearst had been after Foley, not Fallon, whom he did not even know. It was Watson who, hunting for headlines, had pressed the assault on Fallon. Furthermore, it was indeed a moot question what all this hubbub about a Hearst plot had to do with the question at issue—whether Fallon had bribed a juror. But Fallon had gauged the jury shrewdly. The *American* had been giving Fallon merciless headlines, bearing out the idea of persecution. In a travesty on justice, the jury acquitted him and he drew an ovation. It set up a legal anomaly, with Rendigs in prison for having accepted the bribe from Fallon, and Fallon acquitted of giving the bribe.

One cannot credit the claim of Watson and Fowler that Hearst suggested that the sensational Fallon testimony be front-paged like any other news. Succeeding issues of the *American* after Watson telephoned Hearst gave a picture of Editor Watson nervously giving the Fallon story less display than formerly. Watson was trying to squeeze out of the worst editorial pickle of his career. He even descended to using a front-page headline, "HOTTEST DAY KILLS FIVE," while the Fallon trial was handled as a matter that had lost its spark. The *American's* treatment of the climax was a study in evasion. On the day when Fallon made the charges about the illegitimate babies—which the Hearst press would have headlined in billboard type had it concerned any other millionaire-actress couple—the only mention of Hearst appeared on page 4, while no mention whatever was made of "a certain

[7] N. Y. *Times*, Aug. 7, 1924.   [8] N. Y. *Times*, Aug. 9, 1924.

prominent motion picture actress" or of any babies. The story contrived to skip the embarrassing parts and to render it so confusing as to be meaning-less. The part covering all this read:

> The witness [Fallon] said Eidlitz told him he was afraid he was go-ing to be arrested, so he, Eidlitz, told Victor Watson, assistant publisher of the New York American, that Fallon had certain personal information of im-portance. Fallon also quoted Eidlitz as saying that he had told Mr. Watson that Fallon had told him he intended to use the information for blackmail.
>
> Fallon continued:
>
> "And Eidlitz said that a few days after that he, Watson, said he had communicated with Hearst, and Watson said:
>
> " 'We must destroy Fallon at any cost.' " [9]

It will be noted that the American had it that it was Watson, not Hearst, who said that Fallon must be destroyed. The other papers, however, printed the testimony verbatim. It was later said that Mrs. Hearst, irked at having her name dragged into it, suggested that Watson be dismissed. Instead, Hearst transferred him to his smaller Baltimore paper.[10]

The public seemed to take seriously the story of Hearst persecution, for almost overnight the American lost 60,000 in circulation. Smashing the bucket-shop operators also cost Hearst considerably in revenue, as they had been profitable advertisers—another instance where Hearst took a loss in a good cause.

Although the American staff knew that Fallon's story was a fabrication, Ferber took the trouble to go through the birth records and prove to his own satisfaction that there was no record of illegitimate children fathered by Hearst. Fallon's mistress later admitted that he had no birth certificates. Fallon had staged a colossal hoax and got away with it.[11]

III. THE DEATH OF THOMAS INCE

THE Fallon case gave an extra fillip to gossip that had been buzzing for years, making Hearst easily the most rumored-about millionaire in the country. There was a widespread belief that he did have illegitimate children, perhaps droves of them. Gossip being an expanding commodity, he was also credited with other vices generally believed to accompany infidelity. A Hearst legend was being erected that was largely false because the sidewalk analysts sought to define him in ordinary terms. Hearst, being unlike anyone else, was not susceptible to rule-of-thumb judgment. Even in his infidelity he was unortho-dox. He focused on Miss Davies a medieval sort of worship, but at the same time he had great respect and admiration for his wife.

With Mrs. Hearst in Europe and his boys in school, he bent his atten-tion on Miss Davies' film career in California. While her recent pictures

[9] N. Y. American, Aug. 7, 1924.   [10] Nat Ferber, 229.   [11] Nat Ferber, 230–31.

had won praise, it had to be admitted that much of the praise was due to the lavishness of her productions and that in five years as Cosmopolitan's top star she had failed to challenge Mary Pickford as a national heroine. Hearst began negotiations toward an alliance with forty-four-year-old Thomas H. Ince, a former Broadway actor who had become one of filmdom's most eminent independent producers.[1] Ince, producer of such outstanding pictures as *Civilization* and *Anna Christie*, was known in the industry as a maker of stars. Doubtless this accounted for Hearst's interest in him. He was dissatisfied with Miss Davies' status as one of the nation's dozen most famous actresses and was determined to propel her into the No. 1 spot.

In November, three months after the Fallon trial, Hearst gave a yachting party, with Ince one of the guests. Among the others aboard the *Oneida* as she steamed south along the California coast were Miss Davies, Charlie Chaplin, Seena Owen, Theodore Kosloff, Elinor Glyn and Dr. Daniel Carson Goodman, a physician and a Hearst film executive. Ince was seized by acute indigestion on the yacht. Dr. Goodman, who attended him, saw that he was quite ill, so Ince was taken ashore at San Diego and put on a train for Los Angeles. He grew worse en route. His companions removed him from the train at Del Mar and took him to a hotel, where he was given medical attention by Dr. T. A. Parker and a nurse, Jessie Howard. Ince told them that he had drunk some liquor aboard the yacht. He was then taken to his Hollywood home, where he died next day of a heart ailment.[2]

He died almost two days after leaving the yacht. Undoubtedly Hearst, after the recent Fallon sensation linking him with Miss Davies, was anxious to avoid any more of that kind of publicity. Possibly also he was thinking of what the newspapers could do with the story that Ince was taken ill after drinking aboard the *Oneida*. Despite the fact that Hearst strongly opposed excessive drinking at any of his entertainments, such a report would conjure up public speculation about a "wild drinking party" among film people and might even draw ominous attention from the Hays office. In any case, the first newspaper stories concerning Ince's death made no mention of the Hearst party at all. They merely said that Ince had been taken ill while returning from San Diego.[3]

The death certificate was signed by Dr. Ida Cowan Glasgow. A private funeral was held in Hollywood November 21, attended by the family and others including Miss Davies, Mary Pickford, Douglas Fairbanks, Harold Lloyd and Chaplin. Hearst did not attend. The body was then cremated.

If there was an attempt to "hush up" the fact that Ince was taken ill aboard the yacht, it failed, for there were too many people involved. Soon rumors were flying about the "drinking party" preceding Ince's death. A Los Angeles newspaper hostile to Hearst picked them up and demanded an investigation. District Attorney Chester C. Kempley of San Diego made an inquiry and closed it by saying:

[1] N. Y. *Times*, Nov. 21, 1924. [2] Carlson and Bates, 198–99.
[3] N. Y. *Times*, Nov. 20, 21, 1924.

I am satisfied that the death of Thomas H. Ince was caused by heart failure as a result of an attack of acute indigestion. . . . If there is any liquor investigation made it will have to be made in Los Angeles, where, presumably, the liquor was secured.[4]

Despite this statement, and the fact that three physicians and a nurse had attended Ince before he died, the rumors persisted, doubtless augmented by an impression that an effort had been made to conceal the facts about Ince's presence on the Hearst yacht. They built up into what has become a part of the Hearst legend. One can still hear solemn stories in Hollywood today that Ince was murdered, one of the most ridiculous of them being that Hearst found him pressing unwelcome attentions on Miss Davies and shot him fatally.

[4] N. Y. *Times*, Dec. 11, 1924.

4. Castle No. 2

AFTER visiting with Mussolini and with King Alfonso of Spain, and having an audience with the Pope, Mrs. Hearst returned from Europe in December to be met by her twin nine-year-old sons, Randolph and Elbert. (The latter, disliking his name, later changed it to David.) Her eldest son George was now an executive with the San Francisco *Examiner,* while William Jr. and John were both at school in California. Hearst himself still lingered in California, where he bought himself a Christmas present—forty head of buffalo from a Montana herd at $1000 a head. They were shipped to San Simeon to become part of a great zoo he was establishing there.[1]

Now that his film interests were in California, and his beloved castle loomed majestically with twin towers visible for miles, he was loath to return to New York. After much dickering, he agreed to put his Cosmopolitan Productions under the aegis of the newly organized Metro-Goldwyn-Mayer Company. Louis B. Mayer of M.G.M. went to great lengths to lure him into the fold. The film company agreed to finance Hearst's pictures at their Culver City studio, give him a share of the profits and pay Miss Davies a whopping salary—$10,000 a week. This was not so much because they were determined to acquire Miss Davies, most of whose pictures to date had been heavy losers. The main attraction was Hearst and his twenty-two newspapers. Mayer had not been blind to the formidable build-up Miss Davies had received in the Hearst press, and it was understood that M.G.M. and its other pictures would get similarly favorable attention.[2] As usual, Hearst was willing to allow his papers to be used as publicity organs for his enterprises.

Not until April, 1925, did he return east after more than nine months in California. His Clarendon apartment was undergoing redecoration, so he and Mrs. Hearst took a suite at the Ritz-Carlton. He was concerned because Governor Smith, resolved to rid New York of Hearst, announced that he would not back Hylan for a third term as mayor. Hearst countered with a familiar tactic. He threatened to support Hylan on a third ticket if necessary, knowing that Hylan could not win on a third ticket but that it might throw victory to the Republicans.

From England arrived Miss Alice Head, a plump, thirtyish blonde who was in charge of Hearst's two profitable English magazines, *Nash's* and the English edition of *Good Housekeeping.* The Hearsts entertained her at the Ritz, Hearst being interested not only in the magazines but also in her art

[1] N. Y. *Times,* Dec. 16, 20, 1924.   [2] Bosley Crowther, *Hollywood Rajah,* 122–23.

expert, one Mr. Permain, who did much of his buying of art objects for San Simeon. Miss Head had a talk with him and—like all women who worked for him—came away with a flattering impression of the employer she met for the first time. ". . . he listened with close attention to everything I had to say," she recalled, "made friendly comments, told a few funny stories and left me feeling very happy that I was working for so natural and unalarming a person . . .

"The truth is, he is a man of profound learning with an absolutely first-class brain but with a number of engaging boyish characteristics. He is the soul of courtesy . . . . he is always a gentleman, he is quixotically generous, and he has a gay and responsive sense of humor. I have heard it said that his eyes have a cold expression and that he is difficult to get on with . . . He is genuinely shy with strangers, but anyone who treats him as an ordinary human being and is not afraid of him will find him a most interesting and entertaining companion. No one with his love for children and animals could have anything but a kind heart." [3]

One thing Hearst said that startled her. Although he already had a modern castle in California, he was looking for an antique castle in England. In *Country Life* he had seen pictures of Leeds Castle in Kent and St. Donat's Castle in Wales, and was much taken with them. He asked Miss Head to inform him if either was for sale. [4]

After a quick trip to Washington to inspect his newspaper there and to have another luncheon with Coolidge, he tried a new gambit to save his mayor from the avenging Smith. The third-party bluff had failed to intimidate either Smith or George Olvany, the new boss of Tammany who recognized Smith as the real state leader. Hearst, realizing that a third party would get him nowhere, held out an olive branch.

"There are a number of great offices that are going to be filled within the next few years," he wrote in an *American* editorial, "and the Democratic Party is going to fill them if conditions remain as favorable as they are now. The party is powerful and conditions are favorable because of the records of Mayor Hylan and Governor Smith. Consequently these men are naturally in line for some of these offices if the party remains powerful and conditions remain harmonious.

"There is the Mayor of the City of New York to be elected. There is the Governor of the State of New York to be elected. There is a United States Senator from the State of New York to be elected. There is a President to be elected, and very probably a Democratic President. All of these candidates can be supplied by the Democratic Party of the State of New York, and all of them can be elected if there is harmony and the same wise and able leadership that the party has recently had. . . .

"Unquestionably Governor Smith went about his business attending to his duties in his characteristic, capable way, without quarreling with Mayor

Hylan. And unquestionably Mayor Hylan went about his business without quarreling with Governor Smith. . . .

"Who is going to upset the apple cart? Certainly not the gentlemen who are sitting pretty on it." [5]

This sudden Hearst switch, finding good in the governor who before had been so vile, amazed the town. It did not surprise those who read it with the Hearst political code in mind. Deciphered, it meant chiefly this:

That Hearst, recognizing Smith's paramount strength, was suing for peace, for a Smith-Hearst alliance.

That Hearst was asking Smith to return Hylan as mayor.

That in return, Hearst, knowing how badly Smith wanted the Presidency, was suggesting—not promising—that he might support him in 1928 if Smith did not "upset the apple cart" by ousting Mayor Hylan.

The more one reads this editorial, the more one is impressed by its cunning, its reversal of Hearst's previous stand for the political expediency of the moment, its naked maneuvering to maintain power. This was Hearst in his Hyde aspect. It is the apple-cart editorial, not the sex-slaying headlines, that presents Hearst at his worst.

Governor Smith had the code. He knew what Hearst was offering to him. To his credit, he rejected it, doubtless feeling that it could not be depended on anyway. Smith's political fortunes had risen sharply since his first defiance of Hearst, and he was determined to finish the job. He saw to it that Tammany ditched Hylan and nominated the handsome, song-writing James J. Walker, Democratic leader in the state senate, for mayor, despite his own reservations about Walker's affinity for women and night clubs.[6]

From Miss Head, now back in London, Hearst got word that St. Donat's Castle was for sale. "Buy St. Donat's Castle," he cabled her with never a word about the price.[7] With an uneasy feeling about buying a castle which neither she nor Hearst had ever set eyes on, she closed the deal in London for some $120,000. "I felt a kind of sinking . . ." she later admitted naïvely. "I had involved myself in something quite outside the normal duties connected with a publishing house." [8] She later learned that when one worked for Hearst, one's duties were apt to be versatile. Hearst was so delighted that he sent her several cables of congratulation. Then he skipped off to San Simeon and proceeded to do battle with the ungrateful Smith.

Hylan, with $25,000 in campaign money from Hearst, entered the primary against Walker. The Hearst press, editorially and pictorially, began dramatizing the sinister nature of Walker, one cartoon depicting Walker as looking on approvingly as a dope peddler sold drugs to a child. But there was counter-propaganda against the man who was trying to run the city from his aerie in California, with many references to the luxury of his life. "Is William R. Hearst to be continued as the virtual ruler of the biggest city in the Western Hemisphere?" demanded the Women's Democratic Union.[9] The *Times* said

[5] N. Y. *American*, May 25, 1925.
[7] Alice Head, 85.   [8] Alice Head, 86.
[6] Gene Fowler. *Beau James*, 142–43.
[9] N. Y. *Times*, Apr. 30, 1925.

of Hylan, "For him there is but one leader and boss, the Shepherd of St. [*sic*] Simeon." [10] The battle almost drowned the voice of Florenz Ziegfeld, announcing that he and Hearst were planning to build "the largest theater in the United States." Governor Smith unfairly suggested that Hylan was friendly with the Ku Klux Klan, assailed his "blind, obedient subservience to a super-boss," and made much of Hearst's undemocratic predilection for castles.[11] Hearst, already angered at the ruin of his apple-cart scheme, lost his temper entirely. He wrote in part:

> The distinguished Governor of the great State of New York has taken three days laboriously to prepare a vulgar tirade that any resident of Billingsgate or any occupant of the alcoholic ward in Bellevue could have written in fifteen minutes in quite the same style, but with more evidence of education and intelligence. The Wall Street friends of Governor Smith have enabled him to remove his domicile and his refined person from the neighborhood of the Bowery, but he still reverts in manner of thought to the familiar localities of Five Points and Hell's Kitchen, if this may be said without undue offense to these historic localities. . . .
>
>   . . . This political epistle is not issued from my ranch house, which Mr. Smith calls with his usual cheap demagogy "the splendor and grandeur of my palatial estate," but from the fair city of Los Angeles. And let me in this connection recall the pleasing fact that this fair city promptly arrests its crooked politicians and speeds them on their way to jail. New York papers please copy, and Tammany Hall politicians please take notice.
>
>   Furthermore, I might state that my flat in New York and my ranch house in California are not so very different from the prosperous homes of Mr. Smith and Mr. Olvany. The chief difference between my house and the English or Long Island estates of some Tammany leaders is that my house was paid for out of my own funds and not out of subsidies blackmailed from corrupt traction corporations willing to pay high for the priceless privilege of plundering the people of New York City.—William Randolph Hearst.[12]

This ranks high among specimens of unbridled fury set in type. Smith had all the better of it with a homely brand of satire the people understood.

"Hearst is out of the picture," he said. ". . . The owner of the enchanted palace with a thousand hills and a thousand cows grazing. While he and the Mayor were out brushing the flies off the grazing cows on the thousand hills, they were both engaged in shipping the bull to New York." [13]

On election day, Walker overwhelmed Hylan. Hearst called the *American* office that night from California. "How is Mayor Hylan doing?" he asked.

The irrepressible Gene Fowler took the call. "The people have spoken, Mr. Hearst," he replied. "But they needn't have been so loud." [14]

Mayor Hylan uttered a sad swan song. "It seems," he said, "that the people don't want me after all I have done for them." Hearst's *American*, with little originality, said Hylan was the victim of a plot "laid in the inner councils of

[10] N. Y. *Times*, Aug. 13, 1925.   [11] N. Y. *Times*, Aug. 28, 1925.
[12] N. Y. *American*, Sept. 3, 1925.   [13] N. Y. *Herald-Tribune*, Sept. 6, 1925.
[14] Fowler, *Beau James*, 148.

Wall Street." [15] But when the final election came, Hearst supported Walker, Wall Street and all.

Defeat seemed to meet him at every turn. That same year they tore down Stanford White's Madison Square Garden, which must have given a twinge to the sentimental Hearst. How many times had he stood on the platform in that vast arena, looking over a sea of faces that made the walls throb with cheers for him, only to lose, lose and lose again? The wreckers working on the Garden symbolized the wreckage of his own dearest wish, the defeat of his twenty-five years of fighting, speechmaking and string-pulling for the Presidency. Every brick that came tumbling down was a Hearst hope lost in the rubble, a Hearst dream smothered in dust.

Smaller men would have been crushed by such failure. Although Hearst may have thrown a few tantrums, it is a measure of his strength that he was not permanently embittered.

II. A MILK CAN AROUND HIS NECK

EIGHT-hundred-year-old St. Donat's Castle in Glamorganshire was set in 1300 acres of park fronting on Bristol Channel fourteen miles west of Cardiff, and was considered one of the finest Norman buildings in Great Britain. It could be said that Hearst did not really need it, but in a sense his ego did need it. He must have been aware that in buying the castle he made another of the swift moves that appeared in newspapers and astonished people. He loved to astonish people. Perhaps also St. Donat's was satisfying as an emblem of financial power that served as a substitute for waning political power, and certainly he took real pleasure in the prospect of making alterations. An amateur architect of marked talent, he enjoyed creative design. As a medievalist, he could have found nothing better on which to loose this talent than an authentic castle. He did not have time to visit St. Donat's, nor would he for three years, but he took pleasure in the mere sense of ownership, just as he enjoyed owning thousands of antiques he had never seen.

In Washington, a Senate committee complained that the Hearst organization had added rotogravure sections to its newspapers as a separate entity, charged them as a loss and thereby saved $151,000 in taxes. [1] If Hearst was cutting corners on taxes, he also gave money away. He donated $1,000,000 to the University of California for a women's gymnasium as a memorial to his mother. But his public gifts, while not negligible, were rare for a man of his wealth, his three chief ones in twenty-five years being the Lincoln homestead in Illinois, the Greek Theater at Berkeley, and now this second gift to the university. Cynics were inclined to find ulterior motives in his benefactions. This time they noted that he was having trouble maintaining the power of his political machine in California, headed by Hiram Johnson. [2] Since he was on the verge of losing his influence in New York, at all cost he wanted to

[15] N. Y. *American*, Sept. 17, 1925.   [1] N. Y. *Times*, Dec. 15, 1925.
[2] N. Y. *Times*, Aug. 22, 1926.

preserve his strength in his other two political strongholds, California and Illinois.

Although he had greeted Prohibition with joy as the nation's victory over the saloon, and had linked the "wet" Al Smith with the "boozers," he became disillusioned by the triumph of the speakeasy and the rise of dry-era lawlessness. His newspapers conducted a poll among readers. He followed their verdict and came out boldly for the sale of light wines and beer at federal dispensaries—a step that took courage, for Prohibition was one of the hottest of political issues.[3]

He would never forgive Smith, but he took steps to keep the good will of Mayor Jimmy Walker, who was kind enough not to change the name of the ferryboat *William Randolph Hearst*. Smith must have frowned when he read that the mayor had attended a costume ball at the Clarendon on April 29, 1926, which celebrated Hearst's sixty-third birthday and also (a day late) the twenty-third anniversary of the Hearsts' marriage.[4] Soon thereafter, Hearst was off to California while his wife sailed for Europe. Their separations were more frequent now, but they still maintained the façade. From the West he directed another battle with Smith, who ran for his fourth term as governor that fall.

The Republican candidate was Representative Ogden Mills, a wealthy director of banks, railroads and other corporations. Hearst, the one-time corporation hater, backed Mills as he doubtless would have backed W. C. Fields if he were running against Smith. A search was made for an issue on which Smith could be defeated. This was not easy, for the governor had been a good executive. The Mills forces finally resurrected the old Hearst story of 1919 —that in the Smith regime New York City was being flooded with milk so impure as to threaten the health of the population. Again Hearst and Smith locked in combat, Hearst dictating editorials from California, Smith speaking from the stump. Hearst, shrewd psychologist though he was, seemed unable to cope with Smith. His attacks were ably written but bitter, too obviously the work of an angry man. Smith, sticking wisely to the vernacular, said Hearst had given Mills the "kiss of death," and, when experts pronounced the New York milk supply safe, said, "Hearst has hung a milk can around [Mills'] neck and he cannot get away from it."[5]

Smith won in a 257,000-vote landslide. After seven years of intermittent battle he had finally crushed Hearst as a political power in New York State and emerged the one, unquestioned leader.

Phoebe Hearst had said that "every time Willie feels badly, he goes out and buys something." He now bought, sight unseen, a tenth-century Spanish cloister in the province of Segovia, snapping it up for a mere $40,000. He sent Arthur Byrnes, a former curator of the Hispanic Society of New York, to supervise the dismantling of the cloister stone by stone. Byrnes had plenty

[3] N. Y. *American*, Apr. 2, 1926.   [4] N. Y. *Times*, Apr. 30, 1926.
[5] N. Y. *World*, Oct. 25, 27, 1926.

of trouble, for twice his workmen were driven off by irate villagers who said that foreigners were "robbing the community of its greatest treasure."[6] It was then necessary to build twenty-one miles of railway to connect up with the nearest line, and to construct a sawmill to cut wood for the 10,700 crates in which the stones would be packed.[7]

That winter, John Francis Neylan arrived in New York to negotiate a newsprint contract for the Hearst press. Hearst, who was coming to lean heavily on Neylan, picked him up at his suite at the Plaza Hotel and took him to the theater. Neylan remarked on how Hearst's newspaper competitors loved to assail him, which moved Hearst to a story.

"Some of my competitors," he said, "remind me of a tailor named Levy, who had a competitor across the street named Cohen. A good fairy came to Levy and said, 'You have been a hard worker, a good family man. As a reward, name what you want and it will be yours. But remember—whatever you get, Cohen will get twice as much.' Levy thought this over for a moment, then said, 'I want to be blind in one eye.'"

"I think you get credit for devilment you never commit," Neylan observed.

Hearst was silent for a moment. Then he said, "Jack, always remember that Millicent is my wife and the mother of my children. I know I'm the villain of the piece."[8]

III. WHEN HE'S WRONG . . .

In 1926, Lee Ettelson, a tall Chicagoan, arrived to become at twenty-eight the youngest managing editor in the history of the New York *American*. In the Organization this was known as being led to the slaughter. The *American* was an editor-killer. It was Hearst's top paper in the sense that it was the one which for years he had given his closest personal attention and had used as his editorial sounding board. Its skidding circulation had given it the nickname "the vanishing *American*." Although some of this was probably traceable to Hearst's own unpopular political switches, managing editors had come and gone. Even Gene Fowler had been given a whirl at it. Fowler, a sprightly writer but no editor, had lasted a few months and then Hearst had sent him on a Mediterranean cruise, which was his nice way of retiring him as editor. In three years the paper had had six managing editors and a platoon of city editors.[1]

Bradford Merrill, the silver-haired, distinguished-looking general manager of the Hearst newspapers, took Ettelson in tow. With his huge salary and shrewd investments, Merrill had become a reputed millionaire himself. He delivered a short lecture about the peculiarities of the Chief.

"Mr. Hearst is a genius," he said. "Being a genius, he doesn't think the way you or I do. It isn't necessary for him to move from one premise to an-

[6] N. Y. *Times*, Dec. 14, 1926. [7] Aline B. Saarinen, *The Proud Possessors*, 75.
[8] Mr. Neylan to author, Oct. 13, 1959. [1] Nat Ferber, 248.

other to reach a conclusion. He short-circuits all this intermediary thinking and arrives at his solution instantly. Not that he is always right, but in sports terminology he has a terrific batting average.

"But Mr. Ettelson, when he's wrong he's one hundred percent wrong." [2]

This was fairly representative of the attitude of editors in the upper echelons who had occasional personal contact with Hearst. They saw him as a genius in his firm grasp of his mighty enterprises, and they were aware of his prejudices and his capacity for sudden shifts in policy. Hearst editors had to look two ways, keeping one eye on the news and the other on the Chief. Wherever he was, instructions came from him frequently in the form of bulletlike telegrams dispatched by his secretary, Willicombe. An editor whose circulation was rising was likely to get praise along with a suggestion that he might do better. One whose circulation was sinking was under constant pressure. Hearst could find fault with a story's handling, a picture, a headline, a caption, a cartoon. With the success of the tabloids, condensation of the news became a fetish with him. "Nobody likes a long article any more than they like a long speech," he warned.[3]

He could be warm in commendation, and savage in criticism. Once, after looking over an issue of his *Harper's Bazaar,* he telegraphed its editor, Henry Sell, "I find the ads fascinating." [4] He paid well and expected the last measure of devotion. Yet his editors, of whom there were now literally hundreds, had faith in his ultimate fairness. He seemed to miss nothing. He was so appreciative of good work, so ready with a kindly pat on the back, that his criticisms were seldom resented. Hearst, who could be so unfair in politics, was admirably just with his own men. He was careful not to criticize them publicly or over an open wire so that they would be embarrassed. They knew that if a problem arose, they could telephone him and he would listen patiently and deliver a reasonable verdict.[5] He liked to have them telephone him about important matters. He wanted to know what was going on in all of his dozens of offices, and he enjoyed the kingly feeling that he was the actual editor of all his publications—the feeling of control and omnipotence that was so important to him.

It was noticed that a large proportion of his executives were Irishmen and Jews, probably because he liked the aggressiveness and ardor of these races. It took a hardy breed of newsman to be successful in the Organization—men without nerves, men with a sense of adventure and a love of risk similar to that of a mountain climber or tight-rope walker. Hearst seldom discharged upper-echelon men who had proved their value, but if an editor failed circulation-wise in Boston or New York he was likely to find himself working on another Hearst paper in Syracuse or Seattle. At the same time he generally had a colleague or two breathing down his neck, ready to snatch his job away. Hearst encouraged such combat, believing in instilling a feeling of

[2] Lee Ettelson to author, Oct. 9, 1959.
[3] *Selections From the Writings and Speeches of William Randolph Hearst,* 309.
[4] Henry Sell to author, Feb. 24, 1960.   [5] John Dienhart to author, Nov. 12, 1959.

insecurity as a stimulus to greater effort. His editors cringed at some of his crotchets, such as his occasional campaigns against vivisection. But Gene Fowler expressed a general feeling when he wrote, "Mr. Hearst is entitled to a monument for *never having bored* anyone who worked for him." [6]

Yet Hearst had lost the originality that once marked him. He had found what he believed a successful formula thirty years earlier, and had changed little. All of his newspapers had a sameness about them—the splashy head-lines, the sensational pictures, the cluttered makeup, the emphasis on features and comics, and the inevitable typographical errors. Because of the speed at which they were produced, the Hearst papers were notorious for "typos," some of them amusing or obscene. Once, on the New York *American,* the term "battle-scared hero" was hastily corrected in a later edition and came out reading "bottle-scarred hero." [7] The Chief was growing conservative and cautious. His constant watch over his editors, and their fear of making a misstep, robbed them of the spontaneity that comes with independence.

There was a legend that Hearst himself had no nerves, that he was immune to the inner concern of most men. This was merely because he concealed it as he concealed most of his emotions. He worried about his publications, and especially about his *American,* which had sagged to a circulation of about 230,000. Editor Ettelson heard plenty about that.

Hearst had built a large office suite on the ground floor of the Clarendon, to spare his executives the necessity of taking the elevator and cluttering up his living quarters. When in New York he seldom went to the *American-Journal* offices. He sent his men summonses and they came to him. Ettelson occasionally received what was known as "The Call," usually to lunch with a half-dozen other executives. Hearst would speak with each in turn, giving him the most intense concentration, apparently forgetting the others entirely as he discussed a problem and made a decision. Then he would move on to the next, shutting out what he was thinking of a moment before. He kept to the business at hand, forbade any aimless conversation, and settled each matter singly. [8] Every second seemed precious to him, and his executives usually felt rather limp after such a session.

Having great faith in the appeal of attractive typography, he had a plan for reviving the *American* which involved imitating the typography and makeup of the successful Los Angeles *Examiner.* Ettelson felt this a bad policy. He went to work and evolved his own comprehensive plan for re-habilitating the paper, which he presented to Hearst. Hearst, always a good listener, followed him carefully for about forty-five minutes, picking nerv-ously at his hands. At the end he paced the floor in silence for a time, still picking at his hands. Finally he said:

"Mr. Ettelson, you've put a lot of thought into this. If I were a young man we'd do it. But I'm an old man. I have to have results sooner." [9]

At that time, Hearst still had a quarter century of life left in him.

[6] Fowler, *The Great Mouthpiece,* 374.   [7] Nat Ferber, 249.
[8] Lee Ettelson to author.   [9] Mr. Ettelson to author.

5. Building the Legend

I. THE HEARST-MAYER ENTENTE

> I never felt I'd met the real Hearst. Mainly I beheld
> only his outer shell, the protective film behind which lurked
> a secretive, aloof being whose personal convictions were
> not to be fathomed, whose private viewpoints were only
> to be guessed at.   —Irvin S. Cobb [1]

HEARST's failure to achieve the Presidency was a blow from which he never quite recovered. Oppressed though he was by it, he was saved from despondency by his eternal busy-ness, the multitude of projects that kept him looking forward rather than backward. But these, too, took a physical and nervous toll. "Had he not been able to turn to some diversion like the building of San Simeon," said John Francis Neylan, "I think he would have gone crazy." [2] As he grew older, the nonconformist veered somewhat in the direction of conventionality. Although he had poked much fun at the academic world, he was delighted in May, 1927, when little Oglethorpe University in Atlanta conferred on him an honorary Doctorate of Laws.

This came about because his third son, John Randolph, was a student there. Nonsectarian Oglethorpe presumably overlooked Hearst's unorthodox marital status in view of the gift to education that would result. Dr. Thornwell Jacobs, president of the institution, slipped the purple hood around his shoulders with the citation, "William Randolph Hearst, counselor of millions, lover of America, exponent of perpetual peace entente among the English-speaking nations of the world." [3]

Certainly belligerency rather than peaceability had characterized his long-run attitude toward England. However, he had recently executed one of those amazing Hearst switches. Violently opposed to the Versailles Treaty (a Wilson mistake) and the League of Nations (also a Wilson nightmare), he had proposed to restore real peace in Europe through the creation of a combination of English-speaking nations including the United States, England, Canada and Australia. He took pains to insist that this did not mean any of the "foreign entanglements" which he had consistently fought, but his reasoning on this was unclear. The London *Daily News* snapped, "If Mr. Hearst wants to make a permanently peaceful settlement in Europe almost impossible, he has only to raise this spectre." [4] He soon reverted to normal and dropped the idea.

He became a grandfather soon after when his son George's wife had

---

[1] Cobb, *Exit Laughing*, 122.   [2] Mr. Neylan to author, Nov. 5, 1959.
[3] Mrs. Fremont Older, *op. cit.*, 499.   [4] Quoted in N. Y. *Times*, Jan. 24, 1927.

twin children—another reminder that his youth was gone. He had still not *quite* given up hope for office, but after the last trouncing at Smith's hands the hope was feeble. He turned now to two other dreams—the dream of becoming the premier mogul of the films, and the dream of building castles. After 1926, although his legal residence remained in New York, he spent most of his time in California.

In Los Angeles he took a full floor at the Ambassador Hotel, which had gardens with oleanders, poinsettias and cockatoos. At the sprawling Culver City studios of M.G.M. he became something like a king. The top man at the studio was pudgy Louis B. Mayer, a shrewd, ruthless egotist who was not above demanding intimate favors from actresses in return for contracts. Mayer regarded Hearst with sincere although not disinterested reverence. The first photograph transmitted by telegraph wire from California to New York showed Mayer presenting a makeup box to Miss Davies at the Culver City studio.[5] In addition to the priceless publicity of the Hearst press, the arrival of Hearst and Miss Davies had given M.G.M. a magnificence all its own. They brought a splendor unknown even in that fairyland of glitter. Other stars made do with fancy dressing rooms supplied by the studio. For Miss Davies' use between scenes, a fourteen-room "bungalow" costing $75,000 and furnished with Hearst antiques was built on the lot. The cottage, well staffed with servants, became the social center of the studio, the place where visiting bigwigs were taken.[6]

Mayer knew a good thing when he saw it. Maybe Fox and some of the other studios had stars he wanted, but only M.G.M. had William Randolph Hearst and Marion Davies. A former junk dealer who had got into motion pictures via the nickelodeons, aided by a willingness to cozen competitors and friends, Mayer was at first fearful of the impressive Hearst and his silver-spoon background. When he found Hearst genial and friendly, he was charmed. This was at a time when "Hollywood" was thought one of the world's wonders, and visitors were frequent. Mayer saw to it that the important ones were sent to Miss Davies' house, which became known as the Bungalow. In so doing he could impress the important visitors with Hearst, and also impress Hearst with the important visitors. Howard Strickling, then a publicity subordinate, was given the job of taking them to the Bungalow. Hearst was agreeable to being made something of a showpiece. He always greeted the callers pleasantly and treated them to collations prepared by the servants. When Miss Davies was on the set, he was there, watching every move sharply, simply teeming with ideas for improving her scenes.[7] He took special pains to see that Miss Davies had the largest and most active publicity corps of any screen star.

Miss Davies had long since become the fairy godmother of the studio. When an office boy developed an eye ailment, she paid for an operation. She sent a poor studio newsboy to military school for four years. If anyone

[5] Crowther, 126.   [6] Crowther, 123.
[7] Howard Strickling to author, Nov. 19, 1959.

was in trouble, she would help them out, not only with money but with genuine sympathy coming from a sincere heart. Christmas was a colossal occasion, for she would have a party in the Bungalow and give expensive gifts such as watches to all members of the cast, not forgetting the publicity men or the carpenters and electricians and their children. She was one of the most generous and warm-hearted women alive—so much so that horse-players and other chiselers could sometimes wheedle cash out of her.

Naturally, every actor and scene-shifter on the lot wanted to work in her pictures. The pace was leisurely. If she took a few days off, so did everybody else, on full pay.[8] With Hearst around, scenic effects had to be perfect, and time and money were spent to gain perfection. When Miss Davies was making *The Red Mill,* a complete Dutch village was built alongside an artificial canal, each house built to scale from photographs of an actual Dutch town. To freeze the canal for winter scenes, an intricate piping system was built so that the water was frozen with ammonia gas even under the hot California sun, thick enough for several hundred cast members to skate on it. A thousand wooden shoes were manufactured for the players.[9]

Once, while Frances Marion was working on a Davies scenario at Culver City, Hearst and Miss Davies went off on a visit to San Francisco. Two days later, Hearst tried to reach Miss Marion by telephone, failed, and talked to an editor of his Los Angeles *Examiner* instead. Miss Marion must be in San Francisco first thing in the morning, Hearst said. It was a matter of utmost importance. He must get someone to drive her there overnight.

The editor, fearing to trust the job to anyone else, undertook it himself. He called for Miss Marion that evening. She did not know what was wrong, but assumed it had to do with the scenario. The all-night, 400-mile drive over the tortuous roads of the Twenties was an exhausting one. When they reached San Francisco in the morning, Miss Marion, thoroughly fatigued, found Hearst and Miss Davies at the St. Francis Hotel. Hearst greeted her with boyish enthusiasm.

"I heard yesterday that today would be a clear day," he explained, "and it is. So we planned a picnic—just you and Marion and me. We'll go up to Mt. Tamalpais. The view of the city will be splendid!"

The hotel had prepared baskets of delicacies for them, including caviar and champagne. They went off for their picnic, Miss Marion silently marveling at the lengths to which Hearst would go to satisfy a whim and have his own way.[10]

II. KING OF HOLLYWOOD

ON weekends, Hearst often invited the cast, the writers, Mayer and others up to San Simeon. He would have Secretary Willicombe reserve a private car or a whole private train for them on the Southern Pacific—his arch-enemy

[8] Ilka Chase, *Past Imperfect*, 108.   [9] N. Y. *Times*, Feb. 13, 1927.
[10] Miss Marion to author, Aug. 24, 1960.

thirty years earlier—which would take them to San Luis Obispo, where cars from the castle would pick them up. For his special friends, Hearst had an eight-passenger Fokker plane which whisked them up to the ranch from the Burbank airport.[1] A weekend at San Simeon came to be the dream of cinema hopefuls. Once they made it they were in a special class. Hollywood was divided into two castes—people who had been guests at San Simeon and those who had not. The grandeur of the castle, the view, the gardens, the food, the picnics, the glamorous people, the private theater, the tennis, the swimming pools, the horseback riding, the zoo, the name-it-and-Hearst-had-it, was enough to make a starlet's head swim. It was enough even to stagger rich cinema moguls like Mayer and Nicholas Schenck. When Hearst was not in California, he often gave his friends the freedom of the house. On one such occasion the guest list included (among many others) John Gilbert, Buster Keaton, Natalie Talmadge, Hal Roach, Alice Terry, Paul Bern, Aileen Pringle, Schenck, Greta Garbo, Irving Thalberg, Norma Shearer, Edward Goulding, Beatrice Lillie, Eddie Mannix and Morton Downey, all of whom enjoyed the pressed duck, roast guinea fowl and vintage wines at the absent Hearst's expense.[2]

There was only one drawback. Mr. Hearst did not approve of immoderate consumption of hard liquor at San Simeon. A cocktail, yes, but that was all.

Irvin S. Cobb, who wrote for *Cosmopolitan* magazine and also for the films, was one of a group of seventy who spent a weekend at San Simeon. They went up from Los Angeles in a private train supplied by Hearst, complete with refreshment booth and musicians to beguile away the miles. Although Cobb always felt shock at the pipsqueak voice issuing from Hearst's deep chest, he admired the publisher's genuine hospitality, his pungent, witty conversation and his love for a joke, especially on himself.[3] But when Hearst ordered two special trains to take his guests back to Los Angeles, since one group was staying longer, Cobb was staggered at the expense. He could understand private cars, he said, "But why, if I might be so bold to ask, why a whole private train for our batch?"

"Well, I'll tell you, Cobb," Hearst said, "if your group had only private cars they'd be parked on a siding at San Luis Obispo station until the regular train came through and you'd be jerked around while they were hitching you on and getting under way again. I used to use a private car going down from here and just about the time I got to sleep that infernal train would come along and bump into us and wake me up. I hate to be bumped around that way. And I figure any friends I'm entertaining hate to be bumped, too." [4]

Only one thing baffled Cobb. Although he met Hearst many times, it always struck him that the publisher was aloof, on his guard, never revealing his inner self. ". . . I never felt that I'd met the real Hearst," he later wrote, agreeing with hundreds of others who gave up trying to understand the great man and wrote him off as a fascinating mystery.[5]

[1] N. Y. *Times,* June 28, 1927.   [2] C. J. Hubbell to author.   [3] Cobb, 123.
[4] Cobb, 125.   [5] Cobb, 122.

It was no wonder that Hearst speedily became a Hollywood legend, just as he had long been a newspaper and political legend. This was as he willed it, for it seems likely that he consciously sought to make himself a legend. Like an adolescent, he loved to surprise and impress people. There was no longer any concealment of his love for Miss Davies—another sign of his waning political hopes—and the frankness of their attachment amazed even the blasé film colony.

But San Simeon was a good 200 miles from Hollywood, too far for daily commuting, so Hearst planned another castle convenient to Culver City. Mayer, Will Rogers, Joseph Schenck, Harold Lloyd and others of the elect had built mansions along the beach at Santa Monica, making it the gold coast of filmland. Hearst consulted a Brentwood realtor, George S. Merritt, who showed him a large plot of beach land that was available. Merritt was then angered to discover that Hearst's agents were trying to buy the land direct from its owner in an effort to avoid paying the realtor's commission. In his annoyance, Merritt quickly sold the land to another prospect who had been interested. Hearst later called on Merritt.

"I see that land is sold," he said. " 'Fess up. Didn't you buy it yourself so you could resell it to me?"

Merritt, incensed at the implication that he was trying to "hold up" Hearst, told him the facts. "I don't like the way you do business," he said. "I showed you the property, then you tried to freeze me out."

Hearst's gaze was piercing. "When I try to buy anything," he snapped, "the price has a habit of going up and up."

"Mr. Hearst," Merritt said, "there's only one kind of deal I know how to make—an honest one." [6]

Hearst relaxed and smiled. After that the two got along famously. Merritt began buying beach land, keeping it a close secret that Hearst was his client.

III. THE INADEQUATE INCOME

HEARST, whose personal income was estimated roughly as around $15,000,000 a year, was spending money faster than he made it, a bad policy for any capitalist. His utter lack of self-discipline was never more evident than in the helpless, compulsive way he spent, spent, spent. With his political hopes crushed, he grew visibly worse, his ego substituting the pride of acquisition for the power of office. His complaints about taxes reflected his growing removal from reality, his tendency to strike out at anything that hampered his happy spree of spending.

Arthur Brisbane, a one-time socialist who had drifted pleasantly into the profit system, took a hand in helping him spend. Brisbane was in some respects a vest-pocket Hearst—a personal enigma, a workhorse, a madman for circulation, a liberal who had grown conservative, an investor. Brisbane,

---

[6] George S. Merritt to author, Oct. 29, 1959.

however, entirely lacked Hearst's sense of humor and his flights of generosity. He was in the habit of surprising people by telling them the enormous salary Hearst paid him.

Brisbane, who had long plunged in real estate, persuaded his chief to join him in another realty promotion, the Hearst-Brisbane Properties, in which they projected other expensive ventures, among them the construction of the huge Ziegfeld Theater and the Warwick Hotel in New York. Hearst's heavy investments in real estate, invariably at high mortgages, reflected his incurable optimism, his certainty that New York property was bound to rise in value. At the same time he was erecting a mighty building on South Street in lower Manhattan to house his *American* and *Journal,* and was contemplating immense expenditures in radio, applying for licenses to broadcast in eleven cities from coast to coast.[1] Doubtless he regarded his realty investments as money saved, which they would have been had they been held within bounds, if the mortgages had not been so large, and if the market continued to rise. As it was, they constituted a heavy debt burden, and Hearst had little cash reserve against the emergency he refused to believe would arise.

To satisfy the Chief's endless money demands, holding companies of the Organization had floated several bond issues totaling more than $60,000,000.[2] The vast properties once owned solely by Hearst were moving inexorably out of his exclusive control.

The Ziegfeld Theater was one of his pet projects. As the time of its completion drew near, he used to pick up the telephone around midnight whether he was in California or New York and call Editor Ettelson at the *American* to tell him to give the theater a smashing publicity display. The acknowledged musical comedy queen at the time was Marilyn Miller. It was assumed that she would star in the first production at the new theater. One night Ettelson told Hearst that he had heard a disquieting rumor—that Ziegfeld was not going to open with Miss Miller but with something by Edna Ferber called *Show Boat.* Hearst, always annoyed when a specialist moved out of his own field, turned on his iciest voice.

"Suppose we let Mr. Ziegfeld handle that department," he snapped.[3]

Ziegfeld handled it well, for *Show Boat* became one of the successes of all time.

With the vision he often displayed, Hearst recognized aviation as a coming revolutionizer of international travel. His enthusiasm over the 1927 Lindbergh flight to Paris was typical of a man who sought to have America first in everything. Immediately he joined with M.G.M. in drawing up a contract offering Lindbergh $500,000 cash and a percentage of the profits for the right to make a screen story of his life. When the flyer returned to New York to receive a tumultuous ovation, he was later escorted to the Clarendon by Grover Whalen, head of the mayor's welcoming committee. Typically, Lind-

---

[1] N. Y. *Times,* Apr. 25, 1926.   [2] Villard, *Prophets True and False,* 308.
[3] Mr. Ettelson to author.

bergh had to wait a half-hour for Hearst to arrive.[4] When he did, he showed his famous guest his collection of armor, then produced the contract. Lindbergh shook his head.

"You know, I said I did not intend to go into moving pictures," he said.

Hearst reasoned with him. "This is not a moving picture in the ordinary sense of the word. It is not a fiction story. It is the real story of your life. . . . Do not consider it as a benefit to yourself, but as an inspiration to others."

But Lindbergh was firm. The money-minded Hearst, amazed and impressed by this rejection of a fortune, gave him the contract to tear up.[5]

Motivated in part by the great circulation-building possibilities of transoceanic flights and in part by patriotism, he offered Clarence Chamberlain and Charles Levine $100,000 if they would make the westward flight from Europe to the United States. He sponsored an entry in the ill-fated Dole flight to Hawaii, and the plane was lost with its two pilots. This tragedy made him hesitant about another flight he had intended to back, one by Aviators Lloyd Bertaud and J. B. Hill from the United States to Rome. But Philip Payne, his air-minded, circulation-minded managing editor of the New York *Daily Mirror*, was determined to go through with it. Not only that; unknown to Hearst, Payne intended to go along as a passenger.

There was a mournful story of mass circulation methods behind Payne's move. In order to gain readers for the *Mirror*, he had revived the unsolved Hall-Mills scandal in New Jersey, making unsupported charges resulting in the arrest of Mrs. Hall and several others. The case against them blew up, ending in lawsuits against Hearst which he was said to have settled ultimately for a sum in six figures.[6] Payne had made a costly error. Some atonement for this was in his mind as he planned the flight, aware that if the editor of the *Mirror* flew to Rome it would be a Hearst scoop that would gather in more readers. Hearst sent Payne a worried telegram from California, saying that "in view of the recent disasters" he would not take responsibility for the flight unless the government gave it full approval. Payne replied that the plane, *Old Glory*, had government approval. Hearst now decided against it regardless:

> Dear Phil: Please think of my situation. I have had one airplane lost and two fine men drowned. If another such disaster occurs effect would be terrible, not only on my peace of mind, but on public opinion. I telegraph you all this to have you get pilots to accept prize and give up dangerous adventure.—W. R. Hearst.

The tenacious Payne replied:

> Dear Chief: The pilots appreciate your magnanimous offer, but insist they be allowed to fill their contracts to fly. Weather ideal today. . . . Every possible precaution taken. . . . You have been a great Chief to work

[4] N. Y. *Times*, June 6, 1927.   [5] N. Y. *American*, Feb. 20, 1934.
[6] Emile Gauvreau, *My Last Million Readers*, 108.

for. I honor and love you, and I know you will forgive any mistakes I have made.—Phil Payne.[7]

The last sentence was Hearst's first hint that Payne intended to accompany the flight. The *Old Glory* took off from Old Orchard, Maine, and was lost at sea with its three occupants. Hearst financed a search for the bodies by boat that was fruitless.

For his San Simeon zoo, Hearst bought two giraffes, seven zebras, five ostriches and an assortment of other fauna. He bought a newspaper in Pittsburgh, collaborating there with a long-time publishing friend, Paul Block. For a "between-seasons" dwelling, chiefly for Mrs. Hearst, he paid $400,000 for another castle, the Long Island estate of Mrs. O. H. P. Belmont, a "medieval" pile complete with moat and drawbridge.[8] Then he turned to Mexico in the most grotesque adventure of his career.

[7] N. Y. *American,* Sept. 8, 1927.   [8] N. Y. *Times,* Oct. 7, 1927.

6. The Mexican "Documents"

For fifteen years Hearst had worried about his Mexican properties, particularly his Babicora ranch. Villa had looted it of cattle. Carranza had raided it. During the Obregon administration there had been a period of quiet, but under Obregon's successor, Plutarco Elias Calles, there was trouble again. The radical Calles, pressing agrarian reforms, had taken several pieces of the ranch and given them to the peons. Hearst's feeling of the sanctity of his property was outraged. With his compulsion to improve any property he owned, he had been rebuilding Babicora, pouring money into it, sending hundreds of white-faced bulls there for breeding purposes. But he was also concerned about his holdings farther south—his Guanacevi and San Luis mines, his timber and chicle lands.

In 1925, disturbed by the Calles program, he sent one of his magazine executives, Frazier Hunt, to Mexico City. Since he already had representatives there, one of Hunt's duties may have been to snoop and make sure they were on the job. Hunt later wrote that part of his assignment was a "small gumshoeing job," which he did not explain but which also might have included an undercover effort to ascertain how far the government would go in expropriation. Hunt was further instructed to interview President Calles and his Minister of Agriculture and to write laudatory stories about them for the Hearst Sunday papers [1]—another of the many instances of Hearst's use of his newspapers to promote his own interests. If Calles were praised in the Hearst press, perhaps he would be kind to Hearst.

For years, foreign capitalists had exploited Mexico to the detriment of its own people. For example, American and British interests owned 91.5 percent of the nation's oil wealth, Mexicans themselves holding a mere 1.1 percent.[2] Calles stepped up a program of "Mexico for the Mexicans," inaugurating plans for the gradual repossession of properties held by outsiders and also becoming embroiled in a quarrel with the Catholic Church in Mexico. There were quick repercussions in the United States. Religious groups, both Catholic and Protestant, were indignant. Above all, American capitalists whose interests were endangered reacted energetically. Washington was filled with lobbyists branding Calles a "bolshevik" and demanding armed intervention in Mexico. The loudest cries for intervention came from such American holders of Mexican oil and other properties as the mil-

[1] Frazier Hunt, *One American and His Attempt at Education*, 293–94.
[2] Hudson Strode, *Timeless Mexico*, 269.

lionaire Edward L. Doheny. Relations between the two countries became so strained that armed intervention seemed a possibility.[3]

It was with this background that Hearst, whose press had been surprisingly moderate toward Calles, began his Mexican maneuvers. His own career demonstrated that at intervals he could be depended on to do something approaching lunacy. By 1927 he was overdue.

According to later testimony, in the spring of that year, an unnamed American citizen living in Mexico learned that documents were for sale there proving the existence of anti-United States plots. He passed this information on to Edward Hardy Clark, the long-time manager of Phoebe Hearst's finances who was active in the management of the Hearst Mexican properties. Clark told Hearst, who decided to obtain the documents. He assigned his correspondent in Mexico City, John Page, to employ a "trustworthy investigator" to aid him. In Mexico, Page hired one Miguel Ávila, a Texan of Mexican descent, who got busy and soon said he managed by bribery to secure a number of documents from government clerks. Ávila was then brought to the United States, where he proposed to bribe clerks in the Mexican consulate in New York City. Sure enough, he quickly produced further documents which he said came from the consulate and which seemed to corroborate details given in the others. The Organization paid Ávila a total of $20,150 for his gumshoe work.[4]

In July, Victor Watson, who was again with the New York *American*, was summoned to San Simeon. There, along with Page and Ávila, he had a conference with Hearst about the documents. After that, Ávila returned to New York to try to get more papers from the consulate there.[5] It appears that all the papers ultimately secured were in the hands of the Organization by September. However, they were not used at once, possibly because Hearst wanted to wait until Congress convened in December so that they would have maximum impact and draw quick government action.

Meanwhile, Hearst was in an agony of disappointment on September 22 when a rival newspaper chain stole a march on him by getting the rights to broadcast the Dempsey-Tunney fight in Chicago.

On the brighter side, Miss Davies' new film, *Quality Street*, made the Hearst press express wonderment that regardless of how colossal her previous pictures were, her latest one was always greater. "MARION DAVIES HITS NEW FILM HEIGHTS" was the headline over one review which ran a gamut of superlatives and declared, "Miss Davies' performance has the sparkling quality of a gem."[6]

On November 14, all of Hearst's newspapers began a series of sensational front-page stories, under their traditionally easy-to-read headline type, telling of sinister anti-American plots below the Rio Grande. The revelations were based on the alleged official documents, some of which were published

[3] Frank Tannenbaum, *Peace By Revolution*, 64–65.
[4] N. Y. *Herald-Tribune*, Dec. 16, 1927.
[5] N. Y. *Herald-Tribune*, Dec. 17, 1927.　　　　[6] N. Y. *American*, Nov. 2, 1927.

in facsimile. They claimed to expose shoals of conspiracies, some of them sponsored by President Calles himself—plots to foment a Central American war against the United States, plots to colonize Mexico with hordes of Japanese to aid in the war, plots to further Communism, plots to bribe United States newspaper editors, clergymen, legislators and others. Readers were assured that the documents proving these plots were unquestionably official and authentic, coming from Mexican secret archives.[7]

No other newspapers carried the stories. Hearst was so excited about his scoop that he ordered three of his lieutenants to promote it to the limit —Edmond D. Coblentz, editor of the New York *American,* Victor Watson, and V. H. Polachek, in charge of circulation for all Hearst Sunday papers. These three urged Moses Koenigsberg, head of Hearst's International News Service, to send the sensations out over his wires. Koenigsberg, however, apparently smelled a rat, for he declined and I.N.S. avoided the stories.[8]

The revelations raised a furor in Washington. The Mexican Embassy issued an indignant statement pronouncing the documents "utter forgeries." The forger of the documents, it said, had earlier offered to sell them to the Mexican consulate in Los Angeles for $25,000, this being a form of blackmail with a threat to offer them for publication elsewhere if they were not purchased. He was turned down. "Now," said the embassy, "some American newspapers are publishing these very same faked documents, after some months have elapsed, the blackmail having proved a failure." [9]

The Hearst press continued the daily exposures. There was much speculation as to Hearst's motives. President Coolidge had recently sent Dwight Morrow to Mexico as ambassador in an effort to settle United States–Mexican differences. Some thought that Hearst, with his penchant for mischief-making, was trying to embarrass Morrow, who was a Morgan partner. On the other hand, the one-time radical publisher had become a warm admirer of Coolidge. Indeed, he had another of his luncheons at the White House with Coolidge at the very time the sensations were being published.

On December 9, the twenty-six papers of the Hearst press—including the Washington *Herald*—published a document purporting to show that the Mexican government had authorized payment of $1,115,000 to four United States Senators whose names were deleted in the newspaper reproduction. Congress was now in session. Senator David Reed of Pennsylvania, angrily waving a copy of the *Herald,* called for an investigation, pointing out that every Senator stood under a cloud until the matter was aired. The Senate unanimously voted the appointment of a five-man committee to probe the Mexican documents.[10] Perhaps it was significant that the Hearst papers ceased the Mexican extravaganza the next day.

On December 15 the committee started to take the testimony of principals in the matter, bringing out the manner in which the documents had come

[7] All Hearst papers, Nov. 14, 1927, ff.   [8] Koenigsberg, 457.
[9] N. Y. *Times,* Nov. 17, 1927.   [10] N. Y. *Herald-Tribune,* Dec. 10, 1927.

into Hearst's hands. Much of the inquiry was aimed at determining how these explosive documents had been verified as authentic.

It turned out that they had *not* been verified. Hearst and his men had been guilty of incredible negligence. Some of the papers had been shown to the then United States Ambassador James Sheffield in Mexico City, who expressed surprise but could not give an expert opinion as to their authenticity. The counselor of the embassy, Arthur Schoenfeld, also looked them over and suggested that the signature of President Calles, appearing on some of them, should be authenticated. Had this been done? Well, no one seemed sure. It came out that it had not. Hearst believed that his editors, Watson and Coblentz, had carried on some further investigation. It developed that they had not. Watson was taken in by the fact that Ávila produced documents in New York that agreed perfectly with those found in Mexico. Furthermore, in the midst of all this Watson was moved from the *American* to take the late Phil Payne's post on the *Mirror*, and the job of continuing with the Mexican documents was handed over to Editor Coblentz. Coblentz seemed to feel that the verification had been handled by Watson, and went full speed ahead.[11] Watson's testimony, when he was questioned by Senator Reed, indicated a paucity of high-level responsibility.

Q—When you planted Ávila in the Consulate General did it occur to you that Ávila was there for the purpose of corroborating himself?

A—It did not impress me that way at all.

Q—Well, was it not asking a man to get documents to prove the authenticity of documents he himself had procured?

A—Yes, but I see nothing wrong in that, provided he could get the documents.[12]

The documents themselves were handed over to the committee. They named the four Senators who allegedly had received tainted money from Mexico as William Borah ($500,000), George Norris ($300,000), Thomas Heflin ($300,000) and the younger Robert La Follette (a trifling $15,000).[13] The Senators were furious. An examination of the papers showed them to be replete with grammatical errors such as one would hardly expect government clerks to make. President Coolidge had been vacationing in South Dakota at the time the Hearst men were contemplating their scoop. Edward Hardy Clark had been sent there with the documents to show them to the President. This, of course, was not for verification, since Coolidge could hardly qualify as an expert, but to get the attitude of the administration. But when Clark brought up the subject, Coolidge said he took no stock in the papers and decided that it would be unwise even to look at them. Clark returned to New York none the wiser.[14]

The long and short of it was that the Hearst men had depended with

[11] N. Y. *Times*, Dec. 17, 1927.   [12] The same.
[13] N. Y. *Herald-Tribune*, Dec. 16, 1927.   [14] The same.

remarkable naïveté on Ávila. They had made no effort to prove his character and reliability. They had not taken the simple, elementary step of having the documents examined by handwriting experts. They had gone ahead with the publication of documents charging a neighboring country with warlike activity and impugning the character of the Senators *without any real effort to prove their authenticity.*

Hearst, however, still insisted that they were genuine. He testified imperturbably when Senator Joseph Robinson questioned him.

Q—Did you learn of any grammatical errors in these articles which tended, in your judgment, to impeach the validity of them?

A—I believe there are some grammatical errors in the documents, but I am told that is not unusual. . . .

Q—If it should appear that there are twenty or thirty grammatical errors in a single page of the documents, would that tend to impeach the authenticity of a document?

A—I would not answer that for I do not know how frequent grammatical errors are in similar documents. I really would not know.

Hearst went on to say that he felt sure that his revelations of the "plots" would naturally cause an investigation, particularly in view of the charges that four Senators were involved. His testimony on this point laid bare astonishing ambiguities:

Q—Did you investigate whether money had been actually paid to the United States senators?

A—No, sir, we didn't.

Q—Did you go to the senators mentioned and ask them?

A—No; we could not without revealing the contents.

Q—Have you any evidence that any senator received any such money as mentioned here?

A—No. In fact, I do not believe they did receive any money.

Q—Have you ever heard of any evidence to sustain such a charge?

A—No; I do not believe the charge.[15]

If this were to be taken at face value, Hearst in his newspapers had been willing to tell millions of the guilt of Senators whom he privately believed innocent. This was probably not quite true. It appears that Hearst was now beginning to doubt the validity of papers in which he had formerly placed blind trust, and was beating a strategic retreat. He admitted that the reason the Hearst press had deleted the names of the four Senators was "probably" because of fear of libel suits.

Ironically, as this was going on, Charles Lindbergh arrived in Mexico as a "good-will ambassador" in an effort to renew some of the friendly feeling the Hearst publications had wrecked.

[15] N. Y. *Times,* Dec. 16, 1927.

It developed that John Page, the Hearst correspondent involved, was an old hand at "documents." He had earlier tried to interest the editor of the Philadelphia *Public Ledger* in an alleged letter of the elder Senator La Follette to President Calles assuring Calles that a group of United States Senators were opposed to intervention in Mexico. The *Ledger* man suspected the letter was a fake and declined to use it. Page, questioned about this, said he had not got that letter from Ávila but from "a Mexican newspaperman." Although Page said he had talked with the newspaperman four times, he suffered lapses of memory for he could not remember the man's name, nor where he had met him, nor could he describe him.[16] Page's testimony was so evasive that Senator Reed later commented that it appeared he was not telling the truth.

It became evident that in disturbed Mexico, the forging of documents was a common practice among intriguers aiming to discredit the government and feather their own nests. Frank McLaughlin, an American engineer in Mexico, came to Washington to testify that Ávila was "notoriously known as a purveyor of forged documents." Ávila, he said, had also dealt in papers purporting to give American embassy secrets. "This traffic in documents is a business in Mexico City," McLaughlin said. "It's a regular business. You can get any kind of document you want." [17]

II. THE SEWER SYSTEM OF JOURNALISM

SENATOR NORRIS was in a sick bed at the time, but he was not too ill to write an open letter denouncing Hearst in terms dripping with contempt:

To William Randolph Hearst: A fair analysis of the recent articles in the Hearst papers showing an alleged attempt by Mexican officials to bribe United States Senators and editors of various publications, and an analysis of your testimony before the Senate committee, leads to the inevitable conclusion that you are not only unfair and dishonest but that you are entirely without honor.

. . . you are making an attempt not only to besmirch the character of some of our own officials and journalists but . . . you are trying to excite an animosity and a hatred on the part of our people against the Mexican Government, which, if your articles and alleged official documents were true, would inevitably lead to war between the two countries. . . .

The real reason why you pursued this course [of concealing the Senators' names] was to save yourself from a libel suit, and the fact that you took this course shows that you, yourself, did not have confidence in the genuineness of the documents which you were publishing, because, if they were genuine, you ran no risk in their publication. Your admission that in taking this course you had in mind the saving of yourself from damages in a libel suit is an admission that you believed, yourself, that these alleged official documents were forgeries. . . .

The ordinary observer will not cease to take notice that the four Senators

[16] N. Y. *Herald-Tribune*, Jan. 5, 7, 1928.   [17] N. Y. *Herald-Tribune*, Dec. 28, 1927.

mentioned were all prominent in the Senate in their opposition to interference by our government in the affairs of Mexico. It is rather remarkable that it is only this class of Senators whose reputations are attacked. . . .

It is likewise peculiar that Calles, the President of Mexico, would spend his hard cash to bribe Senators who were already advocating non-interference—a policy that he himself was anxious to carry out. . . .

What is your motive, Mr. Hearst? You have testified before the committee that you have very valuable properties in Mexico. It is almost common knowledge that you were in favor of the overthrow of the present government. You evidently believed that if a revolution could be started it would mean financial benefit for your investments in Mexico. . . .

In other words, for the sake of your financial investments, you were not only willing to ruin the reputation of honest and innocent men but you were willing to plunge our country into war with a friendly neighbor. . . .

The record which you have made in this matter is sufficient to place your publications in disrepute in the minds of all honest men, and it demonstrates that the Hearst system of newspapers, spreading like a venomous web to all parts of our country, constitutes the sewer system of American journalism.
—George W. Norris [1]

The Senator could be excused for believing that Hearst's motives were utterly selfish and ruthless. Ever since the strong regime of Porfirio Diaz, the friend of both Hearst and his father, Mexico had been in a state of continuous revolution that threatened Hearst's interests there, and at times he had urged American intervention. His reply seemed evasive:

. . . The plain facts of this whole Mexican matter are that these Mexican documents are *apparently* quite authentic, and that no proof whatever has been produced of their lack of authenticity. . . .

I held these documents for five months, carefully considering what was the best course to pursue. . . .

And it was only when the authenticity of the documents became *almost overwhelmingly established,* that publication began.

It is true . . . that I have property valued at approximately four million dollars in Mexico, which I had possessed in peace and security through the friendship and favor of the Mexican Government.

Certainly nobody but a perfect jackass—and Senator Norris is not that—at least not a perfect one—could imagine that my property holdings were benefited by losing the friendship and favor of the Mexican Government.

As a matter of fact, in publishing these documents there was a strong probability—in fact, the near certainty—that these properties would be confiscated at the earliest possible moment by the Mexican Government. . . .

However, I can stand the loss of these properties through the publication of the Mexican documents better than I could have stood the loss of my self-respect through the cowardly suppression of these documents out of consideration for my own interest rather than the interest of my fellow American citizens.

Finally, as for the alleged evil motives in endeavoring to reflect upon the

[1] N. Y. *Times,* Dec. 20, 1927.

insurgents in the Senate through the publication of these documents, that seems to me to be the most asinine statement that can be picked out of Senator Norris' scrap-heap of misrepresentation and billingsgate.

My papers have always been in the main supporters of the insurgent group of Senators.

Senator Borah I have had occasion to support and commend probably more than any man in the Senate.

I do not know that I have ever supported Senator Norris, but then I cannot recall that he's ever done anything worth supporting. . . . [2]

The italicized words (author's italics) indicate that by the time Hearst wrote this, he entertained doubts that the documents were authentic—possibly even knew they were not—and was trying to save face. His reasoning was specious, the same he had used in 1916 when he urged intervention in Mexico and praised his own patriotism in being willing to risk his own Mexican property for the public good. The flaw was that if United States troops were sent into Mexico, the chances were that American property there would be safeguarded. Furthermore, if American intervention came about as a result of the Hearst disclosures, it would serve notice on any Mexican government that Hearst and his property had better be treated with care.

The documents in question were given to three government handwriting experts for examination. Hearst likewise supplied three experts to join in the scrutiny—something he should have done long, long before. He obviously was forewarned of the result, for he sent this weaseling message to his editors:

If the handwriting experts should all agree that the documents we have produced bear evidence of having been fabricated, I will not dispute that decision further than to maintain persistently, and I believe patriotically, that the logic of events gives every evidence that the essential facts contained in the documents were not fabricated, and that the facts—the political facts, the international facts—are the things which are of vital importance to the American people and to the loyal representatives of the interests of the American people.[3]

Thus Hearst suggested that he was right even when proved wrong. That same day, his experts and those of the government agreed that the "Mexican documents" were forgeries and frauds, every last one of them.[4]

The documents, the experts found, contained more than 200 omitted accents, over 100 misplaced accents, eighty-six misspelled words, and "no regard to punctuation." Ávila, when given a writing test, habitually made an error that occurred repeatedly in the documents. As a Treasury Department handwriting expert said, "Anybody who would pass a consideration for these documents must have been in a very acceptable mood."[5]

[2] N. Y. American, Dec. 20, 1927. [3] Winkler, Hearst—A New Appraisal, 223.
[4] N. Y. Times, Jan. 5, 1928. [5] N. Y. Herald-Tribune, Jan. 7, 1928.

It was a sad commentary on the independence of the United States legislators that they treated Hearst with the utmost kindness and, except for Norris, none of them publicly condemned him as he deserved to be condemned. Possibly they feared his circulation, his power over voters. Norris was from Nebraska, where Hearst had no newspaper—not yet.

Hearst, who owed an abject apology to four Senators as well as to the Mexican government, subsided into silence. As a responsible journalist he was disgraced as he had never been disgraced before. His newspapers suddenly took refuge in headlines about the Hickman kidnap-murder case in California.

Mr. Hyde was in the ascendant in him during this affair. Yet the evidence suggests that Senator Norris was wrong in believing that he deliberately had the documents framed, or knew all along that they were false. Had this been true, it would seem that the forgeries would have been executed with reasonable skill and would not have contained a swarm of absurd grammatical errors. One theory is that Hearst believed in the documents because he wanted to believe in them. They represented a scoop. They would make headlines, stimulate circulation. They contained several of his pet ideas— the corruption of the Calles regime, the Japanese and Communist menace, the cupidity of American legislators opposed to intervention. One finds no proof that he did not seek to start war with Mexico. What Hearst wanted, he was prone to take, be it an antique, a castle or an idea.

Certainly he knew that the charges against the Senators would result in an investigation. He timed the publication of the latter part of the documents so that Congress would be in session and would be forced to investigate. Would he have done all this had he known that in the end it would publicly shame and humiliate him?

The case of the Mexican documents has never been satisfactorily explained, nor is it yet, unless one takes the ground that Hearst was not entirely sane at the time. He could not be defended on the ground of ignorance of Mexican affairs. For years he had kept a watchful eye on Mexico, had lawyers, supervisors and newspapermen representing him there, and was extremely well informed about the situation. Hearstman Koenigsberg blamed it on Hearst's ability to escape from reality, saying, "He suffered the penalty of an excessive faith in what he wanted to believe." [6] Silas Bent, another veteran New York newspaperman, thought it possible that Hearst reacted in an unbalanced way because he had been mortified at being beaten on the Dempsey-Tunney radio rights—so wounded over being scooped that he plunged into the Mexican fiasco out of blind determination to counter with a splash of his own. [7]

Such an exposure would have wrecked any newspaper whose readers depended on it for accuracy in the news. The fact that the Hearst circulation was not noticeably disturbed showed that his readers were not looking

[6] Koenigsberg, 458.   [7] Bent, *Strange Bedfellows*, 222.

primarily for news but were seeking entertainment and escape. A few years earlier, Hearst had said:

"There is one firm principle of mine which . . . to my mind is merely a matter of professional journalistic ethics—of common journalistic honesty.

"That principle is the right of the public to a square deal on all occasions. . . . I consider a newspaper to be the retained attorney for the public, and I believe a newspaper which is faithless to that trust is as much of a traitor as an attorney who betrays the interest of the client who employs him." [8]

[8] *Writings and Speeches*, 302.

7. Castle No. 3

A CONNOISSEUR of inconsistency, a master of the logic-tight compartment, Hearst still regarded himself as a defender of "the people." Even yet he was capable of lashing out at "the trusts." Not long before the Mexican nightmare, his newspapers had run an admirable exposé of the success of the power trust in lobbying and influencing education. But his crusades had lost the roaring zeal of the earlier days, and seemed more subject to his fickle whims. He gave no indication of realizing that he had become remarkably like the bloated, dollar-signed capitalists his cartoonists used to draw and still drew —an owner of corporations, a captain of industry jealously guarding his own interests.

This was most evident in his attitude toward taxes, which he looked on as federal pocketpicking. He fought the income tax every step of the way. Observers who noted his mode of living were unable to sympathize. Now that Citizen Hearst had given up hope for public office, spending was his chief diversion, the most dramatic way of exercising the power he lived by, and any encroachment on his spending struck at his very heart. One reason for his admiration for Coolidge was the latter's dislike for spending federal funds. But the man who became a downright hero to Hearst was exhausted-looking Andrew Mellon, Coolidge's Secretary of the Treasury.

Mellon, a fellow art collector, was a Bourbon capitalist if there ever was one. He had accomplished the miracle of lowering income taxes and surtaxes and at the same time reducing the national debt. True, he had done this at the expense of the low-income bracket, whose taxes were not reduced at all. On the plea of encouraging industry, he had slashed the levy on large incomes, inheritance and gift taxes to an extent that must have saved Hearst a cool $1,000,000 a year over the 1921 rate, and Mellon himself as much.[1] Also, according to the Couzens committee of the Senate, Mellon began his regime by saving Hearst $1,737,096 in taxes and later allowed him other tax concessions.[2] Mellon had large oil holdings in Mexico, and might be expected to do what he could to protect American interests there. Hearst was so charmed that when it became likely that Coolidge would not run in 1928, he began booming Mellon for the Presidency, calling him the "outstanding figure" of the administration.[3]

In the Senate, Alabama's Heflin, not forgetting the Mexican fakes, rumbled, "I understand Mr. Hearst had a [tax] refund of $600,000 or $700,000 in

---

[1] Harvey O'Connor, *Mellon's Millions*, 140–41. [2] Lundberg, 264 ff.
[3] N. Y. *World*, Dec. 9, 1927.

404

the last two or three years, and that he and Mr. Mellon have become exceedingly warm friends." [4] Mellon denied the refund but not the friendship. Later, Senator Caraway, chairman of the lobby investigating committee, said he had many requests to inquire into "the lobbying done by William Randolph Hearst to secure reduction in taxes of swollen incomes." [5] Nothing came of all this, but Hearst's attitude toward taxes was clear. It added to the number of liberals who had once eyed him with respect but now considered him the most transparent of renegades.

From California, Hearst ran his newspaper chain via telegrams dictated to his secretary, Willicombe, which always began, "The Chief says . . ." In Santa Monica his beach palace—legally Miss Davies'—was nearing completion and he was often in consultation with the architect, William Flannery. This palace actually consisted of five connected Colonial houses with a total of 110 rooms and fifty-five bathrooms. The main house in the center was a great three-story, U-shaped building intended for Miss Davies and himself. The other buildings were for the use of Miss Davies' parents, her sisters, other relatives, guests, and the thirty-two servants needed to keep the place going.[6] Before construction was finished, however, Miss Davies' mother, a faded little woman of great sweetness, died.[7]

Hearst, despite his necrophobia, took charge. For the quiet, self-effacing Mrs. Douras he arranged a tremendous funeral that was a theatrical production. There were hundreds of mourners, including many employes of his Los Angeles papers. The coffin was heaped with orchids and lilies of the valley. Among the pallbearers were Hearst himself, Charlie Chaplin and Harry Crocker, Hearst's favorite staff man on the Los Angeles *Examiner*. Hearst did all this to please Miss Davies.[8]

At the same time he evinced swift anger against one of his most trusted lieutenants, Moses Koenigsberg, highly-paid president of six of Hearst's news and feature services. Koenigsberg had gone to Geneva and managed to defeat an effort by other world news agencies to have the League of Nations enact a law that would make news private property. For this feat it was announced in France that he would be made a Chevalier of the Legion of Honor. Although Miss Davies had gratefully accepted the Award of Merit from the French Dramatic Academy, Hearst wrote an angry, full-page editorial suggesting the resignation of any of his employes accepting foreign decorations.

"I am distinctly and definitely opposed," he wrote, "to any representative of our newspapers or news services receiving any decorations or honorarium from any foreign government, except for patriotic services rendered America's allies in time of war." [9]

Koenigsberg, a twenty-five-year man with the Organization, knew the editorial was aimed squarely at him. Hearst's anger at France for failing to pay her war debts was well known, but this sudden spite over a mere decora-

[4] N. Y. *Times*, Mar. 9, 1928.
[6] Hollywood *Citizen-News*, June 18, 1956.
[8] Frances Marion to author.
[5] N. Y. *Times*, Dec. 7, 1929.
[7] N. Y. *Times*, Jan. 26, 1928.
[9] N. Y. *American*, Jan. 30, 1928.

tion stunned Koenigsberg. Possibly Hearst was also resentful because his lieutenant had not been deceived by the fakes that fooled him. Koenigsberg had not yet accepted the ribbon, and could still have refused it, but doubtless he felt his days were numbered anyway. He accepted the honor on February 19 and simultaneously announced his resignation. He was tendered a huge dinner at the Astor Hotel by 1500 friends, an event intended as much as a rebuke to Hearst as it was a tribute to Koenigsberg.[10]

Meanwhile, the acquisitive Arthur Brisbane, who owned millions in real estate in New York, New Jersey, Florida and California, got beyond his depth. He had borrowed $4,000,000 in 1926 to build the forty-one-story Ritz Tower apartment hotel on Park Avenue and Fifty-seventh Street. Groaning under the financial burden, he offered the building to Hearst. Both Martin Huberth and Edward Hardy Clark, already concerned over Hearst's heavy involvement in real estate, begged him not to buy it. The optimistic Hearst brushed off their objections and shouldered another huge mortgage.[11]

"Artie can't write as well with this problem on his mind," he said.[12]

In 1928 appeared the first biography of Hearst, a generally approving one written by John K. Winkler, a former reporter on the New York *American*. Such was the public interest in the enigmatic publisher that the New York *Times* gave the book a front-page review in its Sunday literary section and it enjoyed a brisk sale. A friend recommended it to Hearst, but he shook his head. "If it doesn't tell the truth it will make me mad," he said, "and if it tells the truth it will make me sad." [13]

II. TOURISM À LA HEARST

THE Democrats nominated Al Smith that summer at Houston, which was enough to make Citizen Hearst become a Republican for certain. His friend Louis B. Mayer, a loyal Hoover man, entreated him to get on the Hoover bandwagon, but the publisher had misgivings about Hoover. Tax-cutting Andrew Mellon was his choice when he attended the Republican convention at Kansas City—a blow to Mayer, for Hearst was a potent influence in the California, Illinois and Texas delegations. But when Hearst found that Mellon was out of the running, he swung over to Hoover and saw him nominated.[1]

Enlarging on a free-handed old custom, on July 20 he sailed with Miss Davies and a dozen of her feminine Hollywood friends for a Hearst-financed tour of Europe. In Paris he telegraphed Alice Head, his London magazine director, an invitation to join them for a weekend. Miss Head, properly interpreting a Hearst invitation as a command, packed a small bag and met them at the Hotel Crillon. Hearst rented automobiles for his entourage and

[10] Koenigsberg, 480–81.   [11] Mr. Huberth to author; also, N. Y. *Times*, Feb. 7, 1928. [12] Richard E. Berlin to author, Mar. 1, 1960.   [13] *American Mercury*, Nov., 1930. [1] Crowther, 136–37.

squired them on a leisurely journey to Rambouillet, Chartres, Tours, Blois, Chambord and other places, visiting cathedrals and châteaux as they went. Hearst, the castle builder, was fascinated by châteaux. He combed them for ideas he could use. In Vichy they drove around in horse-drawn victorias, the Hollywood beauties in smart Magnin dresses causing the citizens to goggle. They meandered on by automobile to Grenoble and the Riviera, stopping at Monte Carlo a few days before continuing into Italy. In all the annals of tourism, nothing could compare with a Hearst tour in cuisine, lodging and general splendor. "At each place we stopped at the most delight-ful and luxurious hotels," Miss Head recorded.[2]

She was embarrassed because the weekend had stretched out to well over a month, she had to supplement her wardrobe, and she was worried about affairs at the London office. Hearst took the young women on visits to the Italian art galleries. Despite his own familiarity with such places as the Uffizi and the Pitti Palace, he always hired local guides to aid in their instruction. He was the most intent and appreciative of sightseers. Ascending the hilltop basilica of San Miniato, he took in the splendid view of Florence and said with real enthusiasm, "One simply can't help feeling sentimental!"[3]

After six weeks, Miss Head pleaded that she must get back to her job, to which he consented. With his party he then traveled via Munich to Bad Nauheim to take the cure. Later they sailed down the Rhine to see the castles that so intrigued him, then returned to Paris.

Although some Parisians resented Hearst's newspaper attacks on France for its war-debt delinquency, Foreign Minister Aristide Briand welcomed him and Miss Davies at the Quai d'Orsay on September 19. The French achieved a realistic acceptance of wealthy men with mistresses unknown in America. Briand was one Frenchman with whom Hearst saw eye to eye, for he had criticized the Versailles Treaty, which Hearst loathed, and was working for closer ties with Germany. Two days later, Hearst was on his way to London. Simultaneously the Hearst press in America scored a clean beat by the exclusive publication of another "secret international docu-ment."[4]

Unlike the Mexican documents, this one was authentic. It was a confiden-tial French memorandum outlining the terms of a proposed Franco-British pact agreeing to a mutual naval strengthening unknown to the United States. Its publication, embarrassing to the British and French, caused an uproar in Paris. Hearst was out of reach, but the Sûreté began to probe the activities of Harold J. T. Horan, the Hearst correspondent in Paris.

In London Hearst had joined Miss Head and Richard E. Berlin, an execu-tive of his magazines who also happened to be in London. Neither Miss Head nor Berlin mention that Miss Davies and her retinue were with him at this point, whether through delicacy or the fact that they had separated is not known. In any case, Hearst had not yet seen the Welsh castle he had

---

[2] Alice Head, 117.   [3] The same.   [4] Carlson and Bates, 233.

bought three years earlier. "Let's go down to St. Donat's and look it over," he said.[5]

His intention was to restore it to medieval perfection, at the same time incorporating modern conveniences. He retained the most able and expensive architect-antiquarian-decorator available, Sir Charles Allom. Allom, a friend of Duveen's, had won knighthood for his redecoration of Buckingham Palace for George V. Hearst, Allom, Miss Head and Berlin drove the 160 miles to St. Donat's, reaching there late in the afternoon.

A servant couple lived in the small part of the castle that was habitaLie. The party got lanterns. Hearst led the way enthusiastically, going from room to room, examining dungeons, climbing turrets and becoming covered with cobwebs. He was so delighted that he refused to stop until he had traversed all of the castle's 135 rooms.[6] Villagers in the vicinity were talking about the wraith of a woman, clad in "flowing white robes," seen wandering around the castle grounds since Hearst bought it. It was assumed to be the ghost of Lady Eileen Stradling, who had lived there from 1510 to 1540 and had vowed to haunt the castle if it ever changed hands.[7] Lady Stradling did not confront the Hearst party, though they did not have dinner until 10 P.M. In the morning, Hearst was driven to Southhampton, where he caught the *Berengaria* for New York. Berlin, recalling an astonishing example of Hearst's photographic memory, says that a few weeks later Hearst, without benefit of diagrams, wrote Allom a detailed letter of twenty-five pages giving instructions for the alteration of the castle.[8]

Landing in New York, he told reporters that he favored Hoover over Smith, but spoke tolerantly. "Prohibition is a senseless issue and should not be considered in the Presidential campaign. Neither candidate has any influence on the issue. . . . Religion has so little place in politics that I refuse to discuss it. . . . I think we should have at least some regard for the framers of the Constitution, who believed in a spirit of tolerance and freedom of thought." [9]

This was Hearst at his best, enunciating principles he actually lived by. Prejudiced though he was in other respects, he was remarkably free from religious bias.

He discovered that his Paris man, Horan, had been arrested on the Rue de la Paix on October 8 and questioned rigorously for hours about the theft of the secret memorandum. The publication of the proposed treaty by the Hearst press had caused such an international furor that the treaty itself was never consummated. There was a suspicion that Foreign Minister Briand, himself opposed to the treaty, had deliberately "leaked" it in a successful effort to defeat it. Horan was quickly expelled from France, and the French police seized Monsieur de Noblet d'Anglure, a young diplomat, and Roger Delaplanque, a Paris newspaperman, charging them with passing the docu-

[5] Mr. Berlin to author.
[7] N. Y. *Times*, Nov. 25, 1928.
[9] N. Y. *Times*, Oct. 6, 1928.

[6] Mrs. Fremont Older, *op. cit.*, 460.
[8] Mr. Berlin to author.

ment to Hearst or Horan. Since Hearst was in Paris at the time of the incident, and his predilection for secret documents was well known, the Paris press angrily recalled the friendly reception given him and accused him of a "breach of hospitality." Horan denied stealing the document and said Hearst had assumed all responsibility for its publication.[10] Hearst himself later admitted that Delaplanque and de Noblet, who were ultimately acquitted, had secured the treaty for him. He insisted, however, that it had not been taken by stealth or bribery but by "good American go-and-get-it methods."

This phrase, when used by Hearst, may well be pondered, along with the fact that the Anglo-American Press Association on Paris voted to expel Horan for "unprofessional conduct." Jules Sauerwine, writing in *Le Matin*, called Hearst "this indelicate megalomaniac" and urged that he be barred henceforth from France.[11]

Hearst moved on to Washington to have another chat with Coolidge and with Secretary of State Frank Kellogg—not about the French commotion, he made plain.

"I consider Mr. Horan's arrest and expulsion a domestic matter," he said. "There is nothing, in my opinion, that the United States can do in the circumstances. I think, however, that the French authorities are acting like spoiled children." [12]

He may have discussed business with the President, whose term was drawing near its end and who would soon write for Hearst's *Cosmopolitan* the story of his life and other pieces, including an explanation of his famous phrase, "I do not choose to run." Hearst admired Coolidge although they disagreed on one point. Hearst, always in favor of the soldiers' bonus, could never convince him that the bonus was not a raid on the treasury.

Indeed, Hearst was becoming a confirmed President-visitor. Ten weeks after the inauguration, he and Mrs. Hearst were White House luncheon guests of the new President and Mrs. Hoover. Hoover could scarcely have forgotten that Hearst had never been enthusiastic about him, possibly in part because he had lived for a time in England, and because he had served under Wilson. In 1924, when Hoover was Coolidge's Secretary of Commerce, the Hearst press had accused him of turning valuable government fisheries in Alaska over to a friend, which he angrily denied. Perhaps these things were in the President's mind, for he was not his usual genial self at the luncheon. He did not seem really glad to see the publisher, who left with wounded feelings.[13]

III. GOD BLESS AMERICA!

In California, Hearst found both of his local castles progressing well. Until he built in Santa Monica, the beach homes of Joseph Schenck and others had been considered the ultimate in splendor. Perhaps he derived a puckish glee out of erecting a pile that made his neighbors' places seem like summer cot-

[10] N. Y. *Times*, Oct. 10, 11, 12, 1928.
[12] N. Y. *Times*, Oct. 12, 1928.
[11] Quoted in N. Y. *Times*, Nov. 14, 1928.
[13] Mrs. Hearst to author.

tages. Seventy-five woodcarvers had worked for a year on the balustrades alone of the Hearst-Davies place. As he did at San Simeon, Hearst followed a practice of building to accommodate antique rooms he had imported bodily from Europe. The main dining room, reception room and drawing room, each more than sixty feet long, all came from Burton Hall in County Clare. Most of the thirty-seven fireplace mantels were from stately English homes. A rathskeller on the lower level had been an inn in Surrey, dating back to 1560.[1]

It took a special kind of skill and imagination to embody old rooms in new construction, and Hearst had it. His penchant for display also came out. It was said that the main building had "more columns across the back than the Supreme Court building in Washington," and they reflected in a 110-foot swimming pool lined with Italian marble. The Pacific Ocean was on the other side of the house, but it was impossible to keep the sea at an even temperature. The mural wallpaper in the Marion Davies suite alone cost $7,500.[2]

It happened that Will Rogers owned a small piece of adjacent land that Hearst wanted for a tennis court. Hearst, who had known Rogers since the *Follies* days, sent Realtor Merritt to ask the price. It was impossible in this instance to conceal the fact that Hearst was the one interested. Rogers said he did not want to sell, and backed this up by putting an outrageous $25,000 price on it. Merritt told Hearst of this. "Well, offer him $20,000," Hearst said.

Merritt did so, whereupon Rogers raised the price to $35,000. Hearst then made a bid of $30,000. The humorist went up to $45,000. One wonders whether Rogers was annoyed with Hearst for some reason, but at any rate it was apparent to Merritt that Rogers was having a game at Hearst's expense and he urged Hearst to do without the land. But Hearst was determined to have it. He kept making bids until at length he got the plot for $105,000.

"Pleasure is worth what you can afford to pay for it," he said philosophically to Merritt.[3]

Still seeking a workable plan that would do away with the lawlessness of Prohibition and yet assure reasonable temperance, he conducted a contest for such a plan in his papers, awarding a $25,000 prize to the winner. For his pains he was assailed by the Anti-Saloon League's Rev. F. Scott McBride, who said, "The so-called Hearst plan is no more than a liquor-selling plan." [4]

Herbert Hoover, out of gratitude to Louis B. Mayer for his support, had the Mayers as his first informal White House guests after the inaugural, and Hearst gave the Mayer visit a full column in his New York *American*. This was the sort of treatment that delighted the publicity-loving Mayer. It made up for certain disadvantages in his arrangement with Hearst. Of the films Miss Davies had made since coming to M.G.M.—*Lights of Old Broadway, Zander the Great, Beverly of Graustark, The Red Mill* and *Quality Street*— only the first had made money. It was growing hard to coax exhibitors to

[1] Los Angeles *Examiner*, Mar. 4, 1951.   [2] Hollywood *Citizen-News*, June 18, 1956.
[3] Mr. Merritt to author.   [4] N. Y. *Herald-Tribune*, June 4, 1929.

take her films. At a Culver City sales meeting, Mayer gave one of his fiery pep talks and then asked if there were any questions.

"Yes," said one of the salesmen. "I would like to ask why do we handle the pictures of Marion Davies?"

To Mayer, this was near treason. Nonplussed for a moment, he spoke of Miss Davies' artistry, of her friendship with Hearst, and of the valuable publicity the Hearst press was giving all M.G.M. pictures. This set him off on a ringing speech about the greatness of Hearst. He told how Hearst's father had survived hardships in the gold-rush days to end up with honors and a seat in the Senate. He traced Hearst's own history, from his turbulent boyhood to his ownership of the nation's greatest chain of newspapers, and became carried away by his own enthusiasm.

"This," he told the salesmen, "is what I want to impress upon you gentlemen. This is the spirit that has made America great. We live in a land of opportunity! God bless America!"

His eyes dampened. "Does that answer your question?" he demanded.

"Yessir," the offending salesman said hastily.[5]

While most critics agree that Miss Davies did not have talent of the first rank and that her acting was often studied, it is likely that Hearst unwittingly destroyed the gay spontaneity that made her so charming in real life. He viewed her as his own creation. He was insistent about her roles. He wanted her to play nothing but romantic young heroines and to appear in a succession of gorgeous or appealing costumes before spectacular sets. He could make directors tear their hair, stopping action and cameras as he went up with suggestions for making Miss Davies appear to better advantage. His weakness for mawkish sentimentality, and his refusal to let Miss Davies grow up, was a frequent trial to the scenarist, Frances Marion. Miss Marion had a heart-to-heart talk with him about that. She pointed out that Miss Davies was a grown woman and that she must play mature roles.

Hearst seemed to agree in principle, but he could not shake off the little-girl conception. Sometime later, he said, "Don't you think it would be a cute little scene if we showed Marion milking a cow?"

Miss Marion lost her patience. "Marion is no longer a little girl milking a cow, W. R.," she snapped. "We can't go on dreaming up these silly things for her." [6]

Although Miss Davies was nearing thirty, he denied her maturity, nor would he allow her to portray a mother. She had to fulfill his virgin image of her. Occasionally she grew restive under this restraint. She had a wistful feeling that she could portray certain dramatic roles, and once she made a strong effort to coax him to let her play Sadie Thompson in *Rain*. Hearst threw up his hands in horror. He would not permit her to play a prostitute.[7]

Her screen career was his property, but she had her way in most other respects. She called Hearst "Pops," and in her uninhibited way would tousle

[5] Crowther, 125-26.   [6] Miss Marion to author.   [7] Evelyn Wells to author.

his hair and fling affectionate insults at him, which amused him greatly. Ilka Chase, who had a role in one of the Davies pictures, noted Miss Davies' attractive habit of blinking as she stuttered, and her informal attitude toward Hearst, whom everybody else on the lot treated with deference and some awe. Once, when she was having lunch with a group of friends at the Bungalow, she telephoned Hearst, who was in Mayer's office, urging him to join them. "Oh, c-c-come on over, W. R.," she said, "and I'll give you a b-b-big k-k-k-kiss." She hung up, saying pleasantly, "The old b-b-bum," and Hearst dutifully made his appearance.[8]

While it would be an exaggeration to say that he mistrusted her, it was noted at the studio how excessively he *worried* about her when she was out of his sight. It was usual for him to telephone frequently to assure himself that she was where she was supposed to be, a surveillance that she took with good humor. Once, when she was in conference with a writer, Hearst telephoned. She passed a few words with him, then said cheerfully to the writer, "Well, Hearst come, Hearst served." [9]

When the Graf Zeppelin made its world flight in 1929, Hearst supplied most of the financing—a promotional scheme he plugged hard in his newspapers. After crossing the Pacific from Japan, the zeppelin made it a point to fly low over San Simeon en route to Los Angeles. In Los Angeles on August 27, Hearst gave a congratulatory banquet to Dr. Hugo Eckener and his passengers, with President Hoover as one of the honored guests.[10] Hearst, who at times could be extremely thin-skinned, seemed unable to forget the unfavorable impression he had got at the Presidential luncheon, and he never held the warm esteem for Hoover that he held for Coolidge. Neither of the two men knew that prosperous America was on the brink of its most disastrous business depression.

Big-domed Arthur Brisbane, whose salary was now $200,000 a year, was likewise unaware of it, although many believed that he knew everything. In his column *Today*, read devoutly by millions, he gave an impression of erudition and infallibility. On October 4, he wrote, "Uncle Sam continues to be prosperous. . . . It is a big, rich country." [11] He sounded another cheery note on October 22, when Wall Street took a sudden skid. On October 24 the bottom dropped out of the market. Brisbane wrote brightly three days later, "Stock gamblers may worry, but there is nothing the matter with national prosperity." [12]

IV. BRISBANE WAS WRONG

It seemed that Brisbane was wrong, for once. Hearst himself joined the army of experts who felt they knew the answer to the paralysis gripping the country. In an open letter to President Hoover printed in all his newspapers, he said, "Lack of confidence is contagious; but, on the other hand, so is con-

[8] Ilka Chase, 108.   [9] Private source.   [10] Mrs. Fremont Older, *op. cit.*, 479.
[11] N. Y. *Journal*, Oct. 4, 1929.   [12] N. Y. *Journal*, Oct. 27, 1929.

fidence contagious." He urged Hoover to make "some reassuring utterance," along with taking "vigorous action in stimulating the legitimate activities of the Federal Reserve . . ."[1]

He had gone through panics in 1893 and 1907, and probably saw no reason why this one should be any worse. It did not seem to enter his mind that the depression could affect him personally to any degree. His inborn optimism excluded that kind of doubt. He had never saved a dime for a rainy day. He had been the world's biggest spender and he continued being the world's biggest spender, a colossus marching straight for the abyss.

In New York he added the Hotel Lombardy to his ownership. Hardly a month passed that did not see him increase his realty holdings, continuing right on into the depression. By now he held title to almost $50,000,000 in New York real estate alone.[2] The mortgages he was meeting were vast. He was advised against this, but his financial men had always advised him against overextending himself and he had come to regard their warnings as the groundless fears of little men. Even the warm-hearted but tough John Francis Neylan, who was high in his confidence and was known as his only "No" man, could not say "No" loudly enough to stop him. "Hearst and I had innumerable quarrels about his expenditures," Neylan later said.[3]

In gratitude to Oglethorpe for his LL. D., Hearst gave the university 400 acres of land and a gift of $100,000.[4] In Wales, Sir Charles Allom was pouring a fortune into St. Donat's Castle with the installation of an enormous banquet hall, Elizabethan and Jacobean paneling, bathrooms by the dozen, a swimming pool and three tennis courts. Special attention was given to Hearst's own room, a study in scarlet with antique red paneling, lacquer cabinets and a great bed bearing an engraved silver plate attesting that Charles I had slept in it in 1645. The silver service at the castle cost a quarter million dollars.[5] Many antique pieces that had earlier been shipped to the United States for possible use at San Simeon or Hearst only knew where, were now sent back across the ocean for use at St. Donat's. Jokesters said a large part of the world's tonnage was used in shipping Hearst oddments back and forth across the seas. As a collector he was never deterred by occasional setbacks. His Spanish cloister, for example, had given him nothing but trouble. After great difficulties, it had been shipped to New York, its 36,000 stones carefully packed in straw in 10,700 crates. In New York, government inspectors quarantined the lot because the straw might carry the dreaded hoof-and-mouth disease. Each crate had to be destroyed, the straw burned, and the stones later repacked in hygienic material. By this time the project had cost almost $500,000, and Hearst did not know what to do with the cloister, so it was stored in his Bronx warehouse, where it remained for years.[6]

Miss Davies' beach palace at Santa Monica had finally been finished, at

[1] N. Y. *American,* Nov. 15, 1929.   [2] M. F. Huberth to author.
[3] Mr. Neylan to author, Jan. 21, 1960.   [4] N. Y. *Times,* July 7, 1929, May 19, 1930.
[5] Mrs. Older, *op. cit.,* 461–63.   [6] Saarinen, 75–76; N. Y. *Herald-Tribune,* Aug. 17, 1952.

a cost of $3,250,000. With the antiques, silver service and objects of art Hearst installed in it, it was estimated to have cost a total of $7,000,000.[7] In the great dining room he added a touch of his own—a dozen full-length oil portraits of Miss Davies as she appeared in *Knighthood, Janice Meredith, The Red Mill* and the other screen roles on which he had lavished almost as much attention as she.[8] His castle at Wyntoon, in far northern California, had recently been destroyed by fire, and he was planning a better one there. But when all was said and done, it was San Simeon that was nearest to his heart, the childhood dream that he was realizing with his energy and his millions.

Excepting Miss Davies and Mrs. Hearst, the most important woman in his life was a quaint, schoolmarmish little thing of uncertain age who wore Queen Mary hats, horn-rimmed glasses and old-fashioned, rustling clothing. This was Miss Julia Morgan, the architect and Beaux Arts graduate who had been a friend of Phoebe's. Together Miss Morgan and Hearst had worked on San Simeon since 1919. She had dedicated her career to the fulfillment of his dream—not entirely a hardship, for she grew wealthy at it. Yet Hearst was a demanding employer, and she was probably one of the few architects alive who could have submerged her own instincts for design, balance and decoration and made herself an instrument for the accomplishment of his plans. Hearst was fond of her. San Simeon was the supreme challenge of his life, and when she came down from San Francisco for a few days he would give her his undivided attention to the neglect of whatever guests were present.[9]

It was almost as if Hearst subconsciously realized that his newspapers were trashy, his political life a failure, even his motion pictures not entirely successful, and was determined that in San Simeon, if nothing else, he would leave an enduring monument to his greatness.

When he and Miss Morgan had started, Camp Hill was an almost treeless eminence rising 2000 feet above the Pacific. Now the sentimental Hearst had renamed it La Cuesta Encantada (The Enchanted Hill), and its bareness was replaced by four Spanish and Italian edifices containing treasures from all over the world and surrounded by a paradise of horticulture. The three "guest houses," each of them palatial in size and grandeur, were finished first —La Casa del Monte, La Casa del Sol and La Casa del Mar. Now, in 1930, the *pièce de résistance,* the king of castles—La Casa Grande—towered over the three smaller ones. It was not finished, and in fact never would be. Hearst, a man fascinated, would continue to add to it as though it were impossible for him to stop.

Since 1919 there had always been from twenty-five to 150 men working at San Simeon. In warm weather Hearst was concerned lest the workmen overexert themselves, and would occasionally send a couple of servants out with pitchers of lemonade which the crew would drink gratefully as they took a breather.[10] According to his lights, he sought perfection

---

[7] Providence *Journal,* Jan. 3, 1960.
[9] Richard E. Berlin to author.
[8] Irene Castle, *Castles in the Air,* 215.
[10] Peter Sebastian to author.

regardless of cost. Once as he drove up his private road from the highway (six miles long) he was dissatisfied with the impression he got of one of the sub-palaces as he gained the top of the rise. Although it was well along, he had it torn down and built some distance away.[11] With Miss Morgan he had pored over drawings of the twin towers that would surmount La Casa Grande, and had approved the final plans. When the towers were completed, he was unhappy about them. They were too stark, too severe. The towers were torn down at great expense and replaced by the fretwork-ornamented towers seen today.[12] As in his newspapers, Hearst sought impact and sensation in his architecture. He shunned the sedate, the calm, the classic. He loved the ornate, the baroque, the medieval. One wonders whether at first Miss Morgan had moments of rebellion against his untrammeled flair for decoration. If so, she quelled it, and rightly so, for San Simeon, with all its faults, became an architectural representation of Hearst. It was significant that after he left New York and became a Californian again, his political hopes in ashes, he renounced his sober black fedora and broadcloth and took up with noisy plaid sport jackets, colorful Hawaiian sport shirts and two-toned shoes.

One reason why San Simeon was difficult and expensive was that it was not built from scratch to suit certain living needs, but was a mosaic of Hearst's memories, inspirations and possessions. In his card-index memory he had recollections of decorative schemes and arrangements he had seen in European castles and cathedrals, and which he wished to incorporate in his own palace. In his New York warehouse and in huge basement crypts at San Simeon he had the antique accumulation of years—entire gothic rooms, carved ceilings, choir stalls, paneling, staircases, corbels, stained glass, sarcophagi, mantels, columns, tapestries, a thousand other things—which he was determined to make a part of his castle. Thus, San Simeon was not only a vast construction project but also a complicated assembly job that kept Hearst and Miss Morgan in repeated sessions of close consultation. The castle was not so much a home as it was a museum, a setting for Hearst. The recent addition of a wing gave the Casa Grande alone more than forty bedroom suites, all filled with antiques and works of art. Miss Morgan was on an annual budget that allowed her to do so much work a year, and although the budget was generous there were years of work ahead.[13]

Another budget-eater was the crew of twenty or more gardeners under Nigel Keep, a gnarled Englishman and a horticulture expert. Many of the plantings had to be blasted from solid rock. A whole row of thirty-foot cypresses was moved from Paso Robles, thirty miles over the mountains, a job that required elaborate boxing and took two years before the trees were growing in Hearst's terrace. Hearst could not bear to see a tree cut down. It cost thousands to move each of several oaks that were in the way of construction. By 1930 the once-bare hilltop was an arboretum of countless trees, both

[11] Princess Pignatelli to author.   [12] Nigel Keep to author, Oct. 15, 1959.
[13] N. Y. *Times,* July 1, 1929.

common and rare. Once Miss Morgan sighted along a line of plum trees and shook her head. "That one is three inches out of line," she said. Keep's men moved it three inches. Hearst kept eyeing the bare hill to the landward where the reservoir was located.

"Mr. Keep, that bareness bothers me," he said. "Could you plant pines there?"

Keep knew better than to tell him something could not be done. "I can try, Mr. Hearst," he replied, "but it will be costly."

"Never mind the cost. Do it." [14]

A road had to be built through the wilderness and up the hill, and pines had to be dragged on sleds by tractors. But the job was done, though Keep shuddered at the expense.

Movie moguls by the score had visited San Simeon, but there were also calls by the great and near great. In 1929, Winston Churchill, who was writing for the Hearst papers, visited the M.G.M. studio and also spent a few days at San Simeon. While he was there, Hearst and Neylan, conferring in the assembly room, were startled when a maid rushed in distractedly.

"Mr. Churchill is fainting," she cried as she hurried past them. "He wants some turpentine."

Hearst and Neylan ran out on the terrace. Churchill was sitting there placidly before his easel, puffing at a cigar as he painted a landscape. It turned out that he had asked a gardener for turpentine to thin his oils, and when the gardener relayed the message to the maid she had thought he said Mr. Churchill was fainting, not painting.[15]

When Mr. and Mrs. Calvin Coolidge visited San Simeon in 1930, dress was worn for the first time at the usually informal castle. Miss Davies, Brisbane and Richard Berlin were among those present when a butler brought out a loaded silver tray and Hearst asked the former President if he would have a cocktail or an aperitif.

Coolidge, the soul of brevity, said, "I don't drink."

"Neither do I," Hearst nodded. "But I find that a sip of this wine is an excellent appetizer."

"Is it alcoholic?" Coolidge inquired.

"Not perceptibly. The alcoholic content is slight."

Coolidge took a glass of Tokay, tried it, and his eyes brightened. He had another. "I must remember this," he said.[16]

Miss Davies later admitted that she was bored. All the men talked about, she said, was "their G-G-Goddam circulation." [17] Annoyed by the frequent gossip that she and Hearst had children, she thereafter occasionally astonished guests by referring with apparent gravity to "my son by Coolidge." [18]

One would have thought that if the Yankee Coolidges would accept the Hearst-Davies arrangement, anyone would, but this was not so. There were a few old-fashioned or high-principled souls who refused to visit San Simeon.

[14] Mr. Keep to author.   [15] Mr. Neylan to author.   [16] Mr. Berlin to author.
[17] Ilka Chase, 117.   [18] Private source.

Among them was the Catholic Neylan, who would come alone on business but would not bring his family. Gay as she was on the surface, Miss Davies at heart resented her equivocal position and never would stop resenting it.

Hearst tried to make it up to her by giving her everything she wanted, by surrounding her with a riot of riches and luxury such as no queen or mistress in history had ever known. No one had any suspicion that he was running short of money. In a sense he was not, but that was because he was borrowing just when he should have been retrenching. Already various units of the Organization had borrowed some $60,000,000 in bond issues. Now Hearst Consolidated Publications floated another $50,000,000 in stock.[19] That made a total of $110,000,000 that had been borrowed, much of it to supply the Chief with spending money.

[19] N. Y. *Times,* July 7, 1930.

8. War with France

I. TOURISM À LA HEARST

In June, 1930, Hearst was entertaining a party of friends and associates at San Simeon when he decided on a trip to Europe. Always the perfect host, he invited all of his guests who could do so to accompany him at his expense. What was described as a "large party" took him up on it, among them Miss Davies and some of her friends, Secretary Willicombe, Editor Coblentz and Harry Crocker.[1] Coblentz and Crocker were favorites of Hearst, who set great store by companions who could keep him amused. Crocker was a wit and Coblentz a mimic who could do side-splitting imitations of everything from Coolidge's nasal twang to the linguistic peculiarities of executives in the Organization. What Hearst did not know was that on occasion (when the Chief was not present), Coblentz did devastating imitations of the high-pitched Hearstian voice delivering judgments to his satraps.

The party landed in Southampton June 27, spent the weekend in London, then went to St. Donat's Castle. For the first time, Hearst saw the new interiors and bathrooms fashioned by Allom, and found them good. Never having outgrown his love for fireworks, he ordered a huge assortment of rockets and whiz-bangs for the night of July 4, along with a man to fire them. To the English, July 4 was just another day, and it was later learned that Hearst's rockets had alarmed mariners all along Bristol Channel.[2]

After a month at the castle, the party, joined by Miss Head, crossed to Paris and then went on to Bad Nauheim. Hearst had gained weight until he was noticeably portly. He was counting on the baths to reduce poundage at the same time as the doctors checked his heart. His dozen companions likewise took the baths (at Hearst's expense) and studied German with the help of instructors (provided by Hearst) while waiting for him. The Bad Nauheim treatment included a three-day rest period between sessions in the baths. Hearst made use of this by escorting his troupe on a boat ride up the Rhine to the Drachenfels. Miss Head marveled at his buoyant energy.

"On these trips Mr. Hearst is just like a boy out of school," she wrote. "He makes me feel at least old enough to be his mother. He jokes with the boatmen and the itinerant musicians, does a little yodeling on his own account, and buys wooden animals and carved inkstands, and gaily coloured scarves and sweaters, and sweets and wines and cheeses—whatever there is to buy, in fact, and all the time tells us in the most interesting way the history of all the places that we visit."[3]

Hearst loved Germany. Its medieval atmosphere and its *gemütlichkeit*

---

[1] Mrs. Older, *op. cit.*, 505.   [2] Alice Head, 141.   [3] Head, 143–44.

touched a responsive chord in his own nature and doubtless had much to do with his Germanophile tendencies.

After a month at Nauheim, the doctors gave him the usual instructions—another four weeks of rest and light recreation known as the "after-cure." He went with his companions for a sojourn in the Italian lake district, then returned to Paris to rest at the Crillon. He had hardly registered there on the morning of September 1 when a polite French official arrived to tell him he must leave the country within four days. According to the government announcement, "This measure . . . has as its origin the role played . . . by Mr. Hearst in the obtention and publication of a secret document relating to the Anglo-French naval negotiations." [4]

Hearst had not been molested during his earlier stay in Paris. However, while in Germany he had given an interview to the *Frankfurter Zeitung* in which he characteristically assailed the Versailles Treaty and the "domination" of Germany by France and other countries, which may have increased the Gallic ire. In a huff, he refused to wait four days but took the next boat train with his party for London. He immediately declared a private war on France which would last much longer than the late hostilities, leading off with a satiric manifesto from the Savoy Hotel:

I have no complaint to make. The French officials were extremely polite. They said I was an enemy of France, and a danger in their midst. They made me feel quite important. They said I could stay in France a little while longer if I desired, and they would take a chance on nothing disastrous happening to the Republic.

But I told them I did not want to take the responsibility of endangering the great French nation, that America had saved it once during the war, and I would save it again by leaving it. . . .

The reason for the strained relations—to use the proper diplomatic term —was the publication of the secret Anglo-French Treaty two years ago by the Hearst papers, which upset some international "apple carts," but informed the American people. . . .

I think, however, that the general attitude of the French press toward our opposing the United States entrance into the League of Nations, or any protective pact to involve our country in the quarrels of European powers, is mainly responsible. Also there might have been some slight irritation at the occasional intimations in our papers that France, now being the richest nation in the world, might use some of the German indemnity to pay her honest debts to America, especially because if it had not been for America she would now be paying indemnity instead of receiving it.

But being a competent journalist and a loyal American makes a man *persona non grata* in France. I think I can endure the situation without loss of sleep. . . .   —William Randolph Hearst.[5]

In this epistle, although it had bite to it, Hearst almost gained a lightness of touch that would have been useful in his war with Al Smith. He was far

[4] N. Y. *Times*, Sept. 3, 1930.   [5] N. Y. *Times*, Sept. 3, 1930.

more effective when he poked fun than when he poured acid. The letter was intended mainly for home consumption, for the ejection of a man as prominent as Hearst from France was front-page news in America. He enjoyed being front-page news, and he took steps to stay on the front pages as long as possible. In all conscience he should have gone to St. Donat's for a leisurely after-cure, but he seemed to forget all about the after-cure. His sudden newsworthiness apparently revived a hope for the Presidency that he had all but abandoned. He took the time to have lunch with Lloyd George, also a Hearst writer, and to buy the Elizabethan great chamber of Gilling Castle in Yorkshire, for which he paid "in six figures," and arrange for its shipment to St. Donat's.[6]

He sent not one but two cables to his New York executives insisting that he did not want any "public demonstration" when he returned.[7] When he reached New York on the *Europa,* there *was* a demonstration and he did not appear in the least annoyed. He was met at Quarantine by a steamboat festooned with welcoming signs and containing two bands, a large deputation of disabled veterans, Veterans of Foreign Wars, and legislators including Senator Robert F. Wagner and Representatives Bloom, La Guardia, Celler, Lindsay, Dickstein and Sirovich.[8] Americans, quick to resent any aspersion on the national honor, were almost unanimous in their condemnation of the French for ejecting Hearst, although many were fuzzy on the technicalities involved. Hearst had become an accidental hero. Tears came to his eyes at the cheers, the band music, the warmth of the greeting. He dearly wanted to be popular, and nothing like this had happened to him since long before the war.

"America is the home of truth and light," he told his welcomers. "To tell the truth in France is to be shooed out of the country, and if you tell the truth in Russia you are lucky if you get out with your life." [9] Then he brought out a statement he had just happened to prepare:

> I have said that I did not complain of my exclusion from France.
> I think I should say instead that there is no distinction in my sixty-seven years which has given me more genuine gratification. Moreover, I hope and believe that this distinction is one I have actually deserved.
> For nearly fifty years I have been active in journalism. I take the obligations of my profession very seriously. I think a newspaper owes a great debt to the public, and that the newspaper's first duty is to keep its public fully and accurately informed. . . .
> This I have always tried to do, and the action of France in my case is, I consider, merely conspicuous recognition by a great nation of the honorable fact that I have done my full duty to my own people and to my chosen profession. . . .
> France has tried persistently to seduce the American press . . . [by] the widespread distribution of the little red ribbon of the Legion of Honor.

[6] N. Y. *Times,* Sept. 6, 1930.
[8] N. Y. *American,* Sept. 16, 1930.
[7] Coblentz, *Hearst,* 98–99.
[9] N. Y. *Times,* Sept. 16, 1930.

Many American newspapermen have been caught by this little red ribbon as guilelessly as bullfrogs are hooked by a bit of red flannel, but I have never allowed any members of my organization to accept civil decorations from any foreign country, or to put themselves or my papers under any obligations to any foreign government.

Indeed, I think Congress should forbid the wearing of foreign decorations by American citizens, except military decorations honorably won in war.

If our bourgeois aristocracy wants some recognition of achievements not sufficiently conspicuous to be known without advertisement, let Congress create a Right Royal Brotherhood of Super-Americans, and confer BLUE ribbons, like the prizes at a horse-show, and so keep American loyalty at home. . . .[10]

He said that the secret Anglo-French treaty would have been injurious to America, and that in publishing it and thereby foiling it the Hearst press had done the nation a service. He had a point there, although he was on less sure ground when he said that the treaty "was not secured by any devious or indirect methods."

II. NO PUBLIC DEMONSTRATIONS, PLEASE

THE Hearst press greeted the Chief as a charter member of the Brotherhood of Super-Americans. "W. R. Hearst Welcomed Home By Statesmen and Veterans," read a front-page headline in the *American*, which carried a six-column photograph of Hearst being greeted at the pier and another two-column close-up showing him grinning and holding the American flag.[1] His good friend Senator Copeland said indignantly, "It is clearly the duty of the administration to make effective protest against the action of France."[2] This was not so. It was a well-recognized right of nations to exclude foreigners regarded as undesirable. The United States would have been within its rights to complain, but could go no farther than to lodge formal protest. However, Hearst himself had made no complaint to the State Department. Two years earlier, his man Horan had not only been sent packing. He had been arrested in Paris and subjected to twelve hours of intensive questioning by the police. At that time Hearst had called it "a domestic matter" and said, "There is nothing . . . that the United States can do in the circumstances." Now that he himself was the victim, though treated far more gently than Horan, he conveniently forgot his 1928 attitude and became a happy martyr.

Hard as he tried, Hearst could not avoid the public demonstrations he disliked. He took to the radio for the first time in his life and assailed the Hoover administration for taking this insult lying down. Assuring his listeners that he did not want to "magnify the incident," he added, "I still think that if Theodore Roosevelt had been alive, or Grover Cleveland had been

[10] N. Y. *American*, Sept. 16, 1930.   [1] N. Y. *American*, Sept. 16, 1930.
[2] Hearst, *Writings and Speeches*, 274

alive, you would have heard little of W. R. Hearst, to be sure, but you would have heard much about the value and validity of the American passport and of due and necessary respect for the rights and liberties of the American citizen." [3]

Then, in his anxiety to avoid magnifying the incident, he went on a triumphant cross-country tour. It began in Boston, where he was that city's guest at its tercentenary celebration and was extolled by Mayor Curley. Next came Chicago, where he was feted in the biggest peacetime reception the city ever accorded, although 15,000 Chicago Polish-Americans protested, calling him an "international trouble-maker." Hearst rode with his Anglophobe friend Mayor Thompson in a red touring car at the head of a vast parade, with fifty bands, that ended at Soldier Field, where he addressed 100,000 cheering citizens on the subject of Franco-Hearst relations.[4] Then came a great official reception in Los Angeles, where thousands of "Hearst-for-President" buttons were mysteriously distributed. He professed astonishment at this, saying, "I know nothing about it, and do not approve of it. I am not a candidate for any public office." [5]

Perhaps his most enthusiastic reception came in his natal city of San Francisco. Here, the Board of Supervisors voted down one of their number, cynical Warren Shannon, who opposed extending Hearst a formal invitation, saying, "The idea is ridiculous. All it amounts to is Hearst inviting himself to visit the city. The invitation, of course, has been arranged by his representatives." [6] Hearst was met by Mayor James Rolph, and honored at the city hall and the St. Francis Hotel, where his address was broadcast over an N.B.C. network. Again he extolled the Hearst press for its "public service" in defeating the secret treaty.

"What I want you to understand, my friends," he said, "is that no dishonorable means were employed in obtaining the treaty. . . .

". . . we did not disguise ourselves as plumbers and rifle the government files.

"We did not bribe any public servants.

"We did not slide down any rain-pipes to steal anything.

"We just used some of the good American methods, the good California methods that I had learned in early days on the San Francisco *Examiner. . . ."* [7]

He still had another reception to attend next day, across the bay in Oakland, where he ended his speech by saying, "I am going to board a train and go down to my ranch and find my little hideaway on my little hilltop at San Simeon, and look down at the blue sea and up at the blue sky, and bask in the glorious sunshine of the greatest State of the greatest nation in the whole world." [8]

[3] N. Y. *Herald-Tribune,* Sept. 29, 1930.
[4] William H. Stuart, *The Twenty Incredible Years,* 432.
   [5] N. Y. *Times,* Oct. 17, 1930.   [6] Carlson and Bates, 240.
   [7] San Francisco *Examiner,* Oct. 17, 1930.   [8] S. F. *Examiner,* Oct. 18, 1930.

A little hideaway on a little hilltop . . .

All along his tour his newspapers had boomed him as they had in the earlier days when he was running for office. The *Examiner,* for example, gave him five columns on the front page plus *all* of pages 10, 11, 12 and 13 for the San Francisco celebration alone.

"Hearst for President" buttons now began appearing in St. Louis. Along with his picture, they bore the legend, "100% American—No Foreign En-tanglements—Independent in Everything—Temperance, not Prohibition." [9]

It is not known that Hearst sponsored the buttons. But he did squeeze every headline, every parade, every cheer, every drop of public drama and personal publicity that he could out of what was really a minor brush with French officialdom, to a point where it became more than a trifle ridiculous. At any rate, the French imbroglio was unfortunate in that it came at the wrong time. The next Presidential election was two years off, and not even Hearst could keep this gaseous balloon aloft until 1932.

He retired to his hideaway and was silent for five weeks, as though those very misgivings might be running through his mind. Then he issued a dis-claimer of any desire for office, pointing out that he was sixty-seven and did not want to add to his labors.

"I have had my day in politics," he wrote. "It was not a very long day, nor a very brilliant one, but it was sufficient to convince me that my best oppor-tunity for achievement was in supporting principles and policies and not in holding public office." [10]

Hearst also wrote a little note to his valet, Joseph Yellinek:

"Joseph—Don't ever get me socks or anything else made in France." [11]

Shortly thereafter, at 2 o'clock in the morning, Mortimer Berkowitz got a call from San Simeon at his New York apartment. Berkowitz had taken A. J. Kobler's place as general manager of the immensely profitable *American Weekly* and also was in charge of selling a small amount of advertising that appeared in the eight-page Hearst Sunday comic section. At that time the comic section carried no advertisements except before Christmas, when there were a few insertions by makers of dolls and electric trains.

Hearst's high-pitched voice came over the wire. He never had any qualms about arousing his executives at any hour of the night. He did his best think-ing at night, and was accustomed to translating his thoughts into immediate action.

"Mr. Berkowitz," he said, "why don't we carry advertising in the comic section?"

"We do carry a little, Mr. Hearst," Berkowitz replied. "But there are only a limited number of companies manufacturing merchandise for children."

"Mr. Berkowitz, don't you know that the comics are read by a great many adults?"

Berkowitz paused in surprise. "That never occurred to me, Mr. Hearst,"

[9] N. Y. *Times,* Oct. 23, 1930. [10] N. Y. *American,* Dec. 1, 1930.
[11] Coblentz, *Hearst,* 101.

he admitted. "But now that you mention it, I know that *I* read the comics."

"Look into it, Mr. Berkowitz, please. There's a great advertising potential there." [12]

Berkowitz sent men out to canvass readers. He learned that more than eighty percent of the adult readers enjoyed the comics—a much larger percentage than could be depended on to read other sections of the Sunday paper. He promoted his discovery to advertisers. Within a few years he and his staff were selling $7,000,000 a year in advertising in the comic section, and his salary, plus bonus, exceeded $250,000 a year.

"Mr. Hearst was sometimes difficult to work for," he later remarked, "but most helpful and appreciative. He knew more about all phases of his business than any of his executives." [13]

[12] Mr. Berkowitz to author, Mar. 1, 1960.   [13] Mr. Berkowitz to author.

9. Influences Malign and Benign

I. A WORLD OF MADNESS

To work for a publication in which Hearst was dissatisfied was to enter a world of madness and pressure that had about equal parts of humor and futility. He was always under pressure for money and success, and this pressure poured down through the echelons with hydraulic force. When the New York *Mirror* was trying, and failing, to catch up with the *Daily News,* its top men went through motions that could hardly be reconciled with sanity.

One of the peculiar things about the *Mirror* was that although it was a Hearst paper, it pretended for a time not to be. One reason for this was that there were already two Hearst papers in New York, and advertisers were reluctant to "spend money in the same place"—to duplicate their space in publications under the same ownership. Another was the unpopularity of Hearst among some wealthy advertisers. His ownership was concealed under a fictitious proprietor, as was done in a few other Hearst cities. When Albert J. Kobler was removed from the *American Weekly,* he formally "bought control" of the *Mirror,* but was actually only a front man for Hearst.[1]

Kobler was emblematic of top-level Hearst executives both in wealth and insecurity. He had taken over advertising supervision of the *Weekly* when it was merely a great success and had made it a literal gold mine. Commissions brought his salary as high as $450,000 a year. Shrewd investments made him a millionaire. He built a large apartment building on upper Park Avenue and, like Hearst, made the top floors into his own aerie. Also like Hearst, he collected art, books and autographed letters. He wore English clothes, rode in a Minerva limousine behind a chauffeur, and was afraid of losing his job.[2] There was some sarcastic comment in the Organization that he was setting himself up as a sub-Chief. It may be that Hearst himself was annoyed by this imitation, for Kobler was one of the few top men who suffered the kingly displeasure. Despite his good work, Hearst came to believe that the *Weekly* could do even better in Berkowitz's hands, so Kobler was given the dirty job of breathing life into the *Mirror.* He managed to get the paper out of the red, an achievement in itself, but this by no means satisfied Hearst because the *Daily News* was still far in the lead.[3]

The *Mirror* had frankly announced that it would dispense ten percent news and ninety percent entertainment. The idea was to make it a sort of printed sideshow of curiosities, scandals and sensations.

[1] Koenigsberg, 349–50.   [2] Gauvreau, 137.   [3] Bessie, 144.

Kobler wanted to hire Editor Émile Gauvreau away from the New York *Graphic,* which he had made the wildest counterfeit in American journalism. He took Gauvreau to see Hearst, who was at his wife's Long Island castle opening crates of antiques that had recently arrived. Gauvreau helped him open crates as Hearst drew him out on a variety of subjects, obviously seeking a line on his knowledge and ability. Gauvreau found him keen, quick, decided in opinion, and was immensely impressed. ". . . I had never met a man of more diversified interests," he noted. "He was endowed with a fascinating charm." [4]

Hearst took Kobler and Gauvreau in his limousine to town, where he intended to buy art. Here Gauvreau got a sample of the Hearst pressure when the publisher turned to Kobler and said, "Remember, Albert, that you are in the position of a man who has moved into a house after buying it under a mortgage. And I'm the man who holds the mortgage." [5]

Gauvreau was hired to edit the *Mirror* at a $25,000 salary, and was given a $10,000 bonus. He discovered that Walter Howey, Hearst's favorite newsman from Chicago, was editing the paper and had not been told that Gauvreau was succeeding him. This was one of Hearst's peculiarities—an unwillingness to tell an editor that he was being replaced. He left this up to underlings who were often afraid to do so. Howey, a brilliant screwball, was busily hatching ideas to gain circulation—a yo-yo contest, to be spurred by a photograph of Mayor Walker twirling a yo-yo, and a Blotto contest, in which participants would squeeze blobs of ink between paper. Gauvreau found it embarrassing because he and Howey sat in the same office, each of them thinking he was editor of the *Mirror,* and it was some time before Howey got the drift and was moved to another post in the Organization. [6]

Three men were reading and tabulating all back issues of the *Daily News,* to see what the *News* had that the *Mirror* did not. The *Mirror* launched a $40,000 prize contest in daily picture puzzles. Both Mrs. Hearst and Miss Davies were contributing occasional ideas to gain circulation, Mrs. Hearst suggesting the use of many small newsy items. Miss Davies, however, arranged to get the confessions of Alma Rubens, the silent film star, which scored a 65,000 circulation gain. [7] Gauvreau, who had some lingering fidelity to news as news, found himself furrowing his brow over stunts to attract the public.

"It seemed incredible to me," he wrote later, ". . . that I should be earning a salary approaching $30,000 a year in a pursuit in which I had come to see nothing but a waste of one's time. I had accumulated circulation by pushing into the back of my mind all that I had learned about the value of constructive news. . . . Outsmarting a competitor in a deal involving a comic strip was of greater consequence to mass readership than years of training in interpreting significant happenings. Signing up the exclusive serv-

[4] Gauvreau, 139.   [5] The same, 141.   [6] Gauvreau, 144-45.   [7] Gauvreau, 160.

ices of 'Mickey Mouse' in New York was considered a master stroke. . . ." [8]

Gauvreau, who knew what he was getting into, should not have been surprised. When the Lindbergh baby was kidnaped, Kobler felt that if the *Mirror* could rescue the baby alive, and give the feat proper promotion, it would be the biggest circulation-gainer in history. Gauvreau and some of his newsmen hurried up to Canada to consult with some gangsters who claimed they knew the tot's whereabouts. The plan, which took little account of the distraught parents, was to bring the child back and present him to Mayor Walker on the City Hall steps as *Mirror* cameramen recorded the scene in a deathless scoop. The gangsters, it turned out, were lying. [9] Soon Arthur Brisbane, doubtless needled by Hearst, was breathing down Kobler's neck, demanding more circulation.

Brisbane, now in his sixties, was most famous for his daily column, but actually he was Hearst's No. 1 man on the editorial (i.e., circulation) side, a classic example of a man who had started out with some ideals and had fallen headlong into Wall Street. He had married late and had six children. Money was so much on his mind that on meeting people for the first time, he would often say, "I'm delighted to meet you, sir. Did you know that Hearst paid me $260,000 last year?" [10] He liked to make estimates of the millions he had made for Hearst. He wrote more than 500,000 words a year. Occasionally he could let slip remarks indicating some illogical resentment toward Hearst for dragging him out of journalism's holy upper levels and into its purely merchandising stratum. His old paper, the New York *Journal*, was noted for its Goodie List—people who, on Hearst's orders, were to be mentioned only in flattering terms—and for its S-List of persons to be mentioned only with scorn. At one time the *Journal* had 2000 names on its S-List, Al Smith being always at the top. A reporter, Carl Helms, was kept busy simply reading over each issue and making sure that the two lists were rigidly observed. [11]

Brisbane himself went out to Hopewell, New Jersey, to cover the Lindbergh case, and spoke to Sydney Boehm, a *Journal* reporter.

"Under no circumstances," he told Boehm, "are you to disturb the Lindbergh family."

He then picked up the telephone and called Hopewell 7, the Lindbergh number. "This is Arthur Brisbane," he said over the wire. "I'd like to come over and talk with you." There was a pause. Then he said, "I don't think you heard me. This is *Arthur Brisbane* speaking." A look of amazement came over his face. "Are you sure," he demanded, "that you understand that this is Arthur Brisbane?" There was another pause, after which he slammed down the receiver angrily and turned to Boehm.

"You need not take the order about disturbing the Lindberghs too literally," he said, and stalked out. [12]

There was little love lost between Brisbane and Kobler. When Brisbane

[8] Gauvreau, 174.   [9] Gauvreau, 168.   [10] *Saturday Evening Post*, Feb. 28, 1942.
[11] Sydney Boehm to author, Oct. 29, 1959.   [12] Mr. Boehm to author.

began to "move in" on the *Mirror*, Kobler's days were numbered. He suffered complete disaster. He lost his fortune in the stock market, and then was dismissed from the Organization for his failure to overtake the *News*. Brisbane himself took over the *Mirror*, after which its Hearst ownership was no longer a secret. Kobler, formerly intensely loyal to Hearst, was thereafter an embittered man who could speak of the once-revered Chief only in imprecations.

Now Brisbane was on the firing line, receiving occasional tart messages from Hearst pointing out the slowness of his progress. Young John Hearst, the Chief's third son, was learning the business at the *Mirror*, joining in editorial wrangles about circulation and wanting to know why the *News* was so far ahead. Brisbane worked feverishly to find his old circulation magic. One of the answers seemed to be more columnists. Soon the *Mirror* was crammed with what Westbrook Pegler called "gents' room journalism," containing the daily writings of Walter Winchell and eight others.[13] Still the *News* was far ahead, and Brisbane became a man possessed. With his belief in the superiority of blue-eyed men, he raged because so many *Mirror* staffers had non-blue eyes. Occasionally he would confront Gauvreau and say, "What do you propose to do about circulation?"[14]

Reading of two girl lumberjacks in Idaho who had won a wood-chopping contest, he ordered Gauvreau to arrange their transportation to New York. They were met by *Mirror* men, who took them in hand. Taken to Central Park and given axes, they displayed their prowess to effete New Yorkers while *Mirror* photographers snapped them and *Mirror* reporters faithfully took down their impressions of metropolitan life. Even this failed to bring a noticeable boost in circulation.[15]

Brisbane smashed the desk with his fist and said, "By God, if they want slush today, they're going to get it!"[16] He located and hired Mrs. Marie Manning Gasch, who thirty-five years earlier had run the "Beatrice Fairfax" column with great success in the old *Journal*. Now in her sixties, she was put at the head of a "love and marriage" department to amplify Brisbane's new circulation keynote: "Get married, have a baby and buy a car!" This was unsuccessful, according to a cynical *Mirror* lieutenant, because although the rising generation was excited about cars, it had little interest in babies except in how to avoid them. Brisbane, under constant pressure, left for San Simeon to confer with the Chief. En route with his retinue of secretaries, he peppered Gauvreau with circulation-building ideas, one telegram reading:

Perhaps love and marriage page needs a discussion. Is man or woman more intensely affectionate? Keep away from anything dealing too closely with sex. Find out whether impulse toward other sex and toward marriage and children is stronger in women or in men. I think it ten times stronger in

[13] Bessie, 152.   [14] Gauvreau, 220.   [15] *Saturday Evening Post*, Feb. 28, 1942.
[16] Gauvreau, 221.

women, more insatiable for biological reasons. Get important person, prefera-
bly clergyman, to say that. Put question to well-known men and women,
actors and actresses, motion-picture people. Perhaps some movie lady, divorced several times, could be considered an authority. Perhaps a better
authority would be someone who married and stayed married. Keep this on
high plane. Use pictures of those interviewed but for God's sake don't use
photographs of horrible looking men like Rev. Dr. Cadman or the long-
nosed Mr. Durante. . . .[17]

Brisbane hired more "stars." He discharged people on whims. He fired
Frank Farley, a political writer, on Christmas Eve after writing an editorial
on the wonderful character of Christ. Actually the *Mirror* was doing fairly
well, touching a sizeable 600,000 circulation, but the *News* doubled that and
the theory was that since the metropolitan area had almost 20,000,000 people
there was no reason why the *Mirror* should not snag at least a million of
them. The "love and marriage" theme flopped. Brisbane was catching it
from Hearst, one of his telegrams reading:

"Dear Arthur, you are now getting out the worst newspaper in the United
States." [18]

II. THE HEARST PLAN FOR RECOVERY

THOSE unaware of Hearst's dual nature could not believe that a man who
published such insubstantial newspapers could have a patriotic concern
for the welfare of his country. He did. The depression, which got worse
instead of better, worried him. He retained remnants of his sympathy for
the common man, confused though it often was with self-interest. Always a
man of action, he began to snipe at Hoover for his failure to act.

Hearst had a recovery plan that did him credit, for it was liberal, eco-
nomically sound and opposed to the thinking of most of his fellow millionaires. Indeed, in his sublime inconsistency, it was opposed to much of his
own thinking. He wanted the government to make an immediate appropriation of $5,000,000,000 to give public-works jobs to the unemployed. He took
to the radio to read Mr. Hoover a lesson.

The depression was caused, he said, by enormous over-capitalization
which had stolen billions from small investors when the crash came.

"If profits had been distributed in wages, prosperity would have been
maintained and increased," he went on.

". . . A gigantic appropriation, not for a dole, but for the employment
of a vast amount of labor at the prevailing rate of prosperity wages, would
not only stabilize wages but immediately set the machinery in motion for the
restoration of prosperity.

"Mr. Hoover . . . has discussed the situation understandingly. Still,
neither the procedure nor the proposals of the administration have been on
a scale at all commensurate with the magnitude of the problem. The gov-

[17] Gauvreau, 223–24.   [18] Gauvreau, 236.

ernment has not been devoid of knowledge. It has merely been inadequate in action."

He even took shots at his old tax-reducing friend, Secretary Mellon, whom he now saw as misguided in his continuing efforts to lower the national debt. "[This] is the time to increase the national debt and increase the expenditures of the government in public works in the employment of labor and thereby increase prosperity. Then, out of prosperity, to pay off the debt." [1]

This was the thoughtful, constructive Hearst speaking. Conservatives shuddered at the idea of adding $5,000,000,000 to the national debt, although a few years later five billions would come to mean much less.

The publishing world was astonished in 1931 when Ray Long, editor of *Cosmopolitan* and editor-in-chief of all Hearst magazines, resigned his $185,-000-a-year job.[2] The small, dapper Long had been a Hearst favorite, the most famous and successful magazine editor of the day. The catch was that Long had not really resigned. Insiders knew that he had resented the authority of a magazine board headed by Richard Berlin, and had lost out in a battle of strength with Berlin. It was also known that he could not have been forced out without Hearst's permission.

The departure of Long raised a flurry of nerves among the other magazine editors. Even more than usual in the Organization, they felt insecure in their jobs. Herbert Mayes, then editing Hearst's *American Druggist,* noticed a general feeling of fear, particularly among business personnel, that he later described as "an office reign of terror." [3]

The staff felt duty bound to give Long a farewell dinner. Yet they worried lest this be construed as taking Long's side. All the top magazine executives refused the job of being toastmaster, fearful that it might impair their standing. They handed Mayes the toastmaster job, as Mayes later recalled, "because I was the least important editor at the time and nobody worried much about what might happen to me." [4]

Hearst finally sold his luxury yacht *Hirondelle,* which had been tied up in Brooklyn unused for years. In June he left for Europe, taking with him Miss Davies and a party of friends whose expenses he paid. He would not permit economic troubles to disturb his regal way of life. He took the cure at Bad Nauheim, then went to Rome for a visit with Mussolini, for whom he conceived a great admiration. "He is a marvelous man," he later wrote of Il Duce. "It is astonishing how he takes care of every detail of his job." [5]

He was careful to avoid hostile France, crossing to England via Holland for a stay at St. Donat's. Here he had Lloyd George as a guest, and for a

[1] N. Y. *American,* June 3, 1931.
[2] N. Y. *Herald-Tribune,* July 21, 1931. Three years later, Long, unsuccessful in the movies, shot himself dead in Beverly Hills. Victor Watson plunged to his death from a hotel window. Harry Payne Burton, later editor of *Cosmopolitan,* died of an overdose of sleeping pills.   [3] Mr. Mayes to author, Jan. 14, 1960.   [4] Mr. Mayes to author.
[5] Letter to Mrs. W. J. Chalmers, Chicago Historical Society.

time conducted his American enterprises by cable and transatlantic telephone. It was said that when the exchange operator at the nearby Welsh village of Llantwit-Major got her first Hearst request to call Los Angeles, she fainted.[6] Hearst returned with his entourage in September on the *Europa,* which also had among its passengers Charles Evans Hughes, the man he had called "an animated feather duster" exactly a quarter-century earlier.

He came back gripped by several fixed notions. One was increasing rage at our former Allies—especially France—because of their failure to pay their war debts. Another was that his five-billion pump-priming plan should be effected immediately. A third was the virtual certainty that Europe was preparing for another war. Right or wrong, he acted on his beliefs. Over the radio, he warned the nation that its folly in becoming embroiled in the World War should never be repeated.[7] He began an anti-war campaign in his newspapers, including a "Mothers of America" movement, united against war. To San Simeon he invited Kathleen Norris and her husband. Mrs. Norris, a San Franciscan, had started with Hearst's *Examiner* in 1908 and later had become a "regular" in his *Cosmopolitan.* She was at the table with a large group as Hearst outlined his crusade to prevent another war, including his effort to enlist mothers by the millions. To her, his sincerity was unquestionable.

"Chief," she said, "if there is anything I can do for the movement—any writing or any service whatever—I'll do it."

He smiled. "Mrs. Norris," he said in his high voice, "you've just been made national president." [8]

He became a walking anti-war propagandist. At M.G.M. he became interested in a picture Walter Wanger was making, *Gabriel Over the White House,* and arranged to have it scheduled as a Cosmopolitan production. He dashed off in longhand some extemporaneous dialogue for it, showing an eerie example of the Hearst prescience:

> The next war will be a terrible story of the . . . horrifying destructiveness of modern agencies of war. Navies and armies will be destroyed from the air, and as these airplanes destroy navies and armies, they will destroy cities, they will destroy populations. Peace and faith are necessary among men, not merely for the welfare of nations but for the very existence of nations. The next war will depopulate the earth. Invisible poison gases, inconceivably devastating explosives, annihilating death rays will sweep to utter destruction not only the men but the children who would constitute another generation and the mothers who would bear them. Unless man's God-given faculty for utilizing the forces of nature for beneficent purposes shall surpass their vicious genius for destruction, the race of man shall perish from the earth and the world will be left to the less destructive, less cruel and less stupid wild animals.[9]

[6] Mrs. Older, *op. cit.,* 463–64.
[8] Kathleen Norris to author, Oct. 19, 1959.
[7] N. Y. *Times,* Sept. 13, 1931.
[9] Crowther, 179.

III. A BOMB FOR MISS DAVIES

As Hearst grew older, time became more valuable, life more precious. He had Walter Howey, now back in Chicago, check carefully on all news stories about scientific advancements in the prolongation of life, and send him reports. He was much interested in the monkey-gland transplantations performed by Dr. Serge Voronoff for rejuvenating the elderly. When a Chicago millionaire had such a transplantation, Hearst inquired occasionally to find if it did him any good.[1] An old king with a young consort, he dreaded time, decrepitude, death. He became annoyed as he came down a slow elevator in the Santa Monica beach palace and growled to Willicombe, "Have it torn out and a faster one put in."[2]

Although he did not slow down a particle, he worried about a successor. His three older sons held executive positions in the Organization, but they were still young. The talk had it that he was grooming John Francis Neylan for the purple—Neylan, the only man who could say "No" to him and get away with it. Neylan could say "No," to be sure, but not always successfully, as evidenced by his frequent lectures about easing up on spending.

Hearst could not stop spending. He invited a crowd of screen folk to celebrate July 4 at the beach house, and bought $10,000 worth of fireworks for the event. As it grew dark it also grew chill, and Hearst was in a pet because everybody went inside to dance instead of watching his fireworks.[3] He and Miss Davies ordered a thick rug, specially woven at a New Jersey factory, twenty-four by a hundred feet in size so that it would exactly fit the beach house second-floor theater and improve the acoustics for sound pictures. When it arrived in Los Angeles, Homer Watters, an *Examiner* man often assigned to attend the Chief's wants, drove to the beach house to inform the Chief. Either Hearst had forgotten about the rug or was in no mood to be bothered with it.

"I didn't order any rug," he said. "Please send it back."

Watters sent the rug on its long return trip. Two days later Miss Davies called him, said of course they had ordered the rug, and asked him to get it back. Watters conferred with the Santa Fe Railroad people, who traced the rug, located it in a boxcar in Albuquerque, and brought it back again. It was so large and heavy that a portion of a side wall had to be removed from the house while a derrick hoisted it in.[4]

Hearst decided to enlarge the marble-lined swimming pool at the beach house. Realtor Merritt ventured that the pool was a big one as it was.

"I think it will look better larger," Hearst said, "and it will give work to unemployed men."[5]

The pool was enlarged. One of the laborers on the job was a slightly-built

[1] John Dienhart to author.
[2] George Merritt to author.
[3] Frances Marion to author.
[4] Homer Watters to author, Nov. 6, 1959.
[5] Mr. Merritt to author.

young man of college age. "He's not strong enough for this heavy work," Hearst told the foreman. "Have him report to the gardener." The young man did so and was put to work tending flower beds and was also sent to night school at Hearst's expense.[6]

With his uncanny memory, Hearst could remember scores of individual reporters on his various newspapers, particularly those who had impressed him with their handling of a story. On a Hollywood newsbreak, he called Warden Woolard, editor of the Los Angeles *Examiner,* and asked him to put a reporter named Jack Mitchell on the story. Woolard replied that Mitchell was seriously ill with what had been diagnosed as Hodgkin's disease. At Hearst's expense, Mitchell was sent north to a San Francisco specialist, who confirmed the diagnosis. Mitchell's days were numbered.

"We must make sure that he has peace of mind," Hearst said to Woolard. "See if his insurance is in order, and if he owes on his home or any other bills. We'll take care of it for him." [7]

Like all actresses, Miss Davies received fan mail from admirers all over the country. Far and away her most devoted fan was Clark Alvord, an aging one-time hard-rock miner who had become postmaster of the hamlet of Nelson, Nevada. Alvord had heard of her many charities, which added to his admiration of her as an actress. Although he had never known her except on the screen, he sent her frequent letters couched in misspelled but heartfelt phrases of worship which were duly answered by her secretary.

Because of her endless generosities, she probably had more sincere admirers than any other film heroine. As Christmas of 1931 approached, the usual flood of gifts arrived at the beach house for Miss Davies, who had an impulsive habit of opening some of them in advance. The butler opened one addressed "Personal only to Marion Davies." Smoke issued from it as he removed the outer wrapping. He hastily tossed it outside, where sheriff's officers later examined it and found it to be a crude but dangerous powder-filled bomb that could have killed or maimed had it not misfired.[8]

Coming east that winter, Hearst stopped in Chicago, where C.I.O. union men were picketing his newspapers for some grievance. Pickets soon paraded around the Drake Hotel, where Hearst stayed, bearing signs emblazoned with "Hearst is an Anti-Union Coward" and similar inscriptions. Hearst, clad in a tweed greatcoat, came out the Walton Street door to see a pint-sized young picket, wearing a thin jacket, shivering as he marched with his sign. He walked over to the picket.

"Son, you're freezing," he said. "This trouble will be straightened out, but there's no use your catching pneumonia."

He took off his greatcoat and put it on the undersized youth, engulfing him. Then he strode over to his taxicab.[9]

A few months later, Hearst, who for two years had begged employers not to cut salaries and had not done so himself, laid skillful plans for a combined

[6] Mr. Merritt to author.   [7] Warden Woolard to author, Nov. 4, 1959.
[8] N. Y. *Times,* Dec. 22, 1931.   [9] Harry Reutlinger to author, Nov. 10, 1959.

newspaper-publicity campaign aimed at goading Congress to act for the relief of the jobless. He ordered his editors to get memorials from governors, mayors, legislators and other leaders in all parts of the country, listing the extent of joblessness in their areas. These memorials would be given to Congress and would be backed by a Hearst-paper news and editorial crusade. He wrote to Mrs. Winifred (Annie Laurie) Bonfils, the aging sob sister who would write some of the articles:

> . . . the papers should have . . . articles of a general character calling attention of Congress and the country to the extent of unemployment and the injury to the individual and the nation that this continuing and growing unemployment creates . . . but I do not want to print a great mass of a dispiriting and discouraging kind. I am afraid this would aggravate the situation and alarm the general public. We want the public to be interested and aroused, but we do not want them to become panicky. . . .[10]

This was Hearst definitely in his Dr. Jekyll aspect.

[10] Fremont Older Papers, letter of May 7, 1932.

10. Hearst the President-Maker

1. THE MAN WHO WASN'T THERE

> . . . I have no political ambitions.
> In fact, if anybody tried to give me a political office I
> would murder him and would consider the deed justifiable
> homicide. —Hearst [1]

HEARST meant this. At long, long last, he had given up the dream of office, admitting to himself that he would never be anything more than plain Citizen Hearst. But he would never give up offering the nation and the world the benefit of his counsel, or give up pulling the strings that manipulated power. To the distress of Louis Mayer, he had quit on Hoover. He urged the Republicans to make Coolidge their candidate in 1932, but when it became plain that Hoover would be renominated, he went over to the Democrats and came out strongly for Speaker John Nance Garner, the Texan who had been in Congress with him a quarter-century earlier.

But first he gave Garner a searching examination. He sent his Washington political analyst, George Rothwell Brown, to interview the Speaker about the issues Hearst considered vital. The *big* question, of course, was whether Garner could keep his prominent nose out of Europe. Garner passed the examination with flying colors. He opposed foreign entanglements, opposed canceling the war debts, and was sound on finance and the tariff.[2]

Shortly thereafter, Hearst startled the nation by taking over the N.B.C. network and booming Garner.

"Unless we Americans are willing to go on laboring indefinitely merely to provide loot for Europe," he said, "we should personally see to it that a man is elected to the Presidency this year whose guiding motto is 'America First.'"

Garner, he said, was the man—"a loyal American citizen, a plain man of the plain people, a sound and sincere Democrat; in fact, another Champ Clark." [3]

The address caused a political sensation. No one had previously regarded Garner seriously as Presidential timber. It disturbed Colonel E. M. House, Wilson's old adviser, who was pulling for Governor Franklin D. Roosevelt of New York. House, seeking Hearst's support, declared that Roosevelt was not an internationalist. Hearst demanded proof.

[1] Coblentz, *Hearst*, 123. [2] Coblentz, *Hearst*, 126–28.
[3] N. Y. *American*, Jan. 3, 1932.

"He [Roosevelt] made his numerous declarations publicly when he said that he WAS an internationalist," he wrote.

"He should make his declaration publicly that he has changed his mind and that he is NOW in favor of keeping the national independence which our forefathers won for us; that he is NOW in favor of not joining the League or the League Court.

"I must say frankly that if Mr. Roosevelt is not willing to make public declaration of his change of heart, and wants only to make his statement to me privately, I would not believe him. . . ."[4]

Exactly two days later, Roosevelt in a public speech declared that he did not favor American participation in the League—further proof of the power of Hearst and his press. Joseph P. Kennedy, a leading Roosevelt sponsor, did his best to bring the publisher around.[5]

But Hearst, not quite trusting Roosevelt's lukewarm repudiation of internationalism, was already hard at work for Garner. He had Brown write a glowing biography of Garner, which was published in instalments in the Hearst press. He enlisted William Gibbs McAdoo of Los Angeles and others in an effort to secure the California delegation for Garner—something political observers thought impossible, for the Speaker was little known there while both Roosevelt and Al Smith had strong support. "Hearst was seeking political revenge against Al Smith," wrote one of his colleagues, Thomas Storke.[6] While this was certainly a strong motive, he was not impelled exclusively by his thirteen-year-old hatred for Smith. He would fight to the death the nomination of any candidate tainted by internationalism.

Hearst's leadership alone was responsible for the astonishing feat of capturing California for Garner when the state was considered strictly a battle between Smith and Roosevelt. He contributed heavily to the primary campaign, boomed Garner in his four powerful California papers, and amazed everybody by winning.[7]

At the age of sixty-nine, the Shepherd of San Simeon, widely believed a political has-been, had a rendezvous with history whose profound importance to the nation not even he could realize or foresee. He personally named a President merely by speaking a few words into a telephone—just the way he liked to do things.

In 1932, for the first time in almost three decades, Hearst did not attend any national convention. He stayed at his little hideaway on his little hilltop. But those who thought that he was not at the Democratic convention at the Chicago Stadium in spirit or by representation were mistaken. Damon Runyon and many other Hearst writers were there. More important, Hearst's own alter ego, the efficient Joseph Willicombe, was there. One can be sure that Willicombe was frequently on the telephone, informing the Chief of every move, rumor and ballot.

[4] Hiram Johnson Papers, letter dated Jan. 21, 1932.
[5] Charles A. Beard, *American Foreign Policy in the Making*, 99.
[6] Thomas M. Storke, *California Editor*, 299.   [7] Storke, 301.

George Rothwell Brown, however, was kept in Washington, which surprised and disappointed him, for this was the first convention he had missed in many years. He did not understand the reason until later.

When the convention got under way, Roosevelt had 666 votes on the first ballot, well short of the 770 needed for the nomination. Smith was second and Garner a poor third. On the third ballot, with New York and other delegations holding solidly for Smith, Roosevelt had gained only a trifling sixteen votes. James A. Farley, Roosevelt's campaign manager, was in a sweat. Another deadlock on the fourth ballot, he knew, would mean that many Roosevelt delegates would slip away—would switch to Smith, or to Newton D. Baker, Wilson's Secretary of War.[8]

What Farley needed desperately was the Garner bloc—Texas with its forty-two votes and California with forty-four. Tears were in his eyes as he spoke to McAdoo, leading the California delegation, and several colleagues.

"Boys," he said, "Roosevelt is lost unless California comes over to us on the next ballot." [9]

Farley telephoned San Simeon in an effort to get Hearst to persuade Garner to release his delegates. Hearst refused to talk to him.

The reason was that Hearst already was setting large wheels of his own in motion. From Willicombe's reports it was obvious to him that Garner had little chance but that his eighty-six votes in California and Texas loomed as a deadlock-breaking power bloc that could swing the nomination to Roosevelt or away from him. If Hearst could manipulate the Garner bloc, he could name Roosevelt as the candidate. He was not enthusiastic about Roosevelt, but the alternative—horror of horrors!—was the S-List Smith or the Wilson-loving, internationalist Baker. The question was, would Garner give up his own slim chance?

Over the wire, Hearst first swung his power club over several Roosevelt managers in Chicago. Would Roosevelt, if elected, eschew any meddling in Europe, any internationalism? They assured him almost tearfully that he would.[10] He then telephoned instructions to Willicombe in Chicago. Willicombe relayed them to Hearst's man Brown in Washington. Next morning, Brown visited Garner at his office and and conveyed Hearst's message. Would Garner release his delegates to Roosevelt? It has been denied that Garner was offered the Vice Presidency in return, which would be surprising if true. Garner, of course, knew that he owed Hearst the strength that he had. He thought it over and agreed. He telephoned his decision to Chicago.[11]

Since 1904, Hearst had personally attended a half-dozen conventions of both major parties, sometimes with power and votes on his or his candidate's side, without affecting the outcome in the slightest. Now, in 1932, he stayed away—and decided the convention, the candidate, and the future of the nation.

That evening, on the fourth ballot rollcall, McAdoo strode to the micro-

[8] James A. Farley, *Behind the Ballots*, 21–24.   [9] Storke, 316.
[10] John Francis Neylan to author, Jan. 21, 1960.   [11] Coblentz, *Hearst*, 134.

phone and uttered historic words: "California casts forty-four votes for Franklin D. Roosevelt." [12]

That did it. Hearst, for the first time in his long life, had named a President—one that he did not particularly want. Most observers also believed that he had named Garner as Vice President. Al Smith, an embittered man, took the next train home, possibly wondering whether his remarks years earlier about Hearst and his Mud-Gutter Gazette had cost him the Presidency.

II. A NATIONAL CURIOSITY

THAT fall, Hearst went to Cleveland to have the eminent Dr. George Crile perform an operation on his throat. "Dr. Crile says he has been doing operations like mine for years," he commented, "and has never had a fatality. Of course I do not want to spoil such a good record." [1] From Cleveland he wired Fremont Older (collect) his judgment of the soon-to-be-defeated Hoover:

"Vote for Hoover and lose your job" has been the result of the first four year experiment with that gentleman. There is no reason to think that another four years would bring anything different as long as there were any jobs left from which people could be discharged or any homes left from which they could be evicted.[2]

For a period—very brief—Hearst rose above the suspicion and execration in which he had been held and assumed the aspect of a National Character. He had been a good boy for several years. He put the popular Roosevelt in the White House and continued to support him. Even many who despised his politics and journalism, and disapproved of his well-known arrangement with Miss Davies, came to hold a grudging admiration for his courage, vigor, and freedom from false modesty in his perfect assurance that he knew what was good for the country. For an oldster, it was a caution the way he got around America, around the world—the way he poked his nose into every issue and delivered tart or humorous judgments on them. You never knew where he would turn up next with a sensation, true or false. It might be in America, Mexico or Europe, but you could be sure that somewhere the old rascal would pop up with a headline-maker. He had been vilified, exposed, discredited and humiliated a thousand times, but he had a hide like a rhinoceros, showing not a wound, still considering himself a national leader (as he miraculously was), still ready to fight it out with any enemy. He never straddled the fence. Whether he was right or wrong, you always knew exactly where he stood, and as a phrasemaker he was simply unexcelled.

To most Americans, Hearst was a legend, a mystery, but nevertheless a vivid and eloquent spokesman for Hearst. He was pig-headed, arrogant, cocksure, sometimes wrong. Yet he stood out like Gibraltar in his insistence on

[12] Farley, *Behind the Ballots*, 25.   [1] N. Y. *Times*, Oct. 23, 1932.
[2] Fremont Older Papers, dated Oct. 23, 1932.

independent utterance. He was unique, an American phenomenon. Indeed, there was no one like him in the whole world. Now he had reached a new estate. He *made* news whether he wanted to or not. Competing newspapers, even though mistrust still lingered, followed his wanderings and reported what he did and said because he was invariably interesting even when he was dead wrong.

But Hearst could never go for long without saying or doing something to arouse wrath. His stay out of Coventry would be short.

Later that year, there was an emergency meeting of Hearst executives at San Simeon. The Organization was in trouble. Business had stagnated. Advertising income had sunk from $113,000,000 to $40,000,000 annually, a frightening loss in revenue.[3] With his incorrigible optimism, Hearst had kept thinking that the depression soon would be over.

Now Neylan knew that drastic measures were imperative. He was angered because he felt that Hearst's lieutenants were too willing to "go along" with the Chief. Even though they were in closer contact with day-to-day business and did not really share his optimism, they were reluctant to risk incurring his wrath by advising economy and retrenchment, things they knew he temperamentally disliked. Although he claimed to despise yes-men, they knew how he loved to run his own business, and how unpleasant he could be to an executive who had the temerity to disagree with him.

"Most of Hearst's top executives were cowards," Neylan later said. "They drew enormous salaries, bought homes on Park Avenue, then spread out to country places on Long Island, and before you knew it they became yes-men because they felt they had too much to lose to argue with Hearst. In times of stress, with a few notable exceptions like Tom White [Hearst's general manager] their loyalty was very thin."[4]

Now, while the executives waited in another room, Hearst and Neylan discussed the problem. The tall Neylan, lucid in reasoning and cogent in speech, argued that there was no choice but to practice rigid economy and retrenchment, including a cut in salaries. He later described the scene:

"The idea of a pay cut was absolutely repugnant to Hearst," he said. "He had preached against that very thing. He wanted to stick by his guns. He said, 'Jack, I'd rather go broke than do that.'"

Neylan demonstrated that there was no other solution. He took his own cut first—one-third of his retainer. Hearst reluctantly agreed. A general pay cut was decided on between Hearst and Neylan. Then they joined the waiting executives and told them of the decision that had been made without their help. It was a vivid example of how little influence they had on company policy when the chips were down.[5]

If Hearst himself took a pay cut, it was not discernible. He was conducting a "Buy American" campaign in his newspapers, which caused some ironic comment about the fortune in foreign antiques he had installed at San

[3] John Francis Neylan to author, Nov. 5, 1959.
[4] Mr. Neylan to author, Oct. 13, 1959.   [5] Mr. Neylan to author.

Simeon and his employment of Italian artisans to set the blue-and-gold Venetian mosaic tiles in his million-dollar indoor swimming pool.

When he lacked ready money, he borrowed it as if his resources were limitless. In March of 1933, he went to a Los Angeles bank for a loan of $600,000, putting up San Simeon as security. Roosevelt's bank holiday blocked the loan temporarily. It happened that Harry Chandler, publisher of the Los Angeles *Times* and long a Hearst enemy, was a stockholder in the bank. Chandler put up the cash personally. Hearst got his money, unaware that he had given a mortgage to a formidable rival.[6]

He celebrated his seventieth birthday at San Simeon with Arthur Brisbane and a flock of executives and friends there to honor him. Although he was still at war with France, he bought through an agent $8,030 worth of stained glass from the abbey at Fécamp, which he was embarrassed to discover had been stolen from the abbey, whereupon he returned it and got his money back.[7] His throat was well enough in December of 1933 for him to lace into Al Smith over an N.B.C. microphone handily installed at San Simeon. Smith had criticized Roosevelt's monetary policy, which Hearst proceeded to defend, labeling Smith a "Morgan agent." Referring to Smith's hostility to Prohibition and his skill at vaudeville, he said, "Mr. Smith is all right in some ways. He is wet and he does a good song and dance. But in this instance it would seem that he is all wet and is giving the public the song and dance."[8]

But if Roosevelt thought he was safe, he was soon disabused. Three months later Hearst was on the radio again from Los Angeles to point out to the nation—very gently for him—the peril in the National Recovery Act.

"It would appear that whenever business in the present emergency has succeeded in getting its head above water," said Hearst, "the National Recovery Act, with the best intentions in the world, has alertly thrown it a millstone or a coil of lead pipe as a life preserver, and has promptly sunk it again."

President Roosevelt and General Hugh Johnson of the N.R.A., he said, were asking too much if they expected private business to employ a million more men at higher wages and shorter hours. Industry could not afford it. The plight of business reminded him of that of the young lady in the comedy act of Savoy and Brennan:

"Said Brennan: 'Sam took his sweetheart out in a rowboat and they quarreled, and Sam threw her overboard, and every time she came up he hit her on the head with an oar. Wasn't it awful?'

" 'Sure,' said Savoy. 'But wasn't she the fool to come up?' "[9]

Allow some bureaucrat to tell him how to run his business? Hearst would die first. Another sort of interference was looming—the Newspaper Guild. Hearst was opposed to that too, just as he opposed anything that might reduce the autocratic control he felt his due. It was true that the mo-

[6] John Tebbel, *The Life and Good Times of William Randolph Hearst*, 315.
[7] N. Y. *Times*, Nov. 26, 27, 1933.   [8] N. Y. *American*, Dec. 3, 1933.
[9] N. Y. *Times*, Mar. 11, 1934.

ment newsmen owed allegiance to any group other than their newspaper, the freedom of the press was impaired. However, Hearst's use of this freedom had not always been admirable, and the newsmen had a legitimate complaint. They were tired of seeing stereotypers and pressmen enjoying regular union salaries and benefits while they themselves were on low pay and always subject to instant dismissal. Possibly Hearst's opposition to the Guild was motivated in part by self-interest, but in it also was the inflexible, old-fashioned journalist code he had lived by since 1887. Newspapering, he felt, was a high-spirited, challenging profession, not a trade. With his own uncommon abilities he was apt to harbor scorn for any professional man who could not command a good salary out of his own talent and industry, without depending on the aid of a guild.

Besides—there were Communists in the Guild, and in organized labor generally. Hearst had developed a deadly hatred for Communism.

11. Hearst, Hitler and Fascism

I. TOURISM À LA HEARST

IN May, 1934, Hearst went on another of those sultanesque excursions that made it appear that his own business was not in real danger from the N.R.A., the Guild, or any other source. He gathered a large group including his son George and his wife, and some movie and newspaper people, among them Miss Davies, Eileen Percy, Dorothy Mackaill, Mary Carlisle, Ella Williams, Harry Crocker, Edgar Hatrick, Arthur Lake and William Collier Jr., and headed for Europe. Hearst also had his dachshund Helena with him. The party, traveling by private car, stopped off in Chicago and stayed at the Blackstone Hotel while Hearst had a conference with General Johnson of N.R.A. They proceeded to New York, where they again lingered while Hearst took a side trip to Washington to have lunch with President Roosevelt, to whom Hearst presented an original autographed photograph of Andrew Jackson and a Jackson holograph. The President must have used all his charm on him, for he returned to New York with nothing but kind words for the administration.

He collected four more members for his party—his sons William Jr. and John and their wives—and gave a cheery interview as they all boarded the *Rex* for Spain. Advertising seemed to be picking up a trifle, he said, and he believed conditions were improving.

"I have sympathy for the National Recovery Act," he added, "and all is right with it so long as they don't tell you to do something you can't do. I think we are going to get along, and all should help as much as they can. I am entirely in sympathy with the President."

But he was not in sympathy with the Guild. "Frankly, I do not believe in a newspaper guild. . . . I have always regarded our business as a profession and not as a trade union." He would be delighted to talk to Mussolini again, he said, and although he had no plan to visit Hitler he would like to see him.[1]

In Madrid, Hearst chartered an airliner to take him and his party to England for a visit to St. Donat's. Being still at war with France, he was a trifle annoyed when the plane made an unscheduled stop at Bordeaux for fuel. The French government now sued for peace, saying that he was welcome, but he did not choose to end hostilities.[2] It happened that his friend Louis Mayer was also in Europe that summer. Mayer, concerned about the persecution of Jews in Germany, wired Hearst urging him to visit Hitler and in-

[1] N. Y. *Times*, May 27, 1934.　　　　[2] N. Y. *Times*, June 22, 1934.

442

tercede for the Jews. Somewhat later, Mayer, who was Republican chairman in California, wired Hearst again suggesting that he support Hoover for President in 1936. Hearst gave him the back of his hand:

> Dear Louis: I am sorry but I cannot conscientiously support that man. He is selfish and stupid. He injects himself into the present situation for his own advantage. He will harm his own party, handicap the whole conservative movement, and strengthen the hands of the radicals. He has said nothing which has not been said better before and he accomplishes nothing but to make millions of people feel that the present incumbent [Roosevelt] would be immeasurably better than this discredited failure . . . If you don't suppress this hoodoo, your party will lose its chance, too, of electing a Congress as well as a President. His name is an anathema to the American public.—W. R.[3]

With Mayer and Hoover taken care of, Hearst and his guests left St. Donat's for Germany, going via Belgium and Holland to skirt hated Gaul. They proceeded into Switzerland, then visited Rome and Venice before returning through Austria to Oberammergau and Munich, Orrin Peck's long-time adopted home. Hearst, who knew Europe better than most guides, was passionately fond of Munich's easy-going life and its National Museum.

"What do I like best in Munich?" he wrote. "Everything—the city, the surroundings, the climate, the bright and kindly happy Bavarian people, the shops, the theaters, the museums—and the beer. Let us not forget the beer . . . In fact, [Munich] is such a delightful place that one has to be careful not to want to live here instead of going home and attending to business." [4]

He attended to business even on this pleasure tour, in which he was pouring out a fortune for the entertainment of a score of younger folk. He stayed up at his hotel until far after midnight to do his writing and send orders to his newspapers in America.[5] Since he did not get up until almost noon, the rest of the party perforce conformed their schedule to his. Serving as his secretary on the tour was the witty newsman, Harry Crocker. Significantly, he and Miss Davies had taken with them the "fun group"—the young and joyous set, quick with jokes and larks. Hearst wanted to squeeze every drop of enjoyment out of life, and he wanted Miss Davies to enjoy herself, to forget the occasional embarrassments that her peculiar status brought about.

In Munich they were joined by Ernst "Putzi" Hanfstaengl, the Harvard graduate who was press officer for the Reich and an intimate adviser of Hitler. Hanfstaengl had long operated a Madison Avenue art shop, so Hearst knew him well. He had doubtless read of Hearst's willingness to see Hitler and was ready to make propaganda use of it. According to William Hearst Jr., he "fastened himself to the party" and accompanied them to Bad Nauheim, meanwhile funneling the Hearst utterances to the German press. One of them was, "If Hitler succeeds in pointing the way of peace and order

[3] Crowther, 196–97.   [4] Coblentz, *Hearst*, 113.
[5] Ella Williams to author, Nov. 1, 1959.

. . . he will have accomplished a measure of good not only for his own people but for all of humanity." [6]

Hearst later declared that he had been outrageously misquoted by the German press.[7] Enough time had elapsed for the charm of President Roosevelt and General Johnson to wear off and for him to brood over his two bugbears, taxes and Big Government. Although he had left America speaking well of the administration and the N.R.A., he now delivered a blast against "futile and fantastic experiments" that raised taxes and debts, going on, "We should end once and for all the N.R.A. and its Nonsensical, Ridiculous, Asinine interference with national and legitimate industrial development." [8]

At Bad Nauheim, four storm troopers arrived to tell him that a plane was waiting to take him to see Hitler. This was too good an opportunity for the old newshound to miss, and he went along. During his chat in Berlin with the Fuehrer, who only three months earlier had staged his infamous blood purge, he suggested diplomatically that National Socialism would win more friends in the United States if the persecution of the Jews and other minority groups would stop. Hitler assured him that these measures were only temporary, insisting that National Socialism was entirely democratic. Hearst left the interview convinced that he had accomplished some good.[9]

A photographer was waiting as Hearst emerged, and snapped a picture of the publisher with Dr. Alfred Rosenberg and other Nazis. The photograph was published in America. Along with the statements about National Socialism on which Hearst insisted he was misquoted, it created a sensation.

Crossing the Channel for a short stay at St. Donat's, he got a worried message from one of his New York executives. His hobnobbing with Hitler, it seemed, and particularly the regrettable photograph, had created a bad impression in America. Would he *please* return on a Cunarder, or anything but a German boat? This was just the sort of advice that would put the crotchety Hearst on his mettle. He sailed home on his favorite floating palace, the North German Lloyd liner *Europa*.[10]

II. HE HAS TO POSTPONE HIS DINNER

WAS Hearst, the American flag-waver, a fascist at heart? Was the old Jeffersonian, the worshiper of individual liberty, secretly plotting to destroy liberty for his own ends? The charge was echoed, re-echoed and widely believed during the peculiar ideological frenzy of the Thirties. Those who looked for the bogeyman found it in Hearst. They could tick off all the symptoms of fascism on their fingers.

A one-time radical, he had "gone conservative." He admired Mussolini. He had "turned against the unions." He fought the Newspaper Guild and the N.R.A. His own business was a dictatorship, wasn't it, with all of his

[6] Quoted in N. Y. *Times*, Aug. 23, 1934.   [7] Coblentz, *Hearst*, 111.
[8] N. Y. *Times*, Sept. 2, 1934.   [9] Coblentz, *Hearst*, 105.
[10] W. R. Hearst Jr. to author, Dec. 8, 1959.

executives "heil-ing" Hearst? He was a nationalist, like Hitler. He found common ground with the rabble-rousing Father Charles E. Coughlin. He hated and feared Communism, declared the New Deal was packed with Reds, gave Russia a wide berth, but loved Germany, visited Hitler and was photographed with Brownshirts.

For all of these things he was called a fascist. This was in a time of depression when hardship had caused a distinct leftist turn among millions, a widespread sympathy for Soviet Russia and a burning hatred for Nazi Germany. Many leftist groups were well organized, highly vocal, and happy to fasten the fascist tag on anyone disagreeing with them.

Furthermore, Hearst was unexcelled in his ability to outrage even balanced observers. When he lived like a king, took a score of his friends abroad, paying all their expenses, and came home complaining of taxes, he defied the fundamentals of good public relations.

Since he never openly embraced fascism, he can only be judged by his actions and his record as a libertarian—no easy task with a man as inconsistent as he. He had got on well with the dictator Diaz in Mexico, under whose regime his property there was safe. His operations in Mexico seemed to have been motivated more by regard for his own property than by any concept of liberty and justice to Mexicans. When he wanted to get facts about someone, he had a habit of sending one of his employes to make inquiries at the scene. In 1933, he had sent G. H. Maines, a former Hearst reporter, to Louisiana to inquire confidentially into the activities and character of Huey Long. "Mr. Hearst decided to send me South to get the facts —and facts only—about Huey Long," Maines later wrote. ". . . The Chief and Brisbane . . . wanted to know if Huey Long was basically honest, or a clown or a brilliant politician." [1] Maines believed Hearst looked on Long as a potential Presidential candidate. The Kingfish, who had done much good in Louisiana, had done it at the expense of democratic government, and with his tremendous appeal to the masses was a visible fascist threat.

On the other hand, Adela Rogers St. John, a Hearst writer who was assigned to cover Long for a time, believed her assignment came about because Brisbane had assailed Long, causing the Kingfish to vow that he would never talk to a Hearst writer. As a result, the Hearst press was being scooped by the opposition on Long, who was the most newsworthy man in the Senate. [2] It seems incredible that the property-loving millionaire Hearst would risk his all by backing Long, whose "Share Our Wealth" plan would theoretically erase swollen incomes. Hearst's interest in Long, which never resulted in anything more than a few stories friendly to Long in the Hearst press, remains unexplained.

The fascist-minded Father Coughlin was Hearst's guest at San Simeon in 1932. The Hearst press, while never openly espousing all the Coughlin doctrines, gave him friendly publicity. But this could be explained on the score

[1] G. H. Maines to author, Apr. 30, 1960.   [2] Mrs. St. John to author, Sept. 20, 1960.

of Hearst's agreement with Coughlin on issues not necessarily fascistic—the priest's hatred of Communism and internationalism, and his break with Roosevelt.

Doubtless Hearst saw in fascism a useful bulwark against Communism, which terrified him with its threat to liberty and private property. If he had to choose between the two, he would certainly have picked fascism, but the evidence indicates that he preferred traditional American democracy first of all. One gets a picture of Hearst, his faith in Roosevelt lost, seeing the country floundering in continued depression, eyeing the horizon uneasily, fearful of collapse, for once uncertain of the cure. One liberal observer, Raymond Gram Swing, thought it possible that Hearst entertained fascist ideas without even knowing it.[3]

Hearst was an embattled capitalist grown cautious with age, driven by financial difficulties, fighting for a way of life that could be criticized as selfish but which was no different from the way of life he had always fought for. It was ironical that he was assailed by Samuel Untermyer and other Jewish leaders who did not know that when he spoke to Hitler he interceded for the Jews, and that he later had his Berlin correspondent, William Hillman, intercede again. Soon after the Hitler interview, he wrote his secretary, Willicombe. The letter, which seems authentic, read in part:

> Fascism seems to be spreading over here. We have got to keep crazy isms out of our country.
> If we can keep out Communism we can keep out Fascism. Fascism here [Germany] and elsewhere has sprung up to prevent the control of countries by Communism.
> Both are despotisms and deprive people of the liberties which democracy assures.[4]

When he landed with his party in New York, he did not *sound* like a fascist. "Thank Heaven for one thing," he said, "the nation which has shown the greatest return toward prosperity is England. And England is very definitely a democracy." The *Times* account went on, "While condemning dictatorships, Mr. Hearst added his belief that Chancellor Hitler seemed to be popular with the German masses largely because of 'his advocacy of a united Germany capable of resisting encroachment of injustice from foreign powers.'" He predicted that some Nazi policies would be modified, "particularly with regard to the Jews." He did not believe Hitler a war threat, but said that France and Italy were arming to the teeth.[5]

Hearst put up at the Ritz Tower while he communed with his New York executives. Richard Berlin brought in Herbert Mayes, who recently had been elevated to the editorship of Hearst's *Pictorial Review*. Hearst, his dachshund in his lap, gazed at him with his piercing blue-gray eyes.

"What do you plan to do with *Pictorial Review*?" he asked.

---

[3] Swing, *Forerunners of American Fascism*, 145.   [4] Coblentz, *Hearst,* 106.
[5] N. Y. *Times*, Sept. 28, 1934.

Mayes, nervous at this first meeting with the legendary Chief, said, "Mr. Hearst, I'm barely on the job. I simply hope to make it a credit to publishing."

"What would you say is the decor of this room?" Hearst inquired.

Mayes, no decorator, looked around. "I'd say it has a little bit of everything," he hazarded.

"That's what we want *Pictorial Review* to be," Hearst smiled. "A little bit of everything." [6]

President Roosevelt, who had most of the nation's newspapers against him and was still hoping to get Hearst back on his side, sent a cordial note:

Dear W. R.: I am delighted to hear from Joe [Joseph P. Kennedy] that you are coming down to see me on Monday. If you have not made other arrangements, I hope you will stay with us Monday night at the White House. [7]

Doubtless they discussed Hitler, and it would be surprising if Hearst did not protest against government interference in business.

While he was in Europe, he had taken a strong hand in breaking the general strike that had made the summer violent in San Francisco. Beginning as a longshoremen's strike, it spread until all unions were involved and the city was paralyzed. After receiving telephoned instructions from Hearst, John Francis Neylan conferred with the mayor, set up an office in the Palace Hotel and pooled all five Bay newspapers (three of them Hearst papers) in a united front against the strike. [8] Said Hearst's *Examiner:*

There are many thousands of honest, upright, God-fearing, hard-working union men now part of the so-called general strike.

The total of these against the handful of communistic radicals, who have gotten them into this mess, is so overwhelming as to make us wonder how they have permitted themselves to be led from wise leadership into this revolt against their very selves. . . . [9]

General Hugh Johnson likewise condemned the strike as "subversive." Strikebreakers were brought into action, and there were bloody conflicts between the militia and the strikers in which the leftist *Nation* declared that "literally thousands" of strikers were injured. [10] The strike was ultimately broken, and if Hearst was a fascist for his action he had strong company in San Francisco. He had become impatient with the abuse of power exercised by some union leaders. Bartley C. Crum, then a young attorney on Neylan's staff, defended Hearst's action in the strike years later, long after he had severed all connections with Hearst.

"The most obvious point that most of Hearst's biographers missed was his Americanism," Crum wrote. "Thus when he authorized Mr. Older to fight for freedom for Tom Mooney it was because he was interested in safeguard-

[6] Mr. Mayes to author, Jan. 14, 1960.
[7] Elliott Roosevelt, *F. D. R.—His Personal Letters,* I, 424.   [8] Mr. Neylan to author.
[9] San Francisco *Examiner,* July 16, 1934.   [10] *Nation,* Aug. 29, 1934.

ing democratic procedures; similarly in the general strike . . . he was against attaining a just end by unlawful means—violence. I can assure you that Mr. Neylan, as soon as the general strike ended, did all in his power to correct abuses on the waterfront in San Francisco." [11]

At the same time, his executives had fired Dean Jennings and Louis Burgess, two Hearst newsmen, for their activities in a San Francisco unit of the Guild. Unless the law—which at the time was obscure—said otherwise, he was within his rights in discharging the men and fighting the Guild. His opposition to the Guild was understandable on grounds other than mere selfishness. Brought up in the old school of journalism, he was guilty along with virtually every other newspaper publisher in failing to rescue newsmen from a condition of defenselessness and insecurity which drove them to organize for their own protection.

Hearst hurried westward to engage in another battle that some called fascistic—the defense of California against the invasion of Upton Sinclair and his "End Poverty in California" crusade. Sinclair, he said, "is a perfectly well-meaning man but a wholly impractical theorist," and he blasted the American people for "traipsing after every irresponsible adventurer with a penny whistle to play and a seductive song to sing." [12] Sinclair had astonished everyone by capturing the Democratic nomination for governor when many staunch Democrats refused to admit that he *was* a Democrat. The state had gigantic unemployment and relief problems, with destitute "Okies" still pouring in to augment them. One of the things the socialist Sinclair proposed to do was to tax business—and particularly the movies—to the hilt. While even the moderate Norman Thomas bewailed Sinclair as a visionary whose excessive promises would fail of accomplishment and harm the socialist movement, Hearst may not have seen the matter from this intellectual plane. He was a movie magnate. He was also a rich capitalist who would be hit hard by Sinclair's tax program. He joined with the Republican Louis Mayer and other moguls in a "Stop Sinclair" drive. In the California Hearst papers, Sinclair was no longer "well-meaning" but was assailed as a Communist. The movie industry levied a day's salary from actors and employes for an anti-Sinclair war chest. There were dark threats that the industry would move to Florida, where taxes were nominal. The drive against Sinclair became a panic-stricken crusade. Several studios turned out fake propaganda newsreels showing hordes of grimy vagrants from other states entering California, ready to expropriate private property when Sinclair was elected. The "vagrants" were studio extras. These newsreels were distributed free to movie houses with immense effectiveness. [13]

Hearst's Los Angeles *Herald-Express* ran a huge photograph of a frightening mob of hoboes alighting from a freight train in Los Angeles to help launch the Sinclair revolution. The "hoboes" were recognized as Dorothy Wilson, Frankie Darrow and other actors in *Wild Boys of the Road*, from

[11] Mr. Crum to author, Sept. 25, 1959.   [12] N. Y. *Times*, Sept. 2, 1934.
[13] Upton Sinclair, *I, Candidate for Governor*, 151–52.

which the photograph was a still.[14] It was another in the long line of Hearst fakes. Sinclair was beaten and the Republican Frank Merriam elected, thanks to the cinema industry and the Hearst newspapers.

Hearst's rage at New Deal bureaucracy and the N.R.A. with its Blue Eagle symbol at times grew choleric. "When Mr. Hearst looks at that Eagle," said Brisbane, "he has to postpone his dinner." [15]

[14] Sinclair, 128.   [15] Gauvreau, 229.

12. The King in Residence

I. ANIMALS HAVE THE RIGHT OF WAY

Treat [Hearst] as a modern Louis XIV and you can rationalize his actions. He is the last of his kind in the newspaper business. The days of palaces in Democracy are over. I've tried to tell him that, but he's going to die like a king. . . .   —Arthur Brisbane [1]

ALTHOUGH Hearst was still friendly with Mayer, both he and Miss Davies were dissatisfied with the roles she had been getting at M.G.M. The studio believed her talent best suited for light comedy, and since the advent of the talkies she had appeared in a succession of frothy affairs including *Bachelor Father, Five and Ten,* and *Polly of the Circus,* being supported in the latter by a new young man, Clark Gable. Miss Davies wanted some juicy roles. She had earnestly sought the lead in *The Barretts of Wimpole Street,* only to see Irving Thalberg, with Mayer's support, give it to Norma Shearer, who compounded the crime by making it a smashing success. As a result, Miss Shearer's name went unmentioned in the Hearst press for a time.[2]

Many had believed that Miss Davies, with her speech handicap, would be finished by talking pictures. "Somebody told me I should put a pebble in my mouth to cure my stuttering," she said later. ". . . Well, I tried it, and during a scene I swallowed the pebble. That was the end of that." [3] However, she trained hard with tutors and managed to make the leap, although some felt that there was a hesitation and studiedness in her diction.

After the return of Hearst and Miss Davies from Europe, they found that the screen rights for Stefan Zweig's *Marie Antoinette* had been purchased for Miss Shearer. Their visits to European castles fired them with enthusiasm for the story as a vehicle for Miss Davies. Mayer, however, was vexed at Hearst for visiting President Roosevelt, whom he considered a menace, and at his slandering of Hoover. Mayer stood firm for Miss Shearer. Another impasse was caused by the fact that at M.G.M. Miss Davies was competing for stories not only with Miss Shearer but with such stars as Jean Harlow, Greta Garbo and Joan Crawford, and the friction was growing heated.[4] Cosmopolitan's contract with M.G.M. was about to end, and Miss Davies did not renew it. Instead, Hearst made a deal with the Warner studio in Burbank. It was somewhat like the end of a queen's reign when

[1] Gauvreau, 303.
[2] Crowther, 185.
[3] Los Angeles *Times*, May 9, 1954.
[4] Howard Strickling to author, Nov. 19, 1959.

Miss Davies' famous bungalow was separated into three sections and hauled out of Culver City on its way to Burbank.

At this time Carmel Snow, editor of Hearst's *Harper's Bazaar,* unaware that Miss Shearer was getting the Hearst silent treatment, featured her in a spread of pictures in the *Bazaar.* She was informed too late of her error by perturbed associates, but the Chief himself never complained.[5]

The movement of Miss Davies to the Burbank studio furnished Hollywood with gossip for months. Now she was queen at Warner's, and it was said that she would soon emerge as a dramatic actress. Instead, she was starred with Dick Powell in a couple of light semi-musicals, *Page Miss Glory* and *Hearts Divided.* Powell was now in the position of Gable and others who had appeared opposite Miss Davies and had felt themselves under Hearst's close scrutiny. Some observers had felt that Hearst was actually *jealous* when his lady was addressed in endearing terms, fondled and kissed by some of the most handsome and famous young men in the industry, all in the line of business. Being Miss Davies' leading man could be nerve-racking, if for no other reason than Hearst's immense power of publicity.

"I was nervous at first," Powell later admitted. "I was a struggling young actor, and Mr. Hearst was a man of limitless newspaper power who could make or break me." [6]

The lead members of the cast would be invited to lunch at the Bungalow, where Hearst sat indolently, often feeding scraps to six or eight dachshunds who swarmed around him at the table. Sometimes there was a cocktail before lunch, sometimes not, but never more than one. Miss Davies enjoyed cocktails, whereas Hearst abominated hard liquor, and this sometimes caused disagreement between them. Powell was struck by Hearst's peculiarly possessive attitude, particularly toward Miss Davies. His eyes followed her everywhere. He had security guards all around—doubtless one result of the bomb that had been mailed to her. But despite his taciturnity he was a perfect host, courteous and affable. Miss Davies, the most generous and friendly of women, invariably got an innocent "crush" on her leading man —a fact that gave Powell some concern. He made it a point to tell Hearst that he need have no worries on that score. Hearst just laughed, but he seemed to appreciate the assurance, for he warmed up toward Powell and even took to calling him "Richard," an unusual concession for one so formal.[7]

Sometimes, when a "take" was finished, Hearst would lead a party to the amusement park at nearby Venice and outdo the young people in shooting at moving targets, eating hot dogs and riding a carousel horse.

Of evenings, the cast would often be invited along with other movie and newspaper people to the beach house, where Hearst would employ "name" bands and would join in the dancing himself. Irene Castle, often a guest, was honored there at a dinner party to which seventy-five film notables had

[5] Miss Snow to author, Apr. 4, 1960. [6] Mr. Powell to author, Nov. 5, 1959.
[7] Mr. Powell to author.

been invited. Miss Davies did not appear, for she could find nothing in her vast wardrobe to please her. She telephoned a dress shop proprietor, who unlocked her store and brought dozens of gowns for Miss Davies to try on. Meanwhile, the agitated maid, who had turned on the water in the bathtub for her mistress, forgot it as she helped with the dresses. The seventy-five waiting guests downstairs were aware that something was wrong when water began trickling down the dining room walls, hung with paintings of Miss Davies in her film roles.[8] Miss Castle was one of those who was a good friend of both Miss Davies and Mrs. Hearst, a situation she found occasionally embarrassing. But to her astonishment, Mrs. Hearst showed the ultimate in charity, even commenting favorably on Miss Davies' pictures.[9]

The beach house, which became known as "the Versailles of Hollywood," was the epicenter of a hurricane of social activity. This social milieu was not snobbish or stuffy, as Pickfair had often been. Guests were not selected for their prestige or wealth, but because they were likable or diverting, and the entertainments there were apt to be joyous and unconventional. Miss Davies was a vital creature, entirely impulsive, always flying from room to room, the soul of friendliness and hospitality. Hearst himself had not conquered his shyness and never would, but he had learned to control it and live with it. There were certain members of "the crowd," particularly the funsters such as Harry Crocker, William Haines and Gene Fowler, who could make him break through his reserve. He was at home with Louella Parsons, with Francis Marion, Bebe Daniels, a few others. If ever he became bored or uncomfortable he would simply disappear, join Willicombe in the office wing and begin sending out the instructions to editors that always began, "The Chief says."

There was one incurable drawback to the beach house: It was finished. Hearst, a frustrated architect gripped by a compulsion to build, occasionally tore out a room or two just for the pleasure of redesigning them and installing more paneling from Europe. But this gave only limited scope for his construction craze. He had a splendid time building a "Bavarian village" at Wyntoon—three great buildings plus several smaller ones, facing a green studded with statuary and a fountain imported from Bavaria. But this, too, was almost finished.

He was happiest at San Simeon, for there he was like an eager painter with an acre of canvas only half filled. Over weekends, and when Miss Davies was between pictures, they hurried to the castle, which they called, with some violence to semantics, "the ranch," and to which they invited guests by the hundreds.

Most of the guests arrived on Friday night. Hearst, the specialist in impact, would have floodlights turned on his castle so that the arriving pilgrims could spy the twin towers from miles away on the coastal highway. Conservatives might quarrel with the architecture, but few denied that San

---

[8] Irene Castle, *Castles in the Air*, 216.   [9] Irene Castle, 219.

Simeon was impressive. Sometimes, fog would wreath the lower slopes of the Enchanted Hill, and visitors coming up the six-mile driveway through thick mist would suddenly emerge to see the illuminated Casa Grande looming over them like a fairy-tale illustration by Maxfield Parrish, and to be struck by an eerie sensation that none of this could be real.[10] Adding to the eeriness was the zoo, the largest private wild animal collection in the country, containing thirty species of carnivora and seventy of grazing animals that included everything from elephants, tigers and water buffalos down to ostriches, yak and chimpanzees. The dangerous animals were caged. The antelope and other herbivores were given freedom of a large tract that included part of the driveway, sealed by button-operated electric gates. Always tender toward animals, Hearst gave his chauffeurs stern orders to drive slowly. The driveway bristled with signs reading "Animals Have the Right of Way," and "Reckless Driving Will Not Be Tolerated." Once, when Miss Parsons was being driven up the hill by day, a recumbent moose enjoying the warmth of the sun-baked blacktop refused to budge. She and her driver waited almost an hour until the animal decided to leave.[11]

A guest arriving for the first time was smitten by amazement that was augmented by the wonders of the castle and grounds. Life at San Simeon was strictly casual within a few set rules. Since Hearst's own hours were scheduled, the routine revolved loosely around that schedule. Guests were free in the morning to sleep or explore the facilities of the estate. They could order any kind of breakfast they wanted from a bill of fare as varied as that of a large restaurant. Hearst and Miss Davies never appeared until an hour or so after noon, when luncheon was served buffet style. The master was the most magnanimous of hosts, proud of his barony and eager for his guests to enjoy it to the full. He often went out of his way to put newcomers or "unknowns" at their ease. It pleased him when everybody got outdoors in the afternoon to take part in some sort of group activity, whether it be swimming in one of the two pools, riding, tennis or a picnic.

The tennis tournaments at San Simeon were legendary, taking in everyone from the veriest dubs to such experts as Bill Tilden, Helen Wills, Fred Perry and Alice Marble, who were often guests. Hearst himself had taken up tennis in an effort to keep down his weight, and had grown remarkably skilled although he remained virtually motionless. Once, Miss Davies sought out Dick Powell and said, "Pops wants to play tennis, and you're elected." Powell had brought no tennis gear with him, but found that from a large equipment room he could take his pick of shorts, shoes and a racket of just the right heft to suit him. He contemplated "going easy" on the lord of the manor, but discovered that this was unnecessary. Hearst never ran. He never picked up a ball that passed him, leaving this to the ball boy. But he gave his whole attention to the game, and he was uncanny at placement. "He was then past seventy," Powell later commented, "but he beat me."[12]

[10] Princess Pignatelli to author.   [11] Louella Parsons to author, Nov. 2, 1959.
[12] Mr. Powell to author.

This was perhaps as well, for Hearst hated to lose at tennis or anything else. Afterward, he took Powell to see his kennel, which contained many different breeds of dogs, among them long-haired dachshunds. Powell remarked that he had never seen that breed before.

"Take one," Hearst said instantly, "with my compliments." [13]

An excellent swimmer, he made frequent use of his pools. Never was he far from his work. Sometimes he would come up from submergence in the pool, spouting like a porpoise, to find Willicombe waiting at the edge with a news teletype. He would look it over, give an order and return to his swimming. There was a telephone at the edge of the pool. There were telephones scattered around the grounds, hidden in slabs of stone or sheltered by trees. No one ever counted the number of telephones inside the four hill-top palaces. The incoming and outgoing calls kept three Hearst-employed telephone operators busy. Visitors sometimes amused themselves by estimating how many families could live in luxury on what Hearst paid for his telephone bill.

Probably he was most famous for his picnics. His cousin, Randolph Apperson, the much younger brother of Mrs. Flint, had joined his staff in 1934, taking charge of the huge cattle ranch adjoining the castle. Apperson would be alerted by Willicombe when a picnic was in the offing, for they took preparation equivalent to a safari. On one of them, the guests took off by horse while Apperson and his men loaded sixteen pack mules with provisions, champagne, caviar, sleeping bags, Japanese lanterns and cooking utensils which were carried miles over rugged trails to the picnic spot. Mules also carried the instruments for a hill-billy band Hearst had hired for the occasion, including a bass fiddle, whose owner rode alongside, nervously keeping an eye on the instrument.[14] Frances Marion and Hedda Hopper, being in their thirties, were often chaperones on these outings. Hearst in his seventies was a splendid horseman who enjoyed these overnight affairs to the full, although many of his younger guests returned exhausted.

At the castle, Hearst's schedule called for a late afternoon siesta. He would descend from the Celestial Suite on the third floor by his private elevator, which was hung with paintings, and dinner would be served around 9. However, this was far from ironclad, for if some entertainment was in progress, dinner might be held up for an hour or two. It so agonized the French chef to find his delicacies growing cold that he would dance in a rage. He finally quit in a huff, to be succeeded by a more tolerant Filipino. One—just one—cocktail was served before dinner. Hearst imposed stringent rules about liquor, not only because of his own puritanism but because he knew that otherwise there would be trouble in the convivial movie-newspaper crowd. He did his best to enforce them, while his guests used all their ingenuity to circumvent them. Guests were forbidden to bring their own liquor, but they did. Servants were forbidden to serve liquor at any but the stated

---

[13] Mr. Powell to author.   [14] Randolph Apperson to author, Oct. 23, 1959.

times and in the stated quantities, but there were evasions and there was bootlegging. Frances Marion recalls Errol Flynn literally staggering in to the dinner table, unnoticed by Hearst, who was busy in conversation.[15] Miss Davies, along with her close friend Carole Lombard and others, evolved stratagems for evading the one-drink rule.

"Marion and I . . . head right for the little girls' room," the fun-loving Miss Lombard told a friend. ". . . That's one place Hearst can't get at us." [16]

But Hearst held the line remarkably well, occasionally firing a servant for smuggling liquor and now and then asking a guest who overdrank to leave.[17]

II. SH-H-H—DON'T MENTION DEATH

ALTHOUGH Hearst could discuss obituaries with his editors in the line of business, he had a violent aversion for mortality, and there was an unwritten law never to mention death in his presence. Dick Powell recalls a dinner at San Simeon when someone commented on the death of a friend. Several others at the table immediately shushed him, with warning glances toward the host.[1] Hearst's morbid fear of death, his interest in scientific schemes for delaying the inevitable, were the reverse side of his love for life. He would be depressed for days by the death of an animal in the zoo. He was likewise plunged into gloom by the death of a tree. His janizaries went to great lengths to conceal the demise of anything near him. Once, when a crew of nurserymen planted a row of palms at San Simeon, and one of them died, they made haste to paint the yellowing leaves green, concealing the grim truth until Hearst left and the tree could be replaced.[2] He carried this idiosyncrasy to extremes. Although the San Simeon forests badly needed thinning, and he loved fireplace fires, he would not permit any of his trees to be cut. He had firewood hauled from Paso Robles, thirty miles away over the mountains. Once, Samuel Goldwyn, in leaving San Simeon, backed his car around and struck an oak, rumpling a fender. Although the fault was Goldwyn's and not the oak's, Hearst had the tree moved to safety at a cost of $5000.[3]

He liked to surprise his guests with special dishes, once chartering a plane to fly to Louisiana and bring back several barrels of shrimp. Dress was informal at dinner, which was served at the fifty-four-foot table in the Renaissance refectory under immense chandeliers suspended from the lofty, carved ceiling. Diners were given a menu, which also listed the moving picture to be shown that evening. Hearst sat at the middle of the long table, with Miss Davies directly opposite him and the more important guests surrounding them. The table accommodated forty diners, seated in great upholstered chairs with carved woodwork, from which they could gaze up at colorful medieval Sienese banners or, lower down, at priceless tapestries and choir

[15] Miss Marion to author.
[17] Adela Rogers St. John to author.
[2] *Saturday Evening Post*, Mar. 9, 1940.
[16] Kyle Crichton, *Total Recoil*, 67.
[1] Mr. Powell to author.
[3] Frances Marion to author.

stalls, while they enjoyed vintage champagne and paradisiac food. Hearst himself liked plain foods, being a crank on well-aged beef which he would not touch until it hung for twelve weeks, after which much had to be trimmed away but what was left was prime. He enjoyed German beer with his dinner. He once astonished his Chicago editors with a telegraphed request that they ship him a half carload of Pilsner Urquell—an order they were able to fill only with the help of executives at the Bismarck Hotel.[4]

Guests were surprised that in these baronial surroundings, where the china and silver were precious and attentive waiters were at one's shoulder, the napkins were paper (of costly softness) and Worcestershire sauce and other condiments were set out in their factory bottles. This was not dictated by economy but by sentiment. It reminded Hearst of the early days in the Seventies and Eighties when he came out to this very spot with his father and mother and picnicked in the open, and of the later days—still remote to his younger guests—when he brought his own wife and children to enjoy the same surroundings in tent-houses.[5] The paper napkins and condiment bottles were memorials to his youth, reminders that he was one of the most sentimental men alive.

Another reminder of this was the mice that made the castle a playground. He could not bear to harm a mouse. The butler was instructed to leave tidbits around so that they would not go hungry. Non-injuring wire-basket traps were left around at night, and in the morning it was the butler's first duty to carry the traps outside and release the mice. Once, when William W. Murray, manager of Hearst's ranch properties, was a guest, a mouse scampered along a molding in the assembly hall, descended to the floor, and was pounced on by Helena, Hearst's favorite dachshund. Hearst turned in time to see this. He pursued Helena and caught her, but by that time the mouse was dead. Highly upset, he turned on Murray and other guests in the room and accused them of complicity in the slaying.[6]

His benevolence did not extend to rats. At one period when a few rats invaded the *palazzo*, he permitted snap-traps to be set out, but he was almost in tears when a stray squirrel was caught in a trap, its leg broken. A Hearst car hurried the squirrel to Cambria, where a veterinarian set its leg.[7]

Mayor Hylan had not exaggerated years earlier when he told the story of Hearst rescuing a toad from a jellyfish. It was another aspect of the wide swing of his emotions from cruelty to kindness. His ruthlessness was usually reserved for things in the abstract, people at a distance. Anyone hurt within his immediate ken, be it human or animal, enlisted his sympathy to such an extravagant degree that he seemed womanly and even ridiculous. A pinched finger aroused his tender solicitude. When his dachshund Helena died, he wept and had her buried under a stone engraved with the legend, "Here lies dearest Helena—my devoted friend." [8]

[4] Harry Reutlinger to author.
[6] W. W. Murray to author, Oct. 16, 1959.
[8] Coblentz, *Hearst*, 244.
[5] Mrs. Fremont Older, *op. cit.*, 539.
[7] Randolph Apperson to author.

Thus, those who knew him only as a host were apt to think him the most soft-hearted person in the world, while those who dealt with him in business or politics could see him as vicious. The older Hearst executives who knew both sides of his nature could explain a benevolent or malefic Hearst newspaper campaign on whether the Chief happened to be in his kindly or nasty mood at the time.

The master's sentimentality was also evident in the special store he set by some of his possessions. One of them was the *pozo,* or wellhead he had bought in Verona in 1891 when he was traversing the world with Tessie Powers. It had long been installed at his mother's Hacienda, and when he sold the Hacienda he had the five-ton wellhead shipped to San Simeon and placed in the stone terrace. He never forgot Tessie. When she neared seventy, he learned in some way that she was in need of money; he had Edward Hardy Clark send her a generous monthly check.[9] He venerated his mother's belongings. Occasionally, when there were many guests at San Simeon, her bedlinen, with the huge monogram "P.A.H.," would be used. It had to go on the beds of people Hearst approved as morally fit to use his mother's sheets.[10] Brain-gazers would have found much of the Oedipal in him. At San Simeon there were madonnas everywhere—madonnas in oil, in tapestry, in terra cotta, in marble.

To some visitors, San Simeon was the ultimate in splendor, while a few thought it weird and somehow frightening. The shrieking of leopards and other animals sometimes aroused guests from sleep in the night. Kindly as Hearst was, and seldom as he was seen, his presence pervaded the place. Whenever anyone said "He" at San Simeon, they meant the master. Irene Castle, a dedicated anti-vivisectionist, often discussed with Hearst crusades against cruelty to animals and credited him with putting a stop to the mistreatment of horses and other animals by the movies. It struck her as ridiculous, however, to play Monopoly in a room so huge that one could hardly see the other end.[11]

Although Miss Davies was expert with racy language, Hearst never swore publicly, disapproved of smoking or telling off-color stories, and was considered a prude. He was downright courtly in his treatment of women. At one San Simeon dinner, when Miss Head had arrived from England, Arthur Brisbane was also a guest. Brisbane, who could be rude, glanced at the comely Englishwoman and said, "Miss Head, how is it that you never married?"

Miss Head hesitated. Hearst came to her rescue. "Artie," he said, "don't you think that is a question that should be directed at Miss Head's suitors?" [12]

After dinner, Hearst and his guests would troop into his private theater, where they would sink into luxuriously deep seats to see newsreels and pre-release feature pictures before anyone but a few movie executives had set eyes on them. It was the duty of Ella Williams, an aide at Hearst's Cosmopolitan studio, to get these films and send them by air to San Simeon—

[9] Private source.
[11] Irene Castle, *Castles in the Air,* 218.
[10] Adela Rogers St. John to author.
[12] Richard E. Berlin to author.

a hard chore, for they had to be pre-release, and a new one was shown almost every night. Once or twice a year she would be forced to repeat a picture already seen, which always upset Willicombe, doubtless because it upset the Chief.[13] In the theater, Hearst's reserved seat was in the front row, with a telephone alongside over which he could order the projectionist to adjust the sound. The movie was a nightly ritual attesting to the intensity of Hearst's interest in what Hollywood people called "The Industry." Whenever he became absorbed in something, his absorption went far beyond what in normal people would be called fascination. In his quiet way he went hog-wild. This had happened to him in photography, love, collecting, typography, politics, architecture, aviation and Americanism, but in none of these was his concentration more acute than in the cinema. It had disappointed him, for Miss Davies had never quite gained the pinnacle, nor had he won top eminence as a mogul. But he was still trying. At San Simeon he enjoyed the films, but he also watched them sharply to see what competitors were doing and to pick up ideas that might be useful.

After the movie, which might end around 1 A.M., Hearst went to work, disappearing via the elevator to his Gothic study above the assembly hall. Here, surrounded by a king's ransom in rare books and manuscripts, he had a rack containing the latest editions of all his newspapers and magazines, which were flown in daily. He could not read them all every day, but he kept a close watch on each of them within a week's time, and would send via Willicombe his "The Chief says" memos of approbation or reproof. Now that he was in California most of the time, his contact with all but his Los Angeles and San Francisco papers was remote. He tried to get the "feel" of each office by telephone, spending hours in cross-country conversation, wanting to know what was going on, inquiring into the smallest details. His soft voice, since the operation, was harder to hear than ever. The executives of his morning papers were on duty during those wee hours, but he had no qualms about arousing others from sleep, and indeed sometimes seemed to forget that most people slept at night. Shortly after Randolph Apperson arrived to take charge of the cattle ranch, he was aroused at 3 A.M. by a telephone call from Hearst.

"Randolph," he inquired, "how many elk have we got?"

Apperson, annoyed, replied, "I can't tell you offhand at 3 o'clock. I'll let you know in the morning."

Next day, realizing that he had been sharp with his cousin and employer, he went over to apologize. Hearst laughed.

"You see, I lead a morning newspaperman's life," he said. "I turn the clock around. It struck me later that that was a weird hour to call you. I won't do it again." [14]

Apperson was summoned to the study one day to discuss Palomino horses with Hearst. The telephone rang as they talked. It was one of the Eastern editors, asking the boss for a new press. Apperson waited in silence. Hearst looked at him from the phone and said, "Go ahead." Apperson was astonished, but he resumed his account of the horse situation. Hearst would nod and reply now and then as he continued his telephone conversation. He was discussing types and prices of presses with the editor at the same time as he was getting Apperson's views on Palominos. When Hearst finally hung up, Apperson said, "Cousin Will, surely you couldn't have heard what I was telling you."

"Oh, yes, I did," Hearst replied. He repeated it almost verbatim. "I seem to have two sides to my brain that can function independently," he explained. "One side was on the editor, the other on you." [15]

Miss Davies often joined Hearst in his nocturnal work sessions with Willicombe. She had talked shop with him for so long that she had an intelligent grasp of the business, and he respected her opinions. It would be 4 or 5 A.M. before they retired to their bedrooms in the Celestial Suite, a third-floor apartment in the bases of the towers commanding a sweeping view of the Pacific and the Santa Lucias. Hearst's and Miss Davies' rooms were connected by a large sitting room with a covered balcony overlooking the terrace. The master slept on a massive bed of black carved wood, once owned by Cardinal Richelieu. On the wall were pictures of Senator Hearst and Phoebe Hearst, along with a handsomely-framed quotation from Bulwer's *Lady of Lyons* describing a paradise on earth and headed, "A Description of La Cuesta Encantada, the Home of William Randolph Hearst." Adjoining was a bathroom with black marble fixtures and gold-plated hardware—not solid gold, as some insisted.

III. REVOLT AGAINST HISTORY

SOME derided Hearst, a septuagenarian, for surrounding himself with cinema people most of whom were less than half his age. Actually, the majority were Miss Davies' guests. He indulged her whims, gave her everything, as a tribute of love and also in payment of a debt he could never settle—his failure to marry her, his theft of her bourgeois "respectability," a loss she felt keenly for all her exterior gaiety.

She took a motherly interest in the romance of younger friends, becoming positively ecstatic when they decided to marry and insisting on helping with details. She often took over entire charge. The marriage of William Curley and Mary Grace, and John Considine and Carmen Pantages, were only two of the many held with her enthusiastic collaboration. Often Miss Davies appeared as a bridesmaid, her friends well knowing how she envied the bride.

She and Hearst had intended to marry, but the odds against them had proved too great. Hearst doubtless could have secured a divorce had he sought one with determination. However, Miss Davies herself came to op-

[15] Mr. Apperson to author.

pose a divorce because she liked his sons and recoiled at the unpleasantness that such a suit would cause all around. She and Hearst had become reconciled to the unsatisfactory solution.

They well knew that their unusual relationship was one of the movie colony's choicest sources of gossip. There was a widespread—and mistaken —belief that they had children, and much speculation as to who and where the children were. Hearst's free-and-easy early life was not unknown. There were occasional rumors that he was "keeping" other women. One of these stories got started when Miss Davies, with her usual extravagant generosity, told an impoverished starlet to charge clothing to the Hearst-Davies accounts in Los Angeles shops. When she did so, talk quickly had it that she was "Hearst's woman." [1] Actually, Hearst had long since put all that behind him. His single-minded devotion to Miss Davies was one of the few constants in his inconstant life.

On the contrary, it was apparent to close friends that he was all too aware that she was half his age, a striking beauty, and that it was *her* affections that might stray. She was now a millionaire in her own right. Since he had no legal hold on her, she was theoretically as free as air. Miss Davies had her admirers, including one movie idol who frequently sent her roses, and she could have married a dozen times over had she wished. Instead, she remained steadfast to Hearst despite the occasional embarrassments she suffered, one of them being a Los Angeles radio evangelist who kept assailing her and Hearst for their unconventionality. The striking fact about the Hearst-Davies relationship is that it was Miss Davies who was the free agent, held the whip hand, but chose voluntarily to remain loyal. Had she been otherwise, she undoubtedly could have driven him mad with humiliation. As one of her close friends remarked, "W. R. was the luckiest man in the world in having Marion's loyalty. She held his peace of mind in the hollow of her hand, she knew it and yet she never took advantage of it." [2]

Another rumor swirled around the head of innocent-looking Louella Parsons, Hearst's syndicated movie columnist, who was close to the Chief and who wielded immense power over film people because millions read her pronouncements as though they came from Sinai. Miss Parsons, who was not well grounded in the classics, occasionally made amusing errors when she got out of her element, which was strictly screen gossip, but it had to be admitted that in her true métier—anticipating the vital statistics among movie folk—she was unbeatable. The rumor had it that she "knew something" about Hearst. Although she was indignant at this implication that she held her job through blackmail, there was little she could do except deny it publicly in a book she published. [3]

As at Santa Monica, the gatherings at San Simeon were democratic, including not only stars, directors and producers but unknowns. Stuffiness was not encouraged. On one occasion, Constance Talmadge, Bebe Daniels, Eileen

---

[1] Evelyn Wells to author.   [2] Frances Marion to author.
[3] Louella Parsons, *The Gay Illiterate*, 37–38.

Percy and several others contrived to sneak an extra cocktail, after which they went outside and affixed panties and brassières on the Water Nymph, the Three Graces, and other nude statuary with which the grounds abounded. When the young ladies came in for dinner, they found their place cards at the very end of the long table, far away from the other diners, and on the table in front of them a heap of empty whisky and gin bottles. It was one of the host's little jokes.[4]

The Hollywood people, although not easy to astonish, were impressed by the vast scope and expanse of everything at San Simeon, a place like a great movie set come to life. They could not repress wonderment at the power of this man who, in this one estate, controlled an area about half the size of Rhode Island and had a regiment of servants and workers to keep it going. Few even of the most frequent visitors had seen all of the castle's many rooms, and he was still adding to them. Five vaults under the Casa Grande were bursting with antique paneling, furniture and ceilings. A warehouse down in the village was likewise filled. Still there was often an excess of treasures, so that they would be stored outside in their crates, protected by tarpaulins. Hearst was determined to make use of all of them if he had to extend his castle to a mile.

He owned his own airfield. He owned 10,000 beef cattle, a splendid dairy, one of the top horse-breeding farms in the country that included Arabians, Palominos, Morgans and Appalusas, and a poultry farm with all the standard breeds plus such exotics as Cornish fowl, wild turkeys and several varieties of pheasants. At San Simeon alone were thirty-five Hearst cars. Mrs. O'Brien, the housekeeper, estimated that it cost about $6000 a day to run the palace alone when there was a full complement of guests.[5] The mere job of logistics in bringing in horsemeat for the lions and tigers, fish for the polar bears, and lettuce, carrots, apples and nuts for other animals was a formidable one. On Sunday mornings, a carillonneur made the tower bells spring into musical life. To the rear of the castle was a long, low cottage where Willicombe reigned over a staff of a half-dozen secretaries and teletypers who kept the Chief in touch with all his newspapers and other interests. There was also a radio operator to keep arriving Hearst planes posted on weather conditions. The cigar-puffing Willicombe had been with the boss so long that he could almost read his mind. Willicombe himself answered about ninety percent of the queries that streamed in from editors and executives. The rest he digested into condensed form on a clipboard—Hearst hated wordiness—and gave it to the Chief for decision.[6]

The San Simeon gardens, breathtaking in their beauty and scope, were estimated to have cost a million dollars. Nigel Keep presided over a large crew of gardeners who, on one occasion, worked all night under floodlights so that the next morning, Easter Sunday, the guests were amazed to see the castle surrounded by thousands of blooming Easter lilies. This was the sort

[4] Adela Rogers St. John to author.   [5] Mrs. St. John to author.
[6] *Fortune Magazine*, Oct., 1935.

of lordly surprise Hearst delighted in. Once, on a trip, he smelled a daphne. Charmed, he telegraphed Keep to plant a circle of daphne all around the castle, which Keep did by cornering all the daphne available at California nurseries—$12,000 worth. Sometimes Keep's crew was inadequate, and Hearst would import others. He brought in Charles Gibbs Adams, a noted landscape architect, with forty extra men, for one of his projects. Adams was amazed to learn that he and all of his men had to be photographed (by the San Simeon photographer) and given identification cards without which they would not be admitted at the gate—a precaution followed with all workers. Hearst ordered Adams to plant wildflowers to cover whole mountainsides within view of San Simeon, so that the outlook would be pleasant. He also instructed Adams to plant trees bordering that part of the driveway enclosed by the zoo—trees whose leaves giraffes, gnus and other herbivores would not eat.[7] In total cost, San Simeon dwarfed George Vanderbilt's palace in North Carolina, Biltmore, the Rockefeller estate in Westchester, and all other American mansions, and was seriously compared with Versailles and Frederick the Great's San Souci.

Probably some of the Hollywood visitors realized that what they were seeing was one man's revolt against history, a kingdom that was hermetically sealed against the republic that surrounded it, an oasis of riotous extravagance existing in a desert world of WPA and FERA. Perhaps some knew that this was a way of life that could not continue for long, and that the only thing that held it together even now was the iron will of the master. How long he could wall out reality as it existed in the other forty-eight states, and in his own newspaper offices, depended entirely on his resources. His resources were almost gone, although no one knew it.

Miss Parsons and some few others were "close" to Hearst, but the term is only comparative, for no one but Miss Davies really penetrated the wary defenses with which he surrounded himself. He always remained the grand seigneur, a man who could never come out from behind his mask. Miss Parsons, while devoted to him, never forgot that she was an employee. His cousin, Randolph Apperson, who regularly discussed the ranch with him and was impressed by his grasp of such technicalities as breeding and marketing, became accustomed to his aloofness. Nigel Keep, the horticulturist, called him "a jewel to work for," but knew better than to mention politics, a subject that could enrage him.[8] Dick Powell observed in Hearst a lordly bearing and "attitude of command" even in his more relaxed moments, and thought him "lonely and shy." [9] It puzzled Powell that a man of such intelligence and discrimination could publish newspapers obviously not directed at people of intelligence and discrimination. Adela Rogers St. John, who regarded Hearst as the keenest editorial brain in the world and admired him extravagantly, could chat with him gaily in a group but was surprised to discover that on one occasion, when she rode up to San Simeon alone with

[7] *Saturday Evening Post*, Mar. 9, 1940.   [8] Nigel Keep to author.
[9] Dick Powell to author.

Hearst and his chauffeur, she was tongue-tied with nervousness at the obligation to converse with him and say the right things.[10] Ilka Chase, who was only a casual guest at San Simeon and scarcely knew the owner, thought there was something repellent about him. When he surfaced near her in the swimming pool, he reminded her of "an octopus," and she made haste to get away. In the evening, she overheard a snatch of conversation between Hearst and his movie executive, Edgar Hatrick, that chilled her to the marrow with what she felt were sinister implications.

"I'm afraid, Mr. Hearst, we won't be able to get the rights," Hatrick said, referring to a song they wanted for a picture.

"Well," Hearst replied in his high voice, teetering back and forth on his heels, "I'm afraid that will be regrettable." [11]

To Miss Chase, the words were freighted with menace, as if Hatrick would be visited with terrible vengeance if he failed to get the rights Hearst wanted him to get. She was merely witnessing an example of how strongly he wanted things, and the pressure he would exert to get them. He was always inclined to believe that when his executives said something was impossible, it was only because they were too indolent to make an all-out effort. Chivalric to women, he could be brusque and even savage to his male executives, whom he liked to keep hopping by instilling in them an uneasy feeling that they were on the verge of losing their jobs. Considering this pressure, it is a sign of near-miraculous magnetism that most of his executives worshiped him. "There is good ground to doubt," wrote Silas Bent, "whether any other publisher has inspired in the employes with whom he came in contact a blinder or more devoted loyalty." [12]

There were some, such as actress Marie Dressler, who regarded Hearst as an ogre and were frankly afraid of him. This may have been due in part to his power and reputation for ruthlessness, but probably as much to the piercing, icy-blue fixity of his gaze when spoken to. The Hearst gaze unnerved even friends and colleagues. His secretary, Willicombe, privately advised editors that the best thing to do was to stare right back at him.

Nervousness haunted the lieutenants who were summoned to San Simeon for conferences. These were high-salaried men of prestige and authority in their own spheres, but when they reached the castle their importance was pricked like a balloon. Although Hearst might see immediately someone on urgent business, it was his habit to make others wait from a few days to a week or more. Already intimidated by the grandeur of their surroundings when they arrived, they would feel the remnants of their self-assurance ooze away as hours and days passed and they conjured up reasons why he might be displeased. They could swim or ride or meet glamorous film people, but they could not get drunk, and their enjoyment of all this was marred by the audience with the unpredictable tycoon that lay before them. Some would grow agitated. Occasionally they would wander over to Randolph Apperson's

[10] Mrs. St. John to author.
[11] Ilka Chase, *Past Imperfect*, 111.
[12] Bent, *Strange Bedfellows*, 221.

office down the hill, smoke cigarettes, pace the floor and say distractedly, "Why doesn't he call me?" [13]

The long wait could reduce strong men to a state of acute anxiety. There was speculation in the Organization as to why Hearst made them cool their heels. Some felt it was simply because he was busy, or because he wanted them to review their problems and have them well in hand. Doubtless these reasons were valid, but it seems likely that he also took a perverse enjoyment in it. He knew perfectly well that they were gnawing their nails. Their attendance on his pleasure enhanced his kingliness, underlined their position as courtiers, and it is not impossible that their jitters amused him, tickled his sense of power. His purchases of jewelry for Miss Davies were often conducted on the same basis. The best jewelers in San Francisco and Los Angeles would be alerted to send men to San Simeon with a fortune in gems for him to choose from. They would often wait a week or so before he got around to making a selection, but it was worth it. Miss Davies had one of the most valuable collections of jewelry in the country.

One of Hearst's favorite women was tall, electric, red-haired Eleanor Medill "Cissy" Patterson, the Chicago heiress. Formerly wed to a Polish count, and later to an American, Mrs. Patterson, who had resumed her own name, sought an outlet for her enormous energies and had tried to buy Hearst's Washington *Herald*. One reason, it was said, was her wish to hurl barbs at Alice Roosevelt Longworth, with whom she had feuded. Hearst refused to sell, but on the strength of a series of newspaper articles she had written, he offered her the editorship of the *Herald* at a negligible salary for her, $15,000 a year.[14] She had accepted, often appearing at the office in riding habit or evening gown. She had flung her barbs at Mrs. Longworth and had turned the *Herald* into a society paper with upper-class prestige—the only Hearst paper so blessed. Mrs. Patterson was a cousin of Colonel Robert McCormick of the Chicago *Tribune* and a sister of Captain Joseph Patterson of the New York *Daily News,* and was part owner of these properties. Thus Hearst had an editor who received most of her $1,000,000-a-year income from rival newspapers. He sincerely admired her journalistic enterprise. When Mrs. Patterson, who rode in her own private railroad car, arrived at San Simeon for a visit, he invariably had the other guests out on the terrace to meet her with armfuls of flowers, and hired a band to furnish a musical welcome.[15]

Mrs. Patterson esteemed Hearst's ability and intellect, but did not claim to understand him.[16] He had a host of admirers, but few who felt that they really *knew* him. Frances Marion, after working with him and Miss Davies on many pictures, was impressed by the duality of his nature.

"W. R.," she said, "was the most kindly and appreciative of persons—and at times the most ruthless." [17]

[13] Mr. Apperson to author.
[15] Mrs. St. John to author.
[17] Miss Marion to author.

[14] Rascoe, *Before I Forget,* 246–47.
[16] Harold L. Ickes, *Secret Diary,* I, 648.

13. Hell-Bent for Ruin

I. BUY IT, PRICE NO OBJECT

> Beware of tranquillity. It proclaims the toppling-over
> stage. It is the sleep that precedes dissolution. . . . About
> the time anybody really desires tranquillity he gets it per-
> manently—in death. —Hearst [1]

HEARST shunned tranquillity as if the only alternative were indeed the death he feared. Depression or no, he kept buying art. He could not stop. He had long since become known to dealers in Europe and America as the world's premier push-over. It was understood everywhere that he could not take a normal view toward art, could not appraise a piece according to cold market value, set a top price and stick to it. This arose from two factors: his yearning to acquire things and his contempt for money. When he bid for something, it was seldom with a hard-headed take-it-or-leave-it attitude, but with the idea that he *must* have it. The thought of losing a piece to another bidder was sheer anguish. He was aware of his own weakness, but powerless to correct it. Even when he entrusted the bidding to an agent, he would be bitterly disappointed and often reproachful if he lost an item or two to an-other bidder. Thus, the agents came to understand that with Hearst, though he might set a top price, price was secondary, the primary object being to make the purchase. The result was that most of what he bought was at highly inflated prices. Experts later estimated that he had paid something over twice the actual value of his art holdings.[2]

Mitchell Samuels, the head of French & Company in New York, who often served as his agent, tried earnestly to school him in the economics of wise bidding. The effort was usually futile. Samuels was puzzled at Hearst's promiscuous buying of art objects in such quantities that they were stored in warehouses and he could never use more than a fraction of them. He developed a theory that what Hearst had in mind was the ultimate founding of a great museum of the decorative arts.[3]

He was wrong in this because he was trying to define Hearst in terms of logic. There is no evidence that he had such a plan. He was a compulsive ac-cumulator, fascinated by pictures in art catalogues, driven by an urge to buy and own things he might never set eyes on. The business of collecting made him bubble with good spirits. Once, when Mitchell Samuels introduced him to his son, Spencer, Hearst did a snappy vaudeville tap-dance before thrust-

[1] N. Y. *American,* Oct. 7, 1935. [2] N. Y. *Times,* Apr. 15, 1951.
[3] Spencer A. Samuels to author, Jan. 20, 1960.

ing out his hand to the young man.[4] To him the thrill of mere ownership was an end in itself. The joy of possession was one of his paramount instincts. The same instinct was evident in his purchase of more horses, chickens and wild animals at San Simeon, and his continued additions to a castle already usually half-empty.

Hearst was often slow in paying for art, but Samuels was always glad to take his note for $50,000, $100,000 or more, knowing he would get his money eventually. Hearst was incorrigible at auctions, where his mere presence always boosted prices. He would go the limit for anything he wanted, and some dealers were not above taking advantage of him with the use of dummy bidders. Samuels urged that he let him do the bidding, and Hearst often agreed to this but frequently forgot the agreement. Hearst would fix a top price for something he wanted, and Samuels would stop bidding at that point, whereupon Hearst, horrified at the thought of losing the prize, would begin bidding himself.

He often had Miss Head chasing around England and the continent for antiquities. His memory was usually infallible, but once, when he cabled Miss Head to buy a certain seventeenth-century silver flagon, she replied that she had already bought that item for him. "I am chagrined at my own stupidity, but delighted," he rejoined by cable.[5]

He was much under the spell of the prestigious and foxy Sir Joseph Duveen. To his mind, anything sold by Duveen was worth more than objects sold by other dealers. He once looked at an antique room for sale at $50,000 by another dealer, turned it down, and later paid Duveen $200,000 for the same room.[6] Duveen knew Hearst's weaknesses and played on them, but on another occasion he outsmarted himself. He sold Hearst three pieces of fifteenth-century majolica for $101,000. Knowing that Hearst would sometimes change his mind and send a purchase back for refund, he decided to guard against such a disaster. He told Hearst a few days later that he had another buyer for the majolica and that he could get him a ten percent profit on it. Ordinarily the belief that someone else wanted an object in his possession was enough to make Hearst cling to it for dear life. This time, however, he either needed money or he suspected the stratagem.

"Well, I guess I'll take that profit," he said.

Duveen, appalled, was forced to pay up.[7]

Art critics sneered at Hearst, one calling him "the grotesque gargantua of our collecting era" who collected cigarette lighters as well as old masters,[8] another complaining that he seemed unable to discriminate between "the awful and the awesome." [9] Yet he had broad knowledge and excellent judgment in some specialties, among them armor, tapestries and antiques. Dealers loved him. A few, like Mitchell Samuels, became personal friends who tried

[4] Mr. Samuels to author.
[5] Behrman, *Duveen*, 171.
[6] Douglas and Elizabeth Rigby, **Lock, Stock and Barrel**, 286, 499.
[7] Richard E. Berlin to author.
[8] Spencer Samuels to author.
[9] Saarinen, 75.

to save him from his rash impulses. The fact that Hearst ultimately bought a total of $8,000,000 worth of tapestries, furniture and other art objects from Samuels alone was enough to offset the admitted difficulties in dealing with him. Samuels' firm of French & Company had bought the contents of Hamilton Palace in Scotland, which was sagging because of coal-mining tunnels underneath it. It included many wall panels and one grand double staircase. Hearst bought most of the panels and also the staircase, which were shipped to his Bronx warehouse. Later he reconsidered.

"The price for that staircase is a little high, Mitchell," he said. "You'd better take it back."

This was done. Later he changed his mind and bought it back again. Then once again he sent it back, still uncrated. This happened several more times, the staircase finally winding up at French's.[10]

Hearst's habit of buying from auction catalogues was safe enough in New York, where one of his dealer friends could inspect items for him, but was risky elsewhere in the United States and in Europe. Once in the Thirties, Hearst telephoned Samuels from San Simeon in considerable excitement.

"There's a big antique sale in Rome day after tomorrow," he said. "I just got a catalogue on it."

He asked Samuels to make purchases for him. Samuels was puzzled, for he had heard nothing of the sale, and he made it his business to be informed of all of them. He telephoned his Italian representative, an art dealer in Florence. *He* had not heard of the sale either. At Samuel's suggestion, he went to Rome and made inquiries. He discovered that the sale was a pure racket, drummed up by an unscrupulous dealer aiming at victimizing Hearst and Hearst alone. Knowing the American's weakness for buying sight unseen, he had prepared a beautiful and misleading catalogue solely for the master of San Simeon. Hearst, Samuels decided at length, knew he would be fooled once in a while, but would rather be swindled occasionally than to miss something he wanted.[11]

The Hearst New York warehouses, two five-story buildings at Southern Boulevard and 143rd Street in the Bronx, were mysterious places, the repositories of millions of dollars worth of art. The ground-floor windows were bricked up for greater safety, and no stranger was admitted. A staff of thirty men worked there, under the general supervision of Christy McGregor, who had risen from a ten-dollar-a-week clerkship with the Organization. A dozen clerks catalogued each incoming piece and had it photographed for the master file kept by Hearst, which he could pore over when he wanted to see what he owned. Among the other employees were two cabinet makers who worked full time just walking through the cavernous interior and making repairs on antiques, and a Scots armorer charged with keeping the armor in shape. Here were stored thousands of articles beautiful or curious, among them scores of paintings, statuary, the crated Spanish cloister, many entire

[10] Spencer Samuels to author.   [11] Mr. Samuels to author.

English rooms, and thousands of rare books, one of them being *The History of the Flagellants*.[12]

One would have thought that that cloister, which had cost Hearst $500,000 and for years had gathered dust in storage, would have been a lesson. Not at all. In 1932 he bought *another* one, the ancient Cistercian monastery of Santa Maria de Ovila, picked up near Siguenza in Spain. "As the structure was taken apart, every stone was particularly marked," reads an account. "The stones were carried by mule, crude ferry, ox cart and narrow gauge railway to Madrid. There they were packed with utmost care. Twelve ships took them to San Francisco " [13]

And what happened to the monastery of Santa Maria de Ovila after it got to San Francisco?

There is some mystery here. Possibly Hearst envisioned erecting the monastery, or part of it, at San Simeon. If so, the plan was discarded. He did not know what to do with it. He considered various ideas for disposing of it. No one was in the market for a monastery. Willicombe thought of selling it to a Hollywood studio for scenic purposes, but the cost merely to ship it was prohibitive.

Some years later, Hearst gave it to the M. H. de Young Museum in San Francisco's Golden Gate Park. The crated stones were stacked carefully behind the museum while the institution's directors waited hopefully for someone to furnish funds to erect it. Since then, a fire has damaged some of the crates, but the stones are still there at this writing, still awaiting the donor who will put them together.

Once Mrs. Hearst visited her husband's Bronx warehouse just to look around. She shook her head.

"How could one man buy all these things?" she said rhetorically to an employe. Then she said, "I think he went out and bought things whenever he was worried." [14]

II. NO. 1 RED-BAITER

In November, 1934, two young men called on Professor John N. Washburne, who taught economics at Syracuse University, saying they were interested in enrolling for his courses. They persuaded Washburne to have lunch with them and to discuss the curriculum at Syracuse. A few days later, the Syracuse *Journal*, a Hearst paper, carried a front-page story under the headline, "Drive All Radical Professors and Students From the Universities," quoting Washburne as having made radical utterances and charging that Syracuse University was ridden by Communism. The angry professor, realizing that he had been duped by Hearst reporters, repudiated most of the alleged statements, and the student paper condemned the *Journal*'s secret-police methods.

[12] *New Yorker*, Feb. 1, 1941.   [13] *Pacific Art Review*, Summer, 1941.
[14] *New Yorker*, Feb. 1, 1941.

The *Journal* came back with a demand that eight professors be discharged as Communists. Although it had the backing of the local American Legion, the crusade fizzled.[1]

In New York, Dr. George S. Counts of Teachers' College, Columbia University, received a letter from a young man who said he was desirous of enrolling in order to learn "the real stuff about socialism, communism and capitalism." [2] Counts, having heard of the Syracuse case, was on his guard. He had a stenographer with him when the young man arrived, and soon got him to admit that he was a Hearst reporter. According to Counts, the reporter said, "Mr. Hearst is engaged at present in conducting a Red scare. . . . You realize of course that because of my assignment I will have to select the most sensational statements from the interview in order to make out a good case. That is what Mr. Hearst is expecting." [3]

Another Hearst reporter called on Dr. William H. Kilpatrick of the same institution, also representing himself as a prospective student. According to Kilpatrick, this visitor likewise admitted his real errand.

"How do you feel about doing this sort of thing?" the professor asked.

"Just about as you think I feel," the newsman was quoted as replying. "I don't like it very much. I hope when the Newspaper Guild achieves its complete organization this sort of thing will go." [4]

In Chicago, Dr. Frederick L. Schuman, of the political science department of the University of Chicago, was annoyed when Hearst's local *Herald-Examiner* allegedly misquoted him when he addressed the Student Union Against War and Fascism, giving his statements a Communist flavor. Schuman complained to the editor, who sent a newsman named Charles Wheeler to investigate.

"We do just what the Old Man orders," Schuman quoted Wheeler as saying. "One week he orders a campaign against rats. The next week he orders a campaign against dope-peddlers. Pretty soon he's going to campaign against college professors. It's all the bunk, but orders are orders." [5]

Later, said Schuman, the *Herald-Examiner* misquoted him in another speech and began an editorial campaign demanding his dismissal as a Red.

These were a few samples of the nationwide Hearst anti-Red campaign, which also found evidences of treason at New York University, the University of Wisconsin, the University of Illinois and other institutions, and denounced such educators as Robert M. Hutchins, John Dewey, Frank P. Graham, Charles Beard and many others. The Hearst organization secured the services of a "reformed" Communist who had written for the *Daily Worker* to help sniff out Reds. The Hearst press was solidly behind the Ives bill in New York, which required teachers to take an oath of allegiance, and similar measures elsewhere. It began a series of articles portraying famine, misery

[1] N. Y. *Times*, Dec. 24, 1934; Carlson and Bates, 253.
[2] N. Y. *Times*, Dec. 24, 1934.
[3] *Social Frontier*, Feb., 1935.
[4] The same.
[5] *The Nation*, Apr. 24, 1935.

and brutality in Russia, while it saw less to criticize in the Nazis. Hearst himself spoke over a coast-to-coast network to warn the nation of the horrors sponsored by the Soviet government, ending on a non-Jeffersonian note:

> The truth is that government by the proletariat, government by the least capable and the least conscientious element of the community—government by the mob, government by ignorance and avarice—government by tyranny and terrorism . . . is the fearful failure that it needs must be and definitely deserves to be.
>
> I thought, my friends, that you might like to know the plain, uncensored truth.
>
> I am glad that this free country of ours permits me to tell it to you.[6]

The shouts of "fascist" were pelting him hard. Yet he attacked fascism in a signed editorial with equal vigor:

> In Italy the Fascist Government has suppressed all freedom of thought and expression, has drilled and dragooned all independent industry and all prosperity out of the country, and has utterly impoverished the people in order to gratify the Government's imperial ambition, and to maintain a nation in arms.
>
> In Germany not only is all liberty lost, and all modern ideas of freedom of thought and speech and publication ended, but as further evidence of complete return to the Dark Ages, the Nazi Government has revived medieval methods of execution and political practices of wholesale assassination.

What America had to fear, Hearst went on, was a rise of Communism that would cause a parallel rise of fascism and a death struggle between the two "in which democracy will surely be destroyed." [7]

He kept hammering at this point—that it was the threat of Communism that brought about the rise of fascism. Some enemies, seeing in this only insidious Hearst cunning, said he was deliberately building up a false Red scare so that a fascist party would quickly rise to take over the country and save it from Communism.[8] Liberals in general, thoroughly disillusioned with Hearst and revolted by his methods, saw in him nothing but evil and refused to credit him with a vestige of sincerity.

It is safe to say that this was an injustice, that Hearst's fear and hatred of Communism was sincere to the point of fixation and that he was ready to use any means, fair or foul, to fight it.

There was indeed a leftward trend of thinking, an extreme-liberal reaction after the Coolidge and Hoover regimes, a political turmoil caused by depression. Some members of the New Deal administration made free-wheeling utterances frightening to conservatives. The Communist party in America had polled its biggest vote in 1932. To the dismay of the American Federation of Labor, Communists had gained control of some labor unions. In many intellectual and academic circles socialism had become popular. The Com-

[6] N. Y. *American*, Jan. 6, 1935.   [7] N. Y. *American*, Mar. 3, 1935.
[8] Swing, 150.

munists were now following their new tactic of boring from within, infiltrating into liberal groups of all kinds. There were, of course, a few Communists and fellow travelers among teachers. The American people as a whole were not aware of Communism as a danger.

It is not surprising that Hearst, who considered himself the watchdog of American democracy and who incidentally was guardian of his own tottering capitalistic empire, should have been frightened into becoming America's No. 1 Red-baiter. He deserves credit for being the first influential citizen to recognize the danger even if there is no excusing his method of attack. When the word came from the Chief at San Simeon, hundreds of Hearst reporters were assigned to a Red hunt that smeared many honest liberals and was a negation of the democracy he claimed to defend.

As a result, he achieved something approaching his unpopularity during the World War. He was assailed not only by Communists but by virtually every liberal group in the land. Norman Thomas called him "nearly public enemy No. 1." [9] A group of college editors condemned him. Fifteen thousand spectators booed him at a mass meeting at Madison Square Garden addressed by Dr. Counts and others.[10] The *Nation,* the *New Republic* and other liberal publications excoriated him. A throng of Communists marched to the *Journal-American* building on South Street in New York and staged a demonstration, chanting, "Hearst is a strike-breaker; Hearst is a war-maker." [11] At a National Educational Association meeting at Atlantic City, Dr. Charles Beard, a victim of Hearst-paper charges, had his own innings, saying in part:

> . . . William Randolph Hearst has pandered to depraved tastes and has been an enemy of everything that is noblest and best in our American tradition. . . . There is not a cesspool of vice and crime which Hearst has not raked and exploited for money-making purposes. . . . Unless those who represent American scholarship, science, and the right of a free people to discuss public questions freely stand together against his insidious influences he will assassinate them individually by every method known to yellow journalism.[12]

Hurt by these assaults, Hearst felt that the public misunderstood him. Perhaps it was with this in mind that he asked his old friend Fremont Older to write his biography. The aging Older did not feel up to the job, but he agreed to help with the research while his younger wife, Cora, did the writing. Hearst sent them four trunkfuls of his letters, dating back to his youth, to get them started.[13]

III. CALL IT THE "RAW DEAL"

IN his frantic effort to boost *Mirror* circulation, Brisbane in 1935 hired pipe-smoking Stanley Walker away from the *Herald-Tribune* at a fancy salary

[9] N. Y. *Times,* Jan. 7, 1935.
[11] N. Y. *Times,* Apr. 7, 1935.
[13] Mrs. Older to author, Oct. 18, 1959.
[10] N. Y. *Herald-Tribune,* Apr. 4, 1935.
[12] N. Y. *Times,* Feb. 25, 1935.

despite the fact that Walker's eyes were hazel, not blue. Walker, who made the move as something of a lark, came to realize that Brisbane had lost faith in Gauvreau and was expecting Walker to create a situation that would force Gauvreau to quit, so that his contract would not have to be paid off. Walker wanted no part of this. Seeing him at the typewriter, Brisbane suspected him of writing a book on company time. Soon he eased the newcomer out of the *Mirror* and into the *American* as "a sort of managing editor." [1]

Walker discovered that a large part of his job there was to reduce expenses, mostly by cutting the staff. Fred Eldridge, the editor who thirty years earlier had had a large hand in getting the Standard Oil letters, had been made an "efficiency expert" whose job was to travel from one Hearst paper to another, eliminating waste. Eldridge would meet daily with Walker and other editors, the net result of the parley being that someone would get a salary cut or get fired. Walker conceived a cordial dislike for the axe-swinging Eldridge, who had a strange phobia, a fear of getting close to windows because he might jump out. "When I learned this," Walker later wrote, "I tried always to maneuver him as close to a window as possible, but he was too clever for me." [2]

Being a top-drawer newspaperman with a real respect for the news, Walker was unhappy in the Organization. He was oppressed by the peculiar news exploitation of the Hearst press, by the sinking morale in the office, and by the smells emanating from the nearby fish market. When Eldridge proposed to slash the salary of a veteran editor in failing health, it was the last straw. "If you really want to save money," Walker said, "don't pick on him. Wire Hearst to let me out of my contract." He was glad to get out after less than seven months.[3]

Meanwhile, Émile Gauvreau had published a book, *What So Proudly We Hailed,* the result of an extensive tour of Russia. In it he pictured Russia favorably, at the same time pointing out the racketeering, corruption and unemployment in the United States. This flouted the Hearst line that the enslaved Russians were starving, while America was the land of the free. Hearst promptly got a telegram from a Russia-hater named Frank Pease, asking how he could employ the disseminator of such treason. Gauvreau's head rolled into the basket next day, although the remainder of his contract was paid off. Gauvreau felt, however, that what really angered Hearst was the suggestion of book reviewers that he had satirized his boss.[4]

About this same time, Managing Editor Ray Van Ettisch of the Los Angeles *Examiner* had a heart attack. Hearst promptly sent him to Bad Nauheim for the long course of treatment there, paying all his expenses.[5]

Toward Roosevelt, Hearst had developed a loathing similar to that he had felt for Wilson. He called the Wagner Act, which would protect the Newspaper Guild's organizing activities, "one of the most vicious pieces of class

[1] Stanley Walker to author, Feb. 8, 1960.   [2] Mr. Walker to author, Feb. 15, 1960.
[3] Mr. Walker to author.   [4] Gauvreau, 295–304.
[5] Warden Woolard to author, Nov. 4, 1959.

legislation that could be conceived—un-American to the core." He had so far retreated from his old trust-busting stand that he called the Wheeler-Rayburn bill, which would eliminate holding companies, "PURE VENOM distilled by a PERSONAL and MALIGNANT OBSESSION." [6] All Hearst editors received a Willicombe warning that the Chief wished them to use the term "Soak the Successful" in referring to Roosevelt's tax policy instead of "Soak the Thrifty," and that the New Deal should always be described by the phrase "Raw Deal." [7]

In attack he was blistering, but in humor he was mirth-provoking. Paul Mallon, the columnist, was so impressed by the Hearst felicity with words that he wrote the publisher frankly asking whether he had a ghost in his pocket. Hearst slapped him down gently.

"Would it be discourteous for me," he wrote, "to ask in return if you write all the articles you sign?

"Of course you do, and of course you do not think that you are so much cleverer than other people that you can write and others cannot.

"I am a professional newspaperman, Mr. Mallon, and I have been working at the newspaper business—not playing with it but working at it—day and night for over fifty years.

"Would I not be a 'dumb cluck,' as the saying goes, if I did not know the rudiments of my trade by this time?

"Of course I write my signed articles, and many more that I do not sign. If I do not write them, who does? I wish I knew. I am being sued on one of them now, and if I did not write it I wish the fellow who did would come up like a man and tell me about it and take the rap.

"Furthermore, Mr. Mallon, I do not think it is such a trick to write. Anybody who can think can write. It does not take much practice to put thoughts into words. All you have got to do is to have some thoughts which are worth putting into words . . ." [8]

Always the isolationist, Hearst fought to keep the Senate from passing a bill for United States entry into the World Court—a bill that had the President's blessing and which Hearst regarded as a violation of the pledge Roosevelt's subordinates had given him during the 1932 convention. With the help of his good friend Senator Hiram Johnson, and a flood of "anti" telegrams largely stirred up by Father Coughlin and the Hearst press, the bill was beaten. Hearst had poorer luck in California, where he and Louis Mayer fought hard but failed to beat a stiff boost in state income taxes. He had been in financial trouble for several years, and at last he knew it. The business revival he had long expected had not come. John Francis Neylan had been working furiously to put the Hearst house in order. The strain was telling on him. He handed in his resignation as of the end of 1935, quitting one of the largest legal retainers in the country.

[6] S. F. *Examiner*, May 29 and June 21, 1935.
[7] James MacG. Burns, *Roosevelt: The Lion and the Fox*, 241.
[8] N. Y. *American*, Oct. 20, 1935.

"Why?" Hearst asked him, astonished. "What have I done?"

Neylan explained that he was worn out. He later said, "The strain was so unbearable that had I not resigned I would have been dead before 1940." A rugged man of great vitality, he was amazed that Hearst, who was many year older and subject to at least as much worry, showed few signs of it. Hearst urged him to stay on, offering more money, but Neylan was firm, as he put it, "literally to save my own life." [9]

One way to save money was in taxes. Both Miss Davies and Hearst petitioned for a reduction in federal tax claims.[10] Another way was to get rid of Roosevelt and his New Deal. Hearst astonished politicos by urging his ancient enemy, Al Smith, as a fine independent candidate in 1936 at the head of a "genuine Jeffersonian Democratic ticket." He said he did not care whether he and Smith had been foes for years. "Nor do I care whether he pronounces the word 'radio' in a manner to suit the professors of the brain trust.

"He pronounces the word 'America' properly and patriotically, and that is all that matters in these widely disloyal days." [11]

It seems unlikely that Hearst seriously wanted Smith to become President. He well knew that Smith and other conservative Democrats were bitter against Roosevelt, and it appears probable that he was hoping to split the Democrats so that a Republican could be elected. G.O.P. men were already eying Governor Alf M. Landon of Kansas, who had staged the phenomenal feat of getting reelected in the Democratic year of 1934. Only a month after his Smith puff, Hearst issued another radio rallying cry from San Simeon. Attacking Roosevelt's "foreign, Fascist ideas of personal dictation," he said, "He can be defeated either by a Republican candidate with a convincing record of actual achievement or by a genuine Jeffersonian Democrat, known and trusted by the people," adding, "I am confident that Governor Landon of Kansas could be elected on the Republican ticket." [12]

Fortune magazine sent writers and photographers to Wyntoon to confer with Hearst and to fall prey to deceiving appearances. *Fortune* came out with a lavish story commenting on the shrewd methods Hearst had used to weather the depression unscathed, estimating his assets at $220,000,000, and suggesting that the Hearst Class A stock was one of the safest in the world—this at a time when the Organization was bleeding to death.[13]

"Confiscatory" taxes became a mania with Hearst. Under previous administrations he had been permitted to lump all of his publications together for tax purposes and to gain advantage because of the great losses suffered by some of them such as the New York *American* and the Chicago *Herald-Examiner*. Under Roosevelt this advantage was gone. Besides, Roosevelt *raised* taxes on corporations and high incomes. Hearst's screams were so

[9] Mr. Neylan to author, Nov. 5, 1959.   [10] N. Y. *Times*, July 19 and Sept. 19, 1935.
[11] N. Y. *American*, Aug. 29, 1935.   [12] N. Y. *Times*, Sept. 30, 1935.
[13] *Fortune*, Oct., 1935.

violent that when the President laid out his tax-raising program he grinned at Interior Secretary Harold Ickes and said, "That is for Hearst." [14] Now, under the new California tax laws, Hearst let that state know that he was thereafter forced to live there less than six months a year in order to escape its levy.

"Heaven knows I do not want to leave California," he wrote. "No one does, least of all a native son whose father was a pioneer; but it is utterly impossible for me to remain here and occupy a place like San Simeon on account of the Federal and State tax laws.

"The California income tax goes to fifteen per cent. Add this to the Federal income taxes and the New York taxes, plus many other taxes, and I find that over eighty per cent of my income will go in taxes—in fact, it may be nearer ninety per cent. Under these circumstances it is absolutely necessary for me to eliminate the high income tax in California."

He warned that others, including motion picture companies, might have to move out. To which Louis Mayer added amen, saying that this was "inevitable" and that "Mr. Hearst's leaving evidences the fear in all our minds of the disastrous consequences of reckless and discriminatory tax legislation." [15]

The hearts of few Californians bled for Hearst, whose deprivations did not seem extreme. Governor David Scholz of Florida invited him to move there, and he also received an invitation from the mayor of Atlantic City, where the American Federation of Labor convention had just denounced him as an enemy of labor. However, in November he and Miss Davies arrived in New York, where it was said they were taking "one or two floors" of the Hearst-owned Ritz Tower.[16] This luxurious building would lose him $592,000 in that year of 1935, and Brisbane was chuckling over his good fortune in unloading it on the Chief.[17] Although Hearst was still on friendly terms with his wife, and they occasionally consulted on business and family matters, he had grown accustomed to having Miss Davies at his side wherever he went and had given up the pretense of family life at the Clarendon.

IV. LANDON TO THE RESCUE

> At my time of life, you just sit here and people bring
> you final decisions to make.   —Hearst [1]

IN December, Hearst hurried out of the Ritz Tower to catch his private car for the West. He turned to Coblentz, who accompanied him to the station in a taxicab. "Cobbie," he said, "I just caught a glimpse of the window of that art shop across the street from the Ritz. There's a painting there I liked

[14] Ickes, *Secret Diary*, I, 384.   [15] N. Y. *Times*, Oct. 23, 1935.
[16] N. Y. *Times*, Nov. 8, 1935.   [17] Gauvreau, 211.
[1] *Fortune Magazine*, Oct., 1935.

—the second one on the left. Would you find out who painted it, how much it costs, and let me know?" Coblentz made a note of it. This sort of thing was routine with anyone close to the Chief.[2]

Hearst's companions on the westward trip were Brisbane, Cissy Patterson and Paul Block, the newspaper publisher, a close friend. Doubtless Miss Davies was with them, though this was not publicized. One of Hearst's errands was to "size up" Governor Landon, whom he had already had several of his writers look over. They stopped off at Topeka, where Hearst, Block and Brisbane had lunch with the governor in the executive mansion. "I think he is marvelous," Hearst said afterward.[3] The plain, pleasant-looking Landon, who spoke so simply, struck him as the man to save the nation from Roosevelt. Landon had made a fine record of efficiency as governor, but probably the point that impressed Hearst most was that he *reduced taxes*.

Mrs. Patterson and Brisbane—and inevitably Miss Davies—continued on to San Simeon with Hearst. The attitude of the intelligent, accomplished Mrs. Patterson toward Hearst was ambivalent. She admired him personally and yet was distressed by his ruthless, iron control over his newspapers. She was perfectly aware that Hearst editors were regarded with contempt by most other newspaper people as well-paid but voiceless slaves. She enjoyed the thrill of running his *Herald*. However, at length she decided to refuse the $15,000 stipend he was paying her. She was now working for him gratis, and letting her friends know about it. "You know, don't you, that I don't take any salary from Mr. Hearst," she said to Secretary Ickes.[4] One suspects that while she could not precisely escape the stigma of working for Hearst, she was at any rate salvaging a species of independence by refusing his money.

Hearst was reaching another of his periodic zeniths of unpopularity. Once the *bête noire* of the conservatives, he was now the whipping boy of groups ranging from liberal to extreme radical. Hisses arose in theaters when the Hearst-Metrotone newsreel appeared, causing the Hearst name once more to be lopped off. He was condemned by the American Federation of Teachers, the Farmer-Labor party of Minnesota, the United Auto Workers, the Newspaper Guild, and the League Against War and Fascism. The latter organization, which was tinctured with Communists, published a pamphlet describing him as the "vilest racketeer of them all," "Hitler's man in America," and calling for a boycott of his publications. A Hearst press series of anti-Hitler articles, it declared, was insincere, a mere sop to public opinion. "Spread the boycott against Hearst," it urged. ". . . Buy a paper, but don't buy a Hearst paper!"[5] Other organizations spurred the boycott idea by handing out "I don't read Hearst" stickers. The boycott hurt an Organization that was already reeling. Many influential Republicans, who looked on Landon as a promising candidate, feared that Hearst support would do him harm rather than good.

[2] Private source.
[4] Ickes, *Secret Diary*, I, 648.
[3] N. Y. *Times*, Dec. 11, 1935.
[5] *Vilest Racketeer of All*, pamphlet.

Hearst created a small sensation by hiring Elliott Roosevelt, son of the President, as a $50,000-a-year vice president of his radio enterprises,[6] a move some enemies ascribed to his desire to placate the administration and get favors from it. Landon easily won the Republican nomination at Cleveland in June, with Colonel Frank Knox—a former Hearst executive—as his running mate. Thereafter the Hearst press boomed Landon in a lavish publicity build-up complete with photographs of the nominee and his family in full color. The charge that Landon was "Hearst-picked," however, was untrue, for the publisher had been far from the first to hail him. The year 1936 was also notable for the publication of three biographies of Hearst, one by Ferdinand Lundberg, one by Oliver Carlson and Ernest Bates, and a third by Mrs. Older. The first two, written by liberals who regarded Hearst as a fascist, assailed him savagely. Mrs. Older, who knew him personally and truly admired him, presented him as a great American, delicately avoiding mention of such things as the Mexican fakes and his involvement with Miss Davies. Readers of all three had a right to be confused, for the Hearst Mrs. Older so esteemed obviously was not the same man the others loathed.

Neither the impending crisis in his own empire, another wage cut in the Organization and the layoff of many men, nor his own bitter complaints about taxes, could make Hearst refrain from acting as if money worries were farthest from his mind. On August 8 he sailed for Italy with a party of sixteen, paying all expenses as usual. Among his companions were Miss Davies, his son George and his wife, Mary Carlisle and Mr. and Mrs. Arthur Lake.

"The race will not be close at all," he told reporters. "Landon will be overwhelmingly elected and I'll stake my reputation as a prophet on it." [7]

Doubtless he regarded his European trip as money saved in that it helped him to avoid California for half the year and thus eliminate the state tax. He had contributed $30,000 to the Republican campaign chest, the largest amount given by any individual.[8] By the time he reached Italy, his money-losing Seattle *Post-Intelligencer* had been closed by a Guild strike that threw 650 employes out of work. Hearst had refused to recognize the Guild, and two Guild men had been fired. In Rome, he was quick to blame the Communists.

"It has cost me over $1,000,000 to conduct my paper in Seattle all through the depression and up to date," he said. "If the Communists want to relieve me of that cost and of the duty of supplying jobs to labor, it is not an unmixed evil. I would save money.

"However, there is a greater issue at stake than saving money. There is the issue of a free press and a free country . . . whether anybody else makes the fight against Communism and mob rule or not, I am going to make it; and I am enlisted for the duration of the war." [9]

[6] N. Y. *Herald-Tribune,* Mar. 15, 1936. [7] N. Y. *Times,* Aug. 9, 1936.
[8] N. Y. *Times,* Oct. 24, 1936. [9] N. Y. *Times,* Aug. 21, 1936.

He fought it in his papers, saying that while Earl Browder was the "titular nominee" of the Communists for President, "The real candidate—the un-official candidate of the Comintern—is Franklin D. Roosevelt." [10]

Stung, the President replied through a spokesman assailing "a certain notorious newspaper owner" for the suggestion that his administration was influenced by Reds. Hearst, accepting the "notorious" tag, replied from across the sea with a blast at the "Karl Marx Socialists, the Frankfurter radicals, Communists and anarchists, the Tugwell Bolsheviks and the Richberg revolutionists which constitute the bulk of [Roosevelt's] following." [11]

Arthur Brisbane and his son Seward joined the Hearst party in Italy, as did Miss Head. Brisbane was an ailing and querulous man, so thrifty that despite his multi-millionaire status he did not have a secretary along to help him with his column, which he continued to grind out on tour. The old editor was slipping. His writing had lost its punch. Hearst had rejected a few Brisbane columns, and had even suggested that Brisbane did not necessarily have to appear on the front page. Possibly he was irked at having taken over Brisbane's miserable Ritz Tower, and also at Brisbane's glorious solvency while he, the creator of it all, was facing disaster.

But there is no hint that Hearst was not cordial to his old colleague. Brisbane's malaise stemmed in part from his realization that he was being paid $260,000 a year for being the most glittering stooge in journalism. Once a man of sincere social conscience, he had been caught up in his pursuit of wealth. He had twinges of remorse.[12]

In Italy, both the seventy-two-year-old Brisbane and the seventy-three-year-old Hearst came down with dysentery. Hearst, as tough as a rooster, recovered perfectly, but Brisbane left the party with his son and joined his family in the south of France to recuperate. Hearst had not resumed diplomatic relations with France, and would not set foot on its soil. He traveled with his companions to Bad Nauheim, where he took his usual cure and stayed away from Hitler. Landon, in upstate New York, flouted the Hearst precepts by saying he did not see why teaching should be made into a "suspect profession" by requiring teachers to take a special oath. The Hearst press put him right on this:

> It is difficult to understand how any citizen can embrace the thought that the act of taking an oath of loyalty to his country will make a teacher a member of a suspect profession.
>
> All officials in public service have taken such an oath. The President of the United States takes it. Mr. Landon, twice elected as Governor of his State, twice assumed it.[13]

At the same time came a reminder of the slowness of American justice. The Madison Square fireworks explosion of 1902 had caused eighty-one damage suits against the city, which had been winding their tortuous way

[10] N. Y. *American*, Sept. 19, 1936.   [11] N. Y. *American*, Sept. 20, 1936.
[12] Gauvreau, 150.   [13] N. Y. *American*, Aug. 28, 1936.

through the courts for thirty-four years. The city had held Hearst liable as co-defendant, and in 1917 he had paid a $24,000 judgment. Now the city settled the last case, clearing Hearst of further liability by his agreement to pay another $30,000.[14] It appears that the total damages Hearst paid was only $54,000, but his legal expenses over the years must have been heavy.

In Amsterdam, he visited the Rijksmuseum and was stricken by the inevitable itch. He spent "more than $70,000" for canvases by Joost Van Cleve and George Morland, bought three seventeenth-century cupboards and dickered for two more paintings valued at $30,000.[15] There was an *"après moi le déluge"* air about Hearst, unable to resist his urge to buy. It was said—perhaps rumor—that he had to borrow money from some of his guests. Doubtless he was pleased to be denounced by Earl Browder and by both *Pravda* and *Izvestia*, and to be "tried and convicted" at a huge public meeting in New York's Hippodrome sponsored by the League Against War and Fascism, of "perverting the news, breeding war, breaking strikes, fascism and destroying liberty." [16] After a stay at St. Donat's, he and his troupe sailed home in a brand-new liner, the *Queen Mary*. Landing in New York the day before election, he repeated to reporters his prediction that Landon would of course be elected. One of those who met him was Adela Rogers St. John. "Adela, how is Landon doing?" he inquired. "Mr. Hearst," she replied candidly, "we're going to get our brains kicked out." [17] As a prophet she excelled her boss, for Landon was snowed under, winning only the eight electoral votes of Maine and Vermont.

That night, Roosevelt's son-in-law, John Boettiger, was answering congratulatory telephone calls at Hyde Park. One came from Marion Davies, who was then followed by Hearst on the wire. "Hello, is that you, Boettiger?" he said. "Well, I just wanted to repeat what Marion said, that we have been run over by a steam roller, but that there are no hard feelings at this end." [18]

Hearst likewise did something like public penance in his newspapers.

". . . Roosevelt's victory," he wrote, "is absolutely stunning to those who opposed him, and utterly astounding even to his supporters.

"It justifies very largely the comparison of Mr. Roosevelt to Andrew Jackson, who is the only man in American history who had an equally overwhelming popular appeal and popular victory.

". . . I believe that we should all not only comply cheerfully with the will of the majority but that we should endeavor to understand and appreciate and apply the wisdom embodied in it. . . ." [19]

Soon thereafter he hired Boettiger at $37,500 a year to take over direction of the Seattle *Post-Intelligencer* and settle the strike. Some said that if Hearst couldn't beat Roosevelt with votes, he would beat him with flattery and by hiring away his family.

[14] N. Y. *Times*, Sept. 19, 1936.
[16] N. Y. *Herald-Tribune*, Oct. 23, 1936.
[18] Ickes, *Secret Diary*, I, 704.
[15] N. Y. *Times*, Oct. 5, 1936.
[17] Mrs. St. John to author.
[19] N. Y. *American*, Nov. 5, 1936.

BOOK SIX

THE PHOENIX

1. The Tottering Throne

WHEN Brisbane returned to New York, he suffered several coronary attacks, took to his bed in his mansion at Fifth Avenue and 102nd Street, and kept dictating his daily column as if the world depended on it. Hearst, who thought the Bad Nauheim heart specialists the best anywhere, sent for his own, Dr. Heinz Groedel, who came post-haste from the German spa. For all of Groedel, Brisbane died on Christmas Day, 1936.

The rival press front-paged his obituaries without calling him great. To Hearst, Brisbane's death must have brought a flood of memories of the long-gone days when the two of them were young, fighting Pulitzer, fighting the Spaniards, fighting Hanna, McKinley, the trusts—the dear, dead days when there was no income tax, no Newspaper Guild, no Communists, no New Deal. He wrote a touching tribute to "my close and dear and long time friend," calling him "the greatest journalist of his day," and published it in all his newspapers.[1] And he attended the funeral.

Brisbane left an estimated $25,000,000 while the Chief was scratching for pocket money. The day of reckoning was at hand. The castles, the Van Dycks, the tapestries, the swimming pools, the tourism *à la* Hearst, had taken their toll. The Organization was staggering under a load of debt to stockholders, newsprint companies and twenty-eight different banks. Frantically it tried to borrow more money. In the summer of 1937, Hearst Publications, Incorporated, and Hearst Magazines, Incorporated, filed with the Securities and Exchange Commission for permission to float a total of $35,500,000 in debentures. The S.E.C., after a narrow look at the existing debts, decided that the Organization could not stand this additional load and allowed it to withdraw the application.[2]

There was sheer panic among the executives—and at San Simeon. They *had* to have that money, and the government said, "No."

Ironically, in the midst of this, Treasury officials told a Congressional Tax Evasion committee that Hearst, by a clever shuffling of holding companies, had saved $2,371,133 in taxes in 1934 and $2,740,575 in 1935, and asked that such corporate leaks be stopped.[3]

One of the minor troubles assailing Hearst was a lawsuit for $40,000 by Jesse Zelda, a mechanic at San Simeon, who said that while he worked on a truck an ostrich sidled up behind him, "knocked him down and trampled

[1] N. Y. *American*, Dec. 26, 1936. [2] N. Y. *Times*, Sept. 2, 1937.
[3] N. Y. *Herald-Tribune*, July 17, 1937.

on him," so that he sustained a hernia, concussion, shock, and had never been the same since.[4]

Zelda could be contained, but not the S.E.C. Its action toppled the Organization off a high-flying cloud of financial fantasy and sent it crashing to the street—Wall Street.

Whose fault was it that the Organization, now shrunk to 27,000 employes, had been allowed to drift into ruin before anything was done? No one but Hearst's. He was the Chief, the boss, the man whose word was final. Although he had been warned many times, he was the one who insisted on investing $50,000,000 in New York real estate at high mortgages, on maintaining papers in New York, Chicago, Omaha and elsewhere that lost millions annually, on spending an estimated $50,000,000 for art. He had blithely led the world's greatest publishing combine from riches to wreckage. Unequaled in his technical skill, he had proved himself fiscally the world's worst executive. The editorial and organizational genius was a chump when it came to the ledger. He had always been a chump financially, and it had only taken a few lean years to prove it. He had railed at the New Deal, railed at taxes, and kept on spending. But there was something more than mere folly in the way he had marched straight into catastrophe with his eyes open. There was that same old Hearst weakness, the overconfidence, the refusal to face up to unpleasant reality that was a part of his megalomania, his kingly assurance that he could do what no one else could do and get away with it— a state of mind that verged on irrationality.

The executives who had warned him had not been able to make him listen because (1) they were too fearful of their jobs to make the warnings forcible, (2) he would not have listened anyway, (3) they kept hoping along with him that a business upturn would save the day, and (4) the Old Man had a touchy heart and might die in time to save the situation.

The Organization made strenuous efforts to hide its near-bankruptcy. Hearst *had* to face reality now. It was obvious to everyone that the man who had walked into trouble was not the one to lead the way out. Someone was needed who realized the value of a dollar. There were hurried consultations with the largest and most pressing creditors, and these creditors firmly thumbed the Chief out. In June, 1937, Hearst, said to be thoroughly frightened, went to New York and relinquished financial control of his publishing enterprises to his friend of almost forty years, Clarence Shearn. Shearn, who had once battled the trusts with Hearst, had so far forgotten his dislike for big bankers as to become one of counsel for the Chase National Bank, holder of some of the Hearst notes. For the first time in a half century, the Chief was not final boss, although he retained technical editorial control.[5]

The total debt was a whopping $126,000,000. There was doubt that bankruptcy could be avoided. Shearn worked with the urgency of a physician over an expiring patient. He began doing what Hearst would never do—

[4] N. Y. *Times,* July 4, 1937.   [5] *Time* Magazine, Mar. 13, 1939.

liquidating the losing newspapers that were draining the firm's lifeblood. On June 24 he killed Hearst's own mouthpiece and favorite newspaper, the New York *American,* combining it with the *Journal* as the *Journal-American.* On June 30 he shut down the Rochester *Journal* and *Sunday American.* Soon thereafter he leased the Washington *Herald* to Cissy Patterson and consolidated losing Universal Service with International News Service.[6] Hundreds of men were thrown out of work, hundreds more getting still another pay cut, but there was no help for it.

Among them was Hearst himself, who took the biggest cut of all, from $500,000 down to $100,000. John Francis Neylan, who temporarily rejoined his old client to help him in his travail, told Mrs. Hearst of the crisis.

"Cut my allowance in half," she said instantly. "And tell the boys they'll have to do the same to help out." [7]

At seventy-four, Hearst learned the financial facts of life. He was unable to buy any more objects of art. Indeed—wonder of wonders—he was *selling.* At Sotheby's famous auction rooms in London was placed on sale eighty-three items of precious old English silver whose ownership was unannounced but which experts immediately recognized as a small part of the treasure he had bought for his castle in Wales. Characteristically, he had overbid for them, having paid some $240,000 for the lot. He received only $110,000 for them at the sale. One Elizabethan silver-gilt cup for which he had paid $16,375 brought a mere $2,500.[8]

This was only the beginning. With Hearst's advice, Shearn appointed a "Conservation Committee" composed of seven Organization executives including Thomas J. White, the general manager; Richard E. Berlin, head of the magazines; Martin F. Huberth, and W. R. Hearst Jr., publisher of the *Journal-American* and representing the family.[9] Huberth's role was vital, for he was the real estate expert, and one of the Committee's chief aims was to liquidate Hearst's holdings. His $50,000,000 in New York property had been bought at inflated values. Now, although it was no longer worth that amount in a depressed market, the huge mortgage payments were an impossible weight on a company fighting for its life.

II. END OF AN ERA

1937 was the beginning of a long nightmare for Hearst. The things he loved— power and possessions—were torn away brutally in a process that became even more urgent and relentless as time went on. To add to his worries, Miss Davies received an extortion note reading "If you value your life you will have one thousand $ in small bills in front of the California show [theater]." [1] Detectives nabbed the culprit, but there was little to cheer

---

[6] N. Y. *Times,* Mar. 21, 1938.   [7] Mr. Neylan to author.
[8] N. Y. *Times,* Oct. 11, Nov. 19, 1937.
[9] N. Y. *Times,* Mar. 21, 1938. The committee, however, was appointed in 1937.
[1] N. Y. *Herald-Tribune,* Nov. 14, 1937.

about in this time of unrelieved disaster. One of the cruelest blows of all came when he and Miss Davies were forced to drop a project that was close to their hearts—their movie enterprise.

Eighteen years earlier he had vowed to make her the nation's top star and himself the greatest mogul of the films. He had failed, and some said he had lost $7,000,000 in failing.[2] Only those who understood how badly he had *wanted* success in this, and how confidently he had expected it, could realize the extent of his bitterness and humiliation at shutting up shop in the Hollywood he had meant to rule. If ever Hearst threw one of his famous tantrums, stamping around in a rage, shrieking in his high voice and breaking things, he threw one now.

As if to sound the knell of the bright Hollywood dream, Clark Alvord, the Nevada postmaster who for years had been Miss Davies' most ardent fan, died at Nelson, Nevada. His will read, "I give and bequeath to my beloved Marion Davies all my property, both real and personal . . ." Miss Davies was left with an estate of some $10,000, which she promptly gave to charity, sending roses for Alvord's grave.[3]

The Conservation Committee had been eying the block-square Hearst art warehouses in the Bronx. The thirty-man staff was still there, guarding a king's ransom in European loot the Chief obviously would never use. Among the accumulations of decades were the 10,700 crates containing the stones of the Spanish monastery—the first one—a $500,000 investment that could not be said to be producing a fair return. The Committee did not know whether a monastery was salable, but they knew that millions of dollars worth of other objects in the warehouse were, and a sale would help satisfy some of the creditors plaguing the Organization.

Was Mr. Hearst willing? He had to be. It must have been like tearing his heart out, but his newspapers came first with him and he authorized the sale of two-thirds of his art holdings.

The Organization was still trying to make it appear that all this was dictated not by necessity but by good business practice. It was pointed out that Hearst was nearing seventy-five and he did not want to burden his family with the enormous inheritance taxes levied on works of art. Chairman White said for publication that Hearst, "conscious of the uncertainties of life" was anxious to "place on a more permanent basis a comprehensive plan of management for all his varied enterprises—newspapers, magazines, art objects, mines, ranches and real estate." [4]

The art world pricked up its ears, for this would assuredly be the biggest sale of treasure in years. It was known that Hearst had plenty of junk, but he also had innumerable objects of great value. Among the paintings to be sold were canvases by Rembrandt, Hals, Rubens, and Van Dyck's portrait of Queen Henrietta Maria which Hearst had insisted on taking off Duveen's hands for $375,000. In addition were sixty rare tapestries, endless furniture,

[2] *Saturday Evening Post*, Aug. 27, 1938.   [3] N. Y. *Times*, Jan. 14, 16, 1938.
[4] N. Y. *Times*, Mar. 21, 1938.

majolica and Hispano-Moresque ware and a host of other items including more complete carved-and-paneled rooms lifted from palaces and European country estates than had ever been gathered together before. Although Hearst had used scores of them at San Simeon and Santa Monica, he still had more than fifty left over. The sale was put in the hands of the Fifty-seventh Street firm of Parish-Watson & Company, which hastened to lease a five-story building so that it would have room to display a small part of the array.[5]

Efforts were made to sell the disastrous Ritz Tower, appraised at $6,000,000, but no one seemed interested. Rather than to continue losing a half million a year on it, the Organization discontinued mortgage payments and handed it over to the bank.[6] Hearst and Miss Davies, evicted from their own New York home, made plans to return to California, taxes or no taxes. Mrs. Hearst meanwhile was packing up and preparing to leave her five-floor-and-penthouse apartment at the Clarendon which she had occupied since 1908. She moved to smaller though still regal quarters on Central Park. The Clarendon was sold, its new owners began remodeling it into smaller apartments which sub-millionaires could afford, and an era had ended.

The fight against insolvency was not a matter of months but of years— a siege, a tense, day-after-day defense against importunate creditors and angry stockholders. Sometimes the battle seemed lost. In 1938, when Hearst Consolidated passed its preferred dividend, one group of stockholders sued for an accounting and a receivership, charging that Hearst "dominated" the other directors and ran the show "for his own personal gain." [7] *Fortune* magazine must have been feeling a trifle silly. Shearn and the Committee worked like mad to stave off collapse. They sold seven of the ten Hearst radio stations, three more newspapers, and scrapped *Pictorial Review*. Their only hope was in selling every property that was not showing a good profit. St. Donat's clearly came within that category, but it was known how the Chief loved his castle in Wales. No matter—it was sink or swim. The castle was put on the market.

St. Donat's was one of the Chief's fancies that made the figure-minded gape. Although he had paid only $120,000 for it originally, he had spent an estimated $1,250,000 to restore and modernize it, a total of $1,370,000. Since he had personally occupied it for a bare four months, unless it could be sold his rental there came to $342,500 a month or about $11,400 a day.

The art objects it contained were worth as much as the castle itself. Christie's in London were authorized to begin sorting them out for auction. Another source of potential revenue was Hearst's magnificent collection of rare books, manuscripts and autographs, which he had gathered over fifty years and which touched high points of American history, biography and literature. He was allowed to keep his favorites. The rest were put on sale at the Parke-Bernet Galleries in New York—letters of William Penn, Cotton

[5] N. Y. *Times*, Apr. 21, 1938.   [6] N. Y. *Herald-Tribune*, Apr. 1, 1938.
[7] N. Y. *Times*, Sept. 22, 1938.

Mather, Benjamin Franklin, an enormous collection of Washingtoniana, manuscripts of Poe, Longfellow, Bryant, Cooper, Mark Twain and many others.[8]

Some of the executives must have been reflecting that if only the Old Man had not bought art and literary treasures and zebras and gnus like a drunken maharajah, and if he had not insisted on holding on to all those losing newspapers and radio stations, and if he had been content with only *one* castle, all this misery would have been avoided.

In the midst of all this, Hearst lost one tax suit in Washington and won another. He agreed to pay a 1929 tax deficiency of $243,354, while the government agreed that he overpaid by $242,759 in 1930, so he came out about even.[9]

For William Randolph Hearst, aged seventy-five, the nightmare was long and its end not in sight. He was shorn of financial control, bankrupted out of Hollywood, deprived of a castle, and auctioneers were putting his treasures under the hammer. Above all, he was being forced to do a thousand things he did not want to do. When one recalls how powerfully he wanted his own way, the ghastly wounds to his ego can be approximated. For an ordinary seventy-five-year-old, given these conditions, the blow would have been fatal. That Hearst did not die of chagrin in 1938 or 1939 was a miracle of fortitude.

He had made so many mistakes that it amounted almost to a cosmic comedy of errors, and yet he had the courage to live under the knowledge of them, or to ignore them, and to fight back. Not once did the man who had been king relinquish the illusion that he was still a king. From San Simeon continued a stream of memos to his dwindling staff of editors, dictated to Willicombe and always beginning, "The Chief says." Likewise came a flood of personal letters.

To Lee Ettelson, now running his San Francisco *Call-Bulletin*, he wrote, "The inside pages are so dead they are dismal. Is everybody away on vacation or just not paying attention?" Three days later he wrote, "No squawks today. The paper is very good—especially considering difficulties.—WRH." [10]

Over in Europe, Neville Chamberlain had carried his umbrella to Hitler at Munich. Hearst's friend Churchill was appealing to America to join with England and France in curbing German aggression. To Hearst, suspicious of England and still at war with France, those nations were trying to drag the United States into a war to save them from the folly of their own (and Wilson's) Treaty of Versailles. He spoke from San Simeon over an N.B.C. hookup to warn the nation to avoid the errors that led it into the World War and to keep clear of Europe's troubles.

"It is no part of the duty of this English-speaking nation," he said, "to support the British Empire in her ambitious schemes to dominate Europe, absorb Africa and control the Orient. . . . England has never in our whole

[8] N. Y. *Times*, Sept. 8, Oct. 26 and Nov. 6, 1938.   [9] N. Y. *Times*, June 1, 1938.
[10] To Lee Ettelson, Sept. 6 and 9, 1938.

history extended any aid, comfort or consideration to this United States of ours . . ." [11]

From the White House, President Roosevelt remarked that most of the opposition to his foreign policy seemed to come from the Soviet press, the Nazi press, the Republicans and the Hearst press.

Replied Citizen Hearst: "The Hearst papers are never quite sure whether they can support or oppose the President's policies, because those policies change so much on their way from expression to execution.

"We are quite sure that we oppose Russian communism, German nazism and English and French imperialism. We support American liberty and democracy, American freedom of the press and freedom of speech, including freedom of the President to take a few fireside shots occasionally." [12]

Right or wrong, there was life in the Old Man yet.

III. THE DISSECTING TABLE

THE hard-pressed Hearst borrowed $1,000,000 from Cissy Patterson at five percent.[1] He borrowed another $1,000,000 without interest from Miss Davies, whose financial condition at the moment was better than his. Whether he swung other private loans is unknown, but it appears that he used the money to help the Organization, not for his own personal expenses. He was now living a bit less like a king and more like a powerful baron. He bought no art. Construction at San Simeon came to a temporary stop. He wanted badly to build a modest sub-palace in a sequoia grove near the castle, but the Committee could not see that this was essential to his well-being.

"Do you know," Hearst said plaintively to his cousin, Apperson, "they won't let me build it." Apperson noted that he appeared like a small boy who had been refused a perfectly reasonable request.[2]

The Committee felt that he should be able to struggle along with four palaces—or actually seven, since there were four on the Enchanted Hill, plus Santa Monica, Wyntoon and St. Donat's (not counting Mrs. Hearst's Long Island castle). No buyer appeared for St. Donat's. It was a white elephant, eating up good Organization dollars for maintenance, until the British government requisitioned it for use as an officers' training center. Hearst still owned twenty daily newspapers, and ran them with his old free-wheeling tyranny, telling Americans what fools they would be to become embroiled in Europe's machinations. When Hitler made his amazing pact with Stalin, Hearst was able to excuse Germany's motives and to add to his already shaky reputation as a prophet:

Why did Germany make a peace compact with Russia, its social and political opponent?

Because Germany was unable to make a peace alliance with France and England, its natural . . . associates.

[11] Los Angeles *Examiner*, Oct. 23, 1938.   [12] N. Y. *Times*, Dec. 6, 1939.
[1] Ickes, *Secret Diary*, II, 560.   [2] Mr. Apperson to author.

Germany offered such an alliance to France and England definitely and repeatedly. . . .

Europe will have peace now, but a peace of dictators—a peace of enthroned tyranny. . . .[3]

New troubles plagued the beleaguered Committee. In the old days, Hearst's bargaining power as the world's largest user of newsprint had enabled Neylan, then representing him, to stabilize the price at around forty dollars a ton. Other publishers who snickered at Hearst's financial woes soon discovered that it hit them too. Hearst was still using newsprint by the thousands of tons, but since the Organization owed millions to Canadian paper producers it was in no position to bargain. The price of newsprint rose to forty-five dollars, to fifty and higher, costing the Hearst chain alone an extra $5,000,000 a year. Canadian newsprint and banking interests were in a position to foreclose, but Berlin, one of the stalwarts of the Committee, managed to coax the Canadians into extending credit. Scratching for money, the Committee found that trying to sell the Hearst art collection, with its thousands upon thousands of items, through art dealers was like trying to pour water through a pinhole. Art dealers were not *big* enough, and ordinary people did not go to them. Someone had an inspiration—department stores! A part of the collection was shipped to stores in Chicago, St. Louis and Seattle, where the sale was so brisk that an even greater such operation was planned.[4]

Numerous writers and intellectuals had attempted to assay Hearst as a social phenomenon, usually with indifferent results because he made them too angry for balanced judgment. Now an Englishman, Aldous Huxley, came out with *After Many a Summer Dies the Swan,* a merciless fiction tour de force patterned in part after Hearst. It told the story of an aging American millionaire, Joseph Stoyte, who owned a California castle decorated with art objects and with a lovely young mistress. Stoyte was an eccentric titan, a culture-hater incapable of appreciating the ancient treasures he owned, a bully who was also pathetically eager to be friendly, so fearful of death that he employed specialists working in a Stoyte-owned laboratory in constant efforts to find ways to prolong the master's life. Huxley's portrait, a fictional mosaic, caricatured Hearst's worst qualities, but certain aspects of the tycoon's psychological twists—such as his strange combination of cruelty and kindness—came close to the mark. Speaking of Stoyte, a discerning friend pointed at the castle and said, "That's his monument to a faulty pituitary."[5]

There was a good deal of peering into Hearst's pituitary and other organs. *Time* magazine ran a splashy "cover story" on him, dwelling unsympathetically on his troubles and his friendship with Miss Davies. One of his chief worries now, said *Time,* was to "keep his job," going on:

[3] N. Y. *Journal-American,* Aug. 23, 1939.   [4] Rigby, 499.

[5] Huxley, *After Many a Summer.*

No other press lord ever wielded his power with less sense of responsibility; no other press ever matched the Hearst press for flamboyance, perversity and incitement of mass hysteria. Hearst never believed in anything much, not even Hearst, and his appeal was not to men's minds but to those infantile emotions which he never conquered in himself: arrogance, hatred, frustration, fear.[6]

The Huxley novel typified the scorn of the intellectuals for Hearst, while *Time*'s story reflected the resentment of professional newsmen who had seen Hearst methods at first hand. It even referred to him in the past tense, as if he were through—a signal error. Few sympathized with an old man fighting for survival. Only *Collier's*, once his arch-enemy, came to his defense in an editorial, "The Good that Hearst Did," cuffing the critics who "gather around to kick an old lion" and declaring that while Hearst was "no ideal man," he had once been a crusading liberal "fully as bold as Theodore Roosevelt and possibly more effective." [7] Hearst was stripped of privacy and dissected like a laboratory specimen.

This was because he *was* a unique specimen, puzzling to the dissectors. A living enigma, he challenged men's minds. While he talked of exalted principles, in his own newspapers Popeye, Walter Winchell and the back-street sex murder triumphed over the thoughtful summation of the news. There were no Pulitzer prize winners in the Hearst press, nor was it interested in them. Its many able men were geared to "raise hell and sell newspapers," not to exercise discrimination.

Why then did Hearst so often take up valuable front-page space for his own big-type pronouncements on national affairs? Because he had never become President, and as a frustrated politician this was the only way he could demonstrate the leadership the voters had denied him—and because he truly believed he knew the answers and could help the country. Depending on whether he was Hyde or Jekyll at the moment, he could inspire a grubby, petty-espionage Red hunt, or lead an honest campaign against war. In his later years he spoke with pride of his long and often successful drive for municipal ownership of public utilities, on which he had expended sincere effort.[8]

There were two theories about Hearst the journalist: that he was a double-dyed cynic who knew perfectly well that he was producing penny-dreadfuls, but liked the profit; and that he was so obtuse that he really thought he was publishing fine newspapers. Neither was quite correct. Critics constantly downgraded Hearst, forgot that if he was an eccentric genius he was still a genius. The young man who wrote his father from Harvard urging that the *Examiner* be made to appeal to "the people," that it must depend "upon enterprise, energy and a certain startling originality, and not upon . . . the lofty style of its editorials," knew exactly where he was going. He had clung to the ideal for more than a half century. He aimed at the masses and let

[6] *Time*, Mar. 13, 1939.   [7] *Collier's*, Apr. 29, 1939.
[8] Adela Rogers St. John to author.

others cater to the intelligentsia, but he took pride in the belief that he knew the mass mind and produced papers that suited it exactly, and that this was a laudable as well as profitable endeavor. The picture of Hearst fussing over his newspapers, laboring over everything from typography to effective news condensation, never quite satisfied with them, does not conform with thoroughgoing cynicism. He shrugged off the jibes of "quality" competitors with a remark that became axiomatic: "Nobody likes us but the people." Further proof that he believed in this with at least a part of his mercurial nature was the way he steered his five sons into the business and the joy he evinced when they took hold. Mrs. Hearst later felt that he was too insistent that they follow him in the profession, and that John, who had artistic talent, would have been happier as an architect.[9]

Hearst, being two men, could be cynical one moment and dead serious the next. Being two men, he outraged the logicians and defied the analysts—and torments any conscientious biographer—because what was said of him was only partially true, or only occasionally true, and was often entirely false, and had to be constantly modified and amended and qualified and restated until at last the seeker was apt to throw up his hands and admit that the truth was impossible to find, or, if found, too recondite to explain. His belief in the solidity and value of his newspapers was another aspect of the peculiar taste that made him buy many atrocities as well as works of art, made him install a teakwood Oriental gable between the two Spanish towers of the Casa Grande, made him wear loud and fancy clothing at an age when conservative attire would have seemed more appropriate. One could say that it was poorly chosen, but would have to admit that Hearst liked and believed in it. A champion rationalizer, he was able to feel assured that whatever he wanted and liked must necessarily be admirable. Strangely, once he had hit on the newspaper formula that suited him in the early years of the century, he changed it little thereafter, so that now his papers had a quaint air about them.

Some of his friends commented admiringly that he was never concerned about mere money, suggesting that he was above such considerations. These observers must have been mesmerized by the offhandedness with which he spent it. Hearst occupied about half his waking hours making money and the other half spending money. His need for money was constant. His anguish when he did not have enough money was enormous. The fact that he took money for granted did not make it any less true that money was a basic need. To say that he was not interested in money is to say that a gourmand is indifferent about food, or that a saint is unconcerned about salvation. Why then did he persist in keeping a half-dozen newspapers that were chronic losers? Because he disliked to fire good men, he hated to admit defeat, he optimistically kept thinking he could make winners of them, and because every additional paper he owned increased his influence, his power. He was

[9] Mrs. Hearst to author, May 25, 1959.

human enough to enjoy having Presidents and politicians seek his support and invite him to lunch.

But there was still another reason. Those newspapers, losers though they were, were his property, and thus became sacred. Anything belonging to him became almost a physical part of him, and losing any of it was like losing an arm or a leg.

Hearst's change from radicalism to conservatism, which won him so much hatred, was attributable in part to expediency and in part to the habitually sobering process of maturity. To the young Hearst, money was no problem. He could always make more millions or borrow from his mother, and so— possessed by the bright dream of the Presidency—he championed the income tax, fought the trusts, demanded legislation for the masses. In the Twenties, when he reached the three-score mark, he discovered that reform had two faces. Many of the social advances he had crusaded for had come to being. The electorate had repudiated him. The dream was gone, the future no longer limitless. His empire was making millions, but his taste for luxuries had swollen to such proportions that he was spending more than he earned. He discovered that some of the reforms beneficial to the masses came at *his* expense. The enlightened American democracy which he had helped bring about had a serious flaw—it failed to allow for the citizen who wanted seven castles. He discovered that labor unions, so long his darlings, were not always scrupulous, and that they could hurt *him*. The income tax was a burden on *him*. As a political philosopher, he felt that the pendulum of reform had swung far enough and had better be stopped. As a capitalist beset by money worries he fell in love with the tax-cutting Mellon, the economy-minded Coolidge and Landon, men he would have pilloried in his earlier years.

He would have found friends in his growing conservatism had he observed reasonable discipline in his own life. Many level-headed conservatives were with him in his denunciations of the New Deal, which was often wasteful. But no other conservative bought so many yak, madonnas or Etruscan vases.

Meanwhile, Europe violated his prophesy and went to war. Hearst excoriated Hitler and fell back on the Washington doctrines. "We can keep out of war if we want to. . . ." he wrote. "America has a great opportunity, a great mission, which it can only fulfill if it keeps out of war." [10]

America prepared for the worst nevertheless, embarking on an effort to build 50,000 planes a year, sending the British fifty over-age destroyers, stepping up defense plans. For troop training the War Department bought 164,000 acres of the San Simeon barony—a sale that must have hurt Hearst sorely, leaving him a mere 75,000 acres, but which added two million precious dollars to the Organization's funds. [11]

[10] N. Y. *Journal-American*, Sept. 4, 1939.   [11] N. Y. *Times*, Oct. 25, 1940.

2. The Limited Monarch

WHEN Brisbane died, his syndicated column *To-Day* died with him. He had hoped that his son Seward would carry it on for him, but Seward's writing did not suit the Hearst editors. Possibly this was one reason why Brisbane's estate refused to surrender the copyrighted title *To-Day* to the Organization which had spread it into homes and barber shops all over the country.[1]

Hearst, being unable to go to Europe because of the war, and also deprived of his former delights in art-shopping and castle-building, had more time on his hands at San Simeon than of yore. In 1940 he dashed off a column of his own and gave it to Warden Woolard, editor of his Los Angeles *Examiner*. "I've been thinking of writing a regular column," he told Woolard. "I may not be able to keep it up, but I'd like to try." [2]

This was the beginning of his *In The News* column that first ran only in the *Examiner* but was so interesting that the rest of the chain soon picked it up. At his best, the Chief could write rings around Brisbane. Although he liked the Brisbanian short sentences, he was not a slave to them and could sometimes dangle clauses at intriguing length. But the main difference was that Hearst was infinitely greater and warmer than Brisbane, and that old age, unpopularity, humiliation and disaster had softened instead of embittered him. He wrote out of a fund of lifelong activity, experience, observation and travel such as could be matched by no other living man. He could still hurl thunderbolts, but fully as frequent were his flashes of kindliness, tenderness and sentimentality. Hearst's last years, harried as they were by troubles that should in all reason have killed him, instead brought out his indomitable courage and greatness of heart.

Despite his long campaign against United States involvement in the war, in July 1940 he viewed the portents and much against his will wrote, "The entry of the United States into the war may be considered more than a probability. In fact, it may be set down as a certainty." [3]

This pronouncement by the "anti-English" publisher made headlines in all the London newspapers and created a stir in the War Office. Leaflets were printed, and in the next R.A.F. raid over Berlin they were dropped to inform the Germans that when even Hearst admitted the inevitability of United States participation with the Allies, the outlook for the Axis was dark indeed.[4]

Hearst had always enjoyed scribbling verse. His *Song of the River,* which

[1] Coblentz, *Hearst*, 4.
[2] Mr. Woolard to author.
[3] Los Angeles *Examiner*, July 24, 1940.
[4] N. Y. *Times*, Aug. 27, 1940.

he had actually written seven years earlier, was a significant revelation of his philosophy, his hope for a life after death. He had composed it at Wyntoon, contemplating the roaring McCloud River and likening it to the riddle of existence. Possibly even he would not have called it great poetry, but he thought it good enough to pass on to his readers:

> *The snow melts on the mountain*
> *And the water runs down to the spring,*
> *And the spring in a turbulent fountain,*
> *With a song of youth to sing,*
> *Runs down to the riotous river,*
> *And the river flows to the sea,*
> *And the water again*
> *Goes back in rain*
> *To the hills where it used to be.*
> *And I wonder if life's deep mystery*
> *Isn't much like the rain and the snow*
> *Returning through all eternity*
> *To the places it used to know.*
>
> *For life was born on the lofty heights*
> *And flows in a laughing stream,*
> *To the river below*
> *Whose onward flow*
> *Ends in a peaceful dream.*
> *And so at last,*
> *When our life has passed*
> *And the river has run its course,*
> *It again goes back,*
> *O'er the selfsame track,*
> *To the mountain which was its source. . . .*[5]

Hearst on bullfights and vivisection:

Have you ever seen a bull fight?
If you have not you need not worry about it.
You have not missed anything which would do you any good.
A bull fight, in some countries, does not exhibit the human race in a very admirable light. . . .
Bull fighting is a cruel sport, but at least it is a courageous one.
It is much nobler than our national United States pastime of indiscriminate vivisection.
It takes courage to face a furious bull.
It takes cowardice to carve to pieces a harmless friendly dog. . . .[6]

Hearst on modern art and music:

What have we in American art today to compare with [the] great creations of the Gay Nineties?

[5] N. Y. *Journal-American*, Feb. 25, 1941.   [6] *Journal-American*, Mar. 19, 1941.

Nothing but some meaningless hentracks defacing clean canvas and made by fakers for fools.

If we can laugh at the Gay Nineties, just imagine the convulsions of raucous laughter that will rock the frames of future generations when they look at the pitiful productions of the so-called modernistic art of today. . . .

What is our music of today?

Little but a jitterbug jangle of inharmonies—a distortion of melody made to gear and dovetail with the physical contortion of the modern dance.

The discordant noise known as jazz originated as a joke and has developed into a tragedy.[7]

The iconoclast-turned-conventional also saw American literature and drama as having deteriorated since the Nineties. But he still liked his little joke, as evidenced by a long disquisition on women's dress that began:

The question has often been propounded:
Do women dress for men or for other women or for themselves?
And the answer is:
Yes.[8]

Like many an oldster, but with more reason than most, he viewed the days of his youth through rosy spectacles. In one nostalgic column he revealed much about his disillusionment with unions and guilds when he told of the time, more than fifty years earlier, when he had gone out in a tug with Haxton and other *Examiner* men to rescue the fisherman marooned on a rock:

Those were the wonderful days, and happy achievements of youth. No grandiose performance of later years ever equalled them in satisfaction.

Life was not "one damn thing after another" then. It was one wonderful adventure after another.

The competition of journalism was a glad sport; and yet back of it all was a due sense of responsibility,—a genuine desire to use the powers and opportunities of the press to serve and to save.

There was delight in work, happiness in service, joy in life,—for we were young.

As Kingsley sings:
> "When all the world is young, lad,
> And all the trees are green,
> And every goose a swan, lad,
> And every lass a queen;
> Then hey for boot and horse, lad,
> And 'round the world away.
> Young blood must have its course, lad,
> And every dog his day." [9]

[7] N. Y. *Journal-American*, Nov. 25, 1941.
[8] *Journal-American*, Oct. 15, 1940.
[9] Hearst writings in possession of W. W. Murray, San Francisco.

II. CITIZEN HEARST AND CITIZEN KANE

THE recognition of the world of the arts that the life of Hearst had elements of high drama was further demonstrated as Orson Welles and his Mercury Players worked on the film *Citizen Kane* at the R.K.O. lot. Rumors sifted through screenland that the picture was based on Hearst's life and that R.K.O. was taking elaborate pains to assure its freedom from libel. Louella Parsons, always Hearst's militant defender, demanded to see the picture as soon as it was finished. She brought two Hearst lawyers with her when Welles gave her a private showing, a reporter noted, and "Miss Parsons and the lawyers sat through the picture in silence and left the R.K.O. projection room without bidding goodbye to Welles." [1]

Citizen Kane raised a cinematic storm. Louis Mayer, never a man to throw money away needlessly, showed remarkable loyalty to Hearst when he learned that the picture might wound his old friend. Mayer offered to pay George Schaefer, president of R.K.O., the $800,000 the film cost if he would destroy it. Schaefer, who detested Mayer's ruthlessness, refused. It was said that Hearst angrily threatened to open an editorial attack on the whole film industry unless the picture was censored or suppressed. There were fears that the still powerful Hearst press would make embarrassing disclosures of the private affairs of certain film magnates. The pressure against the release of *Kane* came from top men in the industry who liked Hearst or feared the hurtful assaults of his newspapers. Schaefer learned that he would have to scratch to find theater bookings for his picture. The great Radio City Music Hall in New York City, a part of Rockefeller Center, refused it. Schaefer telephoned Nelson Rockefeller, who said that all he knew was that Miss Parsons had called him to warn that the picture should not be shown.[2]

Schaefer had to lease independent theaters in New York and Los Angeles to give the film its initial showing. Even after its opening, and with an enthusiastic reception from critics and the public, R.K.O. was able to get bookings only in its own theaters. The big theater circuits of Warner's, Paramount and Loew's shunned it. Schaefer, certain that the pressure against *Kane* came from Mayer and a few other moguls, threatened a lawsuit against the Warner firm for conspiracy unless they would book it. Warner's relented, resistance melted, and *Kane* went on to win the "Best Picture of the Year" award against such competition as *Sergeant York* and *How Green Was My Valley*.[3]

The Hearst press refused to review it. On orders from the Chief, Orson Welles went to the top of the S-List. The excommunication was extended to other R.K.O. productions. A review of *Kitty Foyle*, an R.K.O. picture, was jerked out of the Los Angeles *Examiner* after having run in an early edition. R.K.O. had arranged for the newspaper serialization of *Kitty*, and Hearst's

[1] *New Republic*, Feb. 24, 1941.   [2] Crowther, 257–59.   [3] Crowther, 259.

Detroit *Times* had advertised that it would publish the serialization. It suddenly dropped the advertisements and never ran the story.[4]

Although one can understand the seventy-eight-year-old Hearst's objection to having his own private life, along with that of his wife and Miss Davies, spread with thin concealment on the screen, *Citizen Kane* was not wholly unsympathetic and indeed was a brilliant attempt to explain the inexplicable. Charles Foster Kane, heir to millions, was a newspaper publisher and art collector, long on ability but short on principle, driven by political ambition, builder of a great castle called Xanadu. Handsome, engaging, generous, he was also utterly ruthless in his drive for political power, losing his wife in the process and marrying a blonde young singer. Failing in politics, he turned the shattering force of his ambition on his bride, determined to make her the nation's leading diva despite her woeful lack of voice. Despite enormous effort and publicity, he failed in this also. Kane in his old age became a figure of tragedy who had wasted his great talents in meretricious pursuits, had seen his dreams crumble and was left with nothing but his millions, his echoing castle, and his young wife, who worked unhappily on jigsaw puzzles, hated the loneliness of the place, and later took solace in liquor.

One climactic scene showed the frustrated Kane in a towering rage, seizing rare antiques and crashing them to the floor, leaving the room a shambles. In another, one of Kane's oldest friends said of him, "Charlie wanted everybody to love him. He just didn't have any love to give."

This was hardly fair to Hearst, who in his better moments was kindliness itself, and who lavished on Miss Davies a true and unswerving devotion. It was said that angry as he was at the portrayal of himself, he was more incensed at the unflattering characterization of the young woman the public would surely take to represent Miss Davies.

Hearst and Miss Davies packed off to Mexico with two of his sons and their wives, the director Raoul Walsh and several others. After visiting his properties, he stopped to chat with Ambassador Josephus Daniels in Mexico City. He referred with a rueful smile to his Mexican holdings, of which the government had expropriated several portions. "I suppose they will take it all, piece by piece," he said.[5]

Daniels was impressed by his acceptance of what seemed inevitable. However, the ambassador knew that Hearst employed not only American lawyers but several Mexican lawyers who had influence with the government, and that he had lost less to expropriation than other American property owners. Considering Hearst's ghastly fiasco with the forged Mexican documents, Daniels thought he had come off well.[6]

Soon thereafter, Ilka Chase's book *Past Imperfect* was published. It referred candidly to the Hearst-Davies friendship, made much of Miss Davies' stammer, likened Hearst to an octopus and suggested sinister traits in his

[4] *New Republic*, Feb. 24, 1941.   [5] Josephus Daniels, *Shirt-Sleeve Diplomat*, 354.
[6] Daniels, 354–55.

character. Hearst was wounded and angry, particularly because both Miss Chase and her mother had been his guests at San Simeon and had dined at his table. He was getting almighty sick of being exploited, analyzed and satirized in the movies and in print. Undoubtedly he thought of suing, but gave it up. Any lawsuit might result in his own missteps being paraded before the public, and, worse yet, might be embarrassing to Miss Davies. In his newspapers he had seldom been solicitous about the privacy of others. Now he had backed himself and his lady into a corner where their own privacy was a playground of the curious. There was little he could do about it, but he did send out orders to the Hearst picture agency, International News Photos, that no pictures of him or Miss Davies were to be released unless it was ascertained that they would not be used unpleasantly.

On December 7, 1941, when the Japanese rained havoc on Pearl Harbor, Hearst's fifty-year talk of the "yellow peril" was vindicated and his fight against joining the war was cut out from under him. His newspaper-sponsored "Mothers of America" group, united for peace, now numbered more than a million members who promptly forgot all about peace.[7] So did Hearst.

"Well, fellow Americans," he wrote in his column, "we are in the war and we have got to win it."[8]

III. GIMBEL'S EASY PAYMENT PLAN

THE Committee was still under siege. Several more stockholders' groups carried their complaints to the courts, demanding a receivership. Why, demanded one group of plaintiffs, did American Newspapers, a Hearst corporation, sell the Baltimore, Atlanta and San Antonio papers to Hearst Consolidated, another Hearst corporation, for $8,000,000 in 1935 when those three newspapers were losing a total of $550,000 a year? The grimmest crisis of all faced Hearst when he could not pay the mortgage on San Simeon and discovered that it was Harry Chandler who held his note. While it was true that he had his choice of two other California castles to go to, San Simeon was his heart's blood. Luckily, it had a built-in safeguard: no one but Hearst wanted or could use such a pile. Chandler extended the loan, and the place was saved along with Hearst's sanity, which surely would have tottered had he lost the dream of a lifetime.[1]

At Gimbel's department store in New York, boys' clothing, infants' wear and other goods were removed from the fifth floor so that the entire floor—100,000 square feet of space—could be devoted to the Hearst Collection. Hand trucks and four-wheelers rolled in with the art objects Hearst had gathered over decades in Italy, Germany, Spain, France and elsewhere. He had collected in no less than 504 distinct categories. For the first time, the public got a visual inkling of the scope of his purchases. Parts of the collection had already been sold in London, New York and three other cities, and

[7] Kathleen Norris, *Family Gathering*, 284.   [8] Los Angeles *Examiner*, Dec. 8, 1941.
[1] *Time*, Mar. 13, 1939.

yet Gimbel's two-acre fifth floor was jammed to the ceiling. It had to be remembered that even this was far from all of it, since the Bronx warehouse still contained thousands of crated valuables, and of course Hearst was keeping the best third of the collection for himself.

Some art dealers looked down their noses at the spectacle of selling *objets d'art* like underwear or notions. Some Hearst-haters sneered that the Old Man, who had always catered to the mob, had found his true element in a department store. Gimbel's sent out 10,000 engraved invitations to give the sale a send-off, but people from Hell's Kitchen as well as Park Avenue came to gape at the array of wonders. Even the Spanish cloister was on sale there, through the medium of pictures, the stones themselves still being up in the Bronx. A titled guide with a distinctive foreign accent was on hand to impress the mink trade. Gimbel's advertised "Bargains in Del Sartos and Broadlooms," stressed the chic of wearing a Hearst necklace, and invited one and all to use the Easy Payment Plan. The sale, which went on for almost a year, was a smashing success even though no one was interested in the cloister. People who bought a door-knocker, a scarab, a canvas or a set of fire tongs were probably not aware that they were doing their bit to save the Organization from bankruptcy.[2]

One of the many signs that Hearst had been the dealers' greatest angel was Van Dyck's portrait of Queen Henrietta, for which he had paid Duveen $375,000. At Gimbel's it was reduced to $157,500, still did not sell, and later was knocked down to a mere $89,000.[3]

By now the Committee had been fighting with its back to the wall for four years, and the strain was formidable. John W. Hanes, a Wall Street banker and former Undersecretary of the Treasury, was called in to help hold the line. Hanes, astonished to find that there were ninety-four separate Hearst corporations, many of which owed each other money, worked to untangle the snarl. The lot of the average Hearst employe was an unhappy one, for salaries were low and there was an uneasy feeling that the Organization might collapse at any moment. Hearst had finally been forced to recognize the Guild, although he never embraced it with any affection. The combination of the Guild and hard times had a disastrous effect on many Hearstmen who had been drawing substantial paychecks. In the Chicago city room, for example, where fourteen men had drawn from $100 to $200 a week, the Guild minimum of sixty dollars became the maximum and these men took painful cuts.[4]

San Simeon could get hot in the summer, and ordinarily Hearst used Wyntoon only as his summer palace, as the late Spanish Bourbons used San Sebastian. Early in the war, however, he closed San Simeon and moved to Wyntoon for two years, winter and summer. This was done for two reasons —to save money, and because there was a feeling that the Japanese, angered at the long Hearst campaign against them, might appear in submarines and

[2] Rigby, *Lock, Stock and Barrel*, 499–502.   [3] N. Y. *Times,* June 30, 1942.
[4] Roscoe Cornell to author, Nov. 3, 1959.

shell San Simeon, which made a fine target from the bay. Unlike San Simeon, where the horticulture was artificial, Wyntoon, with its 67,000 acres of virgin timber, was the acme of nature. Its big stone-and-timber castle, The Gables, and its three smaller (but still large) subcastles, stood on the banks of the swift McCloud River, surrounded by 200-foot firs. Hearst, who had built the three-unit "Bavarian village," named the houses The Bear, Cinderella and Angel House, and had retained Willy Pogany and a staff of artists to paint on them suitable illustrations from the fairy tales. Even though he was not precisely a bear, The Bear was his diggings and he was not supposed to be disturbed while there.

Miss Davies, hating Wyntoon, had a scornful name for it—"Spittoon." It was 250 miles north of San Francisco, lost in the wilderness, and in wartime it was impossible to people it with the throngs of guests that made San Simeon merry. She took up backgammon, and there were times when she must have been as lonely as the pathetic heroine of *Citizen Kane,* mournfully working jigsaw puzzles.

Hearst himself, preoccupied with his work, was not visibly oppressed by the solitude. What hurt was the shortage of ready cash, his inability to buy paintings and other attractive things. Once he picked up the telephone and called Richard Berlin in New York, who had emerged as the strong man of the Organization. "Dick," he said, "can you send me $50,000?" Things were still tight, but Berlin said, "Mr. Hearst, I'll do my level best." He did it.[5]

The ubiquitous Willicombe was there, sending out the Chief's instructions to a mere eighteen newspapers now, along with orders to various editors to come to Wyntoon for conferences with Hearst. Lee Ettelson arrived there in midwinter to discuss a radical change in the Saturday San Francisco *Call-Bulletin.* He had to wait several days to see Hearst, which was about par. He spent the time in the Wyntoon library, reading precious, Morocco-bound volumes of Dickens and Thackeray.

Finally he was called into the Presence. He had made a careful study of his report, as it behooved anyone dealing with Hearst. He opened his briefcase and explained that he had in mind three possible plans of varying cost for the Saturday paper. He gave the estimated cost for each plan.

Hearst's gaze grew steely. Perhaps he was touchy on the subject of costs, now that costs had to be watched.

"Mr. Ettelson," he snapped, "I didn't ask you up here to spend money. I can do that better in a day than you can in a month. Let's see what your plan is. Then we can discuss costs." [6]

Irene Castle arrived that winter to find Wyntoon a fairyland of snow and evergreens. Although Hearst was by far the oldest of the three, he, Miss Castle and Miss Davies had something in common. They all remembered the glorious days of Ziegfeld and the *Follies.* All had led lives of excitement, travel and glamor, and the great days of all were behind them. Another

[5] Mr. Berlin to author.   [6] Mr. Ettelson to author.

common interest was the fight against cruelty to animals and uncontrolled vivisection, which all took with utmost seriousness. Miss Castle devoted a large part of her time to the crusade, and Hearst was the only big publisher who would give newspaper space to it—a campaign many of his own editors regarded as the Old Man's worst mania. The two spent hours discussing animals, and how to promote their welfare.

On the night before she left, Miss Castle watched the inevitable movie with the host and hostess. Hearst lolled back in a leather chair, a dachshund asleep on his chest. The place was full of dachshunds, and Miss Castle took a fancy to one of them. Since she was leaving in the morning, and Hearst let nothing interfere with his sleep-until-noon schedule, she made her farewell after the movie.

"What can I do for you before you go?" he inquired.

She asked for two things—a photograph of Hearst and Miss Davies, and the dachshund. In the morning, a maid got her breakfast and the butler presented her with the photograph and the dachshund before she got into the Hearst car that would take her to the station. She later discovered that the dog was one of Hearst's best, a blue-ribbon winner.[7]

In the spring, Louis Shainmark, managing editor of Hearst's Chicago *Herald-American*, went to Palm Springs to recuperate from an operation. Hearing of this, Willicombe relayed a Hearst invitation that he spend a week at Wyntoon. A liberal himself, Shainmark was an admirer of the Chief, believing him sincerely pro-labor but victimized by Communist elements in labor. When he arrived, Hearst greeted him with his usual hospitality. "He gave you a feeling of euphoria, his welcome was so warm and enveloping," Shainmark later recalled.

George Hearst and Arthur Lake and their wives, with a few others, were weekend guests, but by Monday Shainmark was alone with Hearst, Miss Davies and the servants. His mornings were his own, since the host and hostess never appeared until after noon. He found Hearst eager to talk shop about the Chicago situation, and ready to turn a quip or two. Shainmark had heard of his purported dislike of the subjects of old age and death, but he had a joke bearing on decrepitude that he thought the Chief might like, and he risked telling it. It concerned the aged Chauncey Depew and the glamorous Mary Garden seated next to each other at a banquet. The diva wore an exceptionally low-cut dress, which Depew eyed so narrowly that she finally asked what he was looking at.

"I was wondering what keeps your dress up," Depew said.

"Your age, Mr. Depew," Miss Garden replied.

Hearst, nearing seventy-nine, laughed heartily. Shainmark told him how much he enjoyed the prune juice the maid served him in the morning, and also the imported Kulmbacher beer. Hearst was able to joke about *Citizen Kane*. "We have it here," he said. "I must run it off again sometime." Miss

[7] Miss Castle to author.

Davies, however, pronounced it grotesque. Hearst related with obvious feeling how, when the bankers refused to loan him a cent, Miss Davies had saved him with a loan of $1,000,000 without a note of any kind. Once at dinner, Miss Davies got something in her eye. It was a minor annoyance which she dabbed at with a lacy handkerchief, but Hearst, greatly disturbed, hovered over her solicitously, saying, "Can't I help you, Marion?"

After Shainmark left Wyntoon, he found six bottles of prune juice and six bottles of Kulmbacher beer tucked away in his bag—a jovial Hearstian touch. Like all those who saw only the angelic Hearst, with not a sign of horns, he was utterly charmed.[8]

When Hearst had his annual birthday party—his seventy-ninth—at Wyntoon, a crowd of executives made the trek into the wilderness to do him honor. It was a sign of their continuing admiration for the Chief despite his reckless fiscal policies which had almost scuttled them all. According to long custom, each of them in turn proposed a congratulatory toast. But not William Murray, who supervised the ranch properties and had a fine tenor voice.

"If you don't mind," said Murray with a twinkle in his eye, "I'll sing my toast."

With his brother, James Murray, accompanying him at the piano, Murray gazed significantly at Hearst and sang, *I'll Get By as Long as I Have You.* The place resounded with laughter, including Hearst's.[9]

IV. CRISIS IN THE NIGHT

WHEREVER Hearst was, he would pick up the telephone and call the nearest Hearst paper for all manner of special services. When he was at Wyntoon, the San Francisco *Examiner* was "under the gun," as the staff called it. When such a call came in, it had a more galvanizing effect than a five-alarm fire or a murder.

These calls usually came late in the evening, when the Chief was getting up steam. They involved nervous strain, for his voice, always soft, was particularly hard to hear over a long-distance wire. Once he called at 11:30 to say that he was having a party for the children of the help at Wyntoon.

"Please send me a dozen fryer chickens," he said. "No pinfeathers, please; two dozen frankfurters and two dozen buns to fit them; two dozen servings of molded ice cream—one dozen in the shape of Mickey Mouse, the other dozen in the shape of Donald Duck; and one bottle of rhubarb and soda."

A rewrite man jotted down the items with care, said, "Yes, Mr. Hearst," then shouted for the city editor. This was crisis. The Old Man had not said *when* he wanted these things, but it was always safest to assume that he was in a hurry. There was a car leaving for Wyntoon at 1 A.M. with newspapers and mail. That gave them an hour and a half to fill the order. The editor

[8] Mr. Shainmark to author, Sept. 3, 1959.   [9] W. W. Murray to author, Oct. 9, 1959.

snapped orders. A reporter hurried to the Fairmont Hotel, where he corralled the chickens. Breen's all-night eatery, just around the corner from the *Examiner,* supplied the frankfurters and buns. An ice cream manufacturer was awakened and coaxed to open his plant to get the molded shapes. The only all-night drug store happened to be out of rhubarb and soda, so a wholesale drug distributor who lived far out on the Peninsula was aroused and implored to drive to the city at top speed so that the last item could be obtained. The deadline was met, and the whole *Examiner* staff breathed a sigh of relief and went back to routine affairs.

For a time Hearst took pleasure in working out the *Examiner's* crossword puzzles. Once he called to complain strenuously that the "vertical" and "horizontal" instructions had been mixed up by the printers so that the puzzle was impossible to solve. A week later came a telegram: "Chief says your crossword puzzle is balled up again this morning. If this continues he is going to stop taking your paper."

Occasionally Hearst would call to ask that women's clothing be sent to Wyntoon on approval—a request that sent reporters to exclusive women's shops next day to urge that Miss Davies' wants be fulfilled. But most of the night calls, without precisely saying so, indicated a need for haste. Cost was no object in satisfying these demands. It became a common thing for *Examiner* reporters to awaken merchants at their homes and drive them to their establishments to get some item for the Chief. When he called for four trivets, an ironworker was aroused. It was later learned that Hearst was having a Halloween party and the trivets were needed for witches' caldrons. When he called for books on Byzantine architecture, the manager of the Emporium bookstore lost sleep. A request for petits fours hauled an official of Blum's confectionery out of bed. One of the queerer ones was a request for a street car gong, which sent a reporter to the street railway shops. To this day, no one knows why the Old Man wanted a street car gong.

The city-room men would curse roundly at these screwball interruptions of their routine. Later they came to regard them with amusement and even genuine interest, for the nocturnal rambles caused by the Chief's calls contained a sportive element similar to the chase, or a treasure hunt. Some wondered whether Hearst knew the commotion he caused, while others speculated that he was deliberately keeping the boys "on their toes."

The latter supposition seems nearer the truth. The bankers had shorn Hearst of some of the power he loved. But he could still, with a mere telephone call, galvanize the *Examiner* office into frantic activity and send reporters on pell-mell errands through the night, and the chances are that he took a certain quiet satisfaction in it.

At the San Francisco *Call-Bulletin* office, an assistant editor who prefers to remain anonymous often talked by telephone with one of his news sources, the assistant to the president of the local Standard Oil Company. The two made something of a comic routine of it. When the editor called the oil official, he would say, "This is Mr. Rockefeller calling," whereupon the oil man would reply, "Go take a dime and stick it in your eye." When the oil man called the editor, he would use a falsetto voice and say, "This is Mr. Hearst," to which the editor would reply, "I wouldn't wipe my hands with your newspaper."

The inevitable finally happened. A call came into the *Call-Bulletin* from a man announcing himself as Mr. Hearst, and the editor gave his stock reply.

"Pardon me?" said the voice on the wire.

It *was* Hearst.

"Mr. Hearst," said the editor swiftly, "someone cut in on our line." [1]

---

[1] All of these anecdotes were related to the author by present or former Hearst employes who asked not to be named.

3. Old Indestructible

IRONICALLY, it was the war that Hearst had so insistently warned America to avoid that rescued his publishing empire. Circulation rose, advertising boomed, and this, plus the heroic efforts of the Committee, saved the Organization. Hearst rose like a phoenix from the ashes of defeat. He and Miss Davies moved back to San Simeon. The Old Man was so anxious to regain full control that he sued in federal court to oust Shearn from his position of financial power. The court refused, for although the Organization was now a going concern, there were still debts outstanding and until these were settled the suzerainty of Shearn could not be ended without the consent of the banks Hearst hated so fervently.[1]

Although Russia was now an ally, never did he relax his suspicion of the Bear. One got an impression that the Hearst press was not overly concerned about the Russian plight at Stalingrad. Hearst was attacked as an "appeaser" who opposed a second front by Vladimir Krushkoff, secretary of the Soviet Information Bureau. He was assailed by *Pravda*, which declared that his newspapers were "spilling poisoned ink to wreck the great cause of the anti-Hitler coalition," and was insanely (and correctly) charging the Russians with an intention to grab the Balkan countries, Poland and other areas. Hearst, said *Pravda*, was Hitler's best friend in America.[2]

"Marshal Stalin, in his controlled press, calls me a gangster journalist and a friend of Hitler's," Hearst replied. "These accusations have their amusing sides, coming from the gentleman who is the head of the Communist press—the only gangster press I know. . . .

". . . Was not the estimable Marshal Stalin, until recently Hitler's best beloved friend and buddy, his accomplice in the invasion of the Baltic republics, his pal in the rape of Finland, his partner in the plunder of Poland?"[3]

Hearst easily had the better of the argument, and in his suspicion of Russia he was ahead of the national trend. He was on less solid ground, considering his own history, when he attacked Bertrand Russell as "the well known immoralist" and cheered the revocation of his appointment to teach at the College of the City of New York. His puritanical side was uppermost when he assailed Russell's defense of adultery and demanded, "Does the Professor consider it PROGRESS to invite the revival of . . . unchastity?"[4] The man

---

[1] N. Y. *Times*, Jan. 12, July 31, 1943.
[2] Quoted in N. Y. *Times*, Oct. 23, 1942; Feb. 26, 1944.
[3] N. Y. *Journal-American*, Feb. 29, 1944.
[4] Hearst writings in possession of W. W. Murray, San Francisco.

who had shocked Harvard, shocked San Francisco and shocked New York was now, in his old age, worried about the morals of the younger generation. One of his pet aversions was young women in bars. He sent out many a warning like the following:

TO THE PUBLISHERS AND EDITORS
OF ALL HEARST NEWSPAPERS:

There is an insidious attempt to change laws in many places and to allow younger people to enter saloons.

Please oppose this vigorously—violently, in fact.

The age limitation should be in the higher brackets—not in the lower.

A 25-year limitation is better than a 21-year limitation.

And young women should be kept out of saloons under any and all circumstances.

To lower the age for promiscuous drinking would be to raise a race of drunkards.

The agitation for a lower age limitation is largely caused by the Communists and the whiskey manufacturers.

It should be strenuously resisted.—Sincerely, W. R. Hearst.[5]

He had a tendency to blame the Communists for many ills.

Hearst's birthdays had always been occasions for celebration, but by now they were marked by special ceremony. If he had never mastered the art of intimate friendship, he nevertheless had a host of admirers. His eightieth birthday was spent at the Santa Monica house, from which dimmed-out beach towns were faintly visible along the curving shore. It was attended by his sons, their wives, his executives and many Hollywood friends. He received messages from all over the world. Although age was shrinking and bending him a trifle, his intellect was as keen as ever. Begrudging the years, he wore a colorful Paisley shirt, a silk Ascot tie and a dashing jacket with notched lapels. He was not overjoyed at being eighty, and in response to many toasts he made a graceful little speech telling why:

I shall not pretend that I am happy to be eighty. I would gladly exchange that marker for two lifetimes at forty—just as a woman, reaching forty, would gladly exchange that milestone for two at the twenty mark. Yet, I am thankful and grateful that I find so much in life that is fresh, stimulating, and dear to me.[6]

Back at San Simeon again, he cracked the whip over his editors, defended America against all comers, and flung himself into his last architectural orgy —the completion of another wing of the Casa Grande. After what was for him an interval of horrid penury, he had money to spend. Adding another wing was not strictly practical, since he was building rooms that would never be used. But his cellar vaults under the castle still bulged with spoils from Europe that he itched to transform into useless living space that suited his own rococo idea of beauty. Miss Morgan, herself grown old in building San

---

[5] From files of Los Angeles *Herald-Express*. [6] Parsons, *The Gay Illiterate*, 98.

Simeon, had retired to San Francisco, and now her assistant, George McClure, was Hearst's architect. Building materials were almost unobtainable in wartime, but he pulled strings, paid enormous prices and got them. "We must finish the job," he said again and again.[7]

The Casa Grande offended classicists because of its extravagant presumption, its hodge-podgery of art and architecture, its violence to tradition, its excesses in decoration. But it suited Hearst perfectly. It was a proper monument to this man of extravagance, violence and excess as no classic pile would have been.

Statisticians could have a field day totting up the total of Hearst's expenditures for housing himself, his family and Miss Davies. The figure would have to include construction or purchase cost, improvements, land and gardens, and art acquisitions actually used in the dwellings. No one ever knew how much he spent on San Simeon, and the estimate of $40,000,000, which seems inflated, might be scaled down arbitrarily to $30,000,000 to give him the benefit of the doubt. The beach house cost him a total of $7,000,000. The Long Island castle cost $400,000, with no allowance for furnishings and art. St. Donat's cost him $1,370,000, while Wyntoon probably ran no more than $1,000,000. This makes a rough total of $40,000,000, which still does not include the huge expenditures at the million-dollar Clarendon, the Ritz Tower, or the smaller houses he purchased in Beverly Hills, or his long-time rental of a floor at Los Angeles' princely Ambassador, nor would it include such odd items as Miss Davies' splendid "bungalow," or the acreage he bought on the Grand Canyon after enjoying the view and planning a residence which he never got around to building. The fact emerges that he spent more for housing and decoration than any man in history, king or commoner.

He and Miss Davies had a new tenant—his twelve-year-old grandson, John R. Hearst Jr., nicknamed "Bunkie," whose parents were recently divorced. John was furnished with a motor scooter and sent to the San Simeon village school six miles down the slope, where there were thirteen pupils and one teacher. This meant that he had to traverse the zoo, where on one occasion he was forced to step lively to escape an angry water buffalo. He took an interest in his grandfather as a human phenomenon. It amazed him that a man so old could wear such uninhibited neckties and clothing, including one suit of a vivid, billiard-table green. "Other men who wore clothes like that would have looked as though they were in the circus," he observed. "But because Grandpop was so dignified, he made the clothes look dignified, too."[8]

This dignity did not prevent Hearst, when he felt good, from doing a snappy vaudeville jig. Bunkie became accustomed to sleeping in a three-century-old bed surrounded by Gobelin tapestries. A warm comradeship grew between the old man and the boy. Hearst took an interest in his grandson's reaction to newspaper comics he read. He once telephoned Editor

[7] Randolph Apperson to author.   [8] John Hearst Jr. in *Reader's Digest*, May, 1960.

Woolard at the Los Angeles *Examiner* to recommend the use of a certain comic strip.

"It is excellent," he told Woolard. "I have had an expert analyze it, and he approves it without reservation. The expert is Bunkie." [9]

Ordinarily indulgent, he was firm in some respects, notably about courtesy. One afternoon, Bunkie got home from school, picked up the telephone in La Casa del Mar, also known as "A" house, and called Joseph, the butler. "This is John, Jr.," he said. "Bring a piece of cake and a glass of milk over to A house."

Hearst, seated nearby, scowled. He strode to the telephone and called the butler. "Joseph," he said, "never mind that cake and milk."

Then he gave Bunkie a stern lecture for addressing an old retainer in such cavalier style, without even saying "please," and made him go to Joseph and apologize in person.[10]

II. STILL THE CHIEF

HEARST still had his own good teeth, a plenteous thatch of gray hair, a good appetite, and he used glasses only for reading. He continued to play a little tennis in his slow-motion way, enjoyed croquet and swimming, and occasionally went for a canter. But his favorite role was that of the Chief. Editors who hoped that the Old Man would retire, as any reasonable patriarch should, and stop bothering them, were disappointed. He could no more stop editing than he could stop building. He still foregathered in the dark hours past midnight in the Gothic library with Willicombe, turning the pages of his newspapers with his feet and finding things to displease him. He still summoned executives to San Simeon for conferences, and made them cool their heels until he was good and ready. J. D. Gortatowsky, general manager of his newspapers, arrived along with the publishers of the various papers for a discussion of the wartime newsprint shortage. It was Gortatowsky's job to apportion the limited amount of newsprint among the Hearst chain. Each publisher arose in turn to complain bitterly of the division and ask for more paper for his own publication. Hearst listened carefully, then turned to Gortatowsky.

"Gorty," he smiled, "you're doing an excellent job. Everybody is equally dissatisfied." [1]

To San Simeon came his second son, W. R. Jr., about to leave for England as a war correspondent.

"The English people are nice people, charming people," the father said. "Just take care they don't charm you off your American perch." [2]

One of his pepperiest men was Managing Editor John B. T. Campbell of the Los Angeles *Herald-Express*. Campbell, who had a temper, felt it rise

[9] Warden Woolard to author.
[1] Mr. Gortatowsky to author, Apr. 27, 1959.
[2] W. R. Hearst Jr. to author, Apr. 27, 1959.
[10] *Reader's Digest*, May, 1960.

when he got one of the Chief's memos finding fault with his newspaper. He wrote a polite but hard-hitting reply, saying he was disinclined to toot his own horn but pointing out that the *Herald-Express* had shown a steady, healthy growth and now boasted the biggest circulation not only in Los Angeles but in the entire West.

"Now, of course this newspaper is susceptible of plenty of improvement," he went on, "but I can't believe in view of the above figures that it is a very bad newspaper." [3]

Hearst took delight in slapping down a sixty-year-old upstart.

"My dear Mr. Campbell," he wrote. "If you are not 'in the habit of blowing your own horn,' you certainly made up in your last letter for any lack of previous practice. . . .

"Everybody agrees that the *Herald-Express* is a good and growing newspaper.

"It has been while you were editor, it was before you were editor, and please God it will be when you are gathered to your fathers,—which I hope will be many years from now.

"Everybody knows, too, that you are a good editor.

"If we did not think so, you would not be editor of so important a paper as the *Herald-Express*.

"Everybody knows that the *Herald-Express* has many good qualities, characteristics and features, and that is the reason we do not want to lose too many of them by inept condensation.

"The point is not these obvious facts above mentioned.

"The point is that the *Herald-Express* can be improved, as you very wisely say.

"Well, then, let us improve it without so much circumlocution.

"I said let you and I improve it, but if you do not like the association, I will assume the responsibility of issuing the instructions.

"Indeed, you have already done so in large degree, as shown by the sample pages submitted to me. . . ." [4]

It was an example of how Hearst could wield the iron hand and show a hint of menace at the same time as he patted a man on the back. It was not wise to talk back to the Chief although, in his isolation at San Simeon, he had lost the personal contact that would have given more substance to his comments. Sometimes his utterances had the ivory-tower ring that came with ignorance of local conditions and problems, but often they were wonderfully pointed, gem-like in common sense and phraseology. They ranged from disquisitions on whether Hatlo's comic box was better on the sports than on the comic page, to discussions of what to do about Winchell, a Broadway columnist who was setting himself up as an analyst of world affairs. And always they gave the editor the feeling that the Chief was looking over his shoulder, never quite satisfied, forever applying pressure, pressure,

[3] From files of Los Angeles *Herald-Express*, dated Jan. 14, 1944.
[4] From files of *Herald-Express*, dated Jan. 15, 1944.

pressure. Undoubtedly his eternal surveillance robbed his editors of spontaneity. But the Chief could not stop being the Chief.

Miss Davies occasionally attended mass at the little Catholic church down the road from the village. She discussed the newspapers with Hearst, found jobs for some of her friends on the two Los Angeles papers, and saw to it that her special favorites in the entertainment world were well publicized. She supplemented her incessant charities with war work, donating to the service hospitals and even sewing quilts and other hospital needs with her own well-manicured hands. The weekend gatherings continued at San Simeon, with Van Johnson, Sonja Henie, Justine Johnstone, James Stewart and Gloria Swanson among the star-studded guests. But during the week the castle could be a lonely place, not unlike the echoing Xanadu of *Citizen Kane*.

The relationship between Hearst and Miss Davies, although always devoted, was not without some tinge of regret at the tricks that time could play. When they first met, Hearst was in his vigorous, masterful fifties, while Miss Davies was hardly more than a girl. Now, although he was an amazingly spry octogenarian, he was nevertheless an octogenarian, while she still brimmed with comparative youth in her forties. They were more than a generation apart. His tall frame had weathered and bent under hurricanes no other man ever withstood. Miss Davies' figure was still slim, her blonde hair still ungrayed, her blue eyes still sparkling. The thirty-odd years that separated them had been easily bridged back in the days of Wilson and Harding. Now, in Roosevelt's third term, it was a barrier. Hearst, who loved life and hated to grow old, hated it all the more because of Miss Davies' youth, and tried to hold back the years by wearing hand-painted neckties and green suits. Still his eyes followed her wherever she went, as if he were afraid of losing her.

He had given her fame, had made her a millionaire in her own right, had showered her with gifts and surrounded her with luxuries such as no other woman in history ever knew. But he well knew that he had deprived her of his name, and of the conventional wifely status that she had yearned for. For a quarter of a century Miss Davies had desperately wanted to become Mrs. Hearst, knowing all the while that it was impossible, that this one gift the king could not give. Inexorable time, which they had not foreseen as an enemy back in the gay Twenties, had betrayed them both. The touching thing was that both realized it, recognized it as a reality they could not escape, and won at least partial victory through their abiding love.

They still followed the routine of showing movies at night, some of them pre-release. But often now, because he enjoyed it so much, they showed Miss Davies' earlier pictures. He could sit by the hour, watching *When Knighthood Was in Flower, Janice Meredith, Peg O' My Heart* and *The Red Mill*. Tears came to his eyes as he watched the scenes he knew by rote— the scenes he had helped fashion himself, the scenes that carried him back over the years to the time "When all the world is young, lad, And all the trees are green . . ." Each of them pounded him with a hundred recollections of irretrievable youth. The days of the unforgettable *Follies,* with Marion in the front row . . . The days when he still had hopes of becoming President . . . The days when he had no doubt that Miss Davies and he together would scale the last, glittering height of cinema glory . . . The gay trips through Europe with a dozen frolicsome companions . . . The nights on the yacht with the late Florenz Ziegfeld, the late Joseph Urban, the late Will Rogers, the late Arthur Brisbane, and so many others who were now only memories of an era that could be recaptured only on film. He had failed in much that he had set out to do, and yet he could reflect that he had had a lot of fun trying. But for Hearst, who loathed failure, who wanted so badly what he wanted, the pleasure he took in watching the Davies films must have been tinctured with pain.

As always, his sons and executives were there to celebrate his eighty-first birthday. They all waited for him in the vast assembly room, and when he came in they began singing *Happy Birthday.* Bunkie Hearst noted that "His face lighted up and when they had finished he did an 'Off to Buffalo,' winding up with a hand outstretched like an old-time vaudeville hoofer. It broke the place up." [5]

Conchita Sepulveda, the Hearst family friend, had long since married Prince Valerio Pignatelli, had separated from him and had become a writer for the Los Angeles *Examiner.* On August 6, 1945, she arrived at San Simeon for a visit. Hearst met her on the terrace, but he was not his usual pleasant self.

"A terrible thing has happened," he said, his face grave.

"What is it?" she inquired.

"They have dropped an atomic bomb on Japan." [6]

He was visibly upset. The prediction he had dashed off thirteen years earlier—"The next war will be a terrible story of the . . . horrifying destructiveness of modern agencies of war"—had come true. The gentle, human side of Hearst was stricken at the thought of a bomb so frightful that it killed thousands of people, even though they were Japanese. He had indeed come a long way. The man who was born before the battle of Gettysburg, who had seen the first railroad built across the nation, had taken more than a week to cross it as a boy on the same railroad, had cheered the air age and feted Lindbergh, had now lived to see the Atomic Age.

III. DOWN THE ENCHANTED HILL

HEARST had never yet found a secretary who could outlast him. His first, George Pancoast, had moved up the ladder to head the mechanical department, and had died in 1939 at seventy-seven. His second, Max Ihmsen, had moved west to become editor of the Los Angeles *Examiner* and had passed

[5] *Reader's Digest,* May, 1960.   [6] Princess Pignatelli to author.

on. His third, L. J. O'Reilly, had gone to his reward in 1922. His fourth, Joseph Willicombe, retired in 1944 before he was utterly played out. Being secretary for Hearst was an exhausting job. The secretary was required to be intelligent and have a broad knowledge of newspapers, be on call night and day, work like a horse, be ready to travel at a moment's notice, be able to withstand the Chief's occasional anger, and to handle a thousand matters ranging from the momentous to the ridiculous—from arranging a special train to alerting the kitchen staff to prepare Mr. Hearst a poached egg. That Willicombe could have done all this satisfactorily for twenty-two years proved his remarkable business ability as well as an ability to submerge his own individuality and keep himself strictly in the shadow of the Great Man. He was succeeded by No. 5, his chief assistant, H. O. Hunter, who continued sending out memos from the Chief.[1]

The war ended—another milestone. A page of more personal history was torn away when Miss Davies decided to sell her beach house, which was little used now. It was difficult to keep it staffed with servants, and the tax drain was heavy. The place was almost as much of an anachronism as San Simeon, for there were few in 1945 who could afford such an establishment. It brought only $600,000 when it was sold to a real estate operator who planned to convert it into a private beach club. This was almost exactly what its thirty-seven imported fireplaces had cost.[2] The silver, porcelain, furniture and other appointments were auctioned in New York, bringing another $204,762.[3]

Hearst had given up his tennis and now swam only occasionally, but his teletype instructions to his editors were as pithy as ever. He seemed in a perpetual chill, and wanted all the castle fireplaces going full blast. But if he felt the aches of old age, he did not complain. He had never been a complainer. He was amused by the mice that traversed the castle, naming one steady visitor Mortimer. For exercise, he often walked in the mile-long pergola, framed by fruit trees, occasionally stopping to chat with the horticulturist, Nigel Keep. Keep noted that although Hearst never went to church, he liked to discuss religion and knew the Bible well. "He was a religious man in his own way," Keep later recalled. "Once I quoted the Twenty-third Psalm. I made a little mistake in the last line and he corrected me."

A quiet understanding had long since developed between the lord of the manor and the botanical expert who had worked for him since 1919. When Hearst was eighty-three, and Keep a mere seventy-three, Hearst presented him with a photograph of the two of them together and inscribed it, "From an old man to a youngster." [4]

Although Hearst's thoughts turned toward religion, he refused to believe that any mortal could teach him about the infinite. The do-it-yourself politician and newspaperman was also a do-it-yourself religionist. Nominally an Episcopalian, he had always shown respect and tolerance toward other forms of worship. Miss Davies was a Catholic. Many of his executives were Jews,

---

[1] Randolph Apperson to author.
[3] N. Y. *Times,* Dec. 9, 1945.
[2] Providence *Journal,* Jan. 3, 1960.
[4] Nigel Keep to author.

a few of them special intimates. In the movie colony he had become friendly with many Jews, among them Mayer and Goldwyn. He admired Christian Science. He regarded Gandhi as "the greatest man of our century." Now that he had money again, he began to scatter it with a generosity never seen in him before, mostly for education, which he poked fun at and yet believed in. He presented large gifts to the University of California, Oglethorpe University, Catholic Notre Dame University, Methodist-founded Northwestern University, and the Jewish Hospital in Denver, among others.[5] Miss Davies meanwhile spent a fortune to found a children's clinic in Los Angeles.

Public opinion had mellowed somewhat toward Hearst, although the Communists and some liberals would never forgive him. March 4, 1947, marked the sixtieth anniversary of the day back in 1887 when, as a pink-cheeked young man, he had officially taken over the San Francisco *Examiner* from his father. Republican Senator Arthur Capper rose in the Senate that day to deliver a eulogy, praising Hearst for his work for labor, women's suffrage and peace.

"Through it all [Hearst's career]," said Capper, "I find a human factor that especially marks him. Nothing engages his sympathy so quickly as the helpless on earth; nothing inflames his anger so much as wrong to those helpless."

At the same time, Republican Representative Edith Nourse Rogers eulogized Hearst in the House where he had served as a Congressman four decades earlier, saying, "Whenever the term of public servant requires a synonym, I believe it will be Hearst." [6]

Possibly the old man's heart, which the specialists at Bad Nauheim had worried about for years, could not stand the shock of hearing praise emanate from both houses in Washington. Shortly afterward, he suffered a painful seizure. It was diagnosed as auricular fibrillation, a serious heart condition. He recovered partially, but he would never be a well man again. His physicians warned him that he must no longer stay at remote San Simeon. He must move to the city where he could be under the care of a specialist.

Miss Davies went house-hunting. She found a place in Beverly Hills that she thought he would like.

Hearst wept as he made the last trip down the Enchanted Hill—through the electrically opened gates, through the zoo—on his way to Los Angeles.[7] One can picture him turning his head on the coastal highway to catch a last glimpse of the far-off twin towers on which he had spent thirty millions— the towers that represented his youthful dream of triumph and mastery, now shattered by age. He was only mortal after all. He knew he would never come back.

[5] N. Y. *Times*, May 19, 1946; Jan. 9, 1947.   [6] N. Y. *Times*, Mar. 4, 1947.
[7] Tebbel, 10.

4. Long Live the King

THE house at 1007 North Beverly Drive in Beverly Hills in which the ailing Hearst and Miss Davies took refuge was a sharp descent for them both, being valued at only some $200,000. But it was substantial, a three-story Spanish stucco house with a swimming pool and surrounded by eight acres of palms and gardens enclosed by a high wall. With them they had taken two dozen of the San Simeon servants—drivers, nurses, cooks, maids and gardeners—some of whom had worked for them for twenty years or more.

Hearst, who had never taken orders in his life, had orders now that he would take if he wanted to live. Plenty of rest. No excitement. Only token exercise, few visitors, careful diet. His heart was subject to sudden and frightening palpitations. His ailment left him with a palsy so that his hands often shook uncontrollably.

Surely, thought a hundred Hearst editors across the land, the Old Man was finished now. Surely they had received the last of those memos from the Chief.

The nation's newspapers had his obituary ready, but he was in no hurry to accommodate them. On the recommendation of Louella Parsons' husband, Dr. Harry Martin, he came under the care of a young Beverly Hills heart specialist, Dr. Myron Prinzmetal. Dr. Prinzmetal, already noted for his researches in heart malfunction, permitted him to continue his work if he felt up to it.[1] He felt up to it. He got a new secretary, No. 6. He was young Richard Stanley, a war veteran who had been a clerk in the Fox production department and was fast at shorthand. When Stanley first appeared at the Beverly Hills house, he was somewhat nervous, having heard of Hearst's eccentricities. Hearst greeted him cordially but without waste of time. A butler handed him a shorthand book and pencil, and Hearst began dictating a memo to the editors from the Chief.

It was only after Stanley had proved himself that Hearst explained the odd circumstances of his employment. Stanley would stay in the guest house, he said in his weak voice, and would be on call night and day.

"I may want you at any time, whenever I feel well enough," he said. "It would almost eliminate your social life. Do you mind?"

"No, Mr. Hearst," Stanley replied. "I'm not married, and I have few friends here."

Hearst sighed. "Young man, when you die, if you can count your friends on the fingers of your two hands, you'll be fortunate."[2]

[1] Dr. Prinzmetal to author, Oct. 31, 1959.   [2] Richard Stanley to author, Nov. 3, 1959.

He invariably had his dog Helena with him—the last of a long line of dachshunds named Helena. He worked several hours almost every day, but his routine was madly irregular, and Stanley might be called at noon, or at 3 A.M., or both. He was struck by Hearst's courtesy to the servants, and by his prodigious memory for details. Although in his weakness he sometimes shook like a leaf, his keen brain was unimpaired and he was possessed by the old idea that without his supervision his newspapers would fall into all manner of foolish error.

Now, in his invalid years, honors were bestowed on the old man which pleased him but which he was unable to accept in person. W. R. Hearst Jr. was kept busy traveling to Washington to accept awards from the army, the navy, the George Washington Carver Memorial Institute, and others. In the United Nations Assembly, Russia's Andrei Vishinsky took cognizance of Hearst's anti-Communist pronouncements by calling him a "warmonger," which Hearst also accepted as an honor.[3] In 1948 he threw himself into a "MacArthur for America" boom, urging the sixty-eight-year-old General of the Armies for the Republican Presidential nomination. It was his last big crusade, and like so many others, it failed.

Now it was Editor Woolard of the Los Angeles *Examiner* who was "under the gun." Hearst occasionally telephoned him with praise or blame, or asked him to come to Beverly Hills for a conference. Once Woolard heard the Chief's faint voice on the wire.

"Mr. Woolard," he said, "I wish you'd do me a personal favor. I don't want you to delegate this, but to do it yourself. I wish you would go into your art department. Open a window. Then gather up all the airbrushes in the art department and throw them into the gutter."

"I'll do it, Mr. Hearst," Woolard agreed. "May I ask why?"

"I am tired of having people's features destroyed by the hideous misuse of airbrushes. Since it is airbrushes that are responsible for these outrages, I see no remedy but to get rid of the airbrushes."

Woolard, knowing this to be an example of the Chief's humorous exaggeration, went into the art department and merely had a serious talk with the art director about the misuse of airbrushes.[4]

Three guards, employes of the *Examiner,* watched the gate and patrolled the walls at the Beverly Hills place to keep out intruders. Some of the statuary from San Simeon was brought to decorate the garden, where Hearst took short walks. He was thumbing through catalogues again, buying art, silverware and other treasures through agents. Occasionally he and Miss Davies would be taken for a short drive in one of his Buick limousines. Very rarely they would lunch at Romanoff's in Hollywood. Mostly, he and Miss Davies ate at home, and—something new for them both—often alone, in the dining room off the central hall where hung the twelve paintings of Miss Davies in her various film roles.

[3] N. Y. *Times,* Oct. 23, 1947.   [4] Mr. Woolard to author.

Although Hearst was embarrassed by his palsy and his steady loss in weight, he was pathetically appreciative of visits from his sons and from the "old-timers"—Miss Parsons, Louis Mayer, Princess Pignatelli, Frances Marion, and others. Mayer often brought a dish prepared by his cook, chicken soup with matzoh balls. An occasional caller was Captain Horace G. Brown Jr., a merchant marine officer, whose second wife had formerly been the wife of Lawrence Tibbett. Brown, once a cop in Richmond, Virginia, sometimes played cribbage with Hearst. It made the older servants stare because Brown, a big, straight-nosed man, bore an amazing resemblance to Hearst in his younger days. Organization executives still came regularly to consult with the Chief. J. D. Gortatowsky arrived from New York to find Hearst gazing at newspapers spread on the floor.

"Gorty," he demanded, "why is it that our pictures on the Notre Dame-Southern California game are not as good as the *Times'?*" [5]

One night Hearst came down the elevator to the dining room to find Miss Davies chatting with her lifelong stage friends, Justine Johnstone and Mrs. Harry (Eileen Percy) Ruby. Justine Johnstone, the lovely blonde of the *Follies*—Marion's *Follies*—who thirty years earlier had rung down the curtain by appearing as Columbia, wrapped in an American flag. Eileen Percy, the movie beauty who had been on one of the gay, Hearst-guided mass tours of Europe. The old man looked at them, both now middle-aged women. He wept and had to return to his room.[6]

But on his better days he felt indomitably that he would see San Simeon again. He even spent $85,000 for fifty Arabian horses which the almost-empty "ranch" could have got along without. Miss Davies sat with him, talked with him, read to him, kissed him goodnight. Often, when he awoke from a fitful slumber, he would dash off a tender note to her and slip it under her door— so often that she eventually had hundreds of them. One of her friends said, "He gave her everything in life except something to live for—everything except his name." [7] It was a debt he could not pay, but he tried. At his bedside was Marion's photograph, inscribed "To W. R. from Marion," to which she had added lines from *Romeo and Juliet:* "My bounty is as boundless as the sea, my love as deep; the more I give to thee, the more I have, for both are infinite." [8] The devotion between these two, triumphing over illness and the ever-present specter of death, made friends marvel even though they knew the absolute loyalty of both. There were times when Miss Davies telephoned instructions to the Los Angeles papers, causing uneasiness among the editors. Were the Chief's faculties slipping? Was Miss Davies taking over unauthorized control?

In New York, the woman who had Hearst's name could only wait.

---

[5] Mr. Gortatowsky to author.
[6] Stanley Flink to author. Mr. Flink, then a writer for *Time* and *Life*, spent many days at the Hearst-Davies home on assignment. He generously made his notes available to the author.   [7] Mr. Flink to author.   [8] *Life*, Aug. 19, 1951.

At times Hearst was seized with spurts of his old energy, driving Secretary Stanley so hard that the young man was limp at the end of a session. Dr. Prinzmetal, who received $60,000 a year for his ministrations, called daily. He found Hearst formal in manner, never making any small talk, but always courteous regardless of his condition. Although he knew his days were numbered, he never asked for an estimate. Once, when he had an attack of nerves, the doctor gave him phenobarbitol.

"I don't want to become a drug addict," Hearst said half humorously, recalling his many crusades against illicit narcotics.[9]

Some writers later made capital of the fact that Hearst, the crusader against vivisection, was kept alive for years by Dr. Prinzmetal, who often experimented on dogs and other animals. Actually, Hearst merely fought for controlled vivisection, for the licensing of experimentation so that the number of animals so used would be kept to a minimum.

The old man failed. He took to his wheel chair but still clung to the reins. He assigned Adela Rogers St. John to write a series for the *American Weekly* on the early days in Hollywood, asking her to show him each instalment as she finished it. He would linger nostalgically over the story. He began drawing on his own recollections and suggesting further instalments. He became so interested that the series lengthened out and ran for almost a year.[10]

On Christmas Eve of 1950, Agness Underwood, the hard-boiled, warmhearted city editor of the Los Angeles *Herald-Express*, picked up her telephone to hear Hearst's feeble voice. "Miss Underwood," he said, "I just wanted to wish you a merry Christmas." He was now so hard to hear that the editors dreaded getting calls from him, but that was one Miss Underwood did not mind at all.[11]

As 1951 rolled around, Hearst had been four years a-dying, all the while clinging with his old impervious will to the life he still loved. He had shrunk to a bony 125 pounds. The house was kept at eighty degrees—any cooler and he shivered. He still dictated letters and orders to Stanley, who wondered how he could hold up, but he seldom got downstairs now. Clad in a plaid wool bathrobe and slippers, he played the Chief in his bedroom. He had delegated much to his sons and executives, but no more than he had to. His voice was barely audible. Many orders now came from Miss Davies, and the Organization was in a state of nerves, wondering if the orders indeed came from Hearst or whether Miss Davies was taking over.[12]

Nigel Keep, who had retired to his old home in Berkeley in 1949, made a trip to Beverly Hills for a last visit with the boss he truly admired. Hearst was deeply touched.

"I won't be with you long," he said. "Let me bless you." [13]

He laid his hand in benediction on Keep's gray head. It was typical of the grand seigneur, with death staring him in the face, to regard himself as a

[9] Dr. Prinzmetal to author.
[11] Miss Underwood to author.
[13] Nigel Keep to author.
[10] Mrs. St. John to author.
[12] Louis Shainmark to author.

sort of secular pope who could bestow blessings. In July, when Miss Parsons and Bebe Daniels called on him, Miss Parsons said nothing of the fact that her husband had died the previous month. Miss Daniels reminded Hearst of the time at San Simeon when Miss Parsons had allegedly put on her riding breeches backward.

"Louella," he smiled, "was always one to do things differently." [14]

Early in August he telephoned Woolard and asked for a good play on a story about the Pasadena Playhouse, in which he took a paternal interest. The call came during the dark hours, and Woolard just managed to get the story in that same morning edition. A day later, Hearst's secretary called him. The Chief wanted to see him, he said, and he seemed furious. Woolard took tear-sheets of the playhouse story with him and drove fast to Beverly Hills. Hearst, in his wheelchair, Helena in his lap, glared at him. Woolard moved close so he could hear.

"Mr. Woolard," he demanded, "who owns the Los Angeles *Examiner?*"

"Why, you do, Mr. Hearst."

"Well, if I own it, and I want something in it, why can't I have it?"

Woolard saw what was wrong. He brought out the playhouse story, which Hearst had not expected would make the previous day's issue. Hearst stared at it, then made the humblest of apologies.

"Mr. Woolard, please forgive me," he said. "I'm an old man, and I'm sick. I don't notice things as well as I used to. Please drop in when you can. I want to keep in touch." [15]

It seemed impossible that he could live more than a few days. W. R. Hearst Jr. and Richard Berlin, now president of the corporation, flew west for the death watch. The old man declined to make their stay a short one. On August 12, he dictated a few letters, then enjoyed a last visit from Frances Marion. To him, Miss Marion was inextricably connected with the days of cinema glory, when all the trees were green. She told him that she was leaving for San Francisco day after next.

"Frances," he whispered, "please stop at San Simeon and look the place over. I want to be sure that everything is all right there."

Miss Marion noticed that even now, with death crowding him close, his eyes never left Miss Davies, following her every movement just as they had years earlier at M.G.M.[16]

Hearst died at about 9:50 on the morning of August 14, 1951, at the age of eighty-eight. Ironically, he died alone except for the presence of one nurse, who did not know the exact moment of his passing but checked his pulse to find it gone. Miss Davies, who had sat up with him most of the night, was at last asleep under a sedative. The nurse passed the word to a servant, who informed those keeping vigil in the guest house.

William Hearst Jr. and David Hearst hurried over with Berlin. Urgent telephone calls were made. A doctor arrived to make death official. Miss

[14] Miss Parsons to author.   [15] Mr. Woolard to author.
[16] Frances Marion to author.

Davies had had Hearst for more than three decades of life, but in death her control was ended with sharp finality. She was still asleep when the hearse from Pierce Brothers, a Beverly Hills undertaker, arrived and took away the wasted body to prepare it for burial in San Francisco. When she awakened, the place was quiet. Helena padded around unhappily.

"I asked where he was," she said later, "and the nurse said he was dead. His body was gone, whoosh, like that. Old W. R. was gone, the boys were gone. I was alone. Do you realize what they did? They stole a possession of mine. He belonged to me. I loved him for thirty-two years and now he was gone. I couldn't even say goodbye." [17]

That same day, several of Miss Davies' friends whom she had placed in jobs at the *Examiner* and the *Herald-Express* were given their severance checks. The delivery of tne two daily Hearst papers at Miss Davies' home ended that day.

An hour or so after Hearst died, Miss Marion arrived by car at San Simeon. The high towers were etched against a blue summer sky. She found Randolph Apperson at the entrance, closing and locking the gate.

"We just heard," he said, "that Cousin Will is dead." [18]

II. STOP THE PRESSES

WHEN Hearst's body was flown to San Francisco, escorted by four of his sons, the plane passed directly over the San Simeon barony, a castle without a king. To San Francisco also flew Mrs. Hearst with her fifth son, John, from New York. Now that her husband was dead, she could resume in sorrow the position that had been hers in name only for decades. One could only guess at the thoughts of this intrepid little woman, still a seemingly ageless beauty, who had first known William Randolph Hearst a half-century earlier, at the time Miss Davies was born, had borne his five children, had held her head high and maintained her principles through years of separation, and now was still Mrs. Hearst in spite of it all, with the widow's mournful privilege of honoring her late husband and seeing him to his tomb.

The honors were great. People were gathering from all parts of the nation. Louella Parsons and Adela Rogers St. John met in the lobby of the Fairmont Hotel and went upstairs to have a "good cry." The body lay in state for a day and a half at Grace Episcopal Cathedral on Nob Hill (which Hearst had never attended since his mother's funeral), only a few blocks from his boyhood home. Hundreds filed past the costly bronze coffin to see the dead Hearst, clad in a dark blue suit, monogrammed shirt with cuff links, and a blue necktie woven with the family coat of arms. Some were the idly curious who had "heard all the gossip"; others were San Francisco *Examiner* and *Call-Bulletin* employes who had never seen the Chief in life but had heard stories galore about the strange requests he used to telephone to the city

---

[17] *Life*, Aug. 19, 1951.   [18] Miss Marion to author.

desk. Fifteen hundred persons heard the brief services read by the Right Reverend Karl Morgan Block, Episcopal Bishop of California, while a thousand more who could not get in waited outside. In Hearst plants all over the country, work stopped as employes observed a minute of silence—the last time the Old Man would stop the presses. Among the honorary pallbearers were the great or eminent—Governor Earl Warren, Mayor Elmer Robinson, Herbert Hoover, General MacArthur, Bernard Baruch, John Nance Garner, Roy Howard, Louis B. Mayer, Arthur Hays Sulzberger, Mrs. Fremont Older, Hugh Baillie and many others.

The competing newspapermen there—among them Howard, Sulzberger and Baillie—must have been repeatedly shocked over the years by Hearst's callous misuse of journalism. Others, such as Hoover, had personally felt the sting of unfair Hearst attacks. Two—Garner and MacArthur—had received virtually nothing but praise from the Hearst press.

All of them, as the bishop droned on, must have pondered the eighty-eight-year paradox that had come to rest in the bronze coffin in the nave—the career that had at times been marked by selfishness, presumption, ruthlessness, arrogance, cheapness and downright error to such an extent that the wonder was that they had gathered here to honor him. All of them, if they carried the thought through, knew that they were not honoring his manifold error, or the millions he had given to charity, nor were they appearing here out of mere respect for the family. They were recognizing a character so prodigious as to be understood only as a flawed accident of nature that would never occur again—a personality of such titanic scope and torrential energy that it deserved recognition on that score alone, error or no error.

After the service, a police motorcycle escort led the hearse and twenty-two limousines to Cypress Lawn Cemetery at Colma, just south of the city. The huge, marble Hearst mausoleum, surrounded by other great San Francisco names, contained Senator George Hearst, died 1891, and Phoebe Apperson Hearst, died 1919. In the committal ceremony, Bishop Block read the church's service, then Hearst's own *Song of the River:*

> *For life was born on the lofty heights*
> *And flows in a laughing stream*
> *To the river below*
> *Whose onward flow*
> *Ends in a peaceful dream. . . .*

Then William Randolph Hearst joined his two immediate ancestors.[1]

Miss Davies, who was not invited to the funeral, remained in Beverly Hills. "I'd thought I might go to church," she said, "but I'll just stay here. He knew how I felt about him, and I know how he felt about me. There's no need for dramatics." [2]

Deadlines, the house organ of the Los Angeles *Examiner,* announced that the Hearst papers would continue unchanged. This was like saying, after

---

[1] San Francisco *Examiner,* Aug. 18, 1951.   [2] *Time,* Aug. 27, 1951.

lightning and thunder had ended, that the weather would continue unchanged. Nothing could be the same with the Chief gone. The Hearst press had entered a new era, and only one aspect of this was the fact that Miss Davies, who had received so many flattering puffs under the old regime, would go unmentioned in the new unless she really *made* news, as she soon would.

III. THE LAWYERS

HEARST's will, filling 125 typewritten pages, disposed of a personal estate of $59,500,000. It provided for the creation of three trusts. One settled $6,000,000 in Hearst Corporation preferred stock on Mrs. Hearst, along with an outright grant of $1,500,000 in cash. The second, for the Hearst sons, contained a hundred shares of Hearst Corporation voting stock and also enough preferred stock to assure an annual return of $150,000, which the five could add to their already handsome salaries as company executives. The third, a residuary trust, was for charitable and educational purposes, the beneficiaries to be the Los Angeles Museum, the University of California, and others to be selected by a foundation Hearst provided for.

His sons were named as trustees of all three trusts. The will directed that a memorial be built to his "beloved mother" containing part of his art treasures, for public use. As executors of the will he chose eight of his executives, including Berlin, Huberth and Howey. True to his instinct for clinging to what he had, he begged his executors to keep the somewhat shrunken but still vast publishing empire intact: "I request my executors and trustees . . . not to part with the ownership or control of any newspaper, magazine, feature service, news service, photographic service or periodical . . . unless it shall, in their opinion, be necessary or prudent to do so." [1]

There was no bequest to Miss Davies in the will. He had provided for her in an earlier trust fund, dated November 5, 1950. This gave her a lifetime income from 30,000 shares of Hearst Corporation preferred, the stock itself to revert to the sons upon her death. In the will he referred to her as, "my loyal friend, Miss Marion Douras, who came to my aid during the great depression with a million dollars of her own money . . ." He did his best to demolish the ever-recurrent rumor that he and Miss Davies had children, writing:

> I hereby declare that the only children I have ever had are my sons in this will named. . . . If any person or persons other than my said sons shall assert and finally establish . . . that he or she is a child of mine . . . then I give and bequeath to each such person the sum of one dollar. I hereby declare that any such asserted claim of heirship or kinship to me is and would be utterly false and wholly fraudulent.[2]

---

[1] *Editor & Publisher*, Aug. 18, 1951.   [2] *Editor & Publisher*, Aug. 18, 1951.

A few days after Hearst's death, Miss Davies' attorneys staggered the executors by presenting an agreement by which Hearst pooled her 30,000 shares with his 170,000 shares and gave her sole voting power in the Hearst Corporation. This involved no further financial settlement on Miss Davies, but gave her something far more important—final control of the Organization. By its terms she would in effect succeed to the Chief's throne. This agreement reflected Hearst's knowledge that there was hostility toward her in the Organization, his fears that she might be victimized in the interminable legal unraveling of the estate, and his desire to protect her.

If there was one thing the executors were agreed on, it was to put an end to Miss Davies' influence and start the Organization out on a clean slate under professional direction. Yet it appeared that the only ground on which the agreement could be attacked was the ground that Hearst was incompetent when he made it. This was a line the executors were reluctant to take, nor did they relish the prospect of a long, expensive and bitter legal quarrel.

There was another way out. In his will, Hearst had admitted that he was without resources when Miss Davies loaned him a million dollars in 1937. According to California law, a husband could not give away community property. It might be judged that everything Hearst had earned since 1937 was community property, and Mrs. Hearst's lawyers, if they wished, could very likely exact the return of many of Miss Davies' possessions gained since that time.[3]

There were tense meetings between attorneys for both sides. In the end, a compromise was arranged. Miss Davies agreed to relinquish all voting rights, and to serve the Organization merely as an "advisor" at a dollar a year.[4]

The free delivery of Hearst papers to Miss Davies' door was then resumed.

IV. THE OBITUARISTS

At the time of Hearst's death, when every large newspaper ran a long obituary article, and the New York *Times* alone printed a summation of his career that totaled at least 20,000 words, they almost unanimously side-stepped hazarding any judgment as to his true stature. The Hearst press alone used such phrases as "the greatest figure in American journalism," which was true in a sense, but the Hearst press was emotionally involved and could not be expected to make a calm appraisal. The opposition press, which could be looked to for some sort of decisive opinion, just as one would expect an opinion of a deceased composer from fellow musicians, seemed remarkably willing to suspend judgment. The New York *Times* likened him to "an elemental force," and said, "few persons ever succeeded in picking the lock of his character." The Los Angeles *Times* felt him similar to "a force of nature" that could only be described "as a physicist describes some phe-

[3] Tebbel, 363–64.
[4] *Time*, Nov. 5, 1951. For Miss Davies' subsequent marriage see Appendix II.

nomenon of the universe." The New York *Herald-Tribune* said, "one cannot assess [his] final influence." The San Francisco *Chronicle*, which had battled him for six decades, spoke of his "tremendous voltage," but backed away and added, "We would not try to outguess history and offer any final appraisal of William Randolph Hearst . . . But we know that he came into American journalism with both fists swinging, that American journalism will never be the same as it was before it felt his hurtling impact, and that the era has been a more colorful, more zestful time to live for his having been part of it."[1]

The truth was, most newspapermen—even many who had hated and assailed him—were sorry to see Hearst go because a great, violent, fascinating chunk of life and news went with him. He was an original, unique, so unusual that no one was even remotely like him, the newsiest figure in the whole world of news, simultaneously the Sphinx and the blabbermouth of journalism. His passing left the scene strangely sedate and dull. The words "voltage," "impact," "force of nature" and "phenomenon of the universe" were telling descriptions of a man who was as powerful and unpredictable as a hurricane. They also reflected honest puzzlement. Hearst's own contemporaries were baffled. They were saying that he was great—somehow—but they could not explain why. The usual formulae for greatness did not work when applied to him. How could a man guilty of so many transgressions possibly be great? It was as confusing as adding two and two and discovering that for once it did not make four. Standards of appraisal which had never before failed were found wanting in the effort to measure Hearst, because so much of his greatness was obscured in error and misunderstanding.

The cautious obituarists must have known that Hearst's influence on journalism was mostly bad. For all his talk about editorial responsibility, he often forgot his own. He turned journalism into a mad, mass-production world combining elements of the peep-show, the Grand Guignol and the foghorn. True, he made millions, but he spent so many millions more that in 1937 he fell flat on his corporate face and would have been a bankrupt had not a group of executives and a war come along to save him.

Would it be wide of the mark to say that journalistically he was a failure?

As a politician, his chief contribution was probably a negative one. He courted voters with money and the greatest propaganda machine yet devised, but the electorate had the good sense to turn him down and vindicate the essential soundness of the democratic system. With his manifold flaws, he could have been dangerous in high office. Rejected, he still retained considerable power as a political oracle and an influence on voters, but he dissipated much of this because of the zigzag course he followed. In his later years he backed an unbroken succession of losers: Landon, Willkie, Dewey, MacArthur. In fact, the public's refusal to follow him was so persistent that he

[1] All four papers for date of Aug. 15, 1951.

himself was dogged by a sense of frustration, and it became almost axiomatic that the candidate he supported would lose.

Was Hearst, then, a failure as a politician also?

In his personal life, he had touched his own heart and the hearts of the two women closest to him—his wife and his mistress—with tragedy.

Was he a personal failure also? And if he was a failure as a newspaperman, executive, politician and husband, wherein lay his greatness and what was all the shouting about?

Indeed, Hearst, the nonconformist who broke all the rules and led analysts a merry chase when he was alive, did it again when he died and confounded observers who tried to judge him by the usual standard of successes achieved. The effort to determine his real stature and put him in a proper niche could lead into obscure bypaths of psychic research and philosophy. Even today, a decade after his death and almost a century after his birth, the lock of his character is still unpickable. One gets only a partial view through the keyhole. Another clue can be found in what the obituarists did *not* say. They did not, for example, stress his unshakable integrity, his unswerving principles or steadfast beliefs.

These qualities he did not have. Had he had them—added them to his awesome vigor, industry, capability and intellect—he might well have been the greatest man of his era. He had integrity, on occasion. He had principles and beliefs which he firmly swore by at any given time but which could fluctuate as wildly as a compass near the pole. His crippling weakness was instability, vacillation, his inability to anchor his thinking to a few basic, rocklike truths that were immovable in his heart. The rocklike truths were missing in him. For all his potency of utterance, he seemed a creature of caprice, lacking real substance. Benevolent one moment, he could be malicious the next. The tragedy of Hearst was that he had all the equipment for first-rank eminence except the most vital ingredient of all. He was a Rembrandt struck color-blind, a Stradivarius out of tune.

Hearst, the worshiper of success, could not be properly measured in terms of success at all. His true splendor lay in fields not always associated with greatness—as a loser, a fearless fighter, and as an eccentric individualist.

He was unrivaled in the magnificence of his failure, the scope of his defeats, the size and succession of his disappointments. This was because he *tried* everything. In his sixty-four years on the boards, he pleaded a thousand causes, dodged not an issue, feared not an enemy. His occasional successes were all but blotted out by the disasters he encountered. A lover of victory, he became instead a connoisseur of catastrophe. No one could dispute his title as the champion loser of his time. The inspiring thing about him was his ability to see himself trounced in one fight and to come back swinging in the next. Like a battle-scarred pugilist sent flying repeatedly to the mat, he won admiration by getting to his feet again and again, bloody but unafraid and still formidable. Hearst had taken scores of blows on chin and midriff that would have knocked out ordinary men. He kept coming back for more, sometimes forfeiting the admiration he won for his courage by his penchant for hitting below the belt. In the American democratic scene he was the eternal critic, dissenter and gadfly, and there was no one in sight who could come close to taking his place.

As an eccentric, a supreme screwball, a serio-comic vaudevillian who took the whole world as his stage and enacted there an endless series of fantastic charades for more than a half-century, no one could touch him. Always denied the lead role, he thundered out from the wings as a heavy or clown. Who but Citizen Hearst could have set himself up as king, owned seven castles, fought for the common man, looted the world of art, squired a bevy of actresses through Europe, chartered a plane to fetch shrimp, carried on a one-man war with France, rescued a toad and bewailed the death of a mouse? Who but Hearst housed two distinct personalities, swinging from one to the other so rapidly that one could never be sure which Hearst he would meet?

The thing that baffled the obituarists was that one obituary would not do for him. He needed two to describe his two selves. One would have to be decidedly unflattering:

> Spoiled as a child, he never reached emotional maturity in eighty-eight years. He spent his life trying to gratify his overwhelming passions for wealth, power and position. Truth and principle seldom bothered him. His venomous attacks on those in office reflected his own envy and frustration. While he spoke piously of ideals in journalism, he left no gutter unexplored. He pushed the United States into war with Spain, sought to do the same in Mexico, but howled against wars that did not have his authorization. An immoralist, he assailed immorality in others. Aloof, driving, ruthless, he terrorized his own executives. In the depression, when Americans were starving, he squandered millions in self-indulgence and had the nerve to complain of taxes. When crossed, he could wallow in blind rage. Selfish, arrogant, distrustful of others, he thought himself so indispensable that he clung to the reins of his empire until death stiffened his fingers.

But the other obituary would show a different man:

> Heir to millions, he had the character to choose work over idle luxury. He had many of the winning traits of a child. Shy, excessively courteous, he was so sentimentally soft-hearted as to be almost womanly. The kindnesses he performed for friends and employes were unnumbered. He could show the same concern for humanity in the abstract. His sympathies were so aroused by the plight of the Cubans that he insisted on saving them. He was so indignant at the exploitation of the common people that he became their defender against privilege. He never sat on the fence. He proved his patriotism by taking strong stands on issues which could not benefit him personally and in some cases lost him money and popularity. In one love he was true and devoted for more than thirty years. Wonderfully optimistic, he was also superlative in his sense of humor. He loved to do things for others, and many who received his bounty at his castles, on his yachts or on his

group excursions to Europe and Mexico, still cherish his memory. He was tolerant of all religions. No miser, he believed in spending his money, keeping it in circulation, paying good salaries. He stood stoutly behind his editors and reporters, and if his executives feared him, they nevertheless venerated him. Gentleness and consideration were a part of his indefinable charm. Two of his warmest admirers were his valet of a quarter-century, George Thompson, and his horticulturist for thirty years, Nigel Keep. During the minute of silence when the presses stopped, thousands of Hearst employees knew that a titan had passed whose like would never be seen again.

Both obituaries are true, though irreconcilable if Hearst had been one man. He was two, a Prospero and a Caliban, and the lucky ones were those who saw only his angelic side.

APPENDICES

Appendices

I

The Hearsts were Scotch and English, with an admixture of Irish from George Hearst's mother. The name, originally spelled Hyrst, was changed to Hurst before taking its present form. The first Hearst arrived in Virginia Colony in 1608. The Appersons were English. The Randolphs, another ancestral family, were also English. Thus William Randolph Hearst, who came to entertain suspicion of the English, was of predominantly English descent.

II

For more than thirty years Miss Davies had resented the circumstances that made it impossible for her to justify her life with Hearst in the eyes of the law and the church. During that time she had seen dozens of her friends marry, some of them several times. She had taken an active role in sponsoring some of the marriages. Surrounded by marriage, often the benefactress of married couples, she had envied them the freedom to marry that was denied her. To this had been added the four-year ordeal of Hearst's illness, then his death and the legal tangle that followed. Although she had many friends, she was a tired, sad, lonely woman.

Ten weeks after Hearst died, on October 31, 1951, Miss Davies ran off to Las Vegas with Captain Horace Brown, the man who looked so much like a younger Hearst. They secured a license at the town's all-night marriage bureau and were married at El Rancho Vegas. The ceremony was informal, Miss Davies wearing dark blue slacks, a blue sweater and a camel-hair coat. She gave her age as forty-five, although her own biography in Who's Who listed the year of her birth as 1900, which would have made her fifty-one. The Los Angeles Times put out an extra headlining the event. The Hearst-owned Examiner issued no extra, though it mentioned the marriage in its regular edition. Perhaps the most arresting line was:

"It was Miss Davies' first marriage."

III

In addition to his personal estate, Hearst left a publishing organization with assets of some $160,000,000. Included were the following eighteen newspapers in twelve cities:

Boston *American*	Detroit *Times*
Boston *Record*	Chicago *Herald-American*
Boston *Sunday Advertiser*	Milwaukee *Sentinel*
Albany *Times-Union*	San Antonio *Light*
New York *Journal-American*	Los Angeles *Examiner*
New York *Mirror*	Los Angeles *Herald-Express*
Baltimore *News-Post*	San Francisco *Examiner*
Baltimore *Sunday American*	San Francisco *Call-Bulletin*
Pittsburgh *Sun-Telegraph*	Seattle *Post-Intelligencer*

Of the many enterprises allied with his newspapers, the biggest were *The American Weekly,* King Features Service, International News Service and International News Photos. There were also nine magazines:

Cosmopolitan	*Motor*
Good Housekeeping	*Motor Boating*
Harper's Bazaar	*American Druggist*
House Beautiful	*Connoisseur*
Town & Country	

Good Housekeeping and *Harper's Bazaar* were also published in England. *Connoisseur,* a deluxe quarterly, was published solely in England and had an American subscription list.

It took a Los Angeles court more than five years to settle Hearst's personal estate, which included items as diverse as two aging Chevrolet trucks and 157 wild-animal skins stored in a Los Angeles warehouse. After the distribution of family bequests, $43,732,407 was left for the William Randolph Hearst Foundation for Charitable Purposes, one of the nation's larger foundations. Evidently he felt he had done enough for his executives and friends while living, for he left no other bequests.

The big question was, what to do with the still unfinished 100-room San Simeon complex? In his will, Hearst expressed the wish that the castle, along with its works of art, might go to the University of California as a memorial to his mother. The regents declined with thanks. They did not have funds to maintain such a place. The Hearst sons and their families visited it only occasionally and did not feel they could afford it. Likewise, the Hearst Corporation directors were unenthusiastic about pouring more money into the late Chief's dream. Nor did any millionaire turn up who thought he could foot the purchase, maintenance and tax bills.

Here was an anomaly—a $30,000,000 castle that could not be sold and apparently could not even be given away.

In 1954, the Hearst sons began a diplomatic effort to present it to the state of California. It had to be done carefully, to forestall suspicions of legislators and taxpayers that a white elephant was being unloaded on the state. Governor Goodwin Knight and his wife were invited to the castle for a weekend. Knight, impressed, had his director of state parks, Newton B. Drury, make a survey to see if it could be incorporated into the state park system. In 1957 the state accepted the castle as a gift, along with 123 acres of the Enchanted Hill immediately surrounding it.

There were some misgivings, but when San Simeon was opened to the public in 1958, tourists at two dollars a head arrived in such numbers that at first many had to be turned away. Motels sprang up at nearby Cambria, which has become a thriving tourist town. Visitors are ushered through the castle in groups of forty. Some inquire about the actress who lived there with Hearst—a matter the guides are instructed not to discuss. By the summer of 1960, more than 500,000 persons had filed through. Instead of losing the state money, the operation is nicely self-supporting.

In 1953, the Mexican government bought the Hearst Babicora ranch for $2,500,000. In 1955, the main building of the Hearst-Davies beach house at Santa Monica, unprofitable as a club, was torn down to make room for a state-owned parking lot. Many of the period rooms and fixtures were bought by film studios to give authentic background to movies. In 1960, St. Donat's Castle, which buyers had long resisted, was sold to a boys' school.

Of Hearst's seven castles, only Wyntoon remains in the hands of the family and the corporation—a property the Organization has made profitable by gradual logging of its 67,000 acres for an estimated $2,000,000 annual return. When Hearst was living, not a tree could be touched.

Bibliography

Unfortunately, the author had access to only a scattering of the thousands of letters Hearst wrote and received, the bulk of which are in the possession of the family. A few interesting letters by or regarding Hearst were found at the New-York Historical Society; in the Victor F. Lawson Papers and the Carter Harrison Jr. Papers at the Newberry Library in Chicago; in the W. J. Chalmers Papers at the Chicago Historical Society; and in the Fremont Older Papers and the Hiram Johnson Papers at the Bancroft Library, University of California, Berkeley.

When Mrs. Fremont Older worked on her biography of Hearst in 1935, she was given five trunkfuls of Hearst's and his mother's letters. Some she used in her biography. Others she copied but was unable to use. These latter she generously sent to the author. Those which are used in this book are cited as coming from the "Mrs. Fremont Older Notes."

The thousands of newspapers consulted, most of them in New York, Chicago, San Francisco, Los Angeles and Hollywood, are cited in the footnotes. Magazine articles concerning Hearst were found in *The American Magazine, American Mercury, Collier's, Cosmopolitan, Editor & Publisher, Fortune, Harper's Weekly, Hearst's International, Life, The Nation, The New Republic, The New Yorker, The North American Review, The Outlook, The Pacific Art Review, Pearson's, Reader's Digest, The Saturday Evening Post, The Siskiyou Pioneer, Social Frontier, Time,* and *World's Work.*

Of the books and longer articles consulted, the following is a list only of those cited or quoted in this narrative.

Abbot, Willis J., *Watching the World Go By*, Boston, 1933.
Andrews, Wayne, *Battle for Chicago*, New York, 1946.
Atherton, Gertrude, *Golden Gate Country*, New York, 1945.
Baker, Ray Stannard, *Woodrow Wilson: Life and Letters*, New York, 1931.
Barrett, James Wyman, *Joseph Pulitzer and His World*, New York, 1941.
Bean, Walton, *Boss Ruef's San Francisco*, Berkeley, 1952.
Beard, Charles A., *American Foreign Policy in the Making*, New Haven, 1946.
Behrman, S. N., *Duveen*, New York, 1952.
Bent, Silas, *Ballyhoo*, New York, 1927.
———, *Strange Bedfellows*, New York, 1928.
Berkeley: The First Seventy-Five Years (anonymous), Berkeley, 1941.
Bessie, Simon Michael, *Jazz Journalism*, New York, 1938.
Bierce, Ambrose, *Collected Works*, 12 vols., New York, 1909–1912.
———, *The Letters of Ambrose Bierce* (edited by Bertha Clark Pope), San Francisco, 1922.
Bleyer, Willard G., *Main Currents in the History of American Journalism*, Boston, 1927.
Bonfils, Winifred Black, *The Life and Personality of Phoebe Apperson Hearst*, San Francisco, 1928.
Bowers, Claude G., *The Life of John Worth Kern*, Indianapolis, 1918.
Brewton, William W., *The Life of Thomas E. Watson*, Atlanta, 1926.
Browder, Earl, *Hearst's "Secret Documents" in Full* (pamphlet), New York, 1936.
Bruce, John, *Gaudy Century*, New York, 1948.
Burns, James MacGregor, *Roosevelt: The Lion and the Fox*, New York, 1956.
Butler, Nicholas Murray, *Across the Busy Years*, 2 vols., New York, 1936–1940.
Cantor, Eddie, with David Freedman, *Ziegfeld, the Great Glorifier*, New York, 1934.
Carlson, Oliver, *Brisbane*, New York, 1937.

Carlson, Oliver, and Ernest Sutherland Bates, *Hearst, Lord of San Simeon*, New York, 1936.

Castle, Irene, *Castles in the Air*, Garden City, 1958.

Chadwick, French Ensor, *The Relations of the United States and Spain*, New York, 1909.

Chambers, Walter, *Samuel Seabury—a Challenge*, New York, 1932.

Chase, Ilka, *Past Imperfect*, New York, 1942.

Churchill, Allen, *Park Row*, New York, 1958.

Clark, Champ, *My Quarter Century of American Politics*, 2 vols., New York, 1920.

Cleland, Robert Glass, *California in Our Time*, New York, 1947.

Cobb, Irvin S., *Exit Laughing*, Indianapolis, 1941.

Coblentz, Edmond D., *Ambrose Bierce, Stepfather of the Family* (pamphlet), San Francisco, 1958.

————, *Newsmen Speak*, Berkeley, n.d.

————, *William Randolph Hearst, a Portrait in His Own Words*, New York, 1952.

Coleman, Harry J., *Give Us a Little Smile, Baby*, New York, 1943.

Cooper, Kent, *Kent Cooper and the Associated Press*, New York, 1959.

Cox, James M., *Journey Through My Years*, New York, 1946.

Creelman, James, article on Hearst, *Pearson's Magazine*, September, 1906.

————, *On the Great Highway*, Boston, 1901.

Crichton, Kyle, *Total Recoil*, New York, 1960.

Croly, Herbert, *The Promise of American Life*, New York, 1909.

————, *Marcus Alonzo Hanna*, New York, 1923.

Crowther, Bosley, *Hollywood Rajah*, New York, 1960.

Daggett, Stuart, *Chapters in the History of the Southern Pacific*, New York, 1922.

Daniels, Josephus, *Shirt-Sleeve Diplomat*, Chapel Hill, 1947.

Davis, Richard Harding, *Cuba in War Time*, New York, 1898.

Decker, Karl, *The Story of Evangelina Cisneros*, New York, 1897.

Dobie, Edith, *The Political Career of Stephen Mallory White*, Palo Alto, California, 1927.

Duffus, R. L., "The Tragedy of Hearst" (article), *World's Work*, October, 1922.

Farish, Thomas Edwin, *The Gold Hunters of California*, Chicago, 1904.

Farley, James A., *Behind the Ballots*, New York, 1941.

————, *The Roosevelt Years*, New York, 1948.

Farnsworth, Marjorie, *The Ziegfeld Follies*, New York, 1956.

Ferber, Edna, *A Peculiar Treasure*, New York, 1939.

Ferber, Nat J., *I Found Out*, New York, 1939.

Filler, Louis. *Crusaders for American Liberalism*, New York, 1939.

Flynn, Edward J., *You're The Boss*, New York, 1947.

Ford, Edwin H., and Edwin Emery, *Highlights in the History of the American Press*, Minneapolis, 1954.

Ford, James L., *Forty-Odd Years in the Literary Shop*, New York, 1921.

Fortescue, Granville, *Front Line and Deadline*, New York, 1937.

Fowler, Gene, *Beau James*, New York, 1949.

————, *The Great Mouthpiece*, New York, 1931.

Gauvreau, Émile, *My Last Million Readers*, New York, 1941.

Gerard, James W., *My First Eighty-three Years in America*, Garden City, 1951.

Hapgood, Norman, *The Changing Years*, New York, 1930.

————, *The Stage in America*, New York, 1901.

Harrison, Carter H., *Stormy Years*, Indianapolis–New York, 1935.

Hart, Jerome A., *In Our Second Century*, San Francisco, 1931.

Head, Alice M., *It Could Never Have Happened*, London, 1939.

Hearst, John R. Jr., "Life With Grandfather" (article), *Reader's Digest*, May, 1960.

Hearst, William Randolph, *Selections From the Writings and Speeches of William Randolph Hearst*, ed. by E. F. Tompkins, San Francisco, 1948.

Hecht, Ben, *A Child of the Century*, New York, 1954.

Hemment, John C., *Cannon and Camera*, New York, 1898.
Holbrook, Stewart, *Lost Men of American History*, New York, 1946.
Hunt, Frazier, *One American and His Attempt at Education*, New York, 1938.
Hunt, Rockwell D., *California and Californians*, 5 vols., San Francisco, 1926.
Huxley, Aldous, *After Many a Summer Dies the Swan*, New York, 1939.
Ickes, Harold L., *The Secret Diary of Harold L. Ickes*, 3 vols., New York, 1953–1954.
Irwin, Will, *The Making of a Reporter*, New York, 1942.
———, *Propaganda and the News*, New York, 1936.
Isman, Felix, *Weber and Fields*, New York, 1924.
Jessup, Philip C., *Elihu Root*, 2 vols., New York, 1938.
Johnston, Alva, *The Legendary Mizners*, New York, 1953.
Kelly, Florence Finch, *Flowing Stream*, New York, 1939.
Klein, Henry H., *My Last Fifty Years*, New York, 1935.
Koenigsberg, Moses, *King News*, Philadelphia–New York, 1941.
Lane, Anne Wintermute, and Louise Herrick Wall (editors), *The Letters of Franklin K. Lane*, Boston, 1922.
Lee, James Melvin, *A History of American Journalism*, Boston, 1917.
Leech, Margaret, *In the Days of McKinley*, New York, 1959.
Lewis, Oscar, *Bay Window Bohemia*, Garden City, 1956.
———, *The Big Four*, New York, 1938.
The Life of William R. Hearst (anonymous pamphlet), New York, n.d. (probably 1909).
Lingley, Charles Ramsdell, and Allen Richard Foley, *Since the Civil War*, New York, 1935.
Logan, Mrs. John A., *Reminiscences of a Soldier's Wife*, New York, 1913.
Long, J. C., *Bryan the Great Commoner*, New York, 1928.
Lundberg, Ferdinand, *Imperial Hearst*, New York, 1936.
Lyman, George D., *The Saga of the Comstock Lode*, New York, 1934.
Mason, Gregory, *Remember the Maine*, New York, 1939.
Maxwell, Elsa, *R.S.V.P.: Elsa Maxwell's Own Story*, Boston, 1954.
McClellan, George B. Jr., *The Autobiography of George B. McClellan Jr.*, ed. by Harold C. Syrett, Philadelphia, 1956.
McWilliams, Carey, *Ambrose Bierce*, New York, 1929.
Michelson, Charles, *The Ghost Talks*, New York, 1944.
Millis, Walter, *The Martial Spirit*, Boston, 1931.
Morell, Parker, *Lillian Russell*, New York, 1940.
Morris, Lloyd, *Incredible New York*, New York, 1951.
———, *Not So Long Ago*, New York, 1949.
———, *Postscript to Yesterday*, New York, 1947.
Moskowitz, Henry, *Alfred E. Smith*, New York, 1924.
Mott, Frank Luther, *American Journalism*, New York, 1942.
Murray, William W., article on Wyntoon, *Siskiyou Pioneer*, Vol. III, No. 1, 1958, Yreka, California.
Musgrave, George Clarke, *Under Three Flags in Cuba*, Boston, 1899.
Neale, Walter, *The Life of Ambrose Bierce*, New York, 1929.
Norris, Kathleen, *Family Gathering*, New York, 1959.
O'Connor, Harvey, *Mellon's Millions*, New York, 1933.
Olcott, Charles S., *The Life of William McKinley*, 2 vols., Boston, 1916.
Older, Fremont, *My Own Story*, New York, 1926.
Older, Mrs. Fremont, *William Randolph Hearst, American*, New York, 1936.
O'Loughlin, Edward T. (editor), *Hearst and His Enemies* (pamphlet), New York, 1919.
Paine, Ralph D., *Roads of Adventure*, Boston, 1922.
Palmer, Frederick, "Hearst and Hearstism" (four-part article in *Collier's*, September 22, 29, October 6 and 13, 1906).

Parsons, Louella O., *The Gay Illiterate*, New York, 1944.

Paxson, Frederick L., *Postwar Years: Normalcy, 1918–1923*, Berkeley, 1948.

Peck, Harry Thurston, *Twenty Years of the Republic*, New York, 1913.

Phelps, Alonzo, *Contemporary Biography of California's Representative Men*, San Francisco, 1881.

Pink, Louis Heaton, *Gaynor*, New York, 1931.

Pringle, Henry F., *Alfred E. Smith: A Critical Study*, New York, 1927.

———, *Theodore Roosevelt*, New York, 1931.

Pusey, Merlo J., *Charles Evans Hughes*, 2 vols., New York, 1951.

Ramsaye, Terry, *A Million and One Nights*, New York, 1926.

Rascoe, Burton, *Before I Forget*, New York, 1937.

Rea, George Bronson, *Facts and Fakes About Cuba*, New York, 1897.

Rhodes, James Ford, *The McKinley and Roosevelt Administrations*, New York, 1922.

Rickard, T. A., *A History of American Mining*, New York, 1932.

Rigby, Douglas and Elizabeth, *Lock, Stock and Barrel*, Philadelphia, 1944.

Roosevelt, Elliott (editor), *F.D.R.—His Personal Letters, 1928–1945*, New York, 1950.

Roosevelt, Theodore, *An Autobiography*, New York, 1925.

Ross, Ishbel, *Ladies of the Press*, New York, 1936.

Rotha, Paul, *The Film Till Now*, New York, n.d.

Rubens, Horatio S., *Liberty: The Story of Cuba*, New York, 1932.

Russell, Charles Edward, *Bare Hands and Stone Walls*, New York, 1933.

———, *These Shifting Scenes*, New York, 1914.

Saarinen, Aline B., *The Proud Possessors*, New York, 1958.

San Francisco: The Bay and Its Cities (anonymous), New York, 1940.

Santayana, George, *Persons and Places*, New York, 1944.

Schlesinger, Arthur M. Jr., *The Age of Roosevelt: The Crisis of the Old Order*, Boston, 1957.

Seitz, Don. C., *Joseph Pulitzer: His Life and Letters*, New York, 1924.

Seldes, George, *Lords of the Press*, New York, 1938.

Sigsbee, Captain Charles D., *The Maine*, New York, 1899.

Sinclair, Upton, *I, Candidate for Governor*, New York, 1934.

Smith, Alfred E., *Up to Now*, New York, 1929.

Smith, Mortimer, *William Jay Gaynor*, Chicago, 1951.

Steffens, Lincoln, *Autobiography*, New York, 1931.

———, "Hearst, the Man of Mystery" (article), *The American Magazine*, November, 1906.

Stoddard, Lothrop, *Master of Manhattan: The Life of Richard Croker*, New York, 1931.

Storke, Thomas M., *California Editor*, Los Angeles, 1958.

Strode, Hudson, *Timeless Mexico*, New York, 1944.

Stuart, William H., *The Twenty Incredible Years*, Chicago, 1935.

Sullivan, Mark, *Our Times*, New York, 1926.

Swing, Raymond Gram, *Forerunners of American Fascism*, New York, 1935.

Tannenbaum, Frank, *Mexico: The Struggle for Peace and Bread*, New York, 1950.

———, *Peace by Revolution*, New York, 1933.

Tebbel, John, *The Life and Good Times of William Randolph Hearst*, New York, 1952.

Thompson, Charles Willis, *Party Leaders of the Time*, New York, 1906.

Tinkham, George H., *California Men and Events*, Stockton, 1915.

Underwood, Agness, *Newspaperwoman*, New York, 1949.

U. S. Congressional Record, Vol. 29, Part 1, 54th Congress, 2nd Session.

U. S. Judiciary Committee (Senate)—*Report and Hearings, 66th Congress, 1st Session, 1919; Brewing and Liquor Interests and German and Bolshevik Propoganda*. Vol. II.

U. S. Privileges and Elections Committee—Campaign Contributions (Senate). 62nd Congress, 3d Session. Vol. I.

Vanderbilt, Cornelius Jr., *Farewell to Fifth Avenue*, New York, 1935.

Vilest Racketeer of All (anonymous pamphlet), New York, 1936.

Villard, Oswald Garrison, *Fighting Years*, New York, 1939.

————, *Prophets, True and False*, New York, 1928.

————, *Some Newspapers and Newspapermen*, New York, 1923.

Walters, Charles H., *Joseph Benson Foraker*, Columbus, 1943.

Weedon, Ann, *Hearst, Counterfeit American* (pamphlet), New York, 1936.

Weems, John Edward, *The Fate of the Maine*, New York, 1958.

Wells, Evelyn, *Fremont Older*, New York, 1936.

Wilkerson, M. A., *Public Opinion and the Spanish-American War*, Baton Rouge, 1932.

Wilkins, Thurman, *Clarence King*, New York, 1958.

Winkler, John K., *W. R. Hearst: An American Phenomenon*, London, 1928.

————, *William Randolph Hearst—A New Appraisal*, New York, 1955.

Wisan, Joseph E., *The Cuban Crisis as Reflected in the New York Press*, New York, 1934.

Woodward, C. Vann, *Tom Watson, Agrarian Rebel*, New York, 1938.

Young, John P., *Journalism in California*, San Francisco, 1915.

Author's Note and Acknowledgments

This does not pretend to be a definitive biography. Because of the amazing extent of Hearst's activities over so many decades in so many different fields, even a moderately complete story of his life would fill a half-dozen thick volumes. This writer, being unable to devote his lifetime to such a work, has sought to give an honest, though incomplete, picture by concentrating on the outstanding events in Hearst's career. Many of his colleagues are dead. Yet, because he associated with younger people, a surprising number are still living who knew him and worked with him. It was my aim to interview as many as possible of these who were willing to discuss him.

There were difficulties. Chiefly because of his long disregard for convention, and the savage attacks on him, I encountered something like a polite conspiracy of silence, including the following:

Friends of the Hearst family who said, "I'd love to help you, but I don't want to exploit these private matters."

Veteran Hearst employes who refused to say a word about the late Chief for the same reason, or because they felt that talking about him for publication might annoy their superiors.

Hearst partisans angry at earlier attacks on him and who scented another hatchet job.

Some who suspected that my real intention was to sensationalize Hearst's personal life, and who wanted no part of that.

Other employes or friends who were willing to speak of Hearst in carefully edited language, avoiding any aspects that might be "embarrassing."

Still others who spoke freely on the condition that their identities be kept confidential—a circumstance that causes some of the sources cited here to be listed as "private source."

However, members of the Hearst family gave most generous cooperation, as did many members of the Organization. I was likewise fortunate in finding a sizeable number of former Hearst employes, associates and friends who looked back over the years and spoke with gratifying frankness and objectivity. A few, such as Edmond D. Coblentz, died before I could reach them. Others, including John Francis Neylan, Bartley C. Crum and Martin F. Huberth, have died since I talked with them.

From literally hundreds of personal interviews, a picture of Hearst the man emerged which is believed to be substantially true and is substantially different from the fashionable opinion of him.

Hearst suffered for fifty years of his lifetime, and still does, from the anger and hatred of opposing editors incensed by his methods and also by his success. Particularly in New York, he became the victim of powerful journals which, whether by tacit agreement or not, "plugged" his weaknesses and errors while they soft-pedaled or ignored his achievements. A master propagandist himself, he stirred up a virulent counter-propaganda that colored, and still colors, the public impression of him. He became something of a newspaper myth compounded of half-truths and untruths. The counter-propaganda rose to its highest fury when he was suspected of fascist tendencies in the mid-Thirties, when liberal newspapers and magazines opened bitter assaults on him and two biographies were published which stressed the diabolical.

Any biographer willing to believe all that was written of him in competing newspapers would often be misled. Since the newspapers are necessarily a prime source, this posed a problem—particularly since the Hearst papers themselves were not then noted for reliability. I decided to rely most heavily on the New York *Times*, which was the most complete and the least biased in its coverage of Hearst, and to balance it when possible with other accounts.

My sincere thanks go to the John Simon Guggenheim Foundation, whose grant made it possible to extend the scope of this work; and to Dr. Thomas C. Cochran of the University of Pennsylvania; Mr. Earl Schenck Miers of Edison, N. J.; Dr. Norman Holmes Pearson of Yale University; Dr. Roy V. Peel of the University of Utah; Mr. Orville Prescott of New York; and Dr. T. Harry Williams of Louisiana State University, all of whom gave encouragement and help.

I am indebted to Mrs. William Randolph Hearst of New York, who told me of her late husband's earlier years, and to Mr. William Randolph Hearst Jr., of New York, who not only reminisced about his late father but arranged other valuable interviews in New York and California and secured for me a specially thorough tour of San Simeon.

I am warmly grateful to Mrs. Joseph Marshall Flint of New Haven, a first cousin of Hearst's who knew him personally, lived with his mother and father for years, and out of her rich fund of recollection furnished priceless first-hand information; to Mrs. Fremont Older of Cupertino, California, an earlier biographer of Hearst, who gave not only her counsel and recollections but also supplied notes and copies of Hearst letters which were available to her when she worked on her book more than twenty-five years ago; to Mrs. Frances Marion Thomson of New Haven, long a friend and co-worker with Hearst and Miss Davies in their movie enterprises; and to the late Mr. John Francis Neylan of Palo Alto, California, for years Hearst's right-hand man, who talked with me for hours even though he was unwell.

Dr. Henry Wexler, a psychiatrist of New Haven, generously gave his time and skill in discussions of the complexities of the Hearst personality. The judgments drawn from these discussions, of course, are my own and not the responsibility of Dr. Wexler.

The Messrs. Burroughs Mitchell and Wayne Andrews of Charles Scribner's Sons rendered editorial and research assistance far beyond the call of duty.

The Misses Constance Smith and Patricia Schartle, both of New York, gave expert aid and advice in research and in the preparation of the manuscript.

Mr. Charles Samuels of New York, a former Hearstman as well as an old Hollywood hand, gave the author expert personal instruction in the matter of finding Hearst lore in the film capital and elsewhere.

Anyone undertaking a work of this kind must resign himself to a relentless course of people-bothering. Among the people I bothered in the New York area, and who responded with kindly help, are the Messrs. Mortimer Berkowitz, Richard E. Berlin, James Boylan, Charles F. Chapman, Kyle Crichton, Emmet Crozier, Bartley C. Crum, John Dollard, Norman Fedde, Stanley Flink, and Rube Goldberg; Mrs. Suzanne Gleaves; the Messrs. J. D. Gortatowsky, Harry Hershfield, the late Martin F. Huberth, George R. Katz, John Kobler, William C. Lengel, Herbert Mayes, Richard O'Connor, James O'Shea, Ira Peck; Miss Julia Ruman; the Messrs. Spencer A. Samuels, Jack Schaeffer, Henry Schnakenberg, Henry Sell, Louis Shainmark, and Mortimer Smith; Miss Carmel Snow; Mrs. Adela Rogers St. John; the Messrs. C. B. Stratton, Charles E. Tebbs, and E. F. Tompkins; and the Misses Sophie Treadwell, Gretl Urban and Evelyn Wells.

In the Chicago area I was aided by Mrs. Irene Castle Enzinger, and the Messrs. John W. Dienhart, Elmer Gertz, Stanley Pargellis and Harry Reutlinger.

In the San Francisco area, the following contributed signally by their help: the Messrs. Ronald Bergman, Eugene Block, Lee Ettelson, Edgar Gleeson, Walter Heil; Miss Anita Day Hubbard; the Messrs. Dean Jennings, Nigel Keep, Gordon Lindberg, Charles Mayer, William W. Murray; Mrs. Kathleen Norris; the Messrs. Gordon Pates, George M. Rascoe, and John Barr Tompkins.

The following residents of the Los Angeles area were equally generous: the Messrs. Jerry Asher, Sydney Boehm, Roscoe Cornell, C. Louis Friedman, Robert Goldfarb, George Hearst Jr., C. J. Hubbell, Vance King, Herbert Krauch, Alf Larsen, Jack Lait, Jr., John Maynard, George S. Merritt, Martin Mooney; Miss Louella Parsons; Princess Pignatelli; Mr. Dick Powell; Dr. Myron Prinzmetal; the Messrs. Richard Stanley, Howard Strickling, Edward S. Sullivan, James Swinnerton, and William Tusher; Miss Agness Underwood; Mr. Homer Watters, Miss Ella Williams and Mr. Warden Woolard.

At San Simeon, Mr. Randolph Apperson, a cousin of Hearst's, reminisced about his years of association with him and gave a vivid picture of the operation of "the ranch" when Hearst was living. State Park Ranger James Whitehead, in charge of the state staff at San Simeon, aided my tour of the castle, and Mrs. Anne Rotanzi, formerly employed there by Hearst and now a member of the state staff, described the inner workings of what was America's most lavish household. At San Simeon village, Mr. Peter Sebastian, the postmaster, told of his younger days when he worked on the construction of the castle.

Others who kindly supplied sidelights on Hearst were the Messrs. G. H. Maines of Flint, Michigan; Westbrook Pegler of Tucson, Arizona; and Stanley Walker of Lampasas, Texas.

Lastly, my thanks to the Hearst employes and friends who, for one reason or another, gave their help but preferred to remain anonymous.

It should be emphasized that the occasionally critical judgments made about the earlier Hearst press in the narrative do not apply to the modern Hearst press of today.

Index